ON THE VIEWING PLATFORM

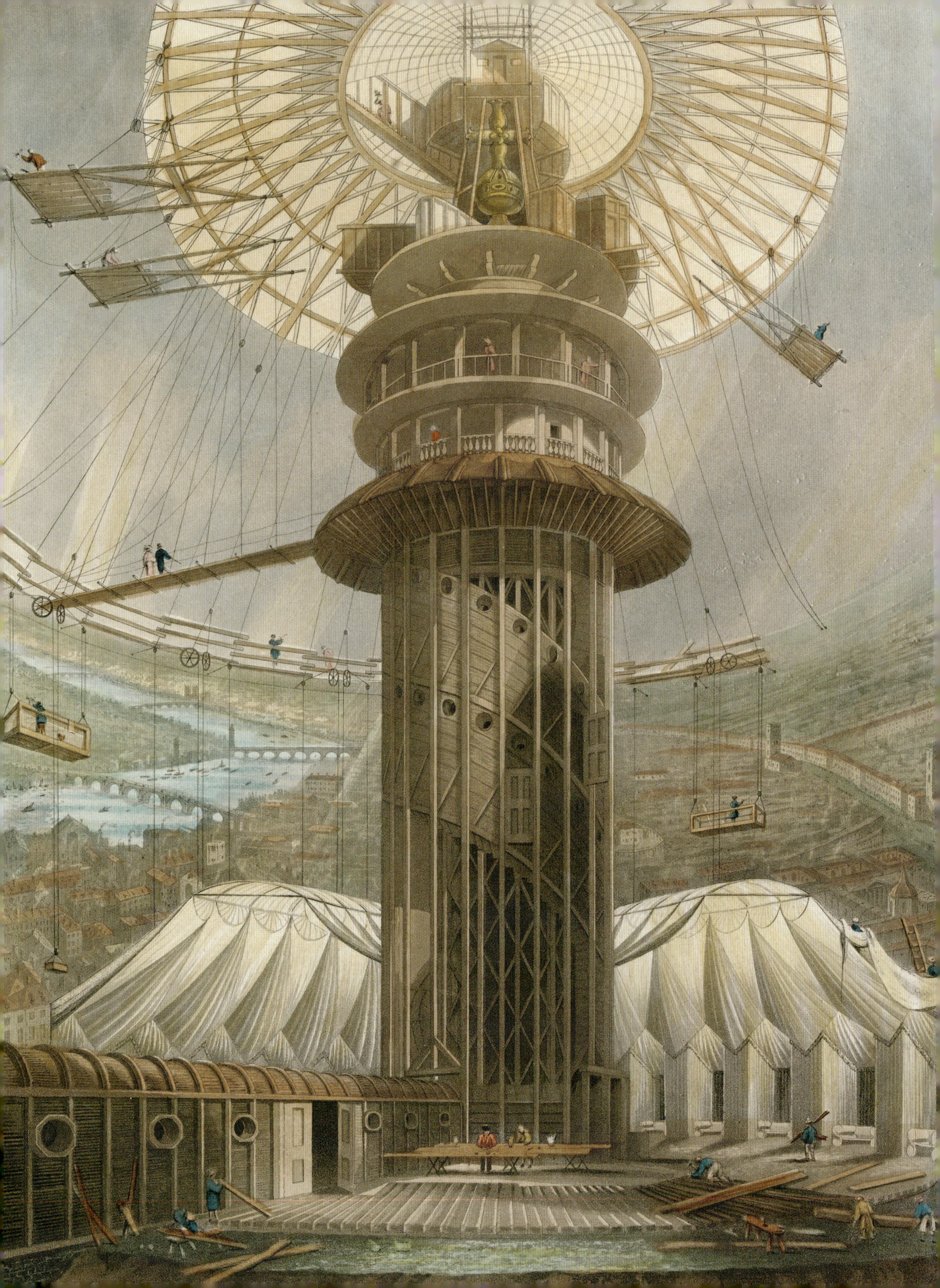

ON THE VIEWING PLATFORM

THE PANORAMA BETWEEN CANVAS AND SCREEN

EDITED BY KATIE TRUMPENER AND TIM BARRINGER

Yale University Press New Haven and London

Published with the assistance of the Frederick W. Hilles Publication Fund of Yale University.

Publication has also been made possible by the generous support of the Department of the History of Art Publications Fund, Yale University.

yalebooks.com/art

Designed by Julie Allred and Leslie Fitch
Set in Crimson and Source Sans Pro type by BW&A Books
Printed in China by Regent Publishing Services Limited

Library of Congress Control Number: 2020936553
ISBN 978-0-300-18479-2

A catalogue record for this book is available from the British Library.

This paper meets the requirements of ANSI/NISO Z39.48-1992 (Permanence of Paper).

10 9 8 7 6 5 4 3 2 1

Jacket illustration: Jeff Wall, *Restoration* (fig. 0.1 detail)
Frontispiece: *The Geometrical Ascent to the Galleries in the Colosseum, Regent's Park* (fig. 1.3 detail)

In Memory of Richard Maxwell (1948–2010)

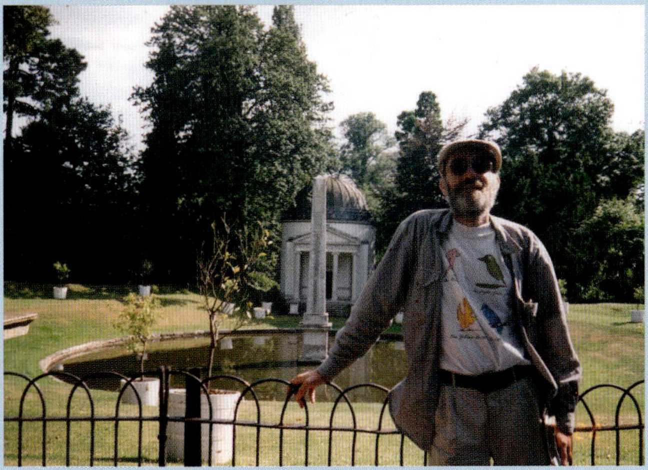

Contents

PART I. THE PAINTED PANORAMA: IMMERSIVE AESTHETICS

PART II. IN (AND BEYOND) THE CINEMA

Acknowledgments

For over a decade, Tim Barringer has been a superb co-teacher, collaborator, interlocutor, and friend. I owe continuing thanks to Mark Sandberg, Martha Ward, Bill Brown, Loren Kruger, and the University of Chicago's former Displaying Cultures workshop, Reading Cultures faculty group, and original Public Culture collective, for years of discussing display practices and exhibition history; to Timothy Hyman, for years of panorama talk (including revelatory discussions in his studio); to Tanya Agathacleous, who gathered New Haven's panorama enthusiasts to co-organize the 2007 Perspectives on the Panorama conference, and to Morna O'Neill, Scott Wilcox, Amy Meyers, and the Yale Center for British Art, for generously organizing and hosting it. The University of Sussex-Roehampton Romantic Nationalism Conference; the American Academy in Berlin; and Francesco Casetti, Craig Buckley, and Rüdiger Campe's Mellon Sawyer Seminar on Genealogies of the Excessive Screen provided fertile frameworks for panoramic thinking. So did both iterations of the Yale History of Art graduate seminars on panoramic painting and film; thanks to our enthusiastic and erudite participants.

Over this book's long gestation, Mal Ahern, Vance Byrd, Francesco Casetti, Oksana Chefranova, Annette Deist, Marta Figlerowicz, Katharina Gerstenberger, Gundula Kreuzer, Thomas LaMarre, Evonne Levy, Alice Lovejoy, Christopher Middleton, John Peters, Brigitte Peucker, Noa Steimatsky, Richard Suchenski, Helen Wilks, and Shamoon Zamir provided crucial panoramic material, insights, and stimulus. Thanks to John Stone, who enabled a prolonged Barcelona sojourn—and repeated MACBA Manon de Boer watchings. In recent years, Alexander Maxwell, Katerina Clark, Jill Campbell, Janice Carlisle, Toni Dorfman, Nancy Glazener, Deidre Lynch, Alison MacKeen, Wendy Olmsted, Kate Orrell, Rita Signorelli-Pappas, and Mollie Sandock lent crucial moral support. Curators in Kansas, Stockholm, and Lucerne answered my questions with erudition and kindness. In Canada, thanks to my brother, John Trumpener (companion on formative childhood planetarium expeditions); to Danielle Baxter and the late James, Ray, and Kathleen Salt, for enabling my adolescent visit behind the scenes to an ornithological diorama being mounted at the Alberta Provincial Museum; to Dennis Theobald, for taking me back to the Chateau Lacombe's revolving restaurant; and to Christine Collinson, for discussing controversial murals by her grandfather, H. G. Glyde.

Above all, I'm indebted to the late Richard Maxwell. On our first date, we discovered a shared interest in Eduard Gaertner and, over the next seventeen years, jointly visited panoramic displays in Switzerland and Thuringia, Prague and Gettysburg, Milwaukee and Los Angeles. In the panoramic as in so many domains, life with him was a joy and an education. KT

This book's origins lie in discussions between Yale colleagues and students over a period of more than a decade. I have had the profound pleasure of co-teaching graduate seminars on the panorama with my friends Katie Trumpener and the late Richard Maxwell. Our teaching relied, as does this book, on the fundamental work of Ralph Hyde, Denise Oleksijczuk, and Michael Charlesworth. I'm grateful to have had the chance to share in Richard's peerless knowledge of nineteenth-century literature and arcana, and to have discussed panoramas and the panoramic over more than a decade with him, Katie, and several generations of outstanding graduate students. Cordial discussions in the classroom and beyond suggest that this volume may be followed by many more on such a richly rewarding topic. I'm particularly indebted to Julia Lum for illuminating discussions of the colonial panorama. Gillian Forrester, formerly curator of prints and drawings at the Yale Center for British Art, has exerted a key intellectual influence on the project throughout. An earlier draft was copyedited with good-humored skepticism by Yale doctoral candidate Gustav Percivall, whose early death alas deprives the field of a highly original mind. We are also grateful to the anonymous reviewers for the press whose comments materially improved the book.

Our discussions at Yale University Press were initiated by the ever-encouraging Michelle Komie. As the book reaches publication, we are grateful to Amy Canonico for her unflagging editorial support, advocacy, tact, incisiveness, and patience; to Raychel Rapazza; to Julie Allred at BW&A Books; and to the entire team at the press. Our thanks to Dan Cohen for his sterling work on picture rights, and to Nicole Chardiet for administrative support. Finally, we remain grateful to the Hilles Fund and to the Yale Provost's Office for their support of this volume. TB

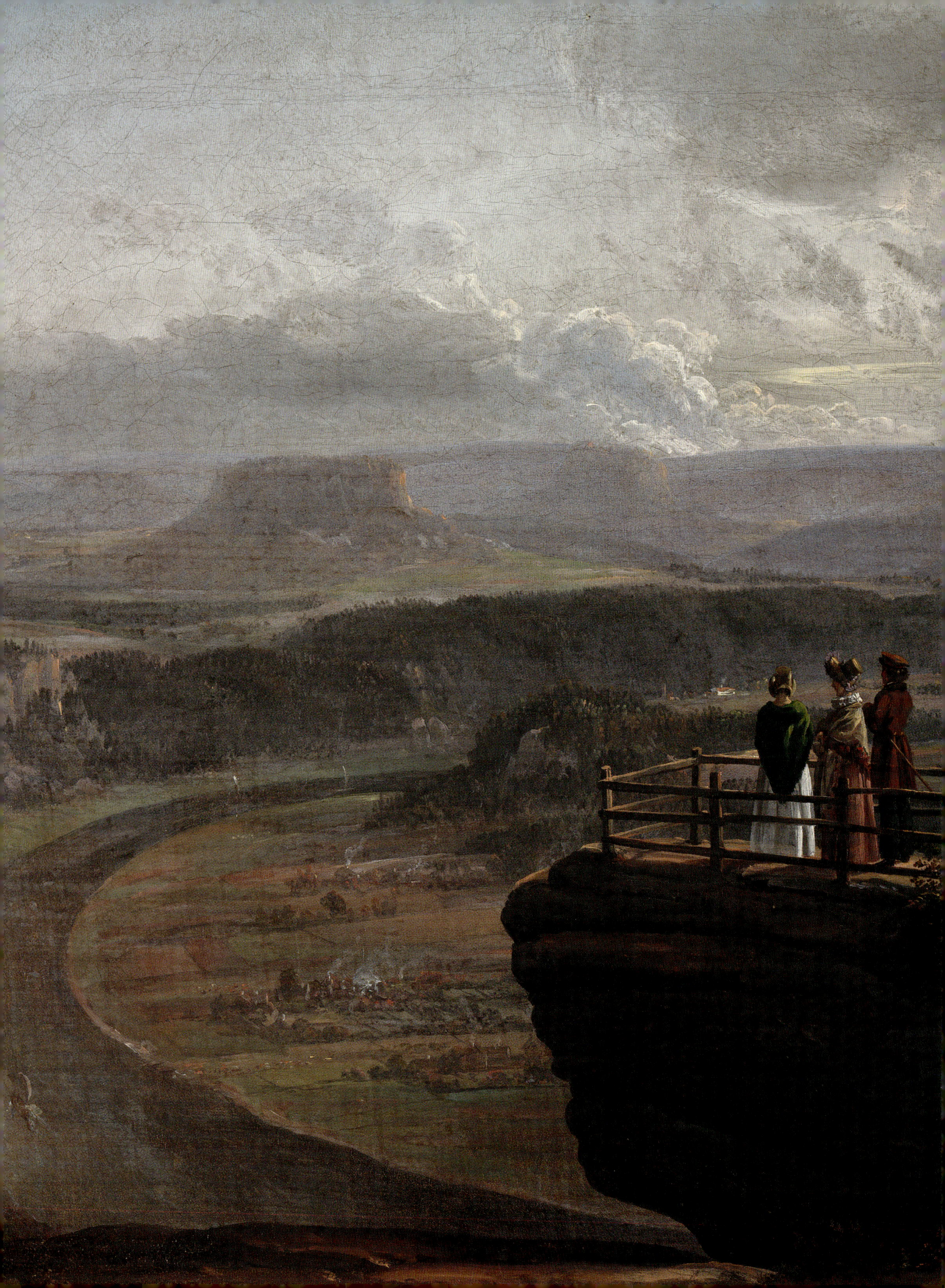

KATIE TRUMPENER AND TIM BARRINGER

Introduction

Setup of the panoramas: Viewed from a raised platform, surrounded by a balustrade, of surfaces lying round about and beneath.

—Walter Benjamin, *The Arcades Project* (written 1927–40)

At the center of a circular Edifice . . . and covered with a conical roof, stretches an isolated platform . . . surrounded by a balustrade; this platform obliges the Spectator to remain, in all his movements, at a certain distance from the circular fortification wall. . . . The first impression one perceives is of an immense view, but confused, with all points-of-view offering themselves simultaneously and without order to the dazzled eye.

—Citizens Vincent, Regnault, et al., "On the Panorama," Report of a Special Commission of the French Académie des Beaux-Arts (28th Fructidor, Year 8 [1800])

Yesterday evening I went to see [Adam Breysig's] famous panorama of the city of Rome. It seems in fact to owe its fame merely to its novelty. . . . The first half of the word [panorama] means something like: *from all sides, round about*; the other half something like *see, to see, something seen.*

—Heinrich von Kleist to Wilhelmina von Zenge (August 16, 1800)

[My fiancé] begged me to put my [racetrack] winnings into the [Sydney] Cyclorama and gold mines; but I had no wish to make my fortune, and merely laughed. The Cyclorama was a large circular structure of canvas. Round the walls were painted scenes of the battle of Waterloo. There was a clear space in the middle of the floor, and old cannons and dummy bodies of dead and wounded soldiers and a lot of rubbish was heaped around you. The trick was that, looking at the walls, you could not tell where the models left off and the painting began. It seemed ever so far away. A man stood on a little platform, with a pointer which he used while following the battle round. Until you had seen the Cyclorama you were nobody, and the shares went up by leaps and bounds.

—Agnes Stokes, *The Autobiography of a Cook*, describing Australia in 1901

Fig. 0.14 detail

You know what a panorama is, don't you? They were one of the attractions that were still extremely popular in Japan when I was an elementary school student. To see it, you first had to pass along a narrow, pitch-black passageway. And the moment you emerged from it, suddenly a field of vision, a world, lay before your eyes. A world completely different from the world the spectator had been living in up to that moment. A perfect, self-contained world as far as the eye could see.

What a surprising trick! Outside the panorama hall, streetcars were running, stalls were selling goods, eaves of merchant houses were lined up, and townspeople were passing to and fro the same way as yesterday, today, and tomorrow. I could pick out my own house. . . . But once I stepped into the panorama hall, all of those things disappeared, and the wide Manchurian plains extended as far as the distant horizon line. And there a gory battle, frightening to behold, was being waged. . . .

There's a world outside the building. And a world inside the building. And the two worlds have their respective grounds and skies and horizon lines. . . . The double worlds of the streets and the plains exist in the same spot.

—"Edogawa Ranpo" (Tarō Hirai), *The Strange Tale of Panorama Island* (1926)

Jeff Wall's 1993 photograph *Restoration*—a luminous transparency some sixteen feet wide—testifies to the spectacular scale of nineteenth-century panoramic paintings and their enormous, complex, fragile apparatus (fig. 0.1). The panorama's purpose was to create, from the viewing platform, a completely convincing illusion of reality. Although enclosed within a rotunda's bounded space, viewers could enjoy vistas reaching to infinity in all directions, an unprecedented immersive experience. In his 1787 patent document, the panorama's Irish inventor, Robert Barker (1739–1806), defines it as providing "an entire view of any country or situation, as it appears to the observer *turning quite round.*"[1] By revealing a nineteenth-century panorama layout, Wall engages in astute media archaeology, paying homage to the significance of the panorama in the interwoven histories of painting, photography, and cinema.

Wall's own image is unmistakably panoramic in scope and format. The panorama's legacy inflects contemporary culture from art installations, film, and digital media to literature, architecture, and landscape design. Yet as Wall himself acknowledges: "A panorama can never really be experienced in representation, in any other medium. I made a 180-degree panorama photograph of a 360-degree picture, so had to show only half of it. The geometry of that struck me as appropriate, harmonic, one to two. It expresses the fact that the panorama was unrepresentable."[2] Unlike Wall's photograph, the panorama cannot be seen all at once. It surrounds and enfolds the viewer. Yet even as it promises a total representation of reality (to quote Jonathan Crary in chapter 2), it "introduces partiality and incompleteness as constitutive elements of visual experience."

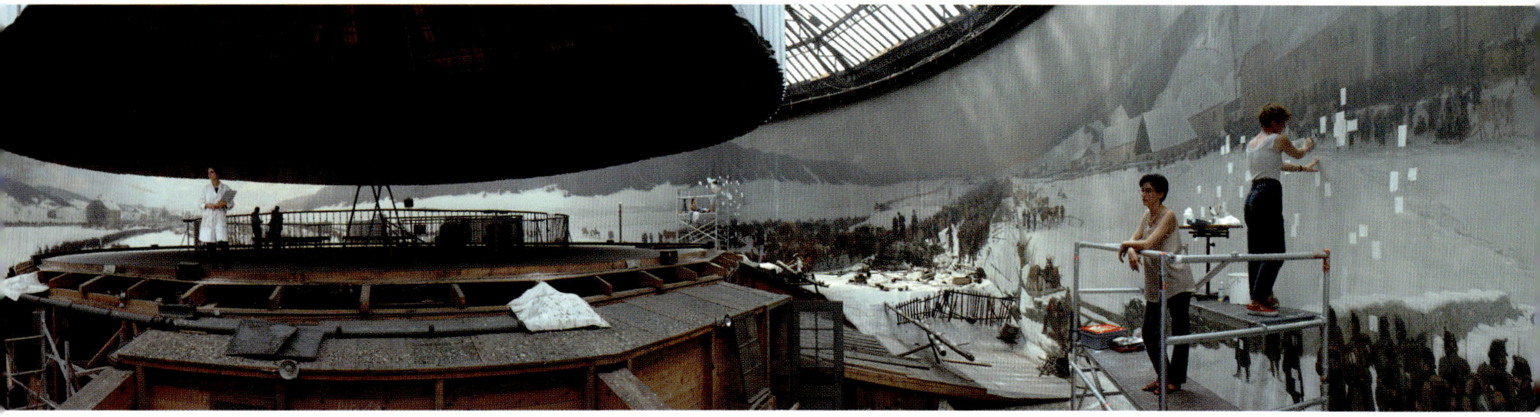

FIG. 0.1. Jeff Wall (Canadian, b. 1946), *Restoration*, 1993. Transparency in lightbox, 119 × 489.6 cm (46 3/4 × 192 3/4 in.).

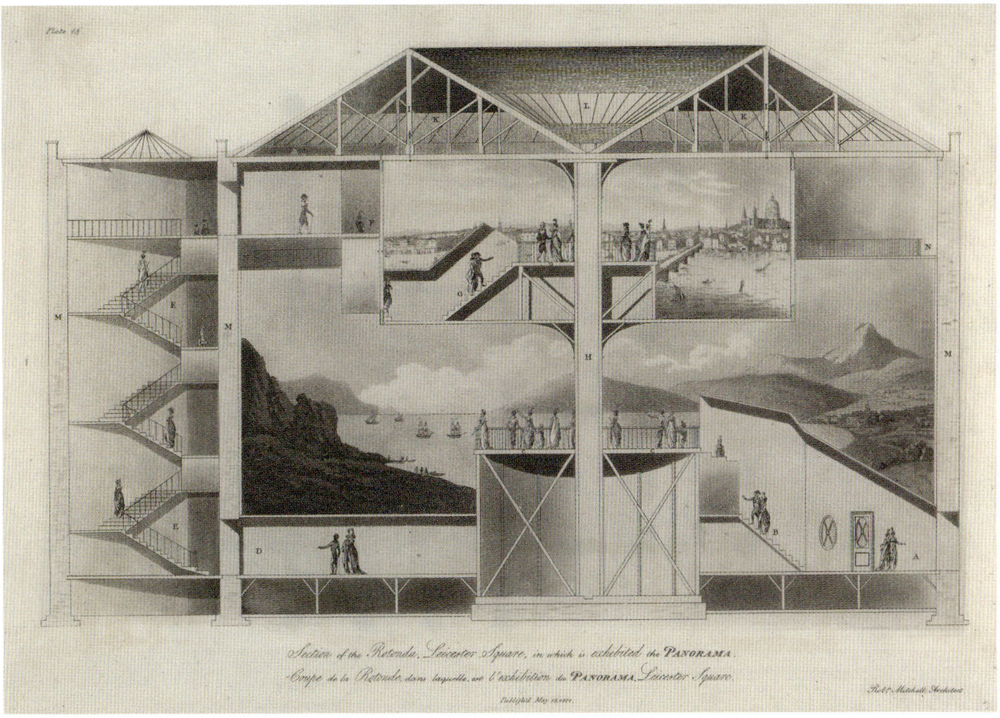

FIG. 0.2. Robert Mitchell (British, active 1782–1809), *Section of the Rotunda, Leicester Square, in Which Is Exhibited the Panorama,* from *Plans, and Views in Perspective, with Descriptions, of Buildings Erected in England and Scotland* (London, 1801). Aquatint. Yale Center for British Art, New Haven, Connecticut, Paul Mellon Collection.

Although a plethora of objects and practices have been described as "panoramas" or "panoramic," the neologism *panorama* (from the Greek *pan,* meaning "all," and *horama,* meaning "view") was coined in 1791 to describe these massive circular paintings, installed in specially constructed rotundas. A paying public viewed them from a central platform. As Wall's photograph deftly reveals, panoramas were lit from above by skylights, screened from viewers by a large, umbrella-like canopy: the view of the painting, through 360 degrees, was unimpaired.

Barker's first panorama was exhibited in Edinburgh in 1787, although the name he initially used—*La nature à coup d'oeil*—did not catch on; the form reached maturity with the opening, in 1793, of a full-scale panorama in London's Leicester Square. In his *Section of the Rotunda, Leicester Square, in Which Is Exhibited the Panorama,* published in 1801, Robert Mitchell (English, active 1782–1809) indicates the ingenious architecture whereby two panoramas could be displayed simultaneously (fig. 0.2).

The panorama is unusual, Franz Schiermeier points out, in its unity of space and content, reliant on its vast, pillarless, circular building to ensure unimpeded sightlines and elicit a sense of sublimity.[3] Fundamental to panorama form, from its beginnings, was the "visual no-man's-land" and the "intervening emptiness" consistently separating platform from canvas and key, Philippe Dubois has argued, in balancing the panorama's simultaneous illusion of distance and proximity.[4]

Yet from about 1830 onward, later panoramas, including the painting Wall photographed—the *Bourbaki Panorama* in Lucerne, executed in 1881 by Édouard Castres (Swiss, 1838–1902) and an army of assistants (fig. 0.3), and restored by 2003 to something approaching its original condition—included "faux terrain" with realia (fig. 0.4), three-dimensional sculptural elements filling the space between canvas and viewing platform. Carefully arranged to accord with the perspectival scheme, these solid forms only added to the reality effect panoramas generated.[5] The influence of Louis Daguerre's dioramas was equally palpable in late nineteenth-century panoramic exhibitions featuring changes in lighting, sound effects, and the occasional introduction of wind, steam, and mist, even mechanically rotating platforms, slowly turning viewers 360 degrees at "imperceptible" speed.[6]

At the panorama's inception, Barker established another crucial element of panoramic experience. Customers would pass through a relatively inauspicious entrance, pay a small fee (one shilling in Barker's establishment), move along a dark corridor, and climb a flight of stairs—before emerging into another world, a virtual reality. On the viewing platform, early panorama visitors were habitually overwhelmed by the wonder of what

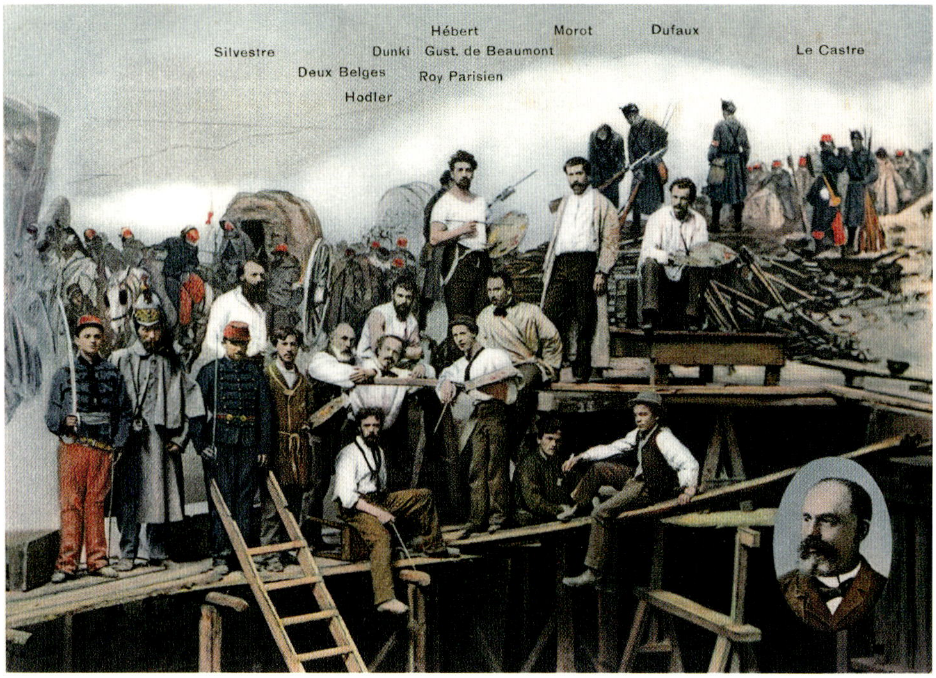

FIG. 0.3. The painters (including Ferdinand Hodler) of the *Bourbaki Panorama* with several models. The inset features the master artist Édouard Castres.

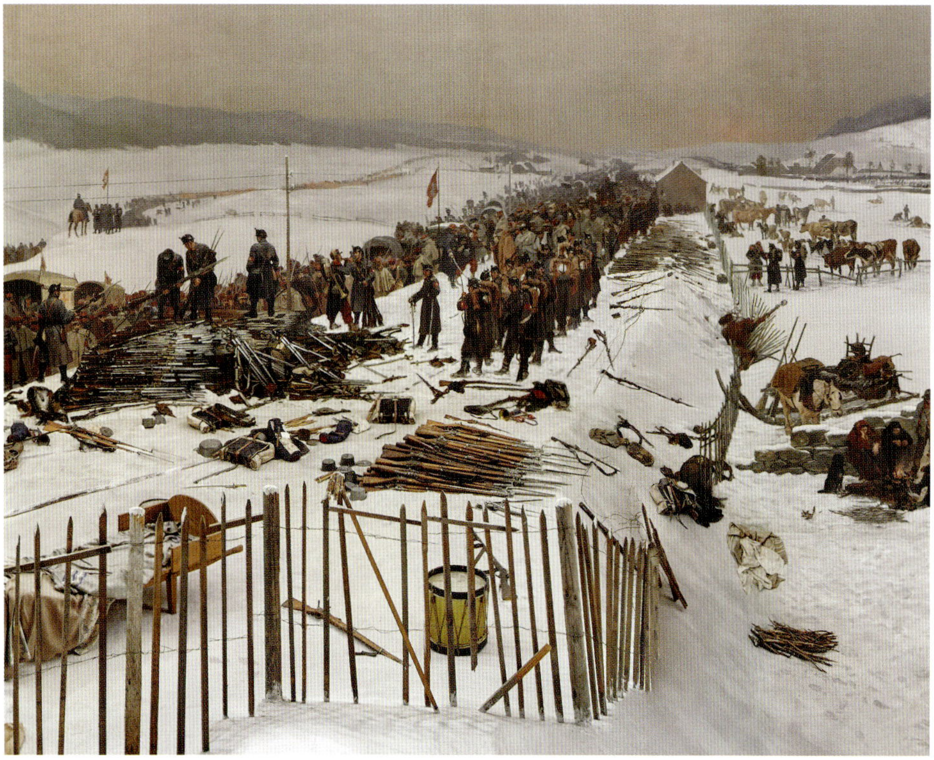

FIG. 0.4. Édouard Castres (Swiss, 1838–1902), *Bourbaki Panorama* (detail), 1881. Oil on canvas, 14 × 112 m (45 × 367 ½ ft.).

they beheld and often subject to strong physiological responses: gasping, fainting, feeling "shackled with iron bands" (the German aesthetician J. A. Eberhard) or (in the case of Queen Charlotte confronting a maritime panorama) seasick.[7]

But such physical and sensory unease was also the result of the panorama's novelty in bringing together different, hitherto unrelated visual protocols and perspectival vantage points. The secure vanishing point and reassuring framing devices familiar from landscape painting are lost.[8] The panorama elicits a sense not so much of mastery as of epistemological uncertainty, despite the artful deployment of trompe l'oeil effects, manipulated lighting, careful perspectival shading, and spacing. The panorama might present picturesque views of distant, exotic places, uncannily detailed views of familiar places, or battlefields and religious sites imbued with patriotic and spiritual meaning.[9] Yet, regardless of its subject, the viewer struggled with the panorama's immensity and circularity, the perceptual uncertainties inherent in its form: as Ludwig Börne noted in 1831, "You hover between shock and admiration [Man schwebt zwischen Schrecken und Bewunderung]."[10] Panoramic form affected some viewers spiritually: Achim von Arnim thus describes his 1809 Berlin visit to Karl Friedrich Schinkel's Sicilian panorama as a "sacred hour in Palermo."[11]

Wall's *Restoration* subtly undermines the essential character of panoramic experience by revealing the artifice creating so persuasive an illusion, making visible the very aspects on whose invisibility the panorama's success was premised. Wall nudges the viewing platform, darkly shadowed, to the left of his composition: two tiny figures are standing within it, surrounded by cast-iron fencing. The white-clad conservators intervene in the space between painting and viewing platform, violating the illusion and revealing the painting's flatness. The authors of this book insist, by contrast, on resituating the viewing platform as the center of analysis, restoring the magical suspension of disbelief that allows even modern audiences, sated with digital-age high-definition and three-dimensional imagery, to marvel at the painted panorama.

A powerful work of art in its own right, the *Bourbaki Panorama* meditates on the futility of war, but also, Katie Trumpener argues in chapter 7, on the moral ambiguities of Swiss neutrality and thus of the viewing platform itself. This collection's title hence calls particular attention to the panorama's ostensibly empty center, the platform with its attendant spectatorial satisfactions, anxieties, ambiguities, immersions, and detachments, its potential for both collective aesthetic and idiosyncratic epistemological experience. One way or another, each chapter explores the visitor's viewing experience, alongside the visual, conceptual, social, and political possibilities of the virtual world perceptible from the platform.

Yet whose vantage point, exactly, does the viewer inhabit, on and from the viewing platform? On one level, that of the panoramic artist himself. From the early modern period onward, artists had sought out hilltops, towers, or promontories from which to sketch (and later to photograph) panoramic views. If no suitable tower existed, panoramists sometimes custom-built one: in the 1880s the Milwaukee panorama studio commissioned to paint a Battle of Atlanta panorama erected a forty-five-foot tower on that Civil War battlefield, from which its German-American artists made preliminary sketches for several months. And in Australia, in 1895, Bernhardt Holtermann (1838–1885) built a tower from which to shoot his panoramic photograph of Sydney Harbor.[12]

By the late nineteenth century, some master panoramists positioned themselves on the viewing platform to supervise teams of fellow painters executing in situ panorama painting or restoration.[13] Max Bernstein's 1887 article "About a Panorama: A Chat" takes viewers behind the scenes, showing them the process by which a panorama—here the crucifixion rendering of Bruno Piglhein (German, 1848–1894)—is commissioned, researched, painted, and exhibited. The accompanying vignettes by Friedrich Wahle (German, 1863–1927) include the mixing of colors (fig. 0.5), the building of faux terrain around the viewing platform (fig. 0.6), viewers "On the Podium" contemplating the finished painting (fig. 0.7), and (as the article's frontispiece) the panoramic rotunda itself, from outside, anchoring an expansive, brisk, but uncrowded sense of the urban flow (fig. 0.8).[14] In Bernstein and Wahle's rendition, the panoramist skillfully directs the construction of a *Gesamtkunstwerk* itself integrating painting, installation, and urban surround, crucifixion and secular city. The panorama and its platform give the fortunate viewer—and now the reader—wide vistas, new prospects.

Twentieth-century panorama theorists, in contrast, have viewed Wilhelmine panoramas, and the viewing platform, with retrospective suspicion, weighing issues of political and military power. Dolf Sternberger (writing in 1938) and Oliver Grau (writing in 2002) both exemplify the panorama genre with the widely toured (although now long-lost) *The Battle of Sedan,* painted in 1883 to designs by Anton von Werner (German, 1843–1915). For both Sternberger and Grau, von Werner's use of the viewing platform evokes the elevated vantage points from which generals typically viewed and directed their battles, high enough to give them an overview of a complex, shifting situation, and far enough away to ensure their own physical safety, even in the heat of combat. For Sternberger, the panoramist creates his illusion in "the expectation of an observer who, as if standing on the generals' promontory, scours the scene with a telescope."[15] Grau further postulates that the viewer implicitly feels the generals' presence or spirit, hovering on the platform. Yet for Grau this does

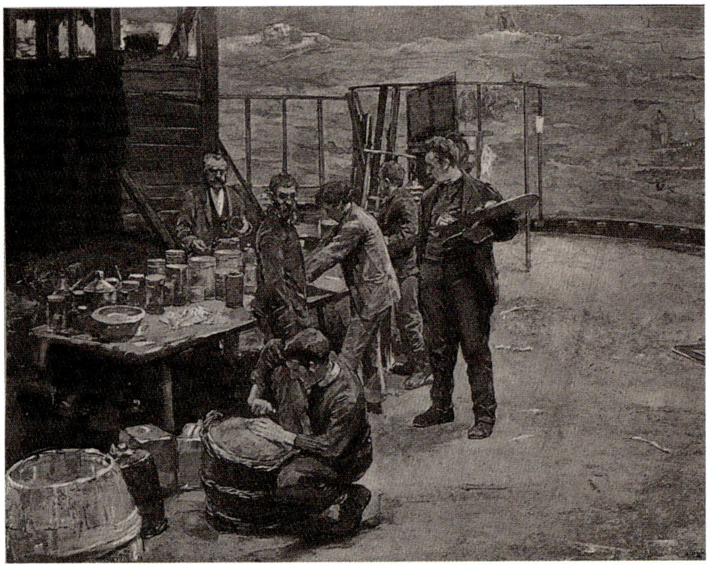

COUNTERCLOCKWISE FROM TOP LEFT:

FIG. 0.5. Friedrich Wahle (German, 1863–1927), *Beim Farbenreiben*, from Max Bernstein, "Von einem Panorama: Plauderei," *Die Kunst für alle: Malerei, Plastik, Graphik, Architektur* 2, no. 7 (1887): 107. Heidelberg University Library.

FIG. 0.6. Friedrich Wahle, *Terrainbau*, from Max Bernstein, "Von einem Panorama: Plauderei," *Die Kunst für alle: Malerei, Plastik, Graphik, Architektur* 2, no. 7 (1887): 108. Heidelberg University Library.

FIG. 0.7. Friedrich Wahle, *Auf dem Podium*, from Max Bernstein, "Von einem Panorama: Plauderei," *Die Kunst für alle: Malerei, Plastik, Graphik, Architektur* 2, no. 7 (1887): 109. Heidelberg University Library.

FIG. 0.8. Friedrich Wahle, *Vor dem Panorama*, from Max Bernstein, "Von einem Panorama: Plauderei," *Die Kunst für alle: Malerei, Plastik, Graphik, Architektur* 2, no. 7 (1887): 106. Heidelberg University Library.

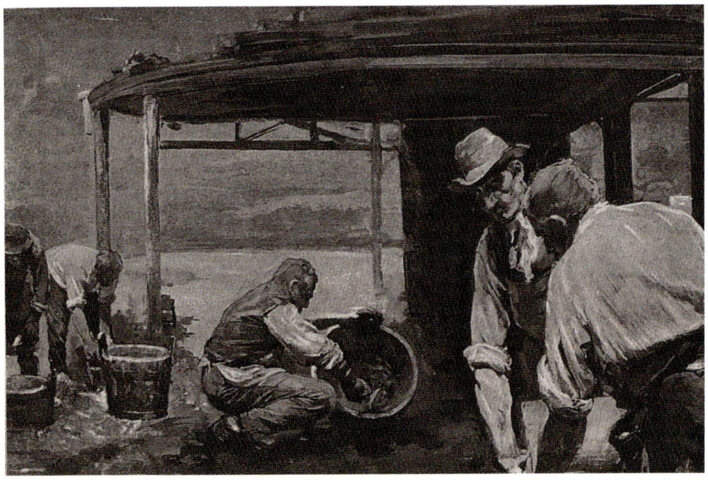

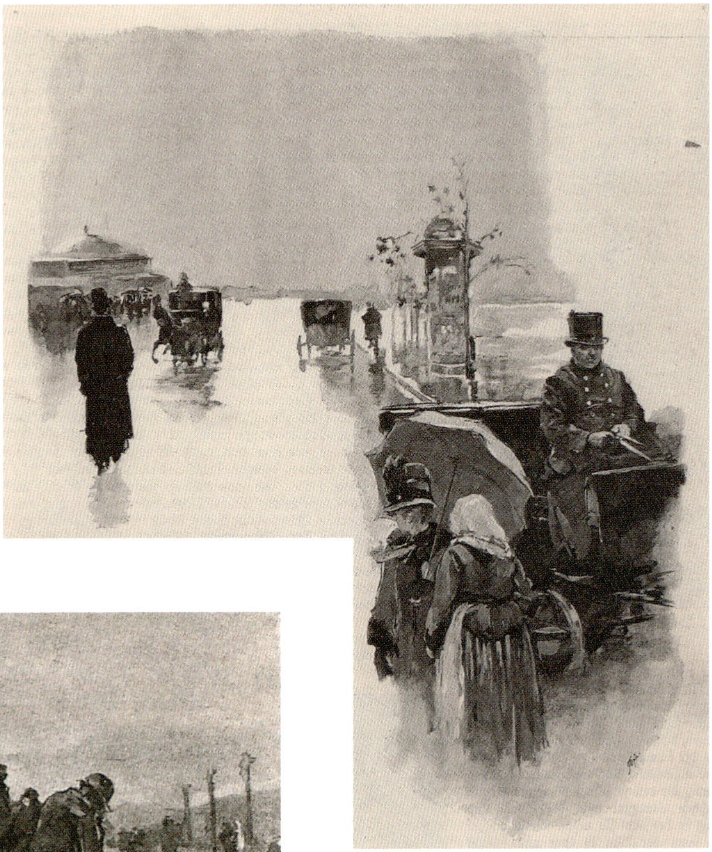

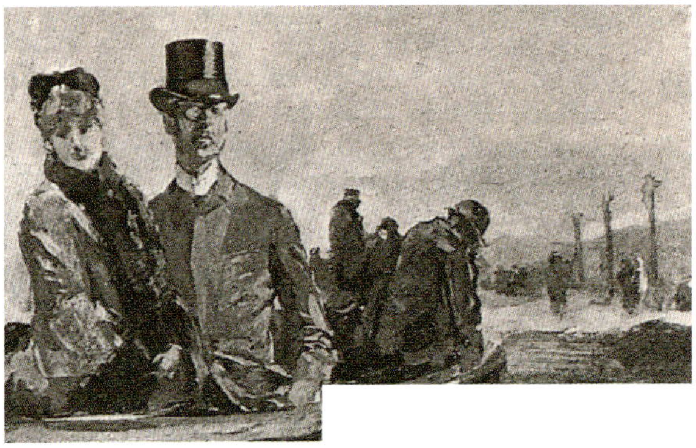

not impart visual mastery to viewers so much as it visually or psychologically reinforces a hierarchical social order in which viewers feel personally watched over by "the supreme commander, the king, with his sovereign view . . . still above him."[16]

The panorama's historic origins include the strategic views drawn by draftsmen, sometimes explicitly for military leaders, to inform troop movement and battle strategy.[17] (Such connections remain fully visible in much nineteenth-century panoramic photography, especially in colonial contexts). Yet the politics and power dynamics of panoramic vision, this book will argue, are nonetheless complex and varied, sometimes shifting, even over the course of a single viewing. Already in two drawings accompanying his 1799 French panorama patent application, Robert Fulton showed male and female viewers leaning over the balustrade and strolling across the viewing platform, while dotted lines showed their potential range and variability of vision from any given position (fig. 0.9). Christian Gottfried Heinrich Geißler's 1815 watercolor of visitors on the viewing platform likewise emphasized viewers' polydirectional gazes: on the left, adults and a boy look straight out at the scene, their pointing fingers reinforcing their lines of vision, while on the right, two additional children stand much closer to the edge of the view, looking downward over the edge. Geißler (German, 1770–1844, himself a sketcher and etcher of panoramic landscape and battle scenes) here presented five viewers all looking at the same vista but from different angles, from varying heights, and in different ways (fig. 0.10).

Unlike framed canvases on museum walls, the panorama encases the viewer within both a performative and a receptive three-dimensional space. Is the panorama visitor merely a spectator or also a performer, expressively treading or pacing the boards of the circular viewing platform?[18] Is the panorama-as-installed a visual and social theater, demanding traversal, consumed actively, in motion, the visitor performing a distinctive dance of discovery? Panorama owners, Vance Byrd emphasizes, sometimes sought to direct and calm viewers' gazes; while faced with an immense picture, viewers were sometimes guided by the presence of a live panorama explainer, as well as by printed keys with numbered views that explicated one vista after the next. Potentially sharpening viewer glances into more pointed gazes, this piecemeal but detail-oriented mode of visual sense making, Byrd argues, had consequences for nineteenth-century reading practices.[19]

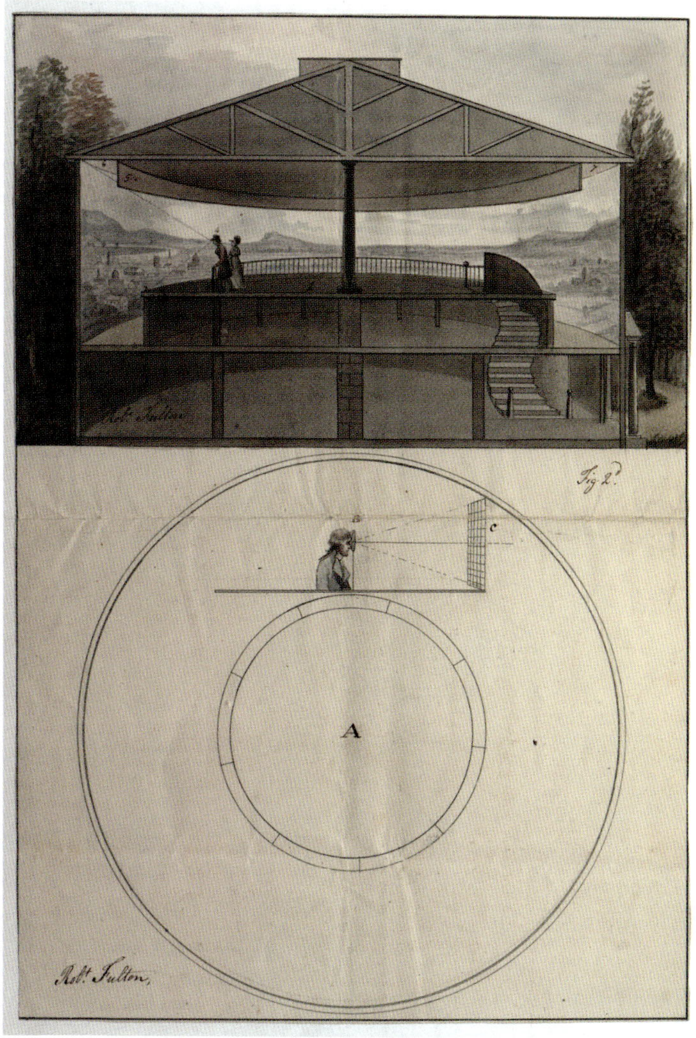

FIG. 0.9. Robert Fulton (American, 1765–1815), *Preparatory Drawing for a Brevet d'Importation: Tableau Circulaire, Nommé Panorama*, 1799. Ink-and-wash drawing. Institut National de la Propriété Industrielle, Courbevoie, France (1BA88).

And yet as John Sweetman argued elegantly in 1981, the panorama as a mode of art succeeds, fundamentally, "by diffusion rather than concentration of interest."[20] "The panorama makes it necessary to move one's head and assimilate a vast, indeed often continuous, area of canvas which defied the logic of any conventional painting with an easily-grasped focus of attention."[21] In this it runs counter to much of the Western art tradition: hence, Sweetman argues, its recurrent stimulus for Western artists over several centuries.

For Dubois, indeed, the panorama's center

> is the spectator (not the painted image). More precisely, it is his gaze around which the whole apparatus arranges itself theoretically, pictorially, and

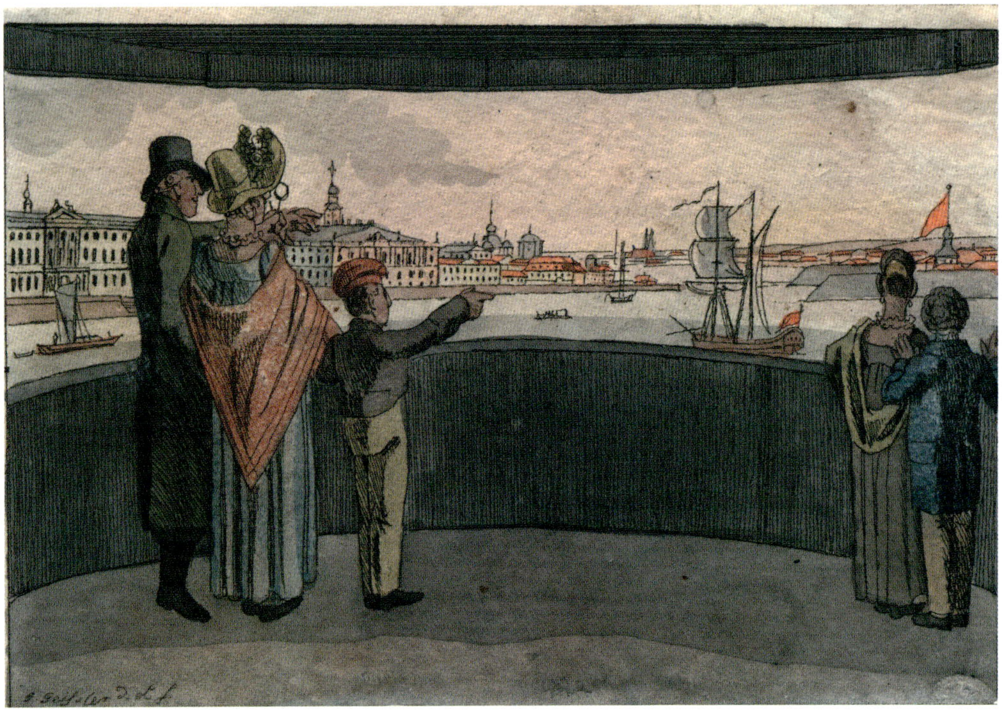

FIG. 0.10. Christian Gottfried Heinrich Geißler (German, 1770–1844), *Das Panorama*, 1815. Colored etching on paper, 11 × 13.8 cm (4 3/8 × 5 15/16 in.). Stadtgeschichtliches Museum Leipzig (Gei II/31 b).

> architectonically. It is a unique point of view constituted as a pivot. The panorama makes the spectator's gaze [*regard*] its central object, literally staging it, on that raised and bordered platform, like a pedestal from which the spectator can exercise his "panoramic view," as if he were in nature, preferably on a mountain, on an observation point from which all the world offers itself up to him in all of its vastness. . . . The spectator, nodal point [*noyau*] of a representation conceived as an apparatus as much as an image, is immersed in an image spectacle.[22]

Yet in an essay rebutting and nuancing Dubois, Michel Frizot also insists on viewers' necessary mobility around the viewing platform: "Visual taking possession cannot occur without perambulation."[23] In excavating the first panorama's popular reception in London, indeed, Markman Ellis quotes a 1793 fictional letter from "Jenny Gadabout" published in the *St. James Chronicle*, which argued "Panorama" should instead be spelled "Pon-a-roam-a," for the invited audience members to "set out upon a roam," exploring distant places rendered oddly proximate.[24]

Eric de Kuyper and Émile Poppe stressed the artificiality of the panoramic view and the "totalizing obsession" of the panoramic apparatus, carefully concealing its own illusionism while banishing the possibility of comparing the scale or content of the view to any other visual surface.[25] Josh Ellenbogen instead emphasizes the panorama's surfeit of visual information. The sequential scanning used to take in a normal-size painting will not work with a painted panorama, for this "does not claim to be organized around a main focus, but instead to hold the infinity of all possible foci available to an observer" (although at any given moment many such foci must in fact be neglected).[26]

Michael Devine argues for the "fundamental communal stability at the heart of the panorama"—the sense of viewers brought and viewing together, in community.[27] Yet because each viewer is potentially ambient, possibly making a circuit of discovery unlike anyone else's, each might also feel perceptually alone, stranded despite others' physical presence, and ontologically uncertain how and where to look next. Indeed, despite its ostensible stasis—its picture freezing a historical moment, its dioramic elements inanimate (fences, piles of rifles), dead (tree stumps), or stuffed (taxidermied mammals)—the panorama can be understood as a mode of theater with the fourth wall removed, enabling and indeed insisting on a mode of transport, visual and psychic engagement that pulls spectators out of their comfort zone, forces them to share the stage, and pushes them to perambulate the platform and in the process to determine for themselves an order of seeing, to reestablish at least a temporary hierarchy of meaning.

ON THE VIEWING PLATFORM

The essays and vignettes gathered here collectively claim for the circular panorama a significance exceeding other early forms of mass culture. Three-hundred-sixty-degree panoramic paintings constitute a pioneering, paradigmatic, visual manifestation of modernity—"one of the places in the nineteenth century," Crary argues in this volume, "where a modernization of perceptual experience occurs." We propose the panorama, moreover, as an early form of installation art, drawing on the emerging conventions not only of art gallery exhibition but of theatergoing, naturalistic staging, scenic wallpaper, touristic sightseeing, recreational hiking, world's fairs, and museal display (in reimagined natural history, ethnographic, and open air museums).[28]

This volume, accordingly, falls into three sections. Following this introduction, a series of short vignettes, each a close reading of an individual work, maps out the terrain of the panoramic, including some important precursors and some limit cases, which define the boundaries of the panorama. The opening vignettes are placeholders for what could be a separate, massive history of proto-panoramic forms. As Timothy Hyman shows, the aesthetic characteristics of the famous Sienese fresco *The Well-Governed City* (1337–40) by Ambrogio Lorenzetti (ca. 1285–1348) foreshadow circular panorama painting's visual effects. Marina Warner examines *The Prospect of Constantinople* (1559), the eleven-foot-long wood engraving by Melchior Lorck (German-Danish, 1526/1527–after 1583). This prospect drawing prefigures the laterally expanded and information-laden vistas of other lands that became nineteenth-century panorama painters' stock-in-trade, containing, like Lorck's work, elements of fantasy and make-believe alongside hard data. We fully acknowledge the presence of proto-panoramic elements across the history of Western art and also (to an extent that defies summary) across world cultures. Chinese and Japanese scroll and screen paintings offer two obvious instances.[29] These storied artistic genres, with their complex history and historiography, fascinated eighteenth- and nineteenth-century Western artists—as they do panoramically minded contemporary painters such as David Hockney (British, b. 1937).[30]

The remaining vignettes hone in on key issues explored in the longer chapters: the relationship between the panorama and imperialism; panoramic photography; and limit cases of panoramic painting, including the sprawling stairway fresco *History of Mexico* (1929–35) by Diego Rivera (Mexican, 1886–1957) and the *Sandham Memorial Chapel* (1926–32) by Stanley Spencer (British, 1891–1959), with its wraparound, visionary army scenes. A final group of vignettes gestures toward the ubiquity of the panoramic in contemporary art, a recurrent theme in this collection.

Two substantial groups of essays constitute the book's main body. Part I, "The Painted Panorama: Immersive Aesthetics," offers expository and interpretative accounts of extant and lost nineteenth-century panoramas while exploring ways the panorama and panoramic modes of seeing became imbricated in nineteenth-century artistic production. These essays pay particular attention to the panorama viewer's subjective experience in relationship to broader questions of nation, empire, and modernity.

Part II, "In (and beyond) the Cinema," examines panoramically inspired film and installation art; early panoramic photography and cinema provide a hinge between the two sections. In its sense of duration, Dubois has argued, the panoramic photograph provides a missing link between the static photograph and time-based cinema: it already represents "cinema in the photograph."[31] This book provides an even longer historical and medial arc. Close examination of the painted panorama's perceptual effects and ideological implications, it demonstrates, can enhance interpretations of more contemporary manifestations of panoramic vision and perception, even as recent developments in film, video, and installation shed important light onto the historical panorama.

PERSPECTIVES ON THE PANORAMA

Recent years have seen a veritable explosion of archival and theoretical scholarship on nineteenth-century painted panoramas. This burgeoning literature rests on a handful of foundational studies, largely by German scholars. Yet so far no account has offered much critical analysis of the shape, agenda, or rhetoric of earlier scholarship. This short sketch can trace only the outlines of that critical history—in hope of catalyzing more sustained scholarly retrospection.

The modern field of commentary begins with two competing critical works, much-cited but perpetually elusive: Dolf Sternberger's *Panorama of the Nineteenth Century* (*Panorama, oder, Ansichten vom 19. Jahrhundert*), published in Germany in 1938, and Walter Benjamin's unfinished *Arcades Project* (*Das Passagenwerk*), written 1927–40, partly in Paris, during Benjamin's self-imposed exile from Germany. The metaphor of panoramic seeing—and "A Panorama," Sternberger's introductory essay on von Werner's *Battle of Sedan*—anchors Sternberger's cultural history of nineteenth-century Europe. At least in retrospect, the essay's interest in von Werner's patriotic, military standpoint, in the complexity of historical timing and placement and in the phantasmagoric, disorienting nature of panoramic viewing, seems linked to Sternberger's uneasy, vertiginous relationship to his own Third Reich context.[32]

Yet more brilliant and capacious, Benjamin's *Arcades Project* likewise takes the panorama as a crucial organizing metaphor for the vastness yet knowability of social life in nineteenth-century Paris—and devotes one of its thirty-six "Convolutes" (folders) to panoramas, in a wide range of nineteenth-century manifestations. *Arcades* is magisterial, yet incomplete, perhaps unfinishable, partially lost, and only partially reconstructable—epitomizing Barker's original description of the panorama as a revelatory series of glimpses, disjointed yet cumulatively coherent.[33]

Sternberger and Benjamin set crucial yet destabilizing precedents for the field. Both strain at the limits of what it is possible to describe and reconstruct. For complex methodological and political reasons, Sternberger meditates on a specific panorama that was widely influential but did not survive, producing an ontological description of the panoramic that ignores empirical viewers and the viewing experience.[34] The actual panorama painting-and-installation as a concrete aesthetic object, indeed, cedes to the phantasmagoric panorama as a vehicle for philosophical speculation.

The next wave of scholarship proved more empirically anchored. Heinz Buddemeier's 1970 German-language sourcebook, *Panorama, Diorama, Photography: The Emergence and Impact of New Media in the Nineteenth Century*, traces the interconnection and cumulative arc of nineteenth-century media forms.[35] Far more influentially, Stephan Oettermann's *The Panorama: History of a Mass Medium* (originally published in German in 1980) offers a well-documented, forcibly argued social history of the panorama, organized along national lines, and particularly effective on the medium's late nineteenth-century Continental manifestations. And on a smaller scale, François Robichon's 1983 "Le panorama, spectacle de l'histoire," mines historical sources to offer both a political economy of the panorama and ideological account of its spectatorship in nineteenth-century France; subsequent French visual theorists (Jacques Aumont, Philippe Dubois, Michel Frizot) would analyze the panorama as *dispositif* (apparatus)—the term used by Michel Foucault to describe institutional mechanisms and structures of knowledge that support the exercise of power in society.[36]

Oettermann links the panorama's rise to the emergence of a hegemonic middle class: following Foucault, he pairs the invention of the panorama with Jeremy Bentham's panopticon prison, that exactly contemporaneous innovation of utilitarian criminology. The overlap has preoccupied panorama theorists ever since. As Dubois stresses, the panorama paradoxically houses its "image without limits" within a "closed structure," and it creates a "total environment" with potentially carceral effects for the viewer.[37] Alan Wallach compellingly reads American landscape paintings in light of a "panoptic sublime":

> Having reached the topmost point in an optical hierarchy, the visitor experienced a sudden access of power, a dizzying sense of having suddenly come into possession of a terrain stretching as far as the eye could see. The ascent of a panorama tower was in this respect a stunning metaphor for social aspiration and social dominance. . . . The panoptic sublime drew its explosive energy from prevailing ideologies in which the exercise of power and the maintenance of social order required vision and supervision, foresight and, especially, oversight—a word equally applicable to panoramic views and to the operation of the reformed social institutions of the period: the prison, the hospital, the school, and the factory.[38]

Yet, as Tim Barringer argues in this volume, Wallach's argument slips between watcher and watched. The panopticon's intrinsic visual logic remains at odds with the panorama: whereas the panopticon subjected a body of criminalized individuals to a regime of surveillance (with a few anonymous servants of the state, mere functionaries, representing the "eye of power"), the panorama affords the mass public a commercial product proffering a euphoric, if potentially deceptive, freedom of vision.[39] Those subject to ideological interpellation by the apparatus of the panorama are not watched or overseen but stand themselves on the viewing platform, perhaps enjoying an illusory sense of authority. Subjective aesthetic experience played no role in Bentham's panopticon: it was intended to transform those being watched, not those looking. Dominant ideologies are promulgated in both cases, but by opposing means. The panorama viewer was a consumer of ideology through visual spectacle, a scenario closer to Adorno and Horkheimer's dystopian "culture industry" than to Bentham's repressively reformist state apparatus.[40]

Bernard Comment's art-historical survey, *The Panorama* (published in French in 1993), concentrated on the panorama's aesthetic, rather than sociopolitical, ramifications, highlighting the role of individual panoramic artists. Comment's publishers served the field well by offering excellent color reproductions of what has become the canon of surviving panoramas.[41] Franz Schiermeier's beautifully designed *Panorama München: Illusion und Wirklichkeit. München als Zentrum der Panoramenherstellung*, published in 2009 by Munich's City Archive, offers a historical survey and political economy of panorama manufacture in one of its European hubs.[42]

Yet it is only with works like Denise Blake Oleksijczuk's 2011 *The First Panoramas: Visions of British Imperialism* that panorama studies began to include sustained close readings of aesthetic form. Oleksijczuk's sophisticated exposition of the painted panorama's early history links the works of Robert and Henry Aston Barker (British, 1774–1856) to the history of the British Empire, whose transition to a position of global dominance was exactly coeval with the new art form's emergence. Oleksijczuk's account is notable for her close attention to panoramas' engraved keys, distributed to viewers to identify topographical and other compositional features (see fig. 1.20). In many cases, these formally innovative engravings constitute our only extant record of particular paintings' appearance.

Scholars have had difficulty accessing such rare materials, which often survive in lone copies. Laurie Garrison's 2013 five-volume anthology, *Panoramas, 1787–1900: Texts and Contexts*, with introductions and explanatory notes, makes available a new wealth of primary information and images, especially for English and American panoramas. Other crucial sources for the study of the early panorama include watercolors, drawings, exhibition guides, and other printed ephemera. Ralph Hyde's 1988 Barbican Art Gallery exhibition catalogue, *Panoramania! The Art and Entertainment of the "All-Embracing" View*, remains the most significant publication dedicated to these graphic sources; Byrd's 2017 *Pedagogy of Observation: Nineteenth-Century Panoramas, German Literature, and Reading Culture* explores the traces panorama culture left in nineteenth-century German journalism and literature.

The medium's later history is chronicled in photographs. Yet there was also a vast, worldwide tradition of panoramic photography, whose nineteenth-century history has been explored, in recent decades, by revelatory exhibitions and publications mounted by key institutions, including the Canadian Centre for Architecture, the Freer Gallery, the J. Paul Getty Museum, Washington's National Archives, and São Paolo's Instituto Moreira Salles.[43]

The 1993 Bonn exhibition *Sehsucht: Das Panorama als Massenunterhaltung des 19. Jahrhunderts* positioned the painted panorama at the center of a richly populated landscape of nineteenth-century optical innovations, devices, and amusements.[44] Two subsequent exhibitions—"Panoramas: The Brazilian Landscape in the Instituto Moreira Salles" (shown in Brazil in 2011) and "J'aime les panoramas: S'approprier le monde" (shown in Geneva and Marseilles in 2015)—explored the panoramic across painted, sketched, and photographic media, juxtaposing unusually wide-ranging historical materials. The Instituto Moreira Salles used panoramic representations of Brazil to meditate on the country's place in the European Romantic painting itinerary and indigenous self-representations, the ideologies of horizon, scale, landscape, and modernization itself: the catalogue's final image, one of the startling 1910 photopanoramas taken in Recife by Francisco du Bocage (Brazilian, 1860–1919), surveys ruined colonial-era buildings, razed to erect modern infrastructure.[45]

"J'aime les panoramas" offered a celebratory, even indulgent amalgam of graphic media, juxtaposing early panoramic technologies with modern work by contemporary artists. Joachim Bonnemaison's 1993 fish-eye lens photographic series thus revealed debts to the history of the panorama, given the images' uncanny similarity to eighteenth- and nineteenth-century circular panoramic diagrams. A plenitude of photography and film stills gave the exhibition a compelling through-line from the eighteenth century to the present; moving seamlessly between periods and cultures, it lacked the historical specificity and close readings crucial, for instance, to Oleksijczuk's account and to historians of early photography.

The "J'aime les panoramas" catalogue achieves brilliant effects through its quirky page size (only 6 ¼ inches wide but 12 ¼ inches high) and layout (two 1790s William Hodges paintings, for instance, sharing a spread with a formally similar montage of NASA photographs from the first moon landing).[46] Such juxtapositions register the insistent presence of the panoramic in contemporary culture and its rootedness in a long history of optical devices and artistic experiment.[47] Yet the exhibition's selections also establish the panorama's direct influence on a wide range of modern artists. As a young man, the Swiss modernist Ferdinand Hodler (1853–1918) worked on the team painting the *Bourbaki Panorama* (painting himself as one of its French soldiers).[48] Even decades later, his own late, horizontally oriented landscapes remain deeply preoccupied with panoramic perspective. Yet so do elongated canvases by artists from Caspar David Friedrich (German, 1774–1840) to Paul Cézanne (French, 1839–1906), Vincent van Gogh (Dutch, 1853–1890), and Gerhard Richter (German, b. 1932), echoing the ways panoramas organized and partitioned their views for the eye.

Recently, Peter Otto and Renzo Dubbini have proposed new critical paradigms for understanding the panorama's cultural meaning. Their form, Dubbini argues, emerged even as industrialization and new metropolitan spaces and movement were shattering the panorama's unified vision.[49] The hyperreality of the panoramic medium, Otto argues, called attention to its status as illusion—leaving audiences with the sense of the contingency of all perceptual worlds.[50] It also weakened viewers' sense of borders.

Media scholars have placed the panorama in equally broad contexts. Vanessa Schwartz's *Spectacular Realities: Early Mass Culture in Fin-de-Siècle Paris* (1999) places the panorama phenomenon within a wide span of cultural entertainments, including the boulevards' social spectacle, the morgue's public presentation of corpses, waxworks, and popular wood-engraved illustrations.[51] Alison Griffiths's *Shivers Down Your Spine: Cinema, Museums, and the Immersive View* (2008) proposes a genealogical investigation into cinema history organized as "case studies in immersive spectatorship." Griffiths's title refers not to the "venerable genre of the horror film but . . . the report of a panorama spectator in 1799 describing his response to the giant circular painting."[52] While careful to avoid a simple teleology in which the panorama becomes merely cinema's linear ancestor, Griffiths offers extended comparisons across time. As in the medieval Gothic cathedral, Griffiths notes, the spectator viewing a Crucifixion "feels co-present at the event," experiencing the scene's "here-and-nowness."[53]

Of the many objects, installations, and devices known as the panorama, scholarly attention—and this volume's first half —has focused primarily on the large-scale 360-degree paintings and their legacy in visual culture.[54] Following Sternberger, Grau's stimulating *Virtual Art* uses von Werner's Sedan panorama to explore the form's aesthetics, ideology, economics, and production history, and it situates painted panoramas within an extended tradition of illusionistic art, stretching from antiquity to present-day virtual reality. (Computer modelers and designers, indeed, are newly interested in the perspectival construction of panoramic spaces.[55]) Beginning with Greco-Roman wall painting, Grau then links the panorama to Baroque trompe l'oeil theatrical spaces.[56] Yet as Oettermann underscored, actual Baroque theaters organized their sightlines for the absolute monarch, in his royal box; the panorama's visual and—to Oettermann, more democratic—political logic refuses to cede the prime viewpoint to any single individual.[57]

Among the questions still awaiting thorough investigation are the ways panoramas (and dioramas) influenced theatrical design and vice versa. As Gustav Solar pointed out, key innovators in a panoramic vein, including Canaletto (Italian, 1697–1768) and Johann Adam Breysig (German, 1766–1831), came from theatrical families or engaged in theatrical design.[58] Dubois compares the void separating the viewing platform from the circular painting with the sunken orchestra pit in Italian theater architecture; Arno Mungen traced panoramic influences on Richard Wagner's *Parsifal* staging.[59] Kurt Forster has explored the way Karl Friedrich Schinkel (German, 1781–1841) moved between architecture, urban planning, panorama painting, and set design; and Wendy Bellion, the movement of Charles Willson Peale (American, 1741–1827) between portrait painting, panoramic sketches, and conceiving the first American museum.[60]

Yet we still may not understand what it meant for Louis Daguerre (French, 1787–1851) to invent the diorama alongside the daguerreotype, for Giovanni Segantini (Italian, 1858–1899) both to paint quasi-panoramic paintings and to design a cyloramic building to hold them, or, indeed, for the Spanish-Venetian designer Mariano Fortuny y Madrazo (1871–1949) both to invent a panoramically inflected theatrical lighting system (the Fortuny cyclorama dome, which gave backdrops apparently infinite depth) and to take panoramic photographs, alongside the avant-garde historicist fashion (and light) design for which he is now remembered.[61]

We might consider the development, for instance, of Romantic or late nineteenth-century painting not only in the context of national schools and institutions but also in terms of the panorama spurring parallel thinking in a range of places, among otherwise disparate artists. In terms of panoramic interest, at least, Peale overlaps with Schinkel, Friedrich, C. W. Eckersberg (Danish, 1783–1853), and Johan Christian Dahl (Norwegian, 1788–1857); and two generations later similar synergies can be discerned between Segantini and Fortuny, Gustave Caillebotte (French, 1848–1894), Edvard Munch (Norwegian, 1863–1944), and even Henri Matisse (French, 1869–1954).

The media archaeologist Erkki Huhtamo has pressed for "excavations of the moving panorama" and the reassessment of this almost forgotten but "true 'multimedia' phenomenon" in the face of what, to him, seems an overemphasis on the circular panorama.[62] The "moving panorama" was an itinerant medium, moving from town to town, yet during each show the audience remained static, seated in an auditorium: "A long roll painting was moved across a 'window' (often with drawable curtains) by means of a mechanical cranking system. The presentation was accompanied by a lecturer, music, and occasionally sound and light effects."[63] Huhtamo details the moving panorama's technological history—and influence as a performative popular culture genre, linked to further forms of dioramic and stereoscopic display, anticipating key visual and narrative characteristics of twentieth-century motion pictures and central dynamics of cinematic spectatorship.

Yet despite their use of a shared term, as Huhtamo himself demonstrates, the moving panorama had a largely separate genealogy from the 360-degree paintings and their descendants discussed in this book. The film theorist Jacques Aumont, too, firmly insisted the genres were "entirely different." The 360-degree panorama offers a deeply immersive experience; for Aumont its crucial innovation is "the history of its apparatus" and the way it "reproduces two major experiences recounted in the travel narratives of the late nineteenth century: that of the horizon and that of the vanishing point."[64] The moving panorama has recently begun attracting serious art-historical attention.[65] Yet for the last two centuries, as this volume details, it is the circular panorama that has retained particularly profound resonances for the fine arts, still haunting the avant-garde.

Especially in its second half, this collection moves beyond the painted panorama to examine analogous forms, including the diorama, the international exhibition building, and the multimedia installation, and to investigate panoramic effects in film and photography whose location is not limited to a single structure. We follow Walter Benjamin in identifying the panorama not only as a key historical phenomenon but also as a significant metaphor for modernity itself. Two panoramas opened in Paris in 1799, followed a year later by Paris's first arcade, the Passage des Panoramas, leading directly to these exhibition spaces.[66]

The arcade thus connected to and extended the panorama. Benjamin placed panoramas alongside Paris's glass arcades as paradigmatic nineteenth-century forms, noting the panorama's cascading influence in twentieth-century visual culture. "The high point in diffusion of panoramas coincides with the introduction of arcades. One sought tirelessly, through technical devices, to make panoramas the scenes of a perfect imitation of nature. An attempt was made to reproduce the changing daylight in the landscape, the rising of the moon, the rush of waterfalls. . . . In their attempt to produce deceptively lifelike changes in represented nature, the panoramas prepare the way not only for photography but for [silent] film and sound film."[67]

In the 1930s Benjamin's own *Arcades Project* gathered a wealth of fragments relating to panorama and cognate forms, enumerated in a list as euphoric as euphonious: "dioramas, cosmoramas, diaphanoramas, navaloramas, pleoramas (*pleō*, 'I sail,' 'I go by the water'), fantoscope[s], fantasma-parastases, phantasmagorical and fantasma-parastatic *expériences*, picturesque journeys in a room, georamas; optical picturesques, cinéoramas, phanoramas, stereoramas, cycloramas, *panorama dramatique*."[68] If this book's contributors look far beyond Paris for an expanded definition of modernity, they nonetheless owe much to Benjamin's pioneering—and tragically incomplete—enterprise in critical cultural analysis and his embrace of the nineteenth century's astonishing and often phantasmagoric plurality.[69]

This book emphasizes the mobile nature of nineteenth-century panoramic experience, building on Benjamin's influential discussion of motion as key to modern urban experience, as on Crary's discussion of "ambulatory ubiquity."[70] The panorama, we have argued above, should not be conflated with the moving panorama—or with the panopticon because panoramic form encouraged viewers not to practice surveillance but to remain physically and psychically exploratory and expansive, if politically compliant.

In 1810, impressed with a panorama he had visited in

Paris, Napoleon instructed his architect to erect several rotundas along the Champs-Élysées to house panoramas honoring his own military victories, paintings that, he imagined, might tour the capitals of Europe as they fell under French domination.[71] This project was never realized, as it was overtaken by actual military campaigns. Had it been, the panorama itself might have become a rather different sort of institution, linked almost from the outset to state ideology and to an official, ceremonial, static monumentalism. Belatedly, indeed, the medium did take on the role of an official state apparatus in fin-de-siècle Japan, the Soviet Union, 1970s Bulgaria, and present-day China and North Korea.[72]

For the most part, however, it continued to be a form conceived, financed, and erected by commercial entities. And the paintings circulated, reaching broad, transnational, even transcontinental audiences. The panorama business itself had transnational overtones: invented by an Irishman in Scotland who found success in London, the panorama was introduced to Paris by Americans (including Robert Fulton, the subsequent inventor of the steamboat). The panoramic painting of Versailles by the American neoclassical artist John Vanderlyn (1776–1852), first shown in New York in 1819 (and now housed in the Metropolitan Museum), commemorates a meeting between European rulers and "suggests an international identity for the visitors on the grounds."[73] In 1885 one enterprising Austrian panorama painter persuaded eight further German and Austrian panoramists to emigrate with him to Milwaukee, which thus became the epicenter of American panorama production.[74]

As André Meyer has argued, the distinctive structure of the panorama building exemplified functional architecture, generally built solely to enhance panoramic presentation, and sometimes temporary in fabrication. By the later nineteenth century, nonetheless, these rotundas were increasingly conceived as quasi-national monuments, historicist shrines to tradition created in self-conscious dialogue with the circular buildings, piazzas, and atria of the ancient and Renaissance world, even as they became showcases for new iron-and-glass construction methods.[75] In these paradoxes, they represent a quintessential, if still understudied, form of nineteenth-century architecture.

Over the twentieth century many cyclorama buildings were repurposed as skating rinks, circuses, or parking garages, their history sometimes visible only in their facades.[76] Worldwide, only a handful of nineteenth-century buildings survived as panoramic display venues. Even in recent years, despite protests from preservationists and the International Panorama Council, high-profile "restorations" of Lucerne's and Innsbruck's panoramas involved fundamentally altering—or abandoning—their traditional buildings, and at Gettysburg prolonged preservationist attempts failed to save the much-admired modernist cyclorama designed by Richard Neutra (Austrian American, 1892–1970). Neutra's rotunda was commissioned by the Park Service in 1958 to display the Battle of Gettysburg panorama by Paul Philippoteaux (French, 1846–1923). It housed the panorama from 1962 to 2005, when the Park Service decided to remove all modern structures from the battlefield. In 2013, after years of pleas, lawsuits, and protests from the National Register of Historic Places, the Park Service razed Neutra's building (fig. 0.11).

Yet the broader legacy of panoramic architecture, Sylvain Malfroy underscores, remains palpable in modernist architectural and urban planning.[77] It has simultaneously influenced many aspects of a widely diffused, now long-naturalized visual culture. Obvious examples include Zeiss projection planetariums (pioneered in 1923), alongside the 1857 British Museum Reading Room designed by Sydney Smirke (British, 1798–1877), the 1928 Stockholm Public Library designed by Erik Gunnar Asplund (Swedish, 1885–1940), and the 1928–31 Viipuri Library designed by Alvar Aalto (Finnish, 1898–1976), with their circular, book-lined conspectuses or allegories of the organic interpenetration of human knowledge, in Aalto's case led up onto by a panorama-like staircase. Further relevant structures include the panoramically circulating moving sidewalk elevated above and around the 1900 Paris Exposition; the projected *Monument to the Third International* designed in 1919–20 by Vladimir Tatlin (Russian, 1885–1953); and revolving theaters (built in Finland and Czechoslovakia from 1959 onward) and revolving restaurants (pioneered in Germany in 1959, popular worldwide in the 1960s and still functioning in Des Moines, Edmonton, Potosí, Tashkent, Abu Dhabi, Iran, and Uganda).

IMMERSIVE EXPERIENCE AND VIEWER RESPONSE

Although the scholarly literature on the nineteenth-century panorama is large and growing, this collection sets different emphases and stages new departures. Some chapters offer pioneering close readings of surviving panoramas, offering extended accounts of what the viewing

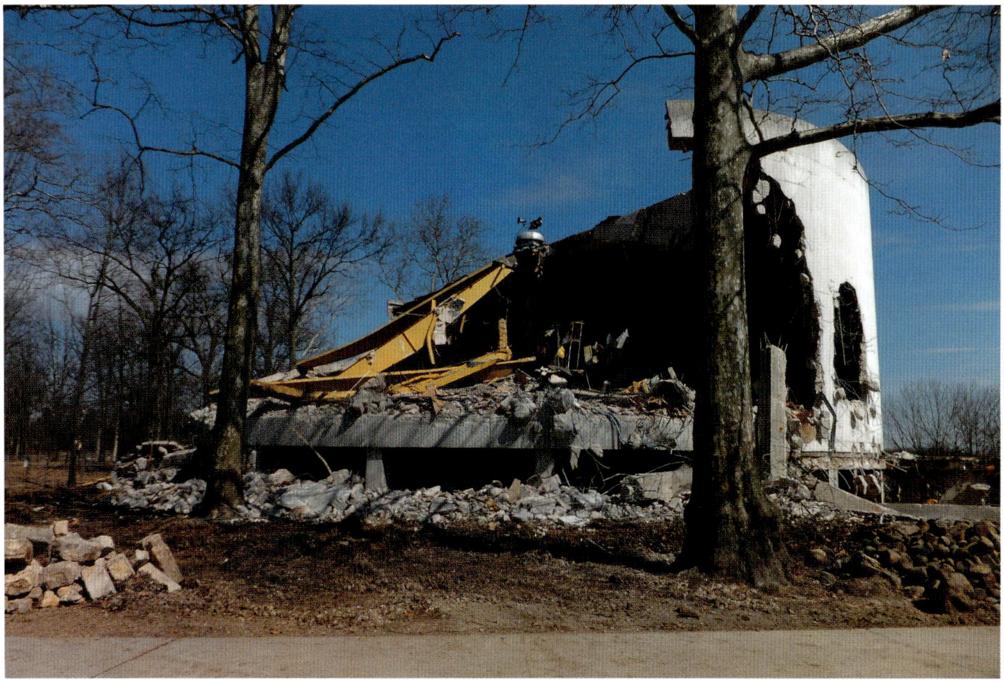

FIG. 0.11. Demolition of the Cyclorama at Gettysburg, 2013.

experience *feels* like to those actually, then as now, in their physical presence, viewing them publicly and collectively. Existing literature has largely ignored the key issue of spectatorship; technical and ideological considerations have tended to overshadow experiential and aesthetic ones, the viewers' feelings of presence and "ambulatory autonomy" on the viewing platform.[78]

Toward the end of the nineteenth century, panoramas began striving for ever-greater verisimilitude effects. In 1901 visitors to Sydney's Battle of Waterloo cyclorama were thus regaled with drumrolls and cannon and gunfire sounds, and they emerged "with their eyes streaming from the thick cloud of gunpowder smoke which filled the tent."[79] And as the French caricaturist (and "panoramic" science fiction writer) Albert Robida (1848–1926) emphasized in his satiric drawing *Panorama de la bataille de Champigny* (1882), viewers of the era's ubiquitous new battle panoramas were subjected to simulated versions of battle conditions, emerging potentially traumatized (fig. 0.12). In Robida's dystopic alternative version of an actually displayed contemporary panorama, viewers were pushed to comprehend siege conditions by being forced to remain on the platform for three days, fed only one herring per day, drenched by simulated rainstorms, and frightened and occasionally even hit by exploding shells. Robida's cartoon is framed by viewers (at top) stumbling through the dark entryway into the panorama, and (at bottom) charging the exit in military formation. But in the middle, as a shell severs a viewer's torso from his legs, fleeing viewers bend and burst through the restraining rail enclosing the viewing platform, itself blasted apart by explosions and reverberation. Viewers who make it to the exit, a note suggests, deserve a military medal. Those responsible for such panoramic display, Robida implies, are as sadistic and irresponsible as those actually waging war.[80] Metaphorically, at least, it is the panoramic effect itself, with its simulation of violence, that impinges violently on the spectatorial space, making it explode and flattening its thin railings, which can no longer even pretend to shield viewers from the abyss of war, the cataclysm the panorama represents and enacts.

For modern-day visitors, the African American poet Yusef Komunyakaa suggests, the experience of viewing nineteenth-century battle panoramas occurs in a register not of active trauma so much as of profound, emotionally moving disorientation. Komunyakaa's 2007 poem "The Panorama" evokes a visit to the Battle of Racławicka panorama in Wrocław, Poland; originally painted for the 1894 National Exhibition in Lemberg (present-day Lviv), Jan Styka and Wojciech Kossak's work depicts a key clash during the 1794 Kościuszko Uprising, in which insurrectionist soldiers and peasants armed only with scythes temporarily defeated the Russian army in their struggle for Polish independence.[81] Thrust into the turmoil,

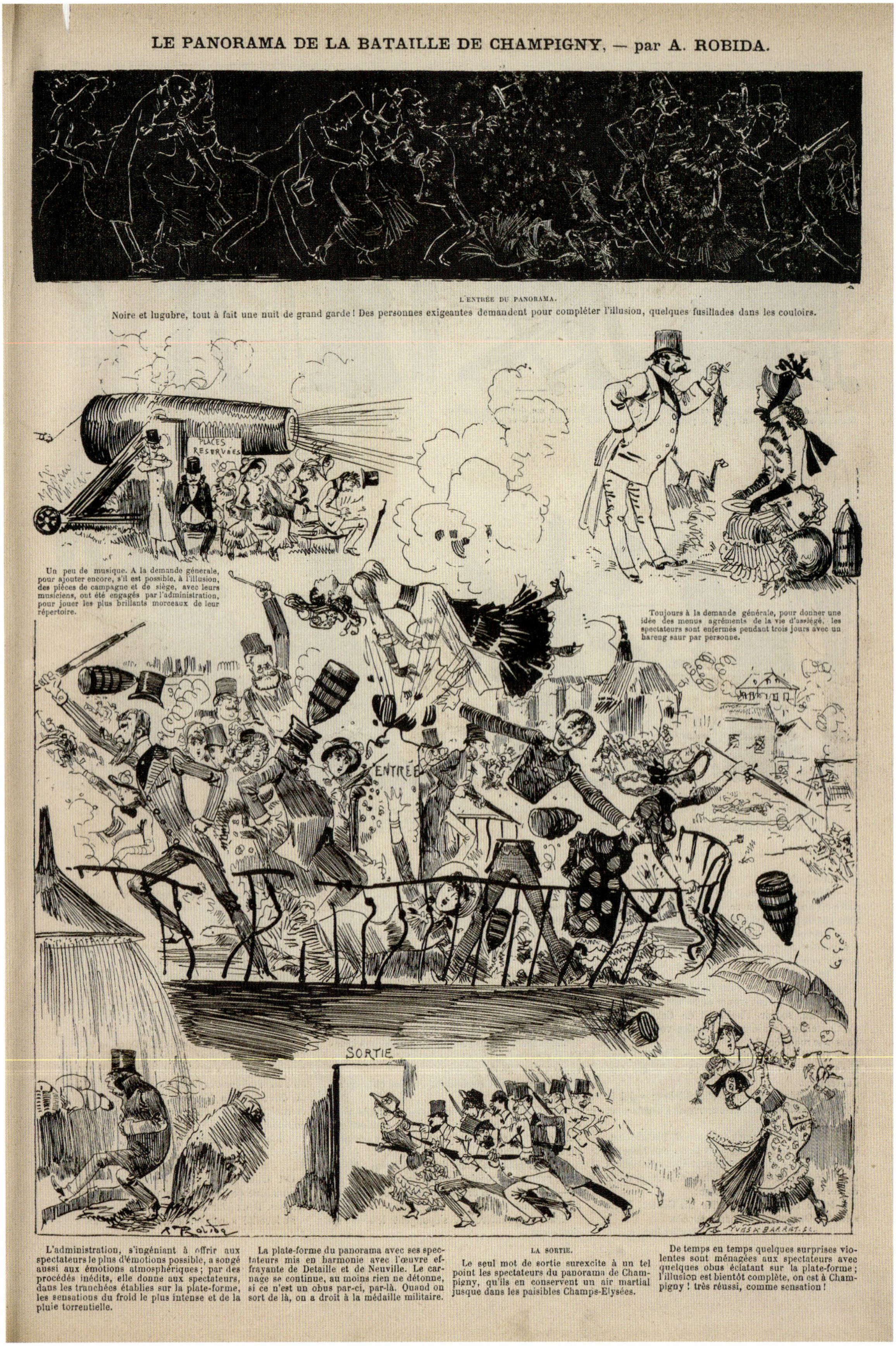

FIG. 0.12. Albert Robida (French, 1848–1926), *Panorama de la bataille de Champigny, La Caricature* 133 (July 15, 1882): 229. Bibliothèque Nationale de France, Paris.

Komunyankaa's viewers struggle to understand what they are seeing.

> It seems we've slowed down the spinning earth,
> standing in this rotunda, holding each other's hand,
> encircled by colors. But there's so much blood
> up there I can't tell where the false terrain begins. . . .
> The open-air light makes it hard to tell if the tall whitish
> birches are real or painted.

Initially, the viewer is drawn into the painting but resists that pull by worrying about how its trompe l'oeil effect is created, how the realia create the illusion of one level of reality yielding to another. That resistance crumbles, however, as the viewer explores the painting's action and suffering, feeling oddly, painfully at one with the "peasants on the canvas wall." The collective experience of viewing becomes subsumed into the feeling of becoming personally embedded in the circular canvas, alongside its historical protagonists. The panorama not only engulfs the viewer but induces powerful if disoriented historical identification, even a moment of synesthesia or auditory hallucination.

> We stand there
> as if attacked from front & rear, from left & right,
> cavaliers caught in a waterfall of hues, momentarily
> silenced, & I can hear only a battlefield trumpet,
> calling & calling, desperately calling.[82]

When panoramas took on nationalist subjects, they potentially became iconic—but also opened themselves to heightened official scrutiny. Thus, attempts to travel to the Racławicka battlefield to make preparatory sketches for the panorama were initially blocked by the Russian military occupiers of the region. Wary of fueling the movement for Polish self-determination; the military later refused to allow publications about the panorama to circulate in areas it controlled, and it impeded travel to view the panorama. Yet this only heightened national reverence for the panorama.[83]

But even when their subject matter and presentation were patriotic, panoramas generally treated paying spectators as discrete consumers and free agents rather than interpellating them as loyal citizen-subjects. Throughout the nineteenth and well into the twentieth century (as the cultural historians François Robichon, Vanessa Schwartz, Mark Sandberg, Alison Griffiths, Jonathan Crary, and Lauren Rabinowitz have detailed), panoramas and panoramic attractions became linchpins of urban visual pleasure districts, and arguably also of a distinctive visual regime.[84] Unlike Oettermann's absolutist theater, in which the king's seat or loge was by design the only vantage point of optimal vision, urban spectacles like the panorama remained ambulatory, opt-in, self-paced, plural, contingent, visited freely and open-endedly.

In recent decades, when surviving nineteenth-century panoramas are reinstalled in new or refurbished buildings, they almost always find themselves surrounded by newer forms of media. Lucerne's new panorama complex houses a separate cinema and multimedia center. And pilgrims to Gettysburg's new Visitor Center can reach the panoramic viewing platform only en masse, by escalator—from a movie theater where an introductory documentary about the battle is projected onto a narrow, semicircular screen. Viewers' actual encounter with Philippoteaux's nineteenth-century painting is thus mediated not only by an accompanying son-et-lumière display but by explicit filmic training in how to isolate details—a far cry from nineteenth-century visitors' unguided, overwhelmed perambulations on the viewing platform.[85]

ART HISTORY, THE PHOTOGRAPH, AND FILM HISTORY

This volume intervenes in fields that, despite their obvious adjacency, have engaged too little with each other's methods and arguments: art history, the history of photography, and film studies. Until recently, art historians eschewed the panorama and the panoramic as manifestations of popular culture, beyond the canon of acceptable subjects of study. The photograph, too, has occupied an interstitial position, troubling categories of high art with a mode of representation that inherently tends toward the demotic. Theatrical and meretricious, the panorama has been thought to represent a corporate pandering to public tastes, in contrast to the ideal of the solitary artist's quest for self-expression under conditions of adversity. We challenge this account, arguing that the panorama was in constant conversation, from its inception, with the genres of high art and, indeed, that many of the pioneering artists of modernity absorbed its lessons.

Like the photograph, the panorama complicates accounts of modern art that are premised on the framed oil painting as the key to the emergence of a market-driven, commodified art world.[86] As a communal experience, the panorama served much as an art exhibition might, to create a new public, but it did so through a shared experience of a single massive image from the viewing platform, rather than through the participation in a market for the acquisition of commodities, such as the individual works shown at the Paris Salon or London's Royal Academy.[87]

And although early panoramas were sometimes the work of a single artist, later panoramas were executed, in most cases, in large ateliers, by teams of painters, even if such collective work was partly mystified behind the name of its leading and titular author.[88] Like film, often celebrated as the creation of auteur directors or great actors, panoramas tended rather to be a studio art, produced for most of their era on an industrial scale.[89]

Film studies has traditionally been concerned with the psychology, ontology, and cognitive processing of cinematic seeing, with the nature of film language, with the work of auteur directors (and cinematographers), and with the economic framing and technological transformation of film production. In recent decades, revelatory new scholarship has explored the emergence of early cinema from nineteenth-century and fin-de-siècle visual culture, along with subsequent paradigm shifts in cinematic production and spectatorship (from the birth of the studio system and the advent of "talkies" to the postwar incursion of television, new forms of virtual reality, the contemporary "death" of celluloid, and the proliferation of new platforms for audiovisual delivery).

The essays here draw on a myriad of important theoretical and historical accounts of film form, social history, and (gendered) viewing practices. Important essays by photographic historians (David Harris, Josh Ellenbogen), art historians (Angela Miller), and film historians and media theorists (Jacques Aumont, Tom Gunning, Philippe Dubois, William Uricchio) have closely examined the continuities—and disconnects—between photographically based medial forms and the painted panoramas that preceded them.[90] Their work has been all the more significant given film studies' relative neglect (with the notable exception of work on avant-garde film) of the many formal and institutional links between cinema and painting, performance and installation art—or even film and photography. This volume thus represents a still rare conjuncture between art, photographical, film historical, and film theoretical work.

Panoramic effects were attempted from the earliest days of photography. Although it was many years before technology allowed photographic prints or projections to grow to a scale rivaling large panorama paintings, early photographers and their audiences were fascinated by the lateral extension of the photographic field, generally by joining prints from different negatives and arranging them to give a single, unbroken panoramic image. The uncanny impression that the camera's unselective indexicality produced on its earliest viewers was only heightened when the field of vision was expanded beyond the human eye's peripheral field. The effect of impossibly multitudinous detail created by the early painted panoramas was now heightened, but on a miniature scale.

The photographic panorama, moreover, could register the operations of capital in their most naked form. As Andrew Vielkind describes in chapter 10, Eadweard Muybridge (British American, 1830–1904) took his 1877 and 1878 panoramas of San Francisco from Nob Hill, from the turret of a mansion still under construction. The land, divided into plots, is undergoing a transformation of astonishing speed and violence: the city is coming into being before our eyes. A more ambitious second panorama was assembled from a series of massive negatives, exposed between 11:00 A.M. and 4:00 P.M. Foreshadowing the motion pictures' conventional direction of the panning camera, Muybridge rotated his camera clockwise, producing thirteen massive negatives. Rather than preserving the scene in a single snapshot, Vielkind notes, Muybridge made his panorama as separate frames with an interval of time between each one and the next, inevitably recording the passage of the sun overhead as it cast shadows at different angles during the day's progression. In contrast to the painted panorama, whose even light purports to depict a single moment (even as the changing light through the skylights animates the scene), Muybridge's panorama chronicles the passage of time, providing a direct link to the moving pictures that emerged in subsequent decades. Vielkind adduces Muybridge as a significant precedent for the experimental films Ernie Gehr (American, b. 1944) has made since the 1970s, in which the movie camera's unblinking eye traverses the city, most spectacularly in *Side/Walk/Shuttle* (1991), from the vantage point of a glass elevator, exploring the same Nob Hill terrain Muybridge had scanned with an earlier form of visual technology.

In chapter 8, Trumpener navigates a related path from panoramic photograph to moving image, noting the close relationship between panoramic modes of seeing and new transportation networks—railroad, steamship, automobile. Like Maria Antonella Pelizzari's discussion of the panoramic photograph that Felice Beato (Italian-British, 1832–1909) took of Lucknow, decimated during a siege in the 1857–58 Indian Uprising (see pp. 52–53), Trumpener's argument explores panoramic photographic techniques in relationship to nineteenth-century imperialist ideologies. Beato adopted one minaret of the Asafi Mosque as a viewing platform, providing a spectacular vantage point from which to survey the Great Imambara palace complex. Only slowly does the viewer notice the despoliation of the city beyond, pummeled to dust by artillery fire. In their unyielding downward gaze, such photographs carry something of the colonial overlord's swagger, even as they are imprinted with evidence of the violence by which empire was sustained. This visual format would metamorphose into the *panning shot* or *pan*, a key technique of twentieth-century cinematic composition.

As Benjamin argues, the nineteenth-century Haussmannization of Paris (followed by similar boulevard constructions in European cities from Barcelona to Vienna and across North and South America) created new bourgeois and commercial sightlines. Another crucial historical development, the advent of motorized vehicles, soon enabled urban panoramic films. As Trumpener argues in chapter 8, these early panoramic films place recurring emphasis on the viewing platform from which filming is occurring. In the Lumière brothers' photopanorama of Rome, likewise, the roof balustrade of St. Peter's Basilica enables unprecedented views of its dome and of Bernini's enormous piazza.

An abiding theme, indeed, is the way architectural features, including Renaissance piazzas and eighteenth-century colonnades, create circular viewing platforms of their own. In their early panorama film *Buxton Skyline* (England, 1901), Sagar Mitchell (British, 1866–1952) and James Kenyon (Britain, 1850–1925) double back on a slow, circular, half-panning shot across Buxton's towers and dome, along its famous Georgian crescent, designed by John Carr (British, 1723–1807), and beyond, to show us the surrounding landscape (trees, cottages, distant smokestacks). The filmmakers angle the camera to avoid any street-level pedestrians walking across the crescent, to focus more directly on the crescent's architectural effects—and to enable film viewers to place themselves implicitly in the landscape and on that large preexisting architectural platform.

Richard I. Suchenski's account of *Napoléon* (1927), the cinematic and panoramic masterpiece of Abel Gance (French, 1889–1981), opens with the "Cinéorama" Raoul Grimoin-Sanson exhibited at the 1900 Paris Exposition. From the center of a circular building, visitors were surrounded by images that ten synchronized 70mm projectors threw onto a 110-yard screen. This initiative was predictive of a whole series of twentieth-century wide-screen and immersive projection experiments. *Napoléon* culminated in two triptych sequences, projecting three images alongside each other on a laterally extended screen more than sixteen yards wide. Although they presented considerable technical challenges, Gance saw the triple screens as the "foundation for a new alphabet for the cinema."[91] Gance was deeply influenced by Victor Hugo, and the sweep of his historical panning shots, capturing landscape and crowd scenes, self-consciously rival the novelist's.[92] The panning shot predates Gance's film, extensively exploited in the films of D. W. Griffith (American, 1875–1948), such as *The Country Doctor* (1909). Yet Gance's extensions, added at either side of the screen to create a panoramic effect, were quite a different gesture.

Ceci tuera cela: the panorama's final decline around 1900 has often been attributed to the rise of the cinematograph. In some panorama buildings, internal rotundas were later literally whitewashed to serve as projection spaces for wide-screen "cinerama."[93] Yet the second half of this book begins to trace a more complicated story. For twentieth-century cinematic form, institutions and spectatorship remain deeply shaped by the precedents of nineteenth-century panorama exhibition, just as the legacies of the panorama and of early panoramic photography and film can be found in contemporary artistic practice across a wide range of media.

In the culminating panning shot in *Riddles of the Sphinx* (England, 1977), Laura Mulvey (British, b. 1941) and Peter Wollen (British, b. 1938) explore the British Museum's Egyptian gallery, camera tracking with methodical rigor in both directions. As Mal Ahern, Vielkind, and Trumpener show, the panoramic has been crucial to experimental film. Fundamentally concerned with women's social, political, and economic dilemmas, *Riddles* is centered formally on the panorama shot. For Ahern (chapter 11), *Riddles* inverts the logic of the panoramic painting, which strives above all to naturalize the scene presented and to erase viewer awareness of the panorama as a technical apparatus. *Riddles*'s thirteen long panning shots use the effect of perspective distortion (so ruinous to the painted panorama) to defamiliarize particular spaces, beginning with the protagonist's kitchen.

In 1966, as part of the New York Film Festival, the American experimental filmmaker Stan VanDerBeek (1927–1984) welcomed a busload of cinephiles and critics to an upstate New York artist's colony and to his Movie-Drome, a curved, custom-built grain silo. While viewers lay on the silo floor, he projected onto the silo's inner planetarium-like dome an overlapping, aleatory mixture of slides, film footage, and live overhead projector drawing. In a 1965 open letter, VanDerBeek envisioned a global network of Movie-Dromes, an orbiting satellite supplying images and transmitting them to multiple sites.[94]

Like Napoleon's idea for a panorama cluster, VanDerBeek's Movie-Drome network remained unrealized. Whereas Napoleon envisioned panoramas as pantheons, as national and imperialist commemoration sites, as historical apotheosis, VanDerBeek's internationalist notion of expanded cinema turned outward. The images VanDerBeek projected in 1966 traversed the entire history of art. The Movie-Drome's form evoked the nineteenth-century painted panorama tradition—even as its content evoked the Lascaux caves, Buddhist statuary, contemporary news photographs, movie clips and collages, cinemas and television, divergent and overlapping traditions of public culture. VanDerBeek's idea of satellite-linked Movie-Dromes envisioned a worldwide web, a universal cultural projection system, an international visual database.

PANORAMIC LANDSCAPES

This book insists on the intermediality of the panorama, on the power of panoramic forms to engage with and transform extant genres. Perhaps the most intimate of these two-way relationships is that between the panorama and the development of landscape painting. In chapter 1, following Michael Charlesworth, Barringer finds precursors for panoramic vision in the military prospect views of Thomas Sandby (British, 1721–1798). Yet plenty of visual evidence also indicates traffic in the opposite direction. While the new medium intrigued established painters such as Joshua Reynolds (British, 1723–1792), Benjamin West (American-British, 1738–1820), and Jacques-Louis David (French, 1748–1825),[95] early landscape painters, including Thomas Girtin (British, 1775–1802), C. W. Eckersberg, and the latter's sometime Copenhagen coeval Caspar David Friedrich, rapidly realized and experimented with its potential. Eckersberg, Denmark's pioneering early nineteenth-century landscape painter, painted at least two panoramas of Copenhagen (now lost), exhibited in 1820s Copenhagen itself. Although art historians long dismissed this as commercial activity, recent scholarship on his surviving panoramic sketches stresses their experimental quality: the true subject of his *Panorama of the Copenhagen Roads* is thus "a horizontal line," the line of the horizon.[96] Eckersberg had studied with David in Paris. Once back in Scandinavia, however, Eckersberg became the region's preeminent champion of plein air drawing and painting. As Karina Lykke Grand argues, Eckersberg's discovery of a widening mobility of gaze shaped his 1844 treatise on perspective—and successive generations of Danish painters (many of them his students). This corpus in turn drove "a picture culture for a new age," even as new technical and optical devices, such as the panorama, "modernized vision and promoted and stimulated the appearance of a new visuality. The perspective of the viewer had now been set free."[97]

Peter Otto's suggestive reading of Friedrich's *Wanderer above a Sea of Fog* (ca. 1817, fig. 0.13) proposes that its famous backview figure may be looking out, from a viewing platform, at a painted panoramic surround rather than a natural scene; this undecidability is one of many instances in which the new institution of the panorama destabilizes rather than consolidates the viewer's sense of the real, inviting the viewer into a state of dream or ecstasy.[98]

Johan Christian Dahl worked alongside both Eckersberg and Friedrich. His *View from Bastei* (1819) self-consciously explores the relationship between the experience of viewing nature and that of viewing a panorama (fig. 0.14). The river and mountains form a massive circumference, enjoyed from a carefully fenced promontory inhabited by middle-class tourists. Dahl's insistent realism, based on a lifetime of sketching from nature, stands in a paradoxical relationship to his embrace of artifice: are we looking at nature or at a panorama? Is there boundless space or a brick wall behind those distant mountains and clouds? If a panorama can replicate nature, can nature replicate panoramic viewing conditions?

The panoramic vista, with its uninterrupted horizon and high viewpoint on an eminence reminiscent of a viewing platform, had a particularly pervasive formal influence on landscape painting. J. M. W. Turner (British,

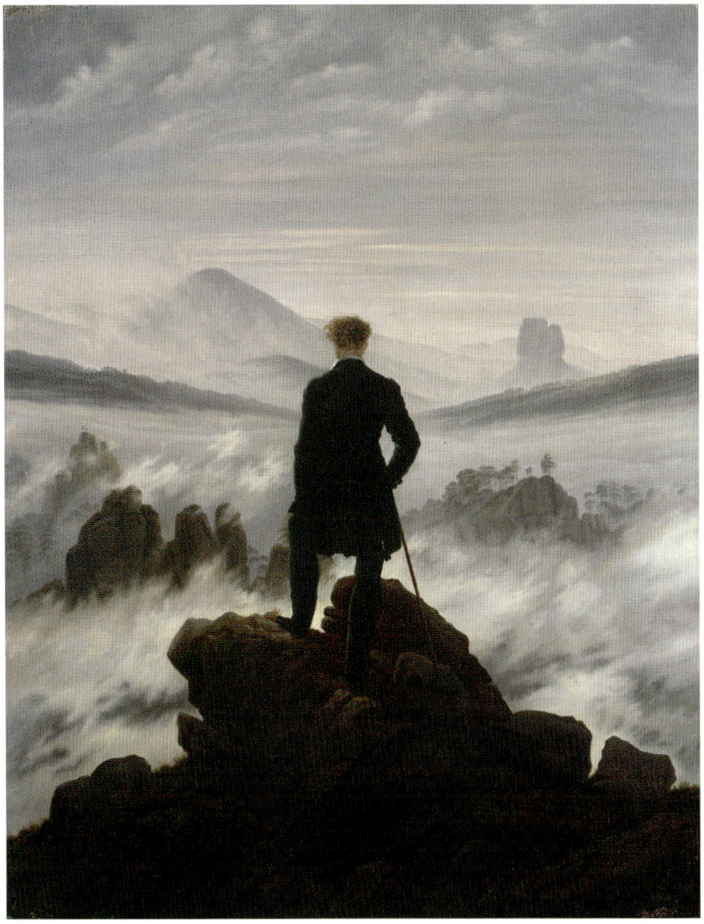

FIG. 0.13. Caspar David Friedrich (German, 1774–1840), *Wanderer above a Sea of Fog*, ca. 1817. Oil on canvas, 94.8 × 74.8 cm (37 3/8 × 29 1/2 in.). Hamburger Kunsthalle, on permanent loan from the Foundation for the Promotion of the Hamburg Art Collections (inv. 5161).

FIG. 0.14. Johan Christian Dahl (Norwegian, 1788–1857), *View from Bastei*, 1819. Oil on canvas, 35.6 × 54.6 cm (14 × 21 1/2 in.). National Museum of Art, Architecture and Design, Oslo (NG.M.02891).

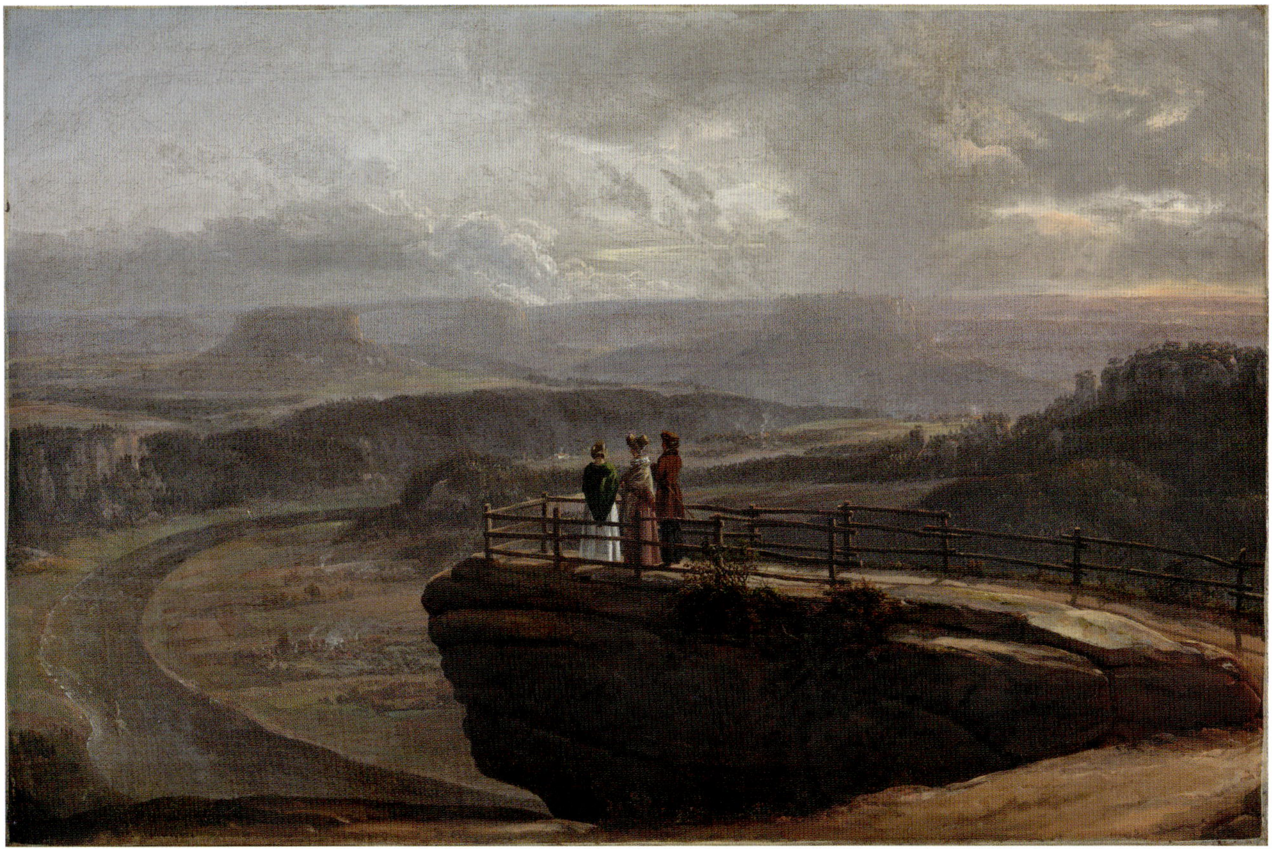

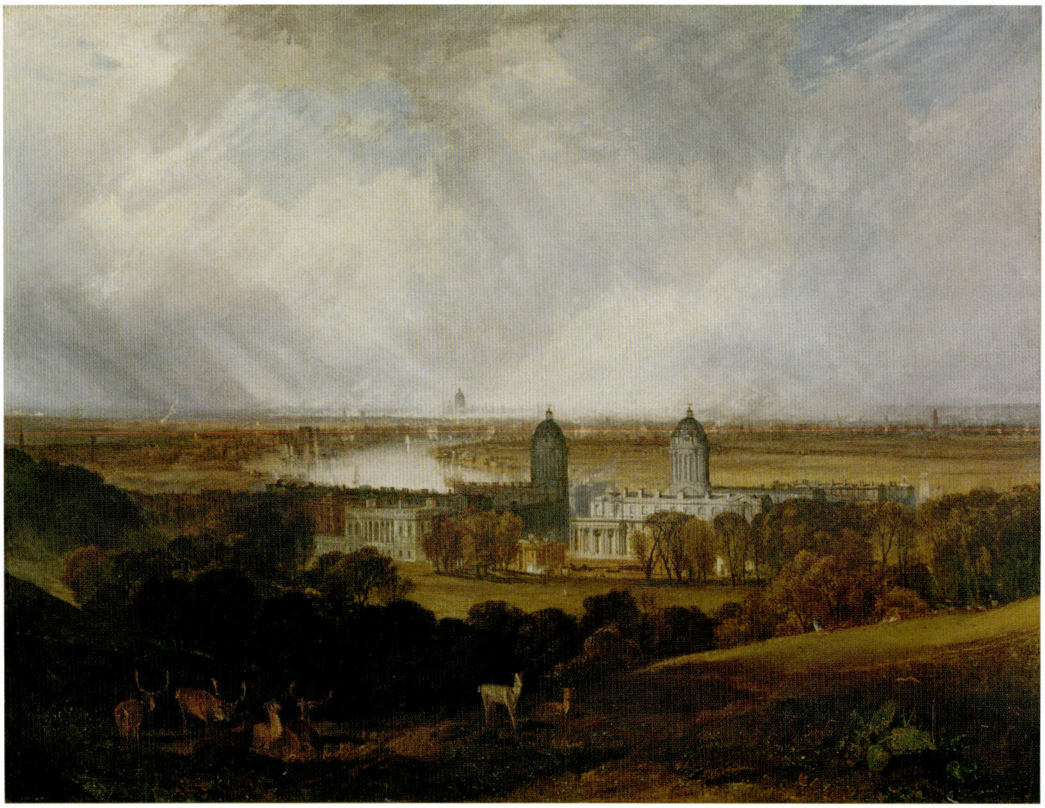

FIG. 0.15. Joseph Mallord William Turner (British, 1775–1851), *London from Greenwich Park*, 1809. Oil on canvas, 90.2 × 120 cm (35 ½ × 47 ¼ in.). Tate, London (N00483).

1775–1851) dispensed with *repoussoir* devices, such as framing trees or architectural elements, in *London from Greenwich Park* (1809), presenting a dramatic city prospect with a flat horizon punctuated only by the towers of the Royal Naval College at Greenwich and, in the distance, St. Paul's Cathedral (fig. 0.15). The London skyline had already been the subject of Henry Aston Barker's celebrated early panorama *A View of London from the Roof of the Albion Mills*, finally installed as a circular panorama in 1793 (see fig. 1.14); a massive panorama of London in the Regent's Park Colosseum would open in 1821. The flat, extensive horizons of the panorama had art-historical precedents: Turner's turbulent city image also sits in a tradition of prospect views with a strikingly flat horizon and vivid cloudscape, which reaches back to Dutch artists such as Philips Koninck (1619–1688) (fig. 0.16). Dahl and Eckersberg were familiar with this tradition, too, from German and Scandinavian collections. Despite its roots in earlier painting, however, Turner's London view bears the unmistakable imprint of industrial modernity. And in planning his work, this culturally most astute artist referenced one of his period's paradigmatic representational technologies.[99]

Rather than taking his place alongside Turner on the viewing platform, John Constable (British, 1776–1837) remained skeptical of modernity and its social effects. In *Hadleigh Castle* (1829) he produced a profoundly pessimistic emblem of the British nation in what he regarded as precipitous decline (fig. 0.17). He sketched the ruined castle on the north bank of the Thames Estuary, the river providing an economic artery into London's docks, connecting the capital with Europe and the British Empire. Visitors to the 1829 Royal Academy exhibition at Somerset House may have visited new panoramas at the Regent's Park Colosseum or, even closer at hand, at Robert Burford's Leicester Square or Strand establishments. Perhaps they speculated that the looming, dark tower—Hadleigh Castle's remains, long used by the coast guard to espy smugglers landing on the banks of the Thames—must command a view of the sunlit water even finer than the one Constable chose for himself. The tower's relationship to the horizon's flat expanse exactly parallels that of the viewing platform and the painted panorama. For like Jeff Wall, 150 years later, Constable seems to have ciphered within his composition the mechanics and ideologies of a visual technology of the modernity whose incursions he so despised.[100]

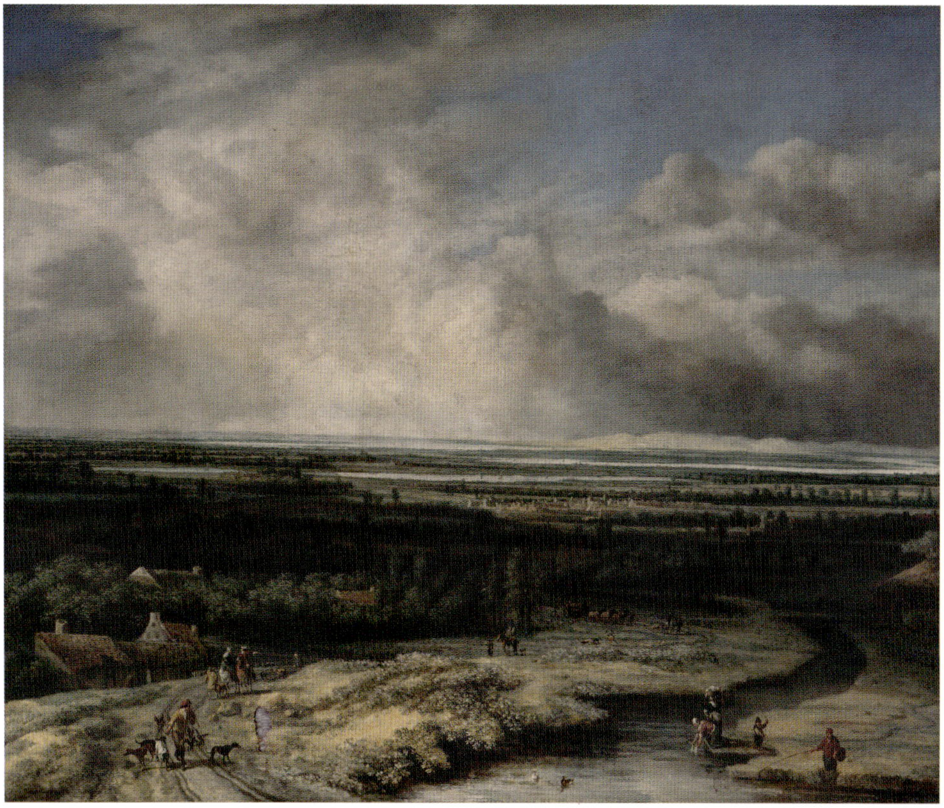

FIG. 0.16. Philips Koninck (Dutch, 1619–1688), *An Extensive Landscape with a Hawking Party*, ca. 1670. Oil on canvas, 132.5 × 160.5 cm (52 1⁄16 × 63 1⁄8 in.). National Gallery, London (NG 836).

FIG. 0.17. John Constable (British, 1776–1837), *Hadleigh Castle, the Mouth of the Thames—Morning after a Stormy Night*, 1829. Oil on canvas, 121.9 × 164.5 cm (48 × 64 3⁄4 in.). Yale Center for British Art, New Haven, Connecticut, Paul Mellon Collection (B1977.14.42).

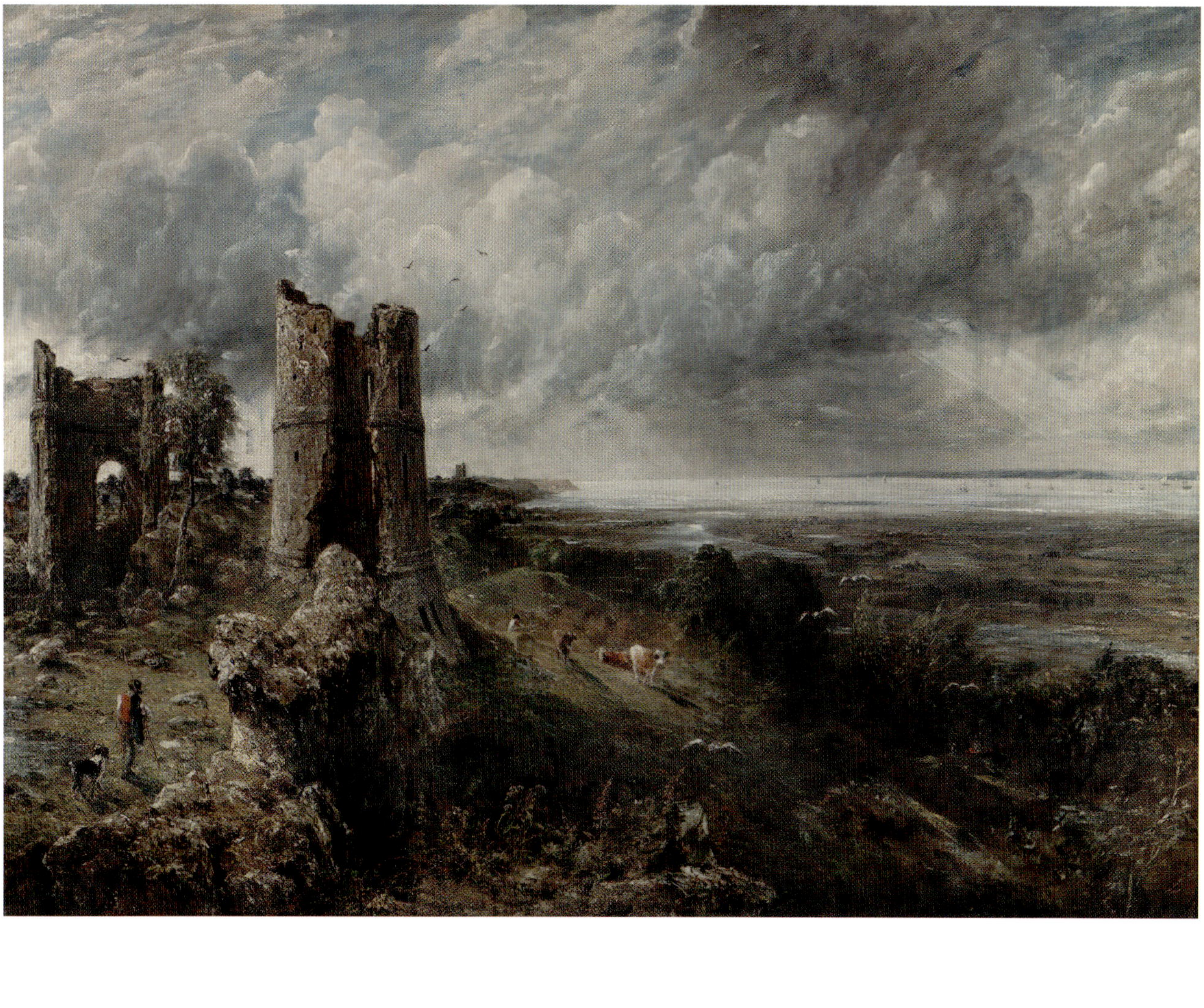

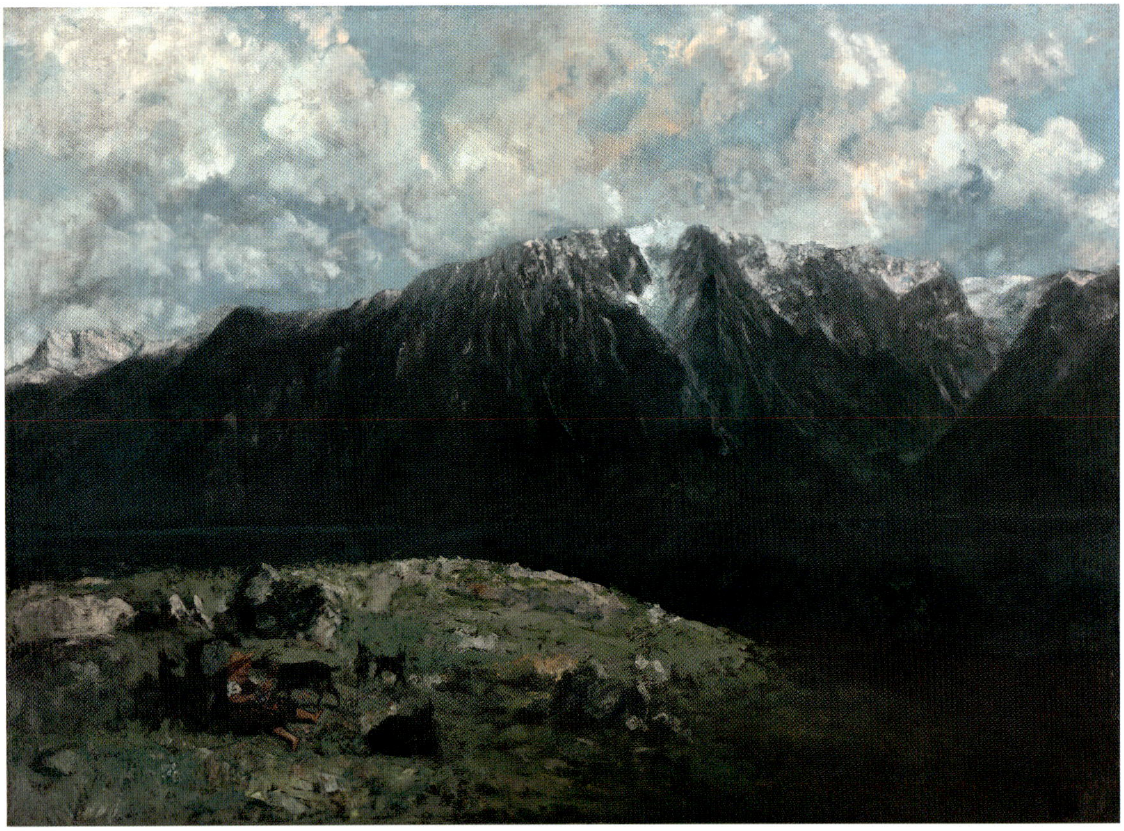

FIG. 0.18. Gustave Courbet (French, 1819–1877), *Panoramic View of the Alps, les Dents du Midi*, 1877. Oil on fabric, 151.2 × 210.2 cm (59 1/2 × 82 3/4 in.). Cleveland Museum of Art, John L. Severance Fund and various donors by exchange (1964.420).

In chapter 2, Jonathan Crary discerns the viewing platform as an equally significant presence within an unquestioned masterpiece in the French history painting tradition, enshrined today in one of the Louvre's grandest rooms: *The Raft of the Medusa* (1818–19) by Théodore Géricault (French, 1791–1824). Paintings, Crary reminds us, were produced and consumed within an expanded field of commodities and attractions; extremely porous boundaries existed between art, the entertainment industry, and various kinds of performance. His chapter strikingly considers the *Medusa*'s despairing dramatis personae as positioned on a viewing platform, scanning the distant horizon, just as Robert Barker's thrilled and disoriented clients might have at Leicester Square.

This volume thus begins to sketch a revisionist history of painting in the age of the panoramic. We reject an account in which the panoramic is a reactionary rejoinder to modernism, as Anton von Werner himself proposed, railing against *The Execution of Emperor Maximilian* by Édouard Manet (French, 1832–1883) as a "weak and nasty piece of work" (*schwächliches Machwerk*), a "dishonest work" compared to the era's historicist panoramic "masterpieces." As early as 1913, however, Werner also lamented the destruction of many panoramic paintings "after the voyeurism of the public was sated," perceptively wondering "whether any art history books of the future will even mention" the genre as more than "a characteristic form of the last third of the nineteenth century."[101]

This book argues that some panoramas were aesthetically powerful works and that the form offered significant possibilities for the century's most innovative artists. Looking beyond Romanticism's interest in the panorama, we argue that later nineteenth- and twentieth-century painters also need reconsideration in these terms. In his 1881 letters, Vincent van Gogh repeatedly praised The Hague's newly opened shoreline panorama by Hendrik Willem Mesdag (Dutch, 1831–1915) as flawless and "deserving of all respect."[102] Other key artists created panorama-inspired works: *Panoramic View of the Alps, les Dents du Midi* (1877, fig. 0.18) by Gustave Courbet (French, 1819–1877), Giovanni Segantini's *Life-Nature-Death*, envisioned for panoramic installation (1898–99), and the 1904 mountain triptych *Panorama of Flims* by Giovanni Giacometti (Swiss, 1868–1933) all evoke panoramas in the scale of their view while delimiting viewing platforms in mountain meadows. In their different ways, Gustave Caillebotte's 1870s and 1880s balcony paintings, Munch's 1891 urban balcony prospect, *Rue Lafayette* (Nasjonalgalleriet, Oslo); and Matisse's *The Windshield, on the Road to Villacoublay* (1917, Cleveland Museum of Art, discussed in chapter 8) lend themselves equally to viewing platform analysis.

Italian futurist *Aeropittura*, interwar aviation paintings, took the viewing platform and viewer into the sky, offering "panoptic viewpoints" and a "sweeping panoramic view of the landscape below."[103] In *Flying over the Coliseum in a Spiral (Spiraling)* (1930, Ventura Collection, Rome), and *Spiraling* (ca. 1936), Tato (Guglielmo Sansoni, Italian, 1896–1974) depicts airplanes circling or in corkscrewing descent, revealing unfamiliar yet implicitly panoramic perspectives on earthbound life. In *Aerial Battle over the Gulf of Naples* (1942), Gerardo Dottori (Italian, 1884–1977) updated the nineteenth-century battle panorama. But the stylized terrain below is itself circular, as if Dottori's airplane flew high above a panoramic representation of the known world or was painted from so high up that the curve of the globe itself was visible.

Michelle Foa's subtle examination of a seascape series by Georges Seurat (French, 1859–1891) explores how panoramic forms shaped Seurat's interest in the seascape's unboundedness and continuing sweep but also how the diorama's interest in the passage of time in a still landscape is echoed by Seurat's own; the series' and neo-Impressionism's profound commitment to seeing and visual sense making is cumulative, processual, time-based.[104] As this book suggests, earlier as well as more modern works deserve equally sensitive analysis attuned to the insistent questions panoramas raised about perception, duration, orientation, and visual protocols.

GLOBAL PERSPECTIVES AND THE HUMBOLDTIAN PANORAMA

Future panorama studies will surely expand on our insistence that the panorama was, from its inception, a global medium. The paintings' very shape alludes to the globe's form and curve; more important, during an era of imperialism and burgeoning international trade, panoramas were a particularly significant medium for representing distant terrain and immersing viewers in exotic locales. Rio de Janeiro, for instance, became the subject of four nineteenth-century panoramic paintings, by French, British, and Brazilian painters; their exhibition variously in Paris, London, Brussels, and—finally, for one panorama—in Rio itself played an important role in establishing Rio within an "international nebula" of capitals.[105]

Like the peep show, Veronica della Dora has argued, panoramas were movable objects that put "the world into a box," rendering landscape portable.[106] From the outset, the panorama exhibition circuit established in Europe's capitals involved sending panoramas to tour the world.[107] Barker's panoramas were very quickly exhibited, in official and unofficial versions, in New York and Berlin. The first panorama displayed in Russia depicted (and originated in) Paris, traveling to St. Petersburg in 1804, soon after its French run had ended.[108] The Scottish painter Robert Ker Porter (1777–1842) made a very early battle panorama of the 1799 storming of Seringapatam. Originally shown in London, Porter's panorama was exhibited in Calcutta as early as 1801. In 1817–18, likewise, a Battle of Waterloo panorama was exhibited in Quebec City and Montreal, only a few years after the events it depicted.[109] And in Austria, Johann Michael Sattler (1786–1847) painted a panorama of Salzburg, devised a portable rotunda, and from 1829 to 1838 toured them together (the thirty-ton load was carried on horse-drawn carts) some 20,000 miles, visiting twenty European cities (including Prague, Berlin, Copenhagen, and Oslo).[110]

In the later nineteenth century, the panorama became very popular in Japan, Australia and Eastern Europe. Japan's 1890s "panorama craze," focused on battle panoramas, culminated with a touring Battle of Sedan panorama previously exhibited in Cincinnati and Toronto.[111] Australia's first cyclorama opened only in 1889 (following a long wave of moving panoramas, moving dioramas, and "modelled panoramas" accompanied by fireworks).[112] As Agnes Stokes recorded in 1901, she and her fellow servants not only flocked to Sydney's cyclorama but joked about investing in it, given its apparently ironclad profitability.[113] By 1910, however, Sydney's panorama, now bankrupt, had closed; Australia's and most of the world's other cycloramas had likewise vanished, apparently for good.[114] Yet later in the twentieth century, Communist governments revived panoramas and dioramas (see chapter 7). Eastern Europe thus saw two (belated) panorama waves, the first during the heightened nationalism of the 1880s and 1890s, the second after 1945.[115]

The last thirty years have belatedly seen a renewed and even broader international panorama "wave." In China alone, more than two dozen large-scale panoramas have been painted—including one designed for export to Los Angeles.[116] New panoramas have also opened in Germany, France, Britain, North Korea, Syria, Egypt, Angkor Wat, and on Australia's Norfolk Island.[117]

Historically, some panoramas attempted to justify colonial expansion. In 1885 Berlin's Colonial Panorama was thus "inaugurated with the display of a bloody punitive expedition to the 'savage landscape' of the new German colony of Cameroon."[118] Yet when panoramas of the Antipodes were displayed in nineteenth-century England, Mimi Colligan has argued, they were sought out not only by viewers seeking pleasurable escape (or feelings of imperial superiority) but by potential emigrants, who scrutinized them carefully to understand what life there might be like.[119] The panorama, Daniel E. White underscores in *From Little London to Little Bengal*, is "a visual technology that set both things and people in motion."[120] Nonetheless, when "leftover" panoramas had a second run in distant European colonies such as British India, their display took on additional meanings, confirming local viewers as a "'little' public," as secondary, nonautonomous consumers of a metropolis-centered visual economy and public sphere—while allowing their viewers to be present in two places at once, on the viewing platform's perspectival center and on the periphery of empire.

This paradoxical positionality is amplified, for White, by the display in nineteenth-century Calcutta of panoramas of London and Dover (the iconic last sight of England witnessed by outward-bound colonial administrators)—but also, formally, by exotic panoramic images that surrounded the viewers with groups of "native" figures (driving home how two groups can become structurally separated by distance and perspective). For White, the panorama embodies colonial ideology not so much in its content as in its form and viewing situation. For metropolitan spectators, being at the panoramic center and in a world center overlaps corporally; for colonial spectators, those sensations can never align.

On the Viewing Platform acknowledges the truly global sweep and influence of the panorama. The medium plays a formative role in how particular parts of the world are represented (and begin to represent themselves) even as it shapes artists', explorers', and travelers' experiences, creating a template for mass touristic experience.

Julia Lum's and Ruth Pullin's chapters examine early painted panoramas of Australia, emblematizing distinct moments in the panorama's history and providing insights into the colony's development. The founding of a prison colony at Botany Bay, following Captain Cook's voyages of discovery, occurred only months after Barker's first panorama opened in 1787. Lum reads the panorama *A View of the Town of Sydney* as a palimpsest of responses to Australasian imperial expansion, inscribing the radically different experiences of the colonial settler, transported convict, and displaced indigene, and revealing the uncertainties and incoherences of Australia's early settler society. Decades later, the Austrian immigrant Eugene von Guérard (1811–1901) stood atop Victoria's Mount Rouse, covering four sketchbook pages with a continuous, meticulously accurate drawing of the view before him, seeking, in Pullin's phrase, "to capture 'everything,'" to create a total portrait of the world before him.

In this, von Guérard betrayed the influence of Alexander von Humboldt's all-embracing vision of the cosmos as a diverse but unified whole. The prolific and influential Prussian naturalist emerges in this book as pivotal to the panorama's history, perhaps the most significant intellect influenced by panoramic vision as an immersive experience. Eduard Gaertner (German, 1801–1877), as Gretchen Bender describes in chapter 4, painted Humboldt into his ambitious Berlin panoramic painting (completed in 1834, figs. 4.1a, 4.1b), telescope perched next to him, discoursing amid an assortment of luminaries positioned atop the roof of a newly constructed Karl Friedrich Schinkel church, surveying Prussia's cultural efflorescence (see fig. 4.3). Over the following decades, Humboldt would develop his own magnum opus, *Cosmos: A Sketch of a Physical Description of the World*, laying out in vivid, accessible style a grand theory of the interrelatedness of every aspect of life on earth. In Gaertner's perceptive conversation piece, Humboldt zealously draws attention to the manifold details of the material world in support of his larger thesis before a group of spellbound spectators. *Cosmos*, too, is a panoramic project, viewing the planet as if from a high viewing platform.

Gaertner's inclusion of Humboldt's telescope alludes to a display strategy sometimes employed by the proprietors of large panoramas: visitors would be lent binoculars, a naval telescope, or simply a cardboard tube, to allow them to isolate details that were carefully inscribed in the painted scene yet could pass unnoticed by the naked eye. The practice of viewing works of art through optical devices was continued by the American painter

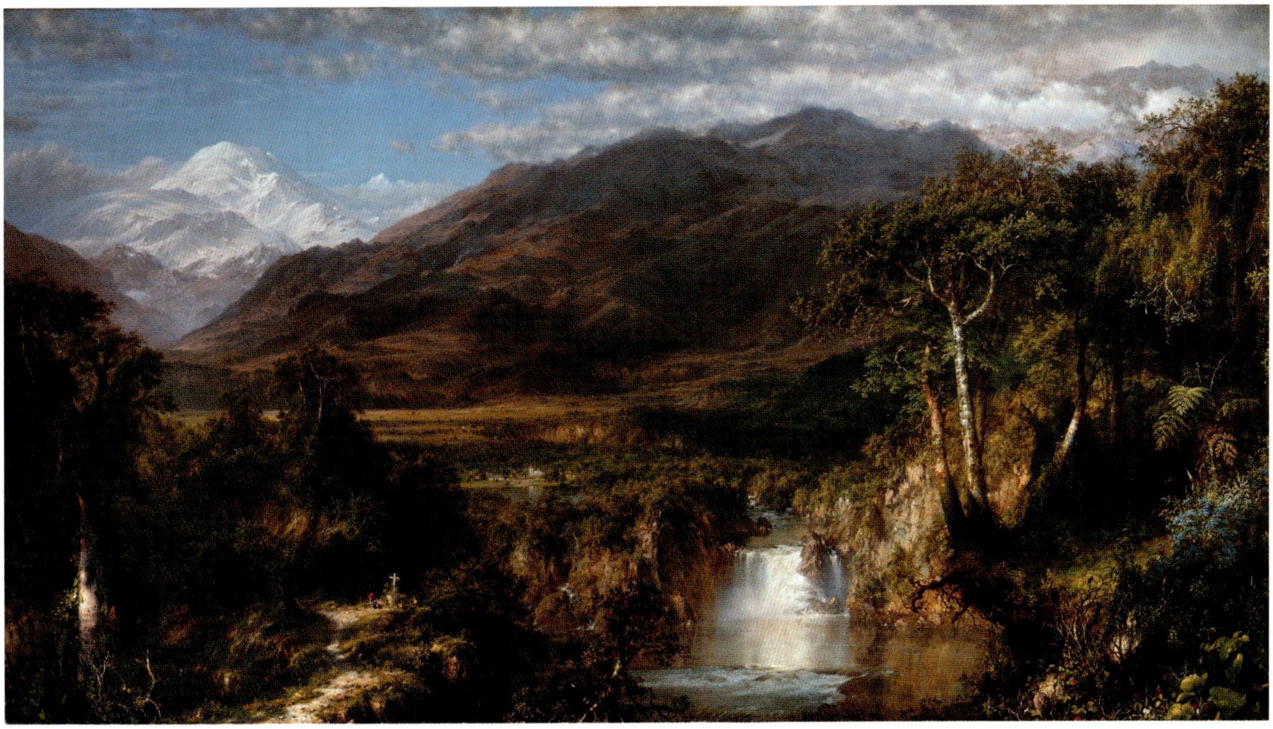

FIG. 0.19. Frederic Edwin Church (American, 1826–1900), *Heart of the Andes*, 1859. Oil on canvas, 168 × 302.9 cm (66 ⅛ × 119 ¼ in.). Metropolitan Museum of Art, New York (09.95).

Frederic Edwin Church (1826–1900), whose large-scale pictorial homage to Humboldt, *Heart of the Andes*, was exhibited in New York as a "Great Picture" in 1859, under circumstances closely resembling those of the panorama (fig. 0.19).[121] Extensive advertising (also a feature of the highly commercialized panorama medium) exhorted visitors to bring opera glasses with them to scan the work for details.

Humboldt was arguably the panorama's most eloquent, most idealistic advocate. Yet when Ferdinand de Saussure evoked the panorama, early in his *Course in General Linguistics* (given 1906–11), to ground his key distinction between synchronic and diachronic, he seemed to push back against the Humboldtian equation of the panoramic with completeness. "It would be absurd to try to draw a panorama of the Alps as seen from a number of peaks in the Jura simultaneously. A panorama must be taken from just one point. The same is true of a language. . . . When the linguist follows the evolution of the language, he is like the observer moving from one end of the Jura to the other in order to record changes in perspective."[122]

Saussure's great-grandfather Horace-Bénédict de Saussure had arguably invented or reinvented the "horizontal panorama," a format already known (and then half-forgotten) in northern Europe from Renaissance cityscape and battlescape etchings. The topographical Alpine panoramas commissioned and supervised by this pioneering eighteenth-century Alpine geologist influenced a distinctive Swiss regional tradition of panoramic drawing, driven by scientific observation and exemplified by Johann Balthasar Bullinger (Swiss, 1713–1793) and Hans Conrad Escher von der Linth (Swiss, 1767–1823), which in some ways anticipated the Barkerian panorama while setting rather different emphases.[123]

Humboldt was equally enthusiastic about panoramas as a pedagogical tool, understanding both the immersive image's affective power and the challenge presented by the new technology of photography (less than a decade old at his writing, yet already experimenting with panoramic formats).[124]

> The improvements in landscape painting on a large scale (as decorative paintings, panoramas, dioramas and neoramas) have also increased the generality and force of these impressions. . . . Barker's panoramas may serve, in some degree, as a substitute for travelling through different regions. Panoramas are more productive of effect than scenic decorations, since the spectator

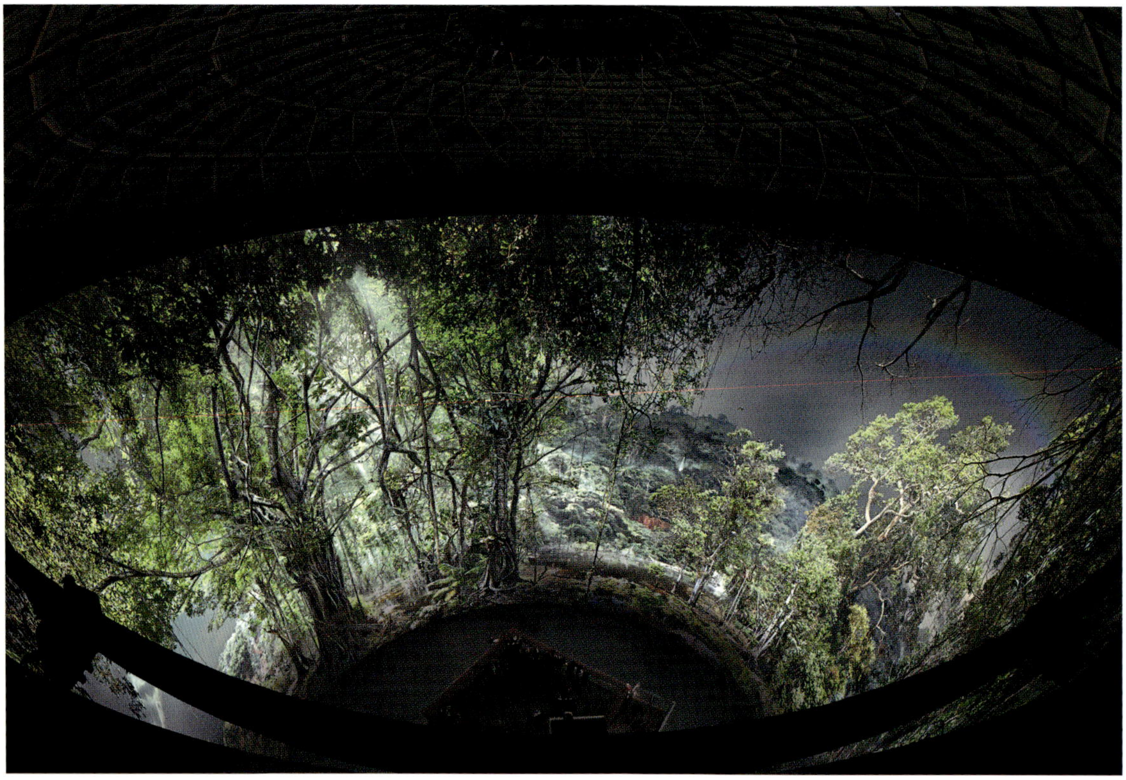

FIG. 0.20. Yadegar Asisi (Austrian, b. 1955), *Amazonien*, 2012.

> enclosed as it were within a magic circle, and wholly removed from all the disturbing instances of reality, may the more easily fancy that he is actually surrounded by a foreign scene. These compositions give rise to impressions which, after many years, become wonderfully interwoven with the feelings awoken by the aspect of the scenes when actually beheld. Hitherto panoramas, which are alone effective when of considerable diameter, have been applied more frequently to the representation of cities and inhabited districts than to that of scenes in which nature revels in wild luxuriance and richness of life. An enchanting effect might be produced by a characteristic delineation of nature, sketched on the rugged declivities of the Himalaya or the Cordilleras, or in the midst of the Indian or South American River Valleys, and much aid might further be derived by taking photographic pictures, which, although they certainly cannot give the leafy canopy of trees, would present the most perfect representation of the form of colossal trunks, and the characteristic ramification of the different branches.[125]

In this volume, Richard Maxwell's "Panorama, Glasshouse, Museum" (chapter 5, completed and expanded by Katie Trumpener after Maxwell's death) draws connections between Humboldt's panoramic vision, with its plenitude of tropical foliage, and emblematic nineteenth-century sites from the palm house to the international exhibition (often likewise housed in a glasshouse or crystal palace). The circus, botanical garden, museum display case, and ethnographic museum's village encampment all belong in a wider history of the panoramic. Such sites—from the world's fairs to fun fairs, from the White City to Coney Island—also became key locations for early cinema, from the outset (as Trumpener and Vielkind argue) obsessed with panoramic form.

In our own day, the large-scale panoramas of the architect, artist, and cultural entrepreneur Yadegar Asisi (Austrian, b. 1955) build explicitly on Humboldt's model of practical panoramic education. His *Amazonien*, exhibited in Leipzig in 2012–13 and intended as an homage to Humboldt, evokes a jungle ecosystem as described in *Cosmos*, with a wealth of flora and fauna on view (fig. 0.20). Extensively sponsored by state and commercial backers and created by a team of sixty under Asisi's direction, this circular pictorial structure self-consciously resurrected the tradition of the educational panorama Humboldt endorsed. The installation's cross section closely resembled those of nineteenth-century panoramas: a multistory viewing platform allowed a large audience to view a 360-degree computer-generated image enhanced by large-scale realia and sound effects.

In the 1980s Asisi exhibited anamorphic reconstructions of ruined Berlin buildings; his 1995 exhibition "Berlin 2005" displayed sketches, maquettes, and panoramic mock-ups of what a future Berlin might look like (new architectural ensembles and new panorama buildings dotted key places).[126] The exhibition catalogue included a historical essay by Oettermann on the panoramic displays of nineteenth-century Berlin (not only in six discrete Berlin panorama rotundas but also in a major train station, in the patriotic recreational center Haus Vaterland, and as the painted backdrop to a plaster replica of a Greek temple).[127]

Twenty-five years later, Asisi has reimagined Berlin not only using panoramic means but also as a future cycloramic hub. His own massive, high-tech, 360-degree images are displayed as popular commercial attractions in Berlin and other German cities, as original panoramas were in their time. Some—including *Rome 312* and *Leipzig 1813*—re-create historical spectacles. Although Asisi himself is acutely aware of the medium's history, and his panoramas seem to function seamlessly in a present-day image ecology, visitors do not perceive them as a self-consciously historicist exercise.[128]

The structures, or "Panometers," created to house these images closely resemble early panorama buildings, and the viewer enters the rotunda in classic panoramic style, through a darkened corridor and up a flight of stairs (although Panometer viewers can generally choose to view the panorama from different floors). Binoculars can be rented. At the Berlin Wall panorama (permanently on view at Berlin's Checkpoint Charlie), the faux terrain separating viewing platform from image is full of viewing figures: the West Berliners looking directly over the Wall from west to east from the low, wooden Cold War viewing platforms erected after 1961 (to facilitate cross-Wall family waving) and the East German border guards, posted in their death-strip watchtower, looking right back, through their binoculars and cameras, at present-day viewers.[129]

Panoramic seeing itself remains a significant component of the modern tourist industry, whose origins lie, like the panorama's, in the late eighteenth century. For Humboldt, as subsequently for Ferdinand de Saussure, Sternberger, and Benjamin, the panorama offers a complex sphere of metaphor and practice with which to think about the nature and limits of cosmic, cultural, and linguistic historiography. Yet Humboldt's model of practical panoramic education also forms part of the ancestry of recent cultural phenomena that, like so much in the medium's history, sits in the interstices between fine art, pedagogy, and commercial enterprise.

In chapter 7, Trumpener discusses Alpine panoramas, examining a range of Swiss and Austrian images from an 1808 view of Thun through the 1896 Innsbruck panorama. Yet elaborate Alpine panorama paintings, now often proudly shown in the locations they represent, are far more than mere adjuncts to the burgeoning tourist industry. In Trumpener's reading, Castres's 1881 *Bourbaki Panorama*, the work Wall photographed during its renovation (see fig. 0.1), testifies to modern warfare's apocalyptic results and self-referentially critiques painting's possibilities. Swiss artists troubled the inviolable status of panorama viewers, demanding they make difficult choices of affiliation. The earlier Thun panorama, produced during the Napoleonic occupation, suggests tensions between a local Swiss tradition of federalism and a Napoleonic worldview rooted in a more abstract sense of the collective. This unstable amalgam of local and global characterizes the panoramic medium as a whole.

THE PANORAMIC IN CONTEMPORARY CULTURE

Even while arguing the panorama's centrality to histories of art and film, this book positions the panoramic within the modern world's wider culture of display. The panorama touches the overlapping spheres of the aesthetic, pedagogical, and performative. By the mid-nineteenth century, Katie Hornstein has shown, French painters and art critics routinely discussed Salon exhibitions by large-format battle painters like Horace Vernet (French, 1789–1863) in relationship to panoramic display and viewer expectations.[130] Meanwhile, Jean-Charles Langlois (French, 1789–1870) added dioramic faux terrain to his panoramic paintings and had viewers ascend to the viewing platform of his first panorama, *The Battle of Navarino* (1831), through a life-size replica of one of the battleships. Climbing through the model ship, through the putative bedroom of the ship's captain, past a diorama of sailors putting out a fire, wax models of sailors' corpses, and seventy-four decommissioned French navy cannons, viewers finally reached the deck, around which the painted scene of battle stretched. Enhancing such effects were the panorama guides, war veterans (many bearing visible war scars or missing limbs) whom Langlois had hired to provide live commentary on the battle's action. Contemporary critics lauded the immersive experience Langlois's stagecraft elicited.[131] It lives on even today—for instance, in Disneyland's Pirates of the Caribbean ride.

Indeed, to take the panorama seriously is to undermine the rigorously policed borders between high and low culture, between the academy exhibition and the fairground, and (historiographically) between fine art, decorative art, and visual culture. *The Raft of the Medusa* is traditionally understood as an unabashed monument of high culture, forever enshrined in one of the Louvre's grandest galleries. Yet, in 1820, Crary notes in chapter 2, Géricault exhibited it at London's Egyptian Hall, during its long life home to numerous amusements, including "natural history, art exhibitions, freak shows, and a vast range of curiosities, versions of panoramas and magic lantern shows, phantasmagorias, ventriloquists, magic shows." The audience for high art also attended all manner of popular entertainments, from freak shows to public executions.

The panoramic has had a dynamic afterlife across contemporary visual culture. The current preoccupation with virtual reality, William Uricchio argues, can be seen as the return of a repressed panoramic sensibility.[132] And there is a panoramic tinge to recent populist murals, cartographic paintings, and photocollages by German, British, South African, and Japanese artists.[133] The *Velaslavasay Panorama*, founded in 2000 by the American artist Sarah Velas as a Los Angeles exhibition space, movie theater, and community center, displays newly created circular panoramic paintings while hosting a wide range of programming on the history of visual culture, proto-cinematic exhibition, and expanded cinema.[134] And recent photo books return to sites of pioneering Anglo-American, Indian, Brazilian, and Afghan photopanoramas to chronicle intervening "horizons of accumulation" or destruction.[135]

Alongside the 1970s "building cuts" of Gordon Matta-Clark (American, 1943–1978), the 2000 *Cyclorama* and 2008 *E-Cyclorama* of Sanford Wurmfeld (American, b. 1942)[136] and the 1998 *Torqued Ellipse* and 2008 *Sequence* of Richard Serra (American, b. 1938), recent ontologically oriented, surround installation works, draw on the expanded "-orama" tradition. So do the chronophotographic collages of Jan Dibbets (Dutch, b. 1941), the 1973–75 *Cones Cojones* series by Bruce Nauman (American, b. 1941), and the installations and film installations of Daniel Steegmann Mangrané (Spanish, b. 1977).[137]

The works of James Turrell (American, b. 1943) and Olafur Eliasson (Danish Icelandic, b. 1967) use light, dark, hue, time (and, for Eliasson, heat and cold) to heighten viewers' sense of the diurnal or evoke viewers' sense of the seasonal, planetary, infinite.[138] Eliasson's work, in particular, negotiates directly with the heritage of the painted panorama, replacing mimetic, painted surface with projected light and allowing the viewer even greater roaming freedom than the traditional viewing platform. His remarkable *Your Rainbow Panorama* (2006–11), permanently installed at Denmark's ARoS Aarhus Kunstmuseum, allows visitors a rooftop view similar to that portrayed in Thun's early nineteenth-century panorama (see fig. 7.3).[139]

Yet Eliasson's view is not a painted panorama but an actual view of the Danish industrial city from a circular cantilevered gantry (allowing a 360-degree peregrination), whose glass walls are tinted every color of the rainbow (fig. 0.21). It rests, in turn, atop a huge square, wooden deck, covering the entire ninth floor, where museumgoers can perambulate to enjoy the urban prospect, sit and sun on deck chairs, or drink coffee in a glass-enclosed café. The view from the rainbow panorama's circular walkway is more striking yet, for its hues shift prismatically panel by panel. Aarhus's largely unremarkable cityscape and harborscape thus continually shift tonality as one walks.

The spectators themselves, moreover, feel imbued by the same colored light that tints the view, so they too may notice subtle shifts in their own appearance and mood as they walk. Certainly as they encounter other walkers, some moving clockwise, others counterclockwise, stopping to admire, take cellphone photographs, and pose in front of the outlook, they see their fellow visitors continually transformed, even transfigured by the color spectrum. Schoolkids race around the top, giggling and roughhousing. Adult tourists stroll or push others in wheelchairs, moving more meditatively through bands and baths of color. Their activity remains fully visible from the streets far below. More distant spectators thus watch watchers watching.

Unsurprisingly, many visitors actually on the walkway film their own partial panoramas on their cellphones, panning or even turning in a 360-degree circle as they move. This panorama is not only a prime space from which to observe viewing behavior but an active panorama generator or breeder. Eliasson's apparently simple installation, then, meditates on the perceptual and public

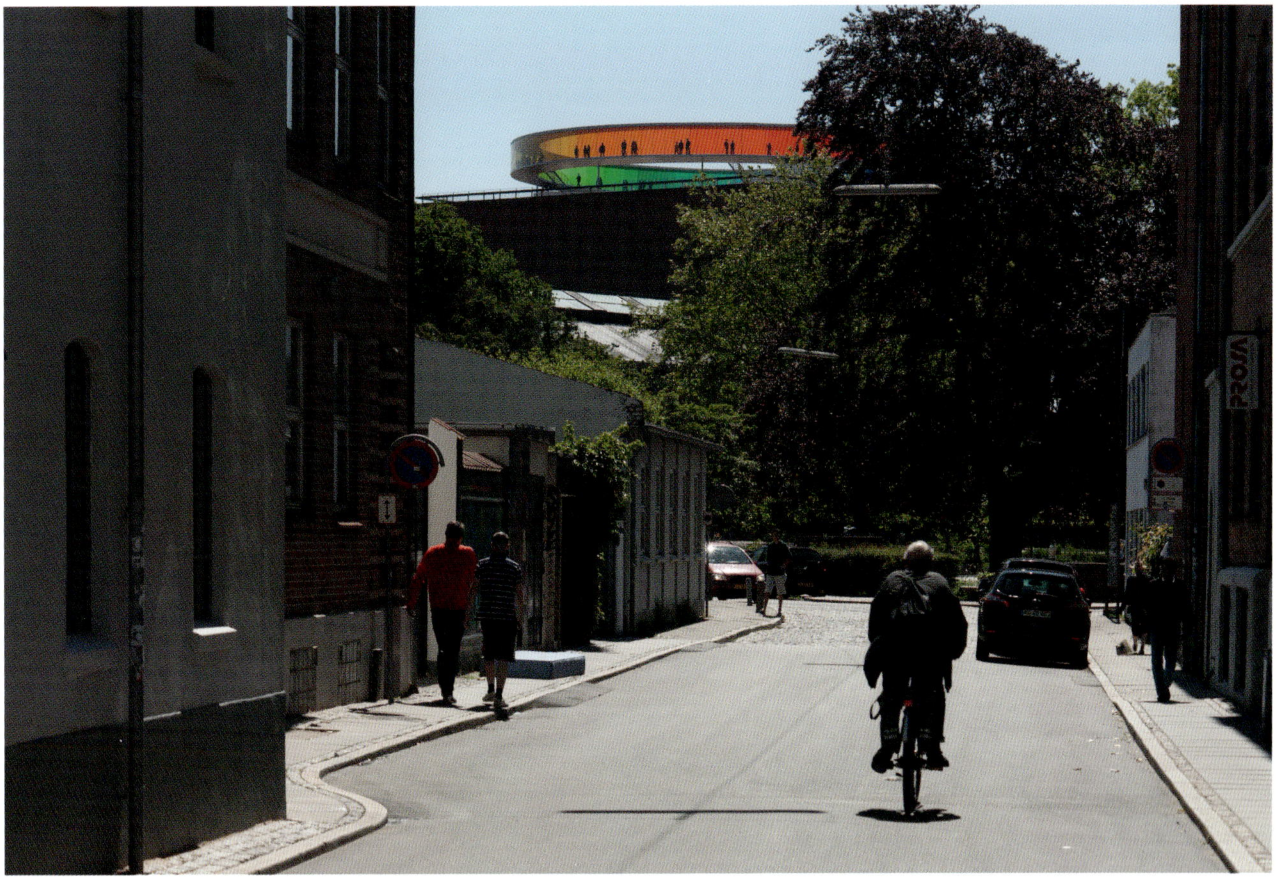

FIG. 0.21. Olafur Eliasson (Danish, b. 1967), *Your Rainbow Panorama*, 2006–11. Installation view, AroS Aarhus Kunstmuseum, Denmark, 2011.

spectacles, the vistas and shifting views, inherent to panoramic experience.

As in the nineteenth-century painted panorama, artifice and verisimilitude, popular thrill and rarefied aesthetic experience are inextricably interwoven. Eliasson's piece took shape in the wake of the walkable Reichstag Dome, designed by Norman Foster (British, b. 1935), opened in 1999 and now one of Berlin's major tourist attractions. In turn, Eliasson's piece is a visible influence on "The Treetop Experience," a spiraling new Danish forest walkway, opened in 2019 in Gisselfeld Klosters Skove, near Copenhagen.

In Aarhus, Eliasson's circular viewing platform approximates the size of some 1960s and 1970s revolving restaurants. But here the viewers, not the platform, move, and here the viewers themselves become a key part of the view, as distance abstracts their figures and movements into a frieze. From this point of view, *Your Rainbow Panorama* is a modern version of the mechanical clocks whose stylized figures emerged and promenaded on the hour or half hour. Here, though, the movement remains perpetual throughout the opening hours of the museum and is ever changing.

In Eliasson's earlier *360° Room for All Colours* (2002), likewise, viewers became an integral part of the spectacle—as perhaps they always have been (fig. 0.22). The tentlike circular structure, its walls washed with light in changing colors, clearly recalls the format of painted panoramas; the experimentation with color suggests Goethe's color theory and moves once again into a Humboldtian realm of Romantic science. Eliasson's artistic genealogy, Pamela Lee argues, includes both the sublime emptiness of Romantic landscape painting (whose links to modernism Clement Greenberg and Robert Rosenblum celebrated) *and* popular nineteenth-century entertainments. As the authors of this volume collectively establish, the painted panorama and fine art have always been closely related; Eliasson's work is only the latest of many instantiations. Drawing on an earlier analysis by Crary, Lee argues the panorama "dramatized the shifting character of the sensorium using

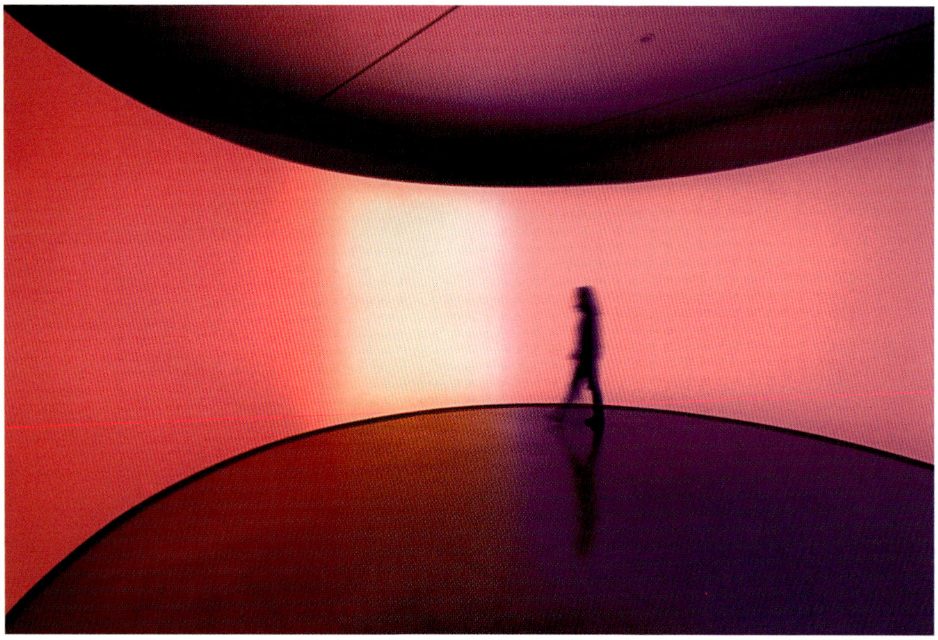

FIG. 0.22. Olafur Eliasson, *360° Room for All Colours*, 2002. Neon lights, light panels, stainless steel, laptop computer with program, cables, and cable controllers, approx. 750 cm (25 ft.) in diameter × 340 cm (11 ft.) high. Installation view, Museé d 'Art Moderne de la Ville de Paris, Paris, 2002.

the techniques of industrialization," and here, too, artists like Eliasson, Turrell, and even earlier minimalists such as Dan Flavin (American, 1933–1996) and Donald Judd (American, 1928–1994) share much with nineteenth-century panoramists.[140]

The 2001 sound installation *The Forty Part Motet* aspires to transcendent, totalizing, yet highly involving spectatorial experience (fig. 0.23). Janet Cardiff (Canadian, b. 1957) creates an aural equivalent of a panorama that helps us visualize a particularly ethereal piece of Renaissance polyphony, Thomas Tallis's *Spem in Alium*.[141] Composed around 1570 in forty parts, the motet groups its singers into eight choirs of five; Tallis's elaborate counterpoint moves back and forth across the circle of singers to create a complex tracery of sound. We have become accustomed, at the cinema or IMAX, to having a wide-screen picture accompanied by Dolby sound, an enhancement of the stereophonic or multichannel sound systems long delivering music in our homes and cars. *The Forty Part Motet*, however, separates the channels still more carefully and visibly. Exploring three-dimensional sound, it enables listeners to develop a spatialized sense of sound and to perceive the defined space within which the sound is unfolding, its contours and reach. In Cardiff's installation the music simply emerges from forty outwardly identical industrial speakers, arranged in a relatively small oval, uncannily recalling the curvature of the cyclorama walls.

Cardiff's installation temporarily transforms the secular museum back into a place of aesthetically anchored worship.[142] And like Eliasson's or Turrell's lightscapes, *The Forty Part Motet* aims to render the spectator's senses sharper, more subtle. Yet this piece also contains a demystifying apparatus, illusion-breaking in plain sight, and a synesthetic aura, rendering sound visible. Recent panorama theory has drawn attention to the way the panorama coordinates planes of vision and ways of seeing, auratic lighting and cosmic omniscience. In Cardiff's work, too, the viewer potentially alternates between a closed-eye apprehension of the whole and an open-eyed sense of the relationship between parts and whole. Such refined meditations on the possibilities and limits of panoramic experience remain prominent in contemporary art.

Yet the panorama's original commercial and ideological exuberance and its mass-market appeal persist as well. From the 1990s onward, new kinds of panoramic images have appeared on a new viewing platform, the worldwide web: virtual real estate "walkthroughs," Google Earth panorama photos—and, from October 2016 onward, the *New York Times*'s interactive website feature "The Daily 360." *Times* journalists worldwide, equipped with panoramic video cameras, were instructed to supplement their print stories with panoramic footage. "See the world from a new angle. . . . Get a first-hand perspective. . . . Transcend boundaries. . . . Demystify the world. . . . Experience elsewhere. . . . See where you stand. . . . To understand the world, see it from every angle. . . . The Daily 360. Be There

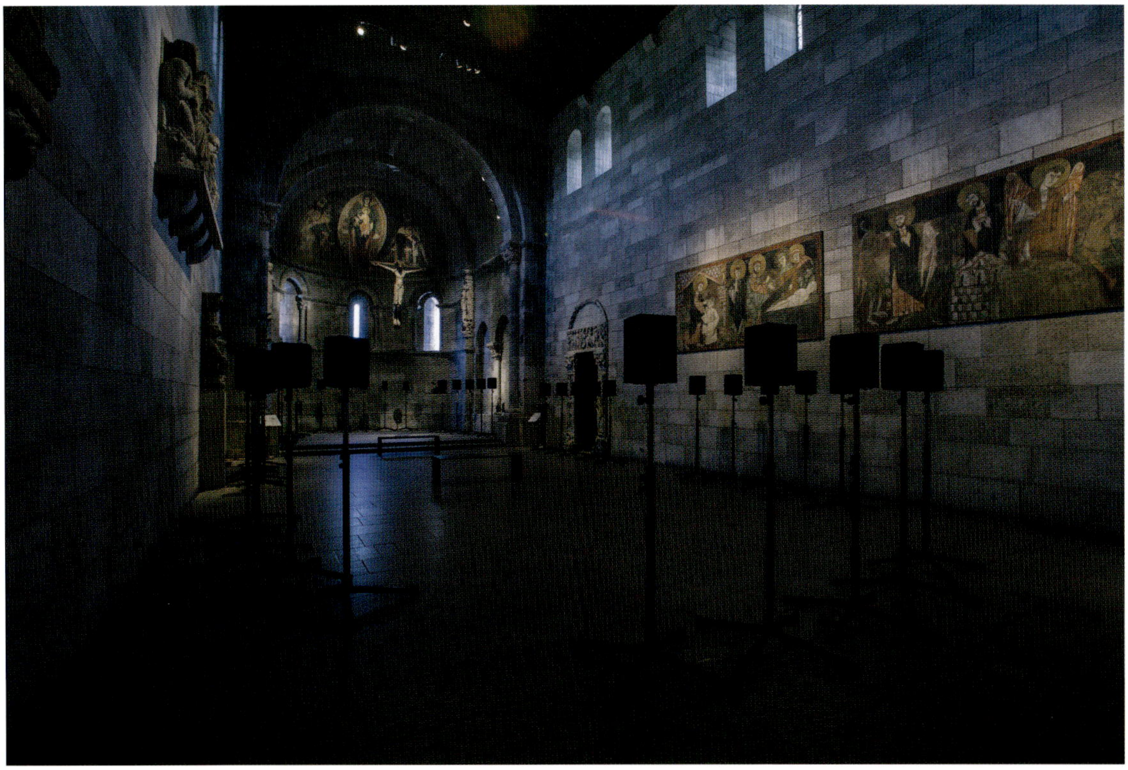

FIG. 0.23. Janet Cardiff (Canadian, b. 1957), *The Forty Part Motet*, 2001, installed at The Cloisters, Metropolitan Museum of Art, New York, 2013. Forty loudspeakers mounted on stands and placed in an oval, amplifiers, playback computer, dimensions variable. Duration: 14-minute loop with 11 minutes of music and 3 minutes of intermission. Sung by Salisbury Cathedral Choir. Recording and postproduction by SoundMoves. Edited by George Bures Miller. Produced by Field Art Projects. *The Forty Part Motet* by Janet Cardiff was originally produced by Field Art Projects with the Arts Council of England, Canada House, the Salisbury Festival and Salisbury Cathedral Choir, BALTIC Gateshead, the New Art Gallery Walsall, and the NOW festival Nottingham.

Now."[143] Such rhetoric echoes the nineteenth-century panorama, just as its sample footage—crowded Middle Eastern and Haitian marketplaces, phantom rides from tugboat and airplane wing, through railway tunnels—evoke fin-de-siècle panoramic films and photography. The picture and sound quality are often indifferent—yet the sense of immediacy is heightened by viewers' ability, with their cursors, to forge their own paths through the image.

"These immersive videos," the *Times* explains, "put you at the center of the scene, allowing you to look left, right, up, down and behind you." More than ever, the viewer is promised personal control over the scene, able to determine personalized, aleatory, ambulatory viewing protocols, invited to "Come face to face with adversity." The first "Daily 360" "offers a rare glimpse of war-torn Yemen," positioning the viewer in the ruins of a Sana reception hall "bombed by a Saudi Arabian airstrike" that killed over one hundred people who had gathered to commemorate a death. The opening tableau is centered on a huge ragged hole left in the hall's middle—a sinkhole, an abyss. Does the "Daily 360" raise critical questions about its own vantage point and the limits of its own knowledge, or does it assume the self-assured stance of the colonial photopanorama, implicitly enshrining New York as the center of a decentered world?

The *Times*'s high-tech panorama update coexists with attempts, in various corners of the world, to revive the painted panorama in something akin to its original, nineteenth-century form. *Splendid Central Plains in Zhengzhou, Central China's Henan Province* was unveiled in 2011 by the Henan Administration of Radio Film and Television at the Tower of Fortune in Zhengzhou City, China.[144] To quote statistics of the kind beloved by Barker, Burford, and their ilk and aptly recorded in the *Guinness Book of World Records*: the painting covers 32,424 square feet and 119 square inches: 536 feet, 5.78 inches long by 60 feet and 5.27 inches wide. Thirteen painters took 345 days to complete it.[145] No individual artist's name is associated with the work, which seems, on the basis of photographic sources, to have been a collective effort. The fact that *Splendid Central Plains in Zhengzhou* decorates the offices of the official television station suggests both the panorama's role in the ancestry of the late twentieth century's ubiquitous visual medium and the complex relationship between the panorama and political power.

The behavior of beholders on the viewing platform, as seen in official Chinese government publicity photographs, reveals the changing image ecology of our own moment. Alongside cameras on tripods, members of the public raise their digital cameras and phones aloft in a forlorn attempt to capture the majestic spectacle surrounding them. Despite Jeff Wall's realization that "a panorama can never really be experienced in representation," they are surely using "panorama" software. If the jostling crowd on Zhengzhou City's viewing platform (or the endless frieze of viewers moving through Eliasson's *Your Rainbow Panorama*, visible from downtown Aarhus) reveals the undiminished visual power of the panoramic, the essays in this collection aim to demonstrate its continuing analytic urgency.

NOTES

1. Laurie Garrison, ed., *Panoramas, 1787–1900: Texts and Contexts*, 5 vols. (London: Pickering & Chatto, 2013), 1:6. Emphasis added.
2. "Restoration, 1994: Interview by Martin Schwander," in Jeff Wall and Thierry de Duve, *Jeff Wall: The Complete Edition* (London: Phaidon, 2009), 86–97; 90.
3. Franz Schiermeier, *Panorama München: Illusion und Wirklichkeit. München als Zentrum der Panoramenherstellung* (Munich: Franz Schiermeier Verlag, 2007), 30.
4. Philippe Dubois, "La question du panorama: Entre photographie et cinéma," *Cinémathèque* 4 (1993): 22–39; 30, translation ours.
5. Later panoramic exhibition sometimes involved additional, variant realia display. In 1828 the British exhibitor of John and Robert Burford's 1823 panorama *View of the City of Mexico* at Harvard College rented "adjacent space" to display his own collection of "Mexican artifacts and curios." Kevin J. Avery and Peter L. Fodera, *John Vanderlyn's Panoramic View of the Palace and Gardens of Versailles* (New York: Metropolitan Museum of Art, 1988), 27. See also Getty Research Institute, "Obsidian Mirror-Travels," https://www.getty.edu/research/exhibitions_events/exhibitions/obsidian_mirror/panoramas.html. Especially since Latin America's wars of liberation were in the news, the double exhibition proved very popular; ethnographic materials doubtless supplemented the panorama's reality claims.
6. Oliver Grau, *Virtual Art: From Illusion to Immersion*, trans. Gloria Custance (Cambridge: MIT Press, 2003), 72. As *Vossische Zeitung* coverage of the 1883 inauguration of Anton von Werner's *Battle of Sedan* panorama noted, the spectatorial platform rotated completely every half hour (Grau, *Virtual Art*, 108).
7. J. A. Eberhard, "Briefe über das Panorama," *Handbuch der Ästhetik* (1807), repr. in *Panorama, Diorama, Photographie*, ed. Heinz Buddemeier (Munich: Wilhelm Fink Verlag, 1970), 172–75; 175; and Denise Blake Oleksijczuk, *The First Panoramas: Visions of British Imperialism* (Minneapolis: University of Minnesota Press, 2011), chap. 3.
8. For Tom Gunning, this redefinition of the frame is a formal problem the panorama bequeathed to photography, then cinema. "Landscape and the Fantasy of Moving Pictures: Early Cinema's Phantom Rides," in *Cinema and Landscape*, ed. Graeme Harper and Jonathan Rayner (Bristol: Intellect, 2010), 32–70, esp. 52–53.
9. Carlos Martin, Sergio Burgi, and Julia Kovensky, "Apresentaçao," in Martin et al., *Panoramas: A Paisagem Brasileira no Acervo do Instituto Moreira Salles* (São Paulo: Instituto Moreira Salles, 2012), 15–16.
10. Ludwig Börne, February 21, 1831, in Börne, *Letters from Paris*, cited in Gustav Solar, *Das Panorama und seine Vorentwicklung bis zu Hans Conrad Escher von der Linth* (Zurich: Orell Füssli, 1979), 43, translation ours.
11. Quoted in Vance Byrd, *A Pedagogy of Observation: Nineteenth-Century Panoramas, German Literature, and Reading Culture* (Lewisburg, Pa.: Bucknell University Press, 2017), 72.
12. Schiermeier, *Panorama München*, 24.
13. In 1908 F. A. Roubaud oversaw restorations of his 1904 *Liberation of Sevastopol* siege panorama in its Sevastopol rotunda. He "directed the work from the viewing platform, by giving instructions to the pupils, standing below at the canvas, on how they could paint a group of soldiers faster, better, by using a unified hue." S. P. Günerfaut, "F. A. Roubaud und seine Panoramen in der Geschichte der russischen und sowjetischen Schlachtenmalerei," in *Tagungsbericht der internationalen historisch-wissenschaftlichen Konferenz "Panoramamalerei in der Weltkunstgeschichte"* (Sevastopol, Ukraine, 2007), 26–33; 28. Translations ours.
14. Max Bernstein, "Von einem Panorama: Plauderei," *Die Kunst für alle: Malerei, Plastik, Graphik, Architektur* 2, no. 7 (1887): 105–10.
15. Dolf Sternberger, *Panorama of the Nineteenth Century*, trans. Joachim Neugroschel (New York: Urizen, 1977), 8.
16. Grau, *Virtual Art*, 107. See also Gabriele Koller, "Panorama und Film in der deutschen Propaganda des deutschen Kaisers Wilhelm II," in *Panorama: Virtuality and Realities. 11. International Panorama Conference in Altötting 2003*, ed. Gebhard Streicher (Amberg, Germany: Verlag Koch-Schmidt-Wilhelm, 2005), 32–37.
17. In 1841, relatedly, Gustav Seeberger (German, 1812–1888) produced a lithographed Munich panorama, drawn from St. Peter's Tower and apparently intended for the use of firemen stationed on that tower. Reproduced in Schiermeier's *Panorama München*.
18. Katja Kwasdek argues that the viewer remains "a spectator, not an actant" ("bleibt aber Zuschauer, nicht Handelnder"). "Sehnsucht nach dem Faux-Terrain—Immersion vom Panorama bis zur Medienkunst," in Streicher, *Panorama*, 20; translation ours.
19. Byrd, *Pedagogy*, 16–28.
20. John Sweetman, introduction to Sweetman et al., *The Panoramic Image* (Southampton, U.K.: John Hansard Gallery, 1981), 7.
21. Sweetman, "The Panoramic Image: The Period to 1850," in *The Panoramic Image*, 10.
22. Dubois, "La question," 27, translation ours.
23. Michel Frizot, "Voir le panorama, ou les yeux sont aussi les pieds," *Cinémathèque* 6 (1994): 94; as Frizot's subtitle insists, "eyes also are feet." Translations ours.
24. Cited in Markman Ellis, "'Spectacles within Doors': Panoramas of London in the 1790s," *Romanticism* 14, no. 2 (2008): 133–48; 142–43.
25. Eric de Kuyper and Émile Poppe, "Voir et regarder," *Communications* 34 (1981): 85–96; 93, translation ours.
26. Josh Ellenbogen, "Inhuman Sight: Photographs and Panoramas in the Nineteenth Century," in Joel Snyder, *One/Many: Western American Survey Photographs by Bell and O'Sullivan* (Chicago: David and Alfred Smart Museum of Art, 2006), 55–73; 62.

27. Michael Devine, "The Whole Thing (and Other Things): From Panorama to Attraction in Stephen Crane's 'The Open Boat,' Ashcan Painting, and Early Cinema," in *Sensationalism and the Genealogy of Modernism: A Global Nineteenth-Century Perspective*, ed. Alberto Gabriele (New York: Palgrave Macmillan, 2017), 217–38; 223.
28. On panoramic wall painting and wallpaper, see Grau, *Virtual Art*, 25–60; Odile Nouvel-Kammerer, ed., *Décor de l'imaginaire: Papiers peints panoramiques, 1790–1865* (Paris: Flammarion, 1990), and her "Wide Horizons: French Scenic Papers," in *The Papered Wall: History, Pattern, Technique*, ed. Lesley Hoskins (New York: Abrams, 1994), 94–113.
29. See, for instance, Wu Hung, *The Double Screen: Medium and Representation in Chinese Painting* (Chicago: University of Chicago Press, 1996); Matthew Philip McKelway, *Capitalscapes: Folding Screens and Political Imagination in Late Medieval Kyoto* (Honolulu: University of Hawai'i Press, 2006); and Michael Komanecky and Virginia Fabbri Butera, *The Folding Image: Screens by Western Artists of the Nineteenth and Twentieth Centuries* (New Haven: Yale University Art Gallery, 1984). On the related Western accordion book tradition, see Alexandre Quoi, "Une vision dé(multi)pliée: Panorama et *Leporello*," in *J'aime les panoramas: S'approprier le monde*, ed. Laurence Madeline and Jean-Roch Bouiller (Paris: Flammarion, 2015), 138–42.
30. See Philip Haas's film *A Day on the Grand Canal with the Emperor of China; or, Surface Is Illusion but So Is Depth*, narrated by David Hockney (Los Angeles County Museum of Art/Milestone Films, 1988).
31. Dubois, "La question," 39; translation ours. Yet see Michel Frizot's rebuttal, "Voir le panorama," 78.
32. Walter Benjamin's unpublished critique links Sternberger's essayism and methodological shortcomings to Third Reich conformity. Benjamin, "Review of Sternberger's *Panorama*" (1938–39), trans. Edmund Jephcott, in *The Work of Art in the Age of Its Technological Reproducibility and Other Writings on Media*, ed. Michael Jennings et al. (Cambridge: Harvard University Press, 2008), 158–65. According to Dietrich Neumann, Benjamin had been annoyed to find the panorama, discussed in his 1935 "Paris, Capital of the Nineteenth Century," adopted by Sternberger as his own reigning metaphor. Neumann, "Instead of the Grand Tour: Travel Replacements in the Nineteenth Century," *Perspecta: The Yale Architecture Journal* 41 (2008): 47–53; 52. On Sternberger's *Panorama* as a model for media histories, see Christian Köhler, "Zyklogrammatik: Dolf Sternbergers *Panorama* as mediale Historiographie," *kultuRRevolution* 68 (May 2015): 52–61.
33. See Andrea von Hülsen-Esch, "Das Panorama und der theatralische Raum bei Walter Benjamin," in *Topographien der Erinnerung: Zu Walter Benjamins Passagen*, ed. Bernd Witte (Würzburg: Königshausen & Neumann, 2008), 123–37.
34. Although fin-de-siècle Berlin school classes frequently visited the panorama, its rotunda was razed in 1908 (a year after Sternberger's birth); the painting came into Kaiser Wilhelm's possession, then vanished. Astrid Weidauer, *Berliner Panorama der Kaiserzeit* (Berlin: Gebr. Mann Verlag, 1996), 26. Thus, it seems unlikely Sternberger ever saw it in person.
35. Buddemeier, *Panorama, Diorama, Photographie*.
36. Stephan Oettermann, *The Panorama: History of a Mass Medium*, trans. Deborah Lucas Schneider (New York: Zone, 1997); and François Robichon, "Le panorama, spectacle de l'histoire," *Le Mouvement Social* 131 (April–June 1985): 65–86. See also Michel Foucault, *Power/Knowledge: Selected Interviews and Other Writings*, ed. Colin Gordon (London: Harvester Books, 1980), 138.
37. Dubois, "La question," 27–28, translation ours.
38. Alan Wallach, "Some Further Thoughts on the Panoramic Mode in Hudson River School Landscape Painting," in *Within the Landscape: Essays on Nineteenth-Century American Art and Culture*, ed. Phillip Earenfight and Nancy Siegel (University Park: Pennsylvania State University Press, 2005), 99–128; 111–13. See also Wallach, "Making a Picture from Mount Holyoke," in *American Iconology*, ed. David Lubin (New Haven: Yale University Press, 1993), 80–91; and Wallach, "The Persistence of the Panoramic," in *Transcultural Spaces: Challenges of Urbanity, Ecology, and the Environment in the New Millennium*, ed. Stefan Brandt, Winfried Fluck, and Frank Mehring (Tübingen: Narr Verlag, 2010), 89–107. On intersections between the panoramic gaze and Western expansionism, see Albert Boime, *The Magisterial Gaze: Manifest Destiny and American Landscape Painting, c. 1830–1865* (Washington, D.C.: Smithsonian Institution Press, 1991); and Jennifer Raab, "Panoramic Vision, Telegraphic Language: Selling the American West," *Journal of American Studies* 47, no. 2 (2013): 495–520.
39. See William Uricchio, "A 'Proper Point of View': The Panorama and Some of Its Early Media Iterations," *Early Popular Visual Culture* 9, no. 3 (2011): 225–38; and Kuyper and Poppe's nuanced panorama-panopticon distinction in "Voir et regarder," 91–92.
40. Max Horkheimer and Theodor W. Adorno, *Dialectic of Enlightenment: Philosophical Fragments*, trans. Edmund Jephcott (Stanford: Stanford University Press, 2002).
41. Bernard Comment, *The Panorama*, trans. Anne-Marie Glasheen (London: Reaktion, 1999).
42. Schiermeier, *Panorama München*.
43. See David Harris with Eric Sandweiss, *Eadweard Muybridge and the Photographic Panorama of San Francisco, 1850–1880* (Cambridge: MIT Press, 1993); Vidya Dehejia, ed., *India through the Lens* (Washington, D.C.: Freer Gallery/Smithsonian, 2000); and Jeffrey W. Cody and Frances Terpak, eds., *Brush and Shutter: Early Photography in China* (Los Angeles: Getty Research Institute, 2011).
44. Ralph Hyde, *Panoramania! The Art and Entertainment of the "All-Embracing" View* (London: Trefoil/Barbican Art Gallery, 1988); and Marie-Louise von Plessen and Ulrich Giersch, eds., *Sehsucht: Das Panorama als Massenunterhaltung des 19. Jahrhunderts* (Basel: Stroemfeld, 1993).
45. Martin et al., *Panoramas: A Paisagem*, 219. The much smaller 2019 New-York Historical Society exhibition "Panorama: The Big Picture" suggests American artists' preoccupation with the panoramic, from the panoramic landscape paintings of John Trumbull (1756–1843) to the cityscapes of Red Grooms (b. 1937), the murals of Richard Haas (b. 1936), and the photomosaics of Claude Samton (b. 1933).
46. Madeline and Bouiller, *J'aime les panoramas*, 83.
47. Scott Wilcox, "The Panorama and Related Exhibitions in London" (M.Litt. thesis, University of Edinburgh, 1976); and Kevin Avery, "The Panorama and Its Manifestation in American Landscape Painting, 1795–1870" (Ph.D. diss., Columbia University, 1995). Richard D. Altick's *The Shows of London* (Cambridge: Belknap Press of Harvard University Press, 1978) remains a classic history of early nineteenth-century London exhibitions and performances.
48. Brigit Kämpfen-Klapproth, *Das Bourbaki Panorama von Édouard Castres* (Lucerne: City of Lucerne, 1980), 89.
49. Renzo Dubbini, *Geography of the Gaze: Urban and Rural Vision in Early Modern Europe* (1994), trans. Lydia G. Cochrane (Chicago: University of Chicago Press, 2002), esp. chap. 2.
50. Peter Otto, *Multiplying Worlds: Romanticism, Modernity, and the Emergence of Virtual Reality* (Oxford: Oxford University Press, 2011), 19–44.
51. Vanessa R. Schwartz, *Spectacular Realities: Early Mass Culture in Fin-de-Siècle Paris* (Berkeley: University of California Press, 1999).
52. Alison Griffiths, *Shivers Down Your Spine: Cinema, Museums, and the Immersive View* (New York: Columbia University Press, 2008), 3.

53. Ibid., 33.
54. This remains the primary focus of the International Panorama Council, a body of panorama proprietors, scholars, artists, and photographers, whose annual meetings—often hosted by extant panoramas worldwide—showcase current scholarly, interpretive, and curatorial work.
55. See Ryad Benosman and Sing Bing Kang, eds., *Panoramic Vision: Sensors, Theory, and Applications* (New York: Springer-Verlag, 2001).
56. Grau, *Virtual Art*, chap. 2. While Jan Blanc, "'Une idée entièrement nouvelle?' Le regard panoramique avant le panorama," in Madeline and Bouiller, *J'aime les panoramas*, 106–14, explores such cross-connections, David B. Clarke and Marcus A. Doel, "Engineering Space and Time: Moving Pictures and Motionless Trips," *Journal of Historical Geography* 31, no. 1 (2005): 41–60, questions putative trans-historical continuities between perspectival systems and viewing conventions.
57. Oettermann, *Panorama*, 23–24.
58. Solar, *Das Panorama*, 29.
59. Dubois, "La question"; and Arno Mungen, *"BilderMusik": Panorama, Tableau vivants und Lichtbilder als multimediale Darstellungsformen in Theater-und Musikaufführungen vom 19. bis zum fruhen 20. Jahrhundert* (Remscheid: Gardezl Verlag, 2006).
60. Kurt W. Forster, "Schinkel's Panoramic Planning of Central Berlin," *Modulus* 16 (1983): 62–75; and Wendy Bellion, *Citizen Spectator: Art, Illusion, and Visual Perception in Early National America* (Chapel Hill: University of North Carolina Press, 2011).
61. Barry Daniels, "Daguerre—Theatermaler, Dioramist, Photograph," in Plessen and Giersch, *Sehsucht*, 36–41; Helmut Gernsheim and Alison Gernsheim, *L. J. M. Daguerre: The History of the Diorama and the Daguerrotype* (New York: Dover, 1969); and Guillaume Le Gall, *La peinture méchanique: Le diorama de Daguerre* (Paris: Mare et Martin, 2013).
62. Grau, *Virtual Art*; and Erkki Huhtamo, *Illusions in Motion: Media Archaeology of the Moving Panorama and Related Spectacles* (Cambridge: MIT Press, 2013), xiii, xviii.
63. Huhtamo, *Illusions in Motion*, 6.
64. Jacques Aumont, "The Variable Eye; or, The Mobilization of the Gaze," trans. Charles O'Brien and Sally Shafto, in *The Image in Dispute: Art and Cinema in the Age of Photography*, ed. Dudley Andrew (Austin: University of Texas Press, 1997), 231–58; 235–36.
65. See Jessica Skwire Routhier et al., *The Painter's Panorama: Narrative, Art and Faith in the Moving Panorama of Pilgrim's Progress* (Hanover, N.H.: University Press of New England, 2015).
66. Schwartz, *Spectacular Realities*, 151. On the longer history of panoramic views of Paris itself, see J. Kugel, *Un panorama de Paris et ses environs: Tableaux-dessins, 1680–1840* (Paris: J. Kugel, 1996).
67. Walter Benjamin, *The Arcades Project*, trans. Howard Eiland and Kevin McLaughlin (Cambridge: Belknap Press of Harvard University Press, 1999), 5.
68. Ibid., 527.
69. The field of the panoramic extends well beyond the visual sphere. Benjamin's celebrated *Charles Baudelaire: A Lyric Poet in the Era of High Capitalism*, trans. Harry Zohn (London: Verso, 1997), uses the phrase *panorama literature* to describe a popular 1840s literary genre assembled from detailed physiological portraits of a range of city types: for Benjamin, a realist panorama, like a realist novel, was built up from a multitude of small sketches. The essay's belated rediscovery sparked a substantial body of literary criticism. On the panoramic roots of realism, see Jonathan Arac, *Commissioned Spirits: The Shaping of Social Motion in Dickens, Carlyle, Melville and Hawthorne* (1979; repr., New York: Columbia University Press, 1989); Richard Maxwell, *Mysteries of Paris and London* (Charlottesville: University Press of Virginia, 1992); Margaret Cohen, "Panoramic Literature and the Invention of Everyday Genres," in *Cinema and the Invention of Modern Life*, ed. Leo Charney and Vanessa Schwarz (Berkeley: University of California Press, 1995), 227–52; Erica Segre, "The Development of *Costumbrista* Iconography and Nation-Building Strategies in Mexican Literary Periodicals of the Mid-Nineteenth Century," *Bulletin of Hispanic Studies* 77, no. 1 (2000): 77–107; Maurice Samuels, *The Spectacular Past: Popular History and the Novel in Nineteenth-Century France* (Ithaca: Cornell University Press, 2004); Tanya Agathocleos, *Urban Realism and the Cosmopolitan Imagination* (Cambridge: Cambridge University Press, 2011); Alison Byerly, *Are We There Yet? Virtual Travel and Victorian Realism* (Ann Arbor: University of Michigan Press, 2012); and Molly Brunson, *Russian Realisms: Literature and Painting, 1840–1890* (DeKalb: Northern Illinois University Press, 2016). On interfaces between panoramic spectacle and literary history, see Robert L. Carothers and John L. Marsh, "The Whale and the Panorama," *Nineteenth-Century Fiction* 26, no. 3 (December 1971): 319–28; Susan Dean, *Hardy's Poetic Vision in The Dynasts: The Diorama of a Dream* (Princeton: Princeton University Press, 1977); Charles Zarobila, "Walt Whitman and the Panorama," *Walt Whitman Review* 25 (1979): 51–59; William Galperin, *The Return of the Visible* (Baltimore: Johns Hopkins University Press, 1988); Jill Wacker, "Sacred Panoramas: Walt Whitman and New York City Parks," *Walt Whitman Quarterly* 12, no. 2 (1994): 86–103; Joseph Moldenhauer, "Thoreau, Hawthorne, and the Seven-Mile Panorama," *ESQ: A Journal of the American Renaissance* 44 (1998): 227–73; Gillen D'Arcy Wood, *The Shock of the Real: Romanticism and Visual Culture, 1760–1860* (New York: Palgrave, 2001); Christopher Oscarsson, "Landscape and the Entangled Bird's-Eye View: Turn of the 20th Century Swedish Culture and the Ecological Imaginary" (Ph.D. diss., University of California–Berkeley, 2006); J. Jennifer Jones, "Absorbing Hesitation: Wordsworth and the Theory of the Panorama," *Studies in Romanticism* 45, no. 3 (Fall 2006): 357–75; Sophie Thomas, *Romanticism and Visuality: Fragments, History, Spectacle* (New York: Routledge, 2008); Laurie Garrison, "Imperial Vision in the Arctic: Fleeting Looks and Pleasurable Distractions in Barker's Panorama and Shelley's *Frankenstein*," *Romanticism and Victorianism on the Net* 52 (November 2008): 1–23; Hsuan L. Hsu, *Geography and the Production of Space in Nineteenth-Century American Literature* (Cambridge: Cambridge University Press, 2010); Nathalie Preiss and Valérie Stiénon, "Sketched by Themselves: The Panorama Tested by the 'Panoramic,'" *Interférences littéraires/Literaire interferenties* 8 (May 2012): 17–24; Helmut Müller-Sievers, *The Cylinder: Kinematics of the Nineteenth Century* (Berkeley: University of California Press, 2012), esp. chap. 8; and Byrd's *Pedagogy of Observation*. It has also informed self-consciously Benjaminian literary, photographic, graphic, and filmic works. Benjamin's *Arcades* quotes earlier panorama-obsessed literary works, from Balzac's 1835 *Père Goriot* onward. Benjamin perhaps grew up reading nineteenth-century (Humboldt-inspired) juvenile "panorama" adventure and travel narratives. Klaus-Ulrich Pech, "Vom Biedermeier zum Realismus," in *Geschichte der deutschen Kinder- und Jugendliteratur*, ed. Reiner Wild, 3rd ed. (Stuttgart: Metzler Verlag, 2008), 131–72, esp. 152–59.
70. Benjamin, *Charles Baudelaire*; and Jonathan Crary, *Techniques of the Observer: On Vision and Modernity in the Nineteenth Century* (Cambridge: MIT Press, 1990), 113. On the panorama's production of newly embodied subjects, see also Kimberly Mair, "Transitory Formations and the Education of the Senses," *Senses and Society* 7, no. 1 (2012): 53–71.
71. Ralph Hyde, "Panoramas—A Brief Introduction to a World-Wide Phenomenon," in *The World of Panoramas: Ten Years of International Panorama Conferences*, ed. Gabriele Koller (Amberg, Germany: SPA Stiftung Panorama Altötting, 2003), 12–19; 14. Philip Shaw powerfully evokes the elevated vantage points Napoleon sought in battle and panoramic

viewing conventions vis-à-vis battle tourism in *Waterloo and the Romantic Imagination* (Basingstoke, U.K.: Palgrave Macmillan, 2002), 67–91.

72. The Japanese government developed guidelines about what panoramas could and could not show, and an implicit mandate to propagandize. Machiko Kusahara, "'We Will Open the Panorama-kan': The Beginnings of the Panorama Craze in Meiji Japan," in *The Panorama in the Old World and the New*, ed. Gabriele Koller (Amberg, Germany: Verlag Koch-Schmidt-Wilhelm, 2010), 76–88; 84. On Soviet panorama painting and exhibition (including more portable "travel panoramas," made to be disassembled and reassembled), see Swetlana A. Argaszewa, "Die Panoramen der Heldenstadt Zarizyn-Stalingrad-Wolgograd," in *Tagungsbericht*, 101–11; on the ideology of czarist panorama censorship and Soviet panorama development, see S. M. Dudikowna, "Das Panorama Verteidigung Sevastopols 1854–1855 als Bildungsquelle der kulturell-historischen Weltanschauung," *Tagungsbericht*, 161–66.
73. Avery and Fodera, *John Vanderlyn's Panoramic View*, 23.
74. Scheiermeier, *Panorama München*, 18.
75. André Meyer, "Das Panoramagebäude: Zweckbau und Monument: Formen und Funktionen einer Baugattung des 19. Jahrhunderts," *Zeitschrift für schweizerische Archäologie und Kunstgeschichte* 42, no. 4 (1985): 274–80. See also Eliana Perotti, "Il cinema della pittura: L'architettura die Panorami in Svizzera," *Kunst + Architekur in der Schweiz* 47 (1996): 258–68.
76. One Chicago cyclorama was repurposed as a velodrome, theater, cinema, and auto showroom. A Boston cyclorama became a boxing arena, flower market, and car manufacture and repair; it currently holds artists', theater, and exhibition spaces. Christine Symchych, "Boston Center for the Arts and Its Cyclorama: An Architectural History," in Koller, *The Panorama in the Old World*, 156–58. Buffalo's Cyclorama was repurposed as a roller rink and a taxi garage; condemned in 1937, then renovated by the WPA, it spent twenty years as a library reading room; since 1989 it has been an office building. Meg Healy, "The Cyclorama Building," *Buffalo as an Architectural Museum*, http://buffaloah.com/a/franklin/369/. Suzanne Wray, "A Fad That Failed," *Panorama* 2 (2018): 55–59, surveys further reuses. Cyclorama closures or reuses often damaged, even doomed, canvases. After a garage was installed in the basement of Lucerne's cyclorama, the viewing platform was twice raised and the top of Édouard Castres's painting twice shortened; eventually, one-third (primarily sky) was gone. Kämpfen-Klapproth, *Das Bourbaki Panorama*, 43.
77. Sylvain Malfroy, "Extensions de l'illusionnisme du panorama dans l'architecture privée," *Zeitschrift für Schweizerische Archäologie und Kunstgeschichte* 42, no. 4 (1985): 311–38. Mair's "Transitory Formations" (63–64) reads Le Corbusier's widely influential horizontal window as panoramically inflected. See also Andreas Luescher, "Inhabitable Illusions and the Panorama" (Ph.D. diss., Pennsylvania State University, 1998).
78. Clarke and Doel, "Engineering Space and Time," 50.
79. Agnes Stokes, *The Autobiography of a Cook*, in *A Girl at Government House: An English Girl's Reminiscences below Stairs in Colonial Australia*, ed. Helen Vellacott (South Yarra, Australia: Currey O'Neill, 1982), 54n.
80. Schwartz, *Spectacular Realities*, 160; see also Philippe Willems, "Albert Robida," *The Sequential and the Panoramic* blog, https://philippewillems.wordpress.com/albert-robida/.
81. Romuald Nowak, "Polnische Schachtenpanoramen," in *Tagungsbericht*, 69–84.
82. Yusef Komunyakaa, "The Panorama," in *Warhorses* (New York: Farrar, Straus and Giroux, 2008), 28–29.
83. Relocated after World War II to the newly annexed and repopulated Wrocław, it remains one of Poland's most frequently visited museums. Anna Baumgartner, "Das Racławice-Panorama in Breslau: Ein Erinnerungsort für die polnische Nation," in *Geschichte im Rundumblick: Panoramabilder im östlichen Europa*, ed. Arnold Bartetzky and Rudolf Jaworski (Vienna: Böhlau Verlag, 2014), 45–64, esp. 50, 57. Following Austria's 1919 loss of South Tyrol and Trentino to Italy, the planned sale of Innsbruck's Tyrol panorama to Americans sparked nationalist pushback. Susanne Gurschler, "Das Innsbrucker Riesenrundgemälde 'Schlacht am Bergisel': Eine Momentaufnahme bewegter Tiroler Geschichte zwischen touristischer Vermarktung und patriotische Vereinnahmung," in Bartetzky and Jaworski, *Geschichte im Rundumblick*, 114–27. Although privately financed (and owned by a Belgian panorama company), von Werner's *Battle of Sedan* panorama was, because of its nationalist subject, "promoted and controlled" by Germany's highest political offices, whose preferences and hints probably shaped politically sensitive nuances of its depiction. Grau, *Virtual Art*, 101.
84. Robichon, "Le panorama," 75–78; Schwartz, *Spectacular Realities*; Mark B. Sandberg, *Living Pictures, Missing Persons: Mannequins, Museums, and Modernity* (Princeton: Princeton University Press, 2003); Griffiths, *Shivers Down Your Spine*; Crary, *Techniques*; and Lauren Rabinowitz, *Electric Dreamland: Amusement Parks, Movies, and American Modernity* (New York: Columbia University Press, 2012).
85. Robert C. Wilburn's "The Campaign to Save Gettysburg" leaves unmentioned the razing of Neutra's modernist rotunda, defensively endorsing the new Visitor Center as ideal for panorama preservation and display, a once-in-a-lifetime pedagogic opportunity. Koller, *The Panorama in the Old World*, 126–28.
86. David H. Solkin, *Painting for Money: The Visual Arts and the Public Sphere in Eighteenth-Century England* (New Haven: Yale University Press, 1993).
87. Compare Thomas Crow's argument about public sphere formation in *Painters and Public Life in Eighteenth-Century Paris* (New Haven: Yale University Press, 1985).
88. Grau, *Virtual Art*, 92, 113–22, instances the *Battle of Sedan* panorama, generally attributed to Anton von Werner. Though von Werner indeed designed and supervised it, every brushstroke was actually painted by a team of fourteen other painters, who received little or no public credit. And even when Paris's Musée Grévin waxworks offered a topical waxwork tableau, "Les coulisses d'une panorama," showing Édouard Detaille putting the final touches on "his" 1883 Battle of Rezonville panorama (a work he had supervised at the Musée Grévin itself), the other inhabitants of the crowded viewing platform are not the actual panorama painters but other well-known contemporary artists, gathered as a kind of pantheon to flank Detaille as artist. Schwartz, *Spectacular Realities*, 104.
89. Robichon, "Le panorama," and Grau, *Virtual Art*, 65–71, 101–5, discuss the panorama as an emerging commodity form (including financing, pricing, rapid studio production, building standardization). Even a panorama's lead painter-designer, Robichon points out (67), retained no legal ownership of "his" creation—for panoramas remained the property of the commissioning joint-stock companies.
90. David Harris, "Eadweard Muybridge and the Photographic Panorama of San Francisco, 1850–1880," in Harris with Sandweiss, *Eadweard Muybridge*, 36–53; Aumont, "The Variable Eye"; Gunning, "Landscape" and "'The Whole World within Reach': Travel Images without Borders," in *Virtual Voyages: Cinema and Travel*, ed. Jeffrey Ruoff (Durham: Duke University Press, 2006), 25–41; Angela Miller, "The Panorama, the Cinema and the Emergence of the Spectacular," *Wide Angle* 18, no. 2 (1996): 34–69; and Uricchio, "A 'Proper Point of View.'"
91. Interview with Kevin Brownlow used for Brownlow's 1968 documentary, *Abel Gance: The Charm of Dynamite* (Rye, N.Y.: Images); excerpts

were reprinted in Roger Icart, ed., *Abel Gance: Un soleil dans chaque image* (Paris: Cinémathèque Française, 2002), 84.

92. On Hugo, see Maxwell, *Mysteries*.
93. Grau, *Virtual Art*, 146–47.
94. Gloria Sutton, *The Experience Machine: Stan VanDerBeek's Movie-Drome and Expanded Cinema* (Cambridge: MIT Press, 2015).
95. Mimi Colligan, *Canvas Documentaries: Panoramic Entertainments in Nineteenth-Century Australia and New Zealand* (Melbourne: Melbourne University Press, 2002), 19–20.
96. Jan Garff, "A Rolled Panorama," in *C. W. Eckersberg's Panorama of the Copenhagen Roads* (Copenhagen: Statens Museum for Kunst, 1983), n.p.
97. Karina Lykke Grand, "The New View," in *Gold: Treasures from the Danish Golden Age*, ed. Grand, Lise Pennington, and Anne Mette Thomsen (Aarhus: ARoS, 2013), 166–99; 176.
98. Otto, *Multiplying Worlds*, 21.
99. See Sweetman's "Panoramic Image," 15.
100. Grau's *Virtual Art*, 63, cites Constable's ambivalent 1803 letter, noting, "Panoramic painting seems all the rage," yet admiring a particular panoramic view of Rome for taking "the greatest care and fidelity."
101. Anton von Werner, *Erlebnisse und Eindrücke* (Berlin: E. S. Mittler, 1913), 373.
102. Vincent van Gogh to Theo van Gogh, August/September 1881, quoted in Neumann, "Instead of the Grand Tour," 51.
103. Emily Braun, "Shock and Awe: Futurist *Aeropittura* and the Theories of Giulio Doubet," in *Italian Futurism, 1909–1944: Reconstructing the Universe*, ed. Vivien Greene (New York: Guggenheim Museum, 2014), 269–83; 270.
104. Michelle Foa, *Georges Seurat: The Art of Vision* (New Haven: Yale University Press, 2015), 7–62.
105. Margareth da Silva Pereira, "The Time of the Capitals: Rio de Janiero and São Paolo: Words, Actors and Plans," in *Planning Latin America's Capital Cities, 1850–1950*, ed. Arturo Almandoz (London: Routledge, 2002), 75–108, 77.
106. Veronica della Dora, "Putting the World into a Box: A Geography of Nineteenth-Century 'Travelling Landscapes,'" *Geografiska Annaler, Series B: Human Geography* 89, no. 4 (2007): 287–306.
107. Yet from the outset, some touring panoramic paintings tore or faded in transit. In 1800 one canvas journeying from Britain arrived in Germany "bleached through." The panorama of London likewise reached Leipzig "so damaged [*abgenutzt*] and bleached out, all figures so blurry and confused," that it took Saxon court flattery to deem it worthy of its "pompous buildup." S. Hausmann, "Die Entstehung der Panoramen," *Kunst für Alle* 5, no. 13 (1889): 201, translation ours.
108. By 1854 two dozen panoramas had been displayed in Russia, including Johann Friedrich Tielke's full and semi-panoramas of St. Petersburg, Moscow, and Riga. Alina Novik, "Rethinking the History of Famous Panoramas: A Russian Perspective" *Panorama* 1 (2017): 17–19.
109. Isabelle Caron, "A Treasure in Canada: Ste. Anne de Beaupré's Cyclorama of Jerusalem and the Crucifixion of Christ," in Koller, *The Panorama in the Old World*, 110–17; 111.
110. Della Dora, "Putting the World into a Box," 300.
111. Kusahara, "'We Will Open,'" 84.
112. Colligan, *Canvas Documentaries*; and Edwin Barnard, *Capturing Time: Panoramas of Old Australia* (Canberra: National Library of Australia, 2012).
113. Stokes, *The Autobiography of a Cook*.
114. Barnard, *Capturing Time*, 15.
115. Bartetzky and Jaworski, *Gechichte im Rundumblick*.
116. Ruby Carlson and Sara Velas, "Shenjing Panorama: A Landmark 360° Collaboration between the Velaslavasay Panorama and Experts of Chinese Panorama Painting," *Panorama* 2 (2019): 77–86.
117. Koller, *The World of Panoramas*.
118. Della Dora, "Putting the World into a Box," 302; see also Schiermeier, *Panorama München*, 51. For French Orientalist/colonialist panorama painting, see John Zarobell, *Empire of Landscape: Space and Ideology in French Colonial Algeria* (University Park: Pennsylvania State University Press, 2010), chap. 1.
119. Colligan, *Canvas Documentaries*, 35–40.
120. Daniel E. White, *From Little London to Little Bengal: Religion, Print, and Modernity in Early Modern British India, 1793–1835* (Baltimore: Johns Hopkins University Press, 2013), 31.
121. In addition to creating an astonishingly elaborate frame, Kevin Avery explains, Church and his colleagues "managed to reproduce the lighting effects created at single picture exhibitions in London. They either painted the walls dark or screened them with dark fabric. Probably, too, they masked the skylight in the gallery in such a way that, though it could not be seen by spectators, its illumination was directed primarily at the painting." Avery, *Church's Great Picture: The Heart of the Andes* (New York: Metropolitan Museum of Art, 1993), 47–53; 35. On Church's response to Humboldt and the paradoxes of detail in large-scale paintings, see Jennifer Raab, *Frederic Church: The Art and Science of Detail* (New Haven: Yale University Press, 2015).
122. Ferdinand de Saussure, *Course on General Linguistics*, trans. Roy Harris (London: Bloomsbury, 2014), 25.
123. Solar, *Das Panorama*.
124. Joseph Puchberger began taking panoramic photographs in 1843, only four years after photography itself was established. Arnaud Frich, *La photographie panoramique* (Paris: Eyrolles, 2004), ix.
125. Alexander von Humboldt, "Landscape Painting," in *Cosmos: A Sketch of a Physical Description of the Universe*, 5 vols., trans. E. C. Otté (London: George Bell and Sons, 1900), 2:457.
126. This follows a long tradition of architects' (and urban planners') use of panoramic photography. The 1911 architectural competition for building Australia's new national capital in Canberra supplied competitors with maps and two 360-degree panoramic drawings. Barnard, *Capturing Time*, 148. In postwar Berlin, urban photopanoramas were taken both to plan and to document massive rebuilding projects. Katie Trumpener, "Stalin Boulevard: Panoramic Vistas and Urban Planning in Eastern European Photobooks," in *Remapping Cold War Media: Institutions, Infrastructures, Networks, Exchanges*, ed. Alice Lovejoy and Mari Pajala (Bloomington: Indiana University Press, forthcoming). Robert Venturi and Denise Scott Brown's landmark 1972 (later revised) *Learning from Las Vegas: The Forgotten Symbolism of Architectural Form* (Cambridge: MIT Press, 2011) reproduces old Vegas panoramic photographs (38) and includes a panorama shot column in its chart (42–43) taxonomizing the resort's famous casinos.
127. Stephan Oettermann, "Imperial Views—Panoramas in Berlin," in Yadegar Asisi, *Berlin 2005: Architektur-Panoramen* (Berlin: Aedes/STERN, 1995), 7–15; see also Asisi, "Das Panorama—ein Dinosaurier des 19. Jahrhunderts," in Streicher, *Panorama*, 92–97, and his "The Rebirth of the Panorama," in Koller, *The Panorama in the Old World*, 136–39.
128. See Asisi's website, http://www.asisi.de/homepage.html.
129. Trailer for *Die Mauer*, https://vimeo.com/56753130.
130. Étienne-Jean Delécluze thus praises Vernet's *The Capture of the Smalah of Abd-al-Kader* (1845) for its unified effect, despite its lack of fixed perspectival vantage point: "The ensemble of this vast scene submits to as many points of view as a panorama." Cited in Katie Hornstein, *Picturing War in France, 1792–1856* (New Haven: Yale University Press, 2017), 121.
131. Hornstein, *Picturing War*, 108.

132. Uricchio, "A 'Proper Point of View,'" 12.

133. Hans Kloss, *Stauferrundbild: Monumentalgemälde im Kloster Lorch* (Gmünd: Einhorn-Verlag, 2007); Titus Matiyane, *Cities of the World* (Rotterdam: 010 Publishers, 2007); Ann Bukantas, ed., *Cityscape: Ben Johnson's Liverpool* (Liverpool: Liverpool University Press, 2008); Ben Johnson, *Spirit of Place: Paintings, 1969–2015* (Southampton: Southampton City Art Gallery, 2015); and Sohei Nishino, *Tokyo* (Tokyo: AMANA, 2015). Felix Topolski's restored panoramic mural, *Memoir of the 20th Century* (1975–89), reopened in London in 2007. Jeffrey Isaac's painted photorealist panoramas and cycloramas touch on many aspects of the medium's history. His 1980s–2000s panoramic paintings reference the Renaissance palazzo, natural history and art museums, Alpine and landscape views, and building scaffolding; they include a David Hockney–inspired photocollage subway panorama, parapet views reminiscent of the Lumières' Photorama (chap. 8), seaside panoramas updating Mesdag's shore panorama, Monet's 1914–26 *Water Lilies* series—and its influential 1927 Paris Orangerie installation—and Henri Matisse's 1952 wraparound cutout *The Swimming Pool*. See Isaac's website at http://www.jeffreyisaac.com.

134. "The Velaslavasay Panorama," http://www.panoramaonview.org/.

135. Ana Luisa Nobre, "Other Landscapes," in Marc Ferrez and Robert Polidori, *Rio*, 2 vols. (São Paolo: Institute Moreira Salles, 2015), 2:229–31; 230. Eadweard Muybridge and Mark Klett, *One City/Two Visions: San Francisco Panoramas, 1878 and 1990* (San Francisco: Bedford Arts, 1990); Jim Masselos and Narayani Gupta, *Beato's Delhi, 1857, 1997* (Delhi: Ravi Dayal, 2000); and Paul Lowe and David Campbell, *Burke + Norfolk: Photographs from the War in Afghanistan by John Burke and Simon Norfolk* (Stockport, U.K.: Dewi Lewis, 2011). Relatedly, see John B. Inglis and Jill Sanders, *Panorama of the Thames: A Riverside View of Georgian England* (London: Thames and Hudson, 2015); Chris Ellmers and Alex Warner, *London's Riverscape: Lost and Found: A Panorama of the River Thames from 1937 and Today* (London: London's Found Riverscape Partnership, 2000); Greg Miller, *Panorama of the Hudson River* (New Paltz, N.Y.: Samuel Dorsky Museum of Art, 2009); and Marin Kasimir, *Éphémère et universelle: Fictions panoramiques* (Paris: Archibooks, 2008). *So weit kein Auge reicht: Berliner Panoramafotographien aus den Jahren 1949–1952, aufgenommen von Fritz Tiedemann; rekonstruiert und interpretiert von Arwed Messmer* (Berlin: Berlinische Galerie, 2009) and Annett Gröschner, Florian Ebner, and Fritz Tiedemann, *Berlin, Fruchtstraße on March 27, 1952* (Ostfildern: Hatje Cantz, 2012), posthumously assemble Teidemann's 1950s East Berlin architectural photographic series into continuous paroramas.

136. Sanford Wurmfeld, "Why a Cyclorama?" in Koller, *The Panorama in the Old World*, 16–17.

137. Erik Verhagen, *Jan Dibbets: The Photographic Work, 1967–2007* (Paris: Éditions du Panama, 2007); for a juxtaposition of Nauman with Horace-Bénédict de Saussure's 1780s mountain panoramas, see Chrissie Iles, "Between the Still and Moving Image," in *Into the Light: The Projected Image in American Art, 1964–1977*, ed. Illes (New York: Whitney Museum of Art, 2001), 33–89; 64–65; and "Daniel Steegmann Mangrané: A Transparent Leaf Instead of a Mouth," Hessel Art Museum, Bard College, 2018, esp. the installation *Spiral Forest* (2017).

138. Molly Catherine Briggs juxtaposes a Turrell light-based work with the nearby Hague shoreline panorama, likewise absorbed with light effects and passing time. Briggs, "Immersion, Chromatics, and Atmospheric Effects: Recalling Period Perception in Turrell's Celestial Vault and Mesdag's *Panorama*," *Panorama* 2 (2018): 60–68.

139. Jens Erik Sorensen, Carsten Thau, and Marie Nipper's innovative exhibition catalogue, *Olafur Eliasson: Your Rainbow Panorama* (Aarhus: ARoS Aarhus Kunstmuseum, 2011), functions as a flip-book, allowing readers to progress around the panorama in quasi-animated style.

140. Pamela M. Lee, "Your Light and Space," in Madeleine Grynszteyn et al., *Take Your Time: Olafur Eliasson* (San Francisco: San Francisco Museum of Modern Art, 2007), 33–49; 38. See also Jonathan Crary, "Visionary Abstraction," in *Olafur Eliasson: Your Lighthouse, Works with Light, 1991–2004* (Wolfsburg, Germany: Kunstmuseum Wolfsburg, 2004), 20–32.

141. The New York Philharmonic's "Philharmonic 360" (2014), in which Karlheinz Stockhausen's *Gruppen* was played in the round (the orchestra surrounding the audience) at the Park Avenue Armory in New York City, likewise referenced the panoramic.

142. In this it resembles the Gothic cathedral in Griffiths's account of "Architectonics, Pilgrimage and Spectatorial Bliss," in *Shivers Down Your Spine, 18–24*.

143. "Introducing the Daily 360 from the *New York Times*," November 1, 2016, http://www.nytimes.com/2016/11/01/nytnow/the-daily-360-videos.html. On photojournalism using panoramic cameras, see Matthew Mirapaul, "The Sweeping View from Inside a Digital Bubble," *New York Times*, September 25, 2003, G5, and Sarah McBride, "The Return of the Cyclorama," *Wall Street Journal*, September 11, 2006, R12.

144. "Splendid Central Plains from C China's Henan Listed on Guinness World Records," Chinese Government's Official Web Portal (gov.cn), April 26, 2011, http://www.gov.cn/english/2011-04/26/content_1852790.htm. For other panorama projects in China, see Xia Shushen, "A Tentative Plan for 'Huai-Hai Campaign' Panorama: Brief Introduction to My Design of China Xuzhou Panorama Gallery in 2003," in Streicher, *Panorama*, 86–88.

145. "Largest Panoramic Painting," http://www.guinnessworldrecords.com/world-records/10000/largest-panoramic-painting.

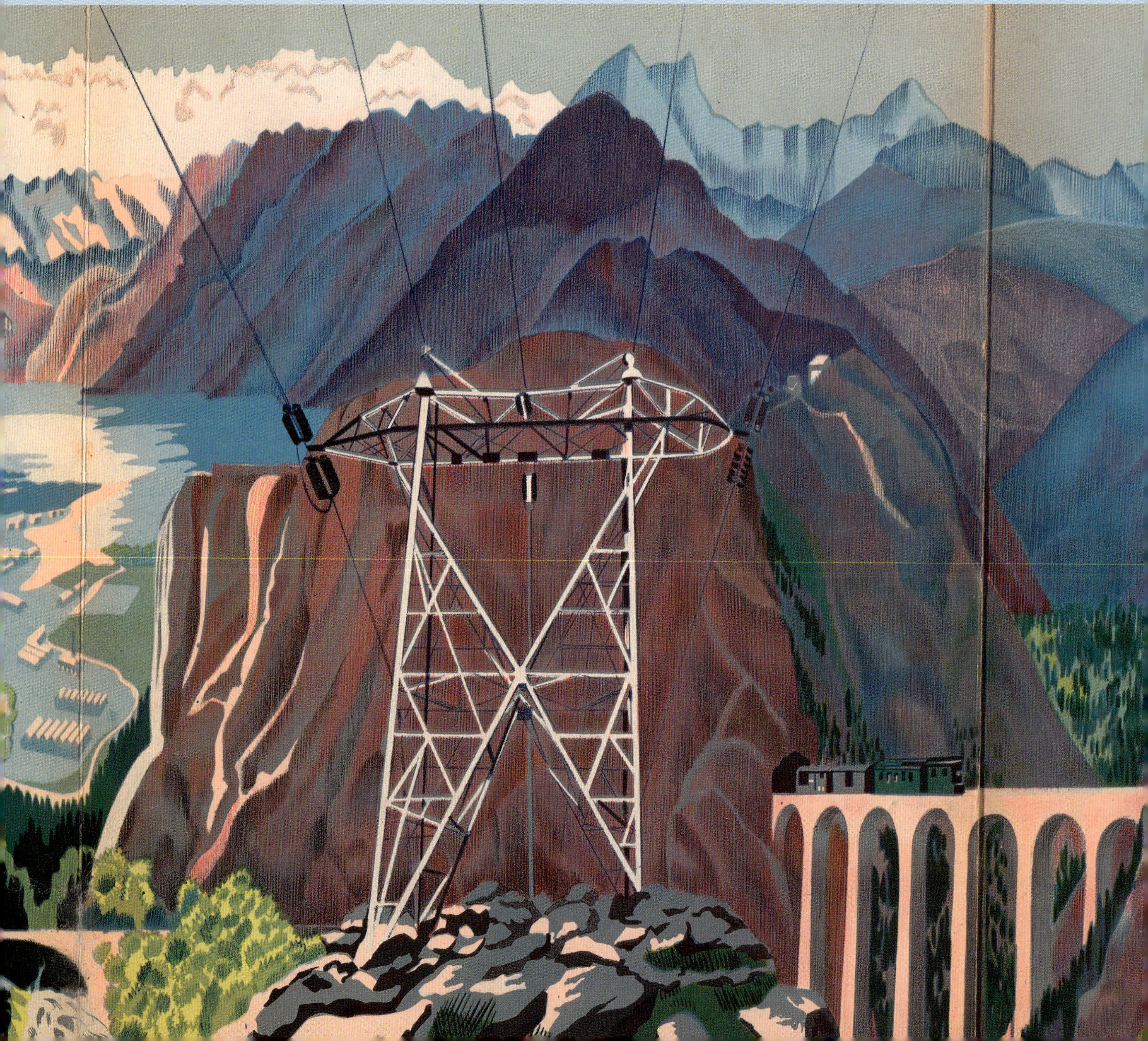

Up Close

Panoramic Vignettes

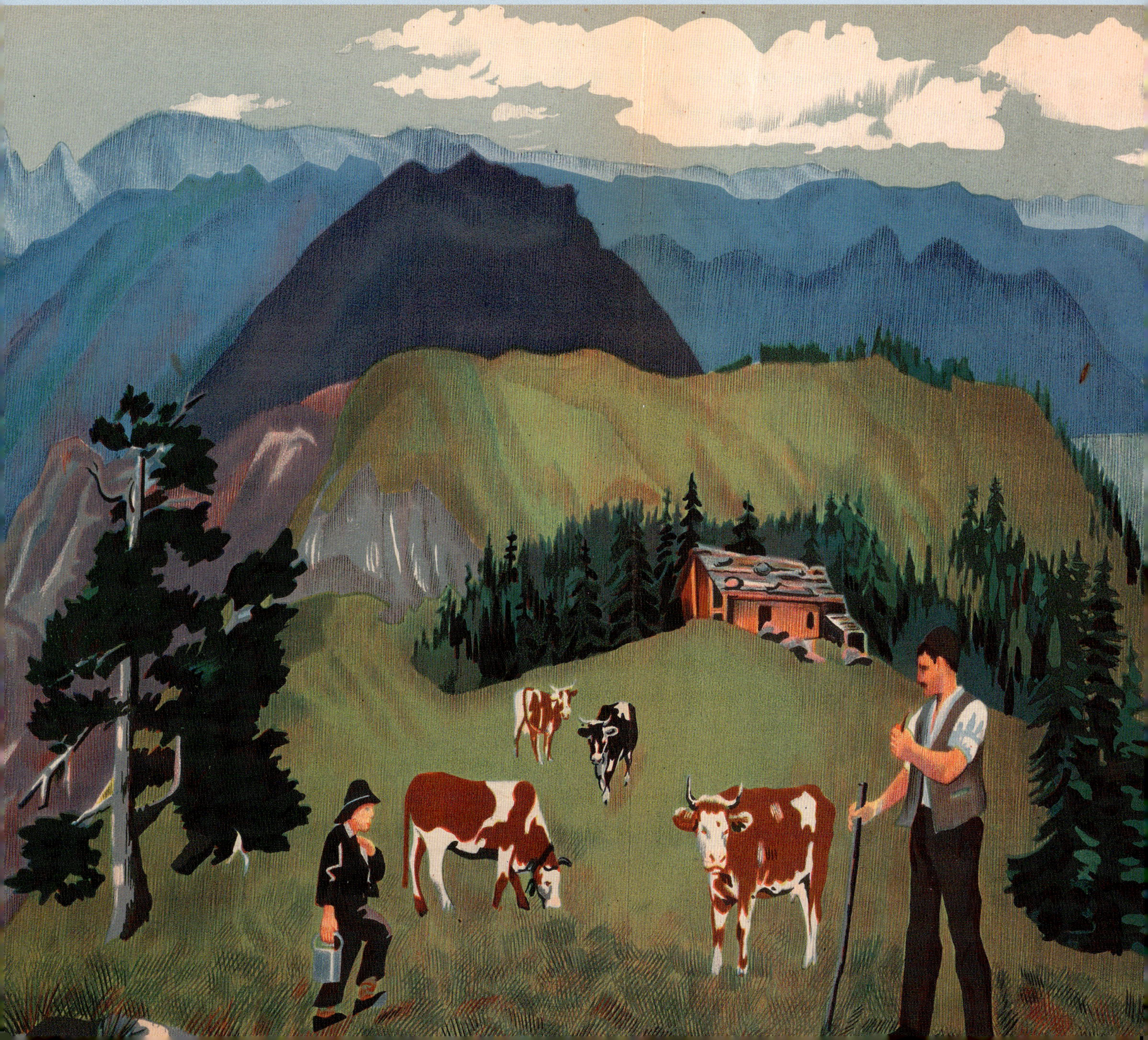

TIMOTHY HYMAN

Ambrogio Lorenzetti, *The Well-Governed City*, 1337–40

The heart of the city-republic of Siena is the frescoed chamber where its ruling body, the Nine, gave judgment. The room's right-hand wall offers a forty-six-foot panorama of a just society at peace. What defines Ambrogio's space as *panoramic* is its extended format, over four times wider than high. We are above the city but see only its right-hand segment; the city wall must continue far below and to the left; the vast tract of countryside under its curving horizon implies an equally grand vista on the city's other side. Two concentric circles: the circuit of city walls, surrounded by its territory.

The panorama has often been seen as a problematic viewpoint, offering us an omniscience, yet holding us at a distance. Ambrogio's pre-perspectival space resolves this dilemma. In an almost magical manner, we are both above *and* inside the city; we see everything yet can participate and move freely (like the "ambient vision" recorded in out-of-the-body experiences or Alain-René LeSage's comic novel *The Devil on Two Sticks*, 1708, where Satan lifts off Madrid's roofs). Near and far can be present simultaneously; at a single glance, we take in the lecturer in the city classroom and glimpse the sea thirty miles beyond. We recognize a kind of seeing truer to our imaginative experience of space (confirmed in reverie and dream) than single-point perspective can ever be.

Ambrogio's masterstroke is the complex construction of gate and wall at the center, which trigger powerful spatial cues. The thin sliver of dark wall reaches down to the right of the nearest zigzag, plunging us back into space; the pale line of ledge behind the castellations—out of sight in the foreground, visible halfway up, then lost again—leads us to a little door in the gate. The pigment is the local burnt sienna, luminously graded to each shifting plane. From the gate we will move left, into the city, or outward along the road. Within the city, the building types are precise (still recognizable in modern Siena). Ambrogio's preparations must have involved far more architectural drawing than most modern painters undertake. But he avoids literal topography—hence, there is no trace of the Campo, Siena's most striking feature.

We are invited to pause at each activity on which our eyes alight: the bookshop behind the dancers, its reader in a carrel; the shoeshop, or hosiery; the rapt lecture audience; the tavern counter, its cured hams hanging much as they do today above Italian bars. Then our eye may travel upward, catching a woman looking out a side window, a vase, a birdcage—and, high above, builders at work on the wooden scaffolding, against a dark sky. Outside the tavern, a peasant goads his donkey; behind, facing the opposite way, another donkey appears in profile, its huge head delicately floating on a golden ochre ground. Everywhere we notice Ambrogio's relish in chance overlaps: the play of partial donkeys, as headless hindquarters disappear behind houses; the incongruous appearance of a sheep's head jutting forward over a young girl's shoulder, as shepherd and flock pass her.

Once we pass through the gate, there is less overlap, and space moves freely around several complete figures. But the scale is not constant. The falconers are much bigger than the peasants working in front of them. As we move down the paved highway, figures diminish in size more or less "correctly," and distance is powerfully felt between road and field. But when we examine the distant figures, the foreground threshers are smaller than the

previous spread: Alexandra Exter, *Panorama of the River/Panorama du fleuve*, detail (see pages 64–65) harvesters behind. We loosely hover over the landscape, passing from one focus to another, invited on a journey through this imagined landscape, where spring sowing occurs alongside summer harvesting. This huge vista, so unlike any other known medieval painting, has prompted speculation that Ambrogio might have seen a Chinese landscape scroll. (Trade between Tuscany and Cathay, along the Silk Road, was at its height during these decades.) Ambrogio's fresco handling is much looser than any contemporaries', more intimate and unplanned. No preliminary design could have anticipated the constant play of calligraphic marks across this enormous surface: the wisps of vegetation, the percussion of a cornfield's stubble, the featheriness of a cockerel's tail. Even after six centuries of damage, it survives as one of European art's greatest "touch paintings," an astonishing feat of sustained improvisation.

When he began to paint the three walls of what is now called the Sala della Pace, Ambrogio (ca. 1288–1348) was almost fifty. He is said to have been a *pictor doctus* (learned painter) and to have "spoken wisely" at one of the chief Sienese councils. He probably contributed to the discussions preceding this important civic commission. The resulting room was perfectly structured to make its statement. The Nine entered beneath an allegory of Justice, taking their seats below. The petitioners facing them saw a stark choice: the "bad" wall on their left, where Tyranny leads to war; the "good" on their right, where the just commune creates a world in harmony.

Despite the everyday, vernacular character of Ambrogio's imagery, its realism is strictly limited. This is a society without wheeled vehicles. The city is surrounded and invaded by allegorical personages. The ring of nine dancers (and tambourine player) dominating the left foreground signify the rule of the Nine; for Ambrogio—as later for Matisse—humans moving together in a circle spell out liberty and communal well-being. In the sky, right of the gate, flies SECURITAS, gibbet in one hand, a cartouche in the other reading (in the still-fledgling Tuscan vernacular), "Every man can travel freely without fear, and each can till and sow, so long as the commune keeps this woman as sovereign, for she has stripped the wicked of all power."

Ambrogio's panorama defines a remarkable moment in European history. The Sienese constitution was by far the most democratic among the Italian communes (self-governing city-states), in place some sixty years, becoming known as *Il buon governo* ("The Good Government"). In Ambrogio's imagery, the Golden Age returns not as pre-urban pastoral, but within a complex modern city. His inclusive, uncentered, fluid space is a truly libertarian idiom; with it he creates a microcosm whose imaginative scope remains unsurpassed.

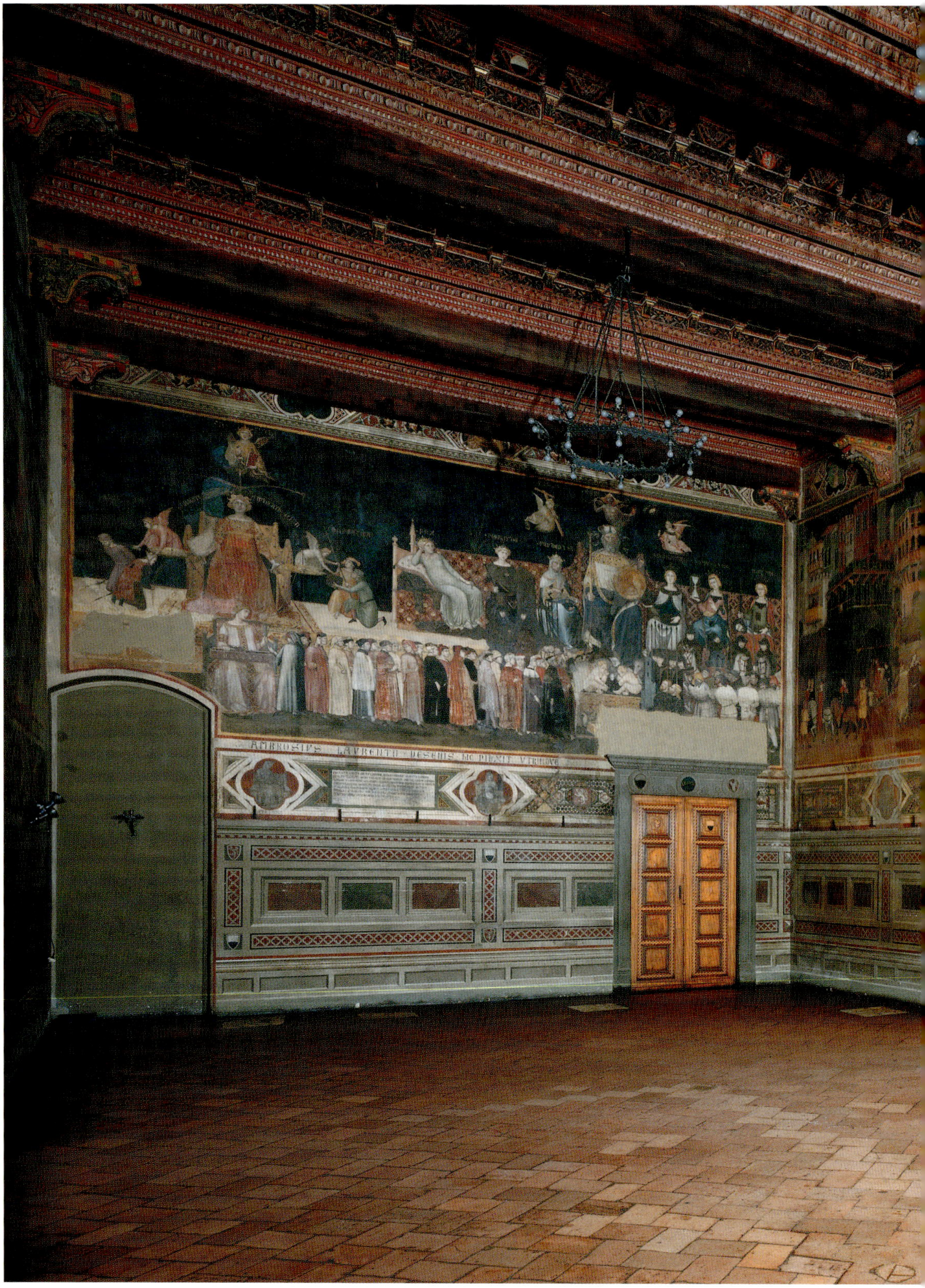

Ambrogio Lorenzetti (Italian, 1285–ca. 1348), *The Well-Governed City*, 1337–40.
Fresco. Sala della Pace, Palazzo Pubblico, Siena.

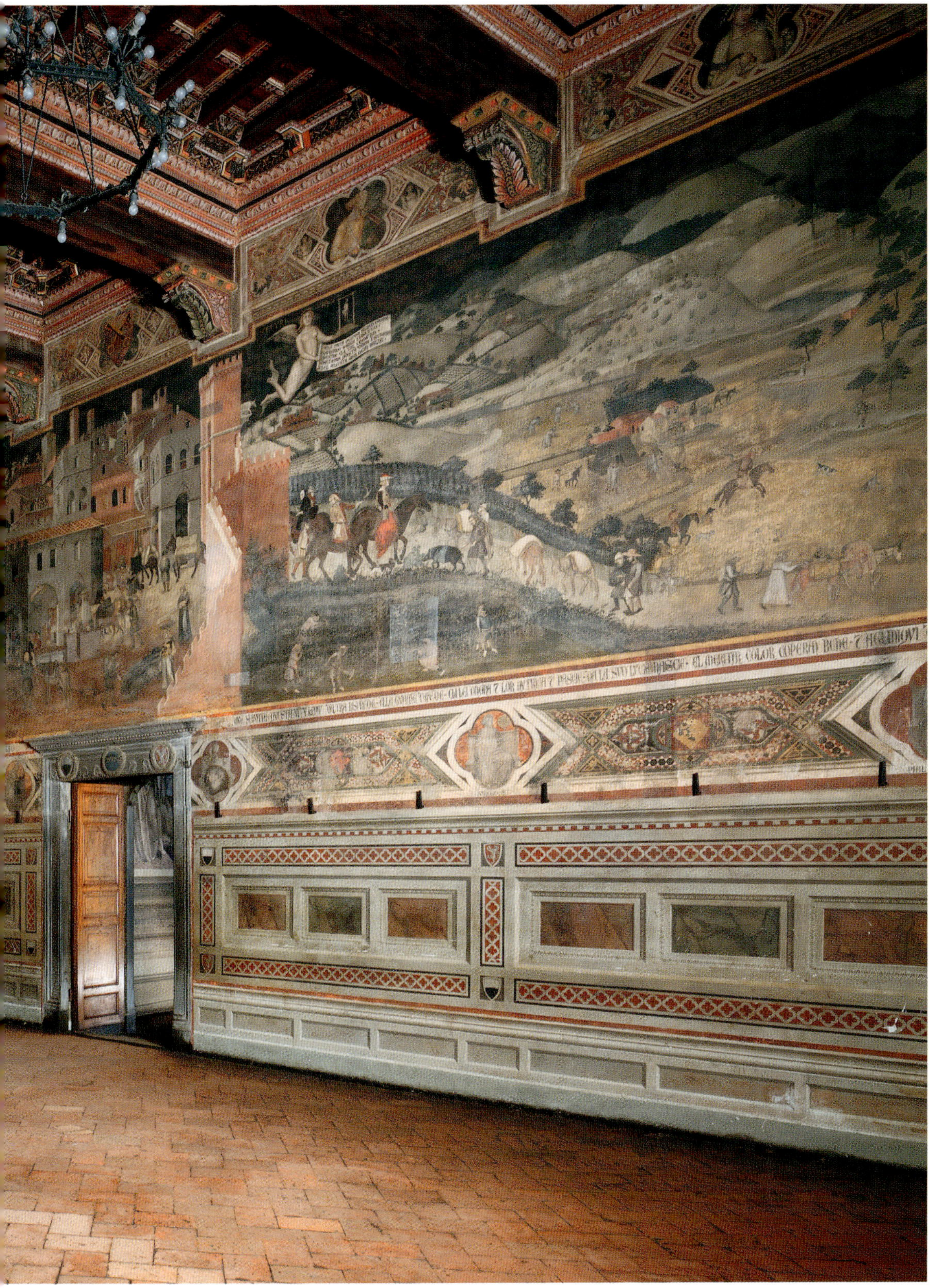

MARINA WARNER

Melchior Lorck, *The Prospect of Constantinople*, 1559

Between 1555 and 1559 Melchior Lorck traveled to Turkey. The Danish-born artist (1526/27–after 1583) was appointed by his patron (and future emperor) Archduke Ferdinand to play a part in the embassy of the Holy Roman Empire, which was sent to negotiate with Suleiman the Magnificent, the Ottoman sultan. Ottoman power was at its apogee; Suleiman's empire stretched across from Algeria to the west, Mecca to the south, Baghdad to the east, and the River Don to the north, all adjoining—and often attacking—the Habsburgs' extensive territories.

The European mission, under the remarkably tenacious Augier Ghislain de Busbecq, aimed to ease the tensions caused by Suleiman's huge possessions, and, in particular, to claim Hungary for his master and confirm him on that country's throne. The prime motive for including an artist in the mission was European curiosity about the Ottomans: Lorck was to create an inventory of data about their little-known culture. One of the first western European observers to travel in the region and record what he found, he produced remarkable intelligence about the mysterious, threatening, unknown realm of Islamic power.

The diplomats returned home with a treaty; they also brought back the first lilac and the first tulip to be seen outside Turkey. Lorck stayed on another four years, the longest visit to that date of any western European artist. During that time, he produced a fabulously rich and rare catalogue of Turkish customs, technology, costumes, and—above all—military arrangements. Born a year or two before Dürer's death, Lorck was an attentive student of the great draftsman's observational powers. Lorck's resulting *Turkish Album* (published in 1626), compiled the detailed, acute reports of an enterprising spy, while creating a marvelous work of artistic skill and imagination.

For several significant works, Lorck adopts the detached omniscience of a narrator's view from above. In the visual arts this translates into an elevated position and a synoptic method, fusing disparate elements into one seamless totality. Yet with startling flexibility, it can also imply a single first-person perceiver uniquely, almost prophetically, equipped to see all. It operates in the manner of the generalized eye of fate, oracular and godlike, and can slip into the persona of an individual investigator, even a peeping Tom, able to uncover things normally hidden from view.

Lorck's greatest work, *The Prospect of Constantinople*, is a panorama drawing, 37 feet long, showing Constantinople and the Golden Horn in a cinematic sweep "from the Seraglio Point to the mountains beyond the walls protecting the city peninsular from the hinterland."[1] The vast, synoptic city vista is magically and microscopically rendered from the heights of the Galata district fortifications on the European side of the Bosporus, which is thronged with the merchants' graceful gaff-rigged dhows, as well as fishing boats, naval vessels, ferries, and skiffs, their sails filling voluptuously in the wind. Lorck details the city's architecture with delicate penmanship, and, in his spiky handwriting, he identifies palaces and stables, churches and mosques, classical antiquities, aqueducts, cemeteries, warehouses, schools, and the city gates. There are washes of green on the trees, of rose-sepia on the battlements on both banks.

The splendors of the classical and Byzantine era are included—Leander's Tower, Constantine's column, and the imposing mass of "S. Sophia"—alongside the Ottoman city's grandeurs. The architect Mimar Sinan's vast Süleymaniye mosque, opened in 1557, dominates the skyline. Lorck's view, dated 1559, is the earliest eyewitness picture of the great Ottoman city, which Sinan and others had built

Yet the Olympian vista he unfolds so convincingly is actually fantastic. The art historian Marco Iuliano has demonstrated how Lorck conflated eight different vantage points to achieve an apparently smooth, unified pan across the Bosporus.[2] This aerial synopsis gives Lorck's penmanship a chance to play wonderfully with the filled sails' crescents and spheres against the stacked cubes and stepped forms of the colossal city. This vision of Constantinople is awe-inspiring in its scale and intensity.

In the foreground, the artist included himself at work, making a flourish on a scroll, which is held for him by an Ottoman grandee, whose huge rolled turban demarcates his status as a mufti or an emir, both positions of authority that defined and upheld the law. The panorama is both a self-portrait and a reflexive celebration of the picture in the process of being made. As in a *mise-en-abyme,* you would see the figure of the artist in the painting he is making were he not blocking the view.

The composition communicates that this commanding overview of the great Ottoman capital has been granted to a uniquely privileged, gifted humanist traveler. Lorck renders himself as a Renaissance courtier with light curls under a velvet cap, a graceful, youthful figure with elongated fingers—Parmigianino, his contemporary, might have rendered him thus—with his elegant outer jacket slung sidewise over his shoulder. Here, the drawing proclaims, is a suitable recipient of a royal bursary, an artist who has studied in Italy. He is executing his art with élan, under the apparently benevolent supervision of a high official, and the relationship discloses the commission's tensions: the Ottoman grandee is being helpful, even admiring, as he holds the lid of a chalice and proffers it, ink-filled, for Lorck to dip his quill. Nevertheless, he is keeping close by, watchfully, no doubt; the visiting European artist has been permitted to record the city—its layout, dwellings, fortifications, trade, shipping—by permission, permission granted because the Turkish Empire has nothing to fear from revealing to foreigners its bustle, magnificence, and power.

Lorck wanted to have his Turkish drawings engraved and published, to make some much-needed money. Instead, the scroll was deposited in the library in Leiden soon after its making, possibly even during the artist's lifetime. It once hung in the reading room of the library, then was put away in the attic, where it suffered much damage, some irreparable, from damp and rats.

NOTES

1. Erik Fischer, *Melchior Lorck in Turkey* (Copenhagen: Royal Museum of Fine Arts, 1990), 9. See also Erik Fischer, Ernst Jonas Bencard, and Mikael Bøgh Rasmussen, *Melchior Lorck*, 4 vols. (Copenhagen: Vandkunsten, 2009), vol. 4. The panorama was originally made up of twenty-one sheets of paper glued together, which have now been separated for conservation purposes.
2. Marco Iuliano, "Melchior Lorck's Constantinople in the European Context," in Fischer et al., *Melchior Lorck*, 4:25–60, 51–60.

OVERLEAF:

Melchior Lorck (Danish, 1526/1527–after 1583), *The Prospect of Constantinople*, 1559. Drawing, length: 11.3 m (37 ft.). Leiden University Libraries (BPL 1758).

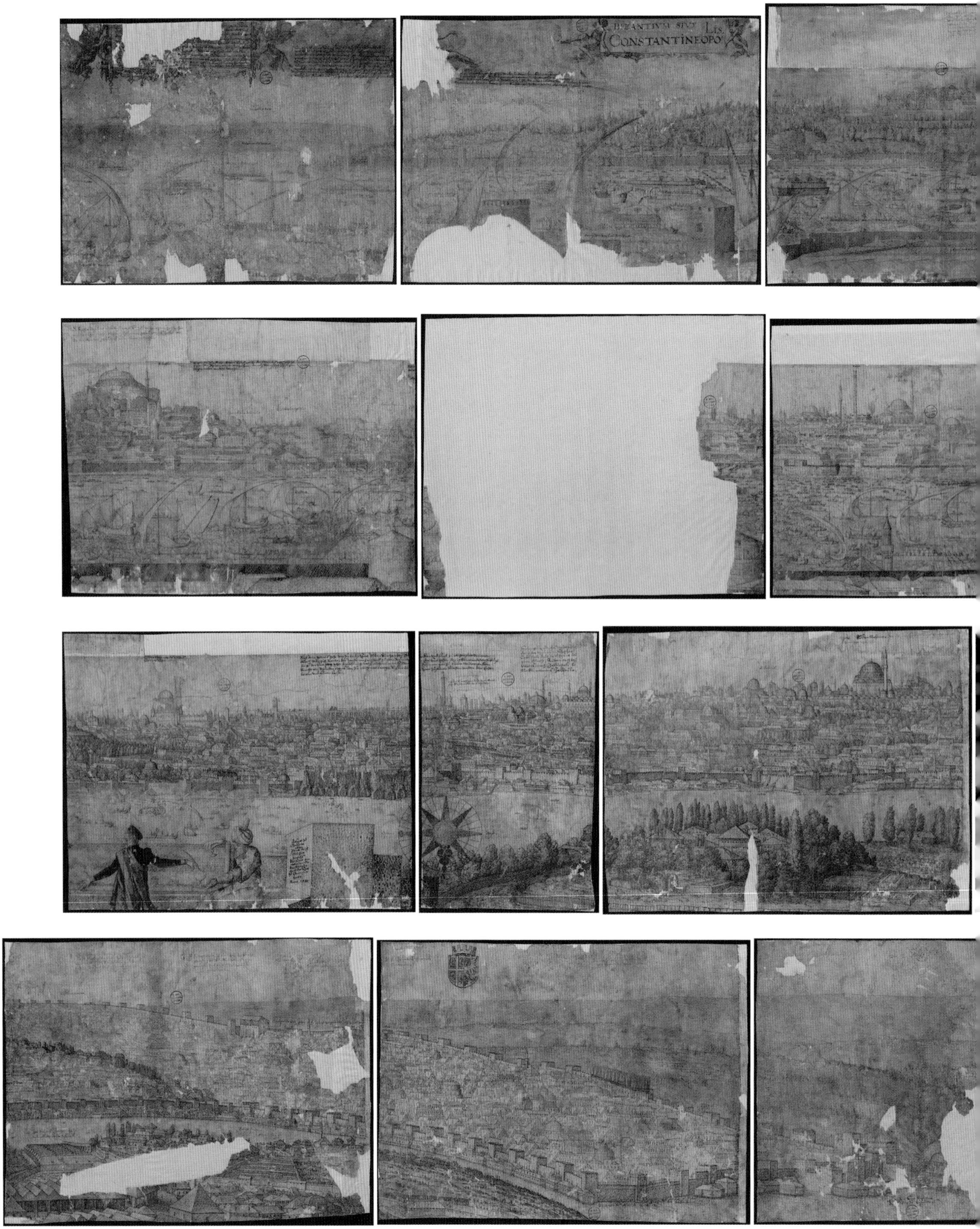
CONSTANTINEOPO

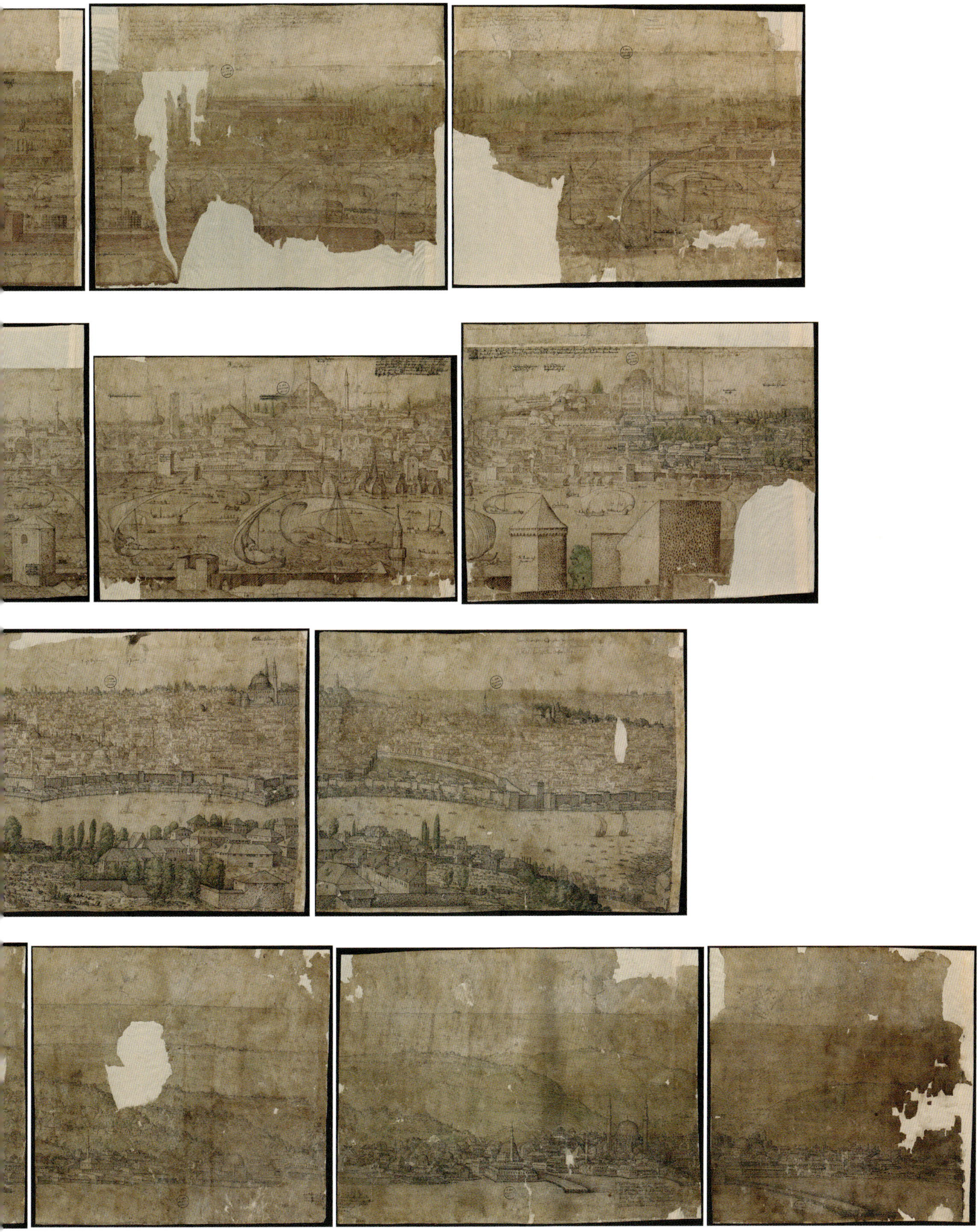

CARLA HERMANN

Robert Burford, *Rio de Janeiro,* 1827

The panorama *Description of a View of the City of St. Sebastian, and the Bay of Rio Janeiro,* a seascape taken from the waters of the Bay of Guanabara, opened to the public on June 25, 1827. Encouraged by the success of a Mexican view, which had closed in May, Robert Burford (1791/1792–1861) decided to remain with Latin America and to display the only panorama of Brazil to be exhibited in London in the nineteenth century. As the object itself has vanished, the print medium is our sole source of information. We gather that the panorama stayed open to the public for more than one year because some papers announced its closure in mid-November 1828. It was successful enough to justify a small tour through the United Kingdom, including Edinburgh and Newcastle.[1] Probably the fragile canvas of the panorama itself disintegrated at the end of its tour. The last we hear of it is an account of the auction of the eight paintings originally produced to serve as the basis for the large canvas.[2]

The crucial surviving source is the engraved key to the panorama. This was sold along with a booklet that included a short historical account and further details of the elements displayed in the view. The image available to us is a simplification of what once was a richly detailed picture. Although the painting exists only as a ghost, the simplified print traces the arrangement of the composition. Divided into two even horizontal parts, it obeys a structure common in Burford ́s panoramic views. In this case, the two-tier arrangement mirrors the difference between the inland city and the bay. Half of what we see is water, and the other half is land. This division enhances the actual geographic distance and makes the city at some times seem distant—as if we had to move halfway into the distance to reach it—and at others, it seems quite close because its presence is mediated through the intermediary forms of boats in front of it.

If the composition ostensibly describes the landscape with ideological neutrality, the representation of three British Royal Navy vessels in the bay denotes an attempt at dominance by stealth. Here I follow Robert Aguirre's notion of an informal empire, which identified Britain's expansionist politics toward cultural domination over countries that were not formally colonies of the British Empire but lay within the British horizon of commercial and trading interests.[3] The imperial influence was not political or military; rather, this dominance was mediated through representations, in the form of art, traveling narratives, and accounts, captured during expeditions and exhibited or published in London.

Instead of a coastal scene simply showing the natural and cultural aspects of the city, Burford preferred a landscape inhabited by ships. They are scattered across the water, in different sizes and shapes. They symbolize the dynamic commercial relationships of trade and commerce that were typical of this historical moment. We see fishing boats, the important Brazilian frigate *Pedro-Primeiro,* and a passenger steamboat. Among them, but differentiated by scale, the huge, richly painted British naval vessel, HMS *Blanche,* embodies a sense of domination.

Such were the efforts to redouble the reality effect of the panorama that the printed commentaries emphasized how detailed and vivid the ship felt, with precisely defined figures: It "strikes on our entry, and so powerful is the effect, that we could scarcely persuade ourselves what we looked at was not reality."[4] As the visitors emerged

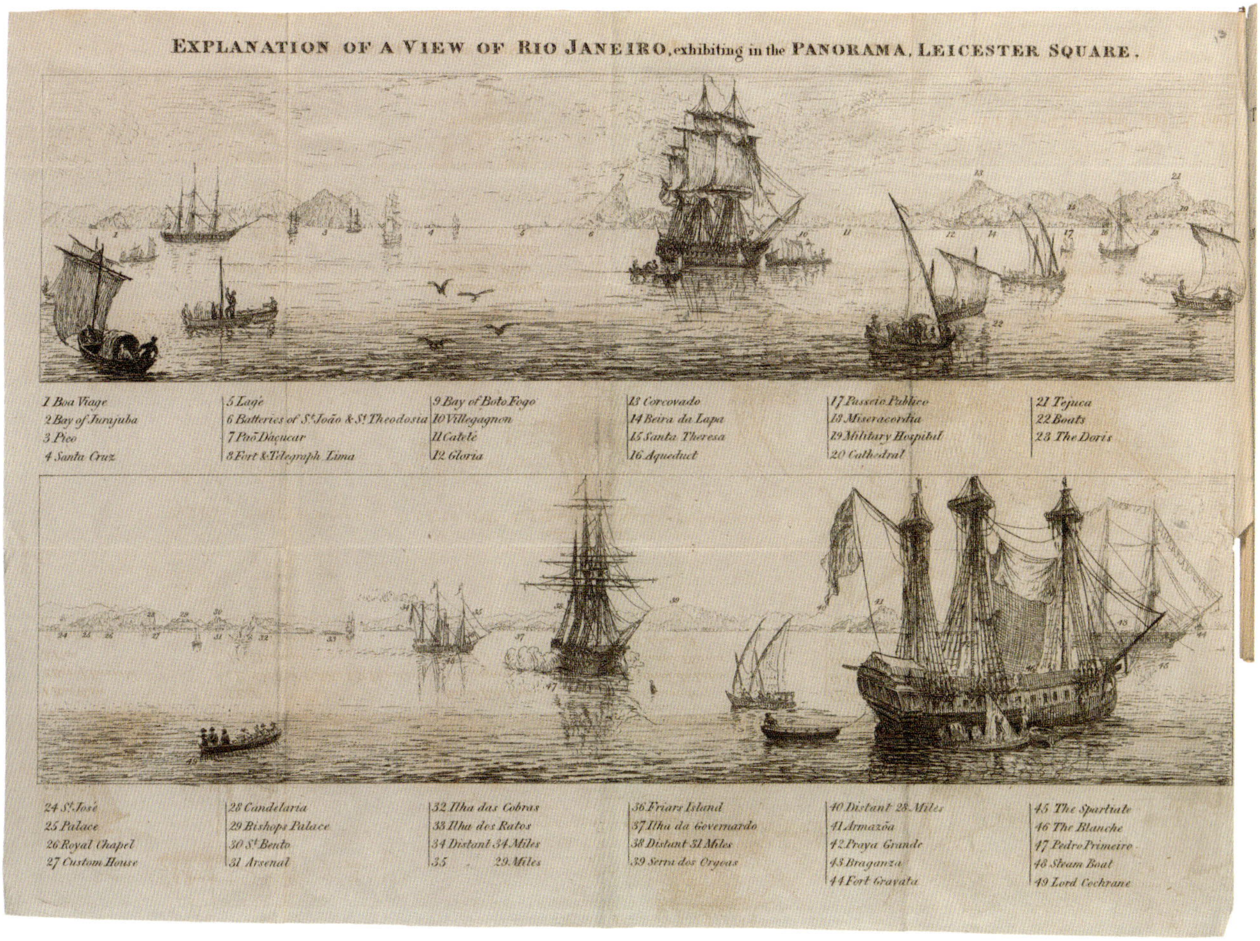

Robert Burford (British, 1791/1792–1861), *Explanation of a View of Rio Janeiro, Exhibiting in the Panorama, Leicester Square*, 1827. Houghton Library, Harvard University, Cambridge, Massachusetts (EC8 B2422 B827p).

in the center of the rotunda, they faced immediately the presence of the British navy in Rio. Furthermore, in one of the smaller boats could be discerned the figure of Lord Cochrane, and the pamphlet text reinforced his importance as the hired commander for the Brazilian fleet. The message is clear: the city that was once a colonial mystery, protected by the Portuguese from any foreign visitors, is now open to world, under Britain's indirect supervision.

The text also adds what is not visible in the image, offering details of the everyday aspects, the kinds of goods and merchants typical of the city, and describing its architecture. More than a presentation or a visiting card, this panorama is propaganda, selling the London viewer a vision of a modern, commodious, and prosperous city. Burford's rotunda showed Rio in succession to over twenty views of other places, including Paris, Malta, Pompeii, Mexico City, Madrid, and Geneva. To place Rio de Janeiro among such a diverse group of cities was to demonstrate that the city was in open contact with the outside world and stood as a participant in the new industrial liberalism. Moreover, by bringing faraway places to London, the panorama put the spectator at the center of the civilized world. From the viewing platform, people could know other places without ever leaving home, and had the idea that the empire—just like the circular canvas—had no boundaries.

NOTES

1. *Caledonian Mercury*, January 7, 1830; *Newcastle Courant*, January 29, 1831.
2. The auction house of W. Bigg announced they were disposed for sale in May 1836; *London Morning Post*, May 17, 1836.
3. Robert D. Aguirre, *Informal Empire: Mexico and Central America in Victorian Culture* (Minneapolis: University of Minnesota Press, 2005), xv.
4. *London Public Ledger and Daily Advertiser*, June 23, 1827.

MARIA ANTONELLA PELIZZARI

Felice Beato, *Panorama of Lucknow from the Great Imambara*, 1858

Felice Beato's sweeping, profoundly sad view of the ruined city of Lucknow has the character of air reconnaissance. Taken from the great height of the minaret of the Asafi Mosque, it surveys the religious and secular buildings of this city, once an opulent court built along the River Gomti in northern India. Lucknow was established in 1775 as the capital of Oudh, and its architectural and artistic splendor blossomed under the governance of the Nawabs, local leaders of Iranian origin. Such majesty was interrupted in 1856, when the East India Company took over the city and deposed the last Nawab, Wajid Ali Shah. Soon after, from May 1857 to March 1858, Lucknow became a theater of war between rebellious Indians and the British colonial authorities (a revolt frequently labeled "the Indian Mutiny").

Most architectural sites in Lucknow, like those in Delhi and Kanpur, were marked and scarred by these battles, and Beato's photographs of the aftermath acted as powerful memorials of the history that swept across northern India. This mode of war photography fueled collective remembrance and shared knowledge; its effect was similar to those of concurrent forms of popular entertainment and public information, including painted panoramas, tourist guidebooks, artists' sketches, newspaper reports, and gazetteers published in the *Times* and the *Illustrated London News*. Beato's fine photographic prints, exhibited at Henry Hering's Regent Street gallery and collected in individual albums, participated in British colonialism's epic stories, stirring narratives of sacrifice, mourning, and military conquest.

Beato's striking panorama transmits these conflicting emotions. In this extensive description mapping out the remnants of *nawabi* architecture, the eye moves left to

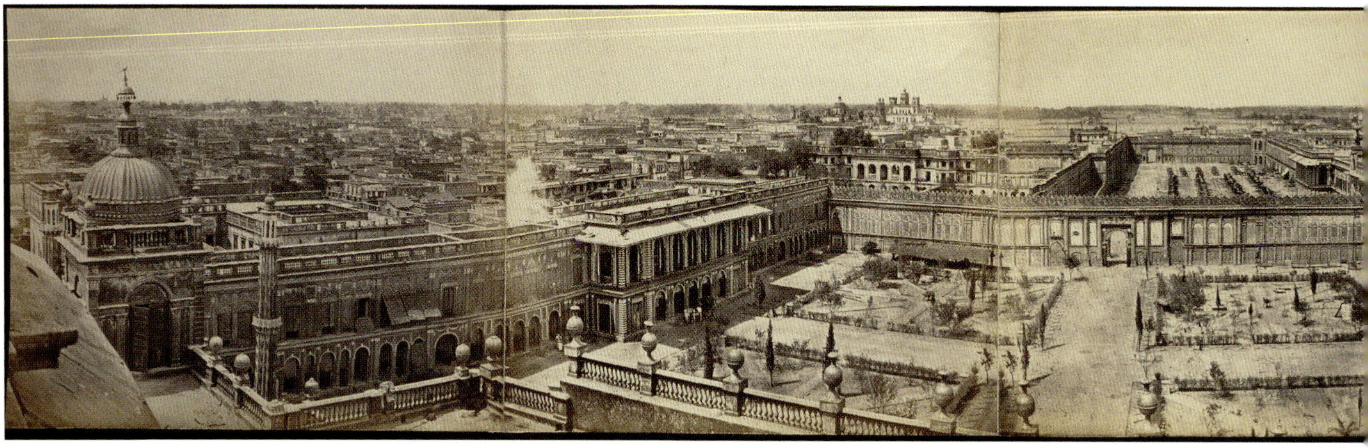

Felice Beato (British, born in Italy, 1832–1909), *Panorama of Lucknow from the Great Imambara*, 1858. Albumen silver print, 25.2 × 30.6 cm (9 15/16 × 12 1/16 in.). J. Paul Getty Museum, Los Angeles (84.XO.421.2.1).

right, looking at the Jama Masjid in the distant east, the city entrance gate, Rumi Dharwaza, the long road leading up to the Macchi Bhawan, a fort built on the hill, above the Gomti banks. Two imposing gateways delimit this fortified building: on the left the Tripolia gate, and on the right the main gate leading to the royal palace, the Panch Mahalla. Each image is perfectly aligned horizontally, and such a seamless sequence of sheets joined together contrasts with the chaotic geometry of buildings below the horizon line—a zigzag of courtyards, fortified walls, and gateways moving in and out of view. The last three plates on the right show the extensive courtyard of the Bara Imambara, the building dedicated to Shia rituals, and reach out to include its extensive terrace. Beato's camera connected the architectural volumes and established spatial relationships.

Panoramic photography found ideal application in India, where large buildings like the Bara Imambara could not be easily grasped in one shot. Western conventions of camera optics often failed to measure up to the intricate articulation of Islamic buildings characterized by multiple courtyards, large plazas, archways, and gateways. Beato took two further Lucknow panoramas (a six-plate Qaiserbagh panorama and a two-part Hussainabad Imambara panorama) and more in Delhi (an eight-plate panorama from the Jama Masjid; a three-plate panorama of Hindu Rao's house; two-part panoramas of the Bastion and Kashmir gate as of the Mori Bastion). He was not alone in his application of panoramic photography in India. John Murray's work in Agra is known especially for his use of multiple negatives that grasped the extent of Mughal monuments like the Taj Mahal and the Pearl Mosque in the Red Fort.

Nonetheless, it is this photograph's military nature that matters most. Beato arrived in Lucknow soon after the British commander in chief of India, Sir Colin Campbell, had reinstated control and chased out the rebels; hence, he was aware of each site's strategic importance. The fort of Macchi Bhawan was in rubble as a consequence of Sir Henry Lawrence's decision to blow it up at an early stage of the campaign, in June 1857. Lawrence, his chief commissioner of Awadh, repaired with his troops to the Residency building, and he was found dead there; his soldiers fought six more bloody months. During the conflict, the Bara Imambara functioned as a secular building quartering the 53rd Infantry Brigade; the tall mosque where Beato's camera was perched became a field hospital.

Hence, the associations of these historic buildings were enriched by current chronicles, and Beato's extensive views participated in a collective trauma back in Britain. While the Leicester Square Panorama presented Robert Burford's painted 1858 *Description of a View of the City of Lucknow, Taken from the Residency*, attesting to the loss of many British soldiers and civilians during the six-month siege, the *Athenaeum*'s June 4, 1862, issue contrasted the painting with the technical excellence and historical resonance of Beato's panoramic views. Deprived of any military action, Beato's eight-plate panorama of the battered city of Lucknow wielded a double-edge sword, which rendered it even more effective. It channeled the force of British control, but it also resonated with grief. Like a military reporter, Felice Beato conveyed these rich and complex meanings to the British audience from Lucknow while remaining at a secure height.

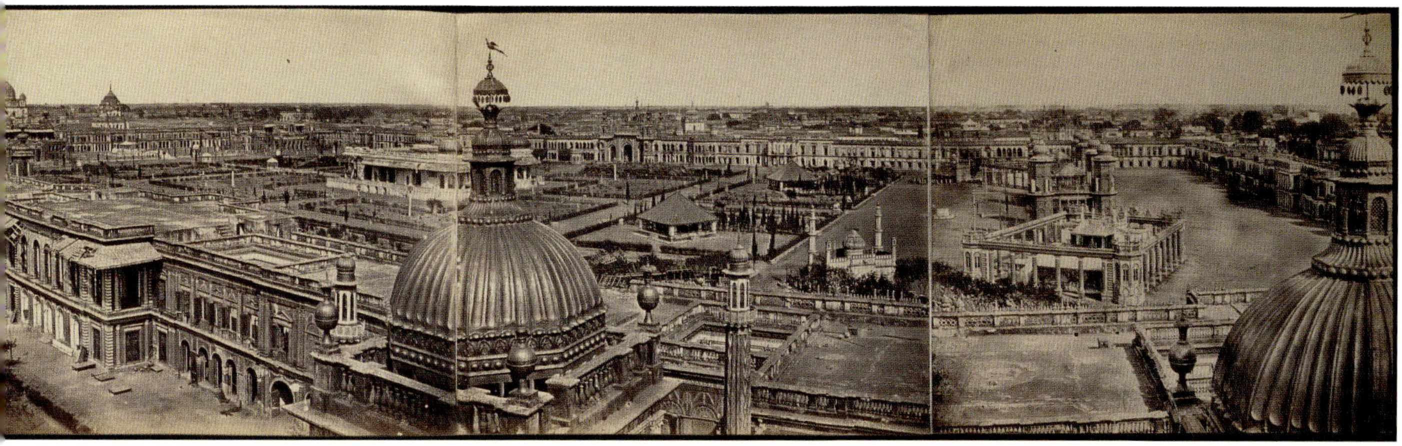

DENISE OLEKSIJCZUK

Oliver Grover, Charles Corwin, Edward Austen, Ernest Gros, and Salvadore Mège, *The Cyclorama of Jerusalem on the Day of the Crucifixion*, 1889

Sunlight, like a circle of fire, appears along the horizon through a narrow opening between earth and black sky. The moon's eclipse of the sun casts the ground in shadow. For anyone emerging onto the raised platform surrounded by the vast painting of a single moment one spring day in AD 30 in Jerusalem, disoriented by the walk up the spiral stairs, the sight of such extreme distance sends a reverberation palpable on the skin and in the bones, like a slight trembling that lingers. The main effect of the panorama's immensity is to energize, have us delight in its vastness, take it in with our breath.

The panorama's strange intensity derives from the elevated view. Open on all sides, the viewpoint is an imagined pinnacle west of the Old City. The painting represents Jerusalem, as it was thought to have looked the year Jesus was crucified, pilgrims arriving on tiny, sinuous roads from Bethlehem, Damascus, and Jaffa to pray at the Temple on Passover. Before the viewer a terrain of green pastures, honey-colored soil, and grazing sheep rises gently toward distant hills on the horizon; to the left lies the city Herod the Great rebuilt, surrounded by enormous sand-colored ramparts; to the right, at the bottom of a rocky escarpment, stands a large, long-robed group, gesturing wildly; and behind is the hill known as Golgotha, where three naked men, nailed by their hands and feet to wooden crosses, are dying in anguish. This panorama's composition deviates little from art-historical tradition. Good Thief on the right, Bad Thief on the left, Jesus is surrounded by a familiar mourners group and a few armored Roman soldiers. The 360-degree format allows the inclusion of things not normally found in a Crucifixion panel painting: the crowd of angry Jews demanding the sign reading "King of the Jews" above Jesus's head be removed, a perspective view of the walled city, including the path Jesus followed with his cross, Herod's dazzling white palace and temple, and, most unusual of all, the surrounding countryside scattered with pistachio and olive trees, grazing sheep, Bedouin *goums*, and caravans. Thus, the panoramic form gave the artists a chance to unleash their technical expertise and imaginative powers to represent the effects of the solar eclipse and the earthquake that, according to the Gospels of Matthew and Luke, took place at Jesus's death.

Opened in 1889, in downtown Montreal, on land rented from the Grey Nuns, *The Cyclorama of Jerusalem on the Day of the Crucifixion* was initiated by the entrepreneur Ernest Pierpoint of Chicago and painted by Oliver Dennett Grover, Charles Abel Corwin, Edward J. Austen, Ernest Gros, and Salvadore Mège.[1] The French panorama artist Paul Philippoteaux may have directed the artists (Mège and Gros assisted him on earlier panoramas). They based their work on Bruno Piglhein's hugely successful, religiously inspired Crucifixion panorama, exhibited in Munich in 1886. Before constructing his historical view, Piglhein and "a group of learned men" conducted extensive research in Palestine, gathering information on the ancient city.[2] By the late nineteenth century, a rise in Christian Holy Land pilgrimage, imperialist competition among various nations in Palestine, and the new scientific archaeology made such panoramas lucrative.[3] Different European and North American teams, aided by ten photographs, painted at least seventeen replicas of Piglhein's painting.[4] Nineteenth-century travel writers famously expressed disappointment upon visiting Jerusalem; most

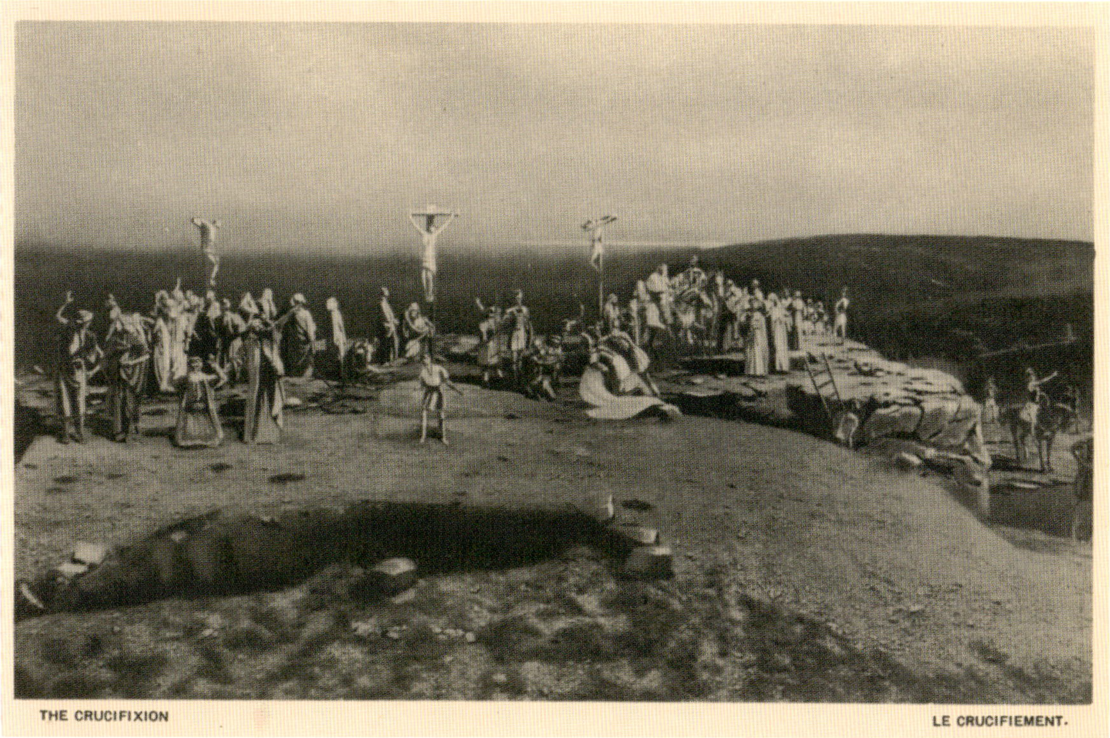

Oliver Dennett Grover (American, 1861–1927), Charles Abel Corwin (American, 1857–1938), Edward J. Austen (American, 1850–1930), Ernest M. Gros (American, 1859–1930), and Salvadore Mège (French, b. 1854), possibly under the direction of Paul Philippoteaux (French, 1846–1923), *The Cyclorama of Jerusalem on the Day of the Crucifixion*, 1889. Postcard, date unknown.

had in mind an idealized city that Jerusalem's reality under the Ottomans could not match. The panorama artists avoided this problem by setting their image in the past. The cyclorama in Montreal was apparently painted in New York by the New York Panorama Company, using 3.5 tons of paint and oils on a canvas fifty feet high, four hundred feet long.[5]

One of the first to visit the panorama in Montreal was Sister Boire of the Grey Nuns, whose published account concentrates on the turbaned man kneeling to the left of Jesus, looking directly at the viewers as if asking them to witness his violent conversion from skepticism to belief: kind-hearted, affluent Joseph of Arimathea placed Jesus in a tomb after his death. Strangely, he occupies the space in front of the canvas like a cutout, two-dimensional silhouetted character fixed to the floorboards. In front of the Crucifixion a large fissure splits the ground, an actual hole in the horizontal surface between the cylindrical painting and the viewing platform. For the devout, the combination of perspectival realism, three-dimensional scenery, and biblical narrative enlivens and intensifies the visual experience. Soeur Boire recalls a biblical passage on resurrection, imagining "the dead leaving their tombs from this opening in the ground, to guide the living in the darkness."[6]

Jesus's head rests on his left shoulder, eyes cast upward, blood flowing down his pale skin from his five wounds. His thin, handsome face bears a humble, weary expression. Potential worshipers are positioned, anomalously, at Jesus's height on the platform where they can better witness and empathize with his suffering than they could while looking up at a Crucifixion scene on a church altarpiece. The painting's form invites viewers to perform the Meditations of Christ, the Catholic spiritual practice in which the faithful methodically retrace Jesus's Passion along the Via Dolorosa. For those who actively participate in imagining the violent physical and emotional pain Jesus experienced on the day of the Crucifixion, the ritual cultivates theological presentness, a sense of the divine, and acute awareness of perceptual embodiedness.

The panorama format not only increases the Meditations' devotional efficacy by visualizing specific places in Jerusalem—and broadens devotional temporality by including visual narratives beyond the scenes of Jesus's

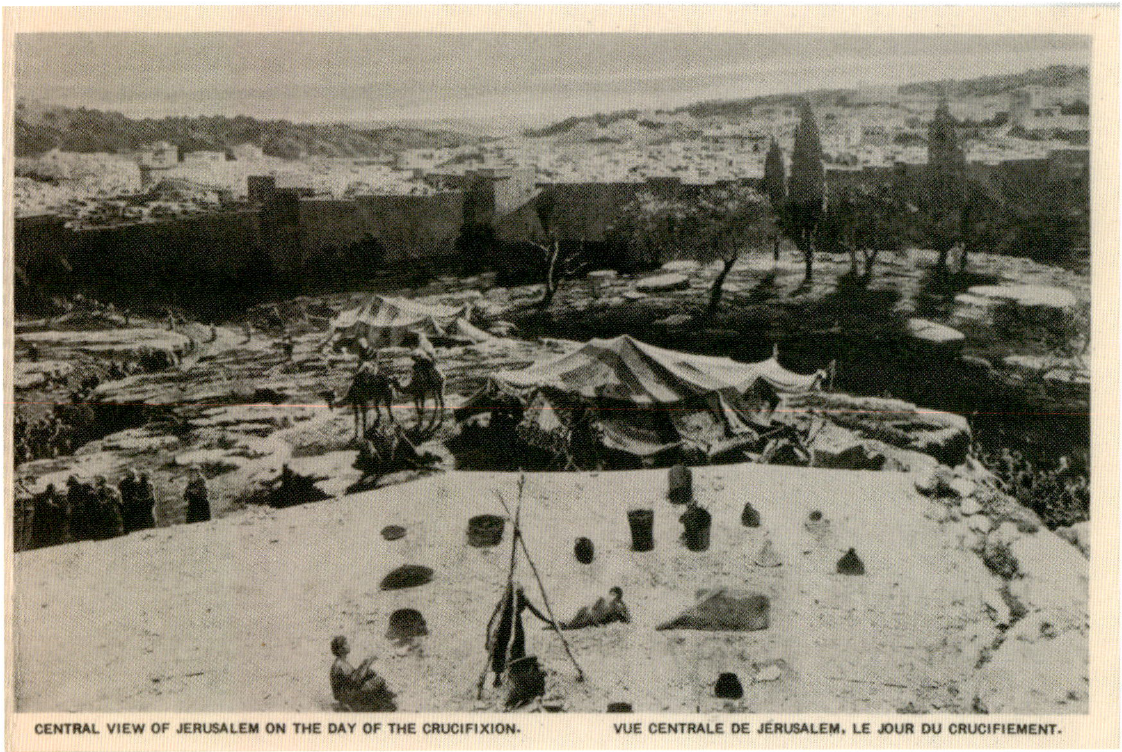

Postcard, date unknown.

Passion. Unlike flat paintings, panoramas have no center; the viewer can choose where to focus his or her attention. The historical view of the city and its environs offers spectators a philosophical opportunity to consider this place's violent history both before and after the painting's fateful moment. To the right of the Crucifixion, not far from Herod's ostentatious white palace, with its gold Corinthian capitals and three huge towers, are the Bedouins' modest dwellings, visible at close range. Two long-bearded, scarf-swathed men stand conversing outside the tent nearest us: one points to Golgotha, the other holds his left hand up against his forehead to shield his eyes to better observe what is taking place there. Slightly behind them, two men on camels look in the same direction. The Bedouins watch carefully.

The two foreground tents are a patchwork of different woolen weaves, some yellowish-brown, others deep red, stitched together to form a large cloth. Draped over five rows of sticks holding it up, the tallest in the middle flanked by two rows becoming increasingly shorter, the wool sags in between them like loose skin on a starving animal. Textures, expertly rendered in paint, make the tent surfaces tactile. The delight of perceiving the fine details of the tents' long nap and deep color appeals to our memory of the smell and feel of woven wool and rough carpets.

Nomads sensitive to the land's seasonal changes, the Bedouins survive in inhospitable conditions without accumulating wealth or possessions. Leading their sheep or goats around the countryside, they take only what their camels can carry. Striking examples of humanity's resilience over millennia, the nomads warn of the weakness of Herod's attempt to establish a kingdom that needed to be protected and fought for, and of similar forms of hubris in our own times. Motivated by kinship, reciprocity, and the will to survive, the prominent inclusion of the nomads in this image of redemption through suffering prompts us to consider Jesus's teachings in light of their earthbound practice of pastoral simplicity.

NOTES

1. *The Cyclorama of Jerusalem on the Day of the Crucifixion* (Montreal: n.p., [1889]), 3. In 1895 the *Cyclorama of Jerusalem* was transported to Sainte-Anne-de-Beaupré, where it remained on display until 2018.
2. Ibid.
3. Simon Goldhill, *Jerusalem: City of Longing* (Cambridge: Belknap Press of Harvard University Press, 2008), 273–75.
4. Stephan Oettermann, *The Panorama: History of a Mass Medium* (New York: Zone, 1997).
5. *Cyclorama: Jerusalem and the Crucifixion, St. Catherine and St. Urbain Sts.*, souvenir (Montreal, 1889), n.p.
6. Soeur Boire, "Jeudi, 21. Février, 1889," Archives des Soeurs Grises de Montréal (ASGM), Administration générale, circulaire mensuelle, vol. 4 (1888–92), 224.

KATIE TRUMPENER

Stanley Spencer, *Sandham Memorial Chapel*, 1926–32

Stanley Spencer's *Sandham Memorial Chapel* commemorates a British officer, Lieutenant Henry Willoughby Sandham, who, having contracted malaria in Macedonia, belatedly died, after being demobilized and reaching home—and hence was not officially considered a World War I casualty. The chapel was commissioned in 1923 by Sandham's family, in the English hamlet of Burghclere, and painted by Spencer over a four-year period. Spencer himself had ended the war at home, on medical leave, after a flare-up of the malaria he too had caught while serving in Macedonia. Drawing on Spencer's own military service there and in Britain, the chapel's antiwar frescoes chronicle army life's petty horrors and small redemptions, focusing not on fighting scenes but the care of the wounded, daily routines at army bases, hospitals, and bivouacs (washing and sorting laundry, mopping floors, moving kit bags, filling water bottles, map reading, tent pitching, assembling stones for road building), surmounted on one end of the chapel by a vast scene of the soldiers' resurrection. Both in individual scenes and as an ensemble, the cycle works with a complex perspectival sense, evoking Giotto's Arena Chapel in Padua and Macedonia's Greek Byzantine chapels, while harnessing Cubist and Expressionist perspectival experiments to new ends. As in the Arena Chapel, the viewer is entirely surrounded by complex narrative cycles in multiple registers, rather than by a single continuous composition; in both, the east end of the chapel is entirely filled with a massive scene of judgment and resurrection that functions as a separate entity. Here, though, in lieu of Giotto's more conventional heaven and hell, sinner and saved, sheep or goats on either side of the central cross, we have an undifferentiated group of resurrected soldiers, arising from their graves—alongside a few Macedonian locals, dressed in sheepskin or goatskin vests, who have died in their midst.

Throughout the chapel, Spencer restates metaphysical categories in texture and textiles. Despite its attention to army life's "domestic routines," Spencer's chapel might be seen as inheriting the pitying emphasis on the horrors of war—including downed mules, collapsing fences, the dying and dead—found in the *Bourbaki Panorama* by Édouard Castres, completed in 1881 and now on display in Lucerne, Switzerland (see chapter 7). Yet in crucial respects, Spencer's chapel functions as an anti-panorama, preoccupied not with circular, seamless sight but precisely with *seams*, the folding, unfolding, draping of cloth and paper: the unfolding of maps and blankets, the way tents collapse from three-dimensional shelters into two-dimensional shapes, trailing guy ropes like octopus tentacles; the texture of towels, mosquito nets, scrubs, aprons, and the "prayer mats" used in floor scrubbing;[1] the signs of folding and unfolding left on convalescent ward tablecloths and fresh hospital bedsheets. Panel after panel, this folding motif is explored so obsessively that the chapel itself—despite its rigid architectural supports—seems a complex piece of origami, meant to be folded into a multisided box. On the micro level, too, folding and unfolding, and the permanent traces both actions leave behind, evoke how war pierces the body, harrows the soul, and yet also how its survivors, pliable as sheeting, burlap, canvas, regain much of their original outer shape.

How can art itself surmount the dematerialization of human bodies in war? By evoking the potential for

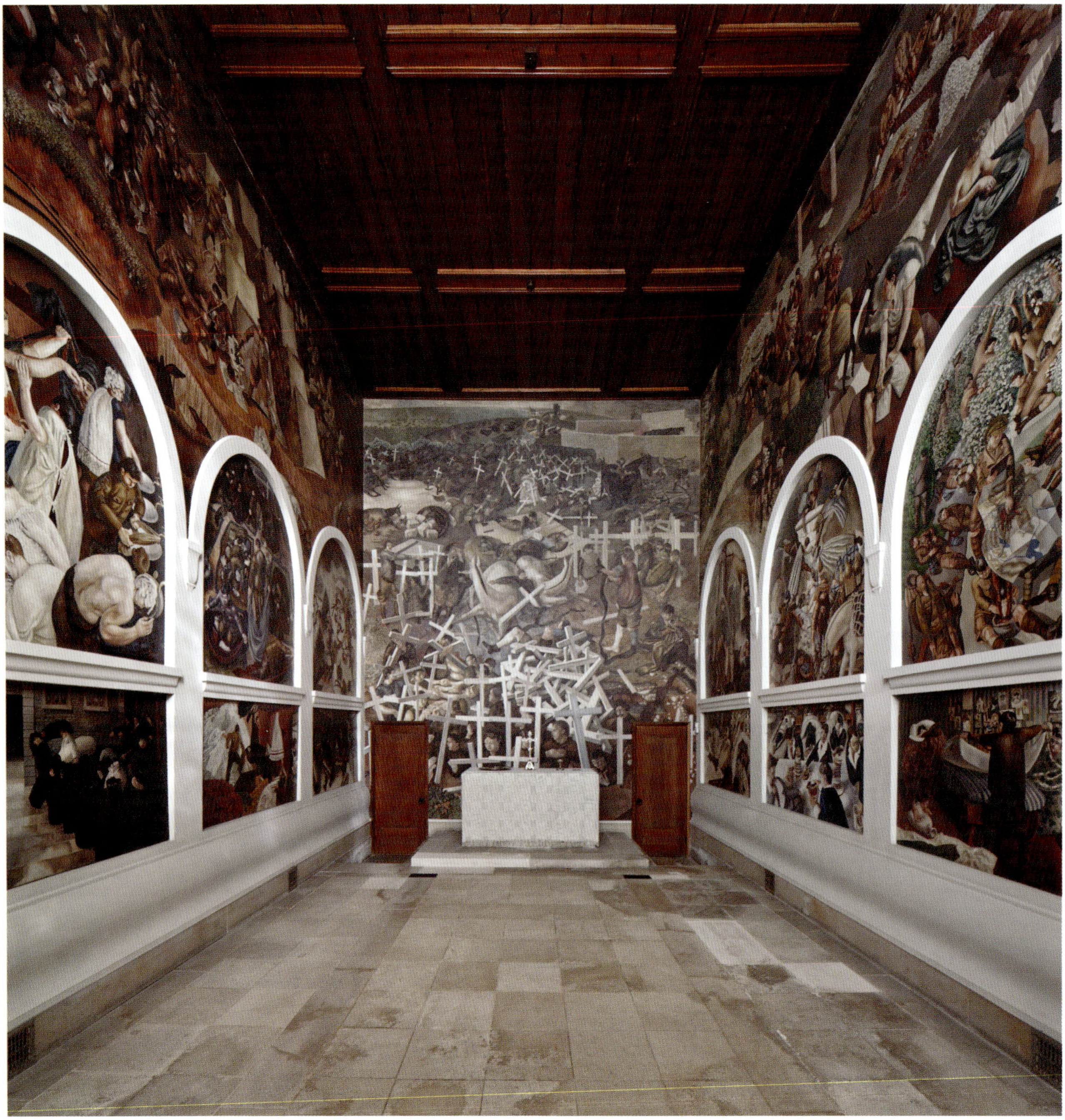

Stanley Spencer (British, 1891–1959), *Sandham Memorial Chapel*, 1926–32. Oil on canvas. Sandham Memorial Chapel, Burghclere, Hampshire, U.K. National Trust Photographic Library.

resurrection in materials—and materiality—themselves. Men are folded and formed by war. And yet their bodies remain separable from the uniforms or textiles that encase them and seem to give them shape and meaning. The gun belts they strap onto themselves as they climb back out of their trenches bear an odd resemblance to giant kidneys—as if they were strapping a prosthetic body over their original bodies. The stiff twill of their uniforms, too, gives the uniforms a life of their own—ironed properly, they will take up their creases anew. So, too, by analogy, soldiers' bodies, toweled, blanketed, bandaged, dried, warmed, swaddled in cloth, can pull back together the souls inside them.

In the hospital wards, wounded soldiers curl or fling themselves into their soft bedding, seeking rest and respite—while frostbite victims' bedding is moved around them on an elaborate hoop, warming them yet avoiding contact with their wounds, allowing viewers to look up onto their prone bodies. During kit inspection, soldiers unfold their blankets and set atop them all personal belongings—including and encapsulated by roll-up portable sewing kits; as the soldiers unfurl or refold their blankets around them, the blankets' coracle shapes suggest they function, psychically, as boats when soldiers are wrapped in them. In the laundry room, however, those sorting and folding laundry drape themselves with large striped towels, which for the moment resemble tallits (Jewish prayer shawls) or shrouds.

In the "Ablutions" panel, some soldiers wash themselves or dry each other, while a medic in a carefully fastened smock paints iodine onto one soldier's stomach. How can painting continue in the midst or aftermath of war? As iodine is painted onto a stomach, to disinfect and purify it. When soldiers wash themselves and wash their clothes en masse, they attempt to purify bodies and uniforms alike, to return them to a state of resilience. And in the "Reveille" panel, the thick crisscrossed mosquito netting protecting men's naked bodies while they dress and shave—and while their comrades rush in to announce the armistice—renders them to the viewer's eye as mosaic tesserae. The war is over: soldiers' bodies are still vulnerable (to mosquitos, to malaria, to war's lingering physical and psychic scars)—but they are also already history, memory, a commemorative frieze.

If the nineteenth-century battle panorama depicted nations' making and breaking on an epic scale, Spencer's panels focus resolutely on individual soldiers in the context of very small groups—ward, work group, platoon. And if the nineteenth-century panorama understood the seamless circle as a guarantor of completeness, plenitude, and national wholeness, Spencer fixes on folds and creases as figures of fragmentation and resilience.

NOTE

1. Stanley Spencer, cited in Duncan Robinson, introduction to *Stanley Spencer at Burghclere: The Oratory of All Souls Sandham Memorial Chapel, Hampshire* (London: National Trust, 1991), 8.

ANNA INDYCH-LÓPEZ

Diego Rivera, *History of Mexico*, 1929–35

Visitors entering Mexico City's Palacio Nacional from its bustling *zócalo* (main square) encounter Diego Rivera's sprawling fresco *History of Mexico* (1929–35) on three massive walls of the entrance stairway. Adorning Mexico's most important political structure, the mural charts an expansive history of Mexico, compressing a sweeping historical view into a finite space.[1] From the Aztecs to Lázaro Cárdenas's presidency (1934–40), *History of Mexico* offers "one of the most compendious visual displays of historical material in near human scale in the history of art."[2] The mural's colossal size—the central wall measures twenty-eight by forty-two feet—and status as a visual representation of national identity place it in the extended field of panoramic images. Rivera mines, adapts, and transforms specific panoramic pictorial conventions—mobile, scanning vision; participatory visuality immersing and activating the spectator; densely layered imagery and abundant details creating visual instability—to create a unique viewing experience. Thinking Mexican muralism in relation to the historical panorama, it cuts to the heart of muralist practice: the politics of space, the nature of realist painting, perceptual and spatial experience, modes of narrativity.

An apparent jumble of scenes on one large surface (flanked by two compositions on related themes), the mural wraps, U-shaped, around the staircase, immersing the viewer in a visual onslaught of historical episodes. Staircase landings serve as viewing platforms, providing partial and fragmented views; especially on the central wall, the mural's dizzying array of events and portraits initially confounds the viewer as an almost illegible large-scale screen, randomly filled with historical characters. Only upon ascending the staircase to a balcony hallway can viewers appreciate a wide, sweeping view of the entire mural, an experience marked by an "instantaneity of vision . . . the all-at-once, nontemporal quality of seeing the mural as a whole image field."[3] *History of Mexico* thus defies normative viewing conditions for Mexico City's mural cycles, in which discrete scenes are dispersed across series of individual panels in large courtyards or covered loggias on several floors of grand buildings. Instead, it embraces the impression of completeness associated with panoramic viewing experience.

Technically a history painting, *History of Mexico* does not obey that genre's typical stylistic, compositional, narrative, or illusionistic coherence. Instead, Rivera's hybrid practice reworks heterogeneous visual modes, creating a radically disruptive package of disparate aesthetic styles: history painting's naturalism; Cubism's overlapping planes; Constructivism's montage effects; stacked figures reminiscent of Dutch seventeenth-century group portraits or Quattrocento painting; the abstracted, flattened forms and spatial ambiguities of the picture writing found in pre-Columbian manuscripts; an overall sense of decorative patterning. The mural's willful disruption of legibility—paralleled by its rejection of clear narrative structure—is surprising given its function, during postrevolutionary reconstruction, as a very public codification of national history. The European panorama, a device for the spatial organization of knowledge, thrived as a spectacle of mass entertainment and consumption; viewed in relationship to the panorama's structural characteristics, the mural offers an ideal means to engage Mexico's emerging postrevolutionary citizenry.[4] European historical and

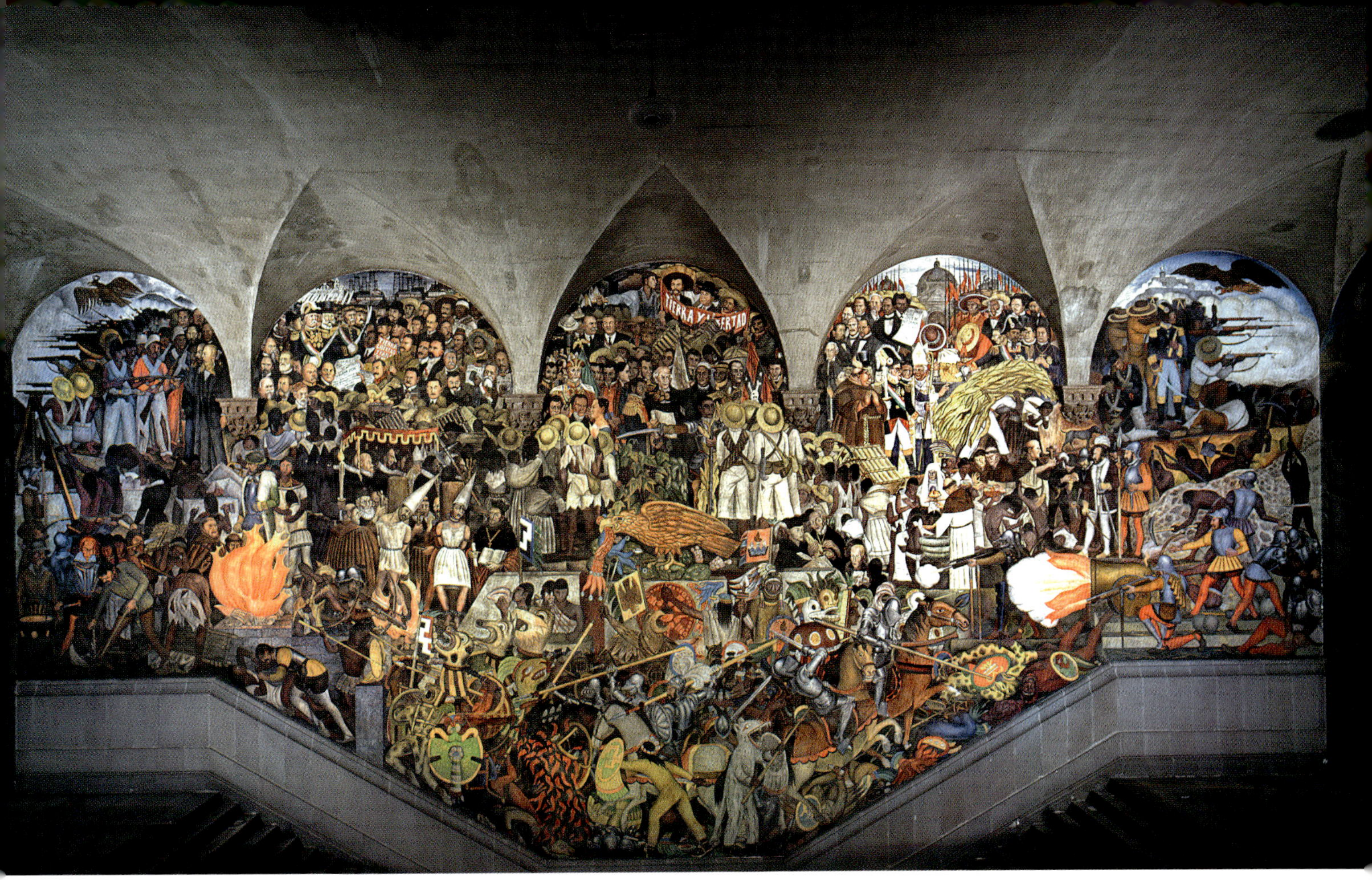

Diego Rivera (Mexican, 1886–1957), *History of Mexico*, 1929–35. Mural. National Palace, Mexico City.

landscape panoramas responded to a bourgeois need for symbolic dominance and possession of the nation and the land; the new Mexican state aspired likewise to legitimacy.[5] Focusing on heroes, momentous events, nationhood, and states-in-confrontation, historical panoramas exploited moments of patriotic fervor as giant propaganda machines.[6] This government-commissioned mural inevitably involves such didactic displays. Yet Rivera also grasped the panoramic format's destabilizing aspects; he created a counter-discourse, upending conventional history painting and challenging government construction and codification of a national narrative.

The central panel's nonlinear compositional and narrative structure conveys visual instability, a scanning form of vision. Designing simultaneously horizontal and vertical reading, Rivera randomly juxtaposed major periods of Mexico's tumultuous history. He packed swarms of figures and centuries of history onto the wall surface, forcing the eye to jump across to make spatial and temporal connections. Episodes depicting the Conquest's violence flow unexpectedly, right to left, along the wall's lower center; stacked above, randomly arranged colonial scenes stretch horizontally across the wall's central portion, veering downward at left. The narrative suddenly jumps to the top far right with the 1847 Mexican-American war, continuing leftward again with the Reform era (beginning 1855), then jumping acutely to the far left, with the 1867 triumph over Maximilian and the French invaders. Moving rightward, for the first time according to conventional narrative, to the regime of Porfirio Díaz (1876–1911), the mural culminates in its uppermost central space in an atemporal (but politically symbolic) mixing of heroes of the early nineteenth-century Independence war and of the twentieth-century Revolution. The complex pictorial organization and antichronological narrative resist the notion of historical progress (except in terms of the Revolution's triumph). It thereby offers Rivera's politicized social history of Mexico through a push-pull dynamic between forces of power, reinforcing a sense of the populace in perpetual struggle and providing a visual corollary to Marxist dialectical materialism. Rather than let events unfold sequentially from left to right, as one might normally expect, Rivera embodied historical tension in the mural's structural logic, implicating the viewer in the process.

This narrative logic, crucially, derives from an ancient Mexican form of panoramic art making: the pre-Conquest codex, generally animal skin or bark panels joined to create an accordion or horizontal screen fold. The Toltec, Mixtec, and Aztec used such tomes to record their history and ritual. Rivera's narrative structure deliberately appropriates the boustrophedon pattern, a snakelike narrative structure found especially in Mixtec genealogical histories.[7] The screen-fold book and its picture writing also became the basis for the post-Conquest codices commissioned by the Spanish to preserve and disseminate knowledge about Mexico's pre-Hispanic cultures. Rivera studied such books and codices. By appropriating pre-Columbian pictorial conventions and visual strategies, he promoted a politicized, indigenist viewpoint celebrating the native past and incorporating non-Western models of vision that challenge false notions of progress. By engaging codices' visual logic—panoramic bookmaking intersecting with Mexico's colonial history—to structure his own history of the nation, Rivera pointed to the book's role as a weapon of colonization.[8] In Rivera's hands, the historical panorama—elaborated by nineteenth-century Europeans as a form of visual power—is used against itself.

NOTES

1. Formerly headquarters of the Spanish viceroys, the Palacio Nacional became the postrevolutionary seat of Mexico's executive branch.
2. Stanton Catlin, "Mural Census," in *Diego Rivera: A Retrospective*, ed. Cynthia Newman Helms (Detroit: Detroit Institute of Arts, 1986), 261.
3. Leonard Folgarait, *Mural Painting and Social Revolution in Mexico, 1920–1940: Art of the New Order* (New York: Cambridge University Press, 1998), 100.
4. Folgarait explores the mural's contradictions, its narrativity in relation to ritual, suggesting the viewer is swept into the social order through various control mechanisms played out through formal aesthetics.
5. Bernard Comment, *The Panorama*, trans. Anne-Marie Glasheen (London: Reaktion, 1999), 19.
6. Ibid., 8.
7. Elizabeth Hill Boone, *Stories in Red and Black: Pictorial Histories of the Aztecs and Mixtecs* (Austin: University of Texas Press, 2000), 61.
8. See Rolena Adorno, "New Perspectives in Colonial Spanish American Literary Studies," *Journal of the Southwest* 32, no. 2 (1990): 173–91; 184; and Elizabeth Hill Boone and Walter Mignolo, eds., *Writing without Words: Alternative Literacies in Mesoamerica and the Andes* (Raleigh, N.C.: Duke University Press, 1994).

KATIE TRUMPENER

Alexandra Exter, *Panorama of the River* (1936), *Panorama of the Coast* (1937), and *Panorama of the Mountain* (1938)

In the late 1930s, the émigré Ukro-Russian Constructivist Alexandra Exter (1882–1949) published three panoramic "novelty books" with the innovative Parisian children's publisher Père Castor. Exter was a modernist painter, an Alexander Archipenko student who participated in overlapping avant-garde circles (French Postimpressionism, Italian futurism, Russian non-objectivism) and designed early Soviet theater sets, ballet costumes, reform fashions, revolutionary street festivities, and the famous futuristic costumes for Yakov Protazanov's science fiction movie, *Aelita, Queen of Mars* (USSR, 1924). Emigrating to Paris in 1924, she taught for years at Fernand Léger's Académie de l'Art Moderne and made Constructivist puppets and illuminated manuscripts.

Exter's panoramas unfurl unidirectionally to form littoral and mountain panoramas. Although Père Castor advertised them as friezes, usable in schoolrooms, Exter's foldout books are two-sided: on one side Exter's topographical images; and on the obverse Exter's small diagrammatic vignettes, punctuating Marie Colmont's poetic geological, zoological, ecological, and technological musings. The pioneering pop-up books of Lothar Meggendorfer (German, 1847–1925), including *A Day at the Zoo* (1884), *International Circus* (1887), and *The City Park* (1890), had been printed on stiff paper, enabling users to set up freestanding panoramic circles to regard from above or crouch alongside, looking in and through. Exter's fanfolds seem designed rather for sedentary, contemplative unfolding, while pushing the codex to its limits. Unlike painted panoramas, they make possible the partition, expansion, and contraction of their views, while drawing attention to color saturation, focal length, and depth of field. Both in the late nineteenth century (the era of Japonisme) and in the early twentieth (the age of Cubism), panoramic artists were obsessed with the Sino-Japanese screen tradition. In his *Water Lilies* cycle (1914–1926), Claude Monet (1840–1926) explored the fluidity and liquidity of perspective; in his *Panorama of Paris* screen (1924–33), Raoul Dufy (French, 1877–1953) explored its malleability, faceting a continuous, wide view. Exter's fanfolds enable readers to undertake related experiments.

Echoing the socialist realist Soviet dockscape of *Port* (1930), the panoramic picturebook of Alexander Nikolaev (Russian, 1897–1957), the triangular city views, riverside car ride, and coastal balloon ride of *The Story of Babar* (1931) and *The Travels of Babar* (1932) by Jean de Brunhoff (French, 1899–1937), and Italian futurist *aeropittura* (exploring earth and sky from aerial removes), Exter's panoramas take us past tranquil landscapes; busy tableaux of agricultural and maritime labor; Constructivist or Cubist cityscapes, elegant in their curving, quasi-organic facades and tram lines. Exter's panoramas visually interlock and overlap: the river rises in the mountains, runs downhill, overflowing its banks, and issues at the shore, near the coastal city where the next panorama begins. *Babar* moved fluidly between African and European terrain; these panoramas likewise compress France's varied topography, traversing seasons and centuries: the river runs from Alps to shore; the coast runs from sunny, beach-faced southern city up the green, rocky Breton coast, from modern wharfs and esplanades to old marine cemeteries and ancient cromlechs.

Like many previous shore panoramas (painted, etched, photographed, filmed), and early nineteenth-century

Alexandra Exter (Russian, 1882–1949), *Panorama of the Mountain/Panorama de la montagne*, 1938; *Panorama of the River/Panorama du fleuve*, 1936; *Panorama of the Coast/ Panorama de la côte*, 1937. From *Albums du Père Castor*. Texts by Marie Colmont (Paris: Flammarion, n.d.). Beinecke Rare Book and Manuscript Library, Yale University, New Haven, Connecticut.

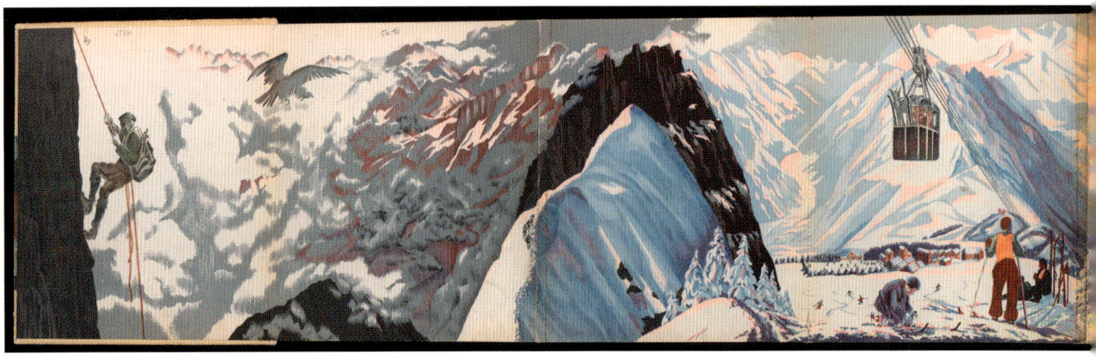

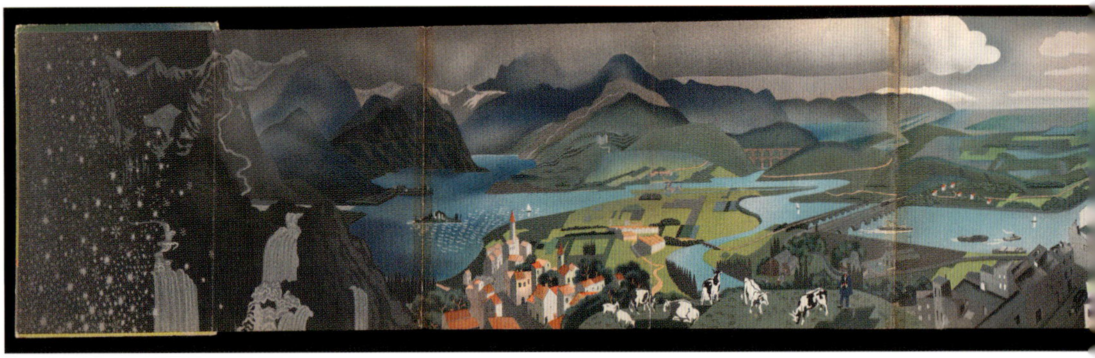

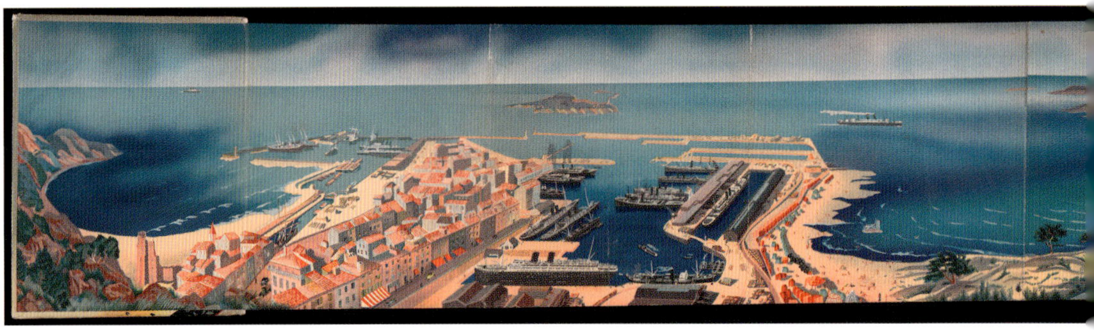

panoramic wallpapers, Exter's first two picturebooks explore the process of vision and the specter of emptiness, undifferentiated stretches of water or sand or storm cloud, spaces without narrative event, dwarfing human presence. Yet between Exter's second and third picturebooks, her panoramas' scale shifts drastically, disconcertingly. Alongside distant and far distant figures, buildings and terrain markers, the mountain panorama includes large spectating figures close to us, sharing or defining our own viewing position or platform: a mountaineer rappelling along a cliff face, skiers ascending by cable car, herders tending flocks in mountain meadows.

While Colmont comments on geological sources of force, waterpower, Exter shows nature's and culture's dynamism: waves pound onto shore; a storm floods the river; harnessed water drives mills; cranes load huge cargo vessels; vast roads, tunnels, and funiculars crisscross the Alps. A huge electricity pylon looms, powering ski gondolas and serving as a symbol of energy. The Symbolist or Fauvist panoramic Alpine meadows of Giovanni Segantini or the Fauvist Giovanni Giacometti and the visual vocabulary developed to celebrate Soviet electrification are here reconciled to showcase an unevenly transformed national landscape.

Exter's panoramas show the inroads of modernization, but also primeval weather systems and apparently intact

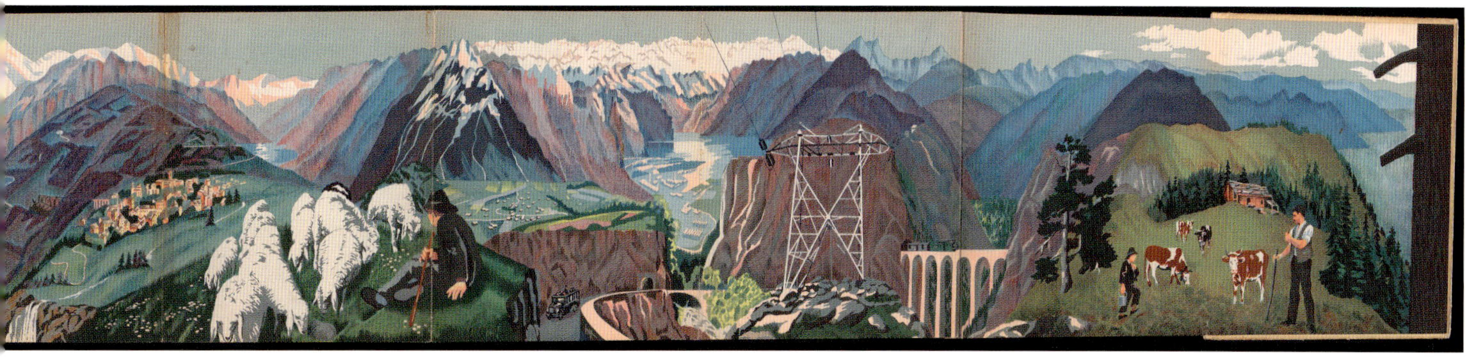

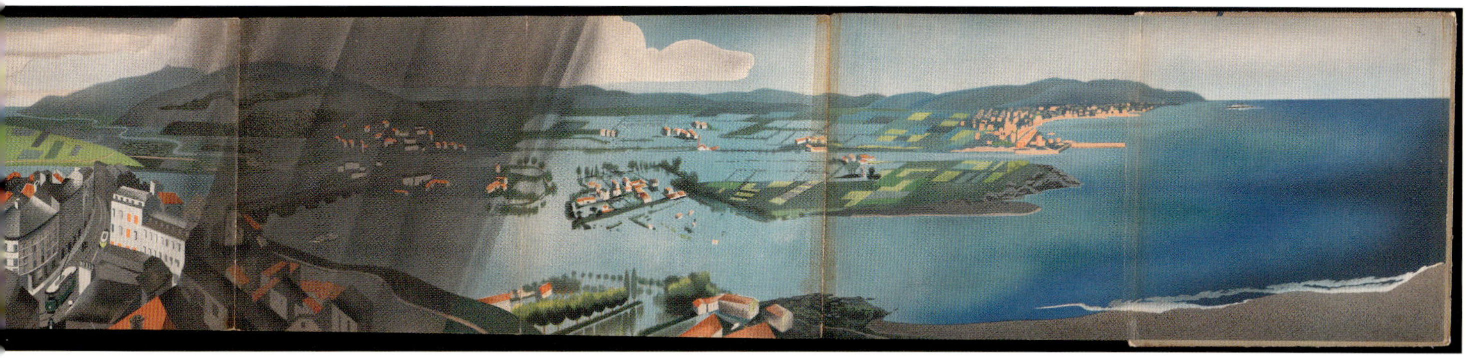

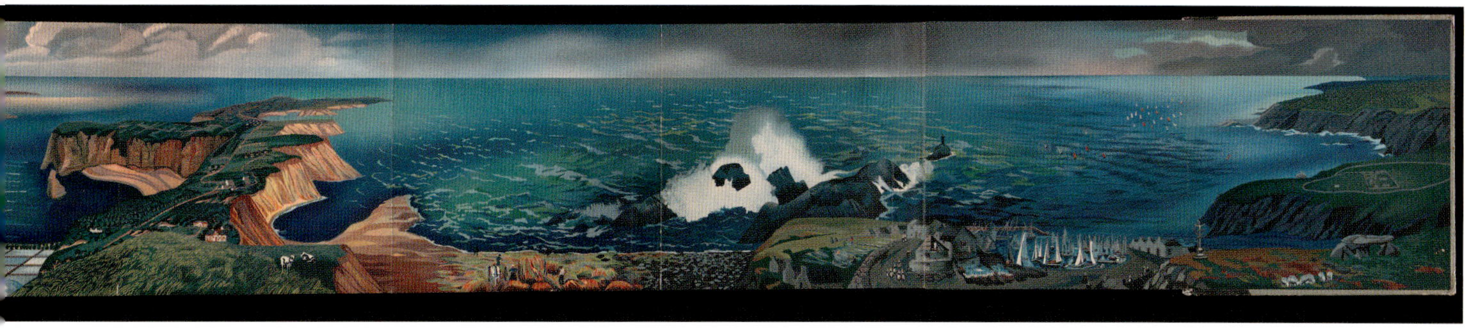

geological formations. If the mountains now contain industrial infrastructure and railway viaducts, the final panorama still ends in the untouched range where the river rises; the shore ends in view of ancient landscapes, archaic sailors' monuments, earthworks; the river descends into the ocean, vast, stunning, empty: modernist pastoral.

Exter's panorama books had a direct afterlife in American picturebooks: the equally wordless 1939 panoramic books *Town* and *Country* by Léger's student Clement Hurd (American, 1908–1988); the 1940 picturebook *Animals Everywhere* by Ingri d'Aulaire (Norwegian-American, 1904–1980) and Edgar Parin d'Aulaire (Swiss-American, 1898–1986); the aerial balloon, kite, and bird's-eye views in the *Curious George* books of H. A. Rey (German American, 1898–1977); *Make Way for Ducklings* (1941) by Robert McCloskey (American, 1914–2003), and later *Madlenka* (2000), *Madlenka's Dog* (2002); and the explorers' tales of Peter Sís (Czech-American, b. 1949). But Exter also fed a tradition of analytic and Constructivist picturebooks—*Hiding Places* (1943) by Louise Woodcock (1892–1957) and Esphyr Slobodkina (Russian American, 1908–2002), Margaret Wise Brown (1910–1952) and Clement Hurd's 1947 *Goodnight Moon*—interested in the faceted nature of vision and perception, tranquil domestic tableaux broken down to reveal the complex disparity of their partial views.

TIM BARRINGER

David Hockney, *Mulholland Drive: The Road to the Studio*, 1980

Mulholland Drive: The Road to the Studio, Hockney's technicolor representation of American landscape on a canvas eight by twenty feet, responds to an American painting tradition little known in Europe: massive, panoramic canvases evoking the sublimity of the great plains, mountains, and deserts of the United States.[1] Epic works by the nineteenth-century painters Frederic Church, Albert Bierstadt, and Thomas Moran of similar dimensions used daring colors and dramatic perspective schemes to represent the Andes, the Rockies, or the Grand Canyon—scenes of Humboldtian natural grandeur. Such compositions derived from the experience of viewing 360-degree painted panoramas, ubiquitous in large American cities during the 1850s. The panorama encouraged artists to experiment with massive, laterally expanded canvases on which could be depicted broad vistas of prairies, deserts, or mountain ranges, with dramatic light effects. Hockney affectionately parodied this work—and the Western movie genre that emerged from it—in early works such as *Rocky Mountains and Tired Indians*, 1965 (Edinburgh, Scottish National Gallery of Modern Art). But he is essentially sympathetic to works of the American sublime largely dismissed by modernist taste. He feels particular kinship with Thomas Moran, born "exactly one hundred years before me not forty miles from [Hockney's hometown of] Bradford," an émigré, like Hockney, to the United States.[2] Moran faithfully rendered topographical detail and atmospheric effects, concerns derived from his close study of Turner and reading of the English critic John Ruskin. By contrast, Hockney asserts, "I'm trying to convey *the experience of space*."[3]

Mulholland Drive evokes the magnificent sweep of the Hollywood hills rising beyond the suburbs of Los Angeles. "Space had been one of the reasons I came to California," he explained; "I am a bit claustrophobic and London . . . seemed to me closed and dark. California, by contrast, was wide open and, of course, filled with light."[4] A spectacular landscape of pleasure, *Mulholland Drive* is inflected by the speed of motion—a picturesque tour at freeway velocity. Appropriately for its Los Angeles subject, Hockney's treatment is informed by cinematic viewing forms. *Mulholland Drive* charts the journey to the studio by car, rather than the view from the studio itself; the eye travels around the canvas as the automobile might weave along the mountain roadway. We enter the composition amid a field of rich purple-blue at the left, follow the road's rise and fall as we move toward the right, our progress tracked by roadside buildings. After a final climb, capped by blue trees dancing against an orange background, we exit the painting at its right margin—only, after a sharp off-camera bend, to reenter it, hurtling past a pylon and a house with three cypress trees in front, before tearing out of the front of the frame, a whiff of burned gasoline left in the air. A mysterious field of vertical red and blue brushstrokes, seeming to rush toward the viewer at center, only emphasizes the tumultuous forward thrust.

The pictorial logic of the composition tracks that of the painted panorama, and the cinematic panning shot that it spawned, moving the eye onward through a circuitous sequence of delights and revelations. This is the West Coast landscape as viewed from an open-top roadster—a favorite Hollywood trope, finding its ultimate referent in the plunging, cliffside landscapes of the Pacific Coast Highway. At the left (in a move familiar from nineteenth-century urban panoramas) we spy a myriad of static details—private spaces that can be seen by us, from the viewing platform, but invisible from the road: rooftops, swimming pool, three Astroturf tennis courts—a landscape of moneyed pleasure in which Hockney himself is at home.[5]

In one respect Hockney deliberately disavows, even parodies, the panoramic heritage. Beyond the horizon, instead of an evening sky, we see the grid plan of the distant flat suburbs, etched as on a street map. This brilliant intervention uncannily matches the experience of staring down from the opulent heights of Mulholland Drive to the flat uniformity of suburbia sprawled at the base of the hills. The disjuncture here is created by the collision of two systems of graphic signification.

Mulholland Drive is not only a journey through an observed, panoramic landscape but a lighthearted, though learned, tour through the history of modern art. If canvas shape and subject suggest precedents in British and American landscape painting, we encounter different forms of mark making, vibrantly re-created from the car window. Hockney references the loaded, parallel brushstrokes of van Gogh; Matisse's exuberant, leaping lines and radiant colors; even Raoul Dufy's evocative, dilettantish palette. The overall composition is reminiscent of late Picasso, the most admired artist in Hockney's pantheon.[6] All these are seamlessly brought together; the heat of the Provençal sun is transformed into an unmistakably Californian vista, the chlorinated swimming pools replacing the Mediterranean. It is a drive-by history of art.

For all its heterodox historical affiliations, the painting is nonetheless marked by a compelling representational link to an observed motif, a wholeness born of many origins. Although we see it through the medium of modernist devices, our eyes can scan and enjoy the full lateral extent of Mulholland Drive, as if we were beholding it across the marvelous totality of a nineteenth-century panorama.

NOTES

1. See, for example, Andrew Wilton and Tim Barringer, *American Sublime: Landscape Painting in the United States, 1820–1880* (London: Tate, 2002).
2. Lawrence Weschler, "Yorkshire and the Grand Canyon," in Weschler, *True to Life: Twenty-Five Years of Conversations with David Hockney* (Berkeley: University of California Press, 2008), 97–114; 26, 112. On Moran, see Nancy K. Anderson, ed., *Thomas Moran* (Washington, D.C.: National Gallery of Art, 1997). This is the catalogue of an exhibition that Hockney saw and greatly admired, though he had known Moran's work previously.
3. Weschler, "Yorkshire and the Grand Canyon," 26, 112.
4. David Hockney, quoted in Lawrence Weschler, "Painting Again in East Yorkshire," in Weschler, *David Hockney: Recent Paintings* (New York: Pace Wildenstein, 2009), 8.
5. For a discussion of *Santa Monica Blvd.*, 1978–80, unfinished, see Andrew Causey, "Mapping and Representing," in *David Hockney*, ed. Paul Melia (Manchester, U.K.: Manchester University Press, 1995), 89–110; 105.
6. See Tim Barringer, "Seeing with Memory: Hockney and the Masters," in *David Hockney: A Bigger Picture*, ed. Marco Livingstone (London: Royal Academy of Arts, 2011), 42–55.

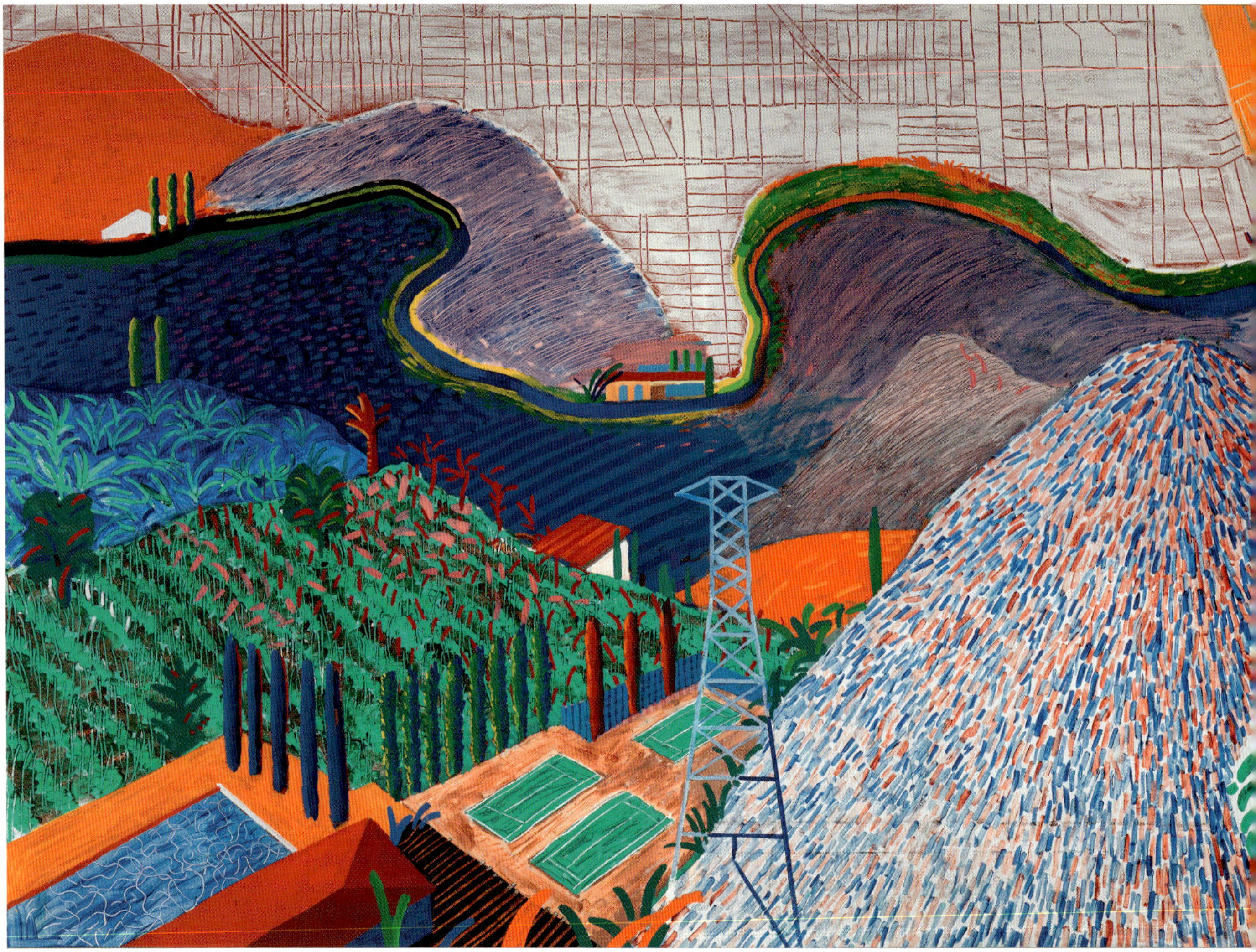

David Hockney (British, b. 1937), *Mulholland Drive: The Road to the Studio*, 1980. Acrylic on canvas, 218.4 × 617.2 cm (86 × 243 in.). Collection of Los Angeles County Museum of Art (LACMA).

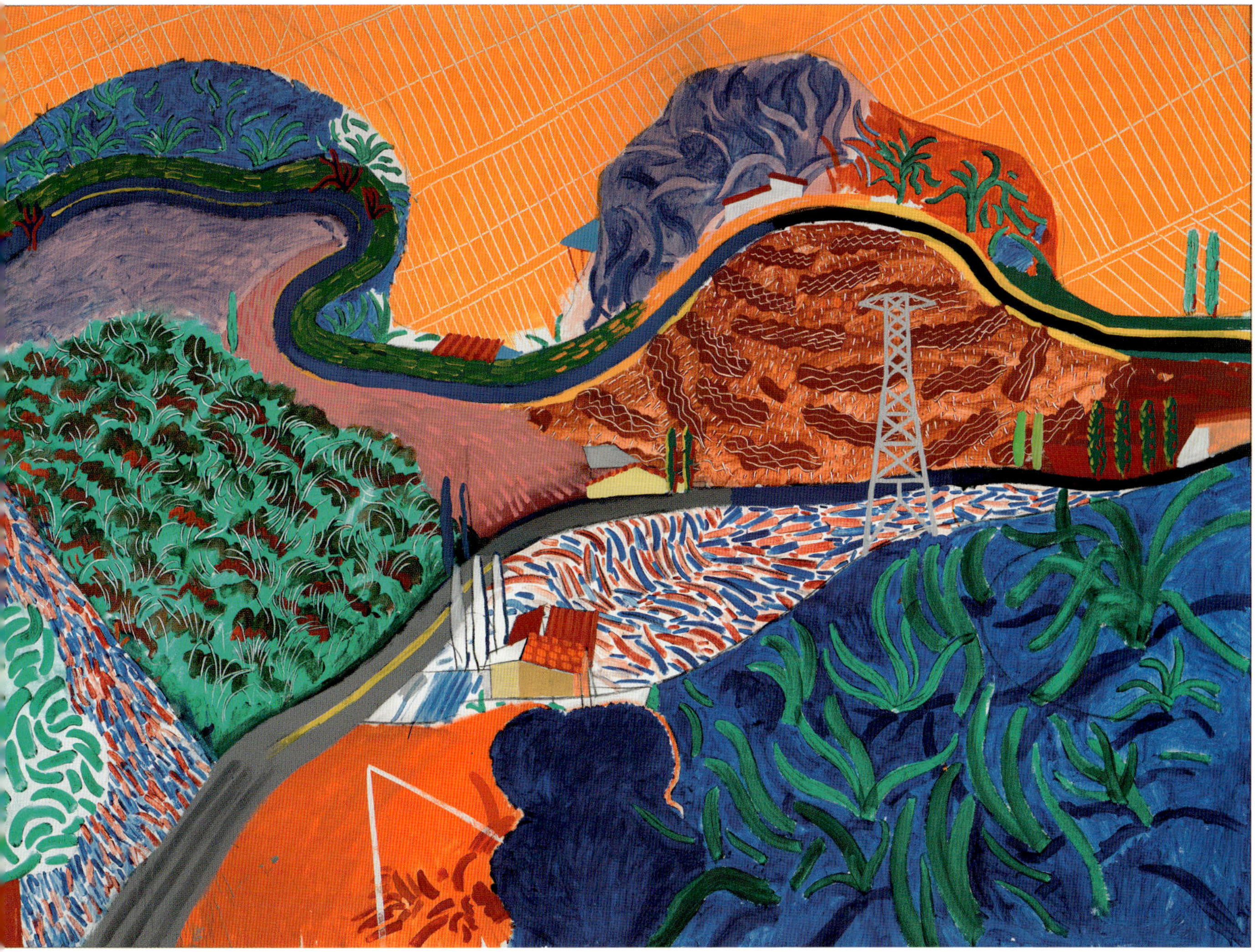

NOAM M. ELCOTT

Stan Douglas, *Panoramic Rotunda,* 1985

In 1985 the Canadian artist Stan Douglas constructed *Panoramic Rotunda,* a circular photopanorama of a swamp, reduced to roughly one yard in height, splayed open, and mounted on a wall in four quarter-circular sections. The result is neither environment, sculpture, nor painting, but rather a curious cross between architectural model, triptych altarpiece (the two central sections are joined comparatively seamlessly), and Monet's water lilies. In Douglas's hands, the immersive, frameless nineteenth-century panoramic canvas becomes a relic that can be studied but not experienced.

At first blush, *Panoramic Rotunda* revisits that media triumphalist moment in 1839 when, over sixty days, the former panorama painter Louis Daguerre announced the invention of photography and saw his diorama burn to the ground. Even as *Panoramic Rotunda*'s vistas are shrunk and dissected, the photographs—three per panel—remain exacting and pristine. Rather than recount the victory of one medium (photography) over another (panoramas), however, *Panoramic Rotunda* isolates the connective tissue between them, the better strike to at it. "I chose a swamp," writes Douglas, "because it can be taken as a metaphor for an eye, it's circular, wet, like an aqueous humour."[1] The circular, wet eye is a potent metaphor for early photography as the union of optics and chemistry. To reduce nature to a continuous series of perspectivally perfect (if not quite uniform) renderings is an even more "natural" transposition of the panorama. Yet the goal is to disembowel, not reconstitute, the unified subject and ocularcentrism of panoramas and photography. "In this piece," Douglas writes, "displayed flayed out on a wall, the subject or central position has been broken open and its individuality has been displaced to the rotunda periphery, broken into three." *Panoramic Rotunda* might be placed in the long line of disgorged and sliced eyes indebted to the renegade surrealist tradition of Luis Buñuel, Salvador Dalí, and Georges Bataille.

But Douglas's title refers less to panoramic images than to the purpose-built structures where they were exhibited. This operative dependence between image and structure has a more familiar twentieth-century counterpart in the film palace. The proleptic relation between panoramas and cinemas is doubly inscribed in the history and immediate critical reception of *Panoramic Rotunda.* The epigraph of its first published review is Walter Benjamin's famous reflections on panoramas: "In striving to produce deceptively life-like changes in their presentation of nature, the panoramas point ahead, beyond photography, to films and sound films."[2] One of the few curators to exhibit the work seemed sure "*Panoramic Rotunda* . . . takes as its subject the desire for cinema."[3] Immediately following *Panoramic Rotunda,* Douglas himself took up cinema as the primary vector of his aesthetic and media archaeology program. But today—as perhaps already in the 1980s—*Panoramic Rotunda* is most striking in its defiance, not its illustration of a technological media progression from panoramas and dioramas to cinemas and other new media and structures.

Panoramic Rotunda occupies a deliberately awkward position between image and structure. It is obtrusive enough to hang uncomfortably on the wall, and its diminutive size fails to live up to its rotunda billing—even if the panels were joined and the circle closed. And unlike the progression from one wildly popular mass medium (panoramas) to another (cinema), *Panoramic Rotunda* was abandoned by both artist and art world without critical success. An admiring critic concluded that its awkwardness "turned what might have been a fascinating ruin into a failed sketch."[4] Douglas himself largely consigned it to oblivion. Rather than teleological, *Panoramic Rotunda* was and remains untimely.

Or perhaps it is best contextualized not in the long nineteenth century, but within the 1980s, a moment producing a surprising number of publications on and restorations of nineteenth-century panoramas. Our current panoramania certainly dates from that moment. If the panorama as mass medium competed with and eventually overtook history painting and later forced painting to conform to its terms, it has, in recent years, become the subject—rather than the medium or technology—of the art-historical gaze. *Panoramic Rotunda* is an early, if somewhat clumsy, artistic instantiation of this renewed historical interest.

Rather than its awkwardness being seen as a liability, its literal disjointedness may be the source of its strength. "The sense I wanted this [piece] to produce theatrically was one of inertia, the rotunda hangs like an artifact in a museum." The stress in Douglas's sentence lies neither on *artifact* nor on *museum*, but on *like*. *Panoramic Rotunda* is not an artifact that could be displayed in a museum of natural history, science, or film and television. (Even art museums have shown next to no interest.) Instead, it hangs *like* an artifact in a museum, complicating every term it touches.

If the first installation of *Panoramic Rotunda*, at Surrey Art Gallery (1986), largely resembled an artifact in a white cube museum, the Art Gallery of Ontario installation (1987) approximated a panorama's conditions of reception: a dark frame deprived the viewer of comparative scale while bright lights brought the image to life. If not quite the nineteenth-century panorama immersive experience, it was also not as inert as Douglas suggests. *Panoramic Rotunda* is a museum artifact that refuses to play dead. This pas de deux with zombie media animates much of the best recent art.

If, as Benjamin famously argues, painting began to outgrow art with the panoramas' first appearance, *Panoramic Rotunda*—among the first museum appearances of historical panoramic technology—marks a rebirth of art from the spirit of media archaeology.

NOTES

1. Mike Hoolbloom, "Stan Douglas Talks at YYZ." *Independent Eye*, Vol. 10, No. 2 (Winter 1989), 36–39; 37. All subsequent Douglas quotations are from this text.
2. Walter Benjamin, "Paris, Capital of the Nineteenth Century," quoted in Scott Watson, "The Afterlife of Interiority: Panoramic Rotunda." *C Magazine*, no. 6 (Summer 1985), 23–25; 23.
3. Barbara Fischer, *Perspective 87: Stan Douglas* (Toronto: Art Gallery of Ontario, 1987), 10.
4. Peter Culley, "Dream as Dialectic: Two Works by Stan Douglas," *Vanguard* 16, no. 4 (1987): 10–13; 11.

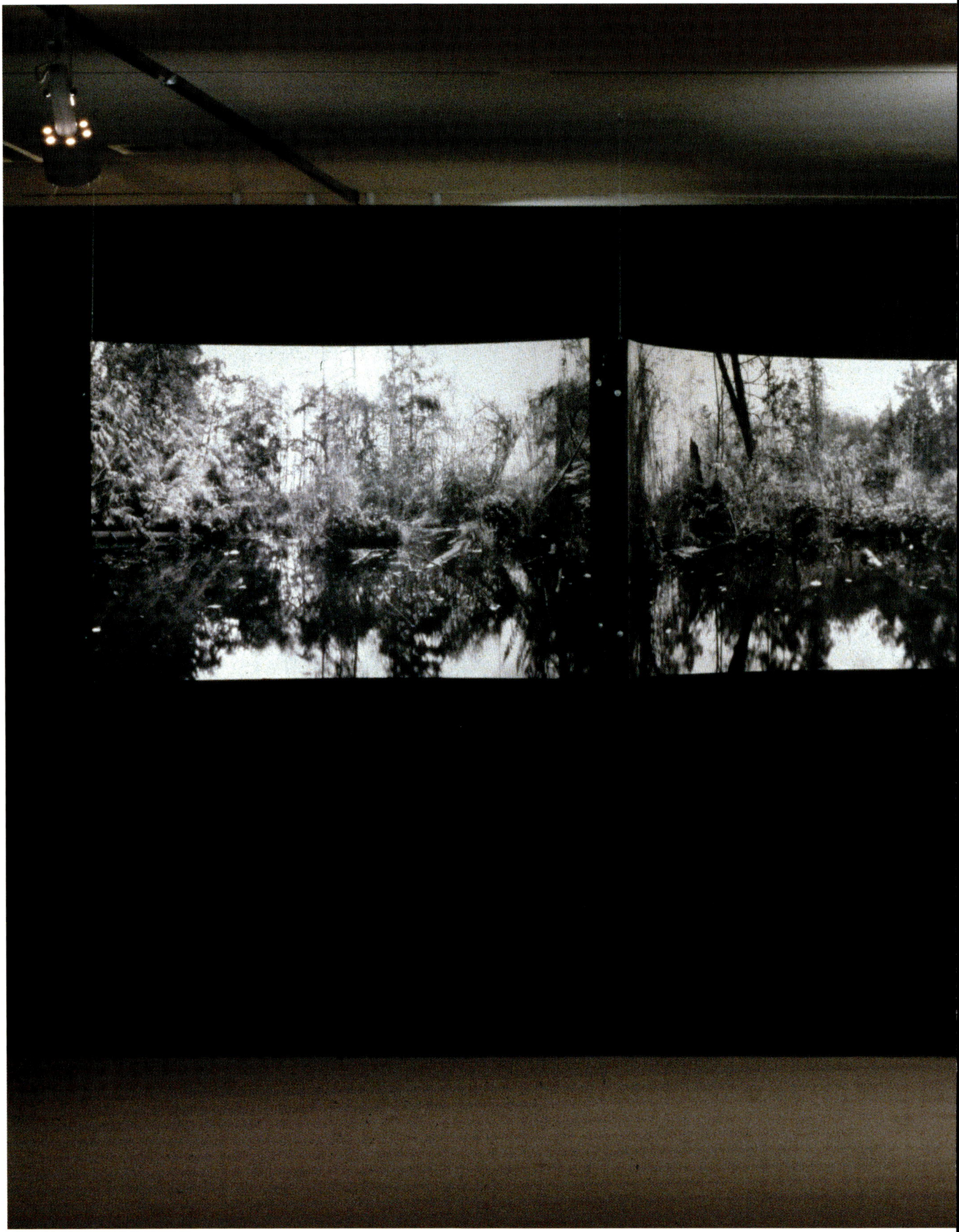

Stan Douglas (Canadian, b. 1960), *Panoramic Rotunda*, 1985. Photo from the 1987 installation at the Art Gallery of Ontario, Toronto.

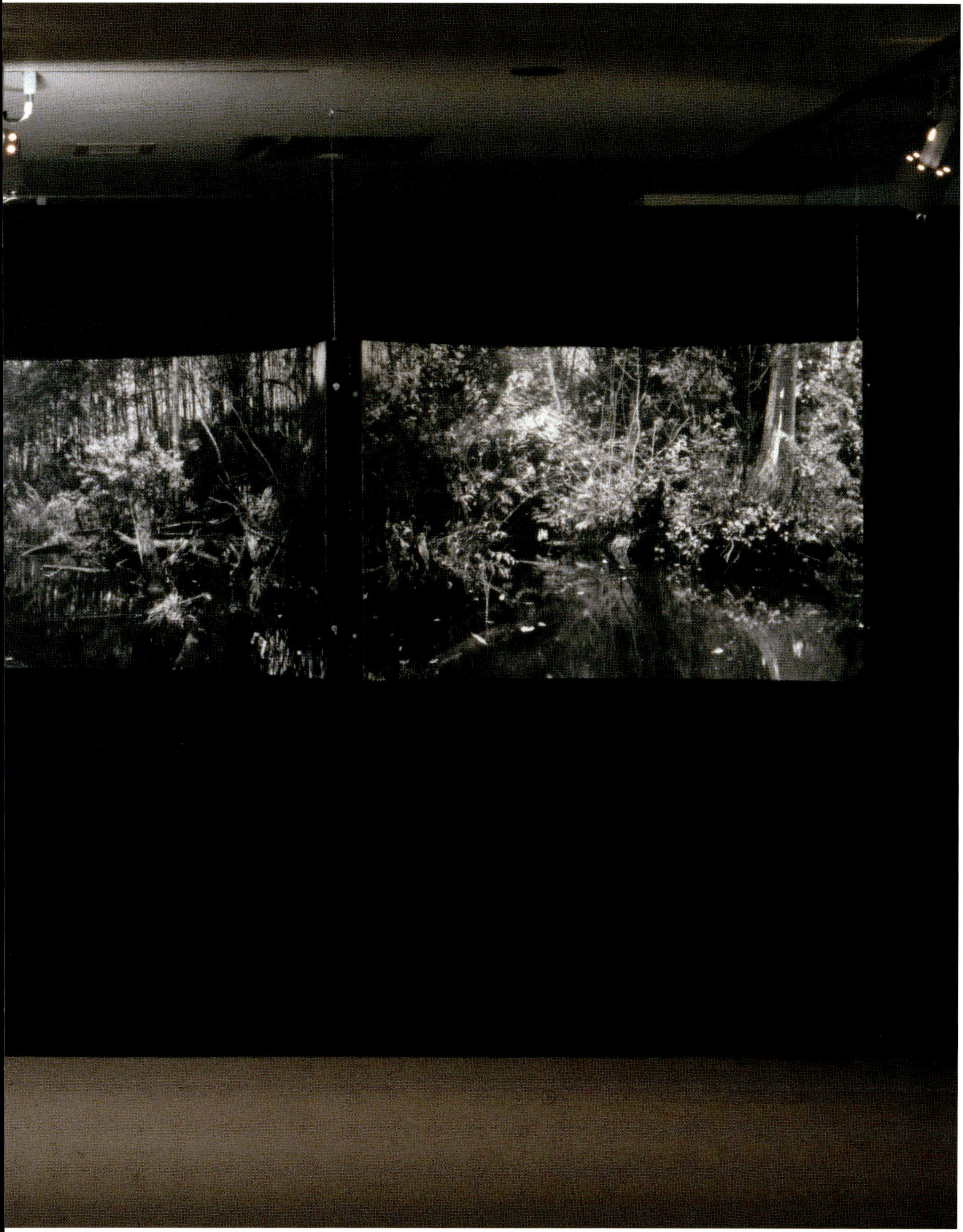

CASSIUS CLAY

Antonio López García, *View of Madrid from the Vallecas Fire Tower*, 1997–2006

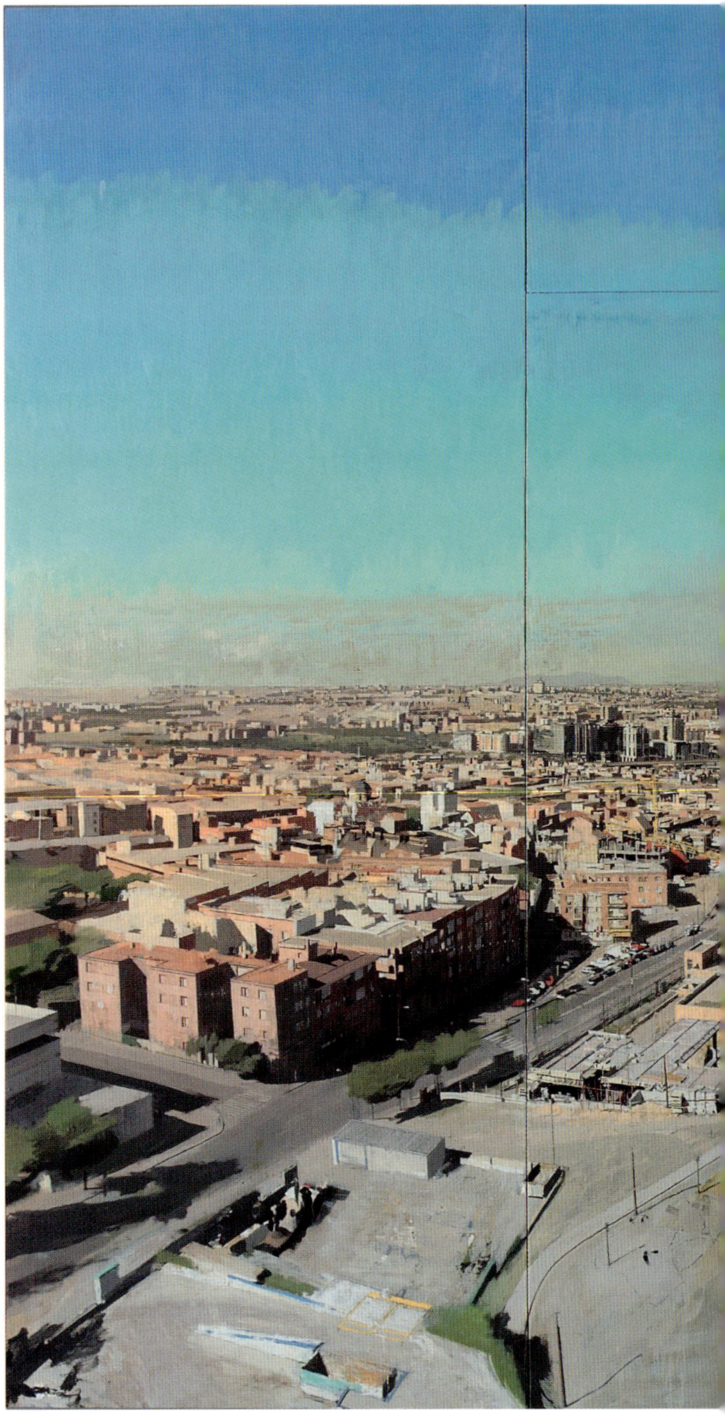

Spanish painting is not known for its landscapes, and the nineteenth-century rise of the European panorama came long after the wane of the seventeenth-century Spanish Empire. Yet in his panoramic views of Madrid and environs, the Spanish painter Antonio López García (b. 1936) suffuses the panorama's customary negotiation between sensory space and rational perspective with meditations on time, light, and urban life. Painted on a grand scale over two decades, with painstaking commitment to the precise details of a sun-bleached cityscape, López García's *View of Madrid from the Vallecas Fire Tower* underscores the panoramic mode's continuing relevance for inquiry into the limits of sight and the limits of art beyond them. The artist himself garnered international attention through Víctor Erice's 1992 documentary *El sol del membrillo* (*Dream of Light* or *Quince Tree of the Sun*), attesting to López García's obsessive study of a single motif, the quince tree, and hard-won realist credentials.

López García first noticed the Vallecas fire tower while painting a different vista of Madrid nearby, realizing that this structure had a ninth-floor terrace offering better city views.[1] Switching projects and prospects, López García began a panel painting from a large tower window. The move highlights the intrinsic anxiety of the panorama as a ceaseless, quixotic quest for the best view and thus its potential to generate alternative vantage points.[2] The panel had to be extended laterally over time, as Madrid crept outward; for the artist, it "emerges and is transformed in parallel with the city."[3] What began as a single board study accreted over sixteen years into a six-panel, profane polyptych of Madrid.

Antonio López García (Spanish, b. 1936), *View of Madrid from the Vallecas Fire Tower*, 1997–2006. Oil on canvas, 250 × 406 cm (98 7/16 × 159 7/8 in.). Asamblea de la Comunidad de Madrid.

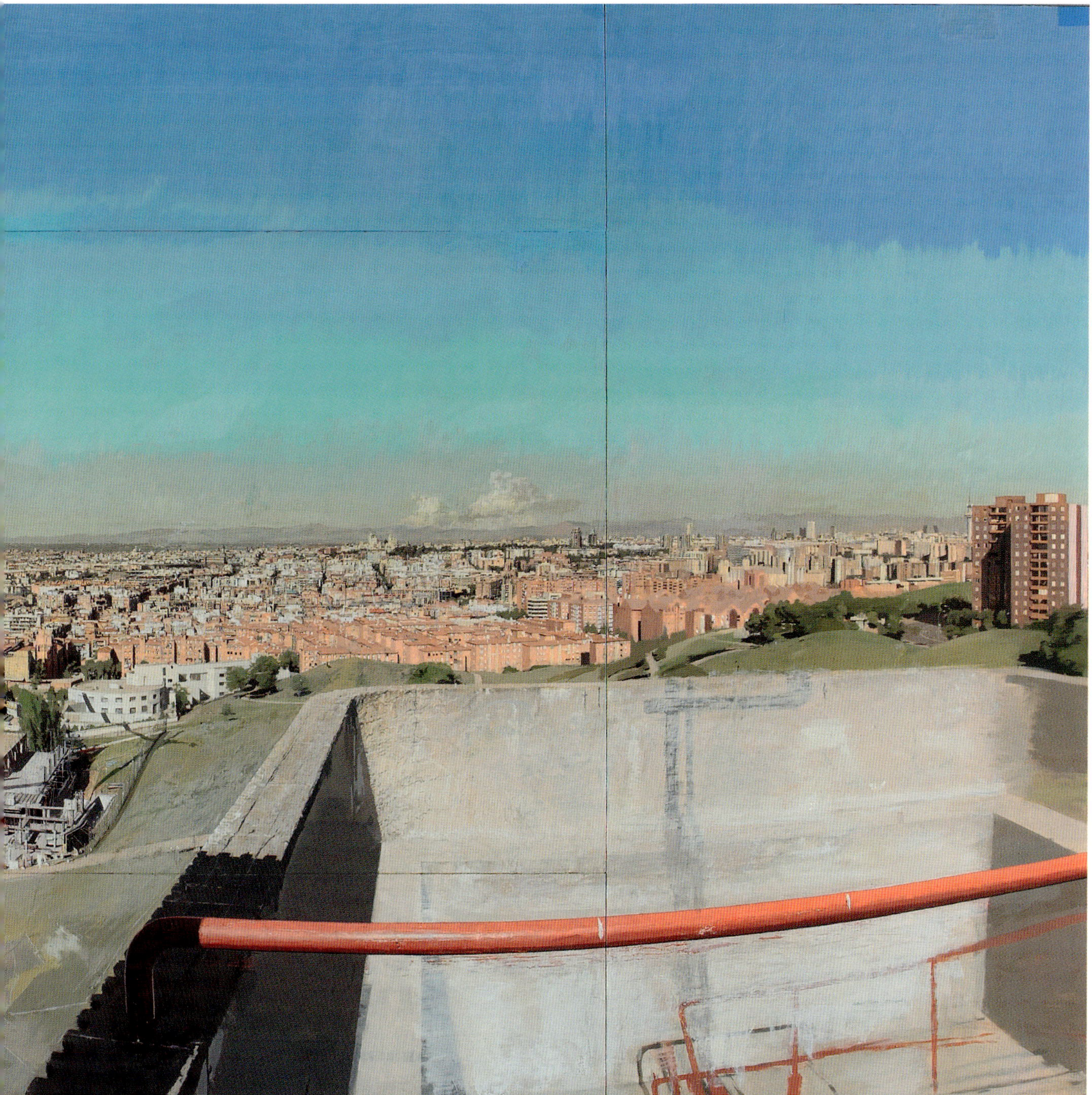

Mystic but mundane, the view is produced by López García's devotion to a particular ritual of capturing light, his reverence for detailing the nondescript. The artist had at most twenty minutes a day, a few weeks of the year, to paint the same seasonal light; this practice in turn demanded decades-long deferrals of finished work, the successive assembly of an image solid in completion yet serial in constitution.[4] More than just the cognitive function of memory and mind, time is coagulated by López García as a key visual pigment and presented as a collaborator to the panoptic eye. Walter Benjamin's assessment of panoramas as "aquariums of distance and the past" finds rigorous execution in López García's rendering of light effects to relate time and distance.[5]

With the sun forestalled, as for Joshua at Gibeon, López García's specific attention to light renders *View of Madrid* emphatically "of the day," and simultaneously engaged with describing the quotidian. His meticulous *veduta* of Madrid presents itself as a domestic, routine image of urban fact, but also as broad allegory. "What I like about Madrid from afar is the profile of a city with nothing characteristic in particular. It is the city, in the general sense."[6]

In this case, natural processes forced a curvature: "Since I left the painting there, the wood support got warped; and as I wasn't able to straighten it I started using another one just like it."[7] By 2004 López García had not only developed the cityscape in detail but also included the fire tower's shadow. The artist inserts it not just as a trace of blocked light but a retracing of sight, suggesting a visual feedback loop in which the shadow becomes both the object of sight and a visual trace of the site affording its view.

López García intensifies this circuit of prospect and referent in later stages of painting. Initially avoiding the fire tower roof because of the antennae, wires, and cables accumulated there, the artist eventually made space for an easel and added the observation deck to the painting.[8] Recalling the physical apparatus of nineteenth-century panoramas, the viewing platform here enables illusions of space but also exposes them as such.

The fire tower's vertiginous immediacy and the quotidian scale of the red guardrail are useful aids in decoding the vast cityscape beyond. The wide purview of panoramic sight makes visible urban information and the networks transmitting it. López García aligns himself with a city's safety infrastructure. There is smoke where there is fire; the pacifying absence of either suggests the city's relative calm. Madrid's bustle fades to stillness at a remove. Other systems are emphasized: housing programs of apartment blocks; parks and green space; and the arterial web of motorways connecting them. The rooftop was also the nexus of various cables, wires, and antennae integrating even freestanding buildings within the larger city grid. And while rooftops are the nether spaces of thermal vents and digital receivers more often than proud observation decks, López García grants prime space on canvas to the dull and unimpressive to enhance the effect of an illusion. The banalities of civic infrastructure wrought in concrete and metal piping are marshaled here in service of the sublime, creating pictorial depth and implications of infinity.

View of Madrid from the Vallecas Fire Tower responds to questions of time, light, and place that had already been raised in the clipped, verbless lines telegraphed by W. H. Auden in "Spain 1937": "Yesterday the shadow-reckoning in the sunny climates."[9] For all the inclusions made available to the panorama, López García stops short of Auden's static "sense of a knowledge encapsulated and possessed."[10] Rather, the most complete view for López García is one determined by change, the aggregate image of ordinary moments in a day, whose tightly defined focus on the instance of light determines its unraveling over years of time, and whose local investment in urban life demands its panoramic view of Madrid.

NOTES

1. Miguel Fernandez-Cid, "The Masterworks," trans. Virginia Pugh Hernandez, in *Antonio López García*, ed. Cheryl Brutvan (Boston: MFA Publications 2008), 144.
2. Ibid.
3. Antonio López García, quoted in Guillermo Solana, "Places and Time," in *Antonio López*, ed. Cela, Garrigues, and Villaverde (Madrid: Fundación Colección Thyssen-Bornemisza 2011), 48.
4. Brutvan, *Antonio López García*, 116.
5. Walter Benjamin, *Gesammelte Schriften*, ed. Rolf Tiedemann and Hermann Schweppenhauser (Frankfurt am Main: Suhrkamp, 1991), 4:240.
6. López García, quoted in Solana, "Places and Time," 47; see also Francisco Umbral, "La verdad de López García" in "Animales sagrados," *La Revista* (December 22, 1996): 76.
7. López García, quoted in Fernandez-Cid, "The Masterworks," 144.
8. Ibid.
9. W. H. Auden, "Spain 1937," in *Another Time* (London: Faber, 1940), 103.
10. W. H. Auden, *The Poetry of W. H. Auden*, ed. Paul Hendon (Cambridge, U.K.: Icon Books, 2000), 94.

RICHARD MAXWELL

Timothy Hyman, *Upper Deck, Rainy Night*, 1991–93

Here comes the painter, entering the upper deck of a Routemaster bus. It looks unstable: the painting's right hand tips up like a ship about to capsize. The painter is the only one standing, the only one holding a support, surrounded by a theater of grotesquely depicted, securely ensconced, self-absorbed characters. If you stare long enough, faces metamorphose into John Tenniel or George Cruikshank replicas.[1] What is Queen Victoria doing, riding a bus, diminutive in the absolute center of things? A giant pumpkin head has floated in from nowhere.

It is all starkly lit, reflected by the cadmium yellow roof. The windows look like paintings, perhaps the huge background canvases in Velázquez's *Las Meninas*. An everyday scene must be fixed as an image before these disquieting perceptions occur to the viewer. And so a rapidly mobile flash of city life is petrified for our edification. The painter is a little reluctant to take center stage: this is too much like a jury of one's peers, or an encircling opera house balcony. Marcel Proust unsettlingly evokes a loge whose occupants are like wax figures; he projects their evanescence and gradual dissolution.

Here they are preserved, solemn, peculiar, self-absorbed, elongated, as the bus goes whizzing along. It is like a glasshouse whose inhabitants take no advantage of looking out the windows. If you look at them from far away, they resolve themselves into coherence like Titian or the Impressionists; if you look at them microscopically, the effect is even more startling: they begin to move through a set of optical illusions, painter's puns. A little man seems to be a photograph on television being interviewed. Look again, and he's Queen Elizabeth. Look again, and he's glancing about nervously. The demonlike figure at the bar seems to lunge forward a little, then withdraw.

The painting's technique foregrounds a contradiction. If you have the big picture, the figures are immobilized. If you have the microscopic picture, they seem to scuttle about. Hyman has a perfect view of the people on the bus and their arrangement and expressions. We see his own comically drawn hand.

In fact, Hyman is everywhere on this vehicle. And this bus, correspondingly, is everywhere in London. It is predictable, a giant mechanical thing that rushes people from destination to destination. In recent years, Hyman has been understandably obsessed with the Ferris wheel, with the London Eye, another mechanical thing that transports people automatically in a mandated order. Hyman knows that he has six minutes at the top, during which he frantically draws London from the heights. Routemaster offers you a different view of the city: street-level, microscopic, hands-on, frighteningly close to all these monstrous travelers.

Routemaster, London Eye: two big machines follow a set itinerary through London with people strapped to them, each one charted toward an inevitable goal, London Eye toward the apex of a circle, Routemaster toward the shifting of responsibility from driver to driver, pushing the passenger face-to-face with the city panorama, the sweep of the River Thames. These large mechanical contrivances trace timed paths, goals shocking even when predictable. The form goes back to the *mappa mundi*; all ambitious, large-scale *mappa mundi* are designed to be turned, evolving like the route of a bus or a Ferris wheel to

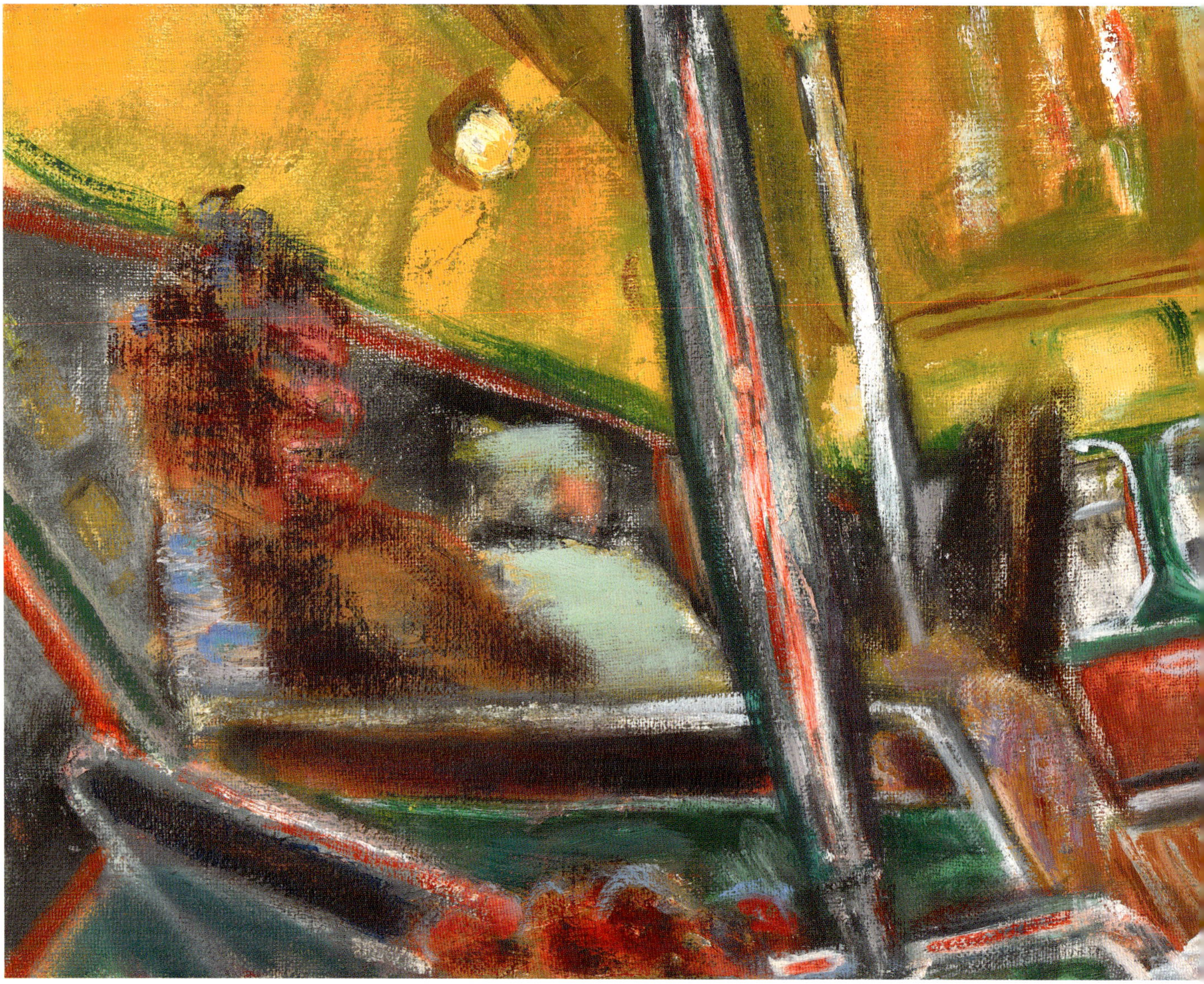

bring the passenger to some surprising, dizzy apex: a panorama, a crowd. The effect strains the viewer.

In Hyman's recent *The Man Inscribed with London* (2009), a red bus makes the turn, its ceiling lit vivid yellow. This is Hyman's heart beating. The same painting shows Hyman in fragments, stacked precariously. Inscribing is a perilous activity, like stacking blocks. Writing is similarly dangerous because it puts one face-to-face with all sorts of revelations, shocks, views. Clearly, one needs protectors along this way. In Hyman's *The Pilgrim Meets Infirmity in Old Age* (1997–2000), the insouciant artist confronts infirmity in old age, not shocked at all, against a background of murky sky. No protector here. Perhaps he is thinking of or invoking buses, an array in which the explorer of London can be swaddled.

This perhaps explains the conspicuously expanded range of vision in the *Upper Deck* picture, whose vivid yellow bus ceiling counteracts London gloom. Formally the line of characters looming or staring at Hyman echoes the array of equally distinctive characters poised supernaturally and larger than life: circular thinking.

Hyman aspires to a body of work that would map out London, Jerusalem, and especially Siena, because of its egalitarian values. This picture explores the way a turning circle shares everything out, yet also the alarming dip in the Routemaster as it tries to turn a corner, apparently nearly capsizing.

Hyman watching Hyman is well placed to note and counteract the shift in the body: to trace that circle by which he is surrounded. He feels no fear then—rather,

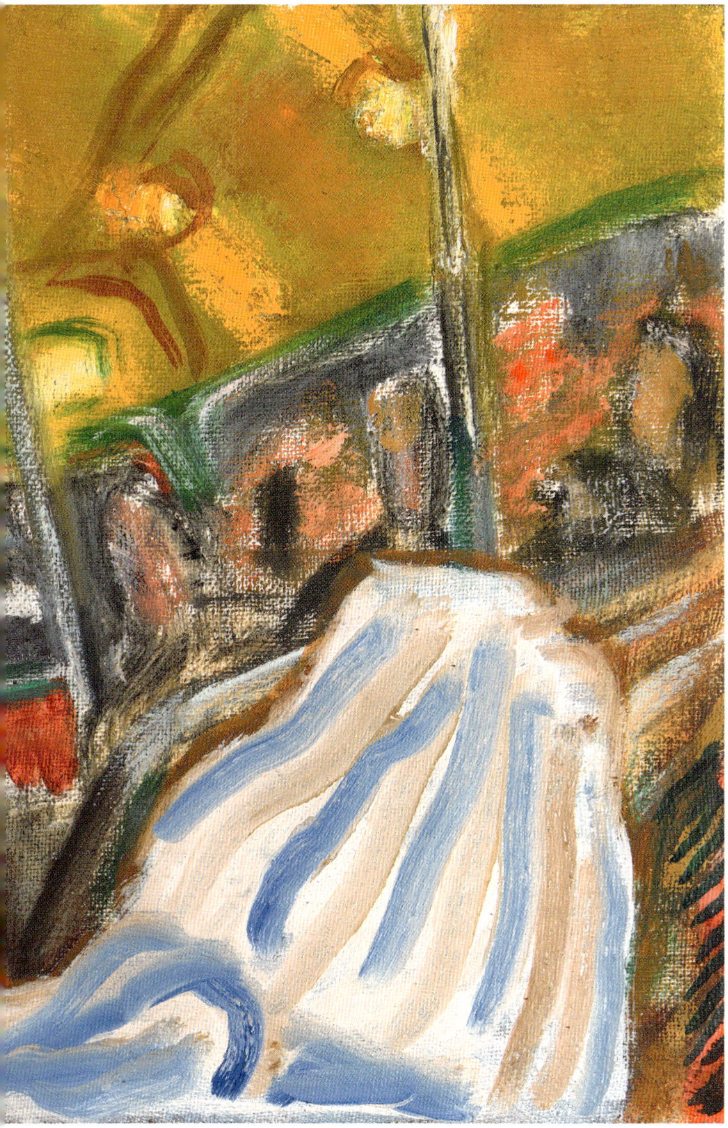

Timothy Hyman (British, b. 1946), *Upper Deck, Rainy Night*, 1991–93. Oil on canvas, 30 × 60 cm (11 ¾ × 23 ⅝ in.). Private collection.

relish and reassurance, as he gets energy from the display. And there is always the little button marked HERE, atop a red stripe, by which the bus's trajectory can be stopped and accident prevented, the artist presented with an opportunity to sketch.

Richard Maxwell dictated this essay in 2010, a month before his death.

NOTE

1. British masters of comic illustration, Cruikshank (1792–1878) began alongside James Gillray, ending in the high Victorian era, whereas Tenniel (1820–1914) worked for the satirical journal *Punch* and created famous illustrations for Lewis Carroll's *Alice's Adventures in Wonderland*.

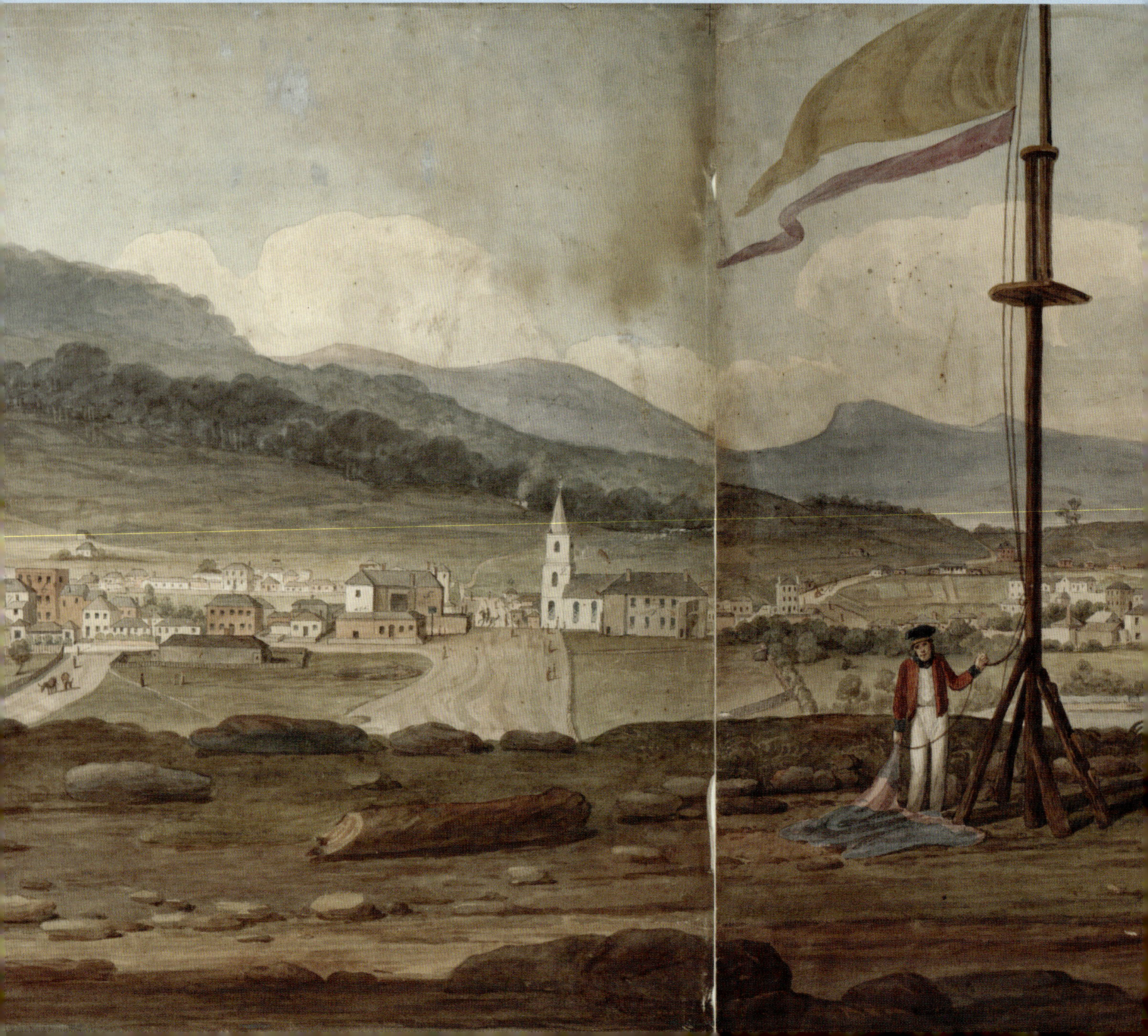

PART I

The Painted Panorama: Immersive Aesthetics

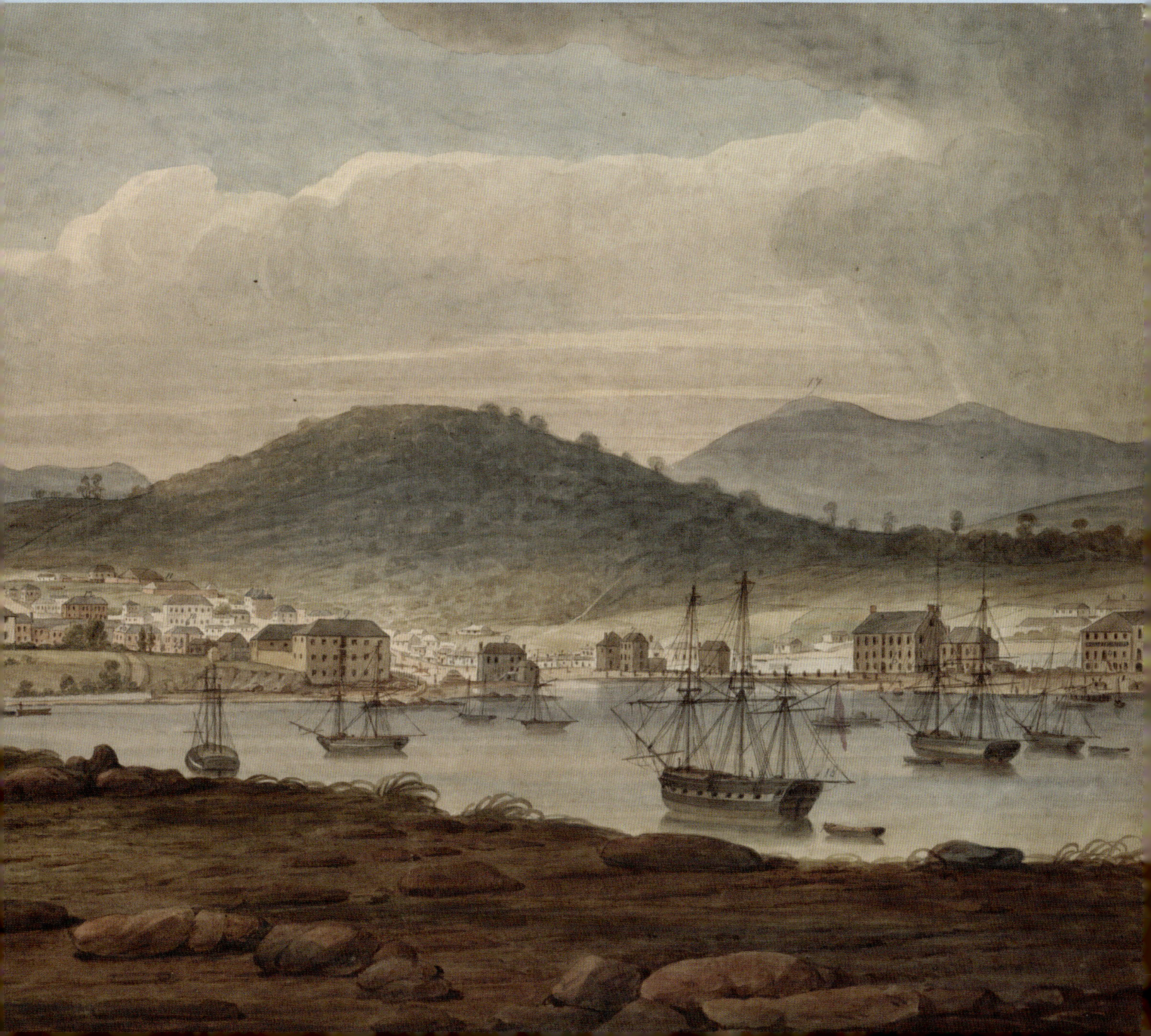

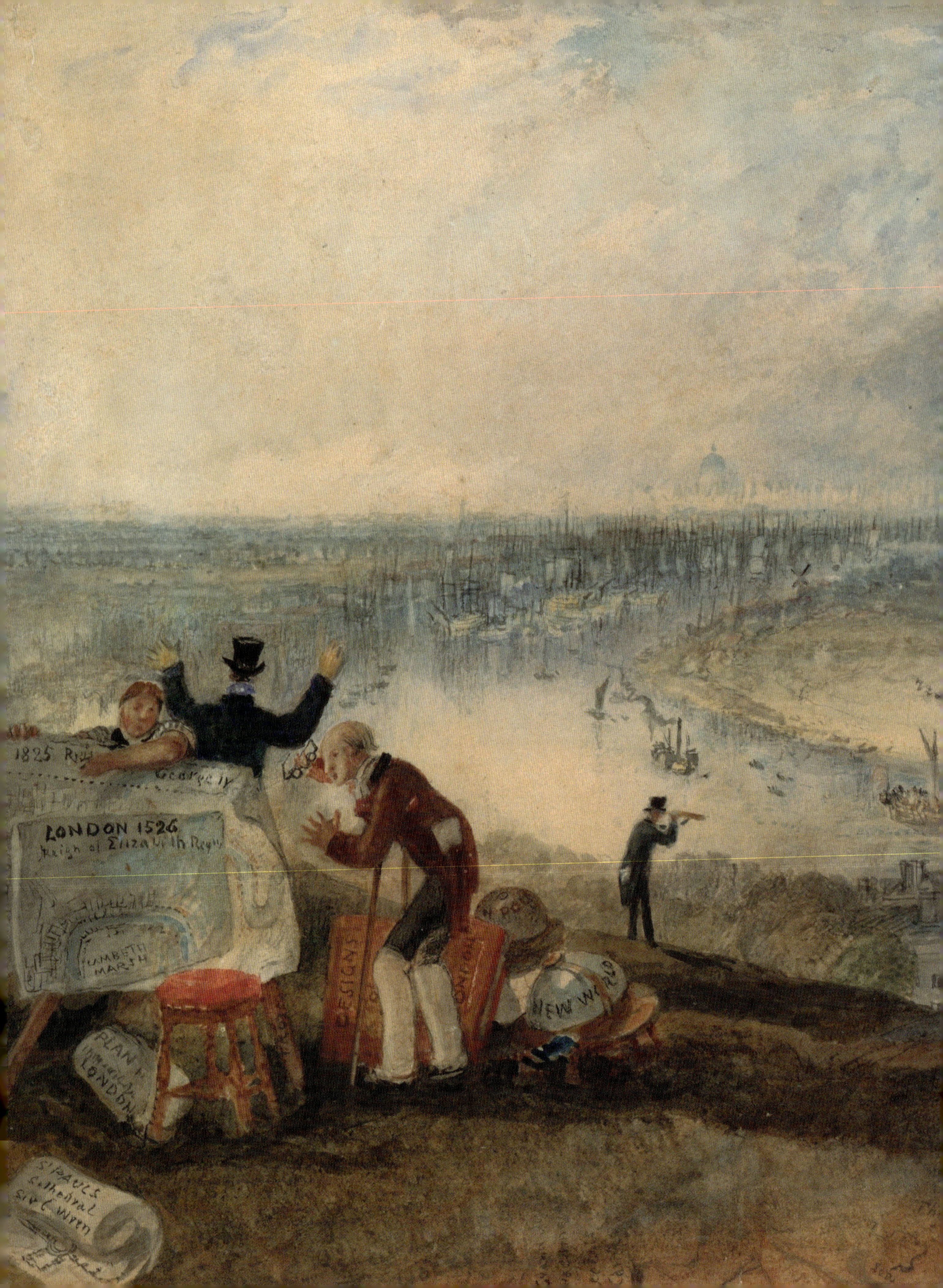

1825
George IV
LONDON 1526
Reign of Elizabeth Regina
LAMBETH MARSH
DESIGNS
NEW WORLD
LONDON
ST PAULS Cathedral Sir C Wren

TIM BARRINGER

1 The World for a Shilling

The Early Panorama as Global Landscape, 1787–1830

From its inception, the painted panorama was understood as a global technology—a manifestation of limitless reach both in visual form and in restlessly changing thematic content. The panorama emerged during a period of warfare between rival empires played out across much of the world and offered nineteenth-century European and American audiences a place at the center of spectacular landscapes and historical events, familiar and unfamiliar. In this chapter I explore the condition of globalism embodied by the panorama's form and argue that through its insistent, phantasmagorical juxtaposition of "here" and "there"—home and abroad, familiar and exotic, imperial center and periphery, metropole and province, civilization and its others—the experience of visiting the panorama formed a paradigmatic viewing experience of modernity.

It is a necessary truism to state that the panorama's inception occurred in the 1780s, at the very moment that historians from Karl Marx to Michel Foucault have identified with the birth of modernity—a period associated with "economic takeoff" and rapid social change.[1] The technology of the panorama was a product of enlightenment scientific thinking and the technologies of the industrial revolution. The gaunt, cylindrical buildings constructed to house early panoramas have more in common, architecturally, with the factory shed than building types (like the theater or picture gallery) traditionally associated with artistic display. Foucault's insights are particularly relevant in relation to Jeremy Bentham's invention in the very same year, 1787, of the panopticon—a prison whose disciplinary regime was based on the regulation of vision and visibility.[2] In the panopticon, the prisoner is subject to constant illumination, and his unseen observers, housed in a tower, are bathed in darkness. Stephan Oettermann describes the panorama as "a complete prison for the eye."[3] I question Oettermann's thesis: for while the panorama undoubtedly served as a powerful mechanism for diffusing the dominant ideologies of the day, notably an emerging global consciousness in the age of empires, it offered, I will argue, an unprecedented, if illusory, sense of freedom to its viewers, who could move through the space and select vistas at will, across hitherto impregnable geographical and social boundaries. In doing so, it inaugurated new possibilities for both the consumption and the production of visual art. This is not to underestimate its ideological power: on the contrary, the panorama's integration of the commercial and artistic seems paradigmatically modern and contrived

facing: Fig. 1.19 detail; previous spread: Fig. 3.8 detail

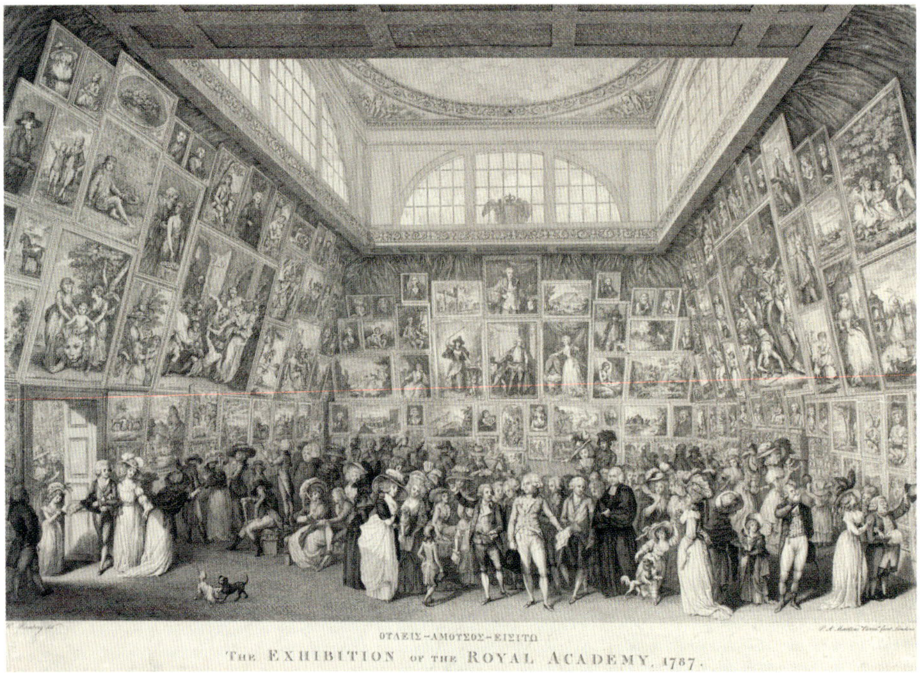

FIG. 1.1. Pietro Antonio Martini (Italian, 1738–1797) after Johann Heinrich Ramberg (German, 1763–1840), *The Exhibition of the Royal Academy, 1787*, 1787. Engraving on paper, 36.1 × 49.9 cm (14 ¼ × 19 ⅝ in.). Victoria and Albert Museum, London (27807).

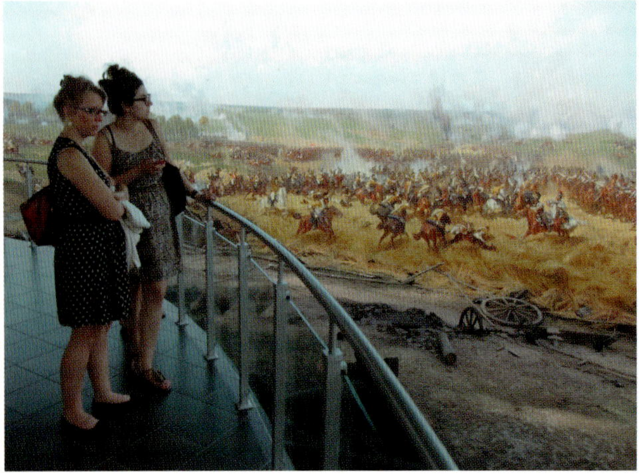

FIG. 1.2. Franz Roubaud (Russian, 1856–1928), *Panorama of the Battle of Borodino*, 1912.

to interpellate (in Althusser's sense) the largest number of individuals. By responding to the demands of a new, prosperous, and ideologically febrile urban middle class, the panorama unmoored pictorial representation from its courtly bounds within the gilded picture frame, offering a more expansive worldview that held liberating as well as repressive potentialities.[4]

THE AMBULANT VIEWER

The central innovation of the panorama was the viewing platform, which profoundly shifted the grammar of visual representation and the perception of art objects. The spectator of the painting created with single-vanishing-point perspective must remain still in order to participate in the illusion and is, indeed, subject to the visual logic of the painting, positioned and conditioned to stasis. In Pietro Martini's (1738–1797) engraving of the Royal Academy, after a drawing made by Johann Heinrich Ramberg (1763–1840) in 1787, the very year the panorama was invented, we see the public consuming one image and moving on to the next as if peering through a sequence of windows (fig. 1.1). Spectators on a viewing platform, however, must move around, choosing the direction of their gaze and the motion of their bodies according to their own will, eventually turning through 360 degrees in order to appreciate, and to take command of, the scene (fig. 1.2). As our introduction notes, Robert Barker's original patent specifies: "My invention is intended, by drawing and painting, and a proper disposition of the whole, to perfect an entire view of any country or situation, as it appears to the observer *turning quite round*, to produce which effect, the painter or drawer must fix his situation, and delineate correctly and connectedly every object which presents itself to his view as he turns round, concluding by drawing a connection with where he began."[5] The experience is one of total immersive illusion, created by the expert manipulation of perspective on the part of the panorama's designer and the teams of artisans employed to create the massive paintings.

Oettermann's proposal that the paying public on the

viewing platform was entrapped in "a complete prison for the eye," I suggest, mistakes, indeed inverts, the panorama's logic; for if we follow the panopticon metaphor, the panorama's viewer is actually positioned as the prison guard, all-seeing and empowered but in darkness, rather than as the hapless illuminated convict in a cell, unable to tell whether he is being observed. Ackermann's aquatint showing the vertiginous viewing platform at the Colosseum Panorama in Regent's Park, London, in 1821 emphasizes this point (fig. 1.3). The viewing platform provides access to a simulacrum of the vista from the dome of St. Paul's Cathedral. For a small payment, the panorama's visitor is empowered to survey London from its highest point, noting the city's landmarks and boundaries, following the lines of the river, roads, and valleys as far as the eye can see. In a telling, self-referential gesture, the Colosseum itself—where the viewers are actually standing—is clearly represented as a distant but nonetheless exaggeratedly prominent structure; Regent's Park beyond it is at London's western extreme (fig. 1.4). This detail suggests the brilliance of panoramic illusion: the viewer's gaze is, in reality, captured by the limits of the building—one is actually staring at a brick wall—but the expertise of the panorama's painters creates an entirely compelling sense of recession into infinity.

The aesthetic power of this sense of boundlessness resonated with the period's dominant aesthetic theory, that of the sublime. Edmund Burke, writing in 1757, placed

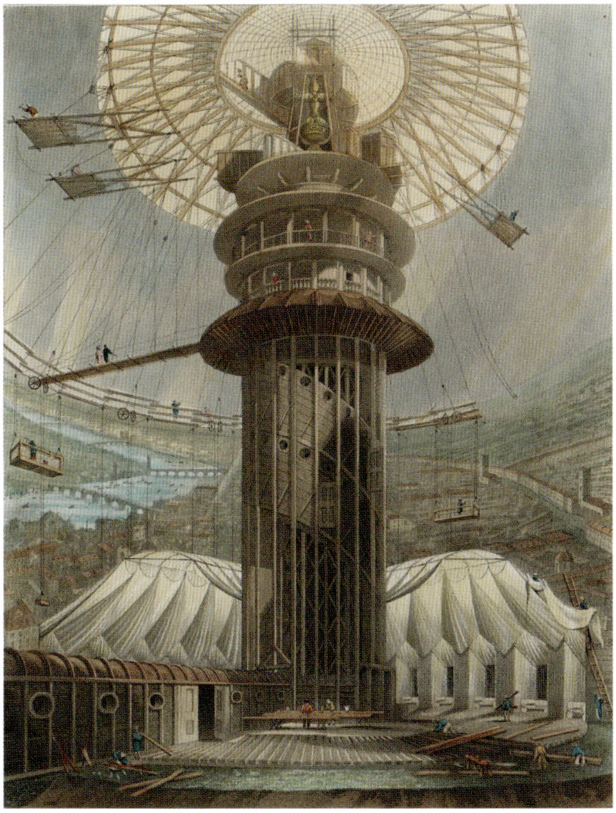

FIG. 1.3. *The Geometrical Ascent to the Galleries in the Colosseum, Regent's Park*, plate IV from *Graphic Illustrations of the Colosseum, Regent's Park, in Five Plates, from Drawings by Gandy, Mackenzie, and Other Eminent Artists* (London: R. Ackermann, 1829). Colored aquatint. Yale Center for British Art, New Haven, Connecticut, Paul Mellon Collection.

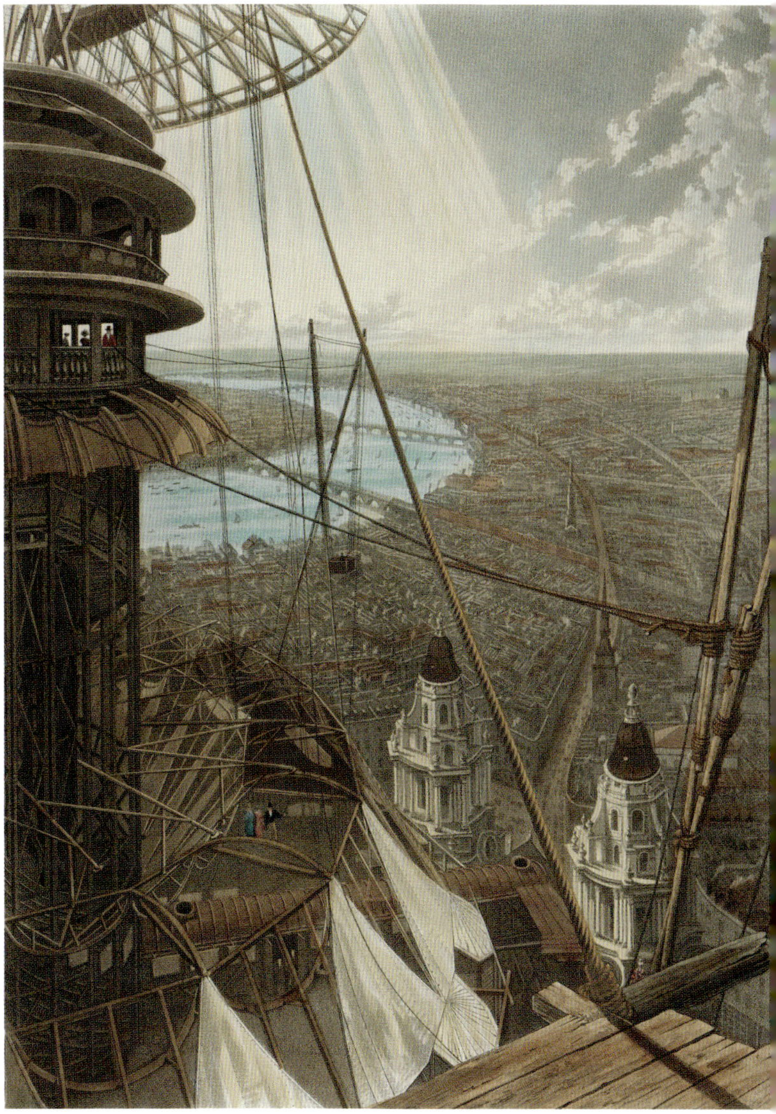

FIG. 1.4. *Bird's Eye View from the Staircase & the Upper Part of the Pavilion, in the Colosseum, Regent's Park*, plate V from *Graphic Illustrations of the Colosseum, Regent's Park, in Five Plates, from Drawings by Gandy, Mackenzie, and Other Eminent Artists* (London: R. Ackermann, 1829). Colored aquatint, 29 × 22 cm (11 1/2 × 8 11/16 in.). Yale Center for British Art, New Haven, Connecticut, Paul Mellon Collection.

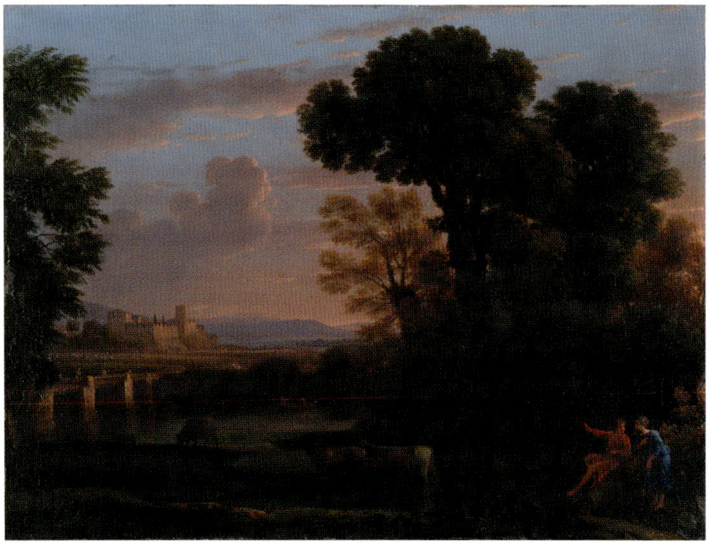

FIG. 1.5. Claude Lorrain (French, 1604–1667), *Pastoral Landscape*, 1648. Oil on copper, 39.4 × 53.3 cm (15 1/2 × 21 in.). Yale University Art Gallery, New Haven, Connecticut. Leonard C. Hanna, Jr., Class of 1913 (1959.47).

FIG. 1.6. Lodovico Caracciolo (Italian, 1761–1842), *Panorama of Rome*, 1824. Oil on canvas, 167.7 cm × 1,335.8 cm (66 × 526 in.). Victoria and Albert Museum, London (1292-1886).

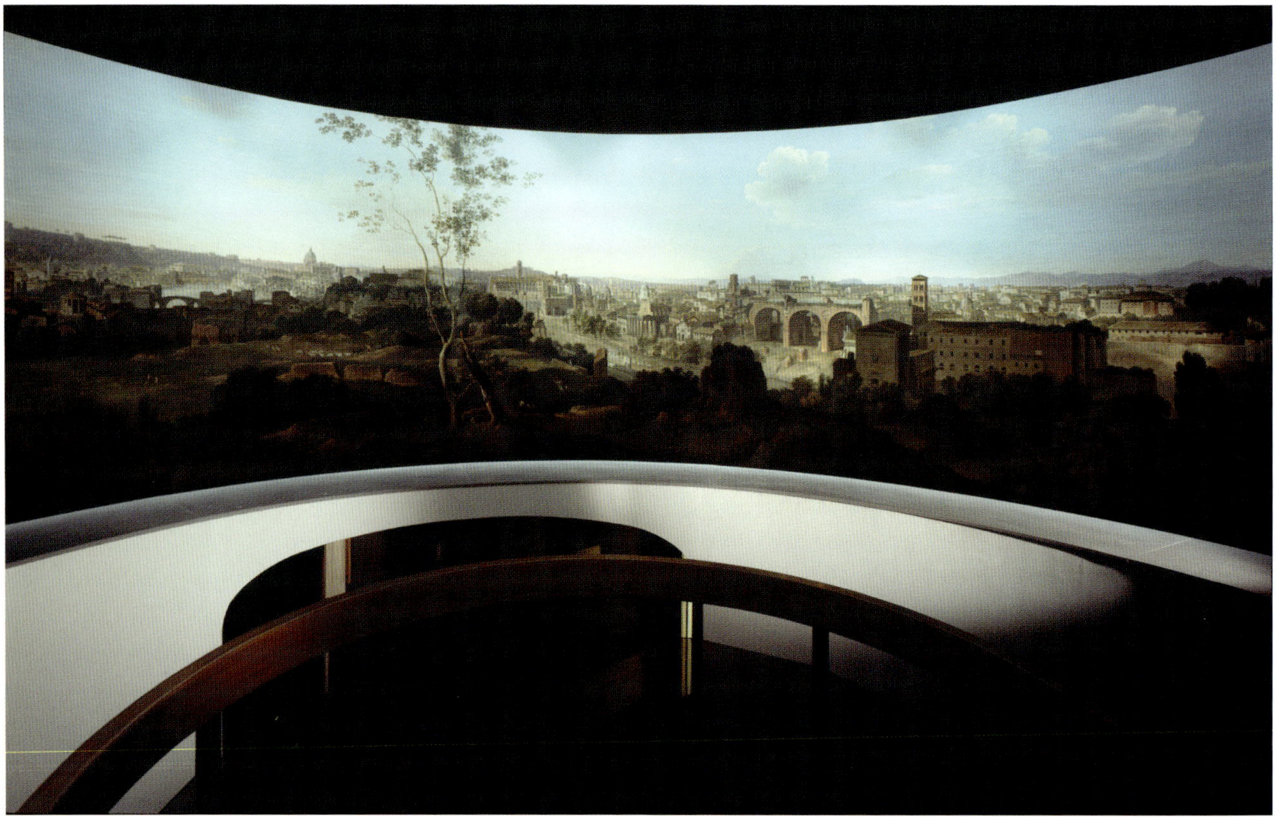

great value on the aesthetic and psychological power of infinity, even seeming in his *Philosophical Enquiry into the Origin of Our Ideas of the Sublime and Beautiful* to prefigure the panorama's effect, when he described "the eye not being able to perceive the bounds of many things, they seem to be infinite." The scale of panorama paintings further ensured their categorization as sublime, for as Burke noted, "Sublime objects are vast in their dimensions, beautiful ones comparatively small."[6] The panorama played into fashionable aesthetics by offering a seemingly endless view of everything.

The aspiration to create a limitless vision of landscape led to fundamental departures from landscape painting conventions. To achieve an unbroken horizon of 360 degrees, painters had to abandon not only the gilded frame, but also the internal compositional devices that had dominated landscape painting at least since the time of Nicolas Poussin (1594–1665) and Claude Lorrain (1604/5–1682), when the genre became established, even if an alternative tradition of the broad prospect view could be found in the work of Dutch artists such as Philips Koninck (1619–1688). The placement of firm vertical elements at both sides of a composition—Claude's famous *repoussoir* trees, for example (fig. 1.5)—had by the early nineteenth century become a trope so ubiquitous that it was hardly even noticed. Yet the panorama could not allow such elements to break up the horizon and draw attention to the composition's artifice. In one striking example, Lodovico Caracciolo's (1761–1842) surviving, relatively small *Panorama of Rome* (1824), the lack of framing devices within the composition allows the vista of the Roman campagna—the very landscape Claude had made his own—to seem endless (fig. 1.6). Only a frail sapling cuts the horizon, a dim memory of Claude. The Claudean landscape (as in fig. 1.5) invites the viewer to enter a carefully staged, severely delimited pictorial space, where the eye navigates a series of firmly positioned signposts before reaching a final payoff at the vanishing point, an exquisite, blue-tinted distance. The panorama's viewing platform, by contrast, allows for a euphoric view of everything that can be seen from a specified viewpoint. The artist widens, rather than narrows, the viewer's range of possibilities. Barker's patrons could wander unfettered through the campagna, taking in its delights according to whim. Briefly, and for a shilling, the metropolitan consumer is the lord of all he—or she, since many of Barker's patrons were ladies of means—surveys.

POLITICAL VIEWS

The freedom of the ambulant viewer to consume the scene at will offers a powerful metaphor for the freedom of the individual subject—those liberties believed to be enshrined in the British constitution after the "Glorious Revolution" of 1688. A powerful emblem of the middle-class subject's emerging empowerment can be found in his or her ability to purchase, for a brief (and avowedly illusory) moment, a kind of magisterial gaze once available only to the aristocracy and the state's military apparatus.

In his insightful discussion of the "Hoober Stand," Michael Charlesworth has located a significant aristocratic precursor to the panoramic form of viewing (fig. 1.7).[7] The "stand," or tower, was built in 1746–68 in the landscape garden of Wentworth Woodhouse, a formidable English country house in West Riding of Yorkshire, as a

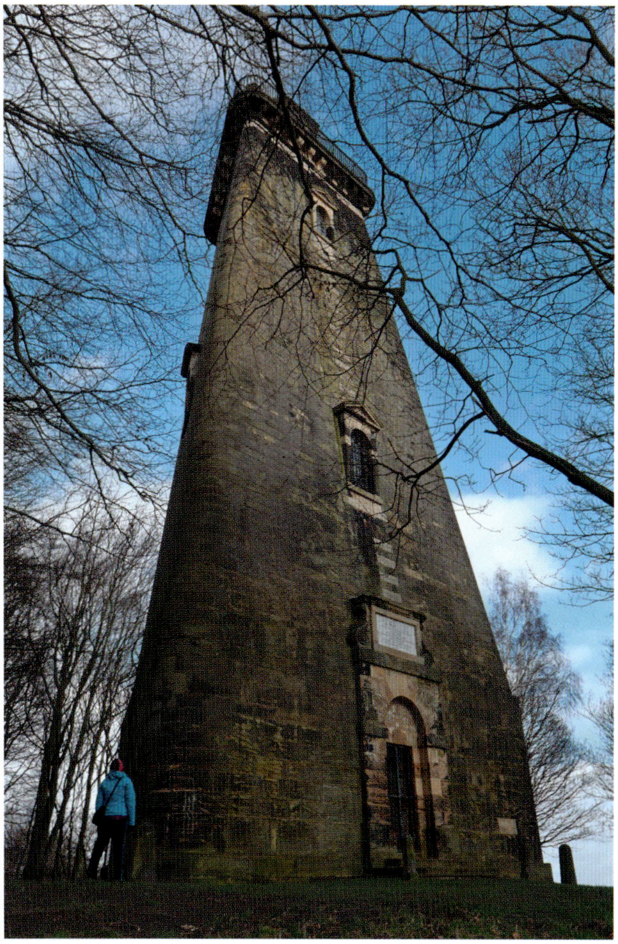

FIG. 1.7. Henry Flitcroft (British, 1697–1769), Hoober Stand, Wentworth Woodhouse, 1746–68.

monument to brutal—though, from a Hanoverian viewpoint, triumphant—suppression of the 1745–46 Jacobite rebellion. It provided a vantage point from which to enjoy views of forty miles and more in each direction. Much of the land belonged to Thomas Watson Wentworth, Earl of Malton, who had commissioned the tower and who delighted in taking groups of visitors—on one occasion including the military artist Thomas Sandby (1721–1798)—to admire the view from the platform at its apex. The relationship between possessing the panoramic vista (even before that term's invention) and political power is transparent here, directly related to a high position in a static social hierarchy conveyed through birth and the inheritance of land, connections with successful military campaigns, and traditional hallmarks of aristocratic authority. In this formulation, the command of visual pleasure and the exercise of inherited authority are indivisible, rooted in the past and projected ineffably into the future.[8] At the Hoober Stand the viewing platform is held exclusively in

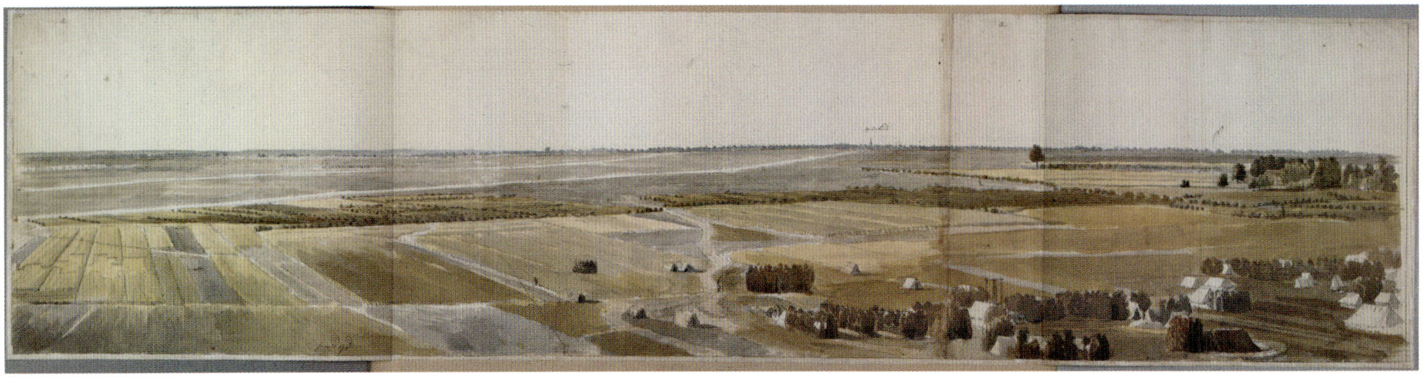

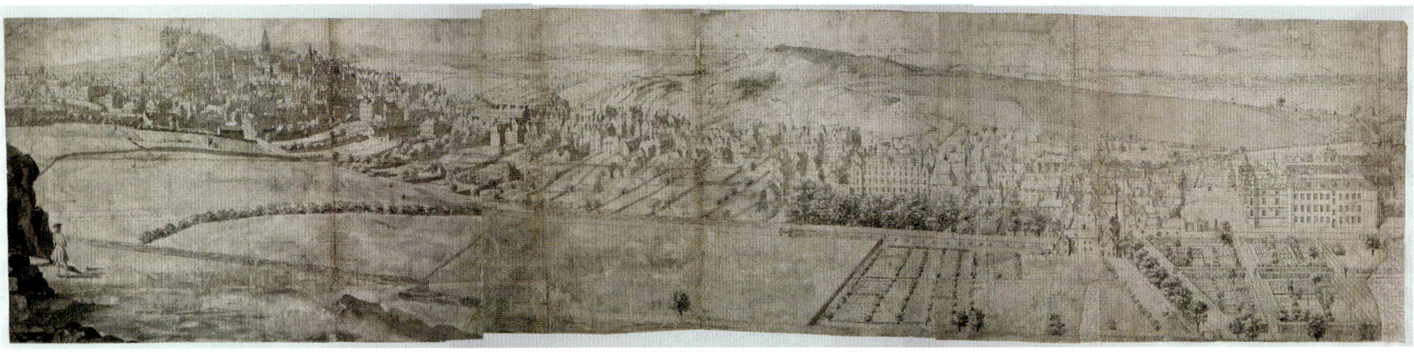

FIG. 1.8. Thomas Sandby (British, 1721–1798), *A Colored Plan of the Encampment of the Allied Troops near Grave, under the Duke of Cumberland and Prince of Orange; the Lines Extending from Zeeland, on the Borders of the Peel Morass, through Heesch, Osch, Ravestein, etc., to the Maes,* June 22, 1748. Pen and watercolor on paper. British Library, London.

FIG. 1.9. Thomas Sandby, *Holyrood Palace and Environs—One of Three Sections of a Panorama of Edinburgh,* ca. 1748–64. Pen and gray wash on paper, 30 × 135 cm (11 13/16 × 53 1/8 in.). National Galleries of Scotland. William Findlay Watson Bequest, 1881.

the "natural" hands of the hereditary landowner: the tranquil vista testifies to peace, the balance of power (between king and aristocracy and among European nations), and the security of the Protestant ascendancy. The views—both political opinions and picturesque prospects—of the Whig elite, challenged by the rebellion, are now firmly in place, held in perpetuity.

After the inception of the panorama as a mass medium in 1793, as we shall see, it was the London middle class that ascended the steps to feel the thrill of taking visual (or virtual) possession, if not of the actual estates and cities of Britain or the imperial territories, then of their vivid and convincing simulacra. There is a palpable, schematic social and political significance in this transition from the hierarchical world of the army and of aristocratic patronage to the anarchic energy of the free market, from aristocratic observance to bourgeois comportment. The shift of audience for global panoramic imagery betokened a significant transfer of imagined—if not yet actual—authority from princes and military men to the shilling crowd.

Yet before attending to the euphoric moment of the panorama's London triumph, it is important to acknowledge the extent to which the technical skill in representation of space in the panorama drew on the skills of military topographers in the service of the state. As Charlesworth has noted, following Bernard Smith and other scholars, techniques for representing the panoramic landscape were developed for instrumental rather than aesthetic purposes among draftsmen associated with, and often employed by, the British armed forces. Thomas Sandby himself created perspective views of battlefields and contested territories, seen from a high viewpoint, as a significant adjunct to maps for use in the planning, execution, and official commemoration of military campaigns. Having served for three years in the Board of Ordnance Drawing Room in Edinburgh, where military maps and plans were prepared, Sandby was employed as "Draughtsman and Designer" by William Augustus, Duke of Cumberland.[9] For the duke he prepared workmanlike studies of potential battlefields, probably based on graphite drawings using a

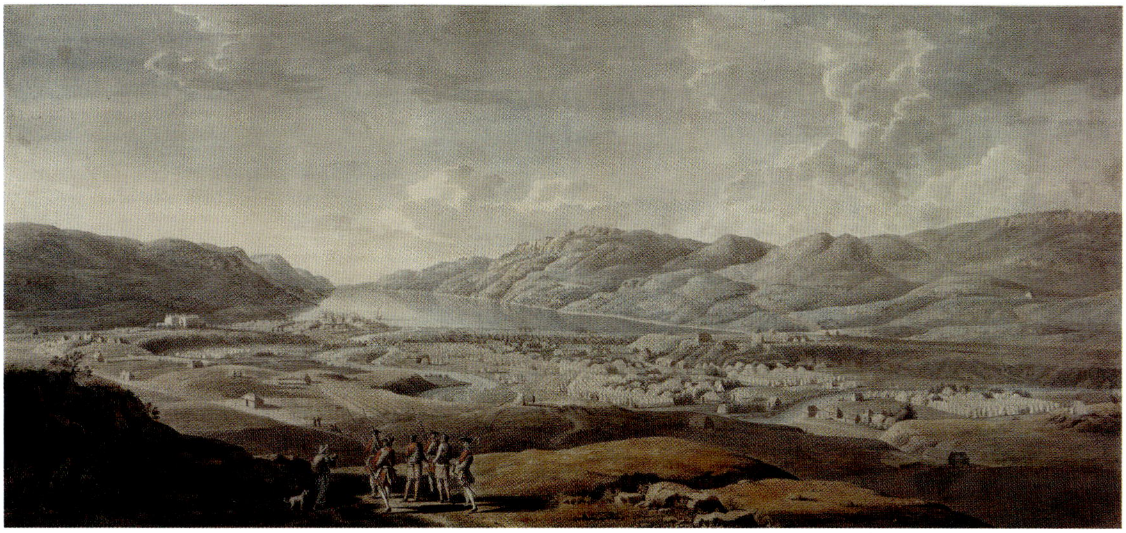

FIG. 1.10. Thomas Sandby, *Fort Augustus*, ca. 1746. Pen, ink, and watercolor, 31.7 × 70.1 cm (12 ½ × 27 ½ in.). Royal Collection Trust, London (914725).

camera obscura, an optical device allowing for swift and accurate landscape transcription. Colored washes emphasized significant topographical elements. In a work created during the duke's maneuvers in the War of the Spanish Succession, with the glorious title *A Colored Plan of the Encampment of the Allied Troops near Grave, under the Duke of Cumberland and Prince of Orange; the Lines Extending from Zeeland, on the Borders of the Peel Morass, through Heesch, Osch, Ravestein, etc., to the Maes*, made on June 22, 1748, for example (fig. 1.8), Sandby's unerring eye surveys the terrain with the concerns of a military commander in mind. Three large sheets of paper are attached to allow a lateral scanning of the horizon and the intervening landscape. Aesthetic concerns and questions of historical association are subordinated to military utility: the primary objective is topographical precision. Penciled inscriptions draw attention to significant features.

Sandby was also present during Cumberland's campaign to quell the Jacobite rebellion of 1745–46, the action the Hoober Stand commemorated. His meticulous outline view *Holyrood Palace and Environs—One of Three Sections of a Panorama of Edinburgh*, surely based on drawings made on-site in 1745–46 (fig. 1.9), references a key site of the rebellion, during which the city was occupied by the Jacobite forces. The Stuart prince, Charles Edward, had briefly installed himself in the Palace of Holyroodhouse, which appears at the composition's right margin. Extended laterally to incorporate a wide field of view, the composition again conforms to the utilitarian rather than the commemorative function. As the cultural geographer Mark Dorrian notes, "In contrast to an approach that displays the city by enumerating and picturing its principal buildings, this view is strategic: its attention is upon the texture of the total urban assemblage and its territory, and the military possibilities and consequences of these."[10]

Cumberland's victory at the Battle of Culloden on April 16, 1746, earned him the nickname "the Butcher." Sandby commemorated the campaign in a meticulously detailed and elaborately finished watercolor, *Fort Augustus*, ca. 1746, probably presented to George II and still in the Royal Collection (fig. 1.10). In contrast to the austere and functional presentation of the *A Colored Plan of the Encampment* and *Edinburgh from Salisbury Crags*, the presentation watercolor *Fort Augustus* includes a sweeping landscape setting, a fully elaborated, cloud-filled sky, and a narrative scene in the foreground. Two Highlanders, wearing traditional plaid, are led away in chains and under guard, as a woman and baby beg Hanoverian troops for clemency toward the prisoners. Although the multitude of tents in the camp, which was the base for Cumberland's military operation, are depicted with preternatural clarity, this refined and valuable artwork (unlike *A Colored Plan of the Encampment*) cannot have been intended for practical field use. Instead, it looks back to a long tradition of commemorative battle painting.[11] Such a work indicates the overlap of, and imbrication between, conventions of instrumental and aesthetic image making, and the applicability of proto-panoramic formats to both.

Thomas Sandby continued in the Duke of Cumberland's service as steward and, eventually, deputy ranger of

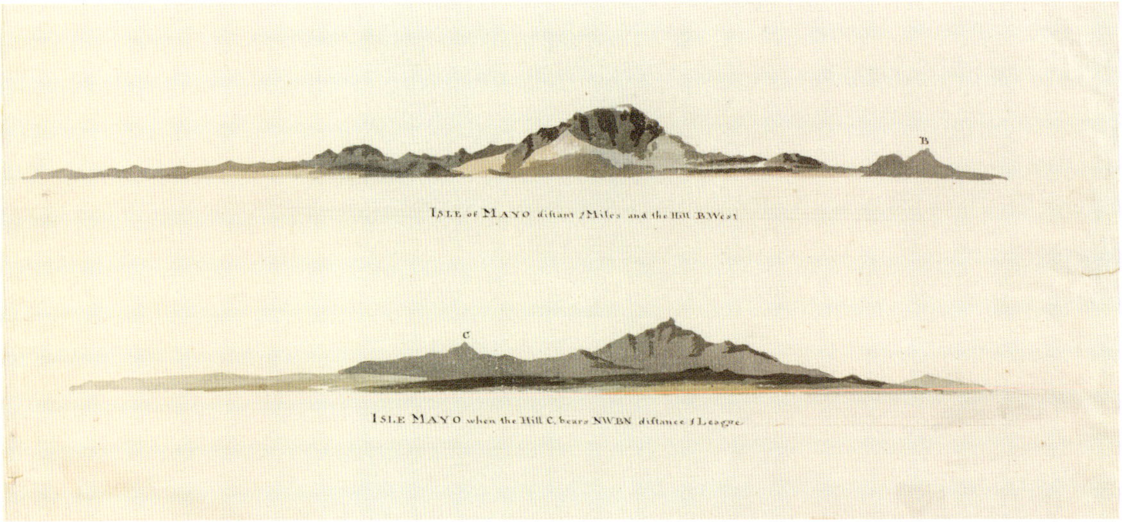

FIG. 1.11. William Hodges (British, 1744–1797), *Two Coastal Views of the Isle of Mayo*, 1772. Watercolor and ink on paper, 33 × 48.3 cm (13 × 19 in.). State Library of New South Wales, Sydney (SAFE/PXD 11).

Windsor Great Park, where he managed the landscape as well as making a series of striking panoramic representations of it. Meanwhile, in 1768, Sandby's younger brother and collaborator, Paul, was appointed chief drawing master at the Royal Military Academy at Woolwich, where he passed on "military science" techniques to a generation of students who applied them in the service of the British Empire. James Pattison Cockburn and George Heriot both made significant early topographical drawings in British North America (Canada). Students at the East India Company's training school at Addiscombe and at the Royal Navy's college at Greenwich learned similar skills. Panoramic viewing, then, became a global visual lingua franca among British colonial forces. The navy's particular need was for rigorously observed and carefully recorded coastal profiles, to aid in recognition of landmasses from offshore, as in examples by William Hodges (1744–1797) from Captain Cook's voyage (fig. 1.11).[12] In many cases, these profiles would have been made with the use of a telescope, a key optical device of imperial navigation. A similar, though much simpler, device played a significant role in relation to the 360-degree panoramic painting: cheap telescopes were often handed to visitors to allow them to scan painted details invisible to the naked eye. The emphasis in all these military forms, as in the later panorama entertainments, was on precision of representation, rather than on artistic self-expression or on cultivating an original style. The nature of the subjects demanded a format that extended laterally.

The panoramic style of topographical draftsmanship merged with the picturesque tradition to produce a hybrid imperial style that combined aspirations to aesthetic merit with practices of rigorous visual surveillance and recording. Typically, views were made from a high vantage point and surveyed a broad swath of territory. A strongly linear representation of physical features of the landscape and of architecture was balanced by a series of washes, in ink or watercolor, to emphasize undulations in the terrain and to add dramatic chiaroscuro effect. Examples can be found in James Wales's *Bombay Views*, painted in watercolor for Sir Charles Warre Malet, the British Resident of Poona, whom Wales met in Bombay in 1791. The compositions appeared as a series of aquatints titled *Views of the Island of Bombay and Its Vicinity*, produced in aquatint in Bombay by Wales himself about 1795 and published posthumously in London in 1800. One plate from the series, *View from Malabar Hill* (fig. 1.12), is made up of two sheets, joined to form a broad, panoramic view. It shows strategically and symbolically significant landmarks such as the flagstaff at Malabar Point (to the extreme right) and, in the distance, Elephanta Island, the location of the already famous cave temples, a significant subject for Wales's work. The territory surrounding Bombay was the subject of a fierce rivalry between the British East India Company and the Marathas, with whom Charles Warre Malet had negotiated a treaty in 1790. Wales's drawings and prints embody the British concern to defend and expand their presence on the west coast of the Deccan: during the nineteenth century Bombay became a mercantile and industrial center. Wales left London for India after Robert Barker's first,

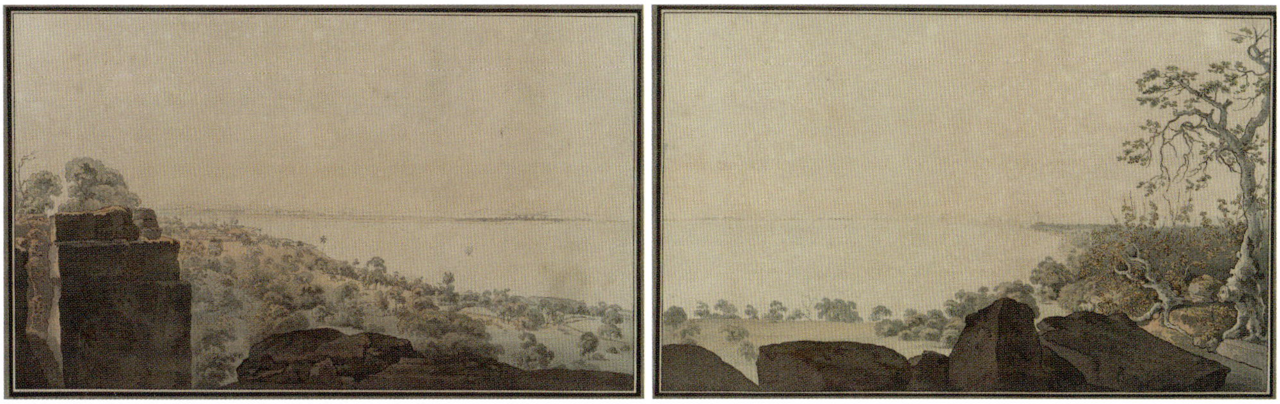

FIG. 1.12. James Wales (Scottish, ca. 1747–1795), *View from Malabar Hill*, ca. 1795. Hand-colored etching. Yale Center for British Art, New Haven, Connecticut, Paul Mellon Collection.

small panorama was exhibited there, and he may have seen it. The dark rocks in the immediate foreground of the *View from Malabar Hill*, part of a crumbling fortification, suggest a viewing platform, cementing the kinship between topographical views of empire and the nascent panoramic form.[13]

VIEW OF EDINBURGH

Barker's first circular painting, *View of Edinburgh and the Surrounding Country from the Calton Hill*, was shown in the Scottish city it depicts in 1788, where the artist undertook some strenuous advertising, insisting that it constituted "AN IMPROVEMENT ON PAINTING, Which relieves that sublime Art from a Restraint it has ever laboured under."[14] Comparison with Sandby's staunchly Hanoverian, and strictly functional, prospect view of the same landscape is instructive (see fig. 1.9). The surviving aquatint version, made in 1789–90 by John Wells after Robert Barker's design (fig. 1.13), suggests a somewhat naive style, lacking Sandby's accomplished rigor yet replete nonetheless with a formidable profusion of detail. Henry Aston Barker (1774–1856) recalled the technical details of this first essay in the panorama as follows: "The circle on which my father painted the first view of Edinburgh was twenty-five feet in diameter; canvas, with paper pasted on it, formed the surface, and the picture was painted in watercolours."[15] The city is situated picturesquely within a broad landscape vista, and the softness of the watercolor medium, amplified by its reproduction in aquatint, suggests a kinship with picturesque views and landscapes of pleasure, which would be less marked in later panoramas.[16]

The world's first panorama opened on January 31, 1788, the very day—though Barker did not know it—that Charles Edward Stuart, the pretender, died in Rome, a coincidence that draws attention to the potentially controversial aspects of the composition. Barker's middle-class Edinburgh audience doubtless included some who lamented the fate of Bonnie Prince Charlie, and the resulting dominion of the Protestant regime, with its German king George II, over Scotland. The Anglo-Scottish elite of the period, by contrast, would have expected any view of the city to function as a celebration of the suppression of the rebellion. Denise Oleksijczuk proposes an ingenious reading of the "secret history of [the panorama's] origins in Edinburgh," noting that the very streets and open spaces now depicted in the new 360-degree panoramic form had, within living memory, been the setting for the rebellion's spectacular events.[17] In a commentary produced to accompany Wells's aquatint versions of his composition, Barker gingerly invites his readers to imagine the moment of the pretender's brief triumph by contemplating the landmarks at which his forces convened.[18] Oleksijczuk reads this as evidence of a hidden Jacobite agenda, linked to the historically Jacobite affiliations of the Archers' Club, in whose hall the panorama was exhibited. Yet Barker was at pains to celebrate the growth of Edinburgh's New Town, laid out since about 1765 on an elegant grid, with wide, salubrious streets. This emphasis confirmed the city's growing prosperity under Hanoverian rule since the rebellion. Moreover, great prominence is accorded to the road from the city to the port of Leith, which connected Edinburgh by sea with the major ports of Britain, Europe, and the British Empire. The vista is replete with the signs of prosperity in agriculture, trade, and industry, the last symbolized by three large blast furnaces smoking energetically by the water's edge. In the foreground, a new observatory

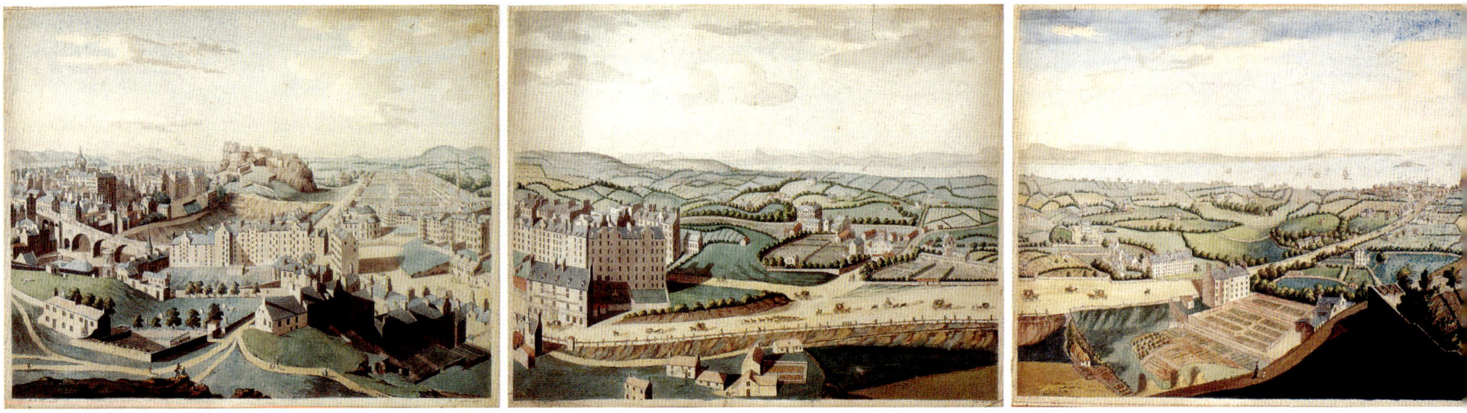

FIG. 1.13. John Wells (British, active ca. 1785–1809) after Robert Barker (British, 1739–1806), *View of Edinburgh and the Surrounding Country from the Calton Hill*, 1789–90. Colored aquatint, each 42.4 × 55.3 cm (16 5/8 × 21 3/4 in.). City Art Centre, Edinburgh Museums and Galleries.

is under construction, symbol of Edinburgh's place at the forefront of the European Enlightenment and of scientific research. The viewer's freedom on the platform—albeit in this case a small one—allowed for possible readings of the painting *either* as representing the site of a heroic uprising against a dominant imperial power, *or* as a demonstration of the peace and prosperity achieved by the Act of Union with England. Unlike Thomas Sandby's rigorously ideological prospects, created ultimately for a single viewer—the Duke of Cumberland—the panorama offered free play to the interpretative instincts of the modern middle class, a body of ideological and social plurality. *View of Edinburgh* could thus encourage and sustain many views, Jacobite and Hanoverian, just as it offered multiple perspectives and vantage points for the delectation of the paying public. If hardly a proto-democratic form of vision (the majority of the population, lacking a shilling, was excluded), the panorama enfranchised a large paying public and allowed for a wide range of views to be expressed and consumed.

METROPOLE

Barker moved the view of Edinburgh to London in 1789. It was displayed at 28 Haymarket until 1791, where, modest in scale, it garnered only fitful interest, lost among the city's myriad entertainments. In that year, however, with characteristic bravado, Barker opened a second painted panorama, exhibited in a circular building erected in his back garden at 28 Castle Street, probably a structure no more elegant than his later painting studio.[19] The new painting, however, was a revelation: *A View of London from the Roof of the Albion Mills* (fig. 1.14), initially a half-circle, soon expanded to a full 360 degrees. Barker placed an advertisement in the *Times* for "a view-at-a-glance of the CITIES of LONDON and WESTMINSTER, comprehending the three bridges, represented in one Painting, containing 1749 square feet, which appears as large and in every respect the same as reality. The observers of this Picture being by painting only deceived as to suppose themselves on the Mills from which the view was taken."[20] The city provided both the location of the viewing platform and the most fascinating subject of the gaze.

London, at the moment the panorama came to prominence, was the world's largest mercantile and political metropolis. By the end of the eighteenth century, the city had become an entrepôt where, through commercial, financial, and imperial networks, proliferating quantities of people, goods, and ideas flowed into and out from around the world. Key to the global nature of the panorama is the medium's unprecedented ability to respond to the condition of the "world city": to present *both* the local and the global—familiar and far-flung parts of the world—with uncanny, persuasive verisimilitude.[21] By making a verifiable transcript of familiar scenery, the panoramic artist could also impute truth value to representations of distant lands for which no authenticating archive was available.

Barker's 360-degree view of London, based on a drawing made in the winter of 1790–91 by his son Henry Aston Barker, was taken from the roof of one of the most prominent buildings on the south bank of the Thames, the Albion Steam Flour Mills, erected between 1783 and 1786. The austere, tiled and glazed surfaces of its roofs and chimneys dominating the panorama's foreground

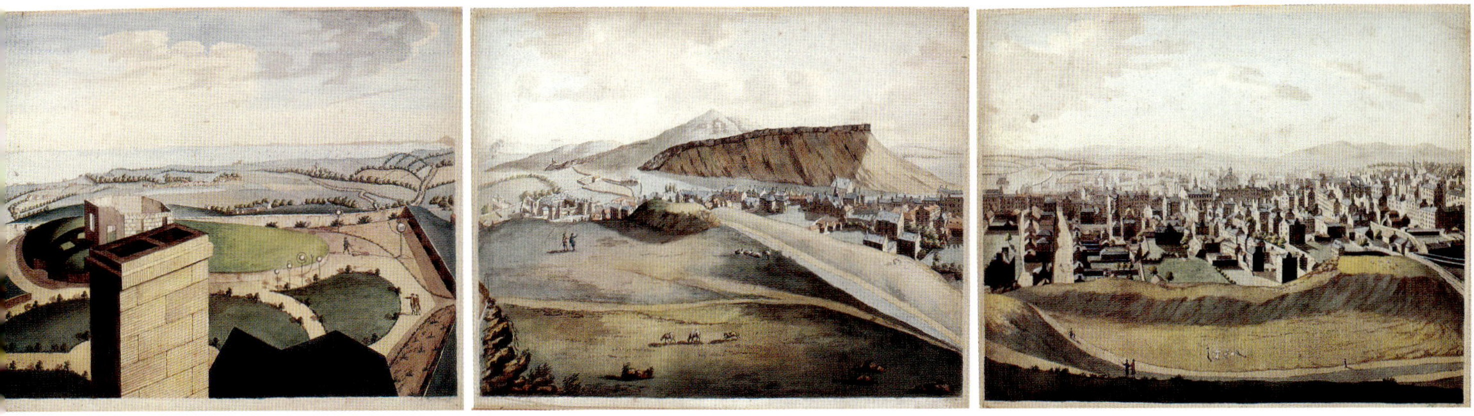

echo the structure of the viewing platform itself (fig. 1.15). This firmly situates the viewer in a privileged location of modernity: Erasmus Darwin described Albion Mills as "the most powerful machine in the world."[22] Celebrated as a marvel of technology by London's financial and intellectual elite—the very epitome of "improvement"—the building housed two new Boulton and Watt steam engines and was capable of grinding flour at a fraction of the previous cost.[23] The panorama's viewing platform, then, sits astride one of the great symbols of modern capitalism, a position that identifies London as the center of a global commerce and co-opts the panorama viewer as a participant in that development. London's poor, by contrast, considered the mill to be a symbol of oppression—raising the cost of bread and taking away traditional jobs. William Blake may have had this structure in mind when referring in the introduction to *Milton* (1804–10) to "dark satanic mills."[24] There was popular celebration when, on March 1, 1791, the entire complex—imperfectly fireproofed and, like panorama buildings, constructed in part from timber—burned to the ground, leaving a wreckage of beams and molten metal.

The large painted panorama of *London from Albion Mills*, the work of Robert Barker and his son Henry Aston Barker, was completed only after the fire, when the building's celebrity was, if anything, enhanced.[25] The composition, recorded in six substantial aquatints by Frederick Birnie (see fig. 1.14), emphasized the harsh, geometric modernity of the mills. This detailed portrait of London celebrated the city's commercial dynamism, rather than its historical or political character. The extreme verisimilitude of representation allowed viewers to see individual figures and read street signs and other details, significant and mundane. The personalia within the composition provide a veritable cavalcade of London types, from gentlefolk to itinerant traders, a chimney sweep and, memorably, several rough men collecting horse manure from the street (fig. 1.16). The joke here is surely that their aroma would not be present within the relatively polite confines of the panorama, any more than their opinions could speak forth on the viewing platform.

In contrast to the wide social spectrum represented, the class address of the Barker panorama of London was quite specific: as William Galperin notes, early announcements of the work were "addressed to 'the public' rather than, like other notices, to 'the nobility, gentry, and the public.'"[26] Barker advertised his panoramas in two venues, the Blenheim Coffee House on New Bond Street and the Chapter Coffee House at St. Paul's, places of entertainment and hospitality frequented by a diverse but literate crowd.[27] This was, then, a middlebrow entertainment aimed at London's middling sort—tradesmen, merchants, and even clerks, and their families, who would feel enfranchised through their visual consumption of the city from the vantage point of one of the great, though already ruined, monuments to commercial and industrial progress. There is a notable formal similarity between the viewpoint from the Barkers' platform and that of the Duke of Cumberland and his forces in Sandby's view of Edinburgh in 1745–46. Yet the politics of vision have shifted drastically. For a shilling public to share in this view—and to identify imaginatively with the implied position of political authority—was to participate in the transformation of the public sphere described by Jürgen Habermas.[28]

The *people*—as opposed to the polite public—who celebrated the demise of the mills had a quite different perception of the vast edifice—a view, in all senses, from below. Some hint of this is discernable in an etching

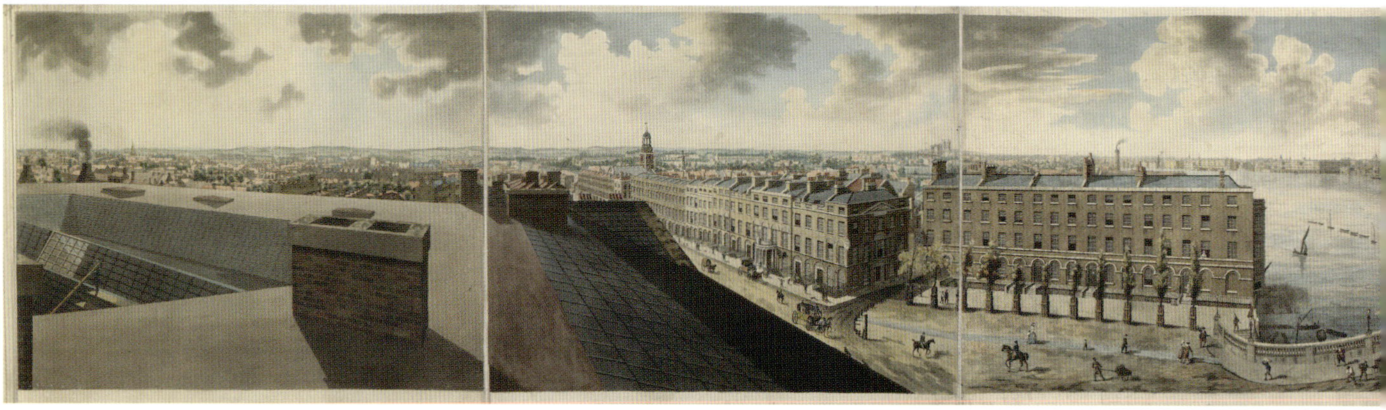

FIG. 1.14. Frederick Birnie (British, fl. 1787–1793), *London from the Roof of the Albion Mills*, ca. 1792–93, after a drawing by Henry Aston Barker (Scottish, 1774–1856) to a design by Robert Barker (British, 1739–1806). Engraving and hand-colored aquatint, one print on six joined sheets, each 49 × 57 cm (19 1/4 × 22 7/16 in.). Yale Center for British Art, New Haven, Connecticut, Paul Mellon Collection.

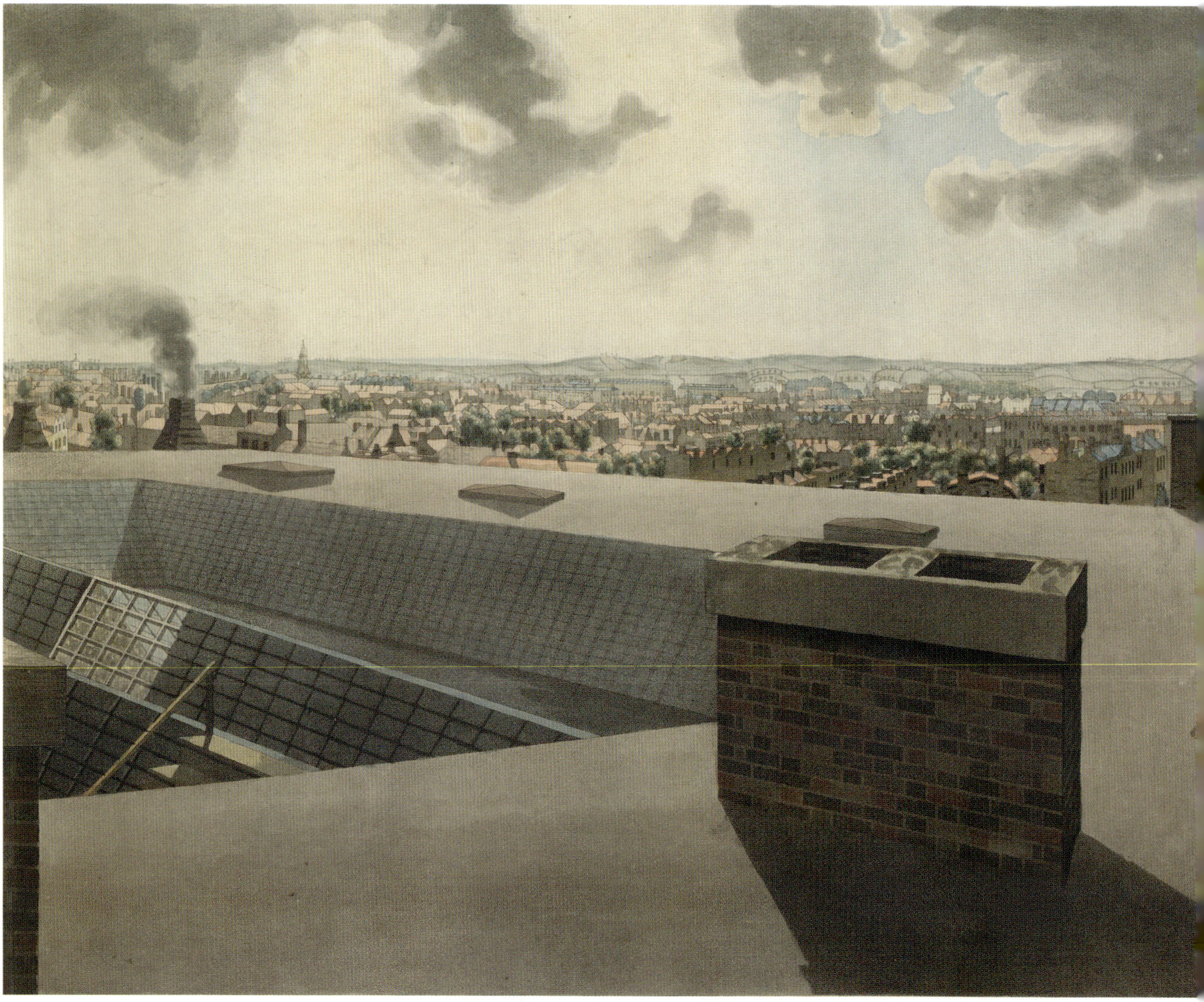

FIG. 1.15. Detail of fig. 1.14.

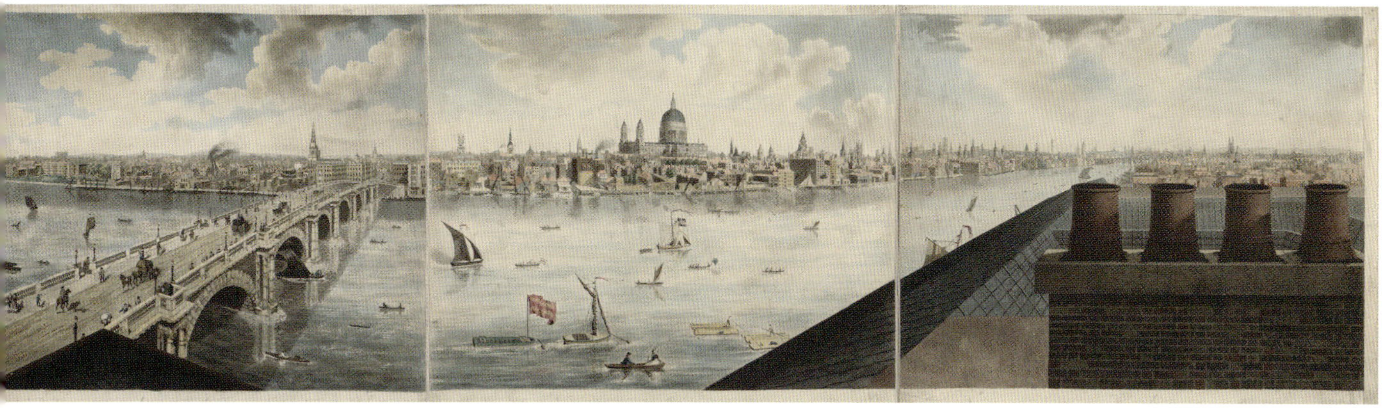

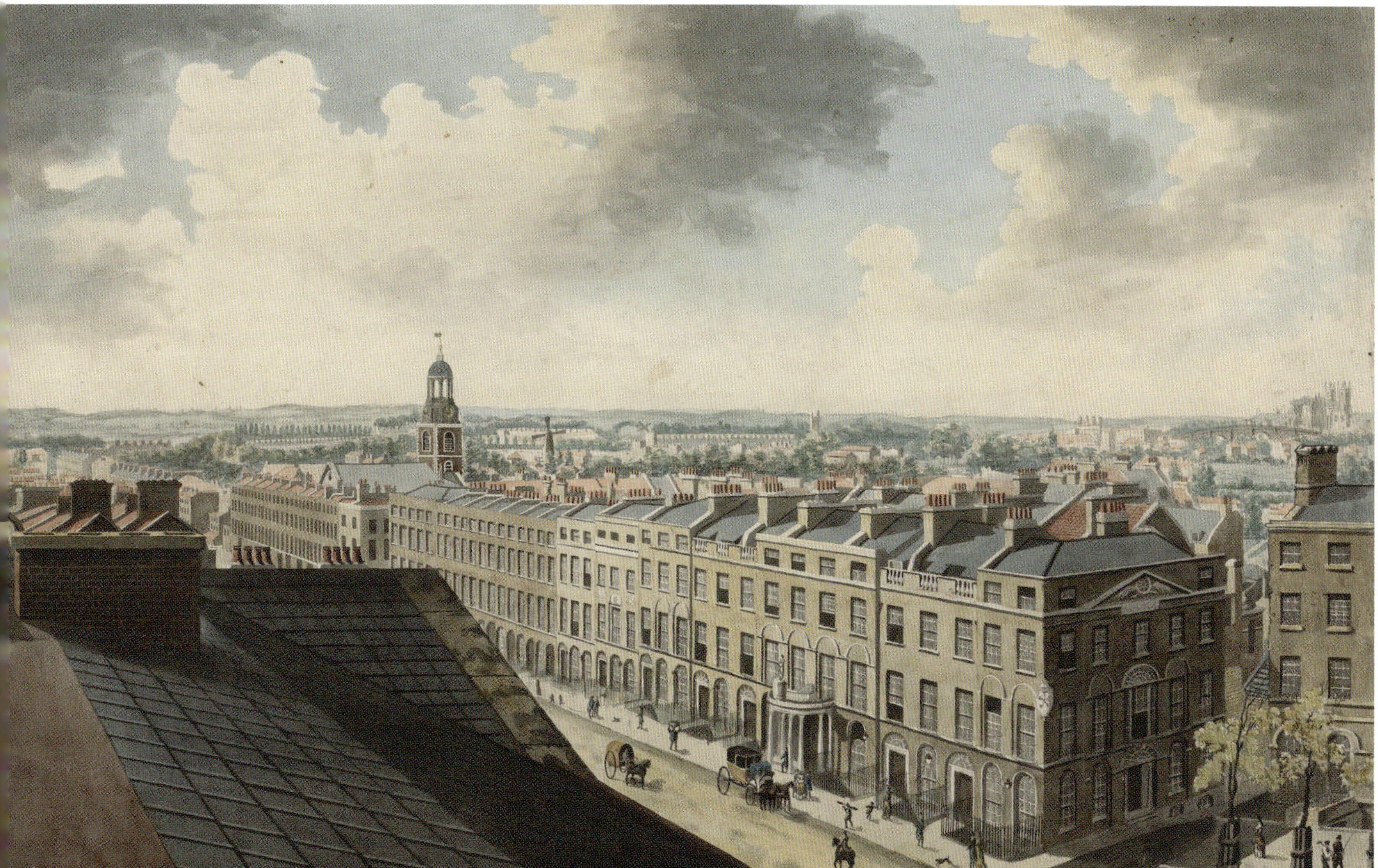

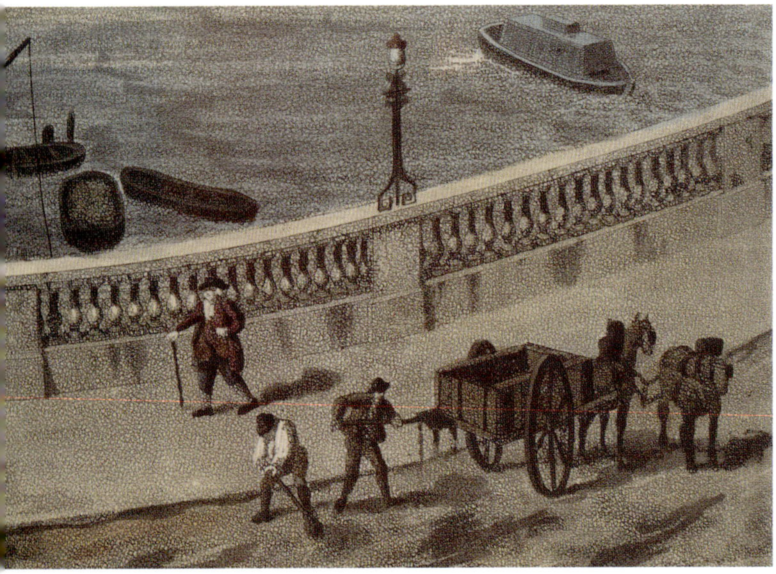

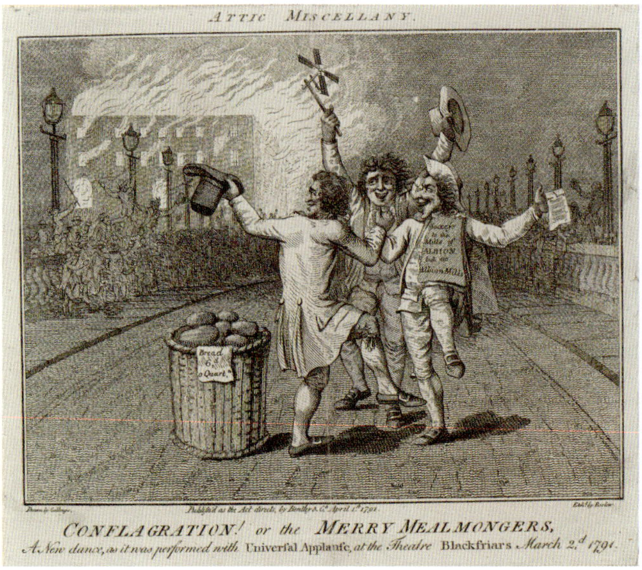

FIG. 1.16. Detail of fig. 1.14.

FIG. 1.17. John Barlow, after Samuel Collings (active 1784–1789), *Conflagration! or the Merry Mealmongers*, 1791. Etching on paper, 19.1 × 22.2 cm (7 1/2 × 8 3/4 in.). British Museum, London (BM 1880,1113.1491).

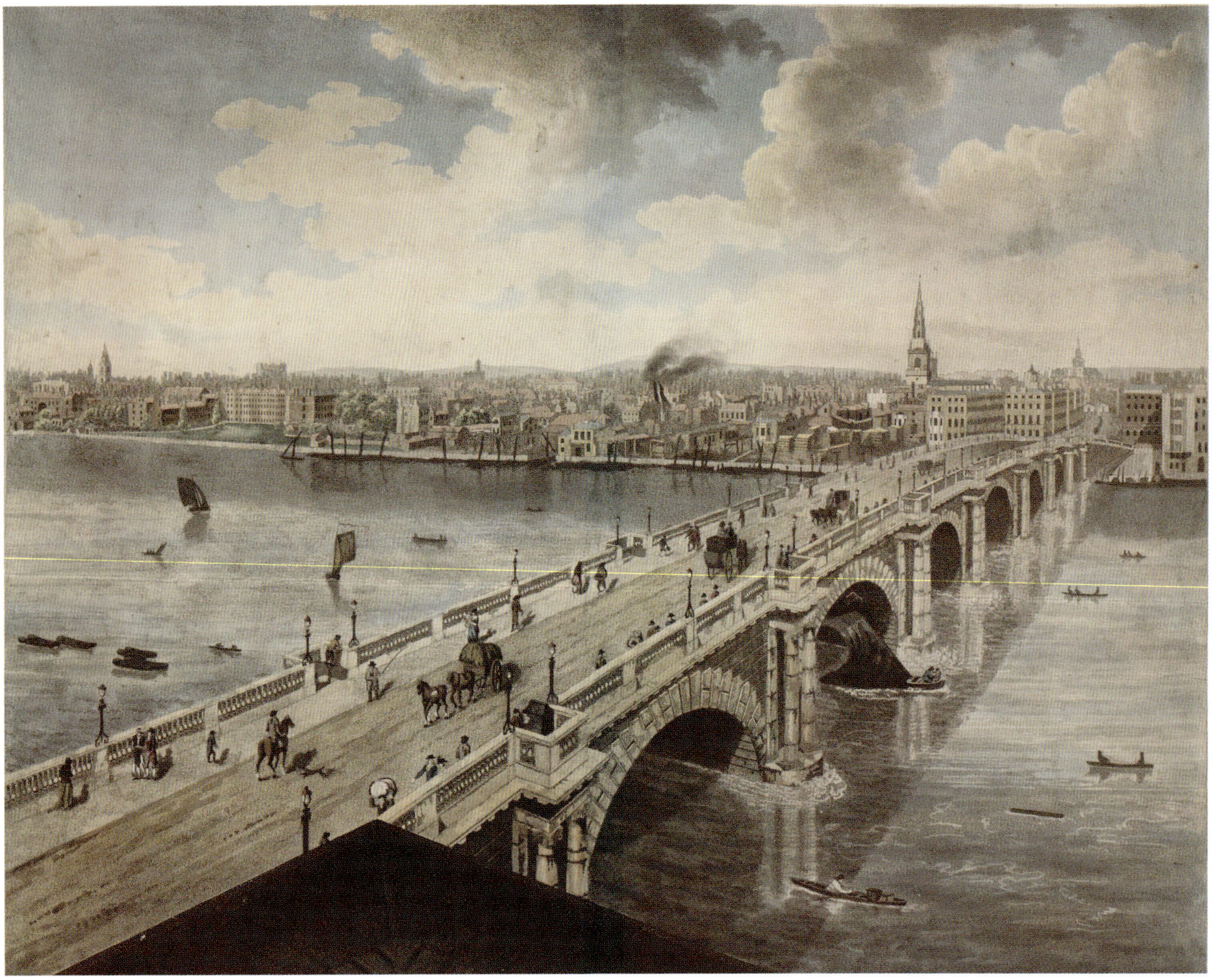

FIG. 1.18. Detail of fig. 1.14.

by John Barlow after a drawing by Samuel Collings, *Conflagration! or the Merry Mealmongers*, published on April 1, 1791, a month after the fire (fig. 1.17), representing the jeering multitude who took to the streets as the mills, rearing up behind them, burned.[29] The three central figures are countrymen, selling bread, whose traditional methods of milling corn are represented by the child's toy windmill held aloft by one of them. Another carries a broadside reading, "Success to the Mills of Albion but no Albion Mills." Their dress distinguishes them from the ragged figures in the rejoicing mob behind; their wild "New dance" and grotesque physiognomies mark them out as belonging to the "people" rather than the "public" and certainly lacking either the financial resources or the social graces to enter Barker's panorama. Their views are from street level.

Barker's panorama of London is dominated by the insistent geometry of transport routes, which slice through the city. The central features are the River Thames and the broad, Italianate Blackfriars' Bridge, which had opened in 1769 (fig. 1.18). Its receding form is the dominant compositional feature of the panorama. A distant forest of masts to the east suggests the East and West India Docks and the Pool of London; the road to the west leads down through Sussex to the South Coast. Across the river, on the Thames's north bank, are institutions of global import; the Palace of Westminster, seat of the imperial parliament, and Somerset House, from which the fleet was administered, and also home of the Royal Academy of Arts. This is the topography of a city at the heart of a matrix of global affairs—and it metaphorically suggests the lines along which power and influence were exerted over the peripheries of the United Kingdom and the great expanses of the British Empire. The panorama itself had a global career. Birnie's aquatints made their way to the United States, where they were expanded once more (and seemingly without permission) onto a panoramic canvas by William Winstanley. Exhibited in 1795 in Greenwich Street, New York City, *London from Albion Mills* became the first panorama to be shown in America.[30]

The influence of Barker's panorama on British artists of the period has been well discussed by Ann Bermingham.[31] Joshua Reynolds, initially skeptical, declared that Barker's panorama "proves it is capable of producing effects, and representing nature in a manner far superior to the limited scale of pictures in general,"[32] and many English landscape painters, including Thomas Girtin, David Roberts, and Clarkson Stanfield, designed panorama paintings. Yet a later watercolor by J. M. W. Turner, *View of London from Greenwich* (fig. 1.19), seems to allude, in the famous vista from atop One Tree Hill, to the viewing platform itself. The subject resembles that of Turner's major oil painting *London from Greenwich Park* (exhibited at the Royal Academy in 1809) (see fig. 0.15), a work whose flat horizon and lack of framing devices within the composition itself suggest the influence of panorama painting.[33] The watercolor of 1825, by contrast, includes a group of near-comical figures gathered on a high eminence examining two maps of London—one dated 1526, the other 1825. They recoil in astonishment at the city's growth. Other documents scattered around them read, "New World" and "N Pole." The processes of history are made visible, as, in Barker's panorama, the economic and imperial functioning of the city is laid bare. In Turner's work as in Barker's, moreover, the Thames is the leading actor in London's historical drama—a highway of commerce linking the metropole with its global mercantile imperium. Map and panoramic view offer two means of charting this phenomenon; four years later, spectators at the Colosseum's massive panorama of London would use telescopes, positioned every few yards, to explore details of the painting invisible to the naked eye from the great height of the viewing platform.[34] Farther afield, a single male figure peers through a telescope attempting to decipher some detail—just as visitors might lean over the rails of the viewing platform and use field glasses to magnify the panorama's minuscule details. Turner's small watercolor, less than a foot in diameter, engages in dialogue with the massive canvases of Leicester Square.

Where Turner's comical figures struggle with maps and other documents, visitors to the Albion Mills panorama were handed a printed sheet intended to aid in identifying the buildings and topographical features arrayed around them (fig. 1.20). With these panorama keys, Barker's panorama generated a significant innovation in graphic culture, in excess of the modifications of perspective and viewer experience in the painted chamber. To provide a legible guide to the scene's monuments and features, the panorama painters created a distinctive form of diagram, which was reproduced as a line engraving.[35] The Barkers and their many imitators experimented with various formats for these documents, which acted as keys, unlocking the panorama's secrets, and as souvenirs. Adopting the emblematic circular shape of the panorama,

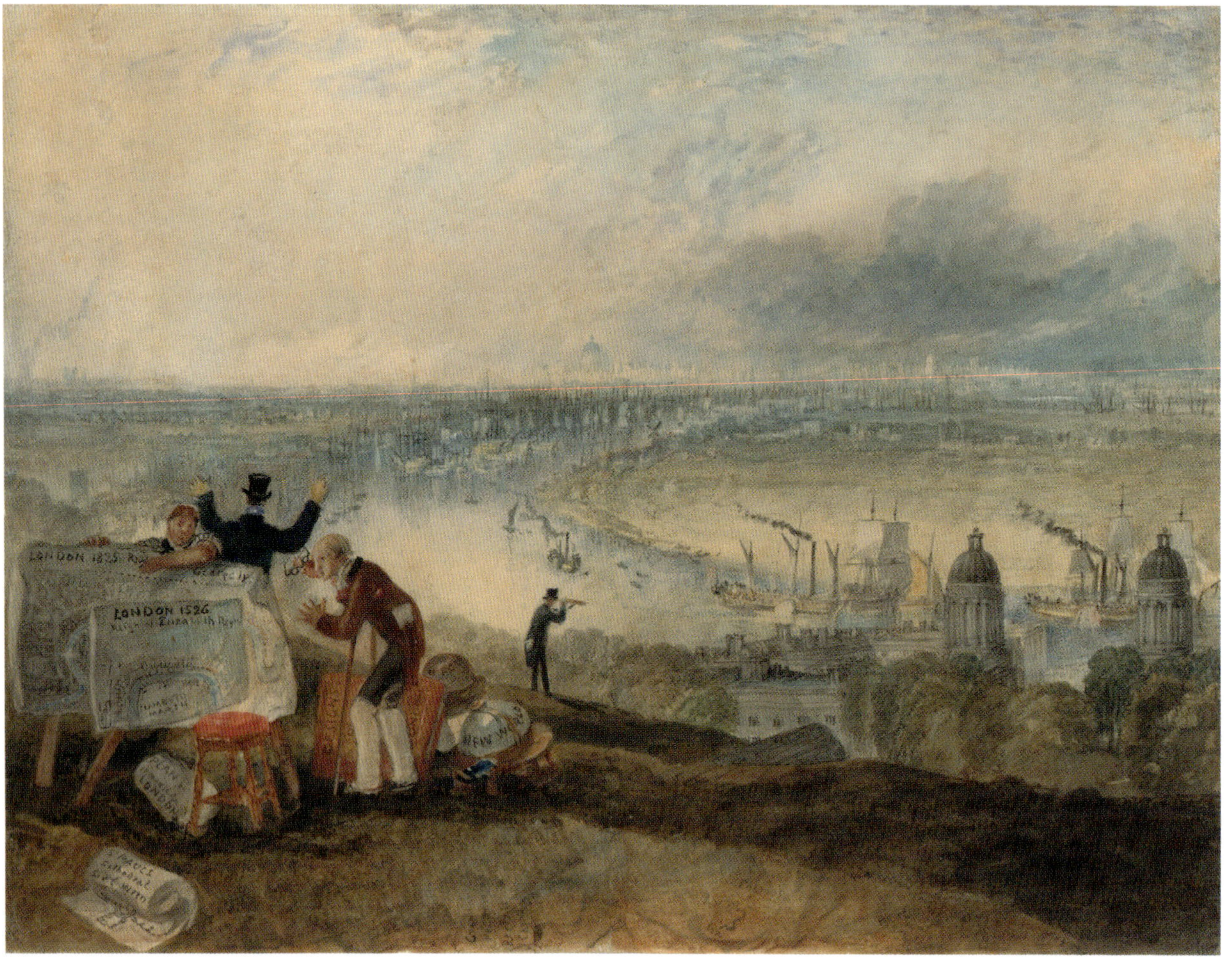

FIG. 1.19. Joseph Mallord William Turner (British, 1775–1851), *View of London from Greenwich*, 1825. Watercolor and ink and traces of graphite, 21.3 × 28 cm (8 3/8 × 11 in.). Metropolitan Museum of Art, New York (59.23.23).

the most striking of these diagrams radiate outward from a small circle in the middle, which effectively represents the viewing platform. The contents of the panorama explode toward the horizon. Once again, then, the viewer is placed insistently at the center, not looking though an Albertian window, but enshrined, or entrapped, at the heart of a dynamic, immersive experience. For this centripetal energy to be exerted, conventional perspective (so effectively manipulated to convince the viewer of the panorama's verisimilitude) has to be abandoned. The resulting visual anarchy, as buildings, trees, and people seemingly hurtle into space, militates against panoramic paintings' careful illusionism, but it captures the excitement of the early audiences on ascending to the viewing platform. These remarkable, ephemeral prints are in many cases all that remains of the great panoramas, so often destroyed by overpainting, by fire, or in transit.

THE PANORAMA IN AN AGE OF WAR

The rise of the panorama correlates almost exactly to the chronology of the French Revolutionary and Napoleonic Wars, begun in 1792 and convulsing Europe and its colonies—with a short break in 1802–3—until their decisive conclusion with Napoleon's final defeat at Waterloo in 1815. Barker's breakthrough with the London audience dated from 1793, and his greatest financial and artistic success, the panorama *Battle of Waterloo*, took London by storm in 1816, earning a profit of more than £10,000. The relationship is by no means coincidental. Barker's most successful subjects were marine battles and other military entanglements; his panoramas undoubtedly participated in the British public's increasing nationalism and bellicosity, the origins of late nineteenth-century popular imperialism. The panorama became a central space in the formation and promotion of a particular strain of national identity, producing a sense of allegiance and belonging, as well as a vantage point from which the great events of world history could be seen and experienced, often within a year of the actual event.[36]

In 1793 Robert Barker opened opulent premises in a prominent position in Leicester Square, designed by the architect Robert Mitchell, who produced a cross section of the building in aquatint in 1801 (see fig. 0.2). In a brilliant gambit, the new Leicester Square building included a second, smaller panorama, inserted above the large one. The first panorama to be installed in this upper space, smaller in scale, was a repainted version of *View of London from the Roof of Albion Mills*. In the larger space below, there appears in Mitchell's aquatint a view of Lake Geneva, perhaps never actually completed. Other forms of documentation, however, show paired with the London panorama *Position of the British and French Fleets, about 9 AM, the First of June, 1794*—also described, with rather more partisan fervor, as *Lord Howe's Victory and the Glorious First of June*. Howe's engagement with the French near Ouessant was the first and largest fleet action of the French Revolutionary Wars, although both British and French sides loudly proclaimed victory. The British aimed to deter a French convoy bringing grain from the United States to France; the battered convoy reached France, but at the cost of seven sunken ships: truly, there was no winner. As Oleksijczuk has demonstrated, Barker's view of the battle exceeded what could be achieved even by a master of the sublime within the bounds of conventional easel painting, such as Philippe-Jacques de Loutherbourg, whose superbly dramatic *Glorious First of June* (1795) places the viewer amid the action, but able to see only a small

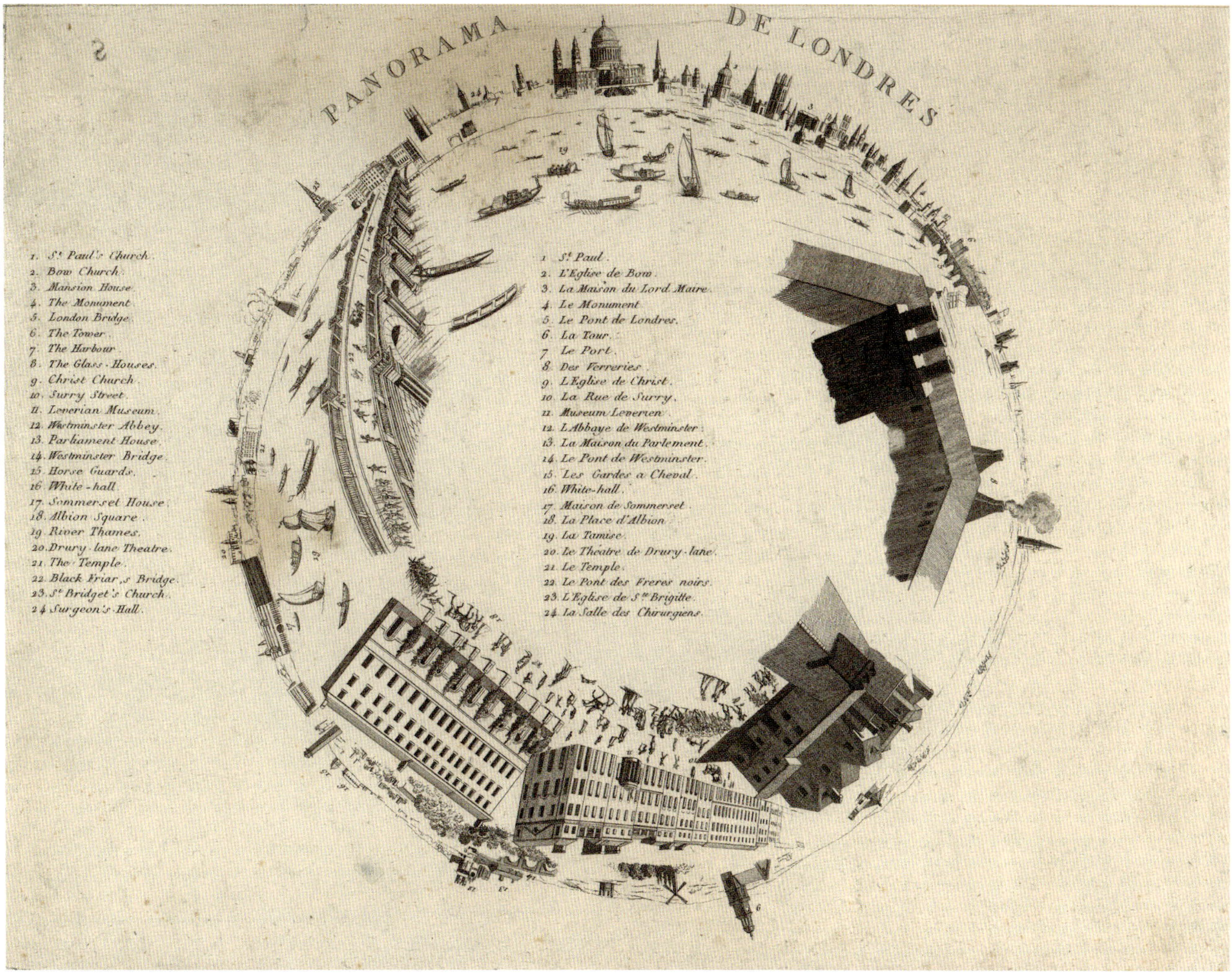

FIG. 1.20. *Key to Barker's Panorama of London from the Roof of Albion Mills; the Highlights Shown in a Circle as They Would Appear on the Panorama, with St Paul's at the Top, Westminster Abbey at the Bottom, Each with a Number from 1 to 24 and Corresponding Key in English and in French*, ca. 1800. Etching and engraving on paper, 30.6 × 40.7 cm (12 × 16 in.). British Museum, London (BM 1880,1113.5509.2).

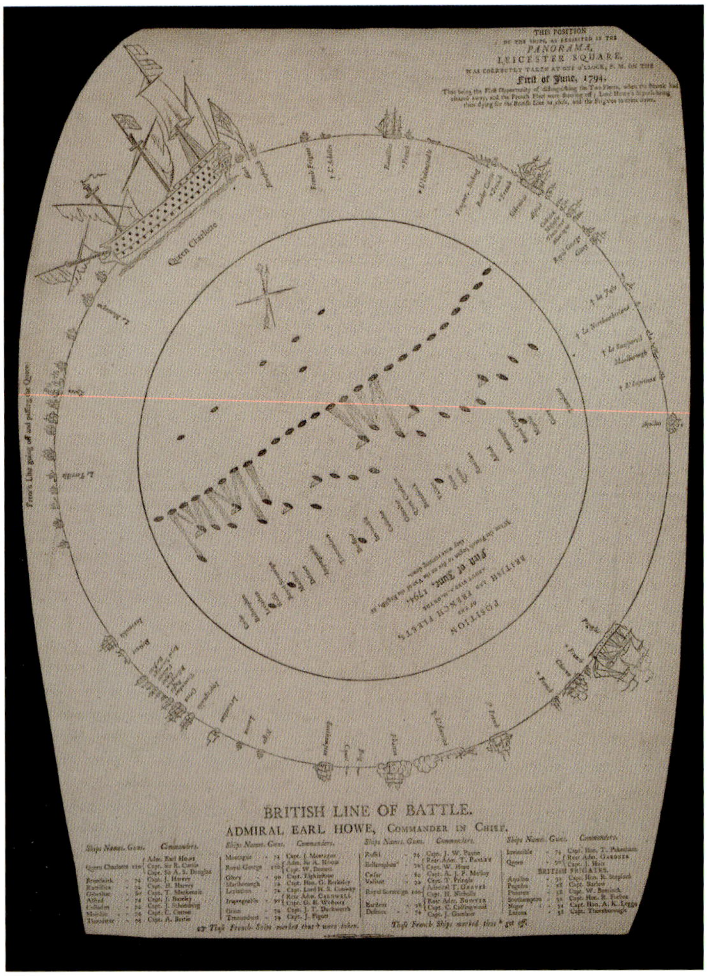

FIG. 1.21. Robert Barker, *Position of the British and French Fleets, about 9 AM, the First of June, 1794*, 1796. Engraving on paper, 38.6 × 29 cm (15 3/16 × 11 3/8 in.). Victoria and Albert Museum, London.

part of it.[37] The massive scale of Loutherbourg's painting may indeed owe something to the influence of the panoramas. By contrast, Oleksijczuk notes, Barker was able to "place the viewer at the *center* of two fleets attacking each other rather than on one side or the other. Thus the panorama gave spectators a unique opportunity to see the action from both sides, to take up a viewing position on the platform that allowed them to see the action from the side of the enemy."[38] The key indicates the extent to which the viewer is embroiled at the center of the conflict, with ships at every angle (fig. 1.21). An extremely complex document, it not only represents the panorama's composition, showing the position of the ships at one o'clock in the afternoon, as HMS *Queen Charlotte* looms large to the north, but also (in a maplike diagram within the inner ring) indicates the earlier state of events, at nine o'clock that morning. By an effort of the imagination, the viewer on the platform could thus re-create the events of the morning. Barker's panorama certainly contributed to the propaganda campaign that proclaimed a victory for Howe's ill-disciplined forces, which had, after all, failed to prevent the American provisions' reaching France.

This exemplified the type of spectacle that remained popular with Barker's audience throughout the Napoleonic Wars, in accordance with what Geoff Quilley has called "a move toward the cult of the maritime in the 1790s that is evident in the multiple representations of naval battles and maritime history in popular culture."[39] The dialogue within the Leicester Square building between the panoramas of patriotic battles and the panorama of London emphasized the direct links between the city's (and the nation's) prosperity and the maritime empire and oceanic trade routes. Barker's ingenious doubling of panoramas made visible the imbrication of metropole, provinces, and empire. Within each panorama, and in the dialogue between small and large rotundas at Leicester Square, the Barkers were able to reveal and emphasize such structural and ideological truths, beneath the mirrorlike stylistic impassivity of panorama painting.

The final conflagration that ended the Napoleonic era was fought on land rather than sea. The world-historical significance of the Battle of Waterloo was unmistakable, and Britons thirsted for information about it; numerous publications, prints, and paintings were produced in the months and years after the battle. Henry Aston Barker hurried with all possible speed to the battlefield to make sketches, which by March 1816 had been transformed into *A Description of the Defeat of the French Army, by the Allied Armies, in Front of Waterloo*. The pamphlet published to accompany the panorama was extremely specific: "The time represented in this painting is about eight o'clock in the evening, when the British and their Allies, having finally repulsed all the attacks of the French, are attacking and routing them in their own position. The representation of the ground was taken while all the wreck of the armies was on the field." The painting was made "from Drawings taken on the Spot." A set of eight etchings, from Barker's "original Sketches of the Field of Battle," was also published. The diagram supplied to visitors follows the established format, positioning the viewer at the heart of the action (fig. 1.22). Dense text panels, squeezed like segments of an orange into the composition, provide a description of the various military units, identified by numbers referring to the centrifugally arranged pictorial

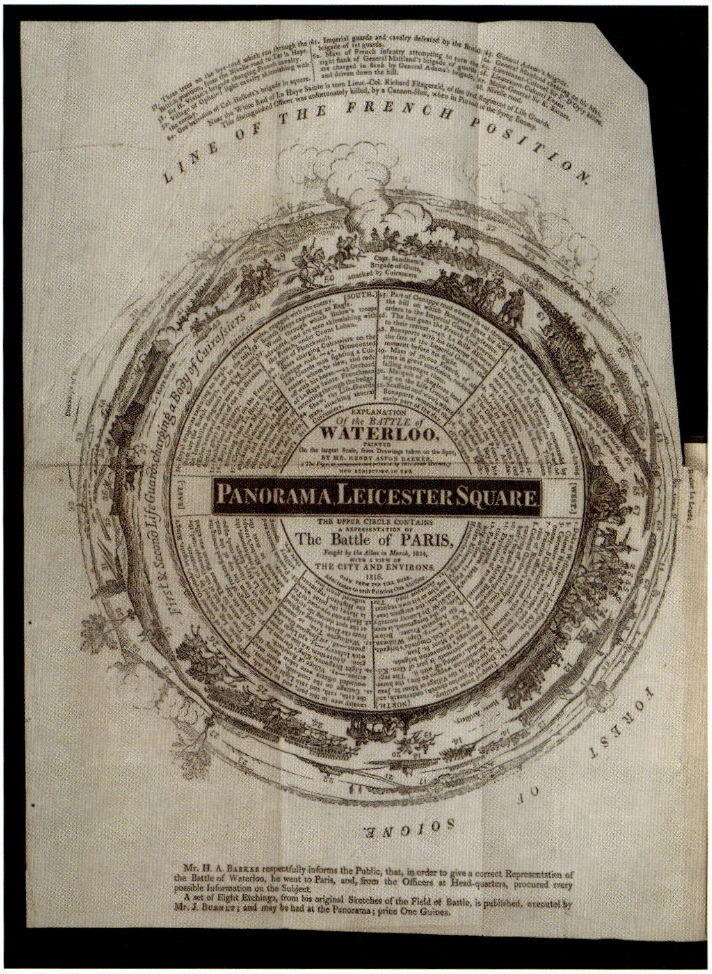

FIG. 1.22. Henry Aston Barker, *Description of the Field of Battle, and Disposition of the Troops Engaged in the Action, Fought on the 18th of June, 1815, near Waterloo: Illustrative of the Representation of That Great Event, in the Panorama, Leicester-Square* ([London]: J. Adlard, 1816), folding plate opposite title page. Cambridge University Library (Pam.6.81.23).

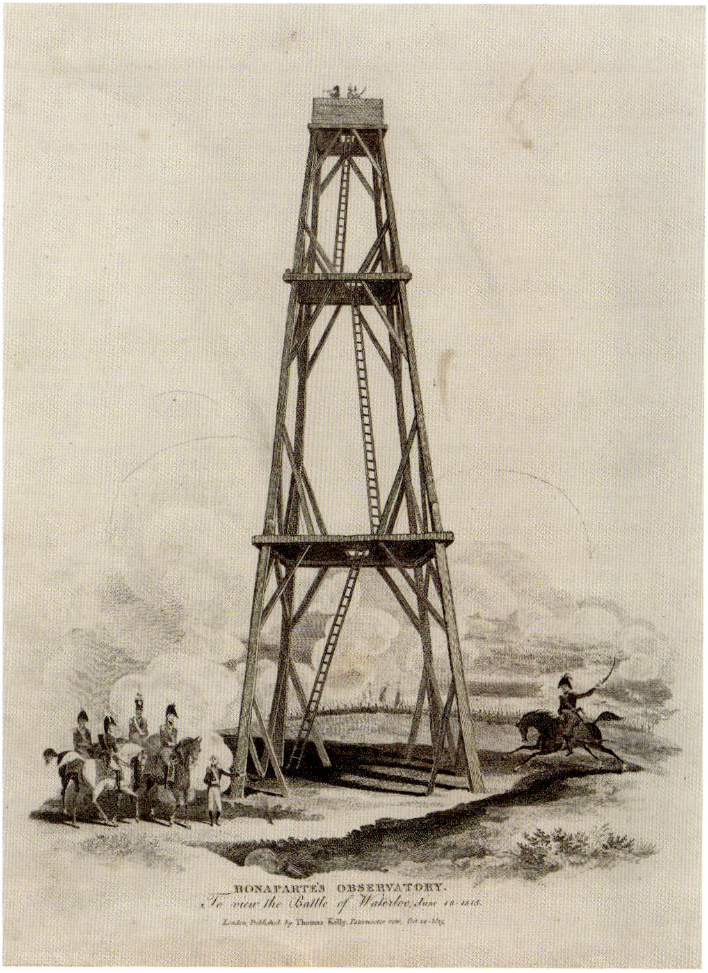

FIG. 1.23. *Bonaparte's Observatory: To View the Battle of Waterloo*, 1815. Engraving on paper, 26.5 × 20.7 cm (10 ⅜ × 8 ⅛ in.). British Museum, London (BM 1875,0612.193).

diagram. Its arrangement suggests a globe, as if the battle, like the conflict of the powers that it brought to a close, reached across oceans to the ends of the earth. No. 1 in the key, inevitably, is the Duke of Wellington, savior of the day, whose heroic gesture can be discerned even in the miniaturized format. Yet visitors to the panorama were not limited to a mere snapshot in time, for the accompanying leaflet included a note that "the following concise account of the battle being read, as it were, on the spot, will convey a general idea of the events of the whole day, as well as the period which this Panorama represents."[40] Henry Aston Barker's place "on the spot" merged with that of the viewer on the platform, reading the pamphlet likewise "on the spot." The panorama experience combined the immediacy of the moment with a longer narrative perspective; unlike the act of reading a published account of the battle, it could simultaneously be synchronic and diachronic.

Sharp-eyed viewers of the panorama key might have noticed, on the remote horizon just west of due south, a small geometrical construction. In the diagram, where it is keyed as no. 51, this is identified, somewhat mysteriously, as a "Scaffold and wood where Bonaparte remained the early part of the day." In fact, this contraption was a kind of viewing platform, providing an elevated, even panoramic prospect of the action. "Bonaparte's Observatory," as it became known, was represented in a lithograph published in Christopher Kelly's *History of the French Revolution* of 1817 (fig. 1.23). As Thomas Southey noted, "In the early part of the day [of Waterloo] he had reconnoitered the ground, and directed the movements from a sort of scaffolding, or

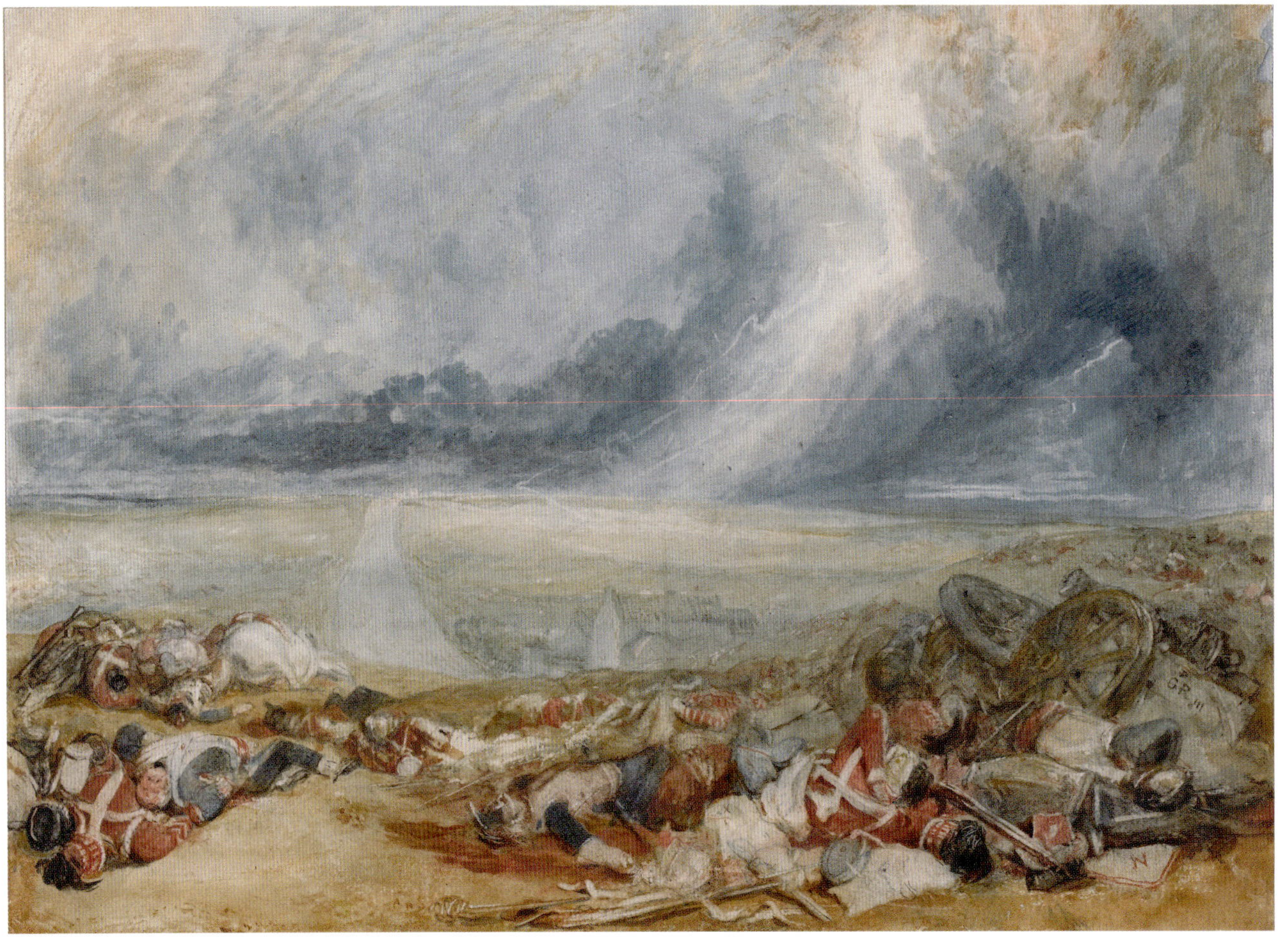

FIG. 1.24. Joseph Mallord William Turner, *The Field of Waterloo*, ca. 1817. Watercolor over graphite with scratching out on paper, 28.8 × 40.5 cm (11 1/16 × 15 15/16 in.). Fitzwilliam Museum, Cambridge, U.K. (2476).

observatory, or telegraph, which had been erected from some ichonographical [*sic*] purposes."[41] The languages of art and battle become inextricably entwined here. Bonaparte's intentions and his viewpoint seem, for a moment, suspiciously similar to those of the shilling public in Leicester Square. But of course, the commanding view was in the hands (as it turned out) of the losing side.

Artists were entirely absent from the scene of conflict, but Henry Aston Barker arrived at the field of Waterloo before the battle's wreckage had been removed. While Barker's panorama, through an effort of historical imagination, reconstructed the fighting as it had been on June 18, his former classmate at the Royal Academy Schools, J. M. W. Turner, visited the site in 1817 and created two works whose major preoccupation was the huge loss of human life—more than 40,000 casualties—and the misery of families and mourners. In addition to a large night scene in oils, exhibited in 1818 at the Royal Academy, of piles of dead bodies illuminated by a flare and the light of burning farmhouses (*The Field of Waterloo*, 1818, Tate), Turner produced a watercolor, also titled *The Field of Waterloo*, that adopts a panoramic viewpoint from high ground (fig. 1.24). No tree breaks the horizon line, and a track hurtles vertiginously away from us. The foreground is piled high with corpses, their glittering uniforms and arms briefly illuminated by lightning. Prefiguring the three-dimensional realia—sculptural figures positioned in front of the canvas—that characterized later nineteenth-century panoramas, the uncomfortable proximity to the viewer of the results of the carnage suggests for a moment that the viewing platform itself has become a scene of bloodshed rather than a safe haven for the consumer of an entertainment.[42]

COLONIAL IMMERSION

In the early years at Leicester Square, the Barkers emphasized Britain's maritime and military prowess and the promotion of imperial designs through the theater of war, yet they generally avoided direct representations of the British Empire. Only later would scenes such as the view of Sydney (1828, discussed by Julia Lum in this volume) and Calcutta (1830) become prominent. Between 1805 and 1820, the Barkers did produce memorable representations of exotic locations such as Constantinople—subject of an important analysis by Oleksijczuk—and others, including Paris, Pompei, Cairo, Messina, Lisbon, Malta, Elba, St. Petersburg, Geneva, and Spitzbergen.[43] Each of these was accompanied by a substantial leaflet, the text lifted from easily available sources giving an introduction to the city, often in spicy and, if appropriate, orientalist terminology. Many of these panoramas were based on sketches made from the motif by Henry Aston Barker, an indefatigable traveler. These panoramas opened up the possibility of a virtual grand tour for an audience whose members could never have afforded to travel abroad—and who, for the period before 1815, were in any case unable to leave England because of the ongoing hostilities.

The most significant imperial image from beyond the theater of European warfare was not produced by the Barkers but by their competitor Robert Ker Porter: *The Storming of Seringapatam*. Not strictly a panorama, this horseshoe-shaped painting was 21 feet high and 120 feet long, its 2,520 square feet of surface surrounded viewers, who stood on a raised platform.[44] When exhibited at the Great Room at the Lyceum in 1800, it was advertised as having been "designed from the most authentic and correct information relative to the SCENERY of the PLACE, the COSTUME of the SOLDIERS, and the various Circumstances of the ATTACK."[45] Its effect on the London audience was considerable—Benjamin West, president of the Royal Academy, declared it "a WONDER OF THE WORLD," language closer to the fun fair than to the museum, but followed up by a wholehearted endorsement.[46] Porter was a rising artist who had studied at the Royal Academy Schools and formed close friendships there with Henry Aston Barker and Turner. In early years, Porter had worked as a scenery painter at the Lyceum Theatre, and his flair for drama is apparent in *The Storming of Seringapatam*, which was painted in a very short time, with the assistance of a fourteen-year-old apprentice, William Mulready, who would become one of the most distinguished figure painters of the Victorian age.[47] The choice of subject was a significant one: Tipu was the Muslim ruler of the largely Hindu state of Mysore in the Deccan. His father, the military commander Haider Ali, had assumed control of the region in the power vacuum created by the decline of the Mughal Empire. Aware of the British East India Company's greed for territorial expansion, Tipu had formed an alliance with the French, and by the 1780s he represented the most significant opponent to British domination of the Deccan. He was defeated in 1789 in the Second Mysore War and subjected to a humiliating treaty that involved the surrender of his sons to the British (an event commemorated in history paintings by Robert Home, Henry Singleton, and Mather Brown), but he redoubled his campaign against the British in the 1790s.[48] His alliance with France continued after the revolution. The defeat of the "inexorable sultan" in 1799 at the Battle of Seringapatam was believed to guarantee British ascendancy in India.[49] These events were closely watched in London, and the news of Tipu's death, at the hands of Sir David Baird's triumphant forces, was greeted with widespread rejoicing. Porter's composition was closely based on verbal reports of the military campaign, and it captures an extraordinary amount of detail. Although the large painting itself was destroyed by fire after an extended tour, an autograph version of Porter's composition survives, finely painted but reduced in size to approximately nine feet in length. This was painted to provide the model for a set of three fine engravings by John Vendramini, each three feet wide, published serially in 1801–2.

The Storming of Seringapatam differs in a crucial fashion from the Barkers' true panoramas: as it was intended to surround the viewer, who looks up at it in the conventional manner as if examining a painting exhibited on a gallery wall, it does not adopt the sweeping perspective from above typical of the panorama. Rather, the viewer, positioned in a ravine, is overpowered by the high walls of Seringapatam, allowing for a high degree of identification with the British soldiers who are in the process of storming the ramparts, a risky and dramatic action. The lack of a significant gap between viewer and painting, as in a panorama (a space that was later mediated by realia or sculptural and other three-dimensional objects), allowed Porter to fill the foreground with narrative detail, which could be examined closely, as in conventional battle painting. Where many representations of the scene focused on the death of Tipu, or the finding of his body, Porter leaves the drama unfinished, as the sultan is not yet in British hands. He stands atop the ramparts, a distant figure identifiable only with the help of Porter's extremely detailed key (fig. 1.25).

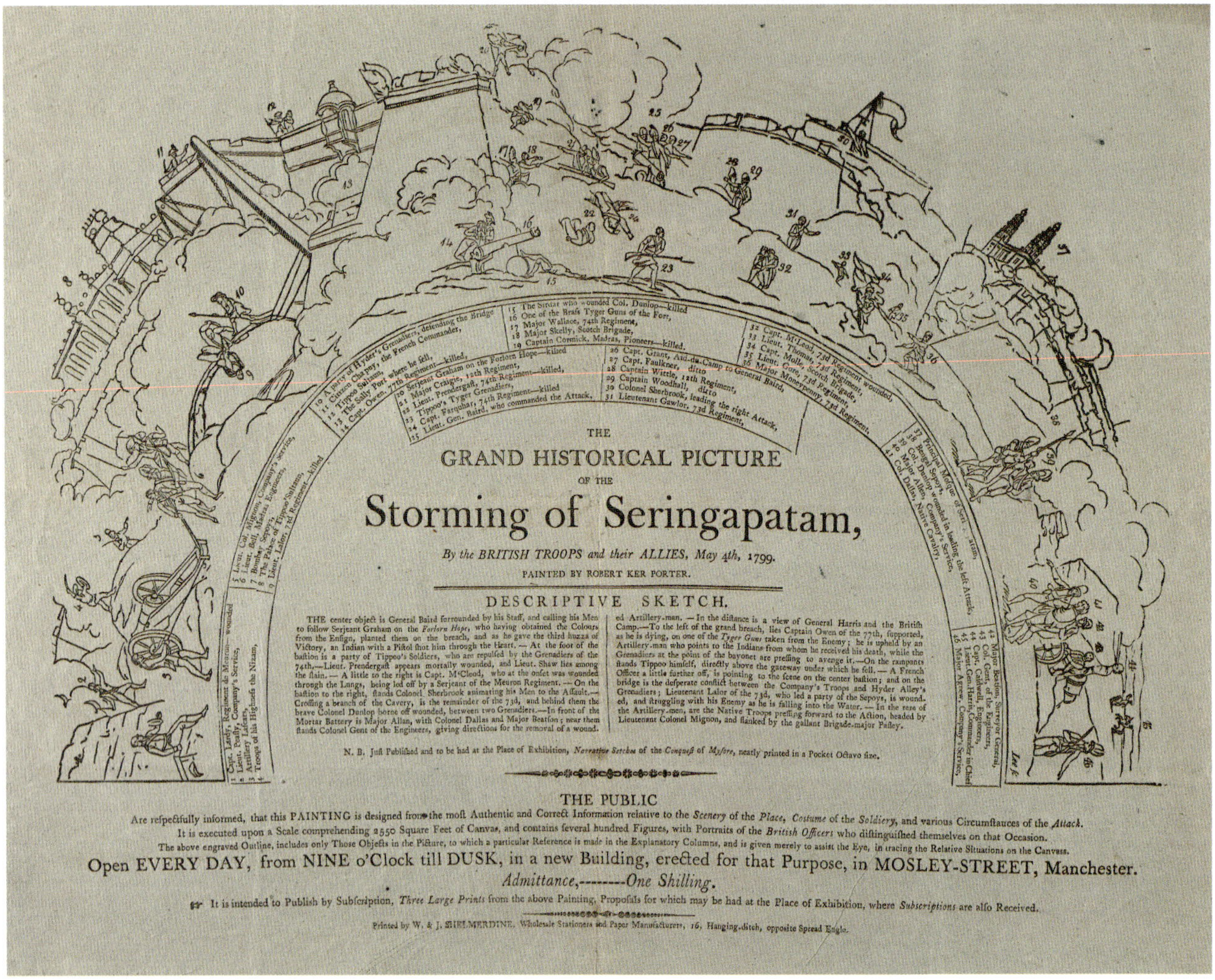

FIG. 1.25. John Lee, after Sir Robert Ker Porter (British, 1777–1842), *The Grand Historical Picture of the Storming of Seringapatam, by the British Troops and Their Allies, May 4th, 1799*, 1800. Woodcut and letterpress, 37 × 51 cm (12 ⅛ × 20 in.). Yale Center for British Art, New Haven, Connecticut, Paul Mellon Fund.

In keeping with its creator's exalted aspirations, *The Storming of Seringapatam* aimed to be more a work of art than an entertainment or a purveyor of information, the terms in which the Barkers' panoramas were largely understood. Porter's work ushered in a new form of immersive Romantic battle painting, whose visceral power was felt by the young Thomas Dibdin:

> It was as a thing dropt down from the clouds—all fire, energy, intelligence, and animation. You looked a second time, the figures moved, and were commingled in hot and bloody fight. You saw the flash of the cannon, the glitter of the bayonet, the gleam of the falchion. You longed to be leaping from crag to crag with Sir David Baird, who is hallooing his men on to victory! Then, again, you seemed to be listening to the groans of the wounded and the dying—and more than one female was carried out swooning. The oriental dress, the jewelled turban, the curved and ponderous scymitar—these were among the prime objects of favouritism with Sir Robert's pencil: and he touched and treated them to the very spirit and letter of the truth. The colouring, too, was good and sound throughout. The accessories were strikingly characteristic—rock, earth, and water, had its peculiar and happy touch; and the accompaniments about the sally-port, half choked up with the bodies of the dead, made you look on with a shuddering awe, and retreat as you shuddered. The public poured in by hundreds and by thousands for even a transient gaze—for such a sight was altogether as marvellous as it was novel.[50]

As Daniel White has recently noted, much of this description is given over to the bodies of the spectators, who shudder, retreat, pour in, and swoon.[51] Evidently the effect of Porter's work on an impressionable and bookish youth was visceral, an authentically panoramic effect. Certainly the painting had the effect of making the physically remote endeavors of empire take on a new level of reality in the minds of the London public.

What the global panorama could do better than any other medium was to supply an experiential equivalent—a sublime simulacrum—of distant events, experienced in the round. It was possible, from the viewing platform, to sense a psychological, even a physiological involvement in events thousands of miles away: to thrill to the smoke and chaos of a naval battle or an imperial skirmish, to be transported by the beauty of a sunset over the bay of Naples, or to be deafened by the roar of Niagara. Yet the viewer on the platform, unlike the consumer of Thomas Sandby's military prospect views, or the art lover presented with a Claudean landscape, was free to explore, discuss, and inspect the scene from any angle, to wander and investigate, to bring preconceptions to bear on the work. The viewing platform, in short, allowed a modern public a new freedom of viewpoint. The panorama's experiential quality; its creation of a heterogeneous, mobile viewing audience; and its deep imbrication in the cultures of modern market capitalism and of commercial and imperial globalization identify it as a founding cultural technology of modernity.

NOTES

1. The classic account is W. W. Rostow, "The Take-Off into Self-Sustained Growth," *Economic Journal* 66 (1956): 25–48. See also E. A. Wrigley, *Continuity, Chance and Change: The Character of the Industrial Revolution in England* (Cambridge: Cambridge University Press, 1988).
2. Michel Foucault, "Panopticism," in *Discipline and Punish: The Birth of the Prison*, trans. Alan Sheridan (New York: Pantheon, 1977), 195–228.
3. Stephan Oettermann, *The Panorama: History of a Mass Medium* (New York: Zone, 1997), 21.
4. This is not to suggest that the framed painting was the only form of visual representation at this (or any other) period. There was a vast spectrum of visual culture from print media to the painted interior and popular forms of paintings such as inn signs. Nonetheless, the framed painting was the key format in the age of exhibitions such as those of the Society of Artists and the Royal Academy of Arts.
5. Quoted in Laurie Garrison, ed., *Panoramas, 1787–1900: Texts and Contexts*, 5 vols. (London: Pickering & Chatto, 2013), 1:6. Emphasis added.
6. Edmund Burke, *A Philosophical Enquiry into the Origin of Our Ideas of the Sublime and Beautiful* (London: R. and J. Dodsley, 1757), 115.
7. Michael Charlesworth, "Thomas Sandby Climbs the Hoober Stand: The Politics of Panoramic Drawing in Eighteenth-Century Britain," *Art History* (1996): 247–66.
8. See Michael Charlesworth, "The Panorama," in his *Landscape and Vision in Nineteenth-Century Britain and France* (Aldershot, U.K.: Ashgate, 2008), 3.
9. John Bonehill, "Thomas Sandby, *Fort Augustus*," in *Paul Sandby: Picturing Britain*, ed. John Bonehill and Stephen Daniels (London: Royal Academy of Arts, 2009), 78.
10. Mark Dorrian, "The Aerial View: Notes for a Cultural History," *Strates* 13 (2007), http://strates.revues.org/5573.
11. See, for example, Adam Frans van der Meulen, *Seizure of Cambrai, 1677*, and *Occupation of Valenciennes*, 1677 (both Versailles, Château).
12. Bernard Smith, *European Vision and the South Pacific* (New Haven: Yale University Press, 1985), 56–57.
13. Holly Shaffer, *Adapting the Eye: An Archive of the British in India, 1770–1830* (New Haven: Yale Center for British Art, 2012), 16. See also Holly M. Shaffer, "Of Men and Gods, and Things: The Making of Maratha Art in India and Britain, 1700–1900" (Ph.D. diss., Yale University, 2016). For a definitive study of Wales's contribution to Thomas and William Daniells' *Oriental Scenery*, see Douglas Fordham, *Aquatint Worlds: Travel, Print, and Empire, 1770–1820* (New Haven: Yale University Press, 2019), 59–117.
14. *Edinburgh Evening Courant*, December 29, 1787, quoted in Scott B. Wilcox, "Unlimiting the Bounds of Painting," introduction to *Panoramania! The Art and Entertainment of the "All-Embracing" View*, by Ralph Hyde (London: Trefoil/Barbican Art Gallery, 1988), 13–44; 21.
15. George Corner, *The Panorama (Leicester Square): With Memoirs of Its Inventor, Robert Barker, and His Son, the Late Henry Aston Barker* (London: Robins, 1857), reprinted in Garrison, *Panoramas, 1787–1900*, 1:16.
16. On the tradition of the prospect view, see Ralph Hyde, *Gilded Scenes and Shining Prospects: Panoramic Views of British Towns, 1575–1900* (New Haven: Yale Center for British Art, 1985); and Caroline Arscott and Griselda Pollock with Janet Wolff, "The Partial View: The Visual Representation of the Early Nineteenth-Century Industrial City," in *The Culture of Capital Art, Power and the Nineteenth-Century Middle Class*, ed. Janet Wolff and John Seed (Manchester, U.K.: Manchester University Press, 1988), 191–233.
17. Denise Blake Oleksijczuk, *The First Panoramas: Visions of British Imperialism* (Minneapolis: University of Minnesota Press, 2011), 23–24. The discussion that follows is profoundly indebted to the pioneering work of Denise Blake Oleskijezuk. Her exemplary study has transformed our understanding of the early years of the medium.
18. See ibid., 36–46. Her discussion centers on Robert Barker, *An Explanation of the Six Plates, Which Contain a Representation of the City and Environs of Edinburgh* (London: A. Grant, n.d.).
19. Oleksjiczuk, *The First Panoramas*, 50.
20. *Times* (London), January 10, 1792, quoted in Oettermann, *The Panorama*, 101.
21. Celina Fox, ed., *London: World City, 1800–1840* (New Haven: Yale University Press, 1992).
22. Erasmus Darwin, Note XI, in the Additional Notes to *The Botanic Garden: A Poem, in Two Parts* (London: J. Johnson, 1791), 22; notes paginated separately from main text.
23. A. W. Skempton, "Samuel Wyatt and the Albion Mill," *Architectural History* 14 (1971): 53–73, 149–52. See also Asa Briggs, *Age of Improvement, 1763–1867*, 2nd ed. (London: Longman, 2000).
24. William Blake, introduction to *Milton*, in *The Complete Writings of William Blake, with Variant Readings*, ed. Geoffrey Keynes (Oxford: Oxford University Press, 1966), 481.

25. See Hubert J. Pragnell, *The London Panoramas of Robert Barker and Thomas Girtin, circa 1800* (London: Topographical Society, 1968).
26. William H. Galperin, *The Return of the Visible in British Romanticism* (Baltimore: Johns Hopkins University Press, 1993), 40.
27. Oleksijczuk, *The First Panoramas*, 51.
28. Jürgen Habermas, *The Structural Transformation of the Public Sphere: An Inquiry into a Category of Bourgeois Society* (Cambridge: MIT Press, 1991).
29. See B. E. Maidment, *Reading Popular Prints, 1790–1870* (Manchester, U.K.: Manchester University Press, 1996), 27–52.
30. Hyde, *Gilded Scenes and Shining Prospects*, 130.
31. Ann Bermingham, "Landscape-O-Rama: The Exhibition Landscape at Somerset House and the Rise of Popular Landscape Entertainments," in *Art on the Line: The Royal Academy Exhibitions at Somerset House, 1780–1836*, ed. David Solkin (New Haven: Yale University Press, 2001), 127–44.
32. Quoted in William T. Whitley, *Artists and Their Friends*, 2 vols. (London: Medici Society, 1928), 2:106.
33. For a pioneering discussion of this recently rediscovered watercolor in the context of the panorama, see Michael Charlesworth, "Subverting the Command of Place: Panorama and the Romantics," in *Placing and Displacing Romanticism*, ed. Peter J. Kitson (Aldershot, U.K.: Ashgate, 2001), 129–45, esp. 136–37.
34. Ralph Hyde, *The Regent's Park Colosseum; or, "Without Hyperbole, the Wonder of the World": Being an Account of a Forgotten Pleasure Dome and Its Creators* (London: Ackermann, 1982), 42.
35. The fullest discussion is that of Oleksijczuk, *The First Panoramas*, 127–71.
36. On national identity in the period, see Linda Colley, *Britons: Forging the Nation, 1707–1837* (New Haven: Yale University Press, 1992).
37. For a full discussion of Loutherbourg's painting in an expanded context, see Geoff Quilley, *Empire to Nation: Art, History and the Vizualization of Maritime Britain, 1768–1829* (New Haven: Yale University Press, 2011), 204–8.
38. Oleksijczuk, *The First Panoramas*, 148.
39. Quilley, *Empire to Nation*, 198.
40. Garrison, *Panoramas, 1787–1900*, 1:112.
41. Thomas Southey, "The Life of Wellington," *Quarterly Review* 13 (April and July, 1815, 2nd ed., 1816): 68, quoted in Philip Shaw, "Re-Placing Waterloo: Southey's Vision of Command," in Kitson, *Placing and Displacing Romanticism*, 106–28; 116.
42. On Turner at Waterloo, see Leo Costello, *J. M. W. Turner and the Subject of History* (Aldershot, U.K.: Ashgate, 2012), 86–87, 92.
43. See Oleksijczuk, *The First Panoramas*, 89–126.
44. For a full discussion, see Pauline Rohatgi, "From Pencil to Panorama; Tipu in Pictorial Perspective," in *The Tiger and the Thistle: Tipu Sultan and the Scots in India, 1760–1800*, ed. Anne Buddle (Edinburgh: National Galleries of Scotland, 1999), 39–54.
45. Key to the panorama engraved by an artist known only as "Lee," 1800. Victoria and Albert Museum, London.
46. Thomas Frognall Dibdin, *Reminiscences of a Literary Life*, 2 vols. (London: J. Major, 1836), 1:143–46.
47. Ibid., 145n.
48. See Buddle, *The Tiger and the Thistle*.
49. The term *inexorable sultan* appears on the tombstone of Lt. Col. John Campbell, died 1784, St. Thomas Cathedral, Mumbai.
50. Dibdin, *Reminiscences*, 1:146–47.
51. Daniel E. White, *From Little London to Little Bengal: Religion, Print and Modernity in Early British India, 1793–1835* (Baltimore: Johns Hopkins University Press, 2013), 31–33.

JONATHAN CRARY

2 Géricault, the Panorama, and Sites of Reality in the Early Nineteenth Century

Even as our present lurches further into the twenty-first century, there is still a pervasive sense that an archaeology of our own rapidly changing perceptual world begins in the nineteenth century amid what Jean-Louis Comolli has memorably described as "the frenzy of the visible."[1] The grounds for claiming this would certainly have less to do with the fact that film and photography were nineteenth-century inventions (the relative transience of these forms is now self-evident). Rather, if it is valuable to insist on continuities between 150 years ago and the present, those links would involve the status of the spectator and the persistence of certain imperatives for consumption, attention, and perceptual competence. Instead of focusing on the development of specific apparatuses or technologies, such as film or photography, I believe it is more important to see how a related group of strategies through which a subject is modernized as a spectator traverse a range of seemingly different objects and locations.

To move quickly from the general to something concrete, consider William Hogarth's *Southwark Fair*, from the 1730s, a work in many ways remote from the more modern problems just outlined (fig. 2.1). It is, however, an image in which we can see forms of premodern and modern culture coexisting. Clearly we are looking at the remains of a traditional social phenomenon in an exhausted condition, at the tail end of its presence within European collective experience. Rather than a literal depiction of a specific fairground, we see here the marginal survival of festival's carnival energies within premodern Europe. Even through Hogarth's own class prejudices, which privileged thrift, conjugality, moderation, and industriousness, we still get a tenuous sense of how the disorder of carnival overturns a distinction between spectator and performer, how it destabilizes any fixed position or identity, how it parodies and profanes official forms with inversions of high and low, how it suggests a teeming mix of sensory modalities, the tactility of bodies mingling, sounds and smells, all at least coequal with vision. At the same time it is clear that carnival's leftover fragments, the vertigo of the topsy-turvy world, had by this time been relegated to the terrain of the fairground, segregated from the city's more rationalized economic life.

One particular component of Hogarth's turbulent scene is the two individuals seated near the right corner, looking into a double-sided peep show.[2] These two spectators are constituted and positioned very differently

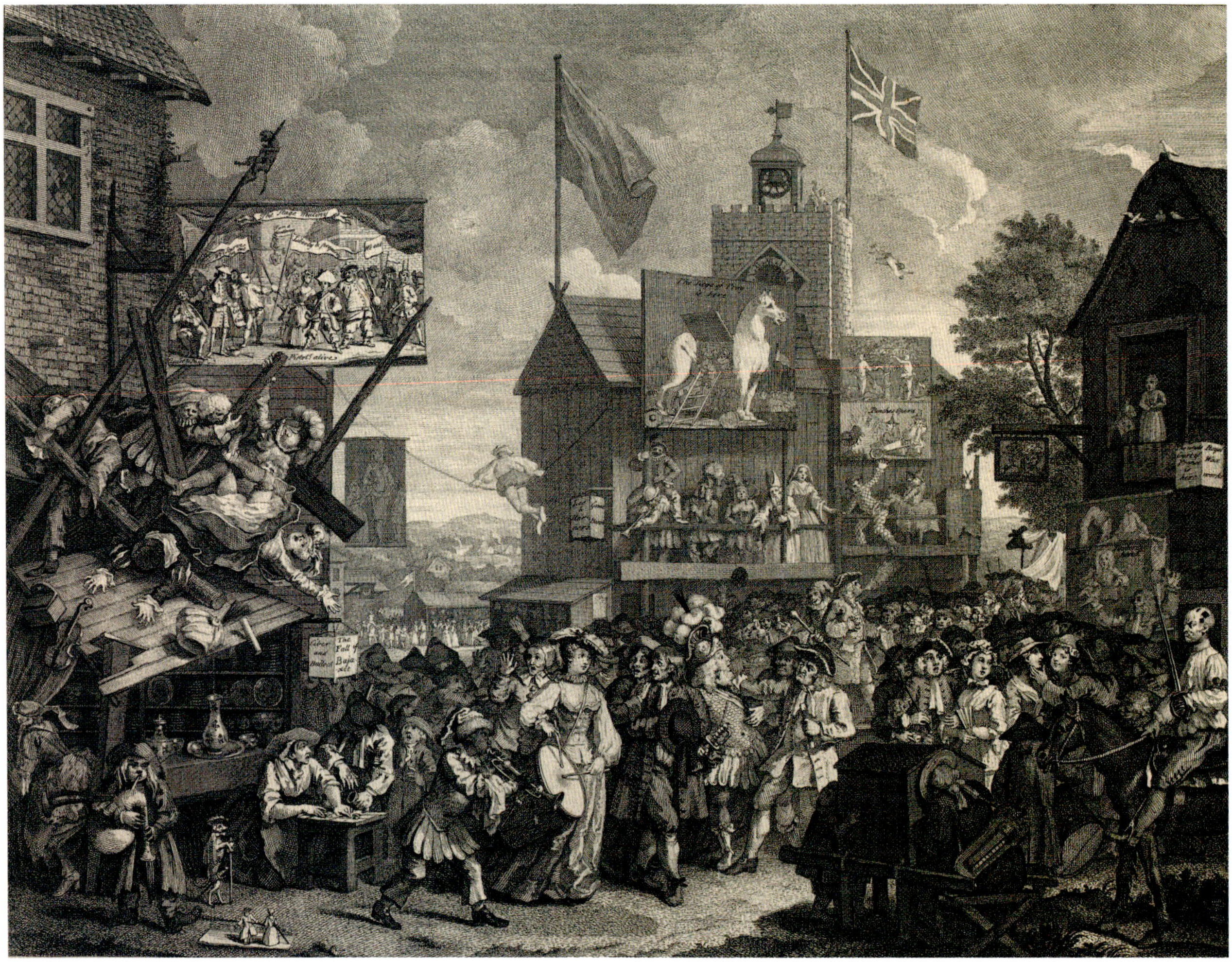

FIG. 2.1. William Hogarth (British, 1697–1768), *Southwark Fair*, 1733/34. Etching and engraving, 34.3 × 45.2 cm (13 1/2 × 17 13/16 in.). National Gallery of Art, Washington, D.C., Rosenwald Collection (1944.5.56).

from anyone else depicted in the print. These immobile and absorbed figures, interfacing with the window of the peep show, anticipate one of the primary pathways that popular culture will trace out of the eighteenth century into the nineteenth and eventually even into our own time, in a process that obliterates or at least sublimates the possibility of carnival. These continuities can be suggested, for example, by considering the peep-show setup of the Kaiserpanorama in the early 1880s, or the related miniature arrangement of the stereoscope, pervasive throughout the second half of the nineteenth century. I am not pointing to any kind of technological lineage or some sequence dependent on the improvement or development of devices, as if the important questions concerned the literal viewing apparatus. Although the form of the peep show can be followed in reverse from the 1730s—back to seventeenth-century perspective boxes and probably further into the sixteenth century—what interests me is the move that began in the later eighteenth century, when the spectator of the peep show conformed generally with Walter Benjamin's account of the novel reader as a new, isolated consumer of a mass-produced commodity. The model of optical apparatus in the corner of Hogarth's fairground shifted from a relatively minor element of early modern popular culture to become a powerful model of what came to characterize dominant forms of visual culture in Europe and North America: the viewer's relative separation from a milieu of distraction and the detachment of an image from a larger background. The physical device is simply a figure for the viewer's broader psychic, perceptual, and social insularity as well as a pervasive privileging of vision over the senses of touch and smell. Mikhail Bakhtin indicates that, after the disappearance of carnival, nineteenth-century experience acquired the character of what he calls a "private chamber," for an enclosed and privatized subject.[3]

As much recent work has shown, a major component of the making of nineteenth-century visual culture was the education and training of both the individuals and collectivities for whom new forms of visual consumption were being produced. The many ways in which this occurred included the spectator's self-disciplining as an occupant of or visitor to interior spaces and institutions, in a sense the formation of modern audiences. The prioritization of visuality was accompanied by imperatives for various kinds of self-control and social restraint, particularly for forms of attentiveness requiring both relative silence and immobility. As Tony Bennett and others have shown, the public museum (whether of art or natural history) emerged as one of the nineteenth-century sites where new kinds of social intercourse seemed to pose possible problems.[4] Amid the democratizing tendencies in postrevolutionary Europe there was concern that an unregulated mixing of social classes could import a fairground disorder to interior public spaces, thereby harming those institutions' pedagogical and ideological agendas. Thus, when the Crystal Palace was under construction, there was considerable official anxiety that this largest-ever indoor space would be threatened by unruly behavior and public drunkenness. For this reason a large security force was recruited and set in place on opening day and on days of reduced ticket prices, but it proved completely unnecessary.[5] In this turning point in the exhibition of manufactured consumer goods, the luster of the commodity radiated its own exhortations for self-control.

Of special fascination to those studying nineteenth-century European visual culture is the Egyptian Hall, in London's Piccadilly neighborhood, operating more or less continuously from 1812 until 1904, when the building, then a hall for early cinematic exhibitions, was demolished (fig. 2.2). Its founder, William Bullock, originally called it the London Museum; given its exterior of simulated Egyptian relief sculpture and hieroglyphs, it quickly became known as the Egyptian Hall.[6] Now physically lost, it remains important as a stratified site through which the historically mutating shape of an exhibition-entertainment milieu can be examined over this long span of time. During the nearly one hundred years of its existence, one could have seen displays of natural history, art exhibitions, freak shows, and a vast range of curiosities, versions of panoramas and magic lantern shows, phantasmagorias, ventriloquists, magic shows, movies, vaudeville, and other music hall–style acts.

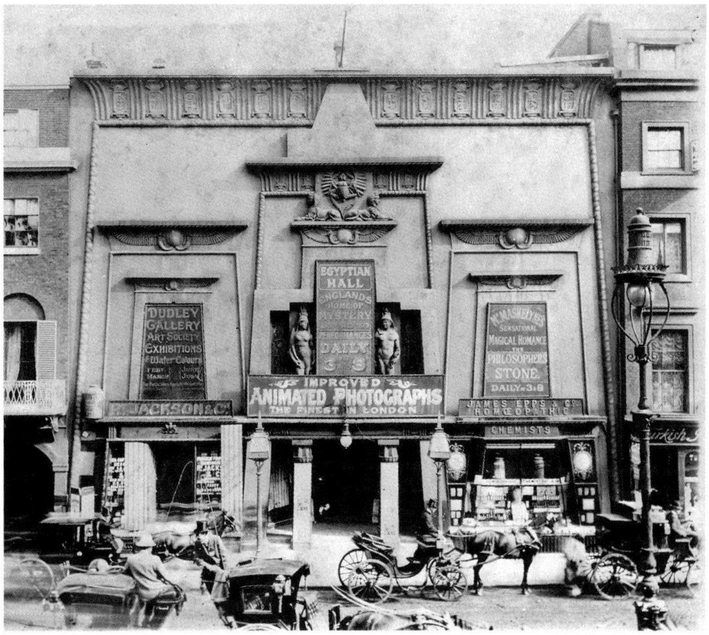

FIG. 2.2. Exterior view of the Egyptian Hall, ca. 1900.

At its opening in 1812, advertisements promised "Natural and foreign curiosities, Antiquities and Productions of the Fine Arts," since its semipermanent display included various spoils taken from Egypt (no doubt alongside a far greater number of fakes): mummies, papyrus texts, statues, gems. There were also exhibits of hundreds of stuffed birds and animals, roughly categorized by types and groups. A plate in Ackermann's *Repository of Arts* represented such a display in Bullock's earlier premises at 22 Piccadilly in 1810 (fig. 2.3). By the late 1810s, the Egyptian Hall was a hybrid of the various possibilities of nineteenth-century organized display, a mix of the obsolete traditions of the cabinet of curiosities with a burgeoning but inchoate inclination to quasi-scientific organization. But it never was to merge into the growth of the modern bourgeois museum; instead, it stayed fully a part of the modern permutation of the older model of curiosities into a nineteenth-century preoccupation with "attractions," in Tom Gunning's term (fig. 2.4).[7] Gunning sees early cinema as an attraction that, like many other nineteenth-century phenomena, relied on the direct stimulation and shock of display, the incitement of visual curiosity and pleasure, and the solicitation of attention through surprise and astonishment, as in magic acts and in shows of giants or Siamese twins in which the mere exhibition of something is self-justifying. The word *attractions*, Gunning explains, operated in Sergei Eisenstein's

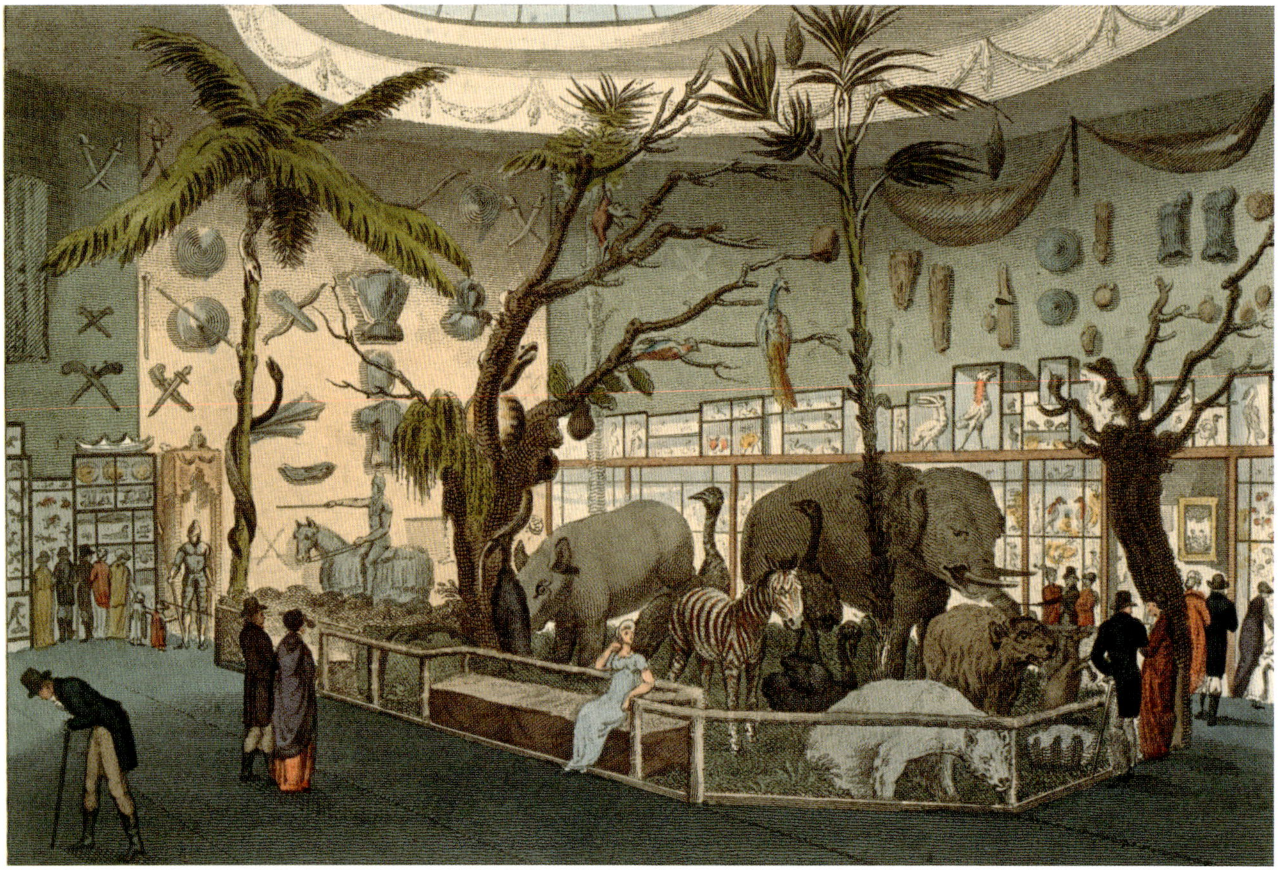

FIG. 2.3. Thomas Hosmer Shepherd (British, 1793–1864), after Peter Frederick Robinson (English, 1776–1858), *Bullock's Museum (Egyptian Hall or London Museum), Piccadilly: The Interior.* Colored aquatint, 12.2 × 19.5 cm (4 7/8 × 7 5/8 in.). (London: R. Ackermann, June 1, 1810). Wellcome Collection, London.

writings to evoke its fairground origins. In this larger sense it is a question of how the premodern fairground's carnival disorder, profuse grotesquerie, and strangeness are deposed on to the peep-show model of visual attraction and how the multifaceted festival *participant* is turned into an individualized, self-regulated *spectator*.

Perhaps the single most important category of nineteenth-century exhibitionary attraction encompasses those various display techniques whose allure was simply their relative efficacy at providing an illusory reproduction or simulation of the real, regardless of what was being shown. In this historical period, there would never be a clear separation between the appeal of a technique of verisimilitude solely as demonstration of its own operation and an attention to the referent conjured up by that apparatus. A site like the Egyptian Hall is thus important for the diversity of "reality effects" that occurred within it. This now-familiar phrase is of course from the late 1960s work of the French critic Roland Barthes, who insisted that a new discursive model of reality took shape in the nineteenth century, that "the real," as modernity came to conceive it, was invented then. He used this term in several different ways. On the one hand, the reality effect was for Barthes a specific device in nineteenth-century literature that had to do with the function of the so-called concrete detail in a fictional text—he called it the "direct collusion of a referent and a signifier, whereby the signified is expelled from the sign."[8] On the other, he insisted that the reality effect was not only textual, linking it to the nineteenth-century emergence of modern assumptions about history, manifested in "the development of the realistic novel, the private diary, documentary literature, the news item, the historical museum, the exhibition of ancient objects and the massive development of photography whose sole pertinent feature is precisely to signify that the event represented has really taken place."[9] Importantly, although photography is emphasized as a reality effect, it is not in any sense a foundational model or prerequisite for it.

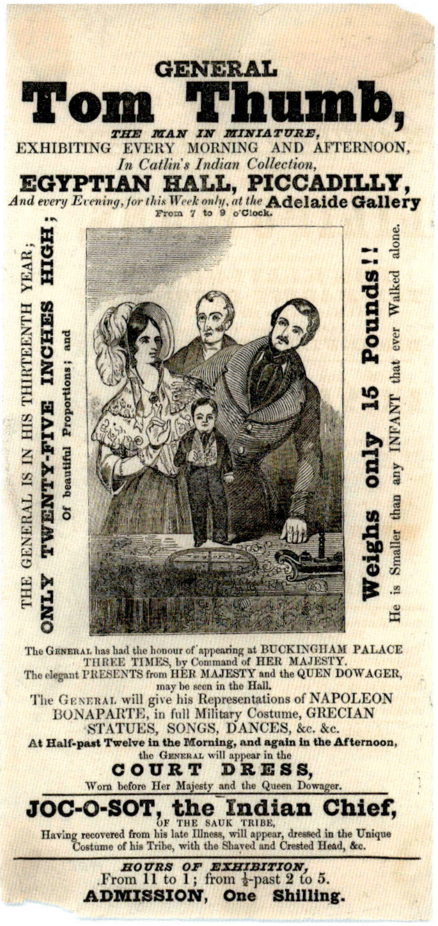

FIG. 2.4. Poster for Egyptian Hall attractions, 1844.

In the Egyptian Hall's early years, one of the most successful exhibits was the display of Napoleon's battle carriage captured after the Battle of Waterloo and shipped back to England. What went on view was not simply a carriage, but a model of the "real" in newly distilled form. Obviously it was of interest because it was luxurious, bullet-proof, and painted dark blue with gold trim and wheels of vermillion—and because Napoleon's wounded, one-armed Dutch coach driver had been brought back to be part of the exhibition. But of overwhelming interest to thousands of spectators was the chance to look inside at the plush drawers and built-in cabinets containing Napoleon's personal wardrobe, bars of soap, pocket watch, liqueur flasks, and numerous other minor articles. In line with Barthes's argument about the concrete detail, these mundane items became a supplementary but vital confirmation of the authenticity of the object itself. After years of exhibition on tour throughout Britain and other parts of Europe, the carriage notably was sold to the then-thriving establishment of Madame Tussaud's in London, becoming part of her permanent display of waxwork figures of Napoleon (for whom she had previously worked).[10] This was a familiar strategy in wax museums, where the simulation was augmented by the adjacency of objects having a literal presence: a wax figure seated at the desk or table actually taken from the person's prison cell, or even more simply, the proximity of illusory wax skin with real clothing that had actually belonged to the subject. But despite the unquestioned popularity of wax museums, it was such "mixed" reality effects that finally were the most problematic in the nineteenth century, usually occupying an outer limit of popular taste or fascination.

Another piece of the Egyptian Hall's heterogeneous visual culture was an object placed on display there in June 1820, Théodore Géricault's *The Raft of the Medusa* (fig. 2.5).[11] Although there are many reasons that the exhibition of this work in this particular venue is of historical importance, there is space here to indicate only a few. For a time, the Egyptian Hall was one of London's most important sites for the temporary exhibition of paintings, usually paintings that either in sheer scale or in subject matter were viable as popular commercial attractions.[12] My larger point is that the nineteenth-century observer of painting was always also an observer who simultaneously encountered a proliferating diversity of optical and sensory experiences. Paintings were produced and assumed meaning not in terms of some cloistered aesthetic and institutional domain but as one of the many consumable, fleeting elements within an expanding field of images, commodities, and attractions.

Thus, with this painting there are two distinct if related problems—the circumstances of its production and of its reception. The fact that Géricault chose for his subject a contemporary news item already made it compatible with a larger social arena in which information was transformed into commodities and attractions.[13] But this is almost incidental to the particular approach Géricault staked out for his representation. And that is why this painting occupies its unstable position between two distinct historical worlds—between the enclosed order of reference organized around the rhetoric of the human body in the art of antiquity and the Renaissance and an unbounded heterogeneous informational field of journalistic, medical, legal, and political sources of evidence, testimony, fact, and other guarantees of the real.

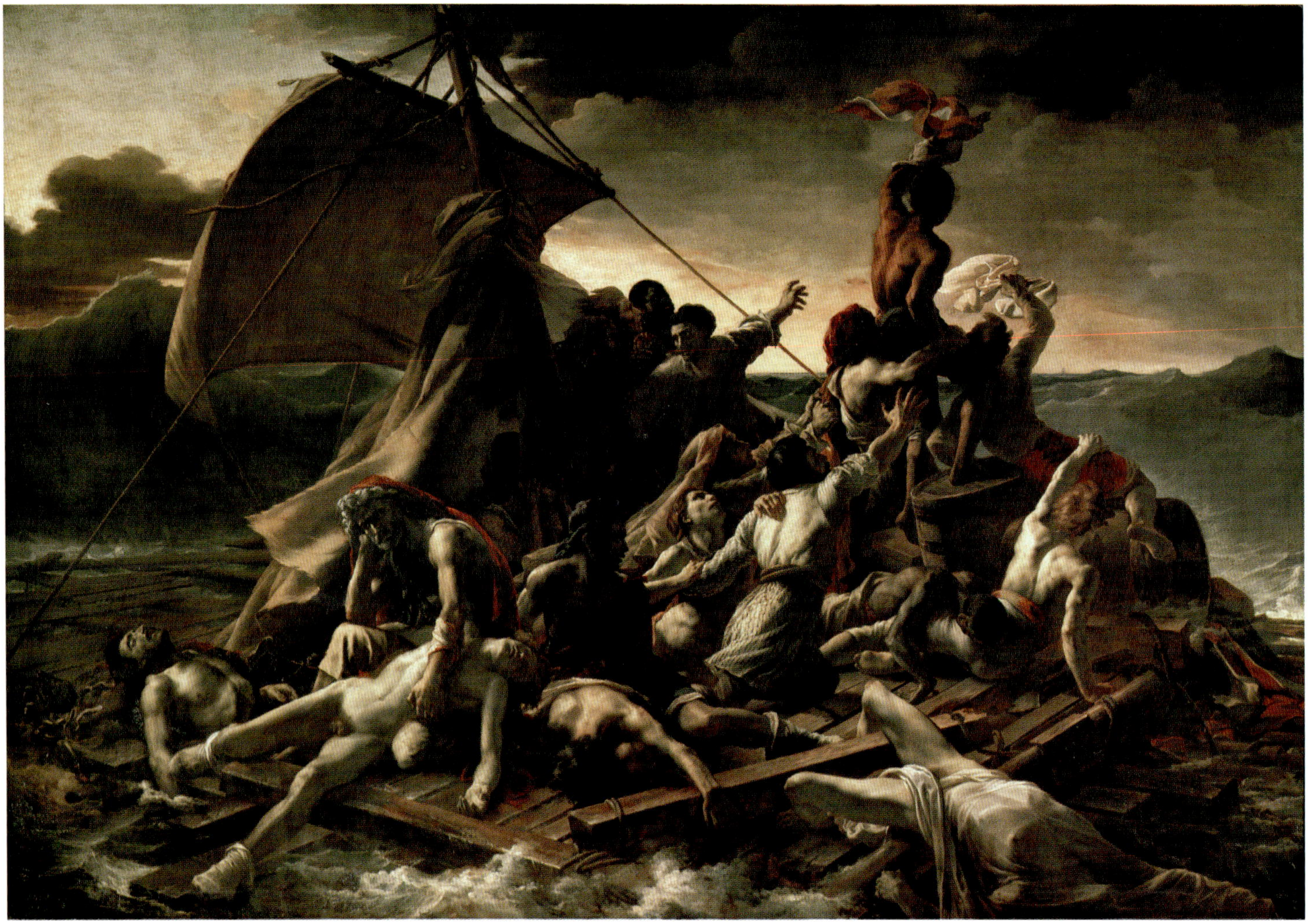

FIG. 2.5. Théodore Géricault (French, 1791–1824), *The Raft of the Medusa*, 1818–19. Oil on canvas, 491 × 716 cm (193 ¼ × 282 in.). Musée du Louvre, Paris (RF 4884).

The procedures through which Géricault arrived at the finished canvas of *The Raft of the Medusa* are well known: the remarkable lengths to which the artist went to master and assimilate the facts, truth, evidence, and immediacy of the horrible event, which had already assumed a multilayered informational existence. Géricault engaged the project as if all this new data could be distilled and forged into a visual experience that would synthesize and transcend its fragmented character. According to his early biographer, Charles Clément, Géricault assembled an immense "dossier crammed with authentic proofs and documents of all sorts," indicating that Géricault attempted to collect every news story and public document about the expedition and shipwreck, every bit of eyewitness testimony, including the best-selling firsthand account by two survivors, J. B. Savigny and Alexandre Corréard.[14] Not only did he assemble all the journalistic images he could find, but he commissioned the *Medusa*'s surviving carpenter to build him a small scale model of the raft, which he tested out in water to see how it floated and maneuvered. He made the acquaintance of Savigny (the ship's surgeon) and Corréard and interviewed them at length, even though their published account was already exhaustive. Géricault also used Savigny and Corréard as models for two of the figures standing near the mast, fastened onto the painting for their stature as eyewitnesses but also as a way of making the representation actual. We should note the utter discontinuity between the semantic status of their images in the painting and the various references to Old Masters' art, whether Michelangelo or Rubens; this is part of the discursive fissure running through the painting. The most extreme and notorious measure undertaken by Géricault to ensure his work's authenticity, however, was his insistence on becoming familiar with the immediacy of death—not death in a narrative, psychological, religious, or symbolic sense, but death as the literal dissolution of the physical body, the body drained of any living coherence. What Clément referred to as the immense documentary dossier of Géricault would finally have to include the corpses and body parts he had delivered to his studio (or studied in hospitals) in order to live with the sights and smells of decaying human bodies, just as the survivors of the raft kept parts of the dead on board for their own sustenance (fig. 2.6). As far as we know, the only thing Géricault did not do, in his immersion into the event, was experiment with cannibalism himself. It is this whole dossier of fact, of evidence, of direct experience that produces, in Barthes's phrase, the work's "referential plenitude." Of course it is not a work that looks real by virtue of its literal correspondence to a specific viewpoint of a specific moment. As critics have noted over the decades, we see no starving, emaciated bodies; we don't see the raft, with its soggy passengers, as it really was, submerged a foot or so below water level. Its verisimilitude is based on its more profound embeddedness in new networks of the real, in which older models of visibility are exceeded.

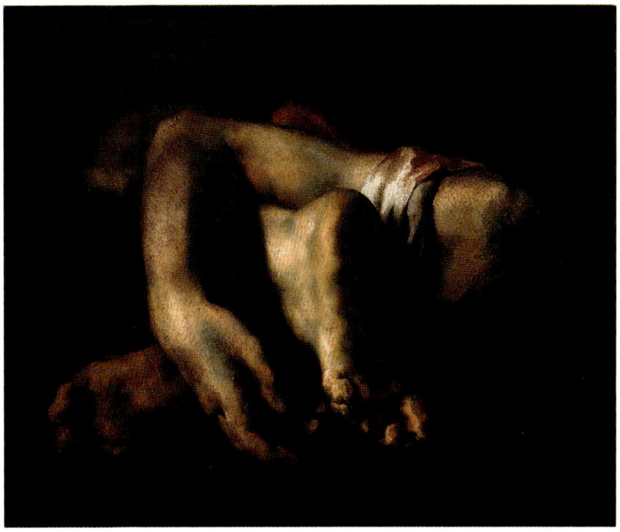

FIG. 2.6. Théodore Géricault, *Study of Feet and Hands*, ca. 1819. Oil on canvas, 52 × 64 cm (20 ½ × 25 ⅛ in.). Musée Fabre, Montpellier.

Working as he did amid this field of effects, Géricault's first inclinations are highly telling. Initially he was convinced that the project could be achieved only through a sequence of several paintings, that the event could be narrated only in terms of its temporal dispersal, its inherent dislocations. But much of *The Raft*'s historical significance lies in how Géricault forced this content and its discursive substructure back within the rhetorical terms of a classical model of representation; that he could not do this seamlessly, that these incompatible projects collide and fracture is part of what made this such a charged object at this threshold of modernity. Even so, as Michael Fried and others have insisted, in his efforts to reduce the event of the disaster to a single image, he chose this moment—a moment in which vision takes on such an exclusive priority, in which the focus of attention is funneled and narrowed to a single point, the barely perceptible top sail of a ship on the remote horizon.[15] To redirect the terms of Fried's argument, the painting incarnates a vision all but cut off from the possibility of a reciprocal exchange of gazes. For reprieve and deliverance in this image would consist in a mutual exchange of gazes, being acknowledged by the ship, that here is tragically denied or at least deferred.[16] But this is fully part of what Bakhtin saw as the "private chamber" character of nineteenth-century experience, where the peep-show model of looking describes both an intensification of visuality and an isolation of the subject from a lived embeddedness in a given social milieu.

We get an even more piercing sense of this new understanding of the privatization of vision in Géricault's late portraits of the insane (fig. 2.7). We are a long way from Goya's nearly contemporary renderings of the madhouse. The line between the normal and the pathological is made disturbingly indistinct. Seen across a room, Géricault's pictures appear more or less congruent with the conventions of middle-class portraiture; only on closer examination does one realize something about them is different. A key feature of these images is the breakdown of a reciprocal gaze, not only the impossibility of a mutuality but a sense of the complete nonidentity of worlds, the loss of a shared objective reality. The music historian Lawrence Kramer, writing on Chopin, thematizes the first half of the nineteenth century as a time when "human subjectivity ceases to be a common field and becomes instead a secret recess. No longer a shared sameness, the self becomes an essential difference, constantly threatened with separation from the outer world."[17] Here Géricault discloses that separation, that difference in extreme form. And it is alongside this shift that the need arises for at least a simulation of a real world experienced in common, that a preoccupation with the real emerges and that whole industries of reality production take shape in a rapidly modernizing West. Yet it is not just that the possibility of our eyes meeting the eyes

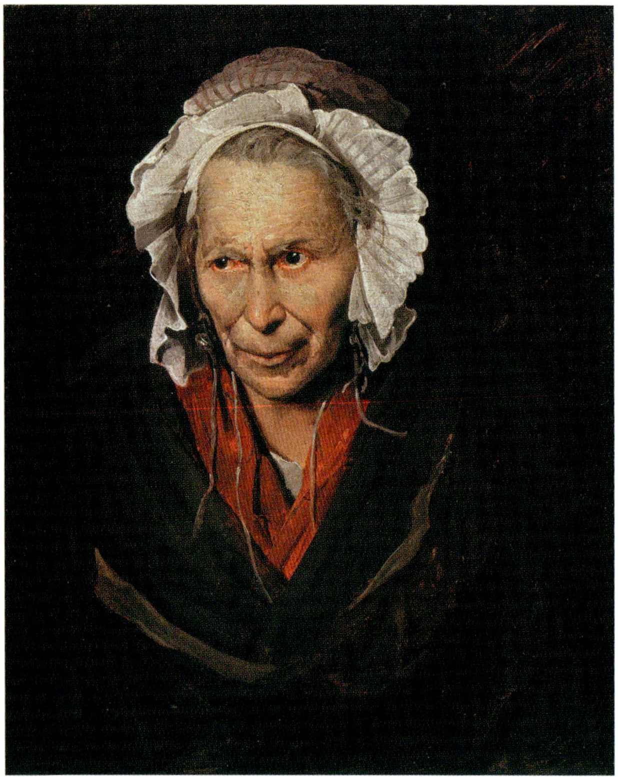

FIG. 2.7. Théodore Géricault, *The Madwoman*, 1819–22. Oil on canvas, 72 × 58 cm (28 3/8 × 22 7/8 in.). Musée des Beaux-Arts de Lyon.

of the insane is unthinkable here, in that any reciprocity would include an unbearable moment of self-recognition and self-differentiation. Rather, it is that Géricault has recorded, with apparent clinical objectivity and detachment, individuals who, in contrast, were perceiving a hyper-delusional world. It is as if they were like optical instruments whose lenses we will never look through but, if we could, would reveal a world radically different from what we assume to be a commonly shared reality. During his stay in England, relatedly, Géricault was repeatedly drawn to architectural motifs that functioned as perceptual "black holes." He showed figures on the verge of entrances into dark unfathomable spaces, which communicated nothing to the observer except the shiver of an annihilating loss of any redemptive possibilities.

In the spring of 1820, a somewhat melancholy Géricault made arrangements for the huge painting to be rolled up, crated, and shipped to London, where it opened in June for public exhibition at the Egyptian Hall. Newspaper advertisements emphasized the painting's grim but sensational subject yet stressed its size as an attraction in its own right. England's public was already well acquainted with the horrific details of the story: when the painting arrived, *The Fatal Raft*, a stage play about the *Medusa* wreck, was showing to sold-out houses a few streets away. Thus, Géricault's work, now extracted from the universe of the Louvre, was made continuous with another network of "actualities," a field of reified current events, which supported its value as an attraction. In the six months *The Raft of the Medusa* was on display at the Egyptian Hall, it drew over 50,000 visitors. The one-shilling admittance price included an abridged edition of the English translation of the Savigny and Corréard book. The availability of this text at the exhibition, of its authority as objective historical discourse, functioned alongside the painting as a reality effect, fully complicit in establishing what Barthes called the authenticity and "omnipotence of the referent."[18]

Following its London run, which at least temporarily eased much of Géricault's financial problems and depression, a deal was struck to give the painting another run in Dublin. Here, standard accounts explain, the painting did less well and, after two months in spring 1821, it was shipped back to France. Why did it not do as well in Dublin as in London? In the Irish capital, in a remarkable historical intersection, Géricault's painting competed for attention with a moving panorama, another artifact of nineteenth-century visual culture, representing precisely the same recent news story and titled *The Wreck of the Medusa*.[19] Sometimes called a peristrephic panorama, this moving panorama involved a long band of canvas painted with a continuous sequence of scenes and unrolled before a seated audience. Colored lighting enhanced the effect of individual scenes, and often a small orchestra added drama to the whole. For roughly the same price, a consumer thus had the choice of seeing over 10,000 square feet of moving painted surface or about 400 square feet of Gericault's motionless canvas. One scene in this moving panorama in Dublin, moreover, was effectively a copy of Géricault's painting, so one really didn't need to pay to see the original as well. If Géricault's painting and the Dublin panorama were rivals for patronage within an economic space around 1820, it certainly should not be seen as some opposition between elite culture and a crude popular form. Rather, it was competition between two types of reality effect that each represented the same event, and the marketplace decided which was the more compelling attraction.

The word *panorama* was used in a variety of ways in the early nineteenth century, and the Egyptian Hall was a place where large mural paintings, billed as panoramas,

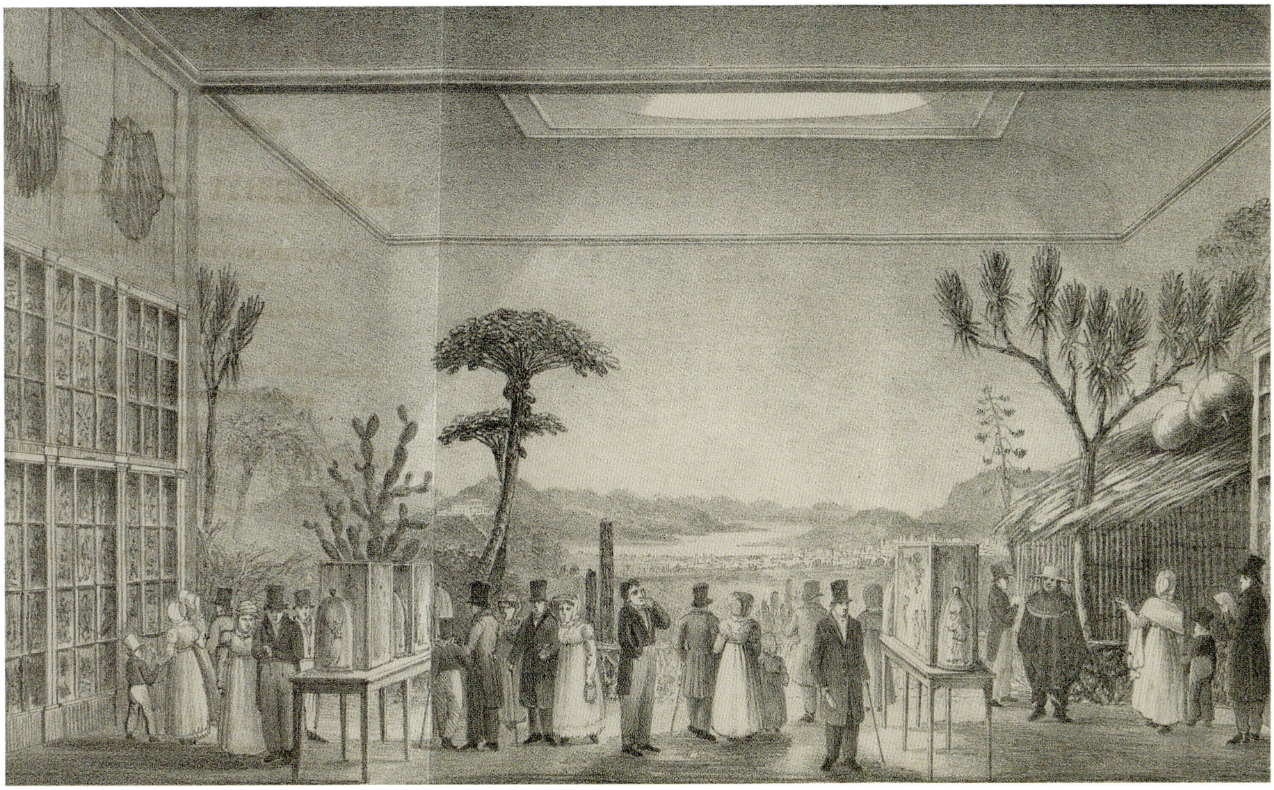

FIG. 2.8. Agostino Aglio (Italian-British, 1777–1857), *Exhibition of Modern Mexico at the Egyptian Hall, Piccadilly*, from William Bullock, *Catalogue of the Exhibition, Called Modern Mexico* (London, 1824). Yale Center for British Art, New Haven, Connecticut. Paul Mellon Collection.

were created as components of exhibitions. One exhibition displayed a large number of objects and specimens Bullock had brought back from a six-month expedition to Mexico (fig. 2.8). These included a mix of real and simulated artifacts: casts of Aztec sculpture such as Montezuma's calendar stone and hundreds of birds and fish, fake plants and fruits, all placed in the context of a large, three-sided painting of a Mexican landscape, like a twentieth-century museum diorama, with a three-dimensional dwelling abutting the two-dimensional painted mural surface. The original referent of the word *panorama* was, of course, a 360-degree circular painting exhibited on the interior of a cylindrically shaped structure.[20] The panorama is a compelling object for historians in that it flourished in a relatively consistent manner for a period coinciding very closely with the nineteenth century itself. A key problem is to explain its historical durability in a time when constant innovation and rapid obsolescence were already integral parts of cultural production and consumption.

This is hardly to imply that the panorama's meaning or effects remained static for over a century. In fact, its status continually mutated in relation to social, technological, and cultural developments. And in the early 1820s, the panorama had an uneasy but relatively uncontested proximity to traditional modes of painting. The situation was very different from that of a few decades later, when the panorama was clearly situated within the terrain of popular entertainment and the term *panorama painter* was an expression of disdain. At least into the mid-1820s there was still a pervasive although often uncertain sense that panoramas were part of the same representational codes as older forms of painting. It was a startlingly unfamiliar format but many writers tacitly assumed that panoramic painting would over time become a conventional way of representing certain kinds of subjects and that major artists would gradually gravitate toward it. Initially many artists and critics immersed in traditional practices were favorably disposed to the panorama. In 1800, in one of the last major academic treatises on perspective, Pierre-Henri de Valenciennes saw it as fully within the terms of classical representation, as just a new twist on familiar problems.[21] In the popular press of both London and Paris, the same reviewers who wrote about conventional art exhibitions would often review the opening of a panorama painting, generally applying the same aesthetic criteria in evaluating success or failure. There is much anecdotal evidence of interest and direct experience of the panorama by artists, including Géricault, David, Ingres, Constable, Turner, and many others. Although such "evidence" means really no more than saying that an artist living in 1920 went to the movies, it also suggests the degree to which panoramas were pervasive and familiar urban phenomena.

The panorama is one of the places in the nineteenth century where a modernization of perceptual experience occurs. The panorama falls into the general category of the phantasmagoric: borrowing from Marx, Theodor Adorno used this adjective to describe any form or process under capitalism that concealed or mystified its actual production or operation.[22] How, specifically, was the panorama phantasmagoric? After purchasing entry, spectators usually entered the rotunda by means of a staircase that led them out onto the central viewing platform. The interior was darkened in such a way that only subdued light entering indirectly from the top of the building illuminated the painting on the structure's walls, leaving the rest of the interior in relative obscurity. Such lighting conditions made the painting seem to radiate its own light; and it was sometimes found that on bright summer days the light would be too strong—enough so that the seams of the separate canvases became visible, revealing the painting's constructed character and thus disrupting the illusion. The elevation was in part purely functional—no doorways could interrupt the continuous surface of the painting. This also meant that spectators could never cast shadows on the image, the effect of which would obviously be anti-phantasmagoric, disclosing it as merely a two-dimensional surface.

Almost all panoramas sought to create a spatial remove from the image, as a moatlike area surrounded the viewing platform. The spectator therefore had nothing like the floor in a museum or gallery interior, which could assist in a subjective rationalization of the intervening distance between eye and image. Accounts indicate audience members occasionally tossed coins at the image as a way of determining how far away it was. Forms as seemingly different as Daguerre's diorama, Wagner's theater at Bayreuth, the Kaiserpanorama, the Kinetoscope, and, of course, cinema as it took shape in the late 1890s are other key nineteenth-century examples of the image as an autonomous luminous screen of attraction, whose apparitional appeal is an effect of both its uncertain spatial location and its detachment from a broader visual field. This is how the panorama can at least be partially associated with the peep-show model: it involves a detachment of the image from a wider field of possible sensory stimulation and creates a calculated confusion about the literal location of the painted surface as a way of enhancing its illusions of presence and distance. At the same time the panorama is another instance of how spectatorship, accompanied by a narrowed focus of attention, produces social docility, even in group circumstances, even for an ambulatory spectator.

But the panorama is unique in that, unlike these other forms, it presents an unbounded image, an image that to the viewer is endless. Departing from the peep-show model, it has no frame.[23] Strictly speaking, it does have upper and lower boundaries. But as one moves one's eyes, head, or body laterally, the image appears as a continuous, boundless field. This is its self-defining feature. In one sense this horizontal orientation is a decisive culmination of a long underway secularization of sight, not only for its refusal of the obvious symbolic resonances of the ceiling and the vertical, but also for its more important evaporation of the vanishing point and residual theological implications. Within this format a popular taste for concrete actuality asserted itself. Developing out of late eighteenth-century enthusiasms for viewing paintings and picturesque landscapes (as opposed to images with mythological, allegorical, or erudite historical themes), the panorama drew audiences that were attracted by cityscapes, landscapes, or recent events they would have read about—battles, sieges, or views of remote regions of the world.

What was it about the panorama that seemed to guarantee a heightened verisimilitude? Barthes's most extensive example of the reality effect is one he himself described with the word *panorama*.[24] Barthes derived this characterization from a textual object, in this case Flaubert's *Madame Bovary*, at a point when Emma has been making regular trips to Rouen to see her lover. She has made the coach ride often enough to know every turn in the road, every landmark along the way, including the crest of a hill from which the entire city of Rouen spreads in full view below.[25] "Then, all at once, the city came into view. Sloping downward like an amphitheater, drowned in mist, it sprawled out shapelessly beyond its bridges. . . . Thus seen from above, the whole landscape had the static quality of a painting."[26] The rest of Flaubert's paragraph is an accumulation of details—the boats anchored in the Seine, distant gray hills, factory chimneys, streets lined with bare trees, roofs wet with rain, and so on. If not specifically the panorama, Flaubert introduces in his text the idea of a visual image circular or round (an amphitheater) and like a painting. There are important affinities here between the strategies of the real at work in panorama painting and in literary realism; it is a pretending or seeming to transcribe the world in a scrupulous fashion while avoiding the trap of what Barthes calls "the vertigo of notation," whereby an authentic realism seems to demand the deliriously impossible inclusion in representation of everything present to sight. Here the "insignificant detail" in the text intervenes as if to proclaim that if this level of minutiae, of narrative irrelevance, is given, then the world is being seen in its completeness, its reality.

If we can speak of the panorama as a reality effect, it is an effect produced through a confluence of many elements. But the overriding way in which a related impression of completeness, of an inexhaustible inclusion of the real, may be achieved is through the image's novel 360-degree format. Like the name itself, the panorama setup presumed to present a total view, characterized by a seemingly self-evident wholeness. And one important definition of the adjective *panoramic*, as used in the nineteenth century, was the notion of a full 360-degree view without obstructions, nothing blocking its optical appropriation. Hence, it provided an imaginary unity and coherence to an external world that, in the context of urbanization, was increasingly incoherent. The viewing platform in the center of the panorama rotunda seemed to provide a point from which an individual spectator could overcome the partiality and fragmentation that constituted quotidian perceptual experience. But while seeming to provide such a simulation of perceptual mastery and identifying the real with that sense of coherence, the panorama was in another sense a derealization and devaluation of the individual's viewpoint.

The panorama's authority was founded on the limitations of subjective vision, on the inadequacy of a human observer. It posed a view of a motif, whether landscape or city, that seemed immediately accessible but always exceeded a spectator's capacity to grasp it. Unlike eighteenth-century topographical painting, the panorama image is consumable only as fragments, as parts that must be cognitively reassembled into an imagined whole. A structure that seemed magically to overcome the fragmentation of experience in fact introduces partiality and incompleteness as constitutive elements of visual experience. Perspective had for several centuries established the pervasive fiction of an adequacy, a congruence between the subjective point of view of an observer and the world. That a perspectival representation allowed only a partial and delimited opening onto that world was offset by the universality and rationality of the laws by which it was composed. Panorama painting, on the contrary, with its cancellation of the vanishing point in the work and its reciprocal loss of a localizable point of view, heightened the disparity between a subjective visual field and the possibility of a conceptual and perceptual grasp of an external reality. It simulated a totality that was necessarily beyond the reach of a human subject. In one sense it became a degraded simulation of the sublime, available to anyone for the price of a ticket; but at the same time perception was transformed into the accumulation of information, of details, of visual facts that finally resisted synthesis into perceptual knowledge. The nineteenth-century proliferation of reality effects coincided with the collapse of the scientific, philosophical, and aesthetic systems that had in various ways posed an imaginary reconciliation of a human observer's limitations with a full possession of a perceivable world.

Two almost contemporary images disclose very different intuitions about the panoramic viewpoint. Caspar David Friedrich's *Wanderer above a Sea of Fog* (ca. 1817) (see fig. 0.13) has long, perhaps excessively, been associated with the panorama's effects; it has been suggested that Friedrich not only was extremely familiar with early panorama painting in Germany but briefly, around 1810, had plans to undertake one himself.[27] In Friedrich's painting the position of this observer and his relation to the surrounding landscape certainly correspond to a panorama's central viewing platform and illusory sense of a distant image. It seems to incarnate the ascendancy of newly released bourgeois aspirations, fantasies of autonomy, and the mastery of a position that transcended local provincial viewpoints and permitted at least an optical appropriation of a natural world increasingly being parceled and abstracted into smaller units of property. Within Friedrich's work, of course, any sense of exhilaration is inseparable from a metaphysical melancholy at the tragic insufficiency of the relation between subject and world. And in a larger European context this image gives a piercing sense of how the panorama coincided with new forms of subjective isolation, of a sensory impoverishment and emotional privatization.

The other image, Géricault's *Raft*, is almost historically simultaneous with the Friedrich work, yet as far as I know it has never been associated with a panoramic viewpoint and certainly does not have the same defining high vantage point of *The Wanderer*. But the perceptual conditions diagramed by Géricault's *Raft* include a group of observers no less situated on what we could call a viewing platform, surrounded by an unobstructed 360-degree view.[28] The sail itself, a curved piece of canvas, hovers on the horizon line like a section of the assembled painted canvas lining the interiors of the panorama rotundas. And the group of spectators on this platform have a far more urgent motivation than Friedrich's mountain climber to scan the perimeter of the circular field. Unlike *The Wanderer*, which suggests the permanence and security of a stable point of view, Géricault's work discloses a very different sense of the conditions of panoramic experience—it is to be uprooted from any point of anchorage, drifting on an amorphous surface like the sea, without markers, without a center, homogeneity and repetition overwhelming singularity. The disparate reality effects Géricault deployed take place within a powerful destabilization of a perceptual field. At stake in the narrative account of survivors desperate for rescue is the primacy of retaining a capacity for visual discrimination and holding on to a position from which that visual capacity could be exercised. But if one of the painting's dominant axes is the famous uplifting sweep of bodies, rising left to right, the other is the implied right-to-left movement of the raft, ominously pushing them away from the object of their looking. So there is a vivid figuration of a damaged and disoriented observer, denied any stable markers of distance or planarity within which a rescuing ship might be discerned. Around this time there was a pervasive awareness among sea travelers about the luminous and meteorological conditions, the mirages and fata morgana, that could play tricks on one's eyes, producing the convincing illusion of ships where there were no ships.

From Jules Michelet to Peter Weiss, the long history of critical responses have often read *The Raft*, in different ways, as an image of the fragility of human bonds and social cohesiveness. As Géricault knew very well from his exhaustive familiarity with the event's details, the monstrous breakdown in human connectedness among the raft's occupants was, at least in part, an effect of the illusory nature of individual perception in these extreme conditions. He knew from firsthand testimony that the raft's occupants, after several days without food or water, experienced visions and fevered illusions of seeing the coastline, of approaching ships, of strolling in beautiful countryside, of meeting old friends, of eating food, like a real-life version of the trance state in Coleridge's *Rime of the Ancient Mariner*. After a certain point, the raft was occupied by people who had, to varying degrees, lost touch with reality. For Géricault, there would have been a direct affiliation between the human content in this project and the portraits of the insane: both were about the precariousness of a shared reality and the vulnerability and malleability of individual perception. The particular event that Géricault finally chose to depict, the moment when an actual ship is seen, is in fact the moment of an incipient breakout of a prior atomized and delusional condition. It is a moment when there is a mounting realization that the sail flickering on the remote horizon may actually not be another hallucination or optical illusion but something perceived in common with others. One of Géricault's enduring achievements here is to have laid bare some of the sensory and cognitive dislocations of modernity, in tracing the tangled and hazardous destiny of a collective subject. At stake in this work is an apprehension of the numbing disproportion between the limits of human perception and the implacable otherness of the exterior world. This is the field on which Géricault's dossier of documents, facts, evidence, images of reality effects drifts, tied together precariously, like the raft itself, never congealing into a reassuring armature of meanings. Whether Géricault meant this shared act of vision on the raft to stand for the redemptive but unachieved possibilities of community is a question whose answer finally depends on the hopeful or catastrophic determinations of our own present.

NOTES

This essay was earlier delivered as a lecture; I am grateful to my hosts and audiences at Brown, Cornell, Princeton, Emory, Yale, University of Washington, and the Whitney Independent Study Program, as well as to the *Grey Room* editors for their help and advice with an earlier version.

1. Jean-Louis Comolli, "Machines of the Visible," in *The Cinematic Apparatus*, ed. Teresa de Lauretis and Stephen Heath (London: Macmillan, 1980), 121–42; 122.
2. On the history of the peep show, see David Robinson, Wolfgang Seitz, et al., eds., *Der Guckkasten: Einblick, Durchblick, Ausblick* (Stuttgart:

Füsslin Verlag, 1995); and Richard Balzer, *Peepshows: A Visual History* (New York: Abrams, 1998).

3. See Mikhail Bakhtin, *Rabelais and His World*, trans. Helene Iswolsky (Cambridge: MIT Press, 1968), 276–77; and Mikhail Bakhtin, *Problems of Dostoevsky's Poetics*, trans. Caryl Emerson (Minneapolis: University of Minnesota Press, 1984), 130–32.
4. Tony Bennett, *The Birth of the Museum: Theory, History, Politics* (London: Routledge, 1995).
5. Jeffrey Auerbach, *The Great Exhibition of 1851: A Nation on Display* (New Haven: Yale University Press, 1999), 136–48.
6. See the extensive factual account of the Egyptian Hall in Richard D. Altick's indispensable *The Shows of London: A Panoramic History of Exhibitions, 1600–1862* (Cambridge: Belknap Press of Harvard University Press, 1978), 235–52. See also Celina Fox, ed., *London: World City, 1800–1840* (New Haven: Yale University Press, 1992), 418–21.
7. Tom Gunning, "The Cinema of Attractions: Early Film, Its Spectator, and the Avant-Garde," in *Early Cinema: Space, Frame, Narrative*, ed. Thomas Elsaesser (London: BFI, 1990), 56–62.
8. Roland Barthes, "The Reality Effect," in *The Rustle of Language*, trans. Richard Howard (New York: Hill and Wang, 1986), 147.
9. Barthes, "The Discourse of History," in *The Rustle of Language*, 139.
10. Ben Weinreb and Christopher Hibbert, eds., *The London Encyclopaedia* (London: Macmillan, 1983), 255.
11. On the exhibition of Géricault's work in England and Ireland, see Lee Johnson, "*The Raft of the Medusa* in Great Britain," *Burlington Magazine*, August 1954, 249–53; Suzanne Lodge, "Géricault in England," *Burlington Magazine*, December 1965, 616–27; Lorenz E. Eitner, *Géricault: His Life and Work* (Ithaca: Cornell University Press, 1983), 209–12; and Rupert Christiansen, *The Victorian Visitors: Culture Shock in Nineteenth-Century Britain* (New York: Atlantic Monthly Press, 2000), 6–41.
12. See, for example, the account of the exhibition at the Egyptian Hall of Benjamin Robert Haydon's enormous *Christ's Entry into Jerusalem*, which coincided with the display of Géricault's painting in 1820, in David Blayney Brown, Robert Woof, and Stephen Hebron, eds. *Benjamin Robert Haydon, 1786–1846* (Kendal, U.K.: Wordsworth Trust, 1996), 12–13.
13. The narrative of the *Medusa* is summarized in Lorenz Eitner, *Géricault's* Raft of the Medusa (London: Phaidon, 1972).
14. Charles Clément, *Théodore Géricault: Étude bibliographique et critique* (Paris: Didier, 1868), 129.
15. Michael Fried, *Courbet's Realism* (Chicago: University of Chicago Press, 1990), 29–31.
16. In creating that "reversed telescope" effect of vast separation between raft and distant ship, Géricault was obviously aware from Corréard and Savigny's book that the eventual rescue occurred because the raft was spotted through a telescope, through the use of a visual technology exceeding the mere human vision deployed on the raft, surmounting the obstacle of distance and space. J. B. Henry Savigny and Alexander Corréard, *Narrative of a Voyage to Senegal in 1816* (1818; repr., London: Dawsons, 1968), 142–43.
17. Lawrence Kramer, *Music as Cultural Practice, 1800–1900* (Berkeley: University of California Press, 1990), 88.
18. Barthes, "The Discourse of History," in *The Rustle of Language*, 139.
19. Nina Athanassoglou-Kallmyer, *Théodore Géricault* (London: Phaidon, 2010), 158–59.
20. Valuable studies of the panorama include Stephan Oettermann, *The Panorama: History of a Mass Medium*, trans. Deborah Lucas Schneider (New York: Zone, 1997); Bernard Comment, *The Panorama*, trans. Anne-Marie Glasheen (London: Reaktion, 1999); Marie-Louise von Plessen and Ulrich Giersch, eds., *Sehsucht: Das Panorama als Massenunterhaltung des 19. Jahrhunderts* (Basel: Stroemfeld, 1993); Ralph Hyde, *Panoramania! The Art and Entertainment of the "All-Embracing" View* (London: Trefoil/Barbican Art Gallery, 1988); and Albrecht Koschorke, "Das Panorama: Die Anfänge des modernen Sensomotorik um 1800," in *Die Mobilisierung des Sehens*, ed. Harro Segeberg (Munich: Wilhelm Fink, 1996), 147–68.
21. Pierre-Henri de Valenciennes, *Éléments de perspective pratique, à l'usage des artistes . . .* (1800; repr., Geneva: Minkoff, 1973), 339–43.
22. Theodor Adorno, *In Search of Wagner*, trans. Rodney Livingstone (London: NLB, 1981), 85.
23. See my comparison of the nineteenth-century optical models deployed by the panorama and the stereoscope in *Suspensions of Perception* (Cambridge: MIT Press, 1999), 295–96.
24. Barthes, "The Reality Effect," 145.
25. Perhaps the most stunning visual treatment of this particular hilltop view of Rouen is J. M. W. Turner's watercolor, and the subsequent engraving by William Miller for the 1834 volume *Wanderings by the Seine*. Earlier, in summer 1829, to promote sales of Turner's engravings, an exhibition of his watercolors was held at the Egyptian Hall.
26. Gustave Flaubert, *Madame Bovary*, trans. Francis Steegmuller (New York: Modern Library, 1957), 299.
27. Oettermann, *The Panorama*, 47.
28. That the rescuing ship, the *Argus*, was named after a one-hundred-eyed mythological creature has struck many as an extraordinary coincidence. Less often remembered is that the full mythological name was Argus Panoptes, accidentally evoking a range of forms through which the capacities of an individual (merely mortal) human observer were exceeded, including the panorama and panopticon. Savigny and Corréard report: "One, among others said, joking, 'If the brig is sent to look for us, let us pray to God that she may have the eyes of Argus,' alluding to the name of the vessel, which we presumed would be sent after us. This consolatory idea did not quit us, and we spoke of it frequently"; *Narrative*, 132–33.

JULIA LUM

3 "Our Transporting Antipodes"

Panoramic Views of Australia and the Works of Augustus Earle

William Heath's satirical print *New Panorama,* or *A Startling Interogation* (1829), depicts a cross section of London society queuing up to attend the latest panoramic attraction (fig. 3.1). "Do you wish to go to *Hell* or *Botany-bay?* Sir," bellows the man at the ticket booth. Heath lampoons Robert Burford's evocative pairing of 360-degree panoramic paintings on view at Leicester Square, London, and the motley crowd queuing to see them. Spanning the larger of the two viewing spaces of Burford's purpose-built rotunda was the circular panorama's first foray into representing a literary theme: *Pandemonium,* an episode from John Milton's *Paradise Lost.*[1] Enveloping the smaller "Upper Circle" was *A View of the Town of Sydney, New South Wales; the Harbour of Port Jackson, and Surrounding Country,* on view from about December 1828 to December 1830 (fig. 3.2); Sydney was the site of the first penal colony in Australia and, to some European imaginations, the equivalent of Milton's underworld.[2] Three months later, Burford mounted another Australian subject at his second panorama theater, located at the Strand; *A View of Hobart Town, Van Dieman's Land and the Surrounding Country* (1831) (fig. 3.3) depicted the swiftly growing settlement in what is now known as Tasmania.[3]

Both painter and proprietor, Burford relied on a more mobile draftsman to prepare the sketches for his antipodean panoramas. The British travel artist Augustus Earle (1793–1838), based in Australia from 1825 to 1828, created the sketches for these first full-scale London panoramas of Australian landscapes. Scholars have linked Earle to the Burford panoramas, but they have never thoroughly addressed the composite structure of these massive paintings in relation to Earle's larger body of work. The striking feature of these first full-scale Australian panoramas was that Earle's original source images (adapted by Burford to create the final paintings) often disobeyed the panoramic format's utopian and illusionistic conventions. The two panoramas discussed in this chapter are infiltrated by Earle's distinctive attitudes; they reveal the dense relational networks that complicate and bring into dialogue two extreme accounts of the colony—a "heavenly" burgeoning utopian settler society on the one hand, the "hellish" amalgam of convict classes and intractable Indigenous populations on the other. Neither vision of Australia was adequate alone. The panoramas are themselves complex, hybrid works of art whose analysis presents special problems. Although their basis lay in

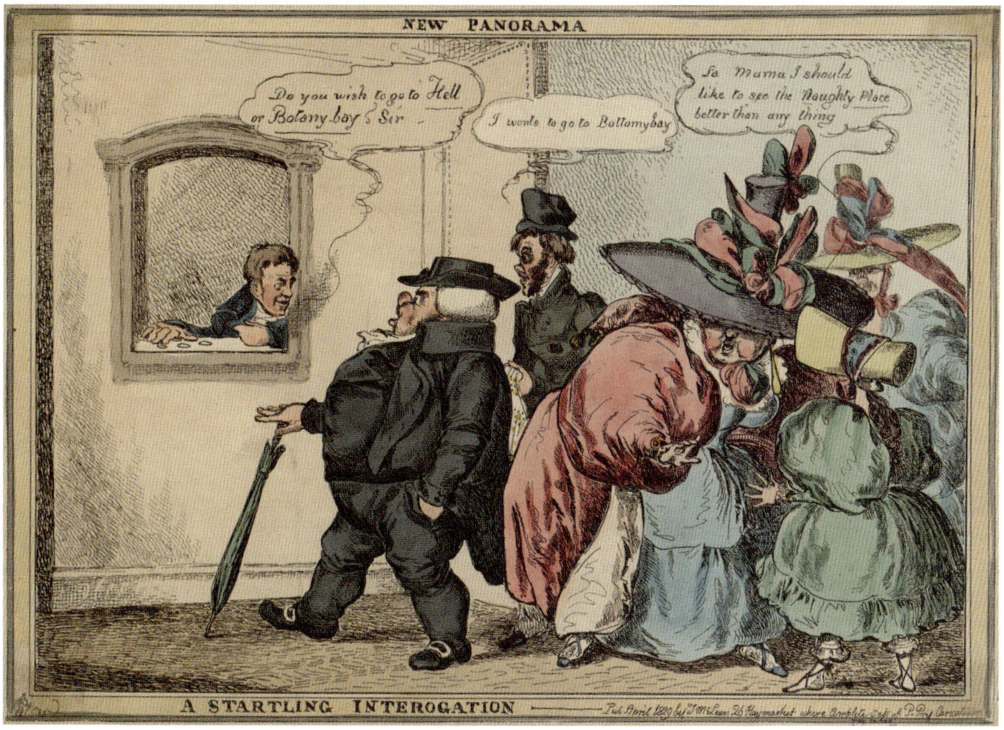

FIG. 3.1. William Heath (British, 1795–1840), *New Panorama: A Startling Interogation*, 1829. Hand-colored etching, 25.4 × 36.2 cm (10 × 14 ¼ in.). National Library of Australia, Canberra. Rex Nan Kivell Collection (nla.obj-13558140).

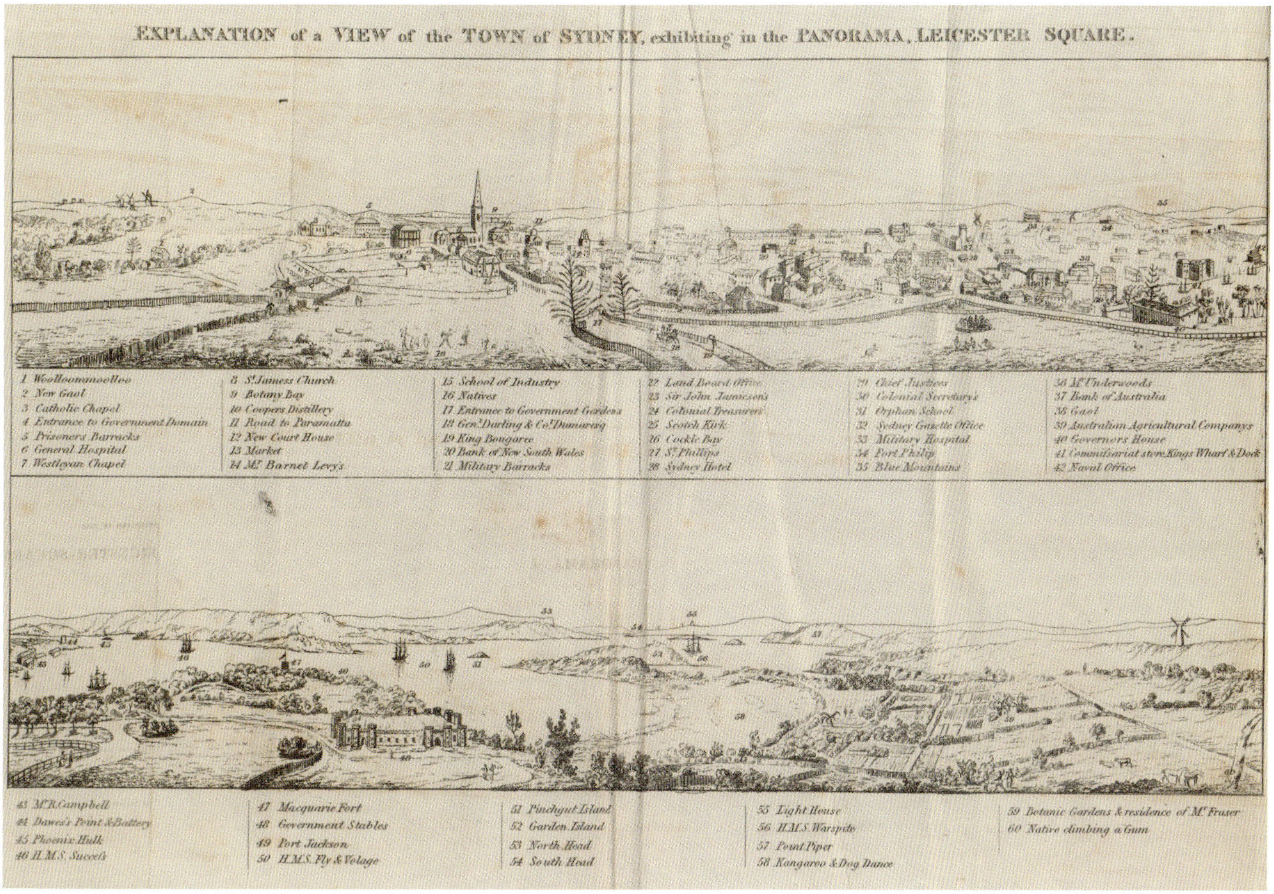

FIG. 3.2. *Explanation of a View of the Town of Sydney, Exhibiting in the Panorama, Leicester Square*, from Robert Burford, *Description of a View of the Town of Sydney, New South Wales* (London: J. and C. Adlard, 1829). Engraving, 24.6 × 37.9 cm (9 ⅝ × 15 in.). National Library of Australia, Canberra. Rex Nan Kivell Collection (nla.obj-135783763).

Earle's preparatory drawings and preexisting imagery, the 360-degree paintings were the work of at least two artists and emerged from a complex chronology of events. Moreover, the final paintings are lost and can be reconstructed only by way of the surviving printed key guides that visitors received with their admittance fees, which presents additional obstacles to analysis.

Like many sweeping New South Wales landscape images produced during the early colonial period, Burford's panorama was intended to challenge prevalent European attitudes toward the "transportation" system as much as to appeal to a metropolitan taste for distant views. London reviewers of the Burford-Earle panorama proclaimed surprise upon viewing the town of Sydney, a thriving urban colonial landscape. This was far from what early maps had marked as an antipodean non-space, a terra incognita. It showed no signs of being a site where European normativity was physically and morally inverted.[4] At first glance, moreover, it revealed anything but the expected environs for the criminal inhabitants of the "world upside down." As a *London Magazine* columnist jested: "Some of our facetious contemporaries have observed that so beautiful a representation of so beautiful a place is calculated to increase the number of 'adepts at irregular appropriation,' or rather that larcenies will be perpetuated . . . for the sole purpose of getting transported to our transporting antipodes."[5] Thus, the ironic play on *transportation*—as punitive displacement and imaginative spatio-temporal projection—articulated the deep conflicts in staging Britain's empire-building projects as topoi of leisure and entertainment.

Yet contrary to the columnist's assumptions, "transportation" and panoramic delights were both imbricated within emerging modern systems of power. The late 1780s saw the rise of three paradigmatically modern phenomena: Jeremy Bentham's panopticon, Robert Barker's panorama, and a European colony in New South Wales.[6] As vehicles of disciplinary regulation and perceptual reasoning—prisons

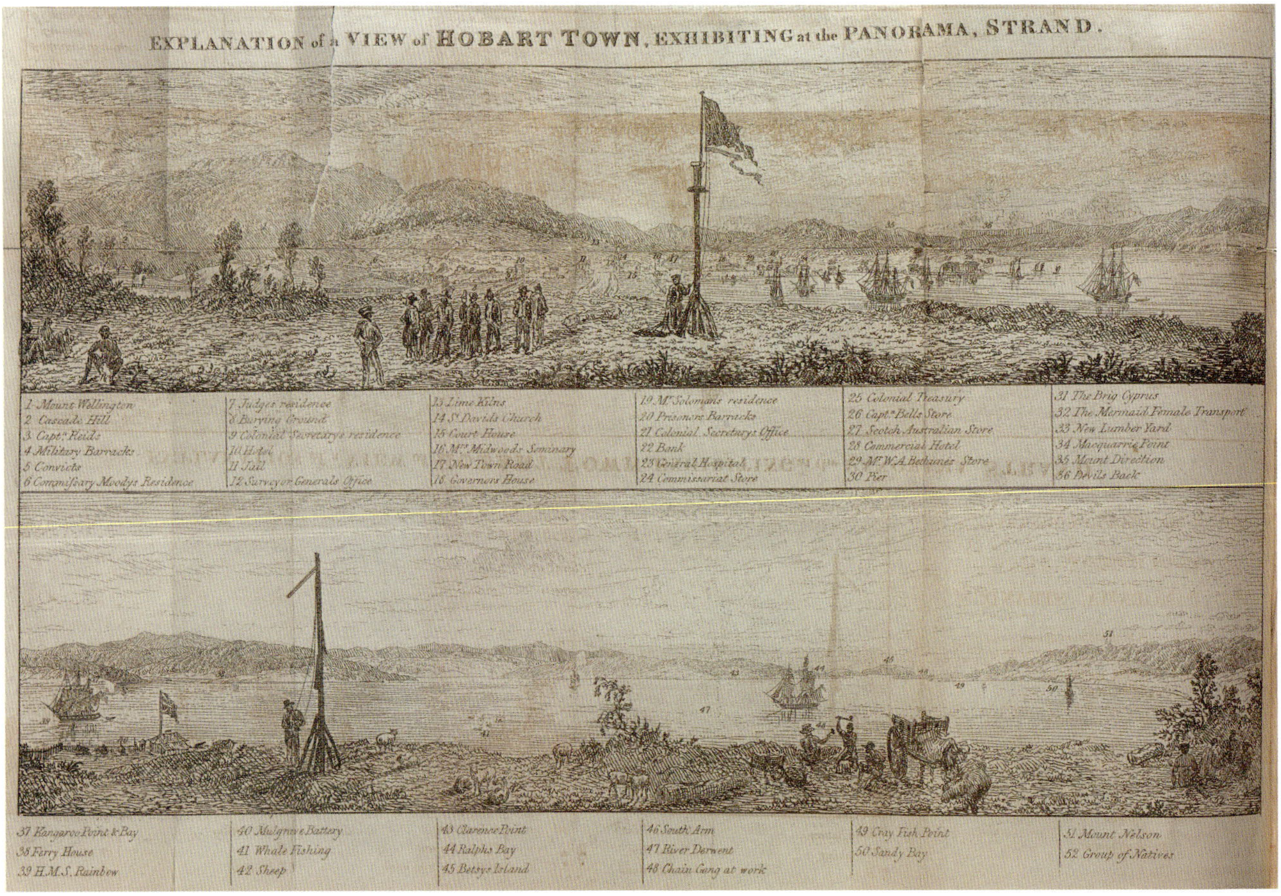

FIG. 3.3. *Explanation of a View of Hobart Town, Exhibiting at the Panorama, Strand*, from Robert Burford, *Description of a View of Hobart Town, Van Dieman's Land* (London: T. Bretell, 1831). Engraving, 28.2 × 44 cm (11 × 17.25 in.). General Collection, Beinecke Rare Book and Manuscript Library, Yale University, New Haven, Connecticut.

of the body and prisons of the eye—all three paradigms of modernity participated, by their respective methods, in the maintenance of state oversight and administrative surveillance.[7] Although it existed as a form of leisure and spectacle, moreover, the panorama influenced how travel artists like Earle recorded the landscape, creating a feedback loop at the heart of the mechanisms of imperial vision.

This chapter explores three colonial subject positions—traveling artist, convict, and Indigenous inhabitant—in relation to the early colonial Australian landscape and settler populations. Earle's work invites the viewer to engage with these multiple subject positions. Making the literal and figurative displacement of each colonial subject visible to the panorama's viewer, Earle exploited his own marginal position to complicate narrative and ideological dimensions of his composition.

The success of Burford's 360-degree panoramic paintings was contingent on accommodating radiating vision, mobile but circumscribed to the raised viewing platform. The illusion had to be sustained seamlessly. While participants were, in fact, enclosed within the bounded space of the rotunda, they were able to survey a vast distance created expressly for their eyes. This paradox has lent itself to abundant comparisons of panoramic mechanisms with Foucault's notions of panoptic vision and disciplinary surveillance.[8] But Burford and Earle's images of Sydney and Hobart challenge any straightforward application of the panoptic metaphor. The process by which Earle's imagery made its way into the London panoramas ensured that no simplistic or triumphalist account of Australia as colonial project would emerge in the final product. While Burford and his collaborators surely intended to tame the latent violence and melancholy of the burgeoning colonial project, conjuring up a palatable entertainment for the London public, their reliance on Earle's artwork as the basis of these compositions complicated any such illusionism. Earle's shifting subjectivity, with its complex narrative entry points and perspectives, became an indelible part of the viewer's panoramic experience.

By the 1820s the 360-degree panorama painting was firmly established as a commercial spectacle, and various offshoots of Barker's invention were emerging all over Europe.[9] By 1827, when Burford took over the Leicester Square panorama, panoramic exhibition was a well-known formula that promised steady audiences.[10] Both Robert and his father, John Burford, had worked under the Barkers (Robert since 1803), and both had exhibited at Academy exhibitions (Robert in 1812, 1816, and 1818). At his father's death in 1827, Robert was left sole owner of two panorama locations, at Leicester Square and the Strand.[11] The Hobart panorama was the final painting exhibited at the Strand panorama before it closed in 1831; the Leicester Square operation continued until 1861.[12]

As Tim Barringer notes in chapter 1, by the 1830s panoramas exhibited in Britain's cities increasingly underscored aims of imperialist expansion.[13] Burford, at the time London's leading panorama proprietor, gave visual form to the headlines describing outlying colonies, inviting visitors to witness progress in the empire's far reaches without having to endure the discomforts of real travel.[14] What emerged was a relay system between far-flung traveler artists and Burford's London-based painters and viewers.

Extant visual evidence of these large-scale representations can be found in the printed key pamphlets handed out to visitors. Denise Oleksijczuk notes a significant shift in key design in 1818. The radiating circular orientation, which provided an "internal viewpoint" (from which viewers could rotate the paper at will to complete their view), was replaced by two rectangular perspective views. Slicing the panorama in half, this invention displaced the emphasis from the novelty of the experiential illusion to one of fixed narrative progression.[15] This new standardized orientation, accompanied by textual labels corresponding to numbered points on the canvas, also narrowed the focus on information management by isolating for the viewer minute geographic details, structures, and landmarks. This was particularly useful when outlining foreign landscapes in colonial development under metropolitan supervision; these became sites of material as well as imaginative investment.

Burford was surely aware of the public interest in the sweeping topographical views of New South Wales, a distinct pictorial tradition that nevertheless shared a set of pictorial and ideological principles with the full-scale London panorama.[16] The long, horizontally oriented landscape view, and topographical art in general, had been formative in the British public's attempts, after the 1788 arrival of the First Fleet, to visualize the new colony. Military men, convict artists, and free settlers produced views of Sydney Cove that circulated both in New South Wales and in England. The English artist Edward Dayes engraved

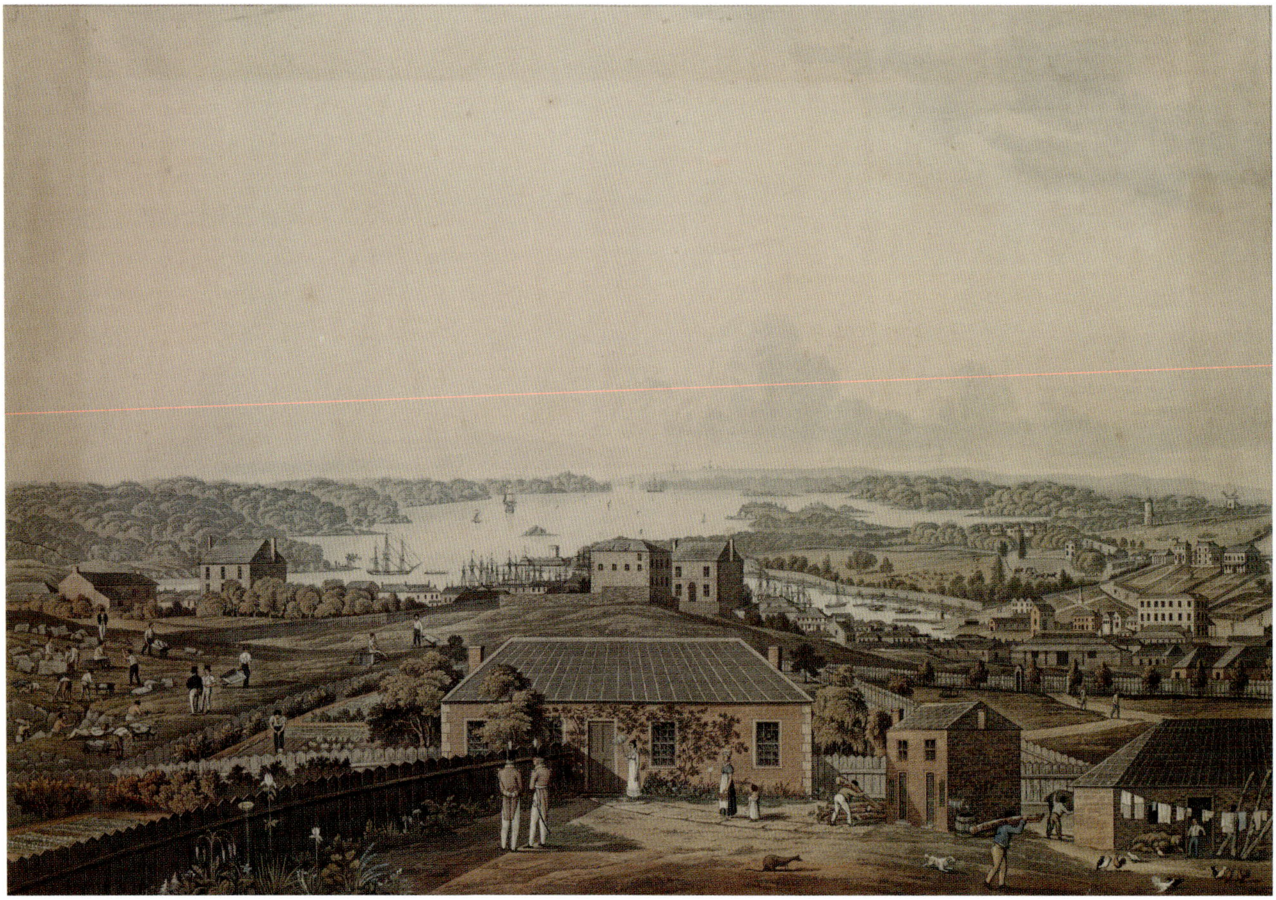

FIG. 3.4. R. Havell & Son after Major James Taylor (Australian, 1785–1829), *The Entrance of Port Jackson and Part of the Town of Sydney, New South Wales*, ca. 1821. State Library of New South Wales, Sydney (V1/ca. 1821/4 | V1/ca. 1821/5 | V1/ca. 1821/6).

some of the earliest prospects of Sydney Cove; in 1805 he wrote that such compositions should include a variety of figures, but that the "low and vulgar should be carefully avoided."[17] Convicts were rarely depicted, but anonymous Indigenous figures became a naturalized feature of the colony's outskirts, signifying a measure of the colony's advancement from its so-called primitive origins.[18]

In 1823–24 Robert Havell, following James Taylor's watercolors, produced one of the most widely circulated sets of engraved panoramic views (fig. 3.4). Taylor, a major in the 48th Regiment, made three views from a single position on what is now known as Observatory Hill, Sydney.[19] Executed during the governorship of Lachlan Macquarie, Taylor's views capture the city newly touched by large-scale civic improvement schemes.[20] With the help of the convict architect Francis Greenway, Macquarie introduced ordered streets and public buildings, including the new leisure space of Hyde Park, the prisoner's barracks, the hospital, St. James Church, and a lighthouse—a signal to incoming convicts and settlers that Port Jackson awaited.[21] Taylor's accompanying texts single out these architectural improvements; they later figure likewise in Burford's 1829 panorama. Government officials were astutely aware of the political gains that artistic views such as Taylor's could yield, especially in response to the recent commission sent from London to investigate the supposed extravagance and leniency of Macquarie's leadership.[22]

Taylor's views were sent to be engraved and published in London, but they probably were never transformed into a 360-degree painting of the kind pioneered by the Barkers and Burfords. Accounts suggest panoramic entertainments did not take hold in Australia until the late 1830s. Yet the colony's settlers had significant stakes in the ways their landscape was represented in England.[23] Offering a broad sweep of terrain on horizontally extended supports, Taylor's landscape images resemble 360-degree paintings in replicating a view beyond the lateral range of vision.

They show the panoramic format as a useful tool to verify colonial progress and military surveillance, an incentive to settlement and capital investment. As propaganda vehicles, such long landscape views allowed London viewers to judge each successive New South Wales governor's progress in developing a wild landscape into well-ordered urban commercial space. For New South Wales settlers, these views also counteracted European stereotypes about a landscape tarnished by its convict population. During an extended trip to England in 1820, Alexander Riley, a Sydney pastoralist and merchant, sent eighteen sheets of drawing paper to his brother Edward, still at Sydney, instructing Edward to search for a competent artist for preparatory work on a full-scale 360-degree London panorama: "We are so largely interested in drawing a public attention to the Colony and in awaking a due degree of Interest toward it that the risk is well worth running for if the plan succeeds. I do not know any measures more likely to certainly call forth the curiosity of all."[24] With their aura of factual accuracy combined with the immediacy of the illusion, such delineations of landmarks were highly effective visually and ideologically.[25]

The merchant's ambition to see a full-scale panorama would remain unfulfilled until Robert Burford successfully mounted his 1829 view of Sydney (based on Earle's drawings).[26] Burford didn't stop with Sydney; embracing increasingly remote subjects, he employed Earle's travel images to depict various stages of colonization in the Southern Hemisphere. Moving on to the more recent settlement of Hobart in Van Diemen's Land (and finishing with the Bay of Islands, New Zealand, Burford's third antipodean panorama based on Earle's sketches), the successive views underscored the progress made by colonial officials in Sydney and retroactively guaranteed the civilizing potential of the incipient settlements.[27] The following discussions of three mobile subject positions contextualize Burford's (and, by extension, Earle's) panoramas in their fraught—sometimes failed—attempts to renovate a terra incognita into a *terra nullius*: an uninhabited land of both "invasion" and "utopia."[28]

Professionally trained yet itinerant in both genre and geography, Augustus Earle has been identified by scholars as one of the first artists to introduce the European romantic landscape tradition to the new colony. And yet his work also complicates the dichotomy between an imported a priori European tradition and the notion of articulating the Australian landscape in its truth (distilled to the problems of *prototype* and *imitation*), a predicament that Rex Butler argues has long beset Australian art historians.[29] Earle's works are of interest to scholars particularly because they often refuse to breach this gap, interested more in enunciating this space than forcing its semiotic closure.[30]

Earle's images differ from those of his traveler-artist predecessor William Hodges, given Earle's lack of interest in using picturesque formulas to shape an idyllic image of the antipodes. His works do reference landscape conventions, yet they often run athwart of them; Earle inserts jarring planar recessions and figures who point mysteriously to compositional voids. And he celebrates those "vulgar" characters so despised by Edward Dayes. Earle's most enigmatic works reveal those charged spaces of cultural collision that can merely be hinted at, not fully articulated through pictorial representation.

As the official artist on the second Cook voyage (1772–75), Hodges was tethered to his commission; Earle, by contrast, remained free from any Admiralty oversight or scientific mandate.[31] His thirst for adventure and artistic subject matter was cultivated from an early age, with transatlantic and artistic roots on both sides of the family. He was born in England to the American portrait painter James Earl (1761–1796) and Caroline Smyth (1759–1838), the widow of the American Tory Joseph Smyth.[32] His uncle Ralph Earl (1751–1801) is best known as an American history painter and portraitist who emigrated to England to study at the Royal Academy.[33] In 1806, while still an adolescent, Earle exhibited *Judgment of Midas* at the Royal Academy, followed by *Battle of Poitiers* (1808) and *Caius Marcius Taking Possession of the City of Corioli* (1809).[34] Along with the American expatriate artists Charles Robert Leslie and Samuel F. B. Morse, Earle perhaps visited Benjamin West's London studio for tutelage.[35] He may have also been influenced by the work of William and Thomas Daniell, onetime Fitzroy Square neighbors whose *Oriental Scenery* (1795–1808) exemplified the transference of picturesque and marine painting conventions onto an "exotic" Indian landscape. During a stay in Madras, Earle himself took up Indian subjects, providing preparatory sketches for William Daniell and E. T. Parris's London panorama *A View of Madras* (1830).[36]

Despite these professional and institutional ties, Earle marked himself almost from the outset as a nomadic

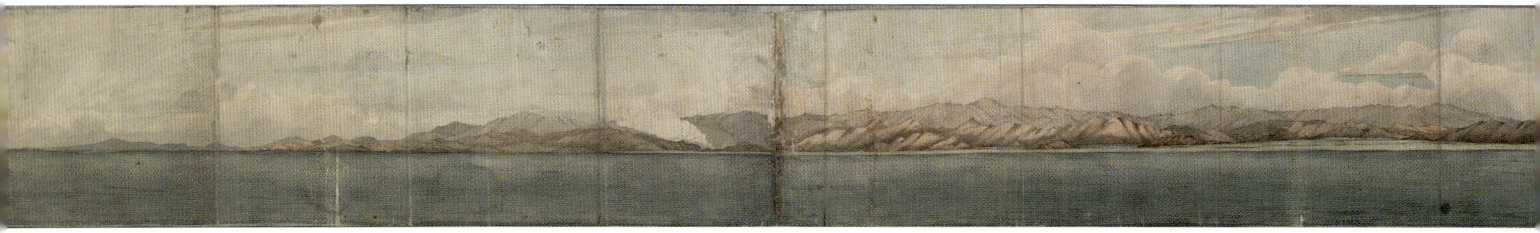

FIG. 3.5. Augustus Earle (British, 1793–1838), *Lima, Callao, Island of St. Lorenzo*, ca. 1820. Watercolor, 14.6 × 54.6 cm (5 ¾ × 21 ½ in.). National Library of Australia, Canberra. Rex Nan Kivell Collection (nla.obj-138471452).

artist.[37] After setting out for the Mediterranean, he traveled in varied parts of the globe, including the United States, Brazil, Australia, New Zealand, the Philippines, India, and Mauritius.[38] His capacity as official artist on the *Beagle* in 1831 (a post declining health forced him to cede to Conrad Martens) was Earle's only "official" voyage commission. Between travels, he exhibited canvases of his travel subjects to metropolitan viewers.[39] He also garnered significant colonial patronage by executing portraits at ports of call such as Sydney, where the colony's elite was eager to sit for a professional artist.

Although he resided in New South Wales only from 1825 to 1827, visiting again briefly in 1828, Earle made significant contributions to Sydney's artistic development.[40] In 1826 he opened Sydney's first art gallery, exhibiting thirty paintings "much visited by the youths of the colony . . . [having] considerable influence in promoting good taste amongst the rising generation," as the Reverend J. McGarvie recalled in his 1829 editorial "On the State of Fine Arts in New South Wales."[41] In 1826 Earle also advertised his intentions of opening an art school, and shortly thereafter he obtained the colony's first lithographic press, on which he produced the series *Views in Australia,* with an accompanying text.[42] Yet despite attempts to integrate himself into Sydney society, Earle remained an outsider. Denied the grant of a tract of land because he had not sufficiently proved himself capable of raising the capital, he once more took up his wandering.[43]

Earle created works inflected by a romantic sensibility and an attentiveness to economic demands; unsurprisingly, he wished to partner with Burford, adapting his work for presentation as a panorama, which would pay him one hundred guineas.[44] The popularity of travel accounts and engravings surely fed the metropole's development of panoramic entertainments. Several of Earle's works seem to anticipate translation into panoramic format, suggesting the panorama's commercial success also shaped the composition of travel views. Possibly under the Daniells' influence, Earle executed many works in a flat, linear format of unusually horizontal height-to-width ratio, often doubling the angle of vision, which suggests many of his works were intended to be adaptable to panoramas. In 1820, well before he knew Sydney, Earle completed a four-section watercolor study, mounted on cloth, of Lima, Callao, and San Lorenzo (fig. 3.5). While the monotonous composition of sea and mountain ranges most closely resembles a coastal profile, a standard form of naval draftsmanship, the annotation and circular extent indicate the image was intended as a study for a full-scale panorama depicting Lord Cochrane's strategic blockade of Callao harbor.[45]

Yet between Lima and Sydney, Earle's panoramic style clearly evolved. Whereas predecessors like Taylor focused on the bustling activity and spectrum of social classes in Sydney's immediate foreground, the Burford-Earle view (see fig. 3.2) telescopes back to a distant Archimedean point. Taylor's view highlights Macquarie's civic improvements; Earle's view vindicates Governor Darling's regime at a time when it too was under attack and endorses Darling's extension of the colony's boundary.[46] Although Burford's panorama is no longer extant, its key outlines a broad, sweeping view of Port Jackson Harbor, the government territories, and the distant mountains from an elevated position, hovering halfway between the traditional "prospect" and the imaginary "bird's eye."[47]

As the accompanying pamphlet explains, the view was sketched from the location of the future governor's house, thus assertively locating its surveying view from the projected center of administrative colonial power. The first governor's house (no. 40 on the key), "the back of which is towards the spectator," is deemed outmoded, given its "rather mean" outward appearance.[48] Earle's view was probably sketched from the top of John Palmer's windmill (which may at one time have been proposed as a site for the future government house; the new governor's

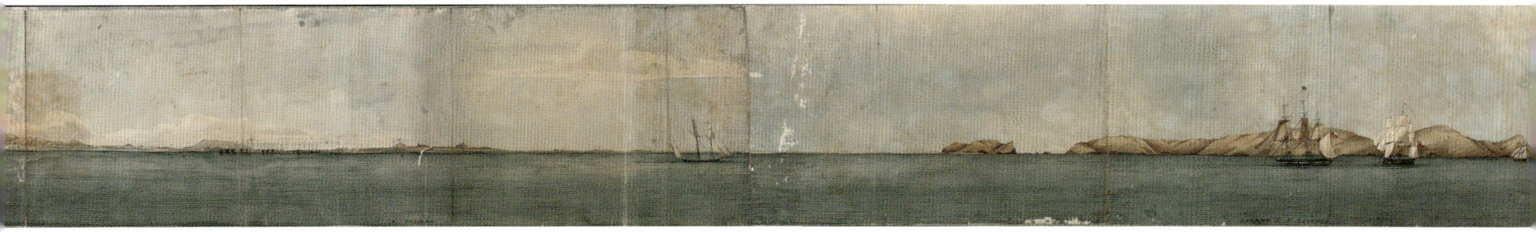

house, built in 1837, would be constructed closer to the water's edge). Palmer, one of the colony's first arrivals, was a wealthy, influential landowner, businessman, and shipowner who leased government land in 1802. Palmer's windmill, the key suggests, was perched on "the highest part of the Government Domain."[49] The windmills dotting the Sydney skyline, along with Palmer's agricultural innovations, became symbols of the colony's efficient food production and rapid progress.[50] Yet the assertive alignment between Earle's viewpoint and the governor's prospect also points to tensions between private landholders and government officials (since Macquarie intended this land for his stables).[51] By the time Earle arrived at Sydney, lease land had been expropriated from Palmer; the distinctive castellated stables (now the Conservatorium) dominate Earle's foreground (no. 48).

If foreground coordinates represented civic progress, a spot sitting on the horizon, at the vanishing point, projected the colony's anticipated expansion. Earle was sketching for the panorama by February 1827 under the supervision of Colonel Henry Dumaresq, who that July took the preparatory work directly to Burford in London.[52] Dumaresq was superintendent of the newly improved roads through the Blue Mountains (no. 35 on the key), which in previous decades were believed impassable. First rendered traversable in 1813 under Macquarie, the Blue Mountains heralded the pastoral paradise of unquantifiable vastness beyond their veil—"a most fertile description to an amazing distance."[53] While ruminating on immediate "improvements," the spectator is also invited to imagine and anticipate territories beyond the realm of vision.

While the Burford-Earle panorama reads as a propagandistic extension of the colonial administration's agenda, an examination of Earle's larger body of Australian works—including a set of enigmatic travel watercolors—challenges this reading of the Burford commission.[54] On a sketching trip to Illawarra and Prospect Hill, Earle depicted the farm of William Lawson, famous as one of the first three surveyors to lead a successful expedition through the Blue Mountains (fig. 3.6). He was rewarded with one thousand acres west of the ranges, on which he established pastoral tracts, effectively opening up the Bathurst region for settlement and growth.[55] Yet Earle's watercolor is not a typical English estate portrait. The foreground is dominated by the roadway leading to the farm, its angular convex fence occupying most of the right half of the image. A figure with tattered clothing and rifle stalks toward the viewer. Bending along the roadway is a fence reminiscent of the enclosures that crisscross the Burford-Earle panorama's foreground. This is no pastoral idyll.

This unsettling work is no exception within Earle's oeuvre, where figures are often situated uncomfortably in relation to their surroundings. Leonard Bell argues that many of the figures within Earle's compositions operate as viewer surrogates. If we accept this proposition, Earle's diverse assemblage of figures opens up multiple narrative possibilities.[56] These spatial and temporal compressions of unfolding social relations in the space of a canvas elicit plural ways of "being in or behaving in . . . landscape," perhaps modeled after Earle's own unmoored relation to his environment.[57]

Before setting foot in Australia in 1825, Earle was stranded for eight months on the remote South Atlantic island of Tristan da Cunha, where he created numerous sketches of a desolate landscape populated by only himself and his dog. Lamenting his experience as the island's "prisoner," he wrote: "From one week's end to another I station myself upon the rocks, straining my eyes with looking along the horizon in search of a sail" (fig. 3.7). Earle's rescue ship transported him to another island—Van Diemen's Land—and a landscape colored by his recent exile at Tristan da Cunha.

A panorama of Hobart Town (Van Diemen's Land) was Earle's second work for Burford. In the surviving

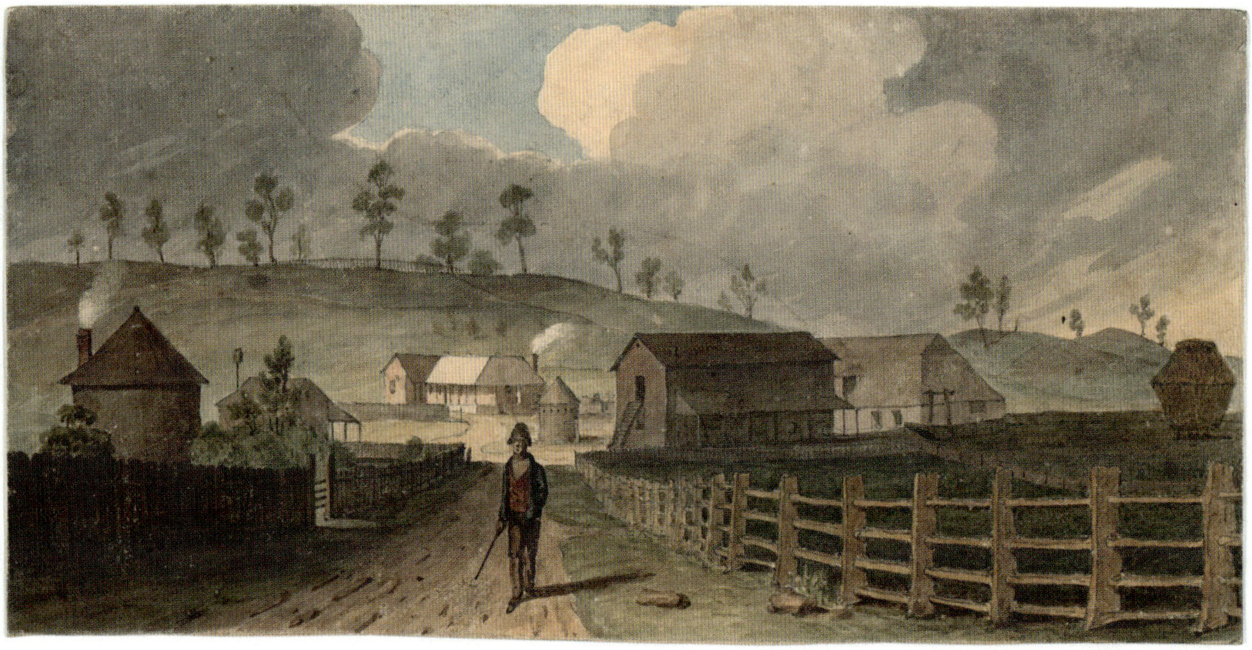

FIG. 3.6. Augustus Earle, *The Farm House of W. Lawson Esqre., N.S. Wales*, ca. 1826. Watercolor, 12.7 × 25.7 cm (5 × 10 1/8 in.). National Library of Australia, Canberra. Rex Nan Kivell Collection (nla.obj-134496573).

preparatory study (fig. 3.8), only two figures are visible in the rocky terrain of Earle's initial composition: a lone sailor changing flag signals, and another figure manipulating the arms of a semaphore station. They command the viewer's attention, while Hobart remains at a distance, partially occluded by a hillside.[58] The privileged foreground and the curtained-off settlement are unusual in contrast to full shipboard views of the settlement from the Derwent River (fig. 3.9).[59]

In lieu of picturesque gum trees, forlorn wooden posts beside the two figures compensate as a *repoussoir*. But they also signify rudimentary, coded communication with the outside world. Scanning the horizon for distant ships, the flag and the semaphore operators are remarkably similar in appearance to Earle's self-portrait in a Tristan da Cunha image, stationing his solitary figure, in seaman's uniform, by a flagpole (fig. 3.10). Given the visual affinities between this image and the sailor in the panorama, and Earle's penchant for including his own figure in landscape imagery, these panoramic passages can be read as self-reflexive quotations of his Tristan da Cunha imagery. Indeed, they gesture toward the coextension of Earle's ontological unmooring and his literal abandonment in the landscape.

The prominent wooden signals themselves contain keys to autobiographical content. Semaphore signals (explained by a chart in the *Hobart-Town Almanack*; fig. 3.11) transmitted information about the movement of vessels from Mount Nelson, where ship activity was most perceptible, to Mulgrave Battery. Depending on the angle of vision—from the panorama viewer's position or, alternatively, from Mount Nelson—the semaphore, with its third arm in the process of being raised or lowered, could read as "vessel seen is a ship," "ditto a brig," "vessel coming in, has got into Storm Bay passage," "The brig seen is gone into [Frederick Henry Bay]," or even "the vessel is from England with prisoners." The red pennant and yellow flag signals more conclusively denote a brig (fig. 3.12).[60] The only brig (smaller vessels with two square-rigged masts) demarcated in the Burford panorama, yet strangely absent from Earle's handwritten annotations, is the government brig *Cyprus*, which conveyed Earle from Hobart to Sydney in 1825.[61] Also visible in the harbor is the HMS *Rainbow*, the ship that took Earle to Madras in 1828, briefly stopping in Hobart that October and November.[62] The inclusion of these two ships in the final painting reveals that Earle's biographical valence has been partially perpetuated by Burford. The associations oscillate between mobility (for Earle and other free passengers) and stasis (for the convicts on shore and locked up in the ships' holds).

With its two lonely figures standing in a barren tract of land, signifying not by words or bodily gestures but wooden symbolic proxies, Earle's Hobart panorama

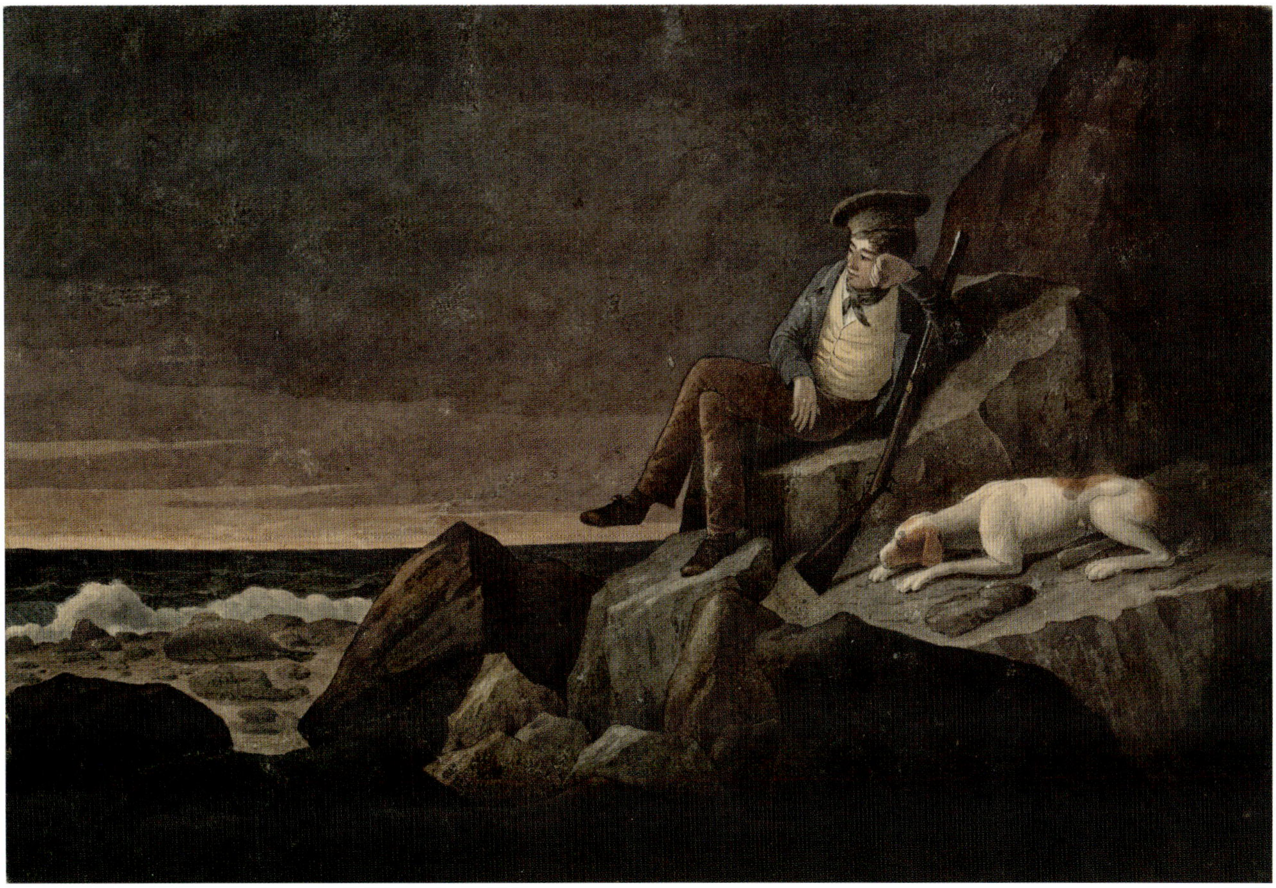

FIG. 3.7. Augustus Earle, *Solitude, Watching the Horizon at Sun Set, in the Hopes of Seeing a Vessel, Tristan de Acunha in the South Atlantic*, 1824. Watercolor, 17.5 × 25.7 cm (6 ⅞ × 10 ⅛ in.). National Library of Australia, Canberra. Rex Nan Kivell Collection (nla.obj-134493611).

conjures up the aesthetics of exile permeating early Australian writing and artistic production. Ian McLean locates Australia's psychology of melancholia in the search for an oceanic utopia, arguing that longing for a horizon paradoxically signifies immobility.[63] Earle may have been familiar with the convict artist Thomas Watling, whose 1794 *Letters from an Exile at Botany Bay* describe the Australian landscape as a pastoral *unheimlich*: "The face of the country is deceitful; having every appearance of fertility; and yet productive of no one article in itself fit for the support of mankind."[64] Watling's observations of Sydney offer a textual analogue to the rocky, brown earth mass dominating Earle's foreground (see fig. 3.8).

Earle was not alone in his ambivalence toward the Australian penal experiment. Since 1787, the British government had dispatched convicted criminals to New South Wales; most convicts were assigned to settlers as free laborers.[65] Security was promised by way of distance: as Jeremy Bentham notes in his pamphlet *Panopticon versus New South Wales* (1802), Australia is "farther from the mother country than the farthest port in the East Indies."[66] From the sixteenth century onward, forced labor in open-air prisons was increasingly seen as a solution to worker shortages and urban poverty.[67] By the end of the eighteenth century, however, the benefits of the transportation "solution" were questioned, and Bentham acted as the major proponent of the "Inspection-House" or panopticon prison model. Railing against the New South Wales penal colony, which he argued violated habeas corpus by illegally detaining convicts after their sentences, Bentham strove to demonstrate that his prison model would reduce costs and would effect reform among the urban population. Bentham contrasted the close, proximate scrutiny his scheme offered with the distant "loose confinement" of the depraved Australian convict population.[68]

Bentham's tract had little effect on colonial administrators. A year later, New South Wales governor Philip Gidley King sent a small party of convicts to establish a

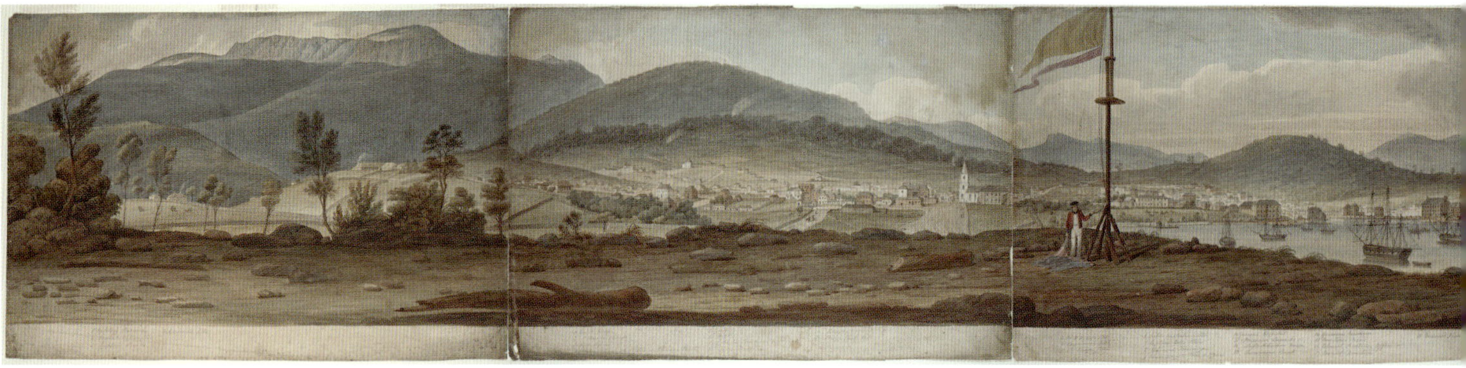

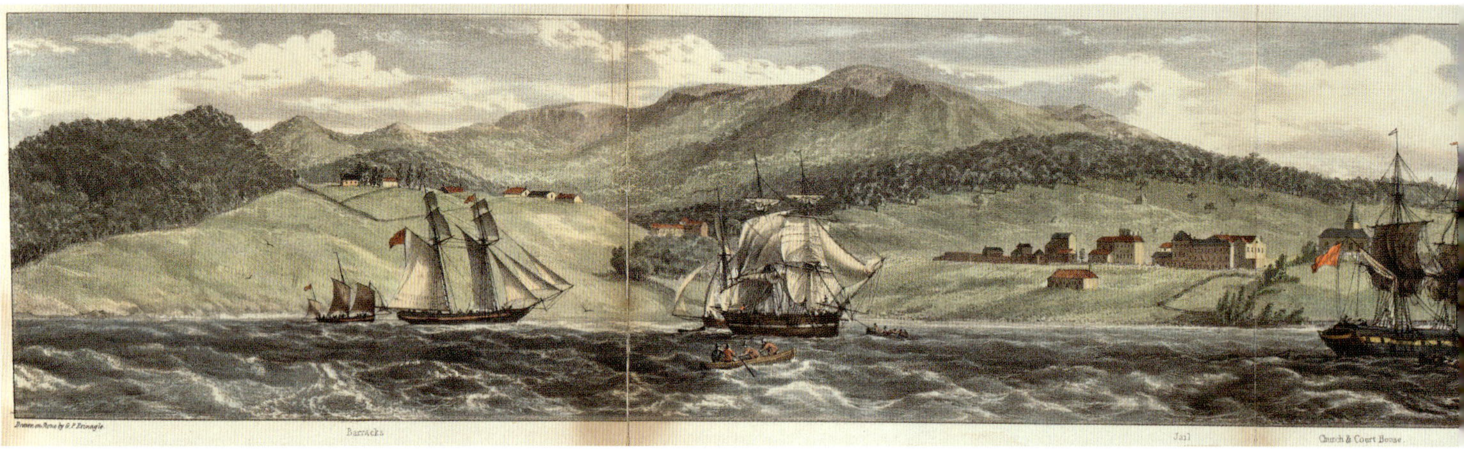

FIG. 3.8. Augustus Earle, *Panorama of Hobart*, ca. 1828. Set of six watercolor drawings, totaling approx. 37 × 222 cm (14 5/8 × 87 3/8 in.). State Library of New South Wales, Sydney (DGD 14).

FIG. 3.9. George Philip Reinagle (British, 1802–1835), *Panoramic View of Hobarton*, from *Princep's Journal of a Voyage from Calcutta to Van Diemen's Land* (London: Smith & Elder, 1833). Lithograph on paper, 15.4 × 79 cm (6 × 31 in.). National Library of Australia, Canberra. Rex Nan Kivell Collection (nla.obj-138469126).

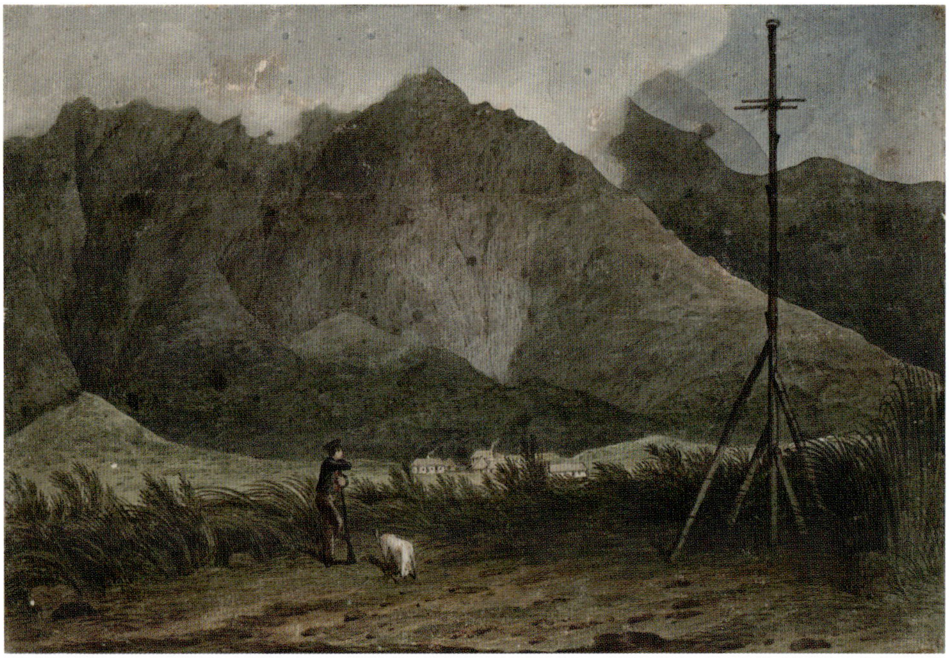

FIG. 3.10. Augustus Earle, *Tristan de Acunha*, ca. 1824. Watercolor, 17.5 × 26 cm (6 7/8 × 10 1/4 in.). National Library of Australia, Canberra. Rex Nan Kivell Collection (nla.obj-134494299).

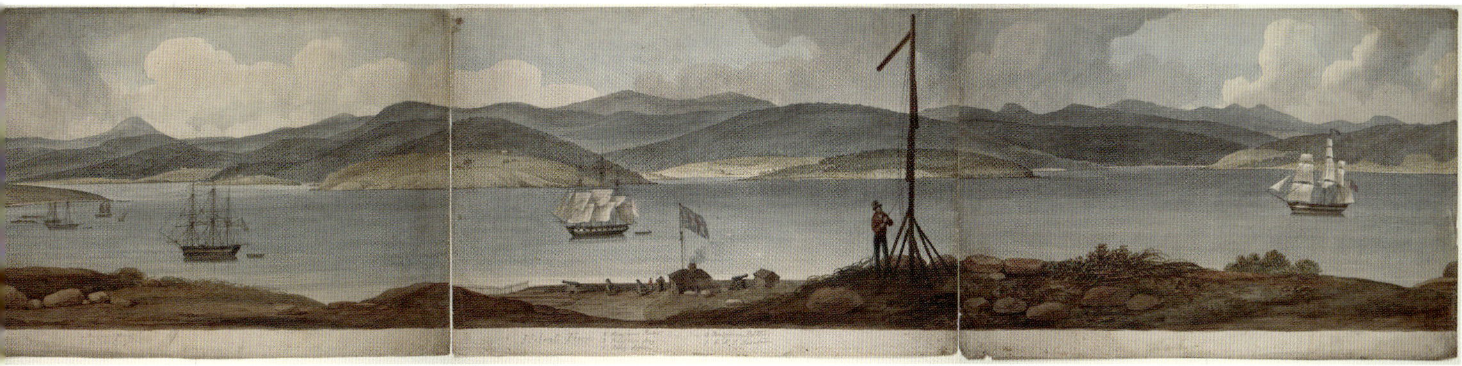

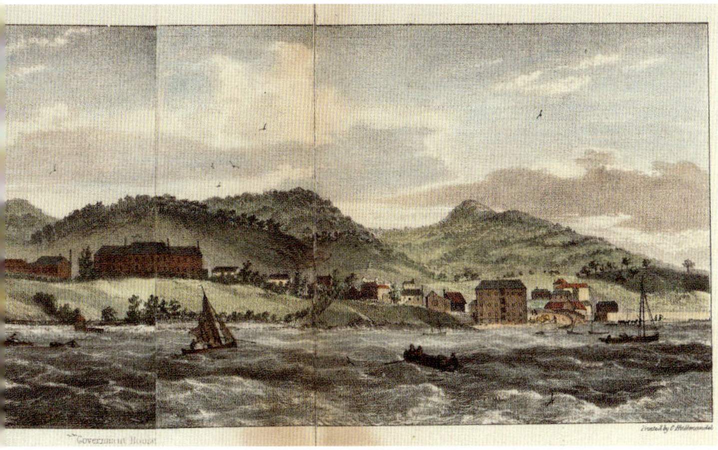

new penal settlement in Van Dieman's Land, on the banks of the Derwent.[69] In the Australian penal system, hardened offenders were sent to Norfolk Island to live out a life sentence; a second class convicted of lesser offenses and deemed capable of reform was sent to New South Wales or Van Diemen's Land to work on roads and public works; a third class was sent to the colonies as free settlers.[70] When Burford's panorama was exhibited, less than thirty years later, Hobart was rapidly developing, its population approximately 6,000 inhabitants, including 2,500 adult prisoners.[71]

Defenders of penal colony reform, including the early Hobart historian Henry Walter Parker, praised the internalized measures of surveillance achieved through the settler-convict relationship. Just as dependent on visual observation as Bentham's panopticism, the assignment system meant a distribution of surveillance mechanisms outside and beyond state control. The convict, Parker explained, "is watched and admonished at every step; he cannot commit the least inaccuracy, but it is remarked and corrected, while at the same time, he has the satisfaction of knowing that if he does right . . . his conduct is observed and appreciated."[72] This model of reform is equally predicated on the convict's sensory intake: "Every thing, indeed, he sees and hears is calculated to make the strongest impressions on him."[73]

If this social system of internal regulation is not evident in Earle's preparatory watercolor, it is certainly visible in Burford's finished version. Burford added Indigenous figures and livestock to the foreground, while transforming the plane of gray-brown rock into undulating pastureland (see figs. 3.3 and 3.8). The city remains in the distance, set into the hills, and retains the majority of Earle's original textual labels of public offices and private stores, with a few additions.[74] Burford also removed a few points of interest from Earle's original drawing, including a man and woman promenading at the outskirts of the settlement (fig. 3.13). Almost directly below the couple the word *Prisoners* appears, perhaps written by Burford or one of his assistants, as this handwriting differs from Earle's.[75] The status of the ambiguous "prisoners" notation remains decidedly unstable, much like convict visibility in the colony's early decades.[76]

"Prisoners" might have been Burford's instructions to transplant a group of convicts and a "chain gang at work" into the scene, superimposed over the pair. Although they leave no doubt about the criminal status of their subjects, these source images—derived from Earle's New South Wales works—complicate the picture of a self-sustaining and self-reforming society.[77] The panorama's row of standing prisoners derives from Earle's lithograph *A Government Jail Gang, Sydney, N.S. Wales* (figs. 3.14, 3.15), an unmistakable caricature of criminal typologies and unreformed personalities, men to be loathed rather than to be considered the basis of a new social order.[78] No prevailing social ranks escape Earle's biting characterization: the barefooted prisoners in their tattered clothing make a mockery of civil society by donning the settler and

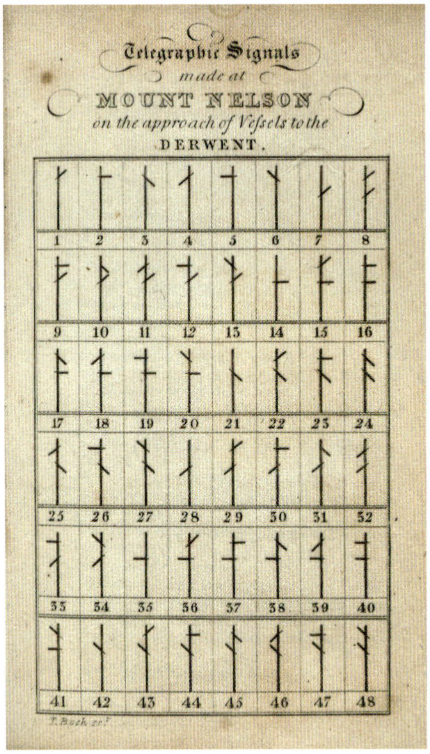

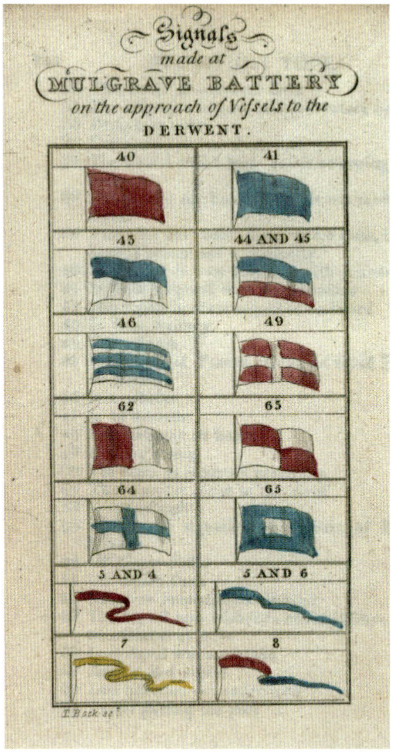

FIG. 3.11. "Telegraphic Signals Made at Mount Nelson on the Approach of Vessels to the Derwent," from *The Van Diemen's Land Anniversary and Hobart-Town Almanack for the Year 1831* (Hobart-Town: Janes Ross, 1831). National Library of Australia, Canberra. Rex Nan Kivell Collection (NK607).

FIG. 3.12. "Signals Made at Mulgrave Battery on the Approach of Vessels to the Derwent," from *The Van Diemen's Land Anniversary and Hobart-Town Almanack for the Year 1831* (Hobart-Town: Janes Ross, 1831). National Library of Australia, Canberra. Rex Nan Kivell Collection (NK607).

sailor castoffs; the unscrupulous-looking turnkey appears no more dignified than the men standing to his right.[79] *A Government Jail Gang* was published in a lithographic series Earle executed upon his 1830 return to England, painting a far more undesirable picture of Australian society than his previous works in the colony.[80]

Burford's "chain gang" group derive from Earle's earlier, unpublished watercolor *View from the Summit of Mount York* (ca. 1826) (fig. 3.16), depicting convicts breaking stones under an overseer's gaze. Their labor, invisible in the Sydney panorama's pamphlet, forged Colonel Dumaresq's roads through the Blue Mountains. Earle's convicts bear the signs of their task's mechanical drudgery, and they break with Claudean conventions. Where followers of Claude such as Richard Wilson allowed Georgic figures to carry out their labor under the benevolent protection of British estate owners, Earle's image shows convict laborers struggling to lift hammers above their heads under a young officer's indolent gaze.[81] By carrying these figures into the panorama, Burford imports the troubling, unresolved oppositions inherent in Earle's New South Wales work.

In this second Australian panorama, Burford invites the metropolitan masses to scrutinize the displacement of its criminal classes—to act, in effect, as both overseers *and* inmates. As a *Literary Gazette* reviewer observed, Burford's "ragged" and "squalid" convicts have "plenty of room for every thing except to commit depredations or run away. We think the panorama ought to be opened gratuitously, or at the public cost, one day in the week, as a moral lesson to 'the Swell Mob.'"[82] The London viewer could be satisfied that the city's petty thieves were now compelled toward self-improvement; another reviewer reminds us that "groups of convicts enliven the picture—we had almost said en*lighten* it, from recollection of the picking propensities to which hundreds of them are indebted for their abode here."[83] The reviewers hoped that the undetected thieves among the crowds of panorama-goers would be sufficiently moved to regulate their own behavior, but as their commentary also reveals, the painting barely served to contain or subdue the convict bodies once "transported."

If the incorporation of convict bodies into a pastoral scene struck a jarring note, the bodies of Indigenous peoples presented an equally alarming breach of pictorial convention: "Why, Mr. Burford, did you introduce into such a paradise, the nasty naked savages, and the fettered gangs of worse than savages!" cried the *Athenaeum*'s reviewer.[84] Although Van Diemen's Land's Indigenous figures are

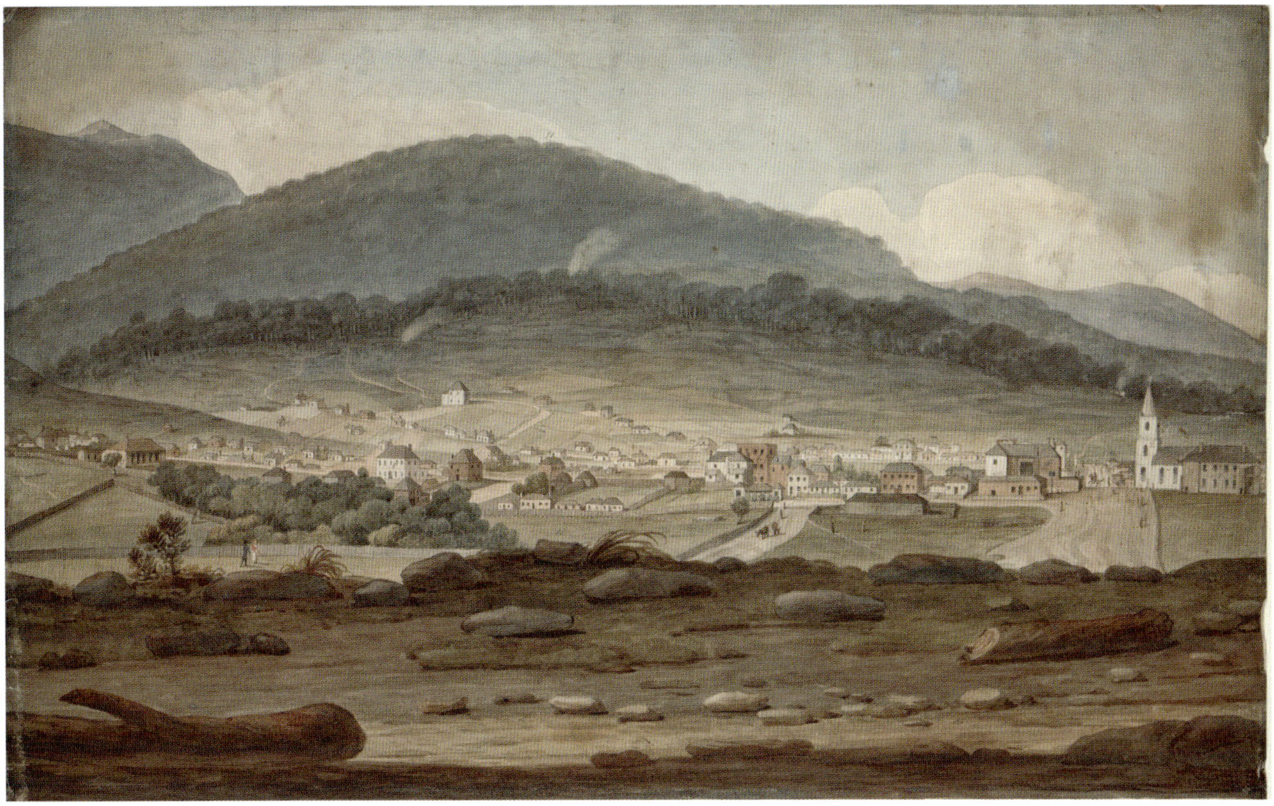

FIG. 3.13. Detail of fig. 3.8.

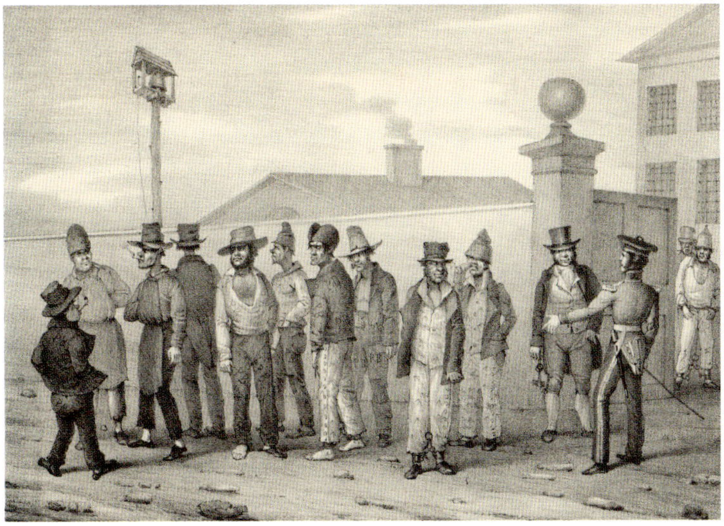

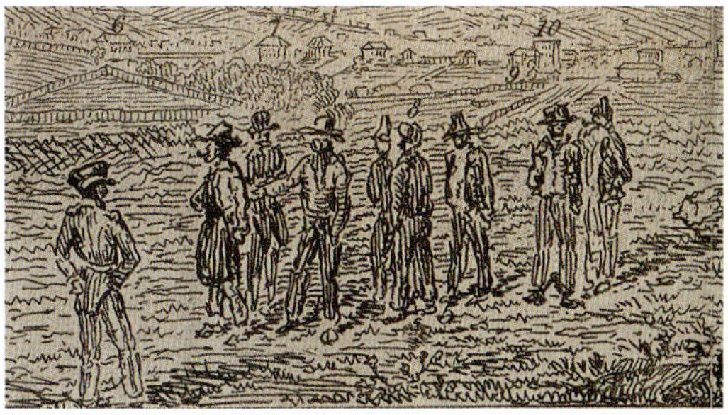

(LEFT) FIG. 3.14. Augustus Earle, *A Government Jail Gang, Sydney, N.S. Wales*, plate no. 3 of part 2 of *Views in New South Wales and Van Diemens Land, Australian Scrap Book* (London: J. Cross, 1830). Lithograph, 28 × 37.6 cm (11 × 14 ¾ in.). National Library of Australia, Canberra (nla.obj-184754078).

(ABOVE) FIG. 3.15. Detail of fig. 3.3.

relegated to an unimportant spot in Buford's composition, their very visibility sets up another discontinuity with a unified, utopian image (fig. 3.17). In reality, Indigenous Tasmanians endured forced expulsion from their homelands. Clashes between British settlers and Tasmania's Indigenous people began in 1804 and reached their height in the 1820s as the rapidly expanding European population expropriated hunting grounds and created competition for resources.[85] Conflict escalated as settlers abducted numerous Indigenous women for sexual exploitation and children for labor. Tasmanian Indigenous nations began full-scale guerrilla warfare in 1826; in the following years, they carried out hundreds of attacks.[86] Declaring martial law in 1828, Governor Arthur effectively legalized mass killings of clanspeople.[87]

In October 1831, while Burford's Hobart panorama

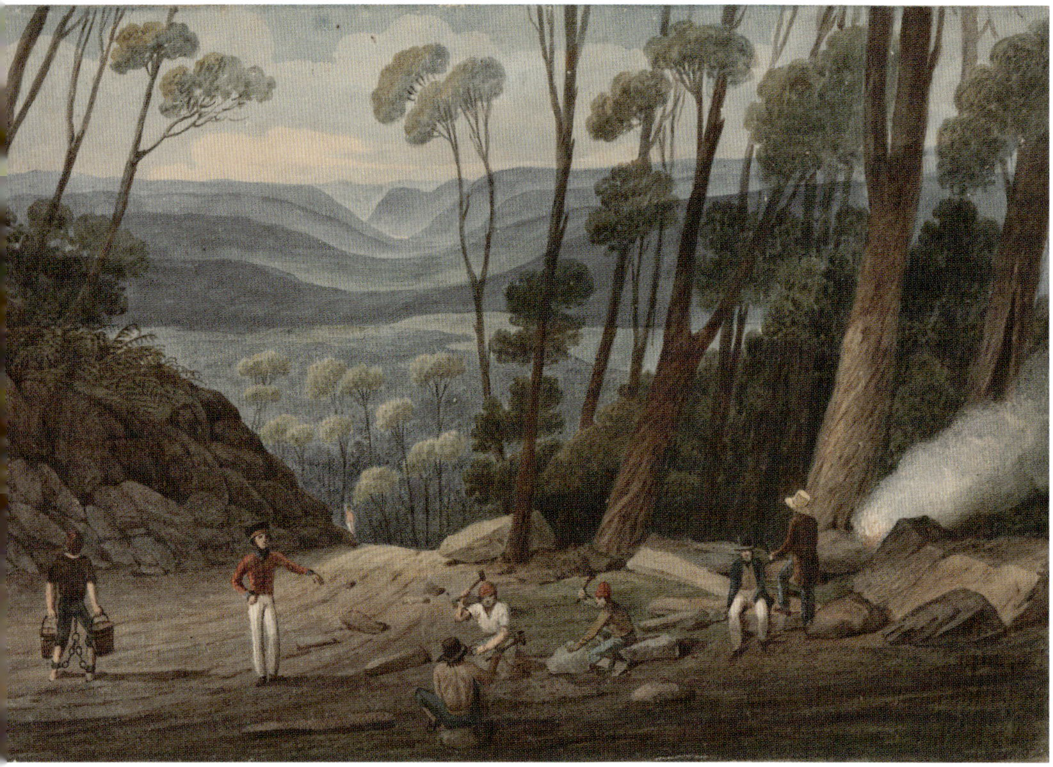

FIG. 3.16. Augustus Earle, *View from the Summit of Mount York, Looking towards Bathurst Plains, Convicts Breaking Stones, N.S. Wales*, ca. 1826. Watercolor, 22.5 × 33 cm (8 ⅞ × 13 in.). National Library of Australia, Canberra. Rex Nan Kivell Collection (nla.obj-134496573).

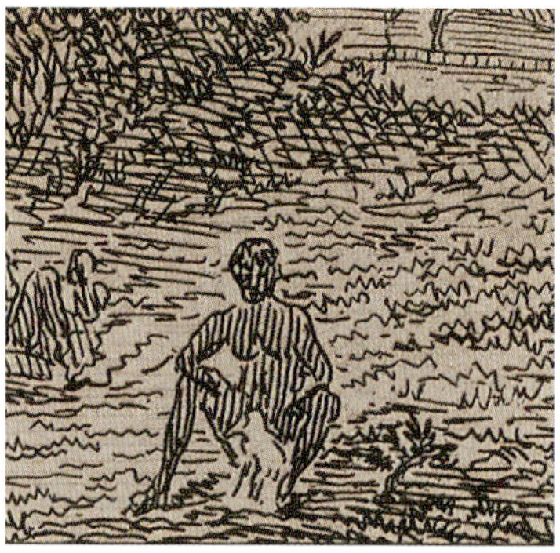

FIG. 3.17. Detail of fig. 3.3.

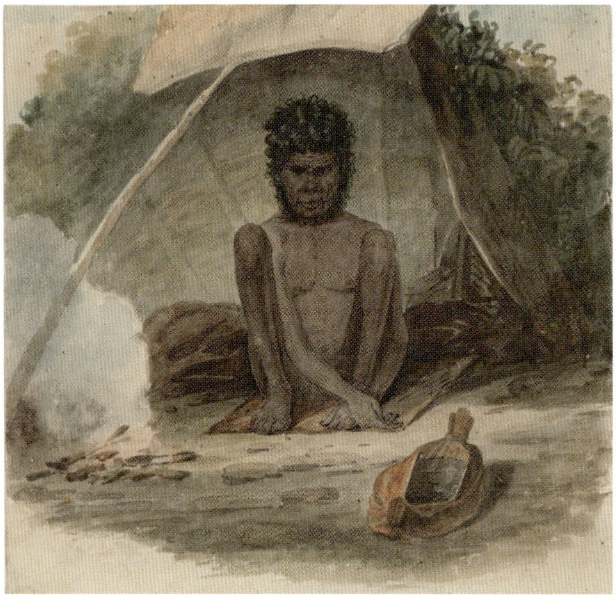

FIG. 3.18. Augustus Earle, *A Native Man, Australia*, ca. 1826. Watercolor, 16.5 × 17.5 cm (6 ½ × 6 ⅞ in.). National Library of Australia, Canberra. Rex Nan Kivell Collection (nla.obj-134501617).

was displayed at the Strand, a military-civilian campaign known as the "Black Line" of three thousand settlers had tried to drive Tasmanian Indigenous people into the Tasman peninsula.[88] The lay missionary George Augustus Robinson was on his "conciliating" mission that would eventually resettle tribes to Flinders Island, where disease and malnutrition quickly ravaged the exiled men, women, and children.[89] Burford's Hobart panorama exemplifies a shift in artistic attitudes toward Indigenous ways of life, coinciding with the removal of Indigenous threat to white settlers. If Earle's initial drawing hinted at an Indigenous presence in the distant plumes of smoke emanating from the hillside, Burford's transposition of Earle's images of New South Wales men (fig. 3.18) is a frightening echo of the historical events in which Indigenous men from New South Wales were employed as trackers in roving parties.[90] While Indigenous bodies were displaced and hunted, their visual proxies invoked passive doubles of their pursuers.

In the first years of European settlement, the Eora peoples of the Port Jackson and Sydney regions also endured irrecoverable population losses and breaks in kinship and territorial ties. By the time Earle arrived in Sydney, the Gadigal, Wangal, and other harbor clans had been pushed from their traditional territories and were living in "black camps" in less populated areas along the Port Jackson

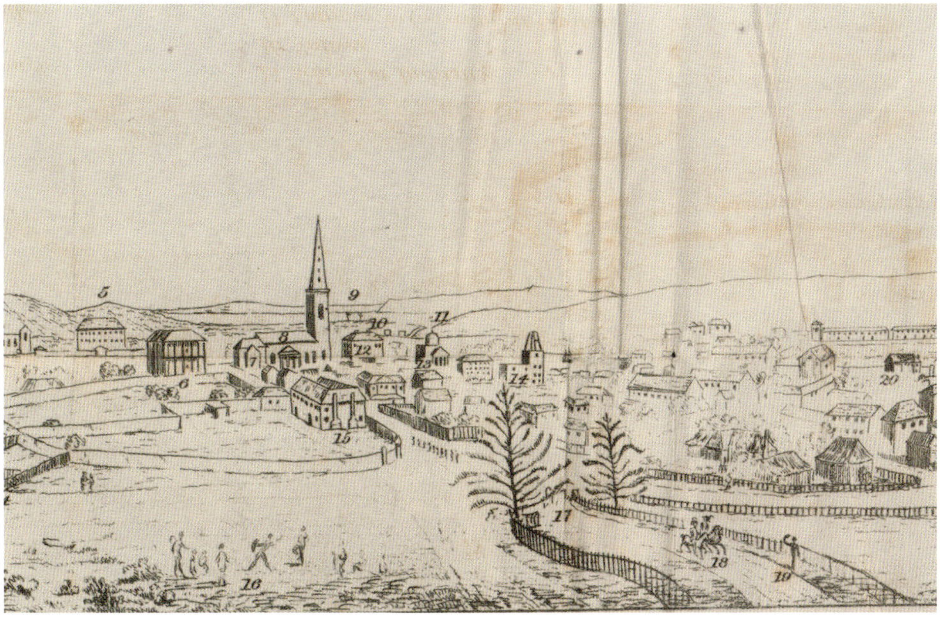

FIG. 3.19. Detail of fig. 3.2.

shoreline.[91] In the Sydney panorama Earle's representation of settler-Indigenous relations most profoundly ruptures the illusion of a utopian colony.

In Burford's first Australian panorama, the closest figures within sight are Indigenous. A group of men perform a spearing ritual (fig. 3.19), while Bungaree, a well-known Kuringgai mediator between the local Indigenous clans and the colonial administrators, stands on the road leading to the governor's domain. Governor Darling and Colonel Dumaresq, Earle's patrons, ride their horses past these two sets of Indigenous figures, symbolizing stereotypes at two extremes: unassimilable savagery and colonial mimicry. Incredulous at the contrast, the *London Magazine* reviewer exclaimed, "We should scarcely conceive that the natives would carry on their trial by ordeal in public, in the out-skirts of the capital, and, as in the panorama, with the governor riding by."[92] By the 1820s a mixture of tribes had settled close to the governor's domain. Bungaree and his Broken Bay clan shared the same grounds as tribes from Newcastle and Port Stephens from the north and Coolangatta from the south.[93]

Uncomfortable collisions between settler society and the original inhabitants who obstinately remained a part of the landscape are not only represented within but seem the main subject of a number of Earle's watercolors. *A View in Parramatta, N.S. Wales, Looking East* (fig. 3.20) presents an Indigenous family resolutely camped next to the road. A military man gestures toward the figures as if in impotent protest, while a figure on the path ahead steals a glance at the disturbance. *Wellington Valley, N.S. Wales, Looking East from Government House* (fig. 3.21) demonstrates the discordant overlap of incompatible cultures.[94] An Indigenous figure stands on the commandant's property, his pose a careful study derived from a prior portrait sketch.[95] His confrontational stare, resolute stance, and lack of engagement with his immediate surroundings draw our attention to his *visibility*; his presence on the land is not just an element of picturesque staffage.

It is hardly surprising, then, that the panorama's image of Bungaree is lifted directly from Earle's oil painting *Portrait of Bungaree, a Native of New South Wales, with Fort Macquarie, Sydney Harbour, in Background*, ca. 1826 (fig. 3.22). By far Earle's most ambitious Indigenous portrait, it also reveals both the artist's and Bungaree's ambivalance toward the colonial settlement. The most widely pictured individual of early Sydney, Bungaree was known for accompanying Matthew Flinders on his circumnavigation of the continent in 1801–2 and for his adoption of English manners, language, habit, and clothing.[96] In a spirit of mockery, the panorama pamphlet calls him "King Boongaree," noting that he is generally the first to board any ship entering the harbor; "his sable majesty, clothed in a gold laced blue coat . . . but neither shoes or stockings, welcomes the arrival of a stranger with much politeness and many bows, and contrives, if possible, to borrow dump or so, to buy for his 'gin' (wife) . . . a little of Cooper's drops."[97] This exaggeration of adopted European mannerisms inadvertently points to the contradictions of the topsy-turvy colonial condition.

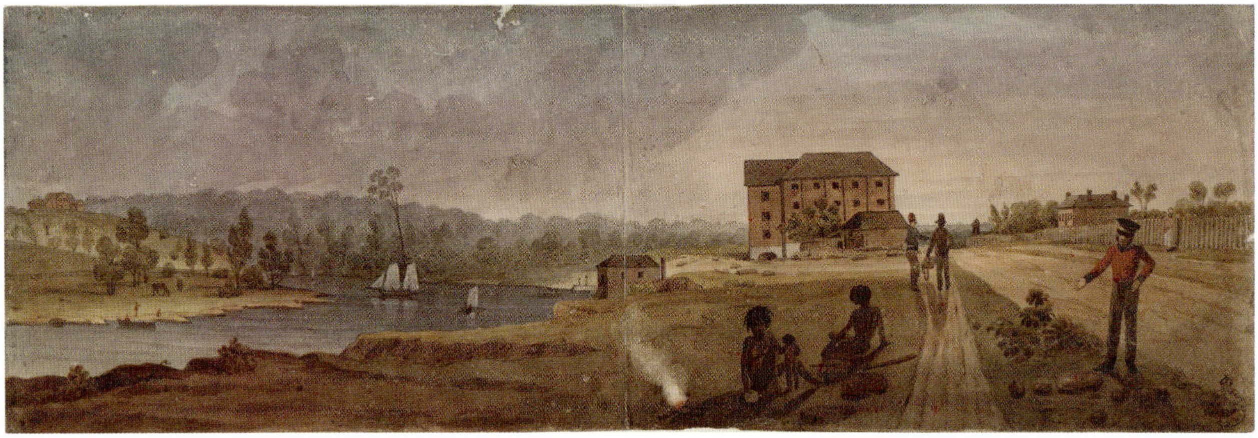

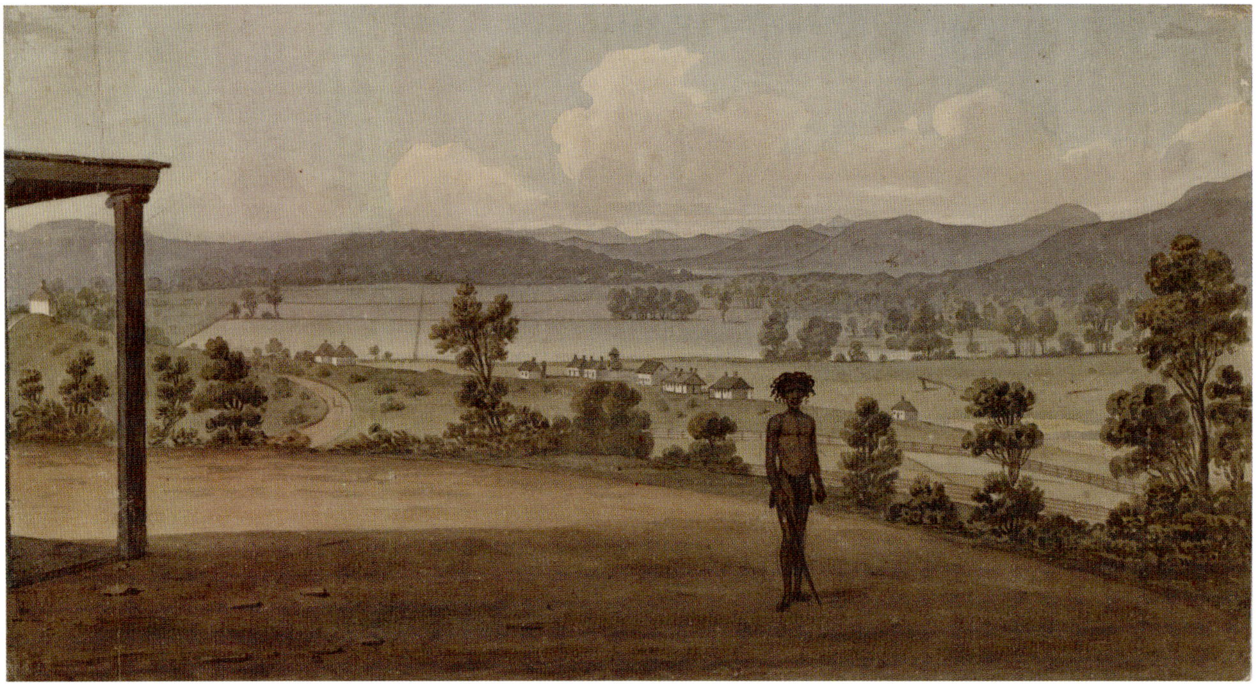

FIG. 3.20. Augustus Earle, *A View in Parramatta, N.S. Wales, Looking East*, ca. 1825–28, from the album *Views N.S. Wales*. Watercolor, 17.7 × 52.1 cm (11 × 20 ½ in.). State Library of New South Wales, Sydney (PXD 265).

FIG. 3.21. Augustus Earle, *Wellington Valley, N.S. Wales, Looking East from Government House*, ca. 1826. Watercolor, 20 × 37.5 cm (7 ⅞ × 14 ¾ in.). National Library of Australia, Canberra. Rex Nan Kivell Collection (nla.obj-134496732).

Bungaree is the first to greet arrivals into the colony, just as he is the first to greet panorama viewers.

Tipping his hat toward the viewer, the panorama's Bungaree addresses the viewer directly, like Earle's earlier portrait. One must assume he is wearing the same uniform of a general's aide-de-camp, and his crescent-shaped metal breastplate or gorget, a gift bestowed on him by Governor Macquarie, is engraved with his name and title, "Chief of the Broken Bay Tribe." While it might be tempting to view Bungaree as a pathetic or comic symbol of the degradation of Indigenous culture, scholars have instead suggested his mimicry strategically bridged incompatible cultural codes.[98] This ritual code of conduct conformed to both Eora and European protocols and was performed to neutralize the cross-cultural encounter.[99]

Earle's formal portrait places Bungaree before a stretch of Sydney Harbor, a small slice of a panoramic view in itself; Burford removes him from his greeting spot to a location within the fenced-in government territories. This displacement may isolate his body within the ordered, manicured environment, but it also positions Bungaree in close proximity to Governor Darling. Bungaree's prominence may well have encouraged panorama viewers to reconsider which figure—Darling or Bungaree—represented the colony's true face. Moreover, this transposition does not suspend alternative readings of Bungaree's gesture, which endure within the residues of Earle's excised depiction.

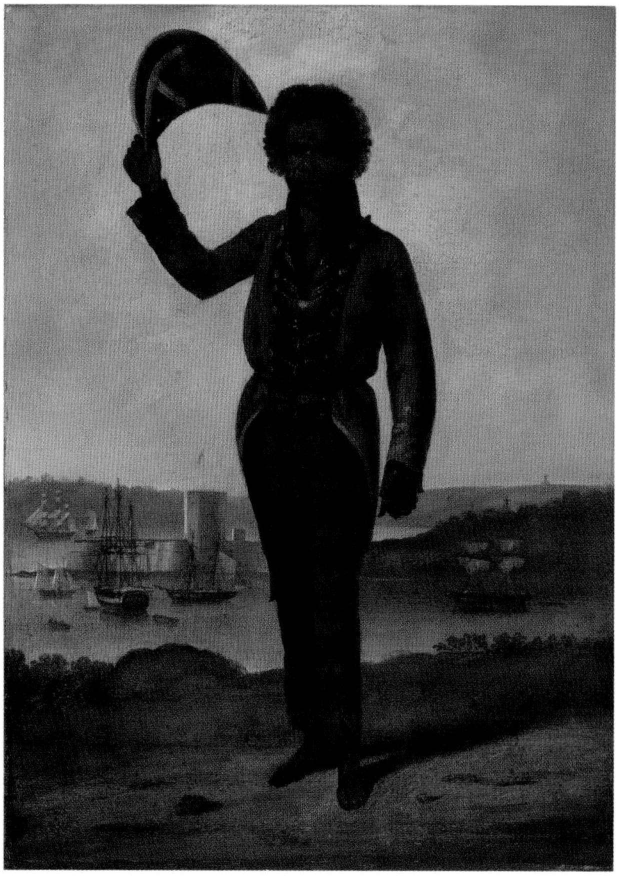

FIG. 3.22. Augustus Earle, *Portrait of Bungaree, a Native of New South Wales, with Fort Macquarie, Sydney Harbour, in Background*, ca. 1826. Oil on canvas, 68.5 × 50.5 cm (27 × 19 ⅞ in.). National Library of Australia, Canberra. Rex Nan Kivell Collection (nla.obj-134114940).

As a colonial observer at the margins of the penal experiment, Augustus Earle viewed Australian society from both inside and outside its social, institutional, and environmental structures. This dual positionality was palpable within the Australia panoramas seen by London audiences between 1829 and 1831. As the key guide and contemporaneous commentary reveal, Earle's oscillating artistic and psychological orientation became part of the viewing experience. Located within Earle's preparatory works and personal studies, which formed the basis for Burford's London panoramas, are the shifting perspectives of an individual standing on the viewing platform watching the scenery unfold before him and those of an individual embedded within the composition. Orderly civic and pastoral European landmarks are rudely juxtaposed with a disorderly wilderness, remnants of Indigenous activity, and the stains of convict society.

Despite Burford's plan to present stable images to entice future investors and emigrants, Earle's peripatetic eyes render the views of Sydney and Hobart simultaneously familiar and alien. While many have theorized panoramic vision in line with the panoptic "eye of power," Earle's unruly representations and Bentham's indictment of Australian penal supervision challenge any straightforward application of a Foucauldian reading. Instead, the various subject positions available to viewers draw a parallel with the ambivalent, unstable "self" of the artist as imperial author, which filters down through Burford's own appropriations of Earle's imagery.[100] These characteristics are not merely the result of the process of transposition from preparatory drawings to painted panoramas but are pervasive to Earle's entire body of "wandering" imagery. These internal contradictions transferred to Burford's view threaten to rupture the picturesque veneer of the redemptive settler colony and to disobey the pretense of *terra nullius*.

Although his fieldwork internalized the compositional, figural, and perspectival strategies of the panoramic, Earle did not settle on a uniform set of identifications or bearings. He operated between genres, subjectivities, and frameworks, adopting elements of the coastal profile, the romantic sublime, the picturesque landscape, the portrait, and the ethnographic field sketch. Earle's ocular displacements coincide with contemporary physical displacements in the colonial world. The wandering artist, convict, and Indigenous Australian: each is transported away from the bearings of "home." London viewers, too, were invited to be "transported" temporarily from their London viewing platform. The viewer's transportation involved stepping into the condition of Earle's social and geographic restlessness, temporarily held captive by the ever-changing landscape of the empire's farthest horizon.

NOTES

I would like to thank Tim Barringer, Mary Eagle, Eleanor Hughes, and Katie Trumpener for their expert guidance and feedback throughout the development of this chapter, and the staff and curators at the National Library of Australia and the State Library of New South Wales.

1. The British-born American artist Thomas Cole may have seen *Pandemonium*, on view concurrently with the Sydney panorama, using it as a source of inspiration for his *Course of Empire* series. Stephan Oettermann, *The Panorama: History of a Mass Medium*, trans. Deborah Lucas Schneider (New York: Zone, 1997), 113.
2. According to Scott Barnes Wilcox's exhaustive survey of *Morning Chronicle* and *Times* coverage, it was shown concurrently with *View of the City and Bay of Genoa*, April 1828–April 1829, and *Milton's Pandemonium*, April 20, 1829–February 17, 1830. Wilcox, "The Panorama and Related Exhibitions in London" (M. Litt.., University of Edinburgh, 1976), Appendix C, 258.
3. Wilcox, "Panorama," 265.
4. "In the sixteenth and seventeenth centuries 'to act the antipodes' had become a proverbial expression"; Ian McLean, *White Aborigines: Identity Politics in Australian Art* (Cambridge: Cambridge University Press, 1998), 14–15.
5. "Diary for the Month of January," *London Magazine*, February 1829, 170.
6. On the rise of the prison in relation to panoptic entertainments, see Oettermann, *Panorama*, 40–44. Gordon Bull was the first to critically examine the relationship among the panorama, the panopticon, and Australia's first penal colony; "Taking Place: Panorama and Panopticon in the Colonization of New South Wales," *Australian Journal of Art: Colonizing the Country* 12 (1994): 75–95. See also Anita Callaway, *Visual Ephemera: Theatrical Art in Nineteenth-Century Australia* (Sydney: University of New South Wales Press, 2000), 139.
7. For convict supervision as a "modernising social structure," and the repression of visual representations of the penal system, see Terry Smith's "Convicts and Capital: The Visual Economy of Surveillance," in *Transformations in Australian Art: The Nineteenth Century—Landscape, Colony and Nation* (Sydney: Craftsman House, 2002), 17–43.
8. See Bull, "Taking Place," 81–84; and Alan Wallach, "Making a Picture of the View from Mount Holyoke," in *American Iconology: New Approaches to American Art and Literature*, ed. David C. Miller (New Haven: Yale University Press, 1993), 80–91; 83. One unverified account claims Robert Barker invented the panorama while in the circular chamber of a debtor's prison. Oettermann, *Panorama*, 39.
9. See Richard Altick, *The Shows of London* (Cambridge: Belknap Press of Harvard University Press, 1978).
10. Henry Barker remained a manager of the Leicester Square panorama until retirement in 1826; Oettermann, *The Panorama*, 113.
11. Wilcox, "Panorama," 100–101. While developing the Sydney panorama, Burford hired a new, young assistant, Henry Courtney Slous (later Selous), who doubtless collaborated on all three of the panoramas after Earle—Sydney, Hobart, and the Bay of Islands, New Zealand; Oettermann, *Panorama*, 113.
12. In 1826 Burford bought out Henry Barker completely and operated both panoramas until his death later that year; thereafter Robert took over the business. The Strand panorama became the Strand Theatre. Oettermann, *Panorama*, 112–13.
13. Denise Blake Oleksijczuk, *The First Panoramas: Visions of British Imperialism* (Minneapolis: University of Minnesota Press, 2011).
14. See Michael Charlesworth, *Landscape and Vision in Nineteenth-Century Britain and France* (Aldershot, U.K.: Ashgate, 2008), 23–24; and Robert D. Aguirre, *Informal Empire: Mexico and Central America in Victorian Culture* (Minneapolis: University of Minnesota Press, 2005), xxvii.
15. Oleksijczuk, *First Panoramas*, 166–69.
16. *Painted Panorama, 1800–1870, 1 to 30 November 1985: Paintings from the Mitchell and Dixon Collections of the State Library of New South Wales* (Sydney: Blaxland Gallery, 1985), 13.
17. Edward Dayes, "On the Principles of Composition as Connected with Landscape Painting," in *The Works of the Late Edward Dayes Inscribed by Permission to Her Royal Highness the Duchess of York* (London: T. Maiden, 1805), 194.
18. Graeme Davison, "The Panorama and the Printing Press," in Susan Hunt and Graeme Davison, *Sydney Views, 1788–1888: From the Beat Knoblauch Collection* (Sydney: Historic Houses Trust of New South Wales, 2007), 14–24; 16.
19. The Mitchell Library (State Library of New South Wales) holds a fourth (watercolor) view, possibly intended to complete the panorama.
20. Callaway, *Visual Ephemera*, 139; and Michael Rosenthal, "The Penitentiary as Paradise," in *Double Vision: Art Histories and Colonial Histories in the Pacific*, ed. Nicholas Thomas, Diane Losche, and Jennifer Newell (Cambridge: Cambridge University Press, 1999), 103–30.
21. Michael Rosenthal, "London versus Sydney, 1815–1823: The Politics of Colonial Architecture," *Journal of the History of Geography* 34 (2008): 191–219, 195.
22. Other early Sydney imagery adapting the "panoramic" format include the sketchbooks of Edward Charles Close (Mitchell Library) and two remarkable Chinese export ware punch bowls picturing Sydney from complementary viewpoints (National Maritime Museum, Sydney, and Mitchell Library, Sydney).
23. On early panoramic entertainments in Australia, see Anita Callaway, *Visual Ephemera: Theatrical Art in Nineteenth-Century Australia* (Sydney: UNSW Press, 2000).
24. Alexander Riley to Edward Riley, April 10, 1820, Riley Family Papers, A 110 / CY 1193 (microfilm), Mitchell Library.
25. For a brief account of artistic patronage in the 1820s, see Patricia Macdonald, "Art, Artists and Patrons," in *Age of Macquarie*, ed. James Broadbent and Joy Hughes (Carlton South, Vic.: Melbourne University Press, 1992), 112–16.
26. Although Gordon Bull has described Major Taylor's image as a full-scale panorama (based on newspaper reports), Mimi Colligan argues the Burford-Earle version was the first panorama of Sydney. Colligan, *Canvas Documentaries: Panoramic Entertainments in Nineteenth-Century Australia and New Zealand* (Carlton South, Vic.: Melbourne University Press, 2002), 33.
27. On the popular notion of Australia as "Imperial Destiny," and the influence of Scottish Enlightenment principles on burgeoning Australian nationalist art and poetry, see Robert Dixon, *The Course of Empire: Neo-Classical Culture in New South Wales, 1788–1860* (Oxford: Oxford University Press, 1986).
28. McLean, *White Aborigines*, 17.
29. Rex Butler, "The Case of Augustus Earle," in *A Secret History of Australian Art* (Sydney: Craftsman, 2002), 114–25.
30. Since 2007, Mary Eagle has argued that Earle's strategy was to juxtapose incommensurate interpretations.
31. Leonard Bell, "Augustus Earle's *The Meeting of the Artist and the Wounded Chief Hongi, Bay of Islands, New Zealand, 1827*, and His Depictions of Other New Zealand Encounters," in *Voyages and Beaches: Pacific Encounters, 1769–1840*, ed. Alex Calder, Jonathan Lamb, and Bridget Orr (Honolulu: University of Hawai'i Press, 1999), 241–64; 242.
32. Jocelyn Hackforth-Jones, *Augustus Earle: Travel Artist* (Canberra: National Library of Australia, 1980), 1–2.

33. Ibid., 2; and Elizabeth Mankin Kornhauser, *Ralph Earl: The Face of the Young Republic* (New Haven: Yale University Press, 1991).
34. Harold Spencer, "Augustus Earle: A Study of Early Nineteenth Century Travel Art and Its Place in English Landscape and Genre Traditions" (Ph.D. diss., Harvard University, 1968), 98.
35. Hackforth-Jones, *Augustus Earle*, 2; and Michael Bryan and George Charles Williamson, *Bryan's Dictionary of Painters and Engravers*, 5 vols. (London: George Bell and Sons, 1909), 2:115.
36. The 1830 panorama was executed at a new building constructed at Coromandel Place, New Road; Altick, *The Shows of London*, 137. A review of the panorama was published in *New Monthly Magazine* 30 (1830), 517.
37. This was the argument of the exhibition catalogue: *The Wandering Artist: Augustus Earle's Travels around the World, 1820–29* (Canberra: National Library of Australia, 1994).
38. Leslie summarized his friend's wanderings: "He had visited every part of the Mediterranean . . . roamed in Africa—rambled in the United States—sketched in South America—attempted to go to the Cape of Good Hope in a worn-out Margate hoy, and was shipwrecked on Tristan d'Acunha, where he passed six months. . . . He then visited Van Diemen's Land, New South Wales, and New Zealand, where he drew from the naked figure. . . . He, by way of variety, proceeded to the Caroline Islands—stopped at the Ladrones—looked in upon Manilla [*sic*], and finally settled himself at Madras, and made money as a portrait painter. Not content, he went to Pondicherry, and there embarked for France, but stopped at the Mauritius, and after some few more calls at various places, found his way home." Bryan and Williamson, *Bryan's Dictionary of Painters and Engravers*, 2:115.
39. *Life on the Ocean* (1837), *Divine Service on Board a Man-of-War* (1837), and *A Bivouac of Travellers in Australia* (1838) were exhibited in London.
40. On January 1, 1827, Earle wrote to the colonial secretary asking to make New South Wales his permanent residence. This request was refused on the grounds that he could not demonstrate sufficient means of cultivating the property. See Eve Buscombe, "A Discussion about Augustus Earle and Some of His Portraits," *Art Bulletin of Victoria* 19 (1978): 59.
41. "On the State of Fine Arts in New South Wales," *Sydney Gazette*, July 30, 1829, 3. A list of the thirty paintings exhibited is enumerated in the Diaries of Rev. John McGarvie, 1825–January 1828. Mitchell Library, State Library of New South Wales, A1332, 235.
42. Earle never completed *Views in Australia*, intended as a multipart lithographic series. Advertisements for the art classes ran in the *Sydney Gazette*, August 18, 1826. When Earle returned to London in 1829, this series, significantly altered to suit a British audience, was published as *Views in New South Wales and Van Diemen's Land, Australian Scrap Book* (London: J. Cross, 1830).
43. Buscombe, "A Discussion about Augustus Earle," 48.
44. Leonard Bell, "To See or Not to See," in *Orientalism Transposed: The Impact of the Colonies on British Culture*, ed. Julie F. Codell and Dianne Sachko Macleod (Aldershot, U.K.: Ashgate, 1998), 117–39; 120. The *Australian*, February 10, 1827, reported that Burford had paid one hundred guineas for eight sketches.
45. Hackforth-Jones, *Augustus Earle*, 56.
46. Darling was criticized for what were perceived as ruthless disciplinarian actions, most notably his harsh punishment of two soldiers, Joseph Sudds and Patrick Thompson. The absence of convict figures in the Sydney panorama is perhaps strategic. See also Hunt and Davison, *Sydney Views, 1788–1888*, 18.
47. A review of E. T. Parris and William Daniell's *A View of Madras* praises Earle's viewpoint from a lighthouse for its appropriate height, while bird's-eye views are "deplored as the grand defect of pictures of a similar class." *New Monthly Magazine* 30 (1830): 517.
48. Robert Burford, "View of the Town of Sydney," in *Description of a View of the Town of Sydney, New South Wales* (London: J. and C. Adlard, 1829), 11.
49. Len Fox, *Old Sydney Windmills* (Potts Point, N.S.W.: privately printed, 2011), 25–28, 42. In the face of food shortages and inadequate equipment, Governor Arthur Phillip first requested the establishment of mills in 1790 to grind wheat for the colony. Three Sydney windmills are visible in Burford's panorama. Fox identifies those visible in the key as Clarkson's mill with post mills, Craigend mill, and Barent Levey's partially erected windmill on the roof of the Royal Hotel.
50. One of the first engraved emblems representing New South Wales (gracing the 1803 cover of the *Sydney Gazette*) depicts a productive landscape marked by civic structures and a windmill (reproduced in Fox, *Old Sydney Windmills*, 12). The accompanying inscription was "Thus We Hope to Prosper."
51. W. E. R. Carter, *John Palmer: Father of the Colony* (Miranda, N.S.W.: John Palmer Society, 1986), 3.
52. The key's description credits Dumaresq with guidance in producing the painting, and articles in the press announced that Earle was engaged in completing the panorama. *Sydney Gazette*, February 9, 1827; *Sydney Monitor*, February 10, 1827; and *Australian*, February 10, 1827. The panorama depicts Dumaresq riding next to Governor Darling. Edwin Barnard, *Capturing Time: Panoramas of Old Australia* (Canberra: National Library of Australia, 2012), 35.
53. Burford, "View of the Town of Sydney," 10.
54. Mary Eagle's forthcoming catalogue will comprise the most comprehensive work on Augustus Earle's oeuvre to date.
55. *Australian Dictionary of National Biography*, s.v. "William Lawson," http://adb.anu.edu.au/biography/lawson-william-2338, accessed December 15, 2012.
56. Leonard Bell, "Augustus Earle: Colonial Eyes Transformed," in *Radical Revisionism: An Anthology of Writings on Australian Art*, ed. Rex Butler (Fortitude Valley, Qld.: Institute of Modern Art, 2005), 134.
57. Ibid.
58. The original watercolor study, housed at the Mitchell Library, appears to be missing a seventh section, which would have depicted Crayfish Point, Betsy's Island, and Mount Nelson.
59. Such as the view of Hobart Town in *Illustrations to Prinsep's Journal of a Voyage from Calcutta to Van Diemen's Land* (London: Smith and Elder, 1833).
60. *The Van Diemen's Land Anniversary and Hobart-Town Almanack for the Year 1831* (Hobart-Town: James Ross, 1831), 135–37, 162–63.
61. In 1829, two years before the panorama's London exhibition, the *Cyprus* made headlines after thirty-one "piratical" convicts mutinied en route to Macquarie penal settlement, taking possession of the ship and steering it toward open ocean. "Piratical Seizure of the Government Brig Cyprus," *Hobart Colonial Times*, September 4, 1829, 3.
62. Earle's second stop at Hobart is rarely mentioned by scholars; many suggest he completed his preparatory drawings for Burford on his first visit, in 1825. Yet the "Whatman 1826" watermark on four drawing sheets, as well as the inclusion of the *Cyprus*, the *Rainbow*, and the *Mermaid*—all docked at Hobart when Earle was there in October–November 1828—suggests that although the panorama may have been begun in 1825, this iteration of the drawing couldn't have been completed until this second brief stopover. Mary Eagle's extensive research supports this, noting the *Rainbow*'s movements gave Earle two short opportunities to complete the sketches: October 19–23 and November

4–11, 1828. Mary Eagle, draft catalogue entry for a forthcoming monograph on Augustus Earle.

63. McLean, *White Aborigines*, 20.
64. Thomas Watling, "Letters from an Exile at Botany Bay to His Aunt in Dumfries," reproduced in *Island in the Stream: Myths of Place in Australian Culture*, ed. Paul Foss (Leichhardt, N.S.W.: Pluto, 1988), 10.
65. Sarah Thomas, "The Wanderer, the Slave and the Aboriginal: Augustus Earle in Rio de Janeiro and Sydney in the 1820s," in *Crossing Cultures: Conflict, Migration and Convergence: The Proceedings of the 32nd International Congress in the History of Art*, ed. Jaynie Anderson (Melbourne: Miegunyah Press, 2009), 331.
66. Jeremy Bentham, *Panopticon versus New South Wales*, in *The Works of Jeremy Bentham, Now First Collected: Under the Superintendence of His Executor, John Bowring*, 6 vols. (Edinburgh: W. Tait, 1838–43), 4:208.
67. McLean, White *Aborigines*, 14–15.
68. John Gascoigne, *The Enlightenment and the Origins of European Australia* (Cambridge: Cambridge University Press, 2002), 126.
69. Henry Walter Parker, *The Rise, Progress, and Present State of Van Diemen's Land with Advice to Emigrants: Also a Chapter on Convicts Showing the Efficacy of Transportation as a Secondary Punishment* (London: J. Cross, 1833).
70. Ibid., 40.
71. *The Van Diemen's Land Anniversary and Hobart-Town Almanack*, 80.
72. Parker, *The Rise*, 47.
73. Ibid., 46.
74. The corresponding numbering has changed, and "Mrs. Midwoods Seminary" and some whaling boats have been added.
75. I believe the word to be "Prisoners"; Mary Eagle agrees, but she also tentatively offers "Prison," since it is beside a mark ("+") added to one of the numbers in Earle's key, apparently an editorial suggestion to drop the Surveyor General's Office from the key (only the roof is visible over the hill in the distance) and move up the next item, the Gaol/Jail/Prison. Eagle, personal correspondence, August 22, 2013.
76. As Richard Neville observes, convict uniforms were not widely enforced in the early decades, which made settler-assigned convicts practically indistinguishable from the free population. Neville, *A Rage for Curiosity: Visualising Australia, 1788–1830* (Sydney: State Library of NSW Press, 1997), 10.
77. Eagle suggests that convicts were brought into the scene to counter London's *New Monthly Magazine*'s editor's comments about the Sydney panorama, which implied that the colony was all too appealing a setting for its criminal transports. Mary Eagle, draft catalogue entry for a forthcoming publication on Augustus Earle.
78. Sarah Thomas, "Witnessing Slavery: Travelling Artists in an Age of Abolition" (Ph.d. diss., University of Sydney, 2012), 156.
79. Michael Rosenthal, "The Extraordinary Mr. Earle," in *The World Upside Down: Australia, 1788–1830* (Canberra: National Library of Australia, 2000), 39.
80. Earle writes in the accompanying text: "The annexed subject is one of the Government gangs being told out of barracks for the daily work, and given in charge of a soldier, who acts as overseer." *Views in New South Wales and Van Diemen's Land*, n.p. (There are no views of Van Diemen's Land; Earle seems to have left the series unfinished.)
81. David Solkin argues that Richard Wilson's paintings ideologically reinforce the nobility's "organic" ties to an ancient landholding class structure. Solkin, *Richard Wilson: The Landscape of Reaction* (London: Tate Gallery, 1982), 130–32.
82. The "swell mob" refers to fashionably dressed thieves and swindlers. "Panorama of Hobart Town," *Literary Gazette: A Weekly Journal of Literature, Science, and the Fine Arts*, no. 739 (March 19, 1831): 188.
83. "Panorama of Hobart Town," *Mirror of Literature, Amusement, and Instruction*, April 16, 1831, 266.
84. "Panorama of Hobart Town," *Athenaeum*, March 19, 1831, 187.
85. Benjamin Madley, "Patterns of Frontier Genocide, 1803–1910: The Aboriginal Tasmanians, the Yuki of California, and the Herero of Namibia," *Journal of Genocide Research* 6, no. 2 (2004): 167–92; 170–71.
86. Ibid., 173.
87. Parker, *The Rise*, 13.
88. See "The Black Line" in Nicholas Clements, *The Black War: Fear, Sex and Resistance in Tasmania* (St. Lucia: University of Queensland Press, 2014), 125–56.
89. Madley, "Patterns of Frontier Genocide," 175.
90. In 1829 John Pigeon, a Warrora man from Shoalhaven, and John Crook, a Johninbia or Yunbai man from Wollongong, were selected by the landowner John Batman to serve as members of a roving party. Alastair H. Campbell, *John Batman and the Aborigines* (Malmsbury, Victoria: Kibble Books, 1987), 30.
91. *Eora: Mapping Aboriginal Sydney, 1770–1850* (Sydney: State Library of New South Wales, 2006), 4.
92. "Diary for the Month of January," 170.
93. *Eora*, 4.
94. Rosenthal, "The Extraordinary Mr. Earle," 39.
95. This is probably taken from a frontal view of the same figure that Earle sketched in *Native of New South Wales from Wellington Valley*, watercolor, Rex Nan Kivell Collection, NK12/33, National Library of Australia.
96. Earle's was one of seventeen portraits of Bungaree. Richard Neville, "Who Is in the Picture?" in *Faces of Australia: Image, Reality and the Portrait*, ed. Richard Anthony ad John Neville (Sydney: State Library of NSW, 1992), 62. *Eora*, 4.
97. Burford, "View of the Town of Sydney," 9.
98. See, for example, Phillip O'Neill, "Putting the English in Drag: Bungaree's Theatre of Mimicry as a Response to Colonialism," in *Aratjara: Aboriginal Culture and Literature in Australia*, ed. Dieter Riemenschneider and Geoffrey V. Davis (Amsterdam: Rodopi, 1997), 69–86.
99. David Hansen, "Death Dance," *Australian Book Review* (April 2007): 32. Citing Bungaree's propensity to mimic English behavior, Sarah Thomas asks, "Who was mocking whom?" in "The Wanderer, the Slave and the Aboriginal," 332.
100. Bell, "To See or Not to See," 123.

GRETCHEN HOLTZAPPLE BENDER

4 Gaertner's Compromise

Spectatorship and Social Order in the *Panorama von Berlin*

Eduard Gaertner's *Panorama of Berlin* is not a panorama. It is not rendered on a curved surface, and it does not completely encircle its viewer. Stephan Oettermann's study of panoramas as the new "mass medium" sees Gaertner's work as of interest as a "special case," yet he ultimately dismisses its significance because of its "return" to the traditional flat surface.[1] Unable for financial and practical reasons to render his work in the round format, Gaertner compromised, completing his work in two separate sections, a view to the south and a view to the north, each painted on three separate canvases mounted in a special frame and hinged together so that they angle slightly around the viewer (figs. 4.1a–b).[2]

This work proves a rich site where contested modes of viewing and competing spatial configurations merge. I emphasize *site* here, for it is not just the cityscape that garners our attention. The true subject of Gaertner's *Panorama of Berlin* is surely the viewing platform itself and the figures displayed on it. Those on the roof configure how viewing is to be done; they structure the city at which they look. The trajectories formed by their gazes and positions across this platform's spatial plane inform the painting's narrative, which attempts to order the urban terrain and the diverse subjectivities that traverse it. Gaertner's painting takes what is typically marginalized in panoramic practice and centers it. As scholarship on the panorama rotunda has elucidated, several structural features and illusionistic devices deceived viewers, directing their attention to the spectacle on the picture's curved surface, directing the gaze outward as they took in a miraculous new world. Alan Wallach argues that this platform was "shrouded in darkness" and a "ghostly or insubstantial realm inhabited by . . . spectators—who . . . became *anonymous* and *invisible* witnesses to the scene."[3] Yet by drawing attention to this typically "insubstantial" realm, Gaertner's painting reverses this dynamic, underscoring that in practice, panorama visitors interested in the broader view also performed on the platform itself, becoming part of the spectacular event.[4] This chapter devotes a close reading and extends a particularizing gaze to this distinctive work, which lies at the periphery of panorama scholarship; it regards the *Panorama of Berlin* as a special opportunity and argues that Gaertner's work should play a central role in the discourse on this important nineteenth-century medium.[5]

Gaertner (1801–1877) began his career in the Royal Prussian porcelain works, where meticulously detailed

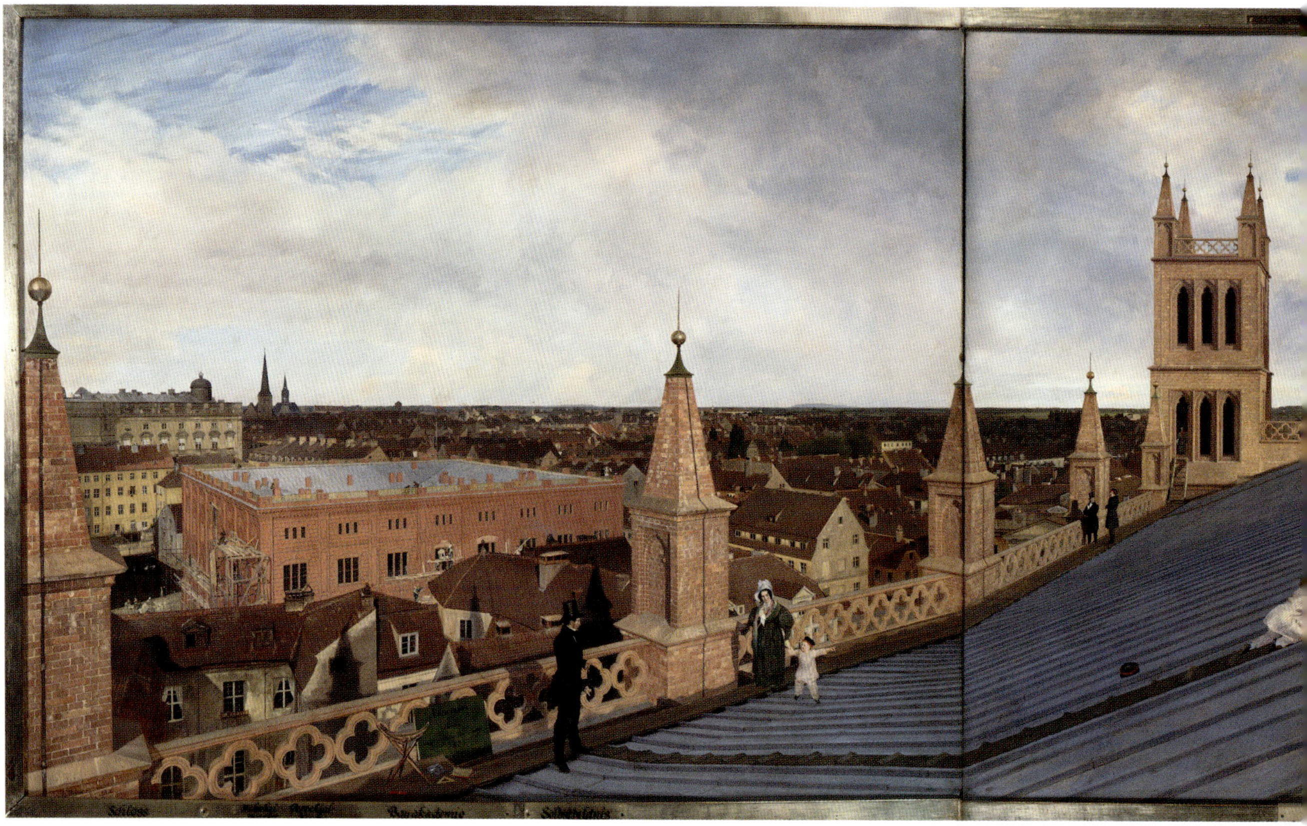

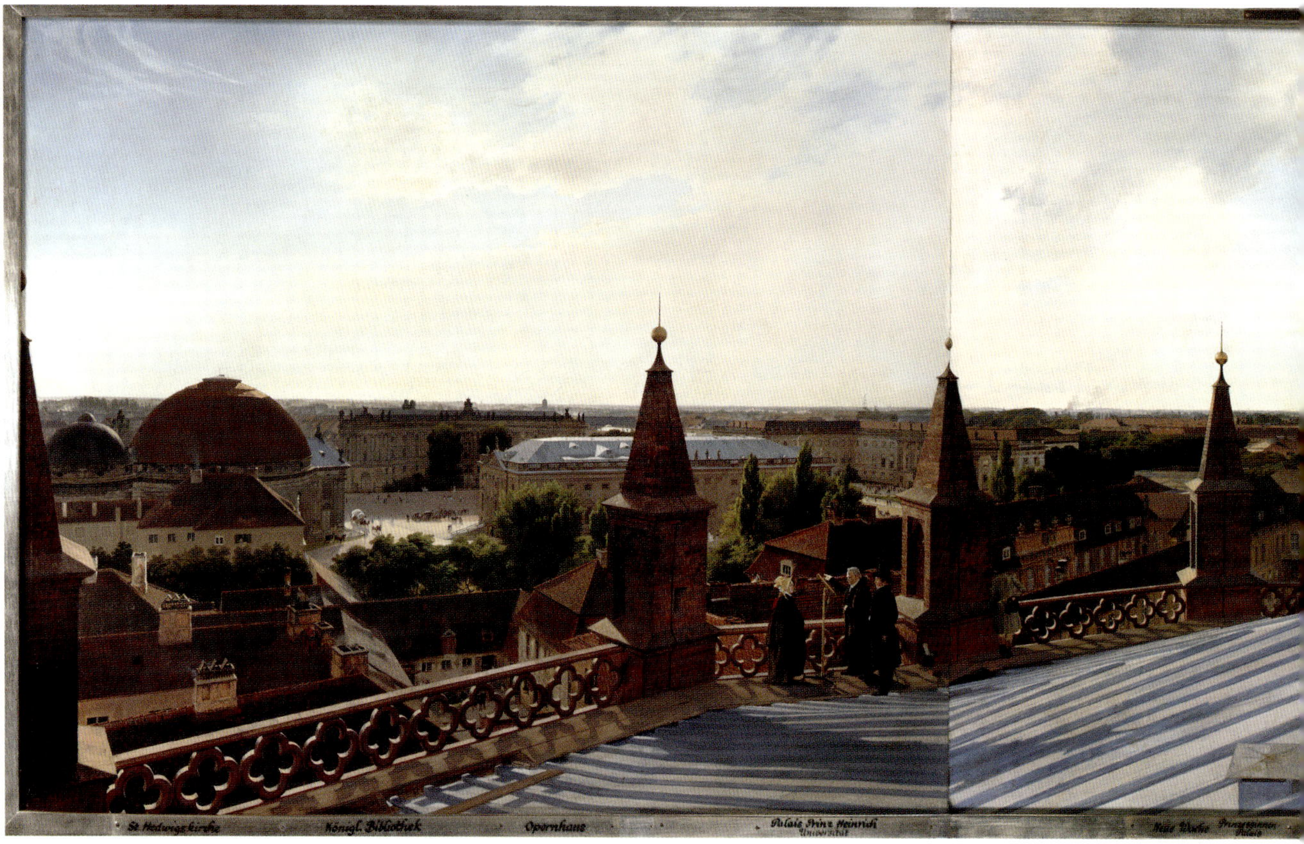

FIG. 4.1A. Eduard Gaertner (Austrian, 1801–1877), *Panorama of Berlin Seen from the Roof of the Friedrichswerdersche Kirche toward the South*, 1834. Oil on canvas, 91 × 313 cm (35 7/8 × 123 1/4 in.). Hohenzollern Family. Neuer (Schinkel) Pavilion, Charlottenburg Castle, Stiftung Preussische Schlösser & Gärten, Berlin.

FIG. 4.1B. Eduard Gaertner, *Panorama of Berlin Seen from the Roof of the Friedrichswerdersche Kirche toward the North*, 1834. Oil on canvas, 91 × 313 cm (35 7/8 × 123 1/4 in.). Hohenzollern Family. Neuer (Schinkel) Pavilion, Charlottenburg Castle, Stiftung Preussische Schlösser & Gärten, Berlin.

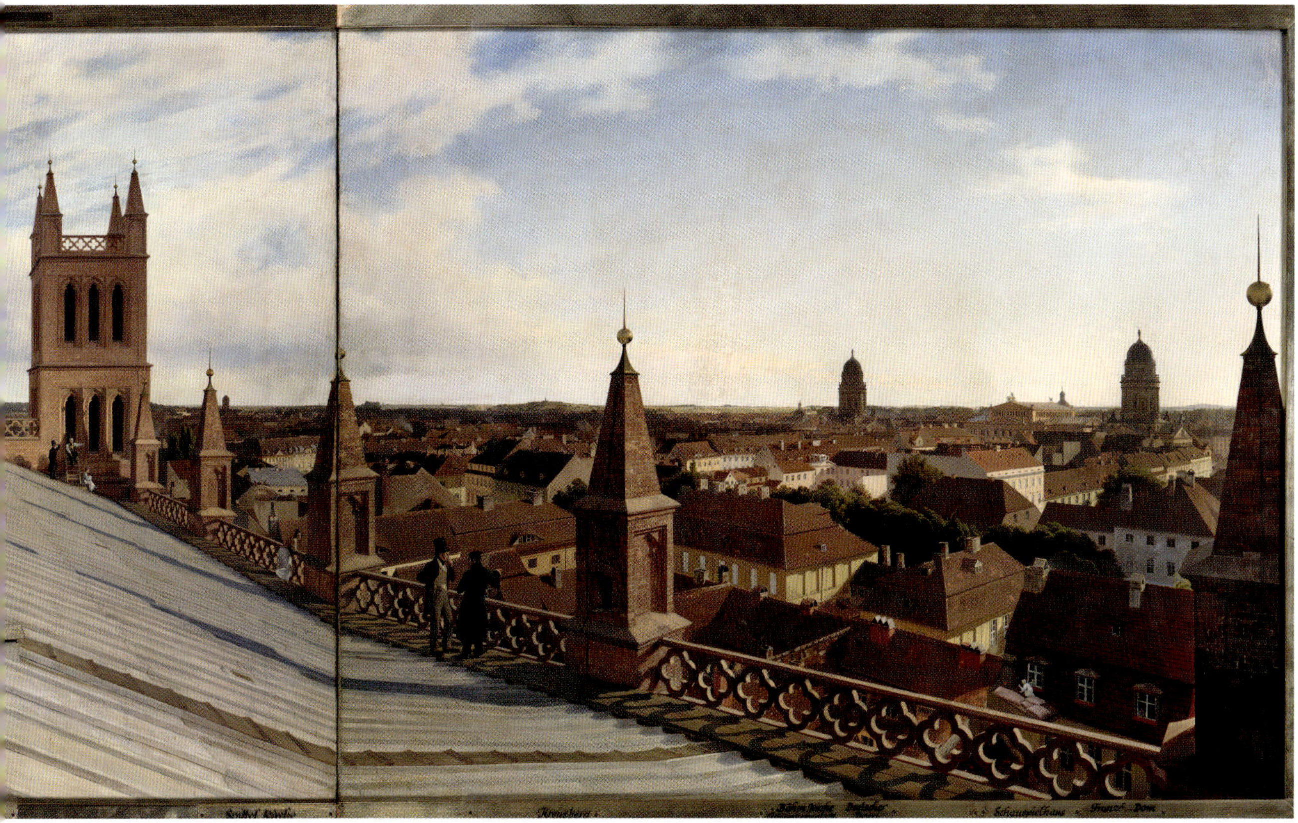
Kreuzberg
Schauspielhaus
Dom

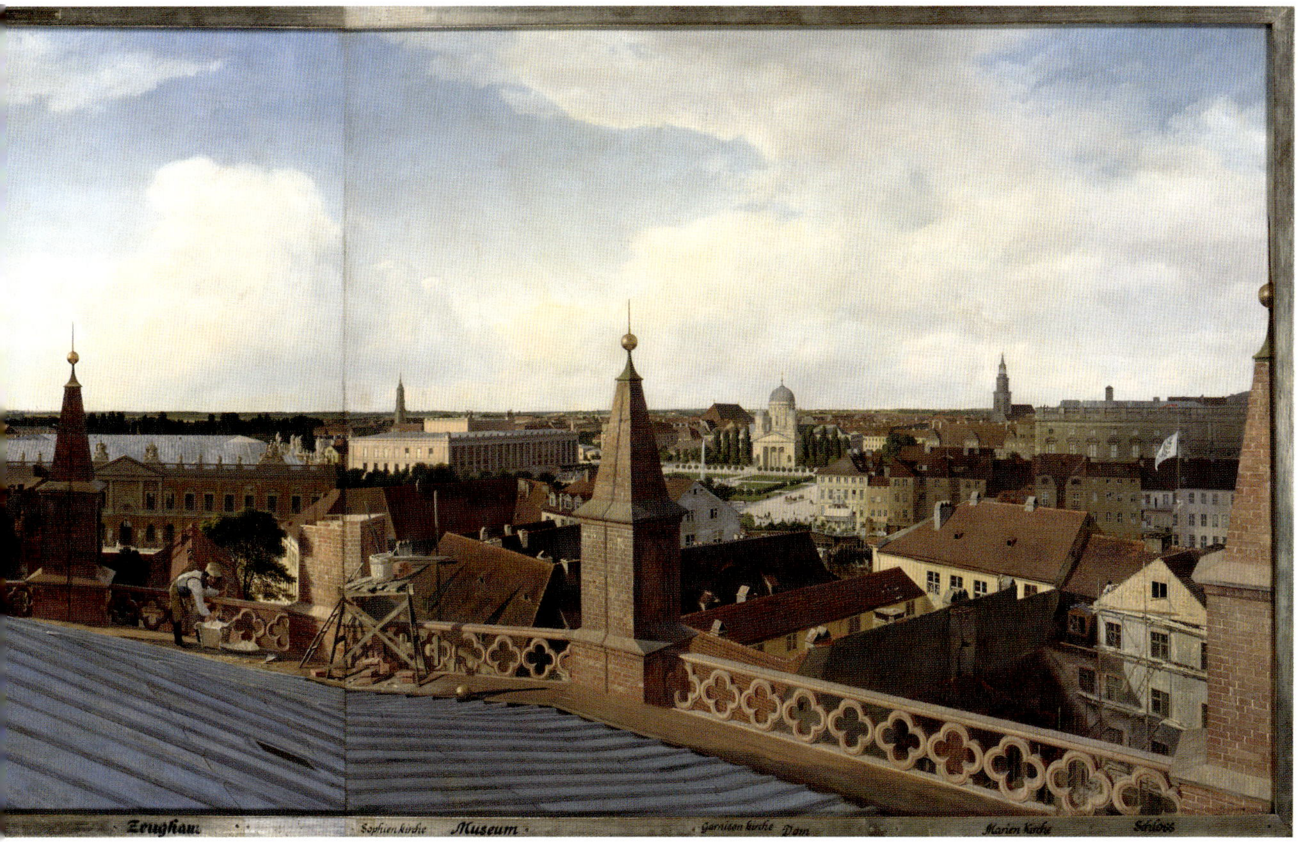
Zeughaus
Sophien kirche
Museum
Garnison kirche
Dom
Marien Kirche
Schloss

views of Berlin edifices were painted on the surfaces of tea sets and large vases.[6] Eventually he became an apprentice theater painter to the Gropius brothers, whose diorama productions brought a key element of modern visual culture to Berlin.[7] Gaertner is often referred to as a leading member of the "Berlin Scene Painters," artists who presented innumerable views of the city's most famous streets and landmarks. Their painted views were often reproduced in published guidebooks, in prints, and on luxury consumer goods.[8] Gaertner's panorama presents an overview of a city to which he dedicated his professional life. Yet in the *Panorama of Berlin*, the city appears as background terrain as the action of the work unfolds in the foreground with several citizens gathered on the roof of the Friedrichswerdersche Kirche. In the southern views, the artist himself is depicted in the left canvas turning back into the space of the picture (fig. 4.2). Gaertner's *Panorama* is also labeled as a self-portrait, "*Selbstbildnis*" inscribed immediately below him on the frame, and his signature rendered on the portfolio leaning against the balustrade: "Panorama von Berlin. Aufgenommen im Jahre 1834 von E. Gaertner."[9] He greets his wife and child while an older son scales the peak of the roof. The *Panorama* is thus also a family portrait.[10] But there are several other spectators, too, including some of Berlin's most illustrious citizens. In the northern views, Alexander von Humboldt is positioned purposefully across from the university that his brother, Wilhelm, founded in 1810 (fig. 4.3). That Alexander rather than Wilhelm is represented here is notable. By this time, Alexander was a senior statesman, scholar, and professor who had returned to Berlin after decades of travel, exploration, and living abroad. His presence on the roof thus becomes a means of signaling the broader terrain of the world beyond the limits of vision here, Berlin's more global aspirations.

The architect Karl Friedrich Schinkel is depicted alongside his colleague Peter Beuth in the southern view across from the Bauakademie, a new edifice under construction (fig. 4.4). In the *Panorama*, Berlin is fundamentally new, as the scaffolding on the Bauakademie in the left canvas of the southern view articulates. The panorama is as much a tribute to Schinkel as a celebration of the city. It originates from the roof of Schinkel's new Friedrichswerdersche Kirche. Aside from the academy and the church, Schinkel's other recent projects punctuate the terrain: the renovated theater on the Gendarmenmarkt, the new museum on the Lustgarten, and the monument to those fallen in the Wars of Liberation, visible on the horizon in the Kreuzberg neighborhood. Gaertner's panorama demonstrates how architecture and public institutions shape urban life. The horizontal expanse of undifferentiated rooftops extending outward is interspersed by the edifices that define Berlin as a new world capital founded on enlightened reason and culture: theater, library, university, museum, each glowing in the afternoon sun. As these structures rise up in the cityscape, they give the topography its "image," to quote Kevin Lynch. Lynch discusses landmarks' centrality as signifiers granting the city recognizability and meaning, "the apparent clarity or 'legibility' of the cityscape . . . the ease with which its parts can be recognized and . . . organized into a coherent pattern."[11] The importance of making the urban terrain legible is underscored by Gaertner's inclusion of text, the labeling of the significant structures on the frame itself.

For Beatriz Colomina, "architecture is not simply a platform that accommodates the viewing subject. It is a viewing mechanism that produces the subject. It precedes and frames its occupant."[12] Gaertner's work, as a portrait of Berlin and its inhabitants and as a physical structure itself, underscores how the built environment actively shapes social space and subjectivity and in so doing encourages us to consider how spectatorship is always and already performed across the spatial terrain of a specific place and time. Gaertner, his wife, Humboldt, Beuth, and Schinkel as the performers, or "spectactors" (to use Peter de Bolla's term), are clearly positioned here, punctuating the city's expanse as their forms vertically match those of the rising spires that segment, order, and regularize the view. De Bolla's study of Vauxhall Gardens notes "the viewer is constantly suspended between two distinct positions, actor and spectator . . . here vision is imbricated within the witnessing of a theatrical event in which we participate and at which we spectate, thereby making us spectactors."[13] Gaertner's figures perform this function, and the narrative of the panorama centers on these gazes—who looks, how they look, how they are positioned as viewers and subjects within the urban terrain.[14]

FRAU GAERTNER, THE BRICKLAYER, AND WOMEN IN WHITE

Prominent in the northern views of the *Panorama* is Humboldt, joined by others, leisurely taking in the view. Also prominent is a bricklayer who works to complete the church's last spire. Just as Humboldt is depicted with

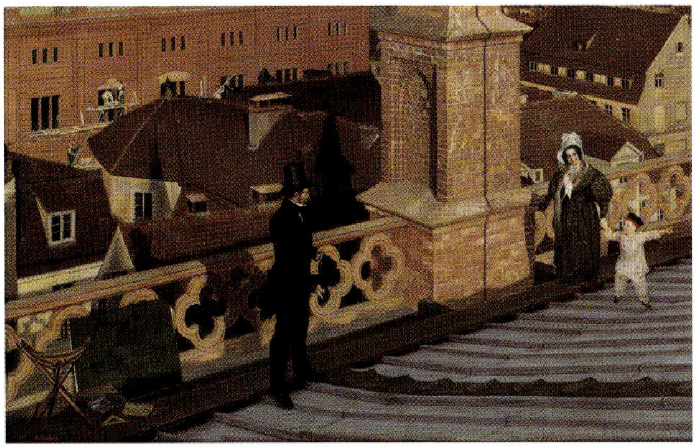

FIG. 4.2. Eduard Gaertner, *Panorama of Berlin Seen from the Roof of the Friedrichswerdersche Kirche toward the South* (detail of Gaertner's self-portrait with his wife and son).

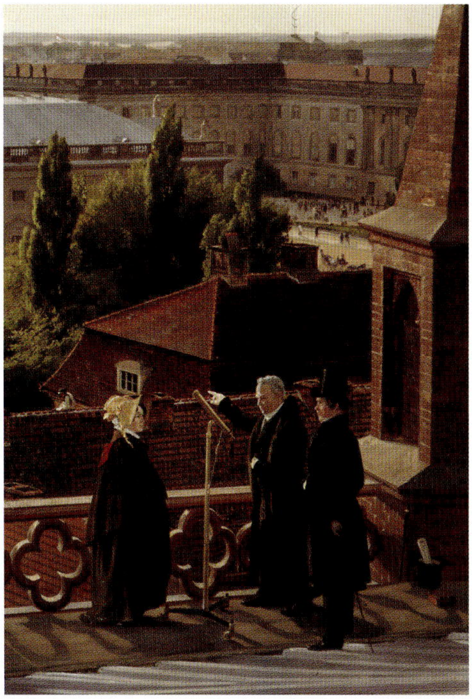

FIG. 4.3. Eduard Gaertner, *Panorama of Berlin Seen from the Roof of the Friedrichswerdersche Kirche toward the North* (detail of Humboldt).

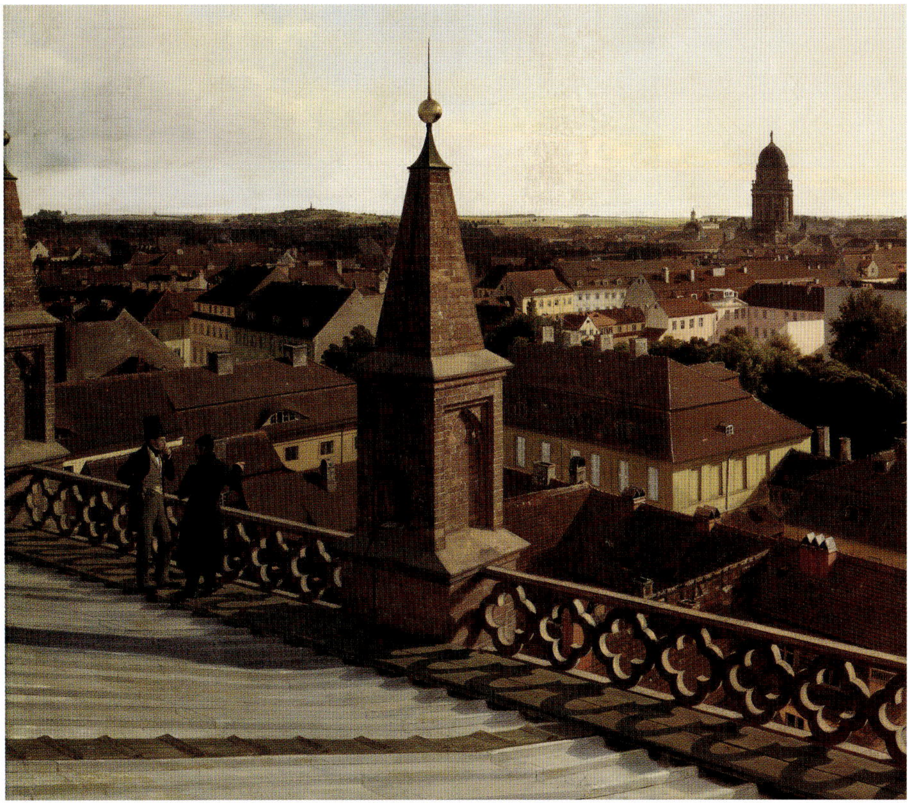

FIG. 4.4. Eduard Gaertner, *Panorama of Berlin Seen from the Roof of the Friedrichswerdersche Kirche toward the South* (detail of Karl Friedrich Schinkel and Peter Beuth overseeing construction of Bauakademie).

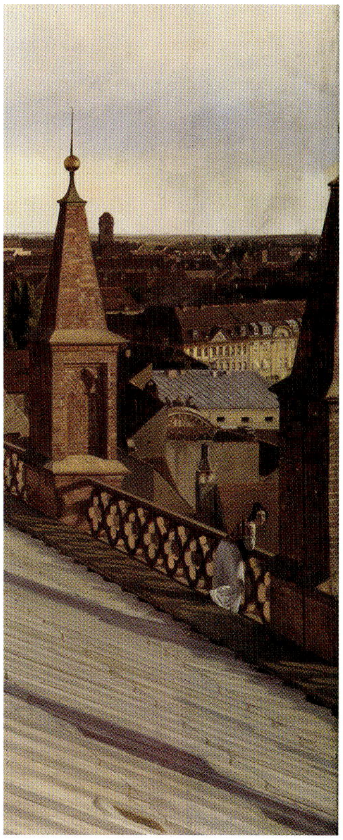

FIG. 4.5. Eduard Gaertner, *Panorama of Berlin Seen from the Roof of the Friedrichswerdersche Kirche toward the South* (detail of woman in white).

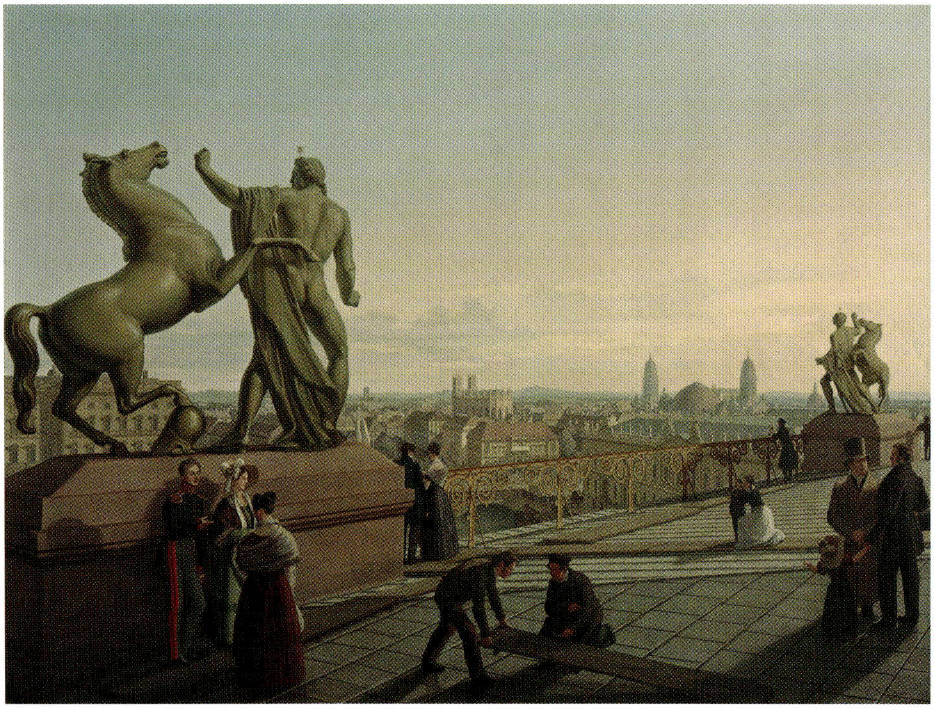

FIG. 4.6. Ludwig August Most (German, 1807–1883), *View of Berlin from the Roof of the Museum*, 1830. Oil on canvas, 79 × 105.5 cm (31 × 41 1/2 in.). National Museum, Poznan (Inv. Nr. Mo 1790).

the tools of his trade (the telescope), the bricklayer mixes his mortar, the physicality of his labor legible in his bent pose. This immediately contrasts with the ease of a finely attired gentleman who stands nearby, leaning against a spire. Elsewhere the division between physical and intellectual labor is repeatedly manifested. Schinkel and Beuth, with their upright postures, survey the Bauakademie work undertaken by numerous workers. Throughout Gaertner's works, the division between intellectual and working classes is legible through attire and bodily deportment, between those who stand tall with ease and those who crouch, strain, bend, or lift. Near the bricklayer, at the far right margin of the northern views, more scaffolding rises against a building as a man repairs a roof. Men with poles guide a small boat along the river, transporting goods. Two women wash clothing in tubs near the river in the far left margin of the southern views and another woman hangs laundry out to dry on the roof of the palace itself. Another crouched and active woman, on the far right edge of the southern view, has hauled a featherbed and pillows out onto a roof to aerate them with a hearty beating.

The detail of the woman beating bedding on the roof represents a moment of permeability between the domestic and the public realm. She and the woman on the roof of the palace are literally airing the laundry, as what is intimate and private is brought into public view. The woman who labors with the bedding on the roof wears a white dress (fig. 4.5). Visually, she serves as a counterpoint to another woman, also dressed in white, standing on the roof in the central section of the southern views. At first glance this unaccompanied middle-class woman in white on the viewing platform does not attract much attention, distanced from the viewer. But as we are positioned on the apex of the roof, our gaze is returned by only three other people: the bricklayer in the northern views, and in the southern views, this woman and Gaertner's wife. Two women meet our gaze, the first clearly a wife and mother as she takes the hand of her son while approaching her husband. By standing alone, the woman in white, in counterpoint to Frau Gaertner, opens the possibility of sexual availability.

That Gaertner's colleague Ludwig August Most was likewise interested in single women occupying urban space is evident from Most's view of Berlin from the roof of Schinkel's Museum, shown at the academy exhibition only two years before Gaertner's engagement in the panorama project (fig. 4.6). Prominent in the left foreground of Most's painting, a young officer divides his attention between two young women. The woman whose back is turned with a fragmented profile is immediately mirrored by the immense nude statue of Castor (or Pollux), whose stance and positioning are very similar.[15] This stark juxtaposition serves as the narrative core of Most's work: her rich, soft, and deep burgundy dress, yielding to pliant bare arms of soft peach, contrasts with the hard, unyielding gray marble of the statue's naked flesh and taut musculature. He towers over her diminutive frame while his actively striving pose counterpoints the quiet, dignified columnar form of her body hidden beneath her dress. The conspicuous placement of the nude rump of this idealized classical hero immediately above her signals a humorous subplot underlying the "demure" exchange between the officer and the proper ladies.

What Gaertner's and Most's Berlin views clearly articulate is that both men and women occupy these spaces and are granted the ability to enjoy the gaze—a gaze not divorced from the sexuality of the bodies housing it. As Denise Blake Oleksijczuk has noted, panoramas enjoyed a particular popularity among women and were deemed acceptable sites for them to visit.[16] Yet with this freedom to move and look came an increasing wariness of the connection between women's presence in public space and the perception of an unbounded sexuality, resulting in middle-class society's desire to associate women with the domestic sphere, where their social role as wife and mother could qualify or safeguard their sexuality.[17] The presence of single women who exercise the freedom of the gaze and wander openly through the public spaces of the city poses a potential threat to bourgeois order. To counteract this, the unaccompanied woman in white is neutralized by the powerful presence of Gaertner's wife and children, conveying the notion that urban public space is sufficiently domestic and thus made safe for the sojourn of single women.

In Gaertner's views, women occupy the public sphere and exercise the gaze because a circumscription of the urban by the domestic allows them to do so. Often Gaertner's cityscapes present Berlin's urban spaces as enclosed and ordered, exteriors taking on the tidy character of Biedermeier interiors.[18] As Peter-Klaus Schuster notes, women and children form a conspicuous presence in Gaertner's cityscapes, even in the most politically official spaces, including the steps of the palace and along Unter den Linden.[19] In his panorama, the city appears as an extension of domestic space as Gaertner's playful son lends the work a sense of ease. At the far end of the roof, immediately under the tower, another woman sits and sews, an activity emblematic of domesticity in scores of contemporaneous Biedermeier paintings.[20] The public spaces of Gaertner's Berlin exude a domestic happiness typically reserved for the home. As the woman with the featherbed emblematizes, domestic work takes place in public view as part of the choreography of daily life.

Most scholarship on Gaertner's *Panorama* names and considers only the illustrious men gathered here: Humboldt, Schinkel, Beuth, Gaertner himself. With the three overlooked figures on the roof as viewing platform, whose gazes triangulate with ours—Gaertner's wife, the bricklayer, and the unaccompanied standing woman—a whole new narrative emerges, a tension established in which Gaertner's actors are positioned and regulated by a reigning social order. The lower classes are present but benignly absorbed in their work, denied the leisurely view. Bourgeois women are granted the power to see and move through city space, but their gaze and movement are framed by a domestic order. Both the single woman and the worker could potentially threaten the middle-class stability of Gaertner's sunny cosmopolitan center, but their potential subversiveness is held in check by the logic of the performance staged by the other bodies who inhabit the roof: the proper wife and the intellectual men.

DIZZYING HEIGHTS, PARTICULARIZED VIEWS, AND HUMBOLDT'S TELESCOPE

Just as Gaertner's panorama attempts to assuage difference, presenting his roof as a stage on which various and diverse subjectivities come together, the work also instantiates and represents multiple and competing modes of spectatorship. Gaertner attempts to signal a corporeal mode of viewing—the tinge of excitement and the dislocation induced by the sensation of dizzying heights, what Stephan Oettermann terms "see-sickness."[21] The woman in white leans her body over the railing, seeing what we, as viewers centered at the apex, cannot, as if she has just been looking over the edge, straight down to the street below.[22] The possibility of being overwhelmed physically by the view was typically gendered as feminine—a weakness inherent to "ladies" and "dandies."[23] In the southern view, the men all stand upright, feet firmly planted. Her pose is more languid and bent, elbows positioned on the railing for support, one leg passively extended. Yet if the viewer associates the corporeal response to the view with weakness, one of the panorama's most prominent figures, Gaertner's eldest son, contradicts this assumption. From his vantage point, the roof does not recede from his eye level, but rather plunges downward to the balustrade. To underscore the child's precarious position, he is depicted crouching on hands and knees, as if afraid to walk upright. Yet with energy and enthusiasm, he boldly reaches his left arm forward, raising a stick that just breaches the line of the apex. The viewer senses his excitement and adventurousness; his corporeal experience remains at odds with the restrained conceptual gaze experienced by the adults. And his bravura counteracts the languid delicacy of the woman in white, a delicacy communicated in part through her dress's transparency—a careful eye notes the balustrade visible through her form.

Oettermann elucidates the ways in which the panoramic medium could instantiate feelings of both liberation and imprisonment, control and weakness, centered and destabilized modes of viewing.[24] Oleksijczuk and Wallach give detail to these tensions; their studies of individual panoramas recognize that the medium accommodated both a fixed, authoritative, and "extensive" gaze—occupying a static center of power—and an "ambulatory," particularizing gaze that focused intensively on details, a gaze temporally protracted and inherently destabilizing.[25] The use of a single vanishing point along the roof's apex anchored around a centered viewer exemplifies Oleksijczuk's fixed position of power and Wallach's "totalizing vision."

What should we make of the telescope positioned next to Humboldt? Hannelore Gärtner and Sybille Einholz read it as a clue to how the viewer is meant to regard the panorama itself.[26] In this volume, Richard Maxwell links it to the worldview expressed in Humboldt's *Cosmos*. It, too, represents a disembodied mode of viewing, anathema to the physical thrill Gaertner's son seeks. The telescope is a tool, a prosthetic with which the gaze disconnects from the body as peripheral vision is eliminated.[27] While viewers of Gaertner's panorama take in the city as a whole, they are also encouraged to draw close and revel in the intricacy of detail, Oleksijczuk's "ambulatory mode" introducing a protracted and distracted experience.[28] Berlin is enjoyed detail by detail, fragment by fragment. As in fully round panoramas, there is no single focal point. But *unlike* the spectator regarding a true 360-degree panorama, the viewer of Gaertner's work can draw close. There is no fenced viewing platform, no intermediary terrain as the viewer is encouraged to step up to the surface. Gaertner began his career as a painter at the royal Prussian porcelain works; his precise attention to the minutiae of lived experience, executed through a steady and careful hand, emerges in the panorama as well, a work that thus aspires to be both monumental (as a "panorama") and miniature in its handling.[29]

The plethora of detail Gaertner presents prods us to linger over the surface—people alight from carriages, men fix roofs, women do laundry, men direct boats on the river. The viewer revels in the play of intricate episodes and fragmented moments, the pictorial *excess* of which Oleksijczuk speaks.[30] The work enacts a powerful pull on the viewer, who cannot help drawing close and, in so doing, performs the "telescopic gaze." Yet is this really a destabilizing moment? Michael Charlesworth has argued that the panorama's eighteenth-century origin can be linked to the military's strategic drawing practices, as panoramic views of contested terrain were deployed to locate points of advantage and weakness on the field of battle.[31] The telescope was an essential tool in this procedure and thus can stand for authoritative control and the exertion of power. Wallach regards the "intensive gaze" as similarly empowering, linked to "social aspiration" and "social dominance." This mode of viewing "drew its explosive energy from prevailing ideologies in which the exercise of power and the maintenance of social order required vision and supervision, foresight, and especially, oversight."[32] The word *oversight* connotes authoritative responsibility; an "oversight committee" exerts watchful and responsible care. Yet it can also mean to not see, to ignore or miss something conspicuous, an inadvertent omission. Both careful attention and careless inattention are implied. Does Humboldt's telescope lure us to distraction or enable us to exert careful control? Ultimately, the latter: as we stand on the roof, looking over (overlooking) the woman in white who beats a mattress on the roof, our gaze is directed to her back. She appears vulnerable and small, just one detail in the broad expanse over which our looking can extend. She is singularly focused on her task as she occupies this small ledge. In the end, we can stare at her while she remains oblivious to our presence.

THE ROYAL GAZE: THE KING AS CENTERED VIEWER

Gaertner's work ultimately recuperates stability over any sense of dislocated vision. By leaving the position of the viewer atop the peak open and anonymous, it may be possible, given the inclusion of the working-class bricklayer and unaccompanied woman in white, that Gaertner allows anyone to step in and enjoy the view. This may be an attempt to "democratize the gaze," as Oettermann claims the panoramic format was inclined to do.[33] Yet given the authoritative stance of the centered viewer, this seems unlikely. While the king is not present in Gaertner's numerous views of Berlin, he is present before them all as their figurative patron.[34] The royal palace is the only monumental structure in the entire cityscape spanning both north and south views.[35]

And the king's favor and patronage proved significant for this work's completion. Gaertner began work on his panorama independently in 1832. For several months, he worked on the sketches, constructing a small hut on the roof of Schinkel's church to complete the painting on-site. Half of the panorama was exhibited in the Academy exhibition in October 1834, to public success. After the exhibition, Friedrich Wilhelm III requested that he bring the panorama to the palace for private display; the appreciative king thereafter funded Gaertner to complete the second half.[36] The freedom of movement and gaze exercised by this work's middle-class citizens clearly did not threaten the king's symbolic authority. The domestic economy constructed by Gaertner's Berlin views accounts for the symbiotic relationship between the monarch and his subjects. The king's laundry, like everyone else's, is aired to dry on the palace roof. The king is not present within these scenes, but he is present before them all as the "father" presiding over this extended family.[37]

The *Panorama* shows people atop the roofs of the building academy and the palace. The palace and the museum serve geographically as especially apt centers for a view of the city, since they are located on the island that connoted the heart of the capital. The museum, too, was used as a viewing platform. Yet Gaertner chose the Friedrichswerdersche Kirche as *the* panorama's central point of focus. Why? Visually, it provides a striking frame for Gaertner's view, which is segmented by its brick spires' vertical rise. In the southern view, the two towers rise up, centered in the main section. The roof's sweeping recession draws the viewer's gaze here, to the towers dominating and contradicting the horizontal expanse. The apex of the roof itself directs the gaze forward, into the picture space and toward the horizon. The roof edges and seams between the zinc shingles serve as traditional orthogonals.[38] Gaertner employs one-point perspective to give his implied viewer, his king, the commanding view over the city in its entirety, which expands from this point as a neatly circumscribed, legible whole. Thus, Gaertner's panorama can be considered more akin to the Baroque theater's absolutist visual strategies, which, as Oettermann argues, posit the sovereign as "the only true spectator"; the orthogonal sightlines and vanishing point are oriented exclusively around his gaze.

Gaertner chose not Friedrich Wilhelm III's palace as the point of origin for his *Panorama* but instead the newly constructed church bearing the king's name. The city is wholly available to the king as he occupies the picture's very heart, floating miraculously above the apex, his presence ordained by a higher divine power. The numerous church towers, visible across the cityscape, their verticality punctuating the view's expansive horizontality, also provide the stabilizing presence of traditional religion to a cityscape otherwise defined by modern public and secular institutions. Using Friedrichswerdersche Kirche itself as the frame for the king's centered gaze, Gaertner aligns Friedrich Wilhelm's authority with God's will, reinstituting, in this modern era, the divine right of kings in a panorama configured as two triptychs.[39]

Gaertner's panorama was painted in the waning years of Friedrich Wilhelm III's reign, years of conservative retrenchment following the Congress of Vienna (1814), the Karlsbad Decrees (1819), and increased censorship imposed after the Hambach Festival (1832). But the *Panorama*'s reference to domestic harmony and familiarity between monarch and subject (as the bricklayer smiles openly and meets the king's gaze) is quite remarkable. Likewise, the panorama's focus on the educated class (Humboldt, Beuth, and Schinkel) and the new institutions they built, which now define the capital city, also testifies to the significant gains toward reform over the preceding decades. Since the 1780s Prussia, in particular, had cultivated stringent educational reforms, enhanced opportunities, and a robust bureaucracy in which men rose into civil service ranks.[40] The Bauakademie, the university, the museum, and the presence of Schinkel and Beuth, both of whom rose from more modest origins to prominent leadership roles, signal that the king enabled modern reform to emerge, even while seeking to remain firmly planted in the center of this new world.

THE BARRICADE

Gaertner's panorama attempts a perfect compromise between tradition and modernity, between middle-class desires for freedom and self-assertion and the royal insistence on control, between the leisure and working classes, between public and private spaces, between urban expanse and domestic confinement, and between competing modes of vision. The picture's realism, its seamless totality presenting Berlin as a rationally ordered space, however, is barely able to conceal very real social discontent and political disenfranchisement. In Gaertner's watercolor of

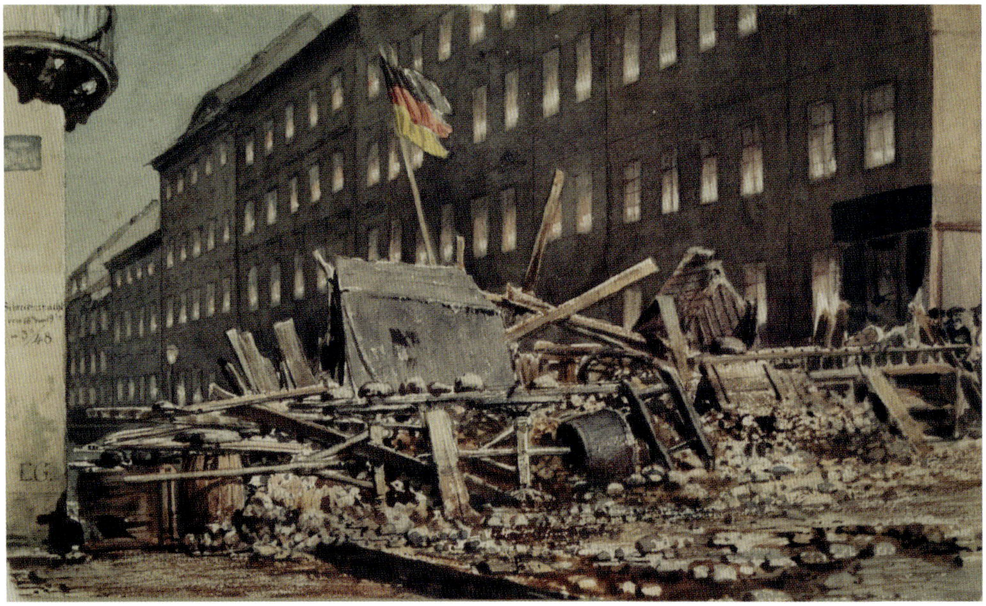

FIG. 4.7. Eduard Gaertner, *Barricade in Breiten Strasse,* 1848. Watercolor and pencil on paper, 14.7 × 24.7 cm (5 ¾ × 9 ¾ in.). Stiftung Stadtmuseum, Berlin.

a barricade, rendered in the middle of the night of March 18, 1848, the sun-filled, harmonious world of class order and contentment gives way to violent frustration, legible in the chaos of the littered street (fig. 4.7).[41] The viewer is now positioned standing firmly on the ground. Rather than enjoying the expansive overview of a prosperous and peaceful city, the viewer of Gaertner's *Barricade* is given a fractured view of a narrow stretch of a single urban street. This is the embodied, partial gaze of the single observer, able to witness the world only as a series of fragmented views, contingent on the parameters of particular subjective experience.

The barricade is constructed hastily from objects once used for more productive purposes: barrels, several pieces of lumber, a wagon wheel, a few doors, bookcases. Aside from the neatly inscribed signature on the edge of the building to the far left of the picture, the watercolor appears hastily made. Pencil lines are legible through the thin wash of gray tones. In the left foreground, a drier brush has left a sense of the texture of the gravel street, and a loose patch of ink fluidly creates a sense of shadow—or blood?—in the far right foreground. The artist, who completed his panorama over years, producing carefully executed studies in order to capture the details of the city in a finished picture, here gives the viewer the sense of working quickly at this particular moment to record this historical event. Gaertner's *Barricade* reveals the very real social discontent and messy upheaval that the panorama so insistently evades. *Barricade* reveals the fallacy of the compromise enacted in his *Panorama,* the balance between middle and working class, king and subject. Now, with a new king—Friedrich Wilhelm IV—fighting to hold on to the crown, Gaertner's viewer stands on the ground, in a street strewn with the detritus of revolutionary violence, as the mundane objects from domestic life spill out into the public space as disorder, as chaos, legible in the artist's desperate attempt to capture this frightening moment when the king vacates the scene, and the city.

POSTSCRIPT: A NEW PANORAMA FOR BERLIN

The German Bundestag asked Norman Foster to reerect a dome over the Reichstag, as a symbol of a resurgent democracy, the new "Berlin Republic" born from the detritus of the collapsed Berlin wall (fig. 4.8). In 1995 Christo and Jeanne-Claude's long-planned wrapping had symbolically purged the semi-ruined Reichstag of its tortured history; now it was to serve once more as the political center of a reunified Germany.[42] Today Foster's glass dome is one of Berlin's most visited and obligatory tourist sites. It serves as a beacon, rising up over the city and visible from many points, a new landmark partially challenging the visual ubiquity of the GDR era *Fernsehturm* (the television tower built in 1964 to anchor East Berlin's otherwise barren Alexanderplatz, still the city's highest structure and visible from many points).

Foster's dome is a remarkable reincarnation of the panorama—an edifice constructed of glass panels that serves as a viewing machine, enabling visitors to partake in an all-pervasive view of the city's reach. But now panorama visitors actually inhabit the skin of the panorama itself. Twin ramps circumnavigate the glass shell, allowing visitors to ascend to and descend from the dome, their movements activating the panorama's "surface." The surface of the panoramic dome, the structure, is both present and absent. The grid formed by the steel supports serves as a frame segmenting the view, but the viewer is supposed to look through and beyond them to the cityscape. The primary picture no longer resides on the panorama's surface.

There is also a secondary spectacle. Like Gaertner's first panorama of Berlin, Foster's dome is left open in the middle. In this case, however, the center cannot be occupied, as it is constituted by an immense mirrored cone rising up and extending outward. Above all, Foster's dome provides an intensive experience, hyperbolically celebrating the acts of looking, seeing, and being seen. Outside the Reichstag, you stand in a tightly packed queue, next to strangers, awaiting admission. In so doing, you stand on the steps of the Reichstag's main facade and hence are yourself on view, on display for everyone passing before the building. After clearing security, where you are subject to surveillance by terrorism-prevention experts, you wait to board an elevator faced with a highly reflective gray surface, its inside walls lined with floor-to-ceiling mirrors. Emerging from the elevator onto the roof platform, you are drawn to the central edifice, the dome that seemingly floats above the roof. Once inside this dome, you find your own image reflected in the monumental mirrored cone not once but over and over, alternative selves repeating in unison the gesture and pose you have assumed. Some views are whole, some fragmented. Your body is intersected by the edges of each mirrored section. Many others join you here, their forms likewise cloned and splintered. Then, as you direct your attention outward and begin ascending the ramps, the act of processing in this communal ritual becomes apparent, becomes conspicuous and internalized as your activity is mirrored by that of the other tourists who process above, behind, and all around you. At the top, you reach a smaller platform open to the sky, Foster's oculus yawning above you. People pause here, rest on the benches, before taking the prescribed downward ramps to return to the base. Waiting at the return elevator, you see yourself reflected yet again in the glass window that overlooks the building's main ground-floor lobby. Then, looking through this glass, you see the tourists standing on the ground through yet another window, waiting outside the building for their turn. Coming full

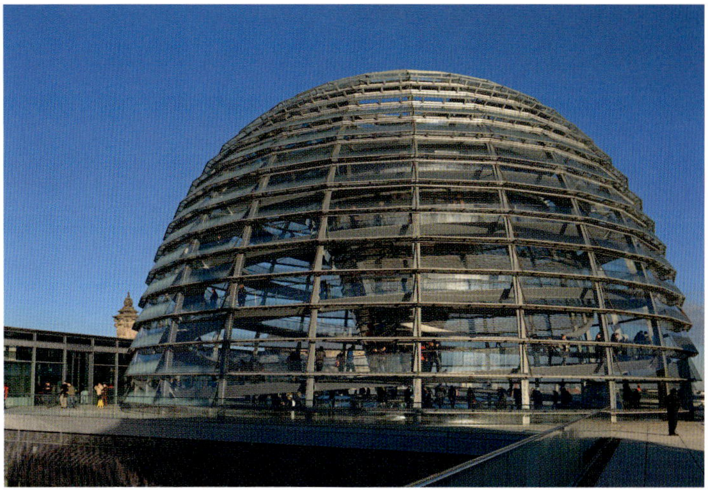

FIG. 4.8. Norman Foster (British, b. 1935), dome atop the renovated Reichstag, Berlin, 1992–99.

circle, you regard your original position in this trajectory. The elevator doors open, you step in, and yet again the mirrors yield your endless reflections, a *mise-en-abyme.*

I detail the totality of this experience as prescribed for, and practiced by, visiting tourists to consider the parallels linking early and recent panoramas in Berlin. Only a stroll down Unter den Linden separates the Reichstag from the Friedrichswerdersche Kirche; both buildings as viewing platforms direct the viewer's attention to Berlin's monumental center, its Mitte.[43] In both, what takes precedence is the performance, the centered activity choreographed across the viewing platform itself. Both induce an intense, narcissistic desire to see oneself as part of a communal whole, joined by others in the act of occupying public space. In both, visitors attend to the view, choosing consciously to visit a special location that regulates, segments, and orders the view. In both, the center is occupied by a politically authoritative body. In Gaertner's panorama, the king is presumed to step in and enjoy the totalizing gaze. In Foster's dome, the center's occupant is ambiguous. Is it the people, symbolically represented by the repeating reflections of visitors gathered around the mirrored cone? Is it the parliamentary body, the Bundestag, whose hall is positioned immediately below the cone and into which one could look, in theory through a circular window (although not actually in practice because of the distance between it and the railing)? The questions raised by Gaertner's *Panorama of Berlin* are still relevant, still applicable, as Foster's panoramic dome continues to fluctuate between the antipodes of liberation and control, empowerment and circumscription. The presence of the "masses" who circumnavigate and thus activate the surface of the dome (hence becoming a panoramic image) stands for a new democracy that adheres to the will of the people. The proliferation of glass stands for a clear, healthy view, utter transparency, and hence an inherently democratic impulse.[44] Yet what do we make of the facts that this route is so narrowly prescribed that the image of the people, and the individual subjectivities who constitute this public body, occupies reflective surfaces so superficially and appears fractured, splintered, and dispersed? Gaertner's compromise still resonates. The yearning for unimpeded movement and the power to look is met with a need to impose a structuring order. Berlin's new panorama still navigates between a fixed, all-pervasive centrality and the fleeting presence of the marginalized subject.

NOTES

1. Stephan Oettermann, *The Panorama: History of a Mass Medium*, trans. Deborah Lucas Schneider (New York: Zone, 1997), 215–16. Since Oettermann's appraisal, others have similarly regarded Gaertner's painting with only passing interest, noting the work's conservative retrenchment in traditional modes of seeing. See Lutz Koepnick, *Framing Attention: Windows on Modern German Culture* (Baltimore: Johns Hopkins University Press, 2007), 54–56, juxtaposing it with Adolph Menzel's 1845 work *Balcony Window*.
2. Each middle canvas is 91 × 93 cm (35 7/8 × 36 1/2 in.), each side canvas is 91 × 110 cm (35 7/8 × 43 1/4 in.).
3. Alan Wallach, "Making a Picture of the View from Mount Holyoke," in *American Iconology: New Approaches to Nineteenth-Century Art and Literature*, ed. David C. Miller (New Haven: Yale University Press, 1993), 83; emphasis added.
4. Denise Blake Oleksijczuk serves as a model here; "Gender in Perspective: The King and Queen's Visit to the Panorama in 1793," in *Gendering Landscape Art*, ed. Steven Adams and Anna Gruetzner Robins (New Brunswick, N.J.: Rutgers University Press, 2001), 146–61; 152.
5. My desire to exert a particularizing gaze on this work at the periphery of scholarly discourse on the panorama is influenced by Derrida's *ergon* and *parergon*, particularly as these concepts are applied to landscape representation in Malcolm Andrews's *Landscape and Western Art* (Oxford: Oxford University Press, 1999), 7. Jacques Derrida, *The Truth in Painting*, trans. G. Barrington and I. McLeod (Chicago: University of Chicago Press, 1987).
6. For a general discussion of Gaertner's professional career and biography, see Ursula Cossmann, *Eduard Gaertner, 1801–1877: Sonderausstellung des Märkischen Museum anlässich des 100: Todestages von Eduard Gaertner* (Berlin: Märkischen Museum, 1977); Irmgard Wirth, *Eduard Gaertner, der Berliner Architekturmaler* (Frankfurt-am-Main: Propyläen Verlag, 1979); Dominik Bartmann, ed., *Eduard Gaertner, 1801–1877* (Berlin: Nicolai, 2001); Edit Trost, *Eduard Gaertner* (Berlin: Henschel Verlag, 1991); and "Eduard Gaertners Berlinansichten," in Gisold Lammel, *Preussens Künstlerrepublik von Blechen bis Liebermann: Berliner Realisten des 19. Jahrhunderts* (Berlin: Verlag für Bauwesen, 1995), 25–32.
7. See Birgit Verwiebe, ed., *Unter den Linden: Berlins Boulevard in Ansichten von Schinkel, Gaertner und Menzel* (Berlin: G. und H. Verlag, 1997), and her essay "Erdenstaub und Himmelsdunst—Eduard Gaertners Panoramen," in Bartmann, *Eduard Gaertner*, 97–112, for a history of Berlin's visual culture at this time, particularly as circulated through the activities of the Gropius brothers.
8. The Berlin Scene Painters include Wilhelm Brücke, Wilhelm Barth, Carl Daniel Freydanck, Eduard Biermann, Johann Heinrich Hintze, Karl Hasenpflug, Ludwig Deppe, Ludwig August Most, Friedrich Wilhelm Klose, and Johann Erdmann Hummel. Lammel, *Preussens Künstlerrepublik*, 13–24; and Irmgard Wirth, *Berliner Malerei im 19. Jahrhundert* (Berlin: Siedler, 1990) 169–232. One such guidebook is Samuel H. Spiker, *Berlin und seine Umgebungen im neunzehnten Jahrhundert: Eine Sammlung in Stahl gestochener Ansichten* (Berlin: Verlag Georg Gropius, 1832).
9. Gaertner's positioning here, albeit less conspicuous and demonstrative than that of Charles Willson Peale's self-portrait in *The Artist in His Museum*, serves a similar function as the artist stands to the side and opens his arms in a gesture revealing the scene to us. Many thanks to the "New Perspectives on the Panorama" audience member who highlighted this connection.
10. But it is only a partial portrait: Gaertner fathered twelve children. See Verwiebe, "Erdenstaub," 106. Most scholars identify the woman here as Gaertner's wife.
11. Kevin Lynch, *The Image of the City* (Cambridge: MIT Press, 1960), 2; for the role of landmarks, see 78–83.
12. Beatriz Colomina, "The Split Wall: Domestic Voyeurism," in *Sexuality and Space*, ed. B. Colomina (New York: Princeton Architectural Press, 1992), 73–128; 83.
13. Peter de Bolla, "The Visibility of Visuality: Vauxhall Gardens and the Siting of the Viewer," in *Vision and Textuality*, ed. Stephen Melville and Bill Readings (Durham, N.C.: Duke University Press, 1995), 282–95; 288.
14. Inspired by Wendy Bellion's "'Extend the Sphere': Charles Willson Peale's Panorama of Annapolis," *Art Bulletin* 86, no. 3 (2004): 529–49, I will explore the "choreography of urban space and power" (531) preceding and structuring the gazes of the diverse subjects who occupy this roof.
15. Catherine Johnston et al., eds., *Baltic Light: Early Open-Air Painting in Denmark and Northern Germany* (New Haven: Yale University Press, 1999), 188–89. Other figures on the roof also seem to correspond, in pose and gesture, to the classical works.
16. Oleksijczuk, "Gender in Perspective," 152.
17. On the increasing separation, in the German context, of public and private spheres and the association of women's roles within the domestic realm, see Marion W. Gray, "Prescriptions for Productive Female Domesticity in a Transitional Era: Germany's *Hausmütterliteratur*, 1780–1840," *History of European Ideas* 8 (1987): 413–26; Peter Petershauer, "From *Hausmütter* to *Hausfrau*: Ideals and Realities in Late Eighteenth-Century Germany," *Eighteenth-Century Life* 8 (1982): 72–82; and Karin Hausen, "Family and Role Division: The Polarization of Social Stereotypes in the Nineteenth Century—An Aspect of the Dissociation of Work and Family Life," in *The German Family*, ed. Richard J. Evans and W. R. Lee (London: Croom Helm, 1981) 51–84. More generally, on women's role in German society at this time, see Ute Frevert, *Women in German History: From Bourgeois Emancipation to Sexual Liberation*, trans. Stuart McKinnon-Evans (Oxford: Berg, 1988).
18. See the brief discussions in Peter-Klaus Schuster, "Eduard Gaertner—die 'Linden' als Bildungslandschaft," in Verwiebe, *Unter den Linden*; and Gotthard Brandler, "Die Stadt als Abbild und Sinnbild: Zur Darstellung der Stadt in der deutschen Malerei des frühen 19. Jahrhunderts," in *Studien zur deutschen Kunst und Architektur um 1800*, ed. Peter

Betthausen (Dresden: Verlag der Kunst, 1981), 187–209. My consideration of Gaertner's work, particularly his *Parochialstrasse*, develops this concept more fully, examining the city as an interior that is specifically domestic, an extension of the bourgeois home. Gretchen Holtzapple Bender, "Interior/Landscape: Placelessness and the Gendered Gaze in the Work of Caspar David Friedrich" (Ph.D. diss., Bryn Mawr College, 2001), 87–97. On the numerous appearances of children and families in the panorama, see Verwiebe, "Erdenstaub," 106.

19. Peter-Klaus Schuster, "Gaertner und die geistige Mitte Berlins," *Jahrbuch Preussischer Kulturbesitz* 30 (1993): 292. See Gaertner's *Treppenhaus im Königlichen Schloss Berlin* (1827) and *Die Neue Wache* (1833).
20. Note Georg Friedrich Kersting's three versions of *The Embroiderer*; in Gaertner's family portrait *Living Room of the Schlossermeisters C. F A. Hauschild*, the eldest daughter is depicted sewing.
21. This is one of the most commonly discussed aspects of Oettermann's study. Oettermann, *The Panorama*, 12–13. See also Wallach, "Making a Picture," 83; and Oleksijczuk, "Gender in Perspective," 148–51.
22. This interpretation is substantiated by Gaertner's preparatory sketch in his diary.
23. See my discussion of the gendering of the gaze in early nineteenth-century visual culture, "Interior/Landscape," 97–109, especially in Goethe's account of climbing the church tower at Strasbourg in his 1811 autobiography, *Poetry and Truth*. Oleksijczuk's "Gender in Perspective" likewise evaluates the gendered implications of the very different responses of the king and queen to Barker's panorama of the assembly of the Grand Fleet of the Royal Navy on May 24, 1793. Both of us refer to a contemporary description of Barker's London panorama in *Privilegirte Wöchentliche Gemeinnützige Nachrichten von und für Hamburg*, September 25, 1799, cited by Oettermann, *The Panorama*, 185–86: while "ladies" and "dandies" complained of physical weakness from the effects of the view because of their "delicate nerves," the author and other hearty Hamburg men do not succumb to this frailty. We refer to this passage originally discussed by Oettermann and point to the significant gendered assumptions on which these contemporary reactions are predicated, elided by Oettermann himself. Oleksijczuk, "Gender in Perspective," 152.
24. Oettermann, *The Panorama*, 6–22.
25. Oleksijczuk, "Gender in Perspective," 148–60; and Wallach, "Making a Picture," 83.
26. Hannelore Gärtner and Sibylle Einholz, "Pro Memoria Romantik: Wanderungen durch Berlin," in *Berliner Romantik: Orte, Spuren und Begegnungen*, ed. H. Gärtner and Annette Purfürst (Berlin: Trescher Verlag, 1992), 12.
27. See Bellion, "'Extend the Sphere,'" 531–37, on the elaborate device Peale invented to complete his panoramic drawings of Annapolis.
28. Oleksijczuk, "Gender in Perspective," 158.
29. Michael Charlesworth also connects monumentality to the miniature in the panorama in *Landscape and Vision in Nineteenth-Century Britain and France* (Aldershot, U.K.: Ashgate, 2008), 16.
30. Oleksijczuk, "Gender in Perspective," 158. See also de Bolla, "The Visibility of Visuality," 198.
31. Charlesworth, *Landscape and Vision*, 4–9.
32. Wallach, "Making a Picture," 84.
33. Oettermann, *The Panorama*, 31.
34. His son, Friedrich Wilhelm IV, assumed the throne in 1840 and continued, albeit to a lesser extent, the patronage of Gaertner and other Berlin scene painters. The high point of Berlin scene painting in the 1820s and 1830s is typically discussed as a consequence of Friedrich Wilhelm III's interest.
35. Verwiebe, "Erdenstaub," 106.
36. Eventually a second copy of the panorama was commissioned so Friedrich Wilhelm III's daughter, now the Russian czarina, could remember her homeland. On the king's role as patron of the *Panorama*, see Verwiebe, *Unter den Linden*, 152.
37. In Gaertner's 1844 interior view of Friedrich Wilhelm IV's unoccupied throne room, the throne sits vacant at the far end, centered along the axis of the room. Both the *Panorama* and the throne room scene display the king's absent presence, enunciated through a prominent central axis and a traditional perspectival system.
38. Verwiebe, "Erdenstaub," 104.
39. The traditional arrangement of the separate canvases, hinged together in a tripartite manner to form a triptych, would also support this religious reading of the work.
40. For Prussia's and Germany's movement toward social and political reform between 1780 and 1840 (and scholars' historiographical views of these tumultuous years), see Joachim Whaley, "The German Lands before 1815," and Christopher Clark, "Germany 1815–1848: Restoration or Pre-March?" in *Nineteenth-Century Germany: Politics, Culture and Society 1780–1918*, ed. John Breuilly (New York: Oxford University Press, 2001), 15–37, 40–65.
41. The period's more famous work commemorating the March Revolution is Adolph Menzel's *Lying in State of the Victims of the March Revolution*. For a detailed discussion of this work and the revolutionary events it references (Friedrich Wilhelm IV's brief loss of control and possession of the city), see Christopher B. With, "Adolph von Menzel and the German Revolution of 1848," *Zeitschrift für Kunstgeschichte* 42 (1979): 195–214; Françoise Forster-Hahn, "'Die Aufbahrung der Märzgefallen': Menzel's Unfinished Painting as a Parable of the Aborted Revolution of 1848," in *Kunst um 1800 und die Folgen: Werner Hoffmann zu Ehren*, ed. Christian Beutler, Peter-Klaus Schuster, and Martin Warnke (Munich: Prestel, 1988), 221–32; Peter Paret, *Art as History: Episodes in the Culture and Politics of Nineteenth-Century Germany* (Princeton: Princeton University Press, 1988), 93–104; Albert Boime, "Social Identity and Political Authority in the Response of Two Prussian Painters to the Revolution of 1848," *Art History* 13, no. 3 (1990): 344–85; and Michael Fried, whose ideas on Menzel's art as an "Art of Embodiment" influence my reading of Gaertner's *Barricade*; see Fried, *Menzel's Realism: Art and Embodiment in Nineteenth-Century Berlin* (New Haven: Yale University Press, 2002), 202–5.
42. For a comprehensive discussion of the history of the Reichstag building, Jeanne-Claude and Christo's project, and Norman Foster's renovations, see Brian Ladd, *The Ghosts of Berlin: Confronting German History in the Urban Landscape* (Chicago: University of Chicago Press, 1997), 83–96; for critical analyses of the political meanings of the new Reichstag dome, see Peter Chametzky, "Rebuilding the Nation: Norman Foster's Reichstag Renovation and Daniel Libeskind's Jewish Museum Berlin," *Centropa* 1, no. 3 (2001): 245–64; and Lutz Koepnick, "Redeeming History? Foster's Dome and the Political Aesthetic of the Berlin Republic," *German Studies Review* 24, no. 2 (2001): 303–23.
43. In so doing, I extend my gaze beyond that of Chametzky and Koepnick, whose accounts focus primarily on the properties of the dome itself. While "panoramic" views were made of Berlin before Gaertner's 1834 painting, I believe his was the first to attempt a fully round, 360-degree view.
44. Both Koepnick and Chametzky consider the facile way Foster's glass dome is connected to a democractic impulse. For a more thorough reading of the use of glass in modern German architecture and its political meanings, see Deborah Barnstone, *The Transparent State: Architecture and Politics in Postwar Germany* (London: Routledge, 2005).

RICHARD MAXWELL WITH KATIE TRUMPENER

5 Panorama, Glasshouse, Museum

Alexander von Humboldt, Franz Boas, Gustaf Kolthoff

Knowledge of the works of creation and appreciation of their guarantor would be powerfully increased if, besides museums, and thrown open like them, to the public, a number of panoramic buildings containing alternating different geographic latitudes and from different zones of elevation, should be erected in our large cities.

—Alexander von Humboldt, *Cosmos: A Sketch of a Physical Description of the Universe* (1845–1862)

Though an entire circle of objects surrounds us, we only notice a certain part of the circle itself, and objects behind us are hidden from our sight, until we turn around.

—C. W. Eckersberg, *Linear Perspective Used in the Art of Painting* (1841)

Maybe one morning, walking in dry, glassy air,
I'll turn and see the miracle occur:
Nothing at my back, the void
Behind me, with a drunkard's terror,

Then, as if on a screen, trees houses hills
will suddenly collect for the usual illusion.
But it will be too late; and I'll walk on silent
among the men who don't look back, with my secret.

—Eugenio Montale, "Maybe One Morning" (ca. 1925)

INTRODUCTION

That a panorama is round, envelops us, constituting a fiction; that it implies the roundness of the world, manipulates two kinds of light; that it can generate the feeling of danger; that it gathers the world's fragments into one circle; that it reconstructs the viewer's vision; that it creates a sense of the world as utopian; that it is dreamlike and encourages action, especially travel: all this has been recognized. This chapter explores less-often acknowledged overlaps between the panorama and the glasshouse, as institutions bringing together and exhibiting the world. The nineteenth century's most iconic iron-and-glass building, Joseph Paxton's Crystal Palace, was a massively expanded glasshouse, based on his earlier Great Stove at Chatsworth. It was created to contain the pioneering Great Exhibition of the Industry of All Nations of 1851, a panoramic display of commodities from across the planet.

The German geographer Alexander von Humboldt (1769–1859), the panorama's most powerful early advocate, envisioned it as an educational scientific tool as well as an art form. In 1827–28, following his South American voyage of exploration, Humboldt delivered "Cosmos," a public lecture series, at the Berlin Academy, describing the universe (including lunar volcanoes, sunspots, meteorites, and southern constellations). In 1834 Humboldt had the further idea of "portraying the entire world, everything we know today about the heavens and life on earth, from nebulae to the geography of mosses and granites, and all this in a stimulating style, that will delight the mind."[1] His eventual *Cosmos* (*Kosmos*, 5 vols., 1845–1862) attempted a comprehensive "physical description of the universe." The book's key concerns, scale, and conceptual ambition also transformed the panorama: thereafter, panoramas became heavier, more immersive, more ambitiously scaled. Humboldt envisioned a world panorama, obsessed with largeness and magnificence, but also the holder of empty space, affirming yet denying the void.

Cosmos lauds a trend-setting recent greenhouse, Karl Friedrich Schinkel's Palm House on Peacock Island (Pfaueninsel), near Potsdam, an innovative glass-and-metal folly transporting a bit of the tropics to a frigid climate. To Humboldt, the glass house and the panorama shared the ability to immerse visitors in an artificial environment while opening the world to them. As this chapter demonstrates, Humboldt's ideas had lasting consequences for museological display conventions and the emotional and aesthetic responses that exhibitions solicit.

BARKER, GAERTNER, HUMBOLDT: THE TURN OF A GLANCE

Robert Barker initially conceived the panorama as "*la nature à coup d'oeil*": nature at a glance. As his 1787 patent application specifies, "The painter or drawer must fix his station, and delineate correctly and connectedly every object which presents itself to his view as he turns around, concluding his drawings by a connection with where he began."[2] Barker emphasized turning motion. Panoramas offer nature not at one glance but in a series of glances spliced together. A panorama composed by Barker's means would resemble a succession of film frames, except that these frames' contents would not overlap in subject matter; composed successively, they would fit together into a single continuous, surrounding view.

Barker's patent also specifies the conditions under which visitors could inspect this view. Barker, Ralph Hyde suggests, believed these viewing conditions to be his real invention. The patent mentions the canvas's circular framing, the top-lighting, the central viewing platform ("inclosure") to prevent viewers from approaching the painting too closely, "interceptions" to block the view of the painting's top and bottom edges, all helping observers, in the patent's wording, "feel as if really on the very spot."[3]

Panoramas' nineteenth-century proliferation attests to their effectiveness at creating that you-are-there feeling. Yet contemporary illustrators also evoked panoramas' demands on viewers, as they proceeded through mazes of tunnels and stairs or gathered here and there around the viewing platforms' edges. When making his image, the panoramist turned systematically, helped by a framing device. While viewing it, visitors perambulated. Sooner or later most would have followed the circle the artist originally inscribed, but on their own time and order—ambling, drawn by curiosity or surprise.[4]

Viewers always stood on the same sort of elevated viewing platform, yet (particularly in city panoramas) this took on many fictive identities. In 1821, during St. Paul's Cathedral's restoration, the land surveyor Thomas Hornor made two thousand sketches from scaffolding atop its dome. These became the basis of his great London panorama, opened in 1829 in Decimus Burton's custom-built Colosseum (see fig 1.4). Like St. Paul's, it offered two galleries from which to observe. "Extending umbrella-like from underneath the lower" gallery, Richard Altick explains, "was a replica of a portion of the outer dome of St. Paul's, so that, bending over the railing, a spectator would see it closest at hand and then, beyond it in the

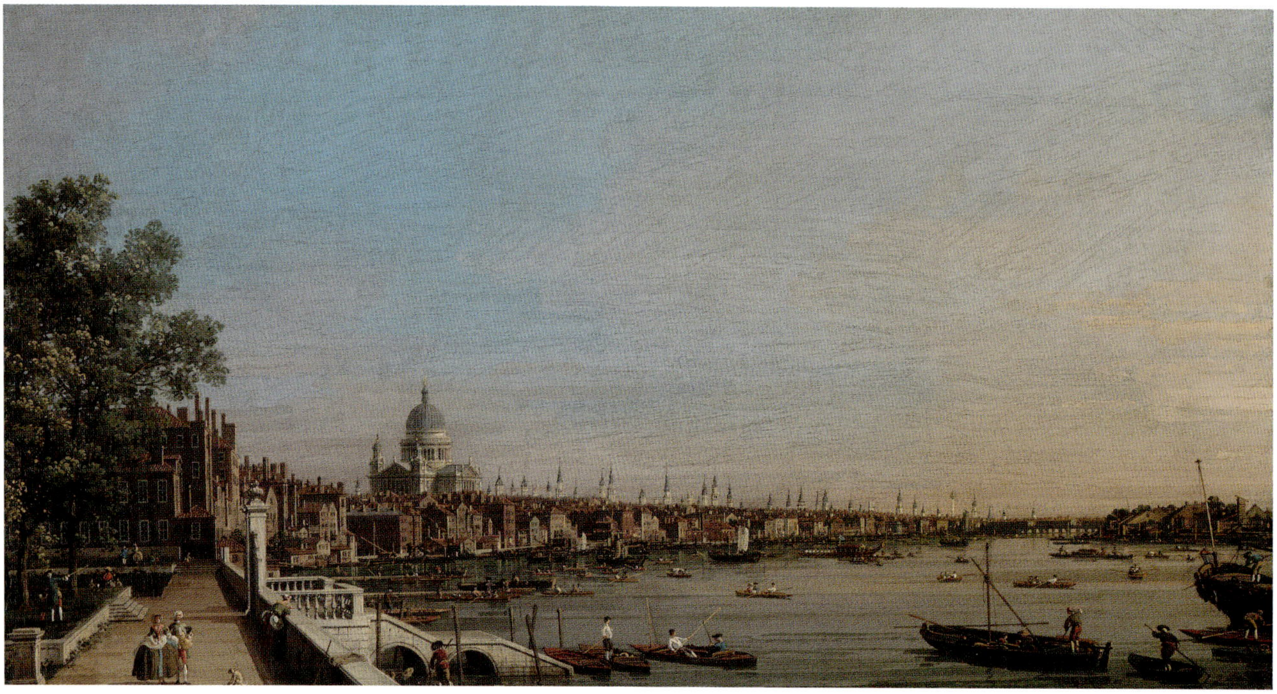

FIG. 5.1. Canaletto (Venetian, 1697–1768), *The City from Near the Terrace of Somerset House*, ca. 1750. Oil on canvas, 38.6 × 72.9 cm (15 3/16 × 28 11/16 in.). Yale Center for British Art, New Haven, Connecticut. Paul Mellon Collection (B1976.96).

immediate foreground—the three-dimensional mockup blending into the painting—those portions of the cathedral's roof and towers which would be seen from the corresponding place on the real gallery."[5] Near the viewer were three-dimensional objects and materials (including the original ball and cross), and a mockup of the scaffold-surrounded St. Paul's summit when Hornor made his original sketches. Farther away were trompe l'oeil architectural elements, especially the two great towers at the cathedral's western front. Visitors commented how seamlessly painted towers blended with three-dimensional architectural elements.

Before the age of the panorama, most city views did not worry about just where viewers were situated: quintessential sixteenth- or seventeenth-century London views were taken from a position hovering impossibly above the Thames, from which the river's north side can be surveyed for miles in both directions. A generation before Barker's patent, however, Canaletto's view of London and the Thames looking from Somerset House Gardens toward London Bridge lets viewers conceive themselves lingering on the terrace a few yards west of the figures promenading up and down, looking onto the river (fig. 5.1). In hindsight, Canaletto's composition seems an ur-panorama of London, paying almost as much attention to *conditions* of display, to situating viewers on an actual, practicable site of observation, as to what they observe.

From Barker onward, this interest remained an integral part of most great nineteenth-century city panoramas. The artist drawing or painting a panorama turned on an abstract, geometric point. He was at a specific locale—Edinburgh's Calton Hill, at the Albion Mills on the Thames's south side, or on a scaffolded platform rigged on St. Paul's dome. But he did not, while making the picture, wander *about* this terrain: he turned 360 degrees, without straying from the chosen center. The viewing platform's material existence was experienced most fully not by the artist in the process of sketching—not by the person who was actually *there*—but by viewers who enjoyed the simulated, reconstructed vista. It is in reconstruction that the original viewing platform's material existence can be appreciated most fully.

The panorama's cultural and formal meaning may reside partly in an implied contrast between the artist's self-discipline, remaining at a single point while turning, and visitors' much greater freedom, piecing the view together through many pieces randomly observed in a rush or stroll about a viewing point more fictive yet more real than the artist's. Yet a third term fills out this contrast between two kinds of motion and of viewing. As we stand on that platform, the view in front of us remains still. One way to preserve the panorama's lifelikeness is not to paint any figures into the cityscape below, or better yet, to render those figures so small that their lack of motion cannot distract the viewer from the lifelike quality of this frameless, engulfing image.

But in this case the panorama's viewing mechanisms are self-subverting. A traditional attraction of panoramas is their abundant detail. Hornor not only surveyed the city from above but subsequently visited the districts he sketched: his panorama reproduces not only a view from afar but an equally insistent set of close-ups. Details contribute to an effect, even though they cannot all be seen sharply. But panoramic entrepreneurs like Hornor added telescopes to their platforms, at the Colosseum and elsewhere, through which viewers could examine the marvels of minutiae on display below and see all those tiny figures close up, breaking the illusion that they were just too far away for their movements to be easily perceived.

The panorama, hence, contrasts not just the artist's disciplined 360-degree turn with the visitor's hedonistic ramble on an illusionistic platform but that rambling with the absolute immobility of the tiny people below. Stillness is crucial to the panorama. When William Wordsworth, a fascinated panorama visitor, composed his own verbal panorama from the vantage point of Westminster Bridge, he observed that all London's "mighty heart is lying still!" in a temporary death, anticipating rush-hour resurrection.[6]

As panorama historians such as Walter Benjamin and Dolf Sternberger have noted, the panorama's success led the term to be used loosely, sometimes meaning any big view, not just one composed by Barker's means and observed under standard panoramic display conditions. Yet even "panoramas" not fully fitting Barker's patent definition have often been shaped by the turning motion allowing the artist to compose the panorama, the related but distinct mode of viewing the finished product, and the contrasting stillness of the streets below, where the whirl of daily routine becomes most evident.

1. A panorama is a view from a height recorded by one person systematically making one 360-degree turn.

2. A panorama is a view from a height observed under certain specified optical and architectural circumstances by many persons circulating erratically, according to whim, around that 360-degree turn previously executed by the surveyor-painter.

3. Many works not literally panoramas—engravings, etchings, framed panel paintings—nonetheless incorporate these panoramic conventions. Such works tend to function as representations of panoramas (strictly speaking) rather than simply as representations of views from above.

The experience of most panoramas, moreover, was mediated by the orientation maps accompanying them, generally taking the same distinctive form. The circular panorama seems reflected in this surface, as in a convex mirror, sometimes with anamorphic distortions, sometimes diagrammatically. On city panoramas, major buildings are labeled. The center of this globelike image is frequently the building from which the panorama has been taken and can now (supposedly) be seen. If urban panoramas are imaginative restatements of a city's appearance from a particularly advantageous viewpoint, the orientation maps accompanying them are further restatements, compressions of views that precisely *cannot* be taken in at a glance into views that can. They encourage us to circulate, wander, see the panorama from many angles—even while they sum up what we would see at a glance from these angles. They encourage us simultaneously to look from a variety of angles, to take in the panorama according to what we might call either (in its dizzying elevation) a bird's-eye or (in its condensed anamorphic turnings) a fish-eye view. The view's circularity is summed up as something we can see all at once, as though we had eyes (a bird's, a fish's, our own somehow multiplied) in the backs of our heads.

Following Gretchen Bender's analysis of Eduard Gaertner's 1834 *Panorama of Berlin Seen from the Roof of the Friedrichswerdersche Kirche* (chapter 4), this chapter briefly returns to Gaertner's two corner panoramas as a representation of Humboldt's Berlin—and hence of Humboldt himself. Though Gaertner's title alludes to the 360-degree panorama-in-the-round, his six panels make no pretense at an engulfing and continuous view (impossible anyway on this intimate scale), nor is there illumination from above. Finally, there is no viewing platform from which to spy out a supposedly distant, "real" spectacle; Gaertner partly returns us to the Albertian territory of panel painting, with its fiction of perspectival view through a window.[7]

Nevertheless, Gaertner's double triptych recuperates important panoramic features, especially in his disposition of viewers on a viewing platform. The panorama is depicted not, as Barker first put it, as a viewing opportunity revealing "nature at a glance" but as requiring many glances by diverse individuals, each making erratic circles around a raised gallery. Gaertner developed the panoramic convention of many viewers on his own terms, by placing tableaux of survey all over the vast church roof.[8]

Yet the Friedrichswerdersche Kirche view is not particularly concerned with rendering Berlin in a frantic state of motion; obligatory antlike beings crawl about, some miles away, but their frozenness can only be emphasized, certainly not hidden, by the leisurely, static scene on the roof above, a frozen tableau in contrast to that mobility which the panoramic viewer normally claims. Gaertner's disposition of his rooftop viewers constructs a panorama of panoramists.

Amid the ontological self-questioning inherent in panoramic form, Gaertner's panorama allegorizes and grounds its own historical moment. Schinkel's church roof (1824–31) is flanked by a narrow walkway on which Gaertner places various characters, including city dignitaries, to look out over the prospect. Humboldt alone has brought a scientific instrument to the church summit and looks out alertly, absorbed by the development of a new Berlin, itself largely Schinkel's work and, as Kurt Forster has argued, conceived in a panoramic mode.[9] From this rooftop, indeed, we glimpse central Berlin's further Schinkel buildings, including the New Watch (1817–18); theater (1818–22); and Old Museum (1822–30).

Schinkel, Forster argues, self-consciously created new urban vistas with spectacular, uplifting sight lines—a process allegorized in Schinkel's 1825 painting *View of Greece in Its Flowering* (now lost, but known from copies), showing workers, high above Athens, hoisting statuary friezes onto the Parthenon. The painting at once celebrates and demystifies the monument, revealing the human labor behind the creation of peerless views while using the workers high on their scaffolding to model the position of future spectators, intent on aesthetic consumption.[10]

Gaertner's painting, in turn, poses Berlin's intelligentsia on Schinkel's scaffolding to admire Schinkel's Berlin. Gaertner's Humboldt appears intense and didactic. He thinks about the educational prospects of immersion in an illusion; he finds himself transported to a panoramic viewpoint where he can observe a metropolis, an ideal city, a *Cosmos* in miniature, growing all around him. Gaertner evokes the grand success of Humboldt's lectures; their stimulating influence on the middle classes; *Cosmos*'s success in expanding awareness and curiosity about the world; the power of Humboldt's intellectual leadership in this burgeoning new Berlin; the possibility of exploration. Berlin's transformation stretches several miles, making the telescope vital. The telescope also evokes Humboldt's observations of South America, that enormous continent he had been the first European explorer to measure adequately. Gaertner's panorama thus dramatizes an important cause-and-effect sequence: Humboldt, stunned by the vividness of what he sees, infused with the confidence to communicate the prospect's extent and intricacy, forging common purpose with his bourgeois listeners, startling some into action.

PEACOCK ISLAND: HUMBOLDT'S DISCOURSES ON THE COSMOS

Circumnavigation opened up the world, allowing a new way of imagining the globe. The panorama's rounded format is a silent reminder of this possibility. It reveals and confirms circumnavigation's pleasures, speaking with particular power to those who stayed home: to know the world is a round globe, that the explorers will return. Increasingly, explorers returned with plants, rare botanic specimens collected in remote places to edify scientists everywhere. The overflow of largely tropical specimens to be stored, displayed, and preserved stimulated several disciplines and encouraged the rise of the greenhouse as an architectural type and of cultural anthropology as mode of inquiry.

To frame his 1809 novella collection *The Winter Garden*, set in a Berlin nobleman's house in the wake of the Napoleonic Occupation, Achim von Arnim imagined a domestic winter garden as an ideal poet's retreat from a politically uncertain world. In this particular winter garden, however, what surrounds tropical plants and animals is not walls of glass but a painted panorama of Humboldt sketching the Andean volcano Chimborazo (which Humboldt himself had climbed). As Vance Byrd points out, the panorama is here taken out of the public sphere to become a centerpiece of "bourgeois sociability."[11] At the same time the panorama represents the wide and distant world, the Humboldtian quest for knowledge.

A decade later, Humboldt himself persuaded King Friedrich Wilhelm III of Prussia to acquire a collection of palm trees, and in 1821 the king commissioned Schinkel to build a palm house on Peacock Island. This royal garden near Potsdam contained a landscape of follies creating a

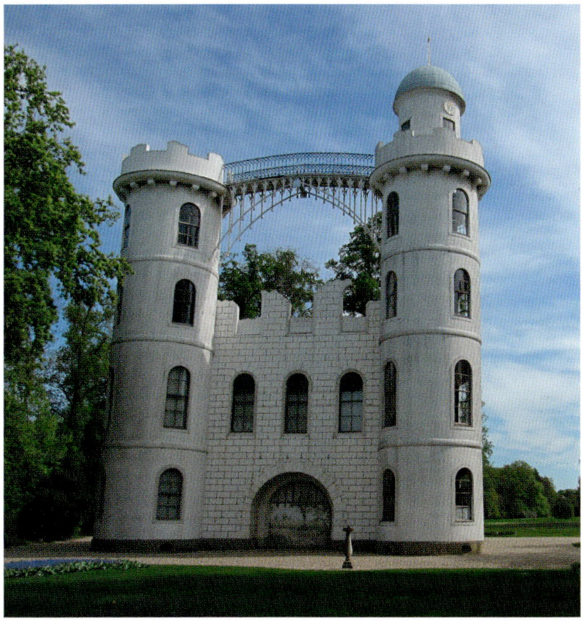

FIG. 5.2. Schloss, Pfaueninsel.

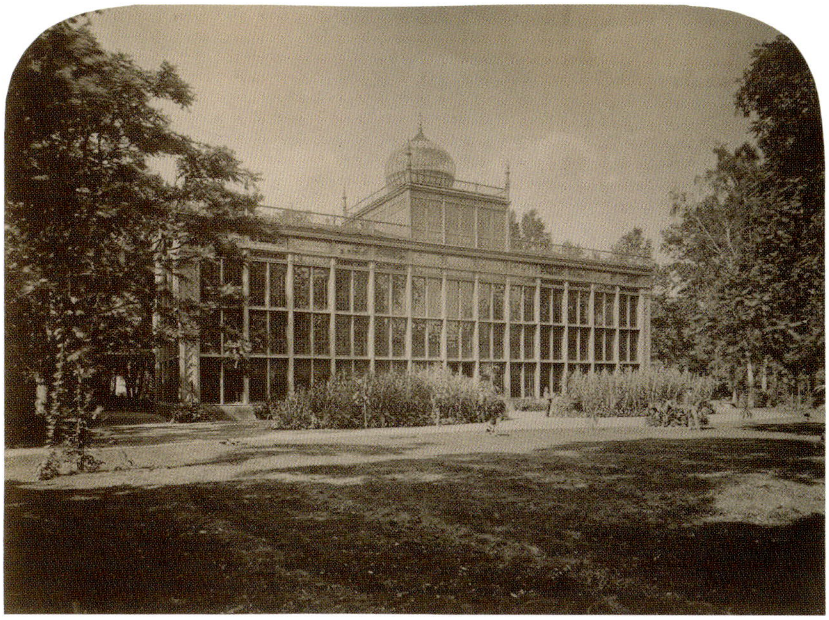

FIG. 5.3. Karl Friedrich Schinkel (German, 1781–1841), Palm House, Pfaueninsel, 1831 (destroyed 1880).

fantasy world to which the king could retreat. Nothing of the Palm House survives today—although visitors to the island are still greeted by a fake castle with a painted prospect through its portcullis, a wrought-iron viewing platform offering panoramic prospects (fig. 5.2), a menagerie, and a gothic dairy. Defying Berlin's frigid climate (and requiring immense upkeep funds), the Palm House accommodated eleven thousand plants the king had purchased, including eighty palm varieties (fig. 5.3). Schinkel constructed its dome based on Thomas and William Daniell's aquatint of the Taj Mahal, and he arranged a performance in the Palm House of scenes from Thomas Moore's 1817 *Lalla Rookh*, with the queen in the starring role.[12] Karl Blechen's vivid paintings of the performance record a vast, enveloping building artfully arranged with palms (fig. 5.4). The view stretches back to surround the viewer by rare, precious plants, brought from other climes, evoked by the grooved columns and their elaborate, organic-looking capitals. Some appear to be growing palm fronds, suggesting the whole building will soon burst into green growth.

Humboldt kept a preserved palm frond on his desk. His work on *Cosmos* as lecture series, then book, forced him to consider how to survey and comprehend vast material. Barker's enclosed panoramas, Humboldt concluded, surpassed any printed texts at defining the zones of nature. These present a distinct "physiognomy," defined especially by native plants; botany was capable of drawing

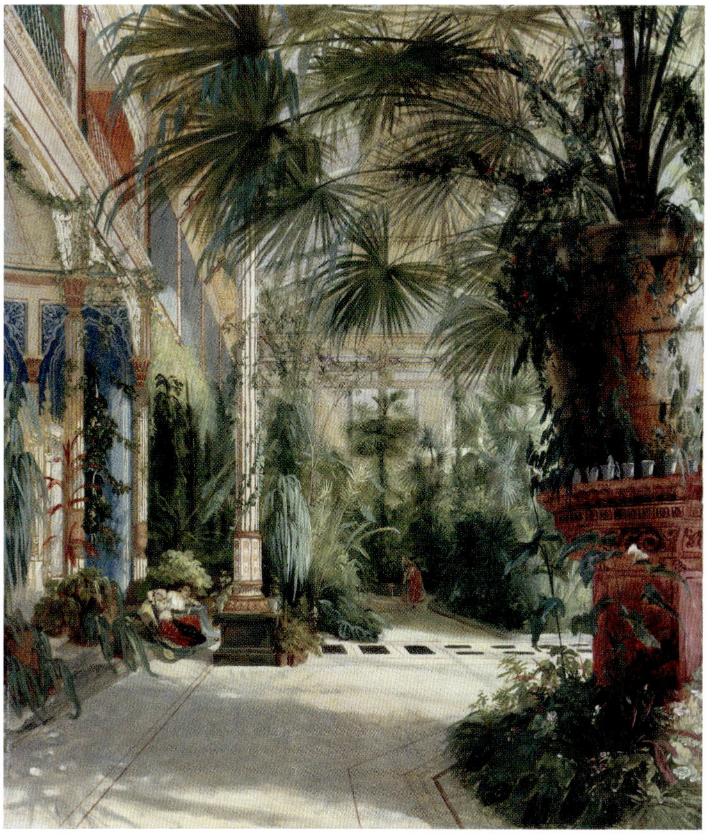

FIG. 5.4. Karl Blechen (German, 1798–1840), *The Interior of the Palm House*, 1832. Oil on paper, laid down on canvas, 64 × 56 cm (25 1/8 × 22 in.). Nationalgalerie, Berlin.

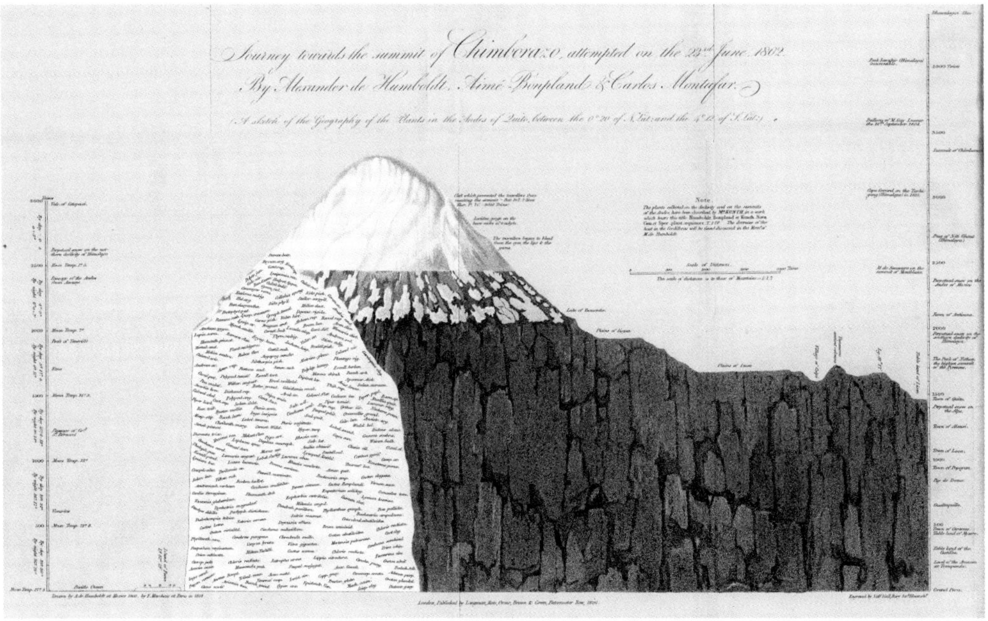

FIG. 5.5. *Journey towards the Summit of Chimborazo, Attempted on the 23rd June 1802. By Alexander de Humboldt, Aimé Bonpland & Carlos Montúfar*, from vol. 3 of Humboldt's *Personal Narrative of Travels to the Equinoctial Regions of the New Continent, during the Years 1799–1804*, trans. from the French by Helen Maria Williams (London: Longman, Rees, Orme, Brown, and Green, 1822). Copperplate profile chart, 24 × 37.4 cm (9 3/8 × 14 3/4 in.). Rare Book Division, Department of Rare Books and Special Collections, Princeton University Library.

lines between different zones.[13] Landscape painting, to Humboldt, was dedicated to differentiating such boundaries; his famous 1834 cross section of Chimborazo showed all botanical zones from the mountain's base to its top (fig. 5.5).

Panorama and cross section offer different ways of penetrating a scene, visualizing it as a whole, seeing the relation between its sections. "Calculated to raise the feeling of admiration for nature," panoramas potentially replicated the effect of Chimborazo's multiple ecosystems, foothills to summit.[14] So did Peacock Island's Palm House, transporting visitors by miraculous immersion in a tropical environment centered by that great traveler's icon, the palm tree.

> When, in the Messrs. Loddiges' palmhouse, or in the *Pfauen-Insel*, near Potsdam (a monument of the love of nature of my noble and departed sovereign), we look down from the high gallery in the bright noonday sun on the luxuriant reed and tree-like palms below, we feel, for a moment, in a state of complete delusion as to the locality to which we are transported, and we may even believe ourselves to be actually in a tropical climate, looking from the summit of a hill on a small grove of palms. It is true that the aspect of the deep azure of the sky, and the impression produced by a greater intensity of light, are wanting, but, notwithstanding, the illusion is more perfect, and exercises a stronger effect on the imagination than is excited by the most perfect painting.[15]

In some respects, nonetheless, Humboldt remains disappointed by the Palm House's lighting effects, unsuccessfully mediated by the building (and Potsdam skies and sun), and unable to integrate two kinds of light.

Through *Cosmos*, Humboldt's Chimborazo image had an indelible effect on the German and world public. The appearance of *Cosmos*'s first volume, in 1845, created a sensation as booksellers and continents competed for copies. For a century it remained a key work of popular science, Humboldt himself the epitome of the heroic scientific explorer. Humboldt had made himself a protagonist of his survey of the universe's immensity: making his way up a river, cutting through Brazil's unknown territory, avoiding Indian tribes with poisonous arrows, becoming his era's most famous volcano climber.

The Humboldt panorama's defining attributes are scope and ambition: Humboldt atop a towering volcano with an immense crater on one side, determined not to be swallowed up; on the other, a view of all Ecuador to learn from. Humboldt tended to think, astronomically, of the viewer surrounded by vast rings encompassing almost unimaginable zones of space, spheres, revolutions. The Humboldt panorama is designed to take in the cosmos: comets, volcanoes, nebulae, stars, jungles. Even if it fails to, it has the potential to include everything. Consequently, the viewer has great confidence there is something behind him: the circle extends, universally, preempting the void.

Cosmos's discussion of the painted panorama concludes with the new medium of photography, yet it wistfully anticipates the botanical dioramas later presented by natural history museums. "Panoramas are more productive of effect than scenic decorations, since the spectator, enclosed, as it were, within a magic circle, and wholly removed from all the disturbing influences of reality, may the more easily fancy that he is actually surrounded by a foreign scene. . . . An enchanting effect might be produced by a characteristic delineation of nature, sketched on the rugged declivities of the Himalayas."[16] *Cosmos* praises—and juxtaposes—panoramas and palm houses. But the panorama comes first because it is popular and commercial, mass entertainment and education. It is not a royal indulgence; it remains open to visits from anyone able to pay. Above all, it simulates a sense of unfamiliar danger from a position of safety. On these terms, the panorama most aptly simulates what was called "Humboldtian science," the observer a participant who placed himself in peril.

Yet Humboldt still included both examples of didactic illusionism. Humboldt was a materialist who opposed Prussia's idealist establishment, and his well-known proclivity for measuring things was one way of resisting idealists' manner of thinking. Humboldt's mention of the Palm House asserted his connections with a royal circle of privilege and self-indulgence. Yet his lectures, conversely, represented a great nineteenth-century effort at mass education, in resistance to court elitism. As Gaertner's Berlin panorama underscores, Humboldt's public lectures and *Cosmos* aimed to place a mass public in imaginative touch with the cosmos and thus transform this public to become adequate to the new Berlin growing up around them.

GREENHOUSE AND CRYSTAL PALACE

Technical innovations from the mid-eighteenth century onward enabled the Victorian greenhouse. The ridge-and-furrow roof; the flexible wrought-iron glazing bar; the new means of manufacturing glass, the cylinder process, which enabled creation of sheets of glass as much as forty-eight inches long; construction by modular unit: Joseph Paxton integrated all these. As head gardener to the Duke of Devonshire at Chatsworth, he managed, between 1836 and 1840, to construct a successful horticultural hothouse, the Great Stove. Paxton used the tropical atmosphere to force a giant Amazonian lily to flower. The enormous amounts spent on such stunts reveal the extent of horticultural training and interest, the frantic effort to amass the most unusual, comprehensive collection: the impulse echoed the seventeenth-century Tradescant family, eighteenth-century circumnavigation scientists like Joseph Banks, and the curators at Kew, an institution whose periodic fight for survival and location amid London's smog never undermined its aspiration to be the world's premier scientific garden.

When the Great Exhibition of the Works of Industry of All Nations was announced for 1851, the building committee accepted Paxton's design, which echoed but was far larger than Chatsworth's Great Stove and boasted ten miles of exhibition space. Paxton's Hyde Park building was seen as either a great experiment or a blot on the urban landscape. The London *Times* dubbed it a "monstrous greenhouse."[17] Yet royal patronage, government funding, and international fame gave it a special status among all iron-and-glass buildings of its time.[18]

The mapmaker James Wyld wanted to erect a model of the world inside the Crystal Palace: he was turned down, so instead he built an enormous, four-story globe in Leicester Square, near Burford's panorama building. Staircases leading upward allowed people to see the earth's surface, especially (no doubt in tribute to Humboldt) its volcanoes, all erupting at once. Wyld's popular Great Globe was held in place by sturdy scaffolding (fig. 5.6) and contained sufficient room to exhibit his wares.[19] The world turned inside out: the Great Globe harmonized with the Great Exhibition's theme.

And the "new and magnificent diorama of Jerusalem and the Holy Land from sketches made on the spot during repeated journeys in the East by Mr. W. H. Bartlett" gave viewers the impulse to travel.[20] Like every subsequent world exposition, the Crystal Palace attracted panoramic exhibitions to its peripheries, reinforcing its original raison d'être. In George Cruikshank's spectacular plate for Henry Mayhew's comic novel, *1851; or, The Adventures of Mr. and Mrs. Sandboys and Family, Who Came Up to London to "Enjoy Themselves," and to See the Great Exhibition* (1851), everybody learned of and hastened toward the Crystal

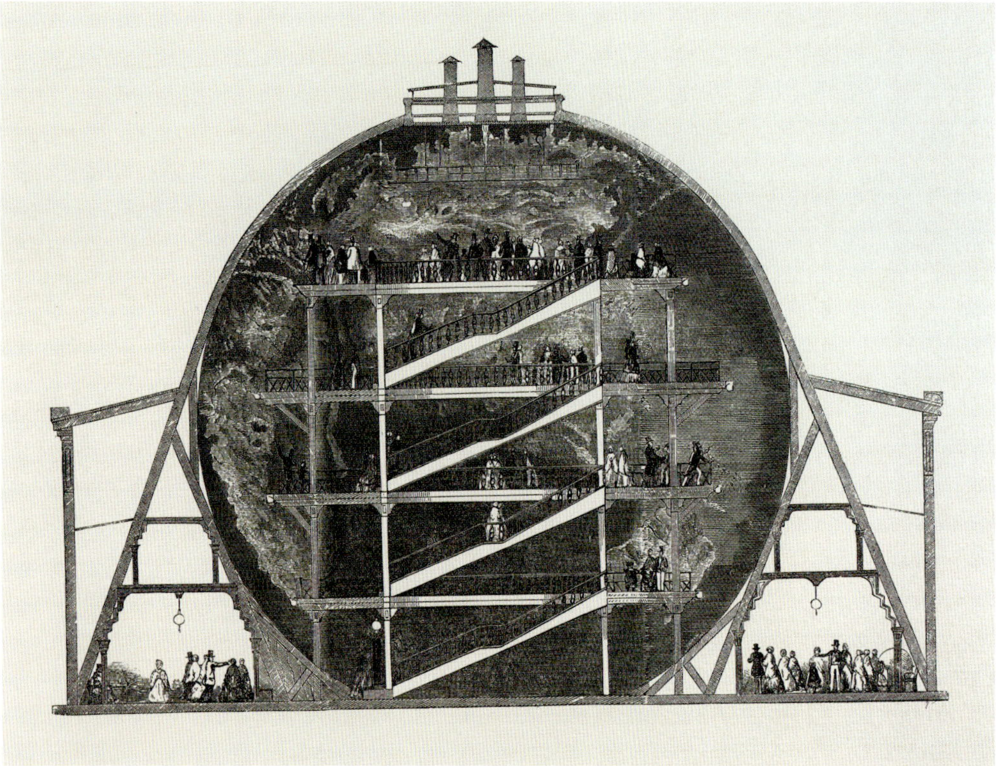

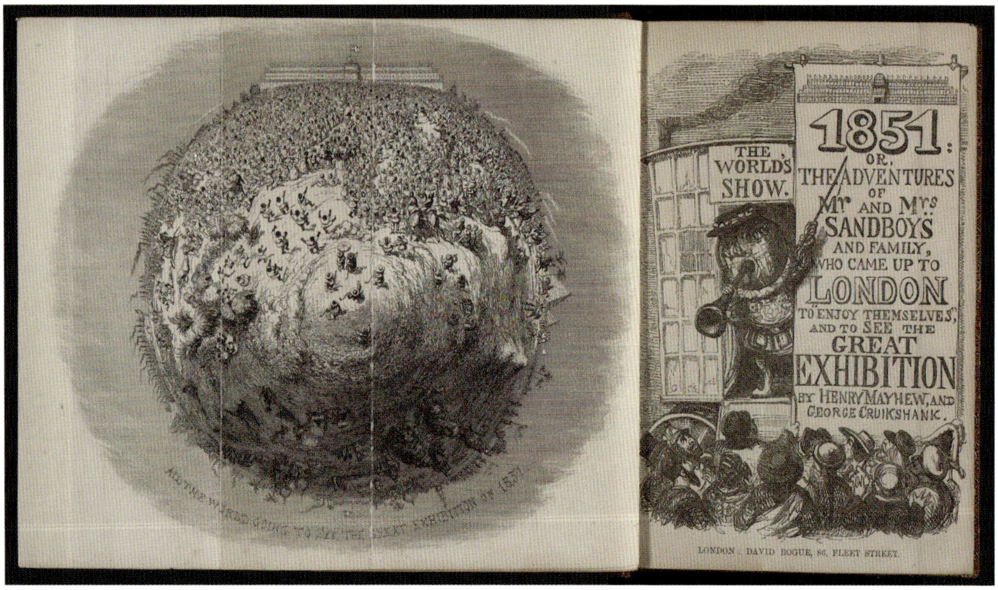

FIG. 5.6. *Mr. Wyld's Model of the Earth—Sectional View, Illustrated London News*, June 7, 1851, 511.

FIG. 5.7. Title page from *1851; or, The Adventures of Mr. and Mrs. Sandboys and Family, Who Came Up to London to "Enjoy Themselves," and to See the Great Exhibition* by Henry Mayhew and George Cruikshank (London: David Bogue, 1851). Wood engraving. Yale Center for British Art, New Haven, Connecticut, Gift of Gloria Scheuer.

Palace, its gargantuan size making it a natural goal for all the world's peoples. Cruikshank's globe-headed showman blows his horn: "the world's show" (fig. 5.7).

Epithets like "this world panorama" refer not to the panorama's form so much as to its inclusiveness and ambition; they are a tribute to British imperialism. They reveal what the Victorians did *not* find essential about the panorama: the sense of teeming plentitude could be created by assemblage rather than by circular form; viewers could feel themselves surrounded by the world without optical effects. Contemporary visual novelty devices nonetheless worked to harness a Crystal Palace effect. These objects, exemplified by scrolling paper panoramas, focused particularly on the pomp of capitals (London, Paris, Berlin) and spaces of leisure, including the circus, fairground, and world's fair.[21]

Popular midcentury Crystal Palace souvenirs thus included "tunnel books" and paper panoramas, which

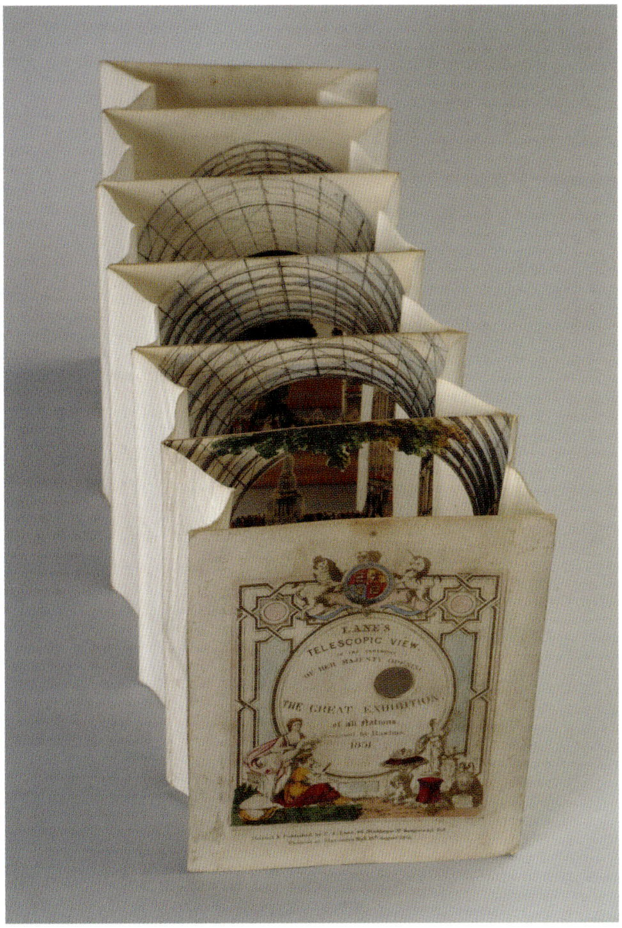

FIG. 5.8. *Lane's Telescopic View of the Ceremony of Her Majesty Opening the Great Exhibition of All Nations*, 1851. The George Peabody Library, Sheridan Libraries, Johns Hopkins University.

allowed viewers back home, long after the fair was over, to reexperience the depth and breadth of fair exhibits. In tunnel (or "peep-show") views like *Lane's Telescopic View of the Ceremony of Her Majesty Opening the Great Exhibition of All Nations* (1851; fig. 5.8) and the contemporaneous *Telescopic View of the Interior of the Great Industrial Exhibition*, viewers looked down a long sequence of pop-up scenes to gain a cumulative view of fair displays.

Such devices, as Rachel Ferguson notes in her 1937 historical novel *Alas, Poor Lady*, had potentially long afterlives, accumulating throughout the nineteenth century in middle-class parlors and nurseries. As late as the 1870s, two decades after the Great Exhibition, playthings still evoked its splendor for a new generation of children. Ferguson's paterfamilias thus "enjoyed his visits to the nursery floor." "He would look indulgently at the newest toys, at Queenie's peepshow, a long elaborate strip of cardboard delicately cut into tinted vistas and dotted with tiny figures of men and women, culminating in the fountain and the park; would humorously wind the tin handle of Aggie's panorama of the Great Exhibition and cause Queen Victoria to pass over one wooden roller and under the other while his children stood about and watched him, affectionate, well-mannered, and sensing accurately that Father was very kindly putting it all on and talking down to them."[22] Ferguson chronicles the breakdown of nineteenth-century mores over sixty years (as impoverished gentlewomen struggle to retain their social or economic foothold). In childhood, however, they still inhabited a paternalistic domesticity replete with the optimism undergirding—and lingering in the wake of—the Crystal Palace.[23]

INSIDE THE GLASS CASE: ETHNOGRAPHY AND NATURAL HISTORY PANORAMAS, 1893

In 1893 Franz Boas, an ardent Humboldt disciple and professor of anthropology at Columbia, brought a group of Kwakwaka'wakw (Kwakiutl) to the Columbian World Exposition from the Pacific Northwest. Their secret initiation ritual, "Cannibal Dance," or Hamat'sa, remained illegal in Canada; when tribe members performed it in Chicago before large crowds (alongside Midway attractions such as Buffalo Bill's Wild West Show), the Canadian Bureau of Indian Affairs tried in vain to prohibit it.[24] Boas oversaw the fair's 16,000-square-foot Hall of Anthropology, and his Kwakwaka'wakw installation included painted backdrops (soon adopted as a convention by natural history museums), and, behind glass, grouped mannequins posed among artifacts of the Kwakwaka'wakw culture. Outside the hall, the Kwakwaka'wakw rebuilt and lived in traditional dwellings shipped from British Columbia, alongside encampments built by other Indian groups. Ever since Carl Hagenbeck's pioneering 1870s and 1880s displays of open-air villages and wild animal displays, open-air presentation had been the default presentation strategy.[25]

Boas's overall display risked harmonizing all too well with the exposition's theme of mankind's evolutionary progress from primitive conditions to advanced modernity. In a detailed *New-York Tribune* report of the live Hamat'sa ritual, the musicologist Henry E. Krehbiel lauded the "ingeniously contrived panorama of the houses of the cliff dwellers"—and read the encampments' ensemble as a *paysage moralisé*, contrasting less and more civilized tribes.[26] Inside the hall, however, Boas made available a contrary view, focused on the glass cases and better harmonized with Humboldt's egalitarian influence.

During the exposition, Boas made drawings, phonograph recordings, and transcriptions and supervised photographs of the visiting Kwakwaka'wakw. The Columbian Exposition and the 1900 Paris World Exposition introduced the broad public to "life groups" of posed mannequins. In 1895, hoping to preserve the gestures of Kwakwaka'wakw ritual for a long-term museumgoing public, Boas himself posed, clothed and semiclothed, for a museum photographer, reenacting ritual Hamat'sa postures. Other contemporary anthropologists, likewise, posed for further life groups, in the attempt to immortalize rituals they had carefully observed in situ.

In 1904, at the Chicago Field Museum, where much of the World's Fair Kwakwaka'wakw collection was reassembled, along with its own life group diorama of the ceremony, an original Kwakwaka'wakw World's Fair dancer visited and reported standing inside the glass case, interpreting the Hamat'sa dance to local museumgoers. By 1906 Boas would become skeptical of life groups and visual reenactments (although he became correspondingly interested in ethnographic cinema as a means to disseminate ethnographic knowledge). Yet his 1890s attempts at embodiment suggest attempted empathy rather than detached observation of a primitive tribe. Like others in the first generation of American anthropologists to undertake fieldwork, Aaron Glass has argued, Boas "may have been promoting the new methodology of participant observation by literally performing their recently acquired embodied knowledge," a feat their "armchair rivals" could not accomplish.[27]

The glass cases were themselves an innovation in museum technology, designed to produce empathy. Their effect was to include the circle of viewers in the reconstructed ritual by an optical illusion of reflection, casting a somatic spell that allowed viewers to dream themselves into the live initiation.[28] The lighting scheme illuminated the case more vividly than the surrounding hall. Any object placed behind glass created desire. (This was the age of great department store displays.[29] Newspapers spoke scornfully of "window-shopping" at the exhibition.) These decisions projected viewers inside the case, adopting the solemn state of the Kwakwaka'wakw actually performing the ritual. By including the viewer in the image, the Boas exhibition completed the panorama's "magic circle." The viewer was enlisted simultaneously as anthropologist and as subject of anthropological scrutiny.

Many natural history museums continued to present dioramic displays of ethnographic life groups (the former place of live enactors now taken by mannequins)—alongside dioramic natural history tableaux of stuffed animals and preserved botanical specimens. These realia, the raison d'être of this approach, are conspicuously Humboldtian, presenting a readable ecosystem, enlivened by flora and fauna.[30]

The museum display case, diorama, and panorama may appear to be categorically different visual technologies. "The framed diorama," Barbara Stafford has argued, "was everything that the monumental panorama was not: a conspicuously mixed genre, both dramatic and fanciful, changeable and above all, intimate." Stafford and Frances Terpak contrast the public nature of the panoramic viewing experience with various dioramic forms (from Daguerre's unfolding dioramic spectacles to the three-dimensional stereoscopic "Kaiserpanorama" peep show), characterized by the "structural tendency to turn attention inward."[31]

Yet historically, panorama and diorama overlap inside both nineteenth-century visual pleasure districts and individual display spaces. Two apparently contrasting visual technologies are brought within a single scopic regime by the geographies of leisure and tourism. In central Berlin, Schinkel had designed an early nineteenth-century complex of art and archeology museums forming a so-called Museum Island. Other northern European cities developed similar educational and leisure districts. In chapter 7, Trumpener details the siting of Lucerne's panorama within a nineteenth-century visual pleasure district encompassing dioramas, natural history museums, and cabinets of curiosities. Educational popular science overlapped with the leisure industry's profitable recreational sites. In nineteenth-century Stockholm, likewise, a former royal game park, Djurgården Island, developed into a (visual) pleasure district, accumulating a popular theater (1801), royal pavilion (1823–27), and amusement park (Tivoli Green Grove, 1883). In 1897 it became the site of Stockholm's world's fair; this General Art and Industrial Exposition's exhibitions ranged from a half-scale reconstruction of medieval Stockholm to demonstrations of new audiovisual technologies (including film and the phonograph).

From the 1870s onward, Artur Hazelius's monumental Scandinavian Ethnographic Collection (housed from 1907 in the vast, custom-built Nordic Museum)

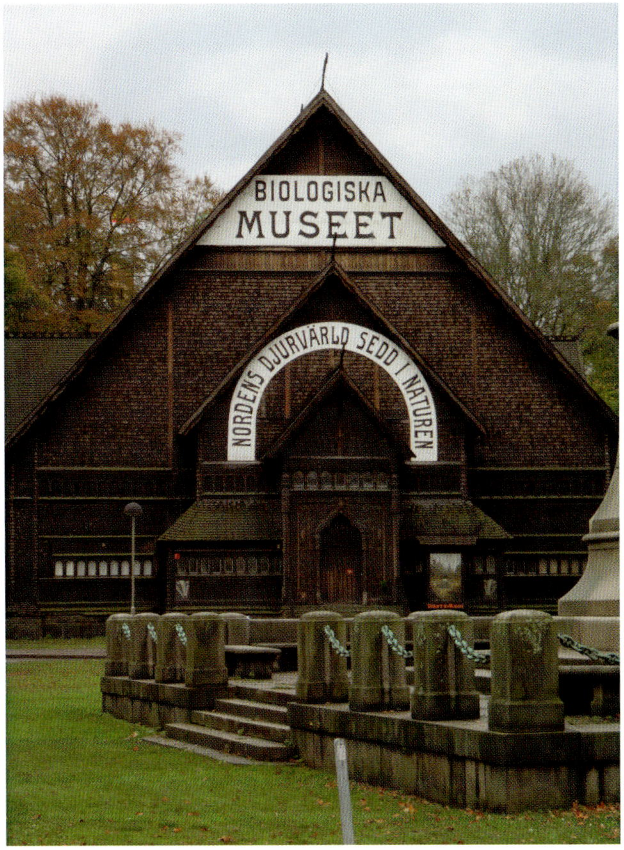

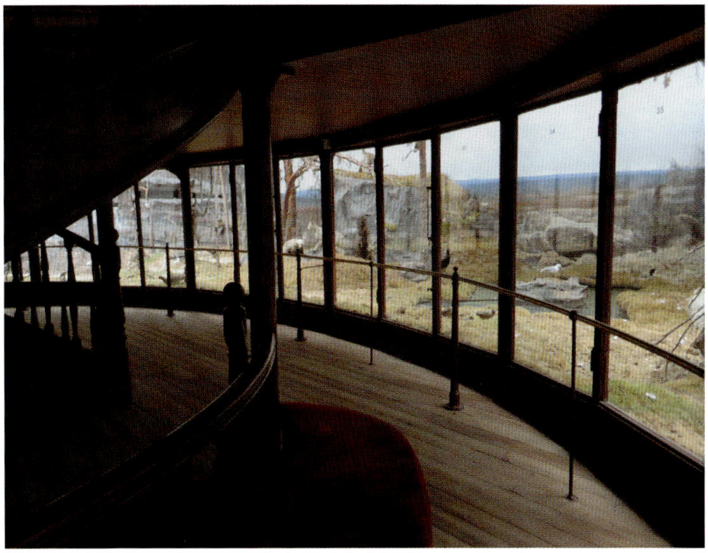

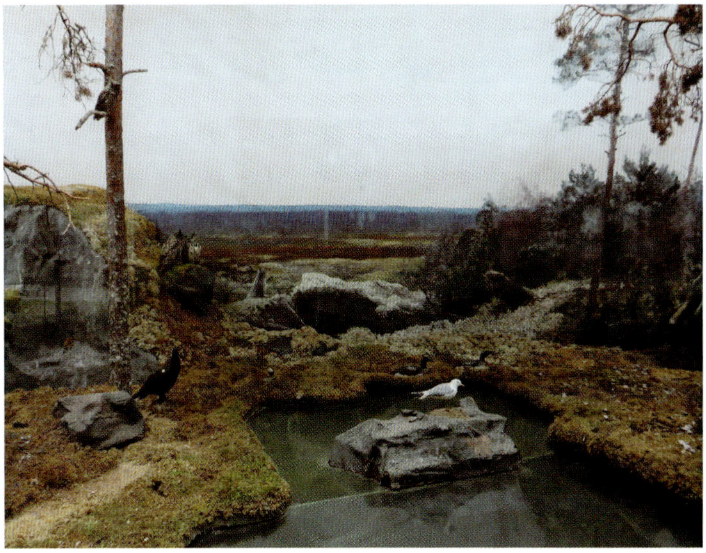

FIG. 5.9–5.11. Biologiska Museet, Stockholm, founded 1893.

anchored Djurgården's subsequent development as a place of encyclopedic pedagogical display. In 1891 Hazelius opened Skansen, the world's second open-air museum, as a nearby extension. And in 1893, at Skansen's gates, the legendary hunter, taxidermist, ornithologist, and Arctic explorer Gustaf Kolthoff opened his Biological Museum (Biologiska Museet, figs. 5.9–5.11).

The Biological Museum's imposing exterior evokes a medieval Norwegian stave church. Yet suspended inside this heavily ornamental, traditionalist wooden building is a full-scale, classic, glass-and-steel panorama structure, unusual only in its use of direct rather than indirect natural light (so changing cloud cover or sunlight registers directly inside the viewing space), in its two-story viewing platform (which enabled spectators to contrast ground-level and bird's-eye views of its scene), and in its fusion of diorama and panorama.[32]

During its first decade, Kolthoff's museum inspired intense local pride, drawing 30,000 spectators its first year, over 100,000 in 1897. As joint-stock company publicity proclaimed, its attraction "far surpassed all the other circular paintings to be found in the capital cities of Europe"; celebrated in the international press, it helped launch natural history museum initiatives in Denmark and Germany. Locally, it was seen as superseding Stockholm's more conventional 1870s battle panorama (in a panorama building thereafter commandeered to house world's fair technological displays, and subsequently torn down). In its turn, the Biological Museum was eclipsed by the Swedish Museum of Natural History (1916), then by Skansen's own zoological garden.[33]

Kolthoff had become interested in panoramas after his first natural history museum was displayed, from 1889 and 1902, at Uppsala University and thus adapted to the cylindrical cupola of its seventeenth-century anatomical theater. Kolthoff followed his Stockholm Biology Museum with further biology museums built across Sweden (and present-day Finland). Without retaining full panoramic shape or scope, these too refunctioned as key elements of nineteenth-century panoramic display, from hidden skylights to darkened access passages, intended to heighten the auratic effect when the spectator finally reached the luminous display windows.

The Stockholm museum grants the viewer both a deeply immersed, embedded dioramic view and a broadly immersed, seamless panoramic survey of the natural world. As Christopher Oscarson stresses, its very name and organization reflect the late nineteenth-century move away from Linnaean biology, organized by phylogenetic classification, toward a more integrative, quasi-Humboldtian vision of species' and habitats' ecological interpenetration.[34] Uniting traditional buildings rescued from Sweden's various regions, of widely divergent styles and purposes, Hazelius's Skansen had offered visitors a metonymic Sweden-in-miniature—and provided an important template for turn-of-the-century world's fairs, whose architecturally distinctive pavilions represented different countries and continents.[35] Kolthoff's adjacent biological panorama, with its invisible fusion of eight distinct landscapes, far northern and arboreal, coastal and inland, likewise offered a natural-historical microcosm of geographically and biologically diverse ecosystems. During the eighteenth century, Linnaeus had compared the earth to a museum and called for natural history museums that, like theaters, showed spectators many dimensions of the world. A century later, when Kolthoff conceived his pioneering natural history museum, he too wished the spectator to have "the whole picture before him," to see "immediately what words cannot describe."[36]

Like Humboldt, Kolthoff was a famed adventurer, traveler, and naturalist; he roamed widely to find and hunt animals in their natural habitats, sometimes accompanied by Bruno Liljefors, Sweden's foremost nature painter. Kolthoff took great pains not only in the tracking and shooting of animals (a process that honed his sense of the interrelationship of species and environments) and in taxidermically preparing and presenting them, but in gathering appropriate dioramic elements—sand, soil, nests, moss, trees, and bushes—from their original habitats. In a completist spirit, he undertook many additional collecting expeditions across Scandinavia, transporting home not only objects such as an eagle's nest but the original edifice of branches surrounding it.[37]

Kolthoff's double viewing platform and its dioramic qualities likewise invited a focus on ecoscape and habitat, the symbiotic coexistence of diverse animal species, birds, plants, and geological formations. At ground level, the viewer confronts both stuffed mammals and a dioramic landscape stretching up to the moss-covered edge of the viewing platform; on the upper level, the view is of cliffs, treetops, birds in movement and repose.

Opening the same year as Kaltoff's Biology Museum, the Columbian World Exposition featured related natural-historical attractions. Chicago's dioramic panorama of Hawaii's Kilauea Volcano (painted by the Chicago artist Walter Burridge) periodically "erupted," loudly re-creating the volcano's explosion; it was situated on the Midway Plaisance, alongside the live encampments of ethnic villages (American Indian, Inuit, Kwakwaka'wakw, Irish, Dahomean, North African, Samoan, Turkish, and so on). Germany's visiting Hagenbeck Zoo displayed live wild animals; ever since the Arctic Panorama at the 1886 Berlin Industrial Exhibit, Hagenbeck's dioramic exhibits had mimicked animals' natural habitats.[38] Kansas State University, meanwhile, mounted a major exhibition of North American mammals (later known as the "Panorama of North American Plants and Animals"), dioramically displaying a wide range of stuffed animals indigenous to the western United States.

Without any evidence of mutual influence, the Kansas Pavilion's semicircular format strongly resembled Stockholm's exactly contemporaneous Biology Museum, half a world away. This pioneering form of habitat diorama, Karen Wonders stresses, arose only in Sweden (shaped by Linnaeus and popular eighteenth-century naturalist culture) and the United States (shaped by eighteenth-century natural history display). As Charles Willson Peale documented in his famous self-portrait, *The Artist in His Museum* (1822, Pennsylvania Academy of the Fine Arts), the first American museum (which Peale opened in 1786) used Linnaean taxonomy as an organizational principle in displaying bird's eggs, stuffed birds, mastodon skeletons, and other anatomical exhibits in dioramic settings. In both the American and the Swedish contexts, potentially abstracting scientific classification coexisted with habitat reconstruction.[39] This display tradition, subsequently adapted by museums across the Western world, demonstrated the potential reconcilability of the scientific cross section, metonymic sample, and artistic evocation and re-creation of a complex life world.[40]

In Chicago, the White City's Kansas exhibition, a collaboration between the Smithsonian taxidermist-zoologist William Temple Hornaday and the University of Kansas biology professor and explorer Lewis Lindsay Dyche, thus blended a range of autumnal habitats, from prairies to Rocky Mountains. A wide range of animal species (including 121 mammals) were arranged in groups, crowded together against a painted backdrop and surrounded by dioramic elements (some brought directly from Kansas); as at a painted panorama, the display was lit by natural light, "admitted by skylights and directed with curtains."[41]

During the planning phase, the decision to center Kansas's state pavilion on dead animals rather than its present-day economy proved controversial: "Very few Kansas people," one newspaper editorialized, "want Kansas known to the world as the stuffed animal state"; others derided the "mummies."[42] Yet the finished exhibition, universally acclaimed for its lifelike staging of nature, was thronged daily by more than 10,000 viewers. In Chicago the diorama was divided from spectators only by a low fence. (It did contain a specially built path along which Dyche sometimes led small visitor groups to see animals and habitat up close.)[43] When the diorama was permanently reinstalled at the University of Kansas, however, it became glass-enclosed, visible through a series of viewing portals; conceived as the core of the new university's natural history museum, it helped consolidate the university's leading role (still ongoing more than a century later) in biodiversity studies.[44]

The Stockholm panorama, in contrast, was conceived from the outset to stand behind glass. In this it differed fundamentally from earlier, painted panoramas. The glassed-in display may have been actuated by practical considerations (the desire to contain preservative smells, the need to safeguard against theft and curious children). Above all, the glass enclosure demarcated it as a museal, pedagogical space, a finite space of dead nature and fixity. Earlier painted panoramas had suggested the eye's virtually infinite capacity; these glass cases both reanimated nature and announced its preservation-in-death. To this extent, at least, the Linnaean classificatory system returned in a new form: abstracting, metonymic presentation of specific specimens standing in for a greater, teeming, more confusing whole.

As building types, both the cyclorama and the greenhouse developed specialized means of making supporting walls disappear or seem something else. Their disorienting if revelatory combination of claustrophobia and agoraphobia shaped a new approach to knowing the world and helped, in Humboldt's shadow, to define the panorama's nature and effect, its aura of danger and materiality, its mass entertainment, its use of intense illusion to connect imaginatively with large groups of people. Humboldt envisioned the panorama's wholesale adoption as a means of mass education. The Crystal Palace has enjoyed an even longer influence, on everything from our trade-based globalization model to the scale and sightlines of modern shopping malls.

In the modern ethnographic museum as in the natural history museum, this essay has argued, these varied forms of transparency are brought together. Some present-day museums follow nineteenth-century precedents in uniting the study of animal and human habitats. Visitors to Chicago's Field Museum of Natural History still find major ethnographic collections alongside halls of birds and gems and dioramic displays of a Pawnee earth lodge, a Pacific Island outrigger canoe alongside animal habitat dioramas. The museum's premiere collection, arguably, remains its "Maritime Peoples of the Arctic and Northwest Coast" display; at its core are many Haida, Tlingit, and Kwakwaka'wakw artifacts that Boas collected for Columbian World Exposition display, and some model Indian village buildings he commissioned as their dioramic surround.[45]

The Field's 1982 reinstallation of this exquisite collection yielded galleries atmospheric as well as informative. A towering totem pole stand, a decorated long-house facade, dioramically presented behind glass: parts of this exhibit present Northwest art as sublime. But the galleries' most powerful effect is much smaller and subtler: as viewers approach each of the wall vitrines, their bodies trigger a shift in lighting level. As they approach each small, discrete object, it is lit up, as if greeting and acknowledging them.

Powerful as it is to stand in close, unmediated proximity to the exhibitions' exceptionally beautiful, enormous, well-preserved totem poles, it is even more powerful to commune with the well-lit objects as they emerge, one by one, from relative darkness. We are far from the vast, sublime nineteenth-century cyclorama view. Yet here, as in the nineteenth-century panorama buildings and Kolthoff's early twentieth-century biological museums, the passage from darkness into light creates a powerful auratic effect. And here, as in Boas's Columbian World Exposition ethnographic installations, a tiny panoramic circle or circuit is established *through* the glass, forging intimate connections between local viewers and objects distant in origin and time. The illumination of these objects solicits our ethnographic empathy, invests them with warmth, restores them somehow to life, to artifactual purpose. In these glass vitrines, as in the nineteenth-century glasshouse, a panoramic effect lives on, as aesthetic and cross-cultural illumination.

NOTES

1. Alexander von Humboldt to Varnhagen von Ense, October 24, 1834, in *Briefe von Alexander von Humboldt an Varnhagen von Ense* (Leipzig: F. A. Brockhaus, 1860), 20; quoted and trans. in Stephan Oettermann, *The Panorama: History of a Mass Medium*, trans. Deborah Lucas Schneider (New York: Zone, 1997), 38.
2. Laurent Mannoni, Donata Presenti Compagnoni, and David Robinson, *Light and Movement: Incunabula of the Motion Picture, 1420–1896* (Gemona: Giornate del Cinema Muto, 1995), 157–58.
3. Ralph Hyde, *Panoramania! The Art and Entertainment of the "All-Embracing" View* (London: Trefoil/Barbican Art Gallery, 1988), 58.
4. Jonathan Crary contrasts their "ambulatory ubiquity" with the fact they were "compelled" to turn head or body to take in the whole image; Crary, *Techniques of the Observer: On Vision and Modernity in the Nineteenth Century* (Cambridge: MIT Press, 1990), 113.
5. Richard Altick, *The Shows of London* (Cambridge: Belknap Press of Harvard University Press, 1978), 149.
6. In René Clair's film *Paris qui dort* (*The Crazy Ray*, France, 1924), similarly, an electromagnetic ray has paralyzed Paris; only visitors arriving by airplane remain unaffected, along with a man stationed atop the Eiffel Tower, where they all take refuge. While the city remains stopped in its tracks, they repeatedly venture down, eventually resetting the ray machine, enabling Paris to resume operations. Clair's fantasy meditates on the relation between unmoving city below and circulating viewers above, a configuration familiar from then-still-extant panorama traditions. To Clair, like Wordsworth, the city *has* to stop in its tracks and the viewers above must descend, *relinquishing* panoramic vision, to start things up again. William Wordsworth, "Composed Upon Westminster Bridge, Sept. 3, 1802," *The Poetical Works of William Wordsworth*. Ed. Thomas Hutchinson, rev. ed. Ernest de Seligcourt. Oxford: Oxford University Press, 1960, p. 214. On the Eiffel Tower as an edifice that produces panoramic vistas and vision, see Roland Barthes, "The Eiffel Tower" (1964), in *A Barthes Reader*, ed. Susan Sontag (New York: Hill and Wang, 1995), 236–50.
7. The six panels hang on two adjacent walls; in the intended presentation, the three left-hand panels are at a 90-degree angle to the three right-hand panels (each of the outer ones at a 45-degree angle to the wall). Describing a 180-degree turn, the physical panels form a half-circle against a right-angled corner. Our first impulse is to imagine the resulting prospect *itself* describing a 180-degree turn, but then the leftmost and rightmost panels would join up to form an imagistically complete circle, could they physically be maneuvered into one. The traditional panoramic arrangement of the completed circle would put the towered entrance to the church opposite the choir and altar end, which would be architecturally correct; as it is—in the 180-degree corner arrangement—choir and entrance appear to be at right angles to one another, an unconventional disposition. So it would be most accurate if we thought of Gaertner's corner panorama as *gesturing to* or *evoking*, not *describing*, a 360-degree turn.
8. The hero of his panoramic view is doubtless Gaertner's pink-striped son, who has crawled (in the middle panel of the southern view) almost to the roof's summit, unaware of losing his rakish red-ribboned hat, enterprisingly wanting to see what is on the other side, excitedly waving a switch as the view looms up. Loose in the panoramic gallery, the child takes in the view through what we must infer is a necessary *succession* of glances, the most active participant in the effort, occurring variously all over that ribbed rooftop, to see Berlin.
9. Schinkel was the great German panoramist of the previous generation, a prolific architect and major scenographer and illusion maker. He painted Berlin's popular 1808 *Panorama of Palermo* and many highly acclaimed dioramas (including those of Constantinople, Jerusalem, and the burning of Moscow), while developing dioramically illusionistic sets for over forty Berlin opera productions (most famously for Mozart's *Magic Flute*). Birgit Verwiebe, "Erdenstaub und Himmelsdunst—Eduard Gaertners Panoramen," in *Eduard Gaertner, 1801–1877*, ed. Dominik Bartmann (Berlin: Nicolai, 2001), 97–111; 97. Gaertner presented an illusion of a new, promising Berlin under construction.
10. Kurt Forster, "Schinkel's Panoramic Planning of Central Berlin," *Modulus* 16 (1983): 64–75.
11. Vance Byrd, *A Pedagogy of Observation: Nineteenth-Century Panoramas, German Literature, and Reading Culture* (Lewisburg, PA: Bucknell University Press, 2017), 74.
12. *The Taje Mahel, Agra*, aquatint, drawn and engraved by Thomas and William Daniell, published by Thomas Daniell, London, 1801 (London: British Library); and Anno Mungen, *"Bilder Musik": Panoramen, Tableaux vivants und Lichtbilder als multimediale Darstellungsformen in Theater- und Musikaufführungen vom 19. bis zum frühen 20. Jahrhundert*, 2 vols. (Remschied: Gardez! Verlag, 2006), 1:132–76.
13. Michael Dettelbach, "The Stimulations of Travel: Humboldt's Physiological Construction of the Tropics," in *Tropical Visions in an Age of Empire*, ed. Felix Driver and Luciana Martins (Chicago: University of Chicago Press, 2005), 43–58; see also Chenxi Tang, *The Geographic Imagination of Modernity: Geography, Literature, and Philosophy in German Romanticism* (Stanford: Stanford University Press, 2008).
14. Alexander von Humboldt, *Cosmos: A Sketch of a Physical Description of the Universe*, trans. E. C. Otté, 2 vols. (London: H. G. Bohn, 1849), 2:457.
15. Ibid., 459.
16. Ibid., 457.
17. Quoted in Jeffrey Auerbach, *The Great Exhibition of 1851: A Nation on Display* (New Haven: Yale University Press, 1999), 50.
18. On nineteenth-century glasshouse architecture, see Georg Kohlmaier and Barna von Sartory, *Houses of Glass: A Nineteenth-Century Building Type* (Cambridge: MIT Press, 1986); and John Hix, *The Glasshouse* (London: Phaidon, 1996). Peter Sloterdijk's "The Crystal Palace," in *In the World Interior of Capitalism*, trans. Wieland Hoban (Cambridge: Polity, 2013), sports a glasshouse on its cover and argues (169–76) that this glass structure staged an "aesthetics of immersion" (170) and became the "prophetic" (indeed globally copied) "building form of the nineteenth century." Even more fundamentally than Benjamin's nineteenth-century arcades, the Crystal Palace "already anticipated an integral, experience-oriented, popular capitalism" featuring "the comprehensive absorption of an outside world in a fully calculated interior" (175).

19. Barbara Black, *On Exhibit: Victorians and Their Museums* (Charlottesville: University Press of Virginia, 2000), 84.
20. *The Holy Land from Original and Authentic Sketches Made on the Spot—New and Magnificent Diorama of Jerusalem and the Holy Land: . . . Painted under the Direction of Mr W. Beverley, from Sketches Made on the Spot, during Repeated Journeys in the East by Mr W. H. Bartlett* . . . (London: W. Beverley, 1851).
21. Terpak reproduces the Spielbudenplatz stretch of Peter Suhr's 1723 scrolling panorama, *Die Reise von Hamburg nach Altona und zurück*, showing tightrope walkers and billboard-like advertisements for acrobats and wild animal exhibits. Frances Terpak, "Panoramas," in Barbara Maria Stafford and Frances Terpak, *Devices of Wonder: From the World in a Box to Images on a Screen* (Los Angeles: Getty Research Institute, 2001), 315–24; 321.
22. Rachel Ferguson, *Alas, Poor Lady* (1937; repr., London: Persephone, 2007), 38.
23. Later works are more skeptical. In Chris Ware's graphic novel *Jimmy Corrigan: The Smartest Kid on Earth* (New York: Pantheon, 2000), an abusive father abandons his son at the top of the main building of Chicago's 1893 Columbian World Exposition, while the son is transfixed by the prospect of the ideal city. Thomas Pynchon's *Against the Day* (New York: Penguin, 2006) surveys the same exposition in the company of Randolph Cosmos, whose hot-air balloon enables panoramic perspectives (and whose adventures showcase many further panoramic machines and locales).
24. Paige Raibmon, "Theatres of Contact: The Kwakwaka'waka Meet Colonialism in British Columbia and the Chicago World's Fair," *Canadian Historical Review* 81, no. 2 (2000): 157–90.
25. Curtis M. Hinsley, "The World as Marketplace: Commodification of the Exotic at the World's Columbian Exposition, Chicago, 1893," in *Exhibiting Cultures: The Poetics and Politics of Museum Display*, ed. Ivan Karp and Steven D. Lavine (Washington, D.C.: Smithsonian Institution Press, 1991), 344–65; 345. But see also Mark Sandberg, *Living Pictures, Missing Persons: Mannequins, Museums, and Modernity* (Princeton: Princeton University Press, 2003). In an influential 1889 lecture, the Smithsonian Institution's G. Brown Goode argued "The Museum of the Future" should be "much more than a house full of glass cases," becoming instead "a house of ideas." Goode subsequently helped conceptualize Columbian Exposition exhibitions. Cited in Robert W. Rydell, *All The World's a Fair* (Chicago: University of Chicago Press, 1984), 45.
26. H. E. K. [Henry E. Krehbiel], "Folk-Music at the Fair: Cannibal Songs of the Indians," *New-York Tribune*, August 6, 1893, 14.
27. Aaron Glass, "On the Circulation of Ethnographic Knowledge," http://www.materialworldblog.com/2006/10/on-the-circulation-of-ethnographic-knowledge/, accessed March 20, 2016.
28. In Marcel Proust's *Du côté de chez Swann* (Paris: Gallimard, 1919), 223, relatedly, young Marcel's Balbec room is lined on three sides with bookcases, whose glass doors reflect the fourth, windowed wall and hence the sea. Through glass surfaces, a bookscape is transformed into a dazzling maritime panorama.
29. As Philippe Hamon argues, the ubiquitous translucent display window shaped both nineteenth-century visual aesthetics and literary realism; Hamon, *Expositions: Literature and Architecture in Nineteenth-Century France*, trans. Katia Sainson-Frank and Lisa Maguire (Berkeley: University of California Press, 1992), esp. chap. 1.
30. On turn-of-the-century ethnographic display practices, see Sandberg, *Living Pictures*, and Alison Griffiths, *Wondrous Difference: Cinema, Anthropology, and Turn-of-the-Century Visual Culture* (New York: Columbia University Press, 2002).
31. Stafford and Terpak, *Devices of Wonder*, 99.
32. Karen Wonders, *Habitat Dioramas: Illusions of Wilderness in Museums of Natural History* (Uppsala, Sweden: Uppsala University Press, 1993), 51, 65–67.
33. Ibid., 56, 63.
34. Christopher Oscarson, "Landscape and the Entangled Bird's-Eye View: Turn-of-the-Twentieth-Century Swedish Culture and the Ecological Imaginary" (Ph.D. diss., University of California–Berkeley, 2006); see also Wonders, *Habitat Dioramas*, 47–48.
35. Sandberg, *Living Pictures*.
36. Wonders, *Habitat Dioramas*, 46.
37. Ibid., 57.
38. Ibid., 41.
39. Ibid., 83–88; chap. 3. Such displays contrasted with more taxonomically organized biology and ethnography museums, common in the late nineteenth century. Surviving examples include Dublin's 1857 Natural History Museum, Oxford's 1886 Pitt Rivers Museum, and Barcelona's Zoology Museum (housed in Lluís Domènech i Montaner's modernist building, constructed for the 1888 World's Fair).
40. Ibid. See also Katharina Dohm et al., eds., *Dioramas* (Paris: Flammarion, 2017).
41. William Sharp and Peggy Sullivan, *The Dashing Kansan Lewis Lindsay Dyche: The Amazing Adventures of a Nineteenth-Century Naturalist and Explorer* (Kansas City: Harrow Books, 1990), 73.
42. Quoted in ibid., 67.
43. Wonders, *Habitat Dioramas*, 124; to safeguard his exhibition during its installation and display, Dyche built and occupied a bedroom hidden beneath the papier-mâché rocks. Sharp and Sullivan, *Dashing Kansan*, 69. Thanks to William Sharp, Kansas State University, for information about the exhibition's history.
44. Chad Lawhorn, "One of America's Treasures," *Lawrence [Kansas] World-Journal*, August 25, 2013, http://www2.ljworld.com/news/2013/aug/25/one-americas-treasures/?print. In 1926 the director of the American Museum of Natural History, Frederic Lucas, praised the resulting panorama for amplifying Dyche's Columbian Exposition ideas about synthetic or life study groups, providing a "composite picture" of animal interactions and behaviors. "In this, the day of moving pictures . . . as the moving picture condenses into five minutes' time the events of days or weeks, so these groups condense into a few feet of space the life and happenings of a much larger area." Quoted in Sharp and Sullivan, *Dashing Kansan*, 141.
45. Douglas Cole, *Captured Heritage: The Scramble for Northwest Coast Artifacts* (Seattle: University of Washington Press, 1985), chap. 5.

RUTH PULLIN

6 Eugene von Guérard

The Panoramic Imperative and the Australian Landscape

On the afternoon of August 6, 1855, the Austrian-born landscape painter Eugene von Guérard (1811–1901) stood at the top of Mount Rouse, a volcanic cone in the western region of the Australian state of Victoria, and surveyed the basalt plains that unrolled to the distant horizon in every direction before him. For the artist, who had arrived from Europe less than three years earlier, the effect of the seemingly limitless space at this site was physical and powerful: he took out his pocket-sized sketchbook and a finely sharpened pencil and recorded, with unerring accuracy and sure cartographic control, the sweep of the landscape from the north to the south, the most striking feature of which is the saw-toothed profile of the Grampian (Gariwerd) Ranges that rise on the horizon to the north (fig. 6.1).[1] The drawing runs over four pages, its continuous nature overtly proclaimed on the fourth page with the inscription *Fortsetzung* ("continuation"), a word that recurs frequently throughout von Guérard's thirty-five extant sketchbooks. Its recurrence, together with the hundreds of drawings that push beyond the constraints of the single page, attest to the compelling panoramic imperative that governed the artist's responses to the Australian landscape.

Like so many of his generation, including a remarkable cohort of German-speaking artists and scientists who settled in Melbourne in the 1850s, von Guérard was inspired by the great German natural scientist Alexander von Humboldt (1769–1859), who understood nature as one vast interconnected and unified whole.[2] In compositions underpinned by a powerful unifying geometry, von Guérard sought to capture "everything," both the expansive breadth of his subject and the miraculously diverse and minute details that were integral to nature's larger scheme. In works such as *Sydney Heads* (1865; fig. 6.2), a canvas that is panoramic in its conception, the overseeing eye and the eye of the miniaturist meet. Viewed from above, and encompassing a geographic breadth that is beyond the scope of the natural field of vision, the complex terrain of Sydney Harbor, depicted in detail and with topographical exactitude, is laid out before the viewer as a complete and "graspable" visual entity.

In his unwavering commitment to the scientifically accurate and detailed depiction of the "botanical or geological features" of the colonies of the Australian New World, von Guérard realized the agenda that Humboldt, on the basis of his own travels in South America, had set

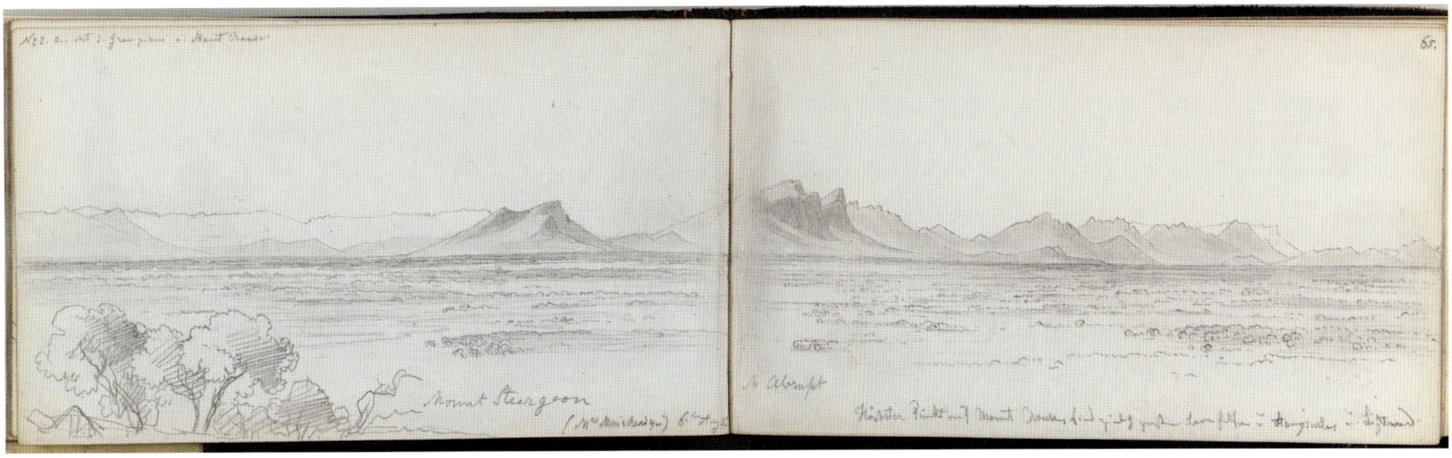

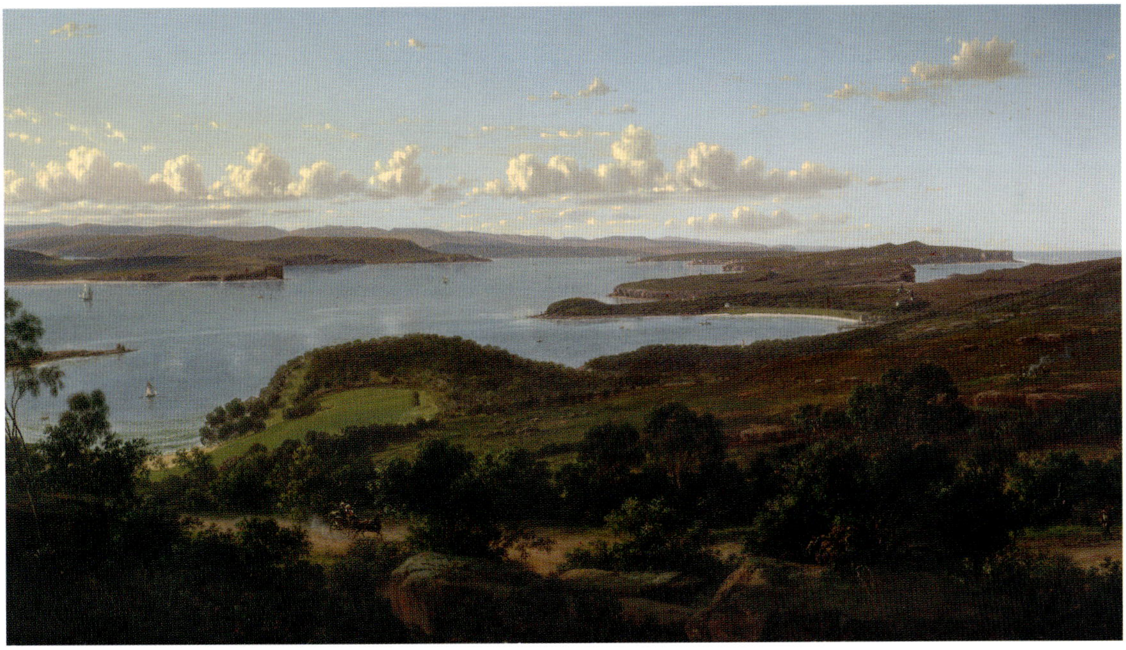

FIG. 6.1. Eugene von Guérard (Austrian, 1811–1919), *No. 2 Ansicht d. Grampians v. Mt Rouse,* August 6, 1855, from Sketchbook 24. Pencil on paper, 10.6 × 30 cm (4 1/8 × 11 7/8 in.). State Library of New South Wales, Sydney (DGB16, vol. 3, 65).

FIG. 6.2. Eugene von Guérard, *Sydney Heads,* 1865. Oil on canvas, 56 × 94 cm (22 × 37 in.). Art Gallery of New South Wales, Sydney. Bequest of Major H. W. Hall 1974 (122.1974).

out for artists in his influential publications.[3] He urged landscape painters to travel "beyond the limits of the Mediterranean" and "to seize . . . on the true image of the varied forms of nature." Humboldt's all-embracing, panoramic vision of the unifying laws that govern natural diversity shaped von Guérard's understanding of the natural world and is reflected in the formal construction of his compositions. Humboldt's vision of nature converged with the visual language of the panorama that had become embedded in von Guérard's imagination during his formative years in Italy and Germany to shape the artist's response to the Australian landscape.

Eugene von Guérard arrived in Australia in 1852, at the age of forty-one, as an experienced and well-traveled artist. His father, Bernard von Guérard (1771–1836), an accomplished and successful miniaturist, was Eugene's first and possibly most influential teacher: an eye for detail and dedication to its depiction, essential skills for a painter of panoramas, became defining and enduring aspects of Eugene's practice of landscape painting.[4] In 1827, when Eugene was fifteen, he and his father had left Vienna for Italy and by 1830 they had reached Rome, where Eugene began his formal tuition under the Italian landscape painter Giambattista Bassi (1784–1852). The von Guérards engaged with the lively community of German painters in the city, and, many years later, Eugene acknowledged the role played by the landscape painters Joseph Anton Koch and Johann Christian Reinhart, and the Nazarene artists then still in Rome in his own artistic development.[5] Eugene and his father lived on the via

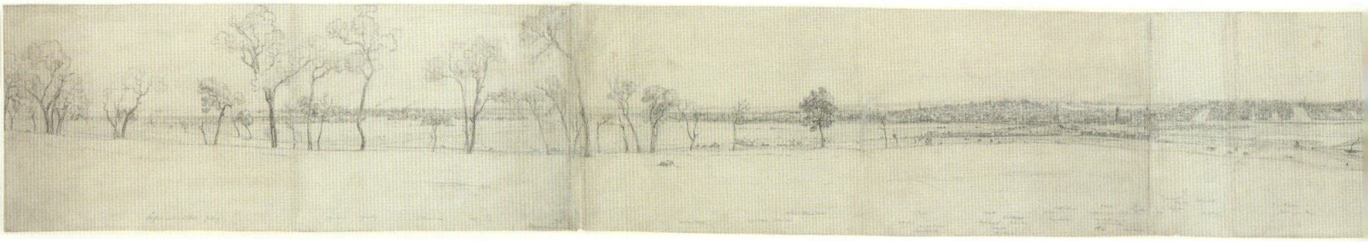

FIG. 6.3. Eugene von Guérard, *Panorama of Melbourne*, February 14–15, March 3, and March 5, 1855. Pencil on five numbered sheets of paper, total 25.5 × 336 cm (10 × 132 1/16 in.). State Library, Victoria, Melbourne (H1547).

Pinciana, just around the corner from the Villa Malta on the Pincian Hill, where Reinhart was working on four large-scale views of Rome, works that make up what is now regarded as one of the great panoramas of Rome. Reinhart's *Four Views of Rome* (1829–35), commissioned by King Ludwig I, recorded the view from the four points of the compass as seen from a belvedere tower in the villa's gardens.[6] The villa itself was a popular subject for northern artists in Rome in the early nineteenth century, to the extent that it became identified with the longing they felt for Italy after returning to their homelands.[7] There can be little doubt that the young von Guérard was aware of the project on which the famous Reinhart—Reinhart's studio was an essential destination for young landscape painters arriving in Rome—was engaged at the equally famous villa. Over the following years, Eugene produced a series of large and meticulously detailed drawings of Italian towns and cities—Naples, Capri, Tivoli, and Florence—executed from elevated vantage points and embracing wide fields of vision.[8] Following his father's untimely death in the 1836 cholera epidemic that swept Naples, von Guérard left Italy in 1838 for Düsseldorf, his father's birthplace and the home of the Düsseldorf Academy, with its progressive and internationally renowned school of landscape painting. There, in addition to his studies in landscape painting under Johann Wilhelm Schirmer, he studied architectural drawing and consolidated his understanding of perspective in Rudolf Wiegmann's *Bauklasse*.[9]

During his years in Düsseldorf (1838–1852), von Guérard traveled both within and outside Germany. Though there is no record of his having seen such famous panoramas as the reworked version of Schinkel's 1808 *Panorama of Palermo* in Berlin in 1844 or the six canvases of Eduard Gaertner's *Panorama of Berlin* (1834) in March 1842, he could hardly have missed the Meister brothers' *Panorama of the Most Beautiful Points in the Middle Rhine Valley, from Ehrenbreitstein to Hammerstein* in Cologne.[10] Von Guérard and his fellow artist (and painter of architectural subjects) Friedrich Arnold stopped over in Cologne on their May 1842 sketching tour of the middle Rhine. The panorama, which reportedly transported viewers "to one of the most charming spots on the Middle Rhine"—the view of Castle Stolzenfels near Koblenz—had obvious appeal and relevance for the artists just setting out on their own *Rheinreise*.[11] Similarly, the famous and huge moving panorama *Mississippi Valley* by Henry Lewis (1819–1904) toured Germany in 1850–51, just as von Guérard's own plans to travel to the New World were taking shape. It is possible that he and Lewis met before von Guérard left Düsseldorf for Australia in August 1852. The precise date of Lewis's arrival in Düsseldorf, where he studied at the Academy, is unknown, but it was between 1851 and 1853.[12] While he was there, he embarked on an ambitious publishing project, undertaken in partnership with the prestigious Düsseldorf lithographic printing and publishing firm Arnz and Company, whose principal was von Guérard's future father-in-law, Heinrich Arnz.[13] Von Guérard was closely associated with the Arnz family of artists and, in the years leading up to his departure for Australia, spent much time at the Arnz family home.[14] Although he was not in Düsseldorf to see the final publication of Lewis's 431-page volume *Das illustrirte Mississippithal* (1854–58), with its seventy-eight color lithographs, he may have seen the lithographs and been aware of the gestation of what was a landmark project for the family business.

Even more relevant for an artist on his way to Australia, particularly for one whose first destination was to be the Ballarat goldfields, was John Skinner Prout's "New Moving Panorama," *The Gold Fields of Australia*. Its opening, at 309 Regent Street, London, in August 1852, coincided with the twelve-day window (from August 5 to 17) during which von Guérard was in London to ready himself for his voyage to Australia on the *Windermere*. During that period, he and the French party with whom

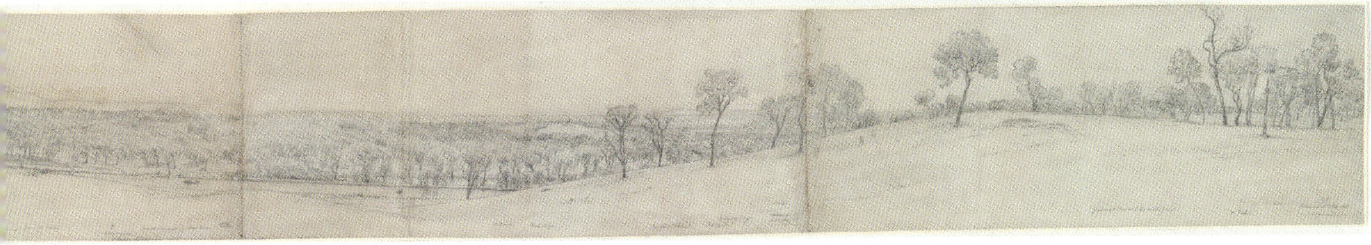

he had teamed up to form a "company" purchased provisions and implements and made all the preparations they could for their life on the goldfields. A review published in the *Illustrated London News* on August 14 described Prout's panorama as "as it were, a matter of business to emigrants, whether they be in quest of gold or pastoral settlement."[15] Although there is no direct evidence that von Guérard and his fellow travelers saw the well-publicized panorama, this timely opportunity to learn about life at their singular destination must surely have been unmissable.[16]

Von Guérard reached Australia in late December 1852; he spent thirteen months on the goldfields and in Ballarat, and then four months in the burgeoning city of Geelong, which, along with Melbourne, was one of the gateways to the goldfields of central Victoria. Among the popular entertainments on offer to the newly moneyed populations of both colonial cities were touring moving panoramas and dioramas, mostly featuring subjects from European history—typically battles or cataclysmic natural disasters.[17] There was a corresponding movement in the opposite direction, to London, of panoramic views of colonial subjects, notably cities. Among them was a three-part aquatint, *Panoramic Views of Port Jackson* (Sydney), engraved by Havell & Son after watercolors by Major James Taylor, shown at Barker & Burford's Panorama Building in Leicester Square in 1824.[18] In December 1828 it was followed by a full-sized panorama, *A View of the Town of Sydney* and, in 1831, in the large circle of the Strand Panorama, *A View of Hobart Town, Van Diemen's Land, and the Surrounding Country,* both after watercolors by Augustus Earle.[19]

In choosing the colonial city of Melbourne as the subject for a 360-degree panoramic drawing, von Guérard was not, like his predecessors, documenting the emergence of a new colonial center. His subject—recorded in 1855, twenty years after European settlement—was the vibrant and fast-changing metropolis of Melbourne. It was a city in which history was being written. Between 1851 and 1854, Melbourne's population more than tripled, from 23,000 to close to 80,000, and the number of buildings in the city nearly doubled in the year 1853, from 4,980 to 9,175. Though it began from a much smaller population base, Melbourne shared the experiences of London and Paris, which were, in Bernard Comment's view, the "only true metropolises of the era to experience extraordinary demographic and territorial explosions."[20] In the case of Melbourne, this experience was intensified by the destabilizing effects of a highly transient population and the uncertain fortunes and unpredictable social conditions concomitant with a society built on gold fever. For Melburnians that instability took tangible form as town planners set out to level the city's terrain, flattening hills and raising street levels over swampy land—a process that required homes to be buried: the earth was literally shifting beneath the feet of the populace.[21] For one new arrival, Melbourne in 1853 had "the noise and confusion of a second Babel."[22] In such circumstances, Bernard Comment argues, the panorama had the potential to play a "compensatory or atoning role," by presenting a reassuringly coherent image of a place experienced as chaotic.[23]

Von Guérard's *Panorama of Melbourne,* drawn from an elevated vantage point (103 feet above sea level) from which the scope of the city becomes measurable and the relationships between its apparently ever-changing elements comprehensible, achieves just that. Begun on February 14–15, 1855, the pencil drawing spreads over five numbered sheets executed in measured increments over several days (figs. 6.3, 6.4, 6.5).[24] When displayed as a linear sequence, the drawing begins and ends looking due south. Von Guérard noted the general area from which he took the view as "Government Reserve hinter d. Bot [Botanic] Garten." The accuracy of the multiple perspectives, however, is such that his precise vantage point, a hillock on high ground on the south side of the Yarra River and to the

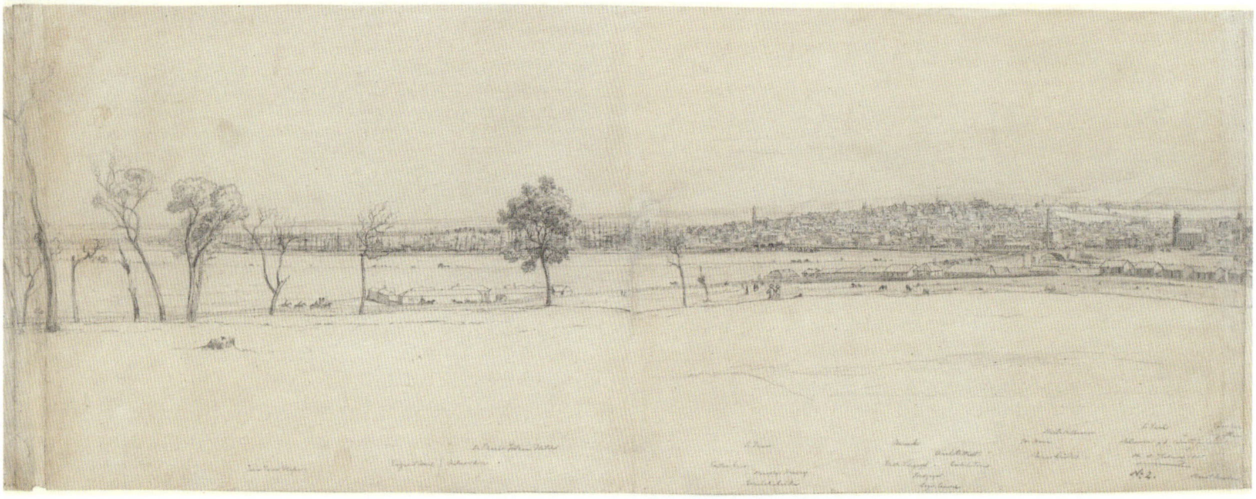

FIG. 6.4. Eugene von Guérard, *Panorama of Melbourne*, sheet no. 2. State Library, Victoria, Melbourne (H1547/b).

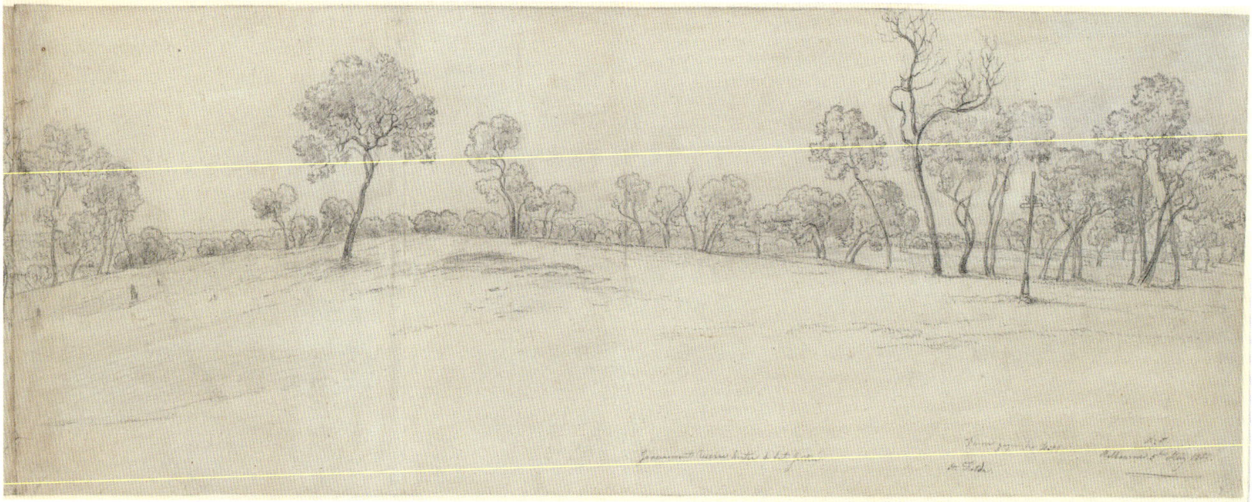

FIG. 6.5. Eugene von Guérard, *Panorama of Melbourne*, sheet no. 5. State Library, Victoria, Melbourne (H1547/e).

northeast of the Botanical Gardens, can be determined. Using an overlay of the 360 points of the compass from this vantage point, the positions of geographical features, streets, and buildings as recorded on James Kearney's 1855 map of Melbourne align almost perfectly with their positions in the drawing (allowing for the historical variation between magnetic north and true north).[25]

From the gardens to the south, von Guérard's view sweeps to the southwest to encompass the distant peaks today known as the You Yangs, near Geelong, before continuing to the busy port of Hobson's Bay to the west. The newly opened rail link from the bay to the city draws the viewer into the built-up city center to the north. The Yarra River continues to the east through Richmond, behind which the Plenty Ranges and then the Dandenong Ranges are visible, before the panorama sweeps back to the gardens to the south. In establishing the south as his starting point, von Guérard positioned the city to the north, in the "center" of the composition if viewed flat. If viewed in the round, the city would face the landscape of gentle hills and eucalypts to the south. The multiple perspectives resulting from the shifting angles of vision required for the panorama are bound together by the line of the horizon and the unifying line of the river in the foreground.

In producing such a drawing, along the base of which geographical features, buildings, and streets were identified on a comprehensive numbered key, von Guérard surely hoped for a commission, perhaps for a series of panoramic views of the city, if not a full panorama. He was almost certainly aware of the interest generated by panoramas like Prout's *Goldfields of Australia,* and, in the context of the "surging civic pride" in "the flourishing city," he would have predicted potential local interest.[26] The story of Melbourne is given dramatic focus in *Panorama* through von Guérard's juxtaposition of the emerging edifices and institutions of a substantial Victorian city—the Town Hall, the University of Melbourne, St. Paul's Anglican Church, the Legislative Council—with Canvastown, a village of tents on the banks of the Yarra that sprang up in response to the lack of available accommodation during the early years of the gold rush. The masts of sailing ships at anchor in the busy ports of Hobson's Bay and the Yarra Yarra Harbor, a deep natural basin in the river near the bottom of the city's King Street, jostle behind that symbol of modernity and progress, the steam train crossing the rail bridge on its way from Sandridge (Port Melbourne) to the Melbourne Terminus; the line had opened only six months earlier and was Australia's first.[27] The grid layout of wide city streets, mapped out by the surveyor Robert Hoddle in 1837, proclaimed the order that was being imposed, both on nature and on the unregulated early development of the city. Von Guérard's comprehensive and "readable" view, taken from a commanding vantage point, gave the rapidly growing city a shape and, with it, a sense of certainty in the face of the sense of chaos that accompanied its hurried and haphazard expansion.

In a young, raw, fledgling city, dominated by recent arrivals still working to establish themselves—and where von Guérard was yet to make his own reputation—no commission was forthcoming, and the drawing remained in the artist's possession until his death in 1901. Von Guérard found other ways to express his panoramic sensibility, ways that could more readily be accommodated by the market that did exist. His career was defined by his extensive travels into some of the most remote and rugged terrain of the colonies of southeastern Australia. The property portraits commissioned by the now well-established landowners of Victoria's Western District and Gippsland are informed by his physical experience of traveling through those regions—of being *in* the landscape. Almost all these works encompass more than could be contained within the frame of one canvas or accommodated within a single field of vision. Some were realized as paired canvases, allowing the stretch of the landscape portrayed to be extended laterally across two canvases or as reciprocal views of the site, looking in opposite directions. Such paired canvases met the needs of patron and artist.

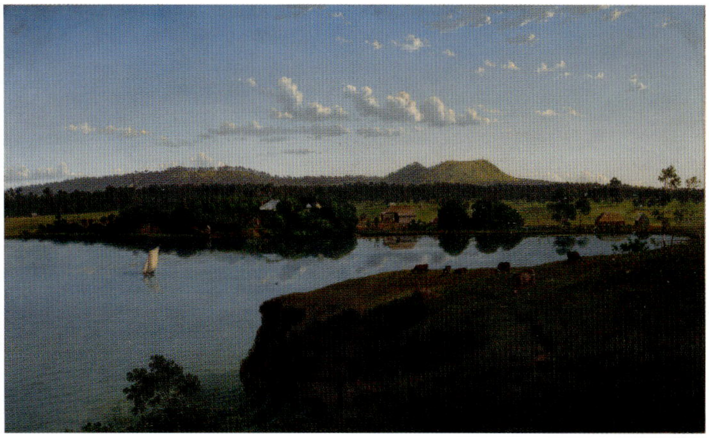

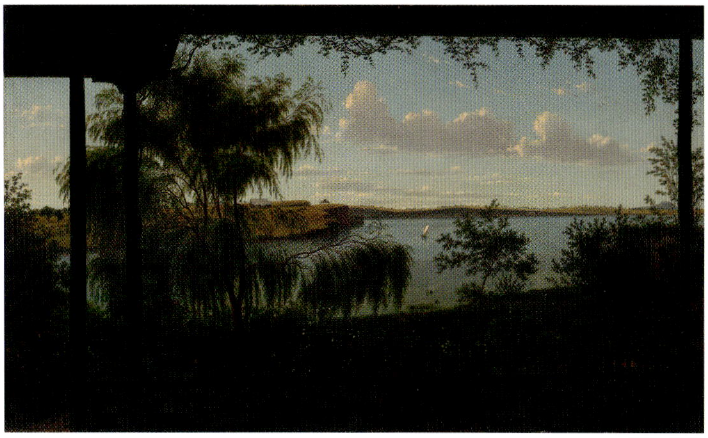

FIG. 6.6. Eugene von Guérard, *Purrumbete from across the Lake*, 1858. Oil on canvas, 51 × 85.5 cm (20 × 33 5/8 in.). National Gallery of Australia, Canberra. Purchased with funds from the Nerissa Johnson Bequest.

FIG. 6.7. Eugene von Guérard, *From the Verandah of Purrumbete*, 1858. Oil on canvas, 51.4 × 86.3 cm (20 1/4 × 34 in.). National Gallery of Australia, Canberra. Purchased 1978.

In the first of von Guérard's paired canvases, *Purrumbete from across the Lake* (1858) and *From the Verandah of Purrumbete* (1858), von Guérard depicted two complementary views of John and Peter Manifold's large and successful grazing property (figs. 6.6, 6.7). In the first the view is to the northwest; its companion looks to the southeast. The artist first visited Purrumbete, situated on Lake Purrumbete, a large volcanic crater lake on fertile grassy plains near Camperdown in Victoria, on April 2, 1857, while on the homeward-bound leg of a two-month expedition through Victoria's Western District.[28] Before sketching the property, he climbed nearby Mount Leura to take in the lie of the land. Over five sequential pages of his sketchbook, he recorded the view from the northeast to the southeast, inscribing the names of geographical features across the top of each page.[29] Later that day, he sketched the view that in 1858 became the subject of *Purrumbete from across the Lake*. In it the viewer looks across Picnic Point and the lake to the homestead, nestled in its well-established garden, and then to Mount Leura on the horizon. The view to the southeast, *From the Verandah of Purrumbete*, framed by the verandah of the homestead in the manner of the trellis-framed views popular with northern artists working in Rome and Naples in the early nineteenth century, looks toward Picnic Point and Mount Porndon on the far right of the horizon. Lake Purrumbete, which lies on an axis between Mount Leura and Mount Porndon, is bookended by the two scoria cones. By depicting the view from the vantage point of the verandah and, in the companion canvas, the view behind that same vantage point, von Guérard effectively offered a panoramic experience of the landscape.[30]

The panoramic effect was achieved quite differently in the paired canvases, jointly titled *View of the Gippsland Alps, from Bushy Park on the River Avon, Victoria*, painted for Angus McMillan, a property owner, in 1861 (fig. 6.8). This time the compelling topographic line of the Alps dictated the form of the work as two continuous long, narrow canvases. Together the canvases encompass an almost 180-degree sweep of the Gippsland Alps from southeast of Mount Baw Baw to northwest of Castle Hill. The horizon line, like a topographic profile between the band of open sky above and grassy expanse below, runs across the midline of the two canvases to unite them. The "'pressure' of the horizon" is described by Stephan Oettermann as the need for completion, the desire for an overview in which "the relationships between details" can be claimed "in one fell swoop."[31] It was a pressure to which von Guérard, for whom topographical and geological accuracy was paramount, was highly sensitive. Carl Gustav Carus (1789–1868), the German geognostic landscape painter and theorist, argued that the landscape painter, through the accuracy of his portrayal of "the form of a mountain range, the quality of the lines that shape its outlines, [and] the gentleness or asperity of its profiles," had the capacity to communicate information about the geological structure and history of his subject.[32] Von Guérard was one of many Düsseldorf artists who, following this advice and the example of the Academy's professor of landscape painting, Johann Wilhelm Schirmer (1807–1863)—and his influential colleague Carl Friedrich Lessing (1808–1880)—undertook extended sketching expeditions into Germany's geologically significant Eifel and Harz regions. The studies he made of rock plateaus and rock formations in the Eifel are distinguished by their precision and the penetrating focus he brought to his subjects.[33]

When von Guérard approached the subject of the Australian Alps in Gippsland, it was from the perspective of an intimate knowledge of the terrain. In the spirit of the Humboldtian *Reisekünstler*, he had trekked into these rugged mountains alongside the scientifically informed explorer Alfred W. Howitt, who had led a government gold-prospecting expedition into the region in December 1860. The area was then so incompletely mapped that the explorer could name "De Guérard's Range" for the artist.[34] Von Guérard's experience of the physical landscape positioned him to present, in the words of Carl Gustav Carus, a "powerful impression of the whole," including the grasses and pond vegetation, observed at close range and from a ground-level viewpoint, in the foregrounds of each canvas.[35] With its clearly identifiable peaks, their geographical relationships accurately recorded from a single vantage point, *View of the Gippsland Alps, from Bushy Park* was, in some ways, like the alpine panorama in Europe.

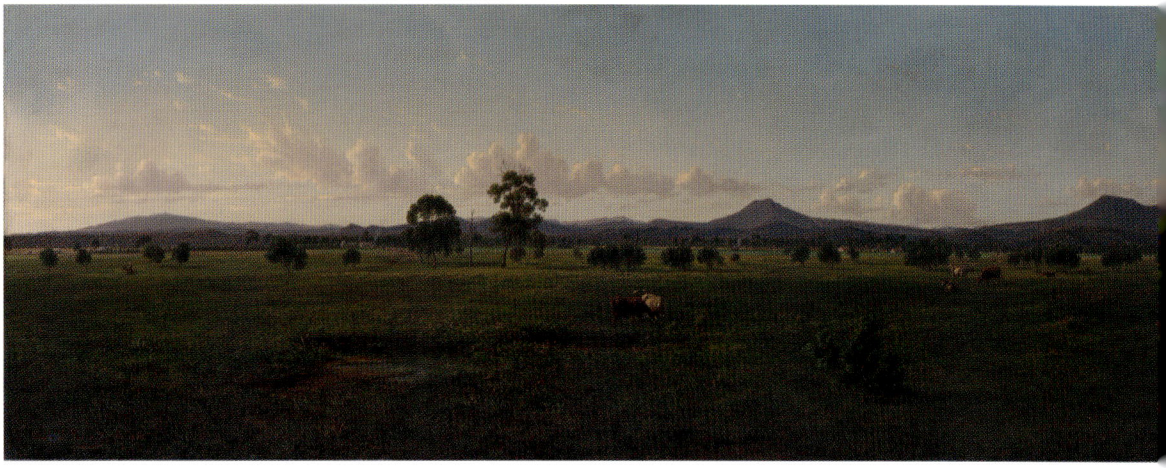

FIG. 6.8. Eugene von Guérard, *View of the Gippsland Alps, from Bushy Park on the River Avon, Victoria*, 1861. Oil on canvas, each 36.2 × 94.1 cm (14 3/8 × 37 in.). National Library of Australia, Canberra. Rex Nan Kivell Collection (nla.obj-134494299).

The "geographic panorama," popular with alpine clubs in Europe and, increasingly, with tourists in the second half of the nineteenth century, was useful to geographers for the information such an image could convey that a cartographic rendering could not, namely the form of peaks from a horizontal projection.[36] The panorama could serve as "an aid to orientation."[37] For von Guérard and Angus McMillan, each of whom had struggled through the notoriously difficult country, the accuracy of this "geographic panorama," one embedded with personal significance for both patron and artist, was paramount.[38]

Though the Bushy Park canvases were exhibited in Melbourne in 1861 at the Victorian Exhibition of the Fine Arts, the audience for these privately commissioned works was, for the most part, restricted. By contrast, when the proprietors of the *Ballarat Star* commissioned von Guérard to produce a panoramic drawing of the city of Ballarat, they intended it to reach the widest audience possible. The artist's 1869 pen, ink, and wash drawing *Ballarat from the Tower of the Western Fire Brigade* was commissioned for a wood engraving, *Ballarat from the Fire Brigade Tower (Looking East)* (fig. 6.9), executed and printed in London. Prints of the engraving were to be presented to the newspaper's subscribers as a New Year's gift in January 1870: "All who have subscribed to the Ballarat Star for three months, or may now pay the subscription for three months in advance will receive a copy of the picture accompanied with the History Gratis."[39] Extra copies of the print could be purchased for between one shilling and sixpence and three shillings, depending on the quality of the paper. The proprietors of the *Ballarat Star* recognized the interest the panorama would generate and advised that prints could be "sent by post to any part of these colonies, or to England for one penny."[40] It was an ambitious project. The scale of the engraving, 48 × 96.7 cm (18 ⅞ × 38 1⁄16 in.), posed significant challenges for the London printers: "The making of the wood occupied three weeks, the drawing on the wood one month, the engraving one month. . . . About twenty persons were engaged on it from beginning to end in merely preparing it for printing," and the cost "amounted to upwards of £260."[41]

Given the growing civic pride felt by the residents of Ballarat—many of whom, like von Guérard, had witnessed the transformation of their city from its early days as an unruly gold-mining settlement into a prosperous, ordered, substantial city with civic buildings, churches, wide streets, and public gardens—a panorama of the city was the ideal choice as the subject of a gift to consolidate and extend subscriptions. In fact, feelings on the subject were so intense that the *Ballarat Star* felt compelled to reassure its readers:

> In giving "a view of Ballarat" we had to consider whether such a view should be a general one, embracing a portion of both the township and some of the more remarkable points of the landscape around, or whether it should be a minute or particular view, bringing into prominence the principal shops and public buildings in some part of the town. The conclusion we came to, was that a general view of the town and neighbourhood would be most acceptable to the public generally, and with this understanding we allowed the artist to choose his own point of view. To those who know how conscientiously Mr Guerard does his work, we need not hardly say that this preliminary step was done most carefully about [*sic*].[42]

Von Guérard had been impressed by the view, looking east from the Western Fire Brigade Tower, when he had

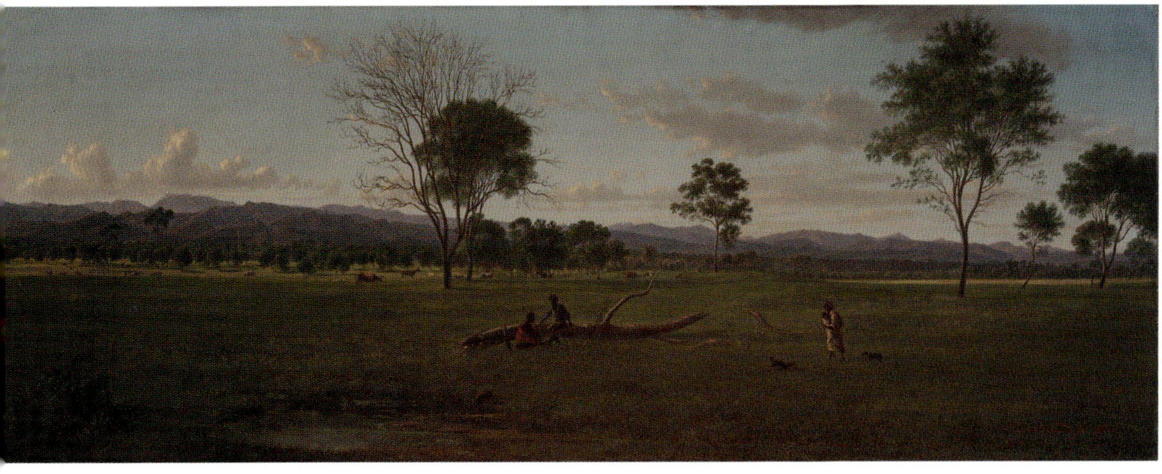

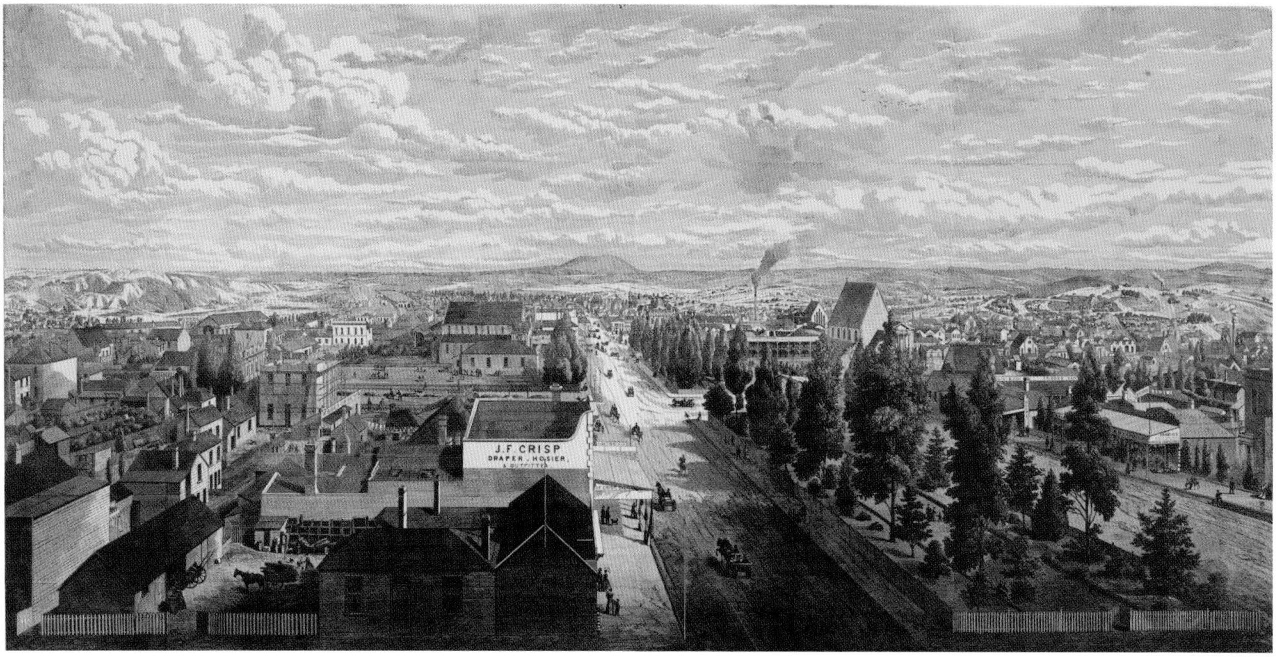

FIG. 6.9. Eugene von Guérard, *Ballarat from the Fire Brigade Tower (Looking East)*, 1870, printed from original block in 1981. Wood engraving on paper, sheet 75.5 × 106.3 cm (29 ¾ × 41 ⅞ in.), image 48 × 96.7 cm (18 ⅞ × 38 1⁄16 in.). Art Gallery of Ballarat. Gift of the Ballarat Historical Society, 1981.

seen it on a visit to the city five years earlier, in 1864, his first return visit since the heady days of the gold rush. In his sketchbook diary, he recorded his amazement at the city's transformation, with its "large railway station, a beautiful theatre" and "beautiful shapes," the forms of the city buildings culminating in the distinctive profile of Mount Warrenheip on the horizon.[43] It was this view, first sketched in pencil and crayon on three sheets of paper over a period of four days on a later visit in February 1867, and titled *Ballarat—Panorama of a City,* that became the subject of the wood engraving. The only change von Guérard made to the composition in his final pen, ink, and wash drawing, *Ballarat from the Tower of the Western Fire Brigade,* from which the engraving was executed, was to include an extra row of buildings in the foreground, which served to anchor the composition.[44]

Nevertheless, the *Ballarat Star* reassured the Ballarat public that the artist had "'viewed' Ballarat from the Eastern and Western Fire Brigade Tower, and also from St Paul's Church Tower on Bakery Hill, and decided that the best for his purposes was the one that is before most of our readers." The resulting work, they continued: "a LARGE PICTURE giving a VIEW OF BALLARAT drawn by E. Von Guérard Esq. Artist, from the top of the Western Fire Brigade . . . takes in all the leading features of the town, and those that send it to their friends in England will be able to point out to them the site of the celebrated Eureka Lead, Golden Point, Black Hill, Warrenheip, Buninyong Mount, the Main Road, Sturt Street, several well known buildings and many other subjects of interest."[45]

It was imperative that, as a fire lookout tower, the five-story Western Fire Brigade Tower should command a complete and uninterrupted 360-degree view of the city and landscape beyond. At the same time, the experience of seeing the view from the octagonal watchtower, with its internal timber staircase, castellated parapet, and (at the time) glazed lookout platform, was in many ways comparable to seeing a panorama from a viewing platform in one of the great panorama buildings in Europe. Von Guérard's personal predilection for viewing towers was such that he incorporated a little tower, with windows on all four sides, into the design for his house in Gipps Street, East Melbourne. From it he painted oil sketches for his own pleasure.[46]

Just over a decade later, in 1881, the Ballarat Council noted the desirability of having pictorial records that would enable future generations to form "a correct estimate" of what Ballarat was like when it was "the premier gold-field in the world."[47] The Melbourne newspaper, the *Argus,* carried a report on the issue, noting that von Guérard "had offered to paint a panorama of the place

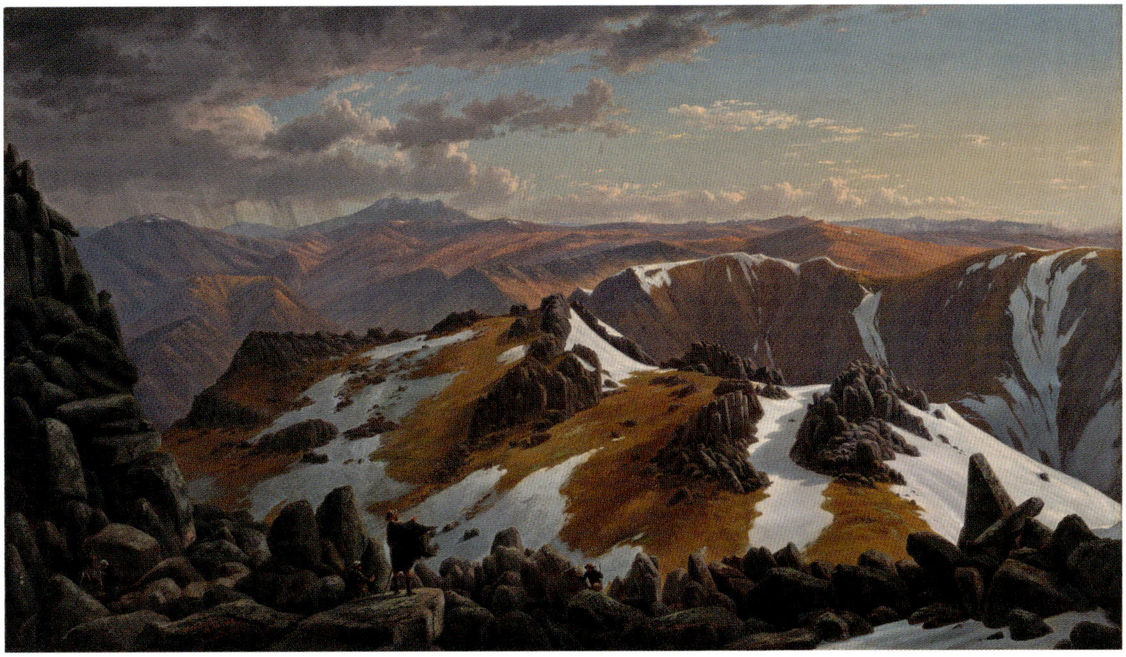

FIG. 6.10. Eugene von Guérard, *North-east View from the Northern Top of Mount Kosciusko*, 1863. Oil on canvas, 66.5 × 116.8 cm (26 × 46 in.). National Gallery of Australia, Canberra.

[Ballarat] but had received no commission," and that he, "one of the best of Australia's painters," was about "to start for Europe," taking with him the three or four hundred drawings made in and around Ballarat in 1853 and 1854.[48] Still no commission was forthcoming, but its importance for the community was now on record. It was not until 1884 that he received the commission for his panoramic canvas *Old Ballarat as It Was in the Summer of 1853–54*.[49] Painted in his Düsseldorf studio from a drawing made thirty years earlier, it was presented to the Art Gallery of Ballarat by his patron, James Oddie, on Eureka Day, 1885.[50]

The extent to which the experience of the panorama had penetrated von Guérard's pictorial imagination is perhaps most potently realized in one of his greatest works, *North-east View from the Northern Top of Mount Kosciusko* (1863; fig. 6.10). His portrayal of the vista from the top of Mount Kosciuszko can be read—as has Caspar David Friedrich's *Wanderer above a Sea of Fog* (ca. 1817)—as "a view of the world as panorama."[51] Von Guérard's windswept figure (the artist himself?), like Friedrich's wanderer, is seen from the back looking over the awe-inspiring vista of mountain ranges and into the pictorial space; the act of viewing is given dramatic emphasis by his exultant gesture (see fig. 0.13). Like both Friedrich's wanderer and the visitor to a panorama, the figure stands on a "platform," here a granite ledge. Like them, he is physically separated from the brilliantly illuminated terrain of the spectacle, in this case by a deep chasm.

But, whereas drifts of fog obscure the physical landscape in Friedrich's work, von Guérard's figure directs our gaze to a painted landscape of unrivaled topographical, geographical, and geological accuracy. For Friedrich, the "spiritual eye" was as important as the "bodily eye," but it was only through the acuteness of his vision that von Guérard could depict the rock formations and mountainous terrain with the accuracy required to convey a sense of their underlying geological character and history.[52] The glacial cirque, the eroded, rounded, worn-down character of the landforms, the granite tors, and the exposed clusters of hard, angular slate along the top of Watsons Crags in von Guérard's *Kosciusko* were recorded, as Carus had required of the geognostic landscape painter, from a scientifically informed perspective together with "the lively apprehension of the artist's eye."[53] Only by introducing the framing device of the wall of rock on the left did von Guérard depart from his absolute commitment to topographical accuracy. Compositionally, this device, a continuation of the rock ledge (the viewing platform) on which the spectator stands, defines—and frames—the view as spectacle.

Following the model of collaborations between artists and scientists of the late eighteenth and early nineteenth centuries, such as those between the painter of panoramic alpine views Caspar Wolf and the amateur geologist Jacob Samuel Wyttenberg and, later, the mathematician and cartographer Daniel Hubor, von Guérard's Kosciuszko expedition was made in the company of the Humboldtian geophysicist Georg von Neumayer. The scientist observed that while von Guérard was recording the landscape in his sketchbook, he and his assistant Brinkmann were "some 40 ft. lower down," taking measurements with a theodolite and barometer.[54] Von Guérard climbed to a higher vantage point so that he could capture the view from Australia's highest peak, a view that at the time had been seen by only a handful of Europeans.[55] The cloaked spectator directs our gaze toward the view but the view he sees is not the view we see. While the dramatic ridge in the foreground dominates his field of vision, we look above and over him, his companions, and the ridge to the expansive vista of mountain ranges beyond. From our privileged perspective, the complex structure of the successive ranges becomes comprehensible. The convergence of viewpoints means that, along with the windswept figure, we experience the landscape at close range and at the same time comprehend its totality.

The resolution of a multitude of minutely observed details of the natural world within harmonious and unified compositions of great breadth is one of the defining aspects of von Guérard's landscape-painting practice. It parallels a central tenet of Humboldt's new vision, his recognition of the unifying laws that govern nature's extraordinary diversity. Humboldt's *Cosmos: A Sketch of a Physical Description of the Universe,* a work in which the scientist set out to encompass "the entire world—everything we know about the heavens and life on earth," exemplifies and parallels the nineteenth-century mode of thinking that produced the panorama.[56] Humboldt was enthusiastic about the capacity of the panorama to "serve, in some degree, as a substitute for travelling through different regions."[57]

From his early days in Italy and Germany, von Guérard had been immersed in the language of the panorama. In Australia the panoramic imperative took on a compelling intensity for him when, as a Humboldtian traveling artist, he encountered the diversity, the vastness, and the grandeur of landscapes still so little known by European audiences. The wonder he shared with Humboldt at nature's beauty and diversity is expressed in the touch of his pencil on paper and his brush on canvas; he looked for ways to capture it all—the intimate details of nature and his experience of the breadth and scale of the landscape around him—within the constraints of the framed canvas. Von Guérard's paintings convey his personal exhilaration at being physically *in* the landscape. They become, as Humboldt observed of the effect of the panorama, "wonderfully interwoven with the feelings awakened by the aspect of the scenes when actually beheld."[58]

NOTES

I am grateful to Dr. Ann Galbally, Professorial Fellow, University of Melbourne, for kindly reading this essay and for her constructive suggestions, and Robert Clinch, a Melbourne-based painter of architectural and panoramic subjects, for his observations on von Guérard's use of perspective in his 360-degree panoramic drawings of Melbourn.

1. Eugene von Guérard, Sketchbook 24, 1855, Dixson Galleries, State Library of New South Wales, DGB16, vol. 3, 64–66.
2. The Humboldtian scientists and artists working in midcentury Melbourne included the botanist Ferdinand von Mueller, the geophysicist Georg von Neumayer, the artist and naturalist Ludwig Becker, and the multidisciplinary scientist and artist Wilhelm Blandowski.
3. Eugene von Guérard, unpublished letter to the *Argus,* Melbourne, June 1870, James Smith Papers, Mitchell Library, State Library of New South Wales, ML MSS 212; Alexander von Humboldt, *Cosmos: A Sketch of a Physical Description of the Universe,* 2 vols., trans. E. C. Otté (London: Henry G. Bohn, 1849), 2:451–58; and Alexander von Humboldt, *Views of Nature,* trans. Mrs. Sabine (London: Longman, Brown, Green and Longmans and J. Murray, 1850), 217–31.
4. Ruth Pullin, *Eugene von Guérard: Nature Revealed* (Melbourne: National Gallery of Victoria, 2011), 1, 44.
5. Von Guérard, unpublished letter to the *Argus,* June 1870.
6. Johann Christian Reinhart, *Vier Ansichten von der Villa Malta auf Rom,* 1829–35, tempera on canvas, Neue Pinakothek, Munich WAF 812, 813, 814, 811.
7. Herbert W. Rott, "Vier Ansichten von Rom vom Turm der Villa Malta 1829–1835," in *Johann Christian Reinhart: Ein deutscher Landschaftsmaler in Rom,* ed. Herbert W. Rott and Andreas Stolzenberg with F. Carlo Schmid (Hamburg: Hamburger Kunsthalle, Neue Pinakothek Munich, 2012), 338–45; 341.
8. Eugene von Guérard, *Camaldoli,* 1836, pencil, 29.0 × 44.0 cm (11 7/16 × 17 5/16 in.); *Neapel,* 1838, pencil, 30.5 × 47.0 cm (12 × 18 1/2 in.); *Capri,* 1838, pencil, 30.5 × 46.8 cm (12 × 18 7/16 in.); *Vedute di Firenze,* 1838, pencil, 29.5 × 44.0 cm (11 5/8 × 17 5/16 in.); *Tivoli,* 1838, pencil, 30.0 × 46.0 cm (11 13/16 × 18 1/8 in). Private collection, Coates, U.K.
9. Von Guérard was enrolled in Schirmer's landscape class from 1841 until 1844 and Wiegmann's *Bauklasse* in 1846–47. Nordrhein-Westfälisches Hauptstaatsarchiv: Transskription der Schülerlisten: Kunstakademie Düsseldorf, Reg. Düss. Präs. Büro, nr. 1559, 1839/40–1851/52.
10. The Meister brothers' panorama was shown in Cologne between 1841 and 1844. Von Guérard's visit in May 1842 is recorded in Sketchbook 14, 1841, 1842, 1846, Dixson Galleries, State Library of New South Wales, DGB14, vol. 4, 17, 18.
11. Stephan Oettermann, *The Panorama: History of a Mass Medium,* trans. Deborah Lucas Schneider (New York: Zone, 1997), 218.
12. Bertha Heilbron suggests that Lewis settled in Düsseldorf in 1851; Bertha L. Heilbron, "Making a Motion Picture in 1848: Henry Lewis

on the Upper Mississippi," *Minnesota History* 17, no. 2 (1936): 143. Later research places him in Düsseldorf by 1853: John Graham Cook, "Artist Henry Lewis: The Case of the Falsified Résumé," *Minnesota History* (Spring 2001): 242.

13. Roger Butler, "Geological and Botanical Exactitude: The Lithographs," in Pullin, *Eugene von Guérard*, 236.
14. His future brothers-in-law included the Düsseldorf School artists Joseph Fay (1813–1875), Oswald Achenbach (1827–1905), Otto Arnz (1823–1860), and Albert Arnz (1832–1914).
15. *Illustrated London News*, August 14, 1852, 114.
16. Mimi Colligan, *Canvas Documentaries: Panoramic Entertainments in Nineteenth-Century Australia and New Zealand* (Carlton South, Vic.: Melbourne University Press, 2002), 38.
17. Ibid., 11.
18. Richard Neville, "Visitors Looked for a Prison, but Beheld a Palace," in *Colony: Australia 1770–1861/Frontier Wars*, ed. Cathy Leahy and Judith Ryan (Melbourne: National Gallery of Victoria, 2018), 75–95; 90. There is conflicting evidence about whether a full-scale panorama of this subject was produced and exhibited. See Gordon Bull, "Taking Place: Panorama and Panopticon in the Colonisation of New South Wales," *Australian Journal of Art* 12, no. 1 (1994): 86. Cf. Colligan, *Canvas Documentaries*, 33; and Edwin Barnard, *Capturing Time: Panoramas of Old Australia* (Canberra: National Library of Australia, 2012), 19.
19. Augustus Earle, [Panorama of Hobart], ca. 1828, watercolor and pencil on six sheets, ca. 37 cm × 222 cm (14 9/16 × 87 7/16 in.), Dixson Galleries, State Library of New South Wales.
20. Bernard Comment, *The Panorama* (London: Reaktion Books, 1999), 137–38.
21. Act 16, Victoria no. 38 (1853), cited by Sharon Lane and Alyssa Gilchrist, "Heritage in Ruins: An Investigation into Melbourne's 'Buried Blocks,'" report to the Heritage Council of Victoria, May 28, 2019, 22, https://heritagecouncil.vic.gov.au/wp-content/uploads/2019/10/Part1-HeritageInRuinsFinalReport-Sections1-3.pdf.
22. Davis Calwell, September 5, 1853, in Miles Lewis with Philip Goad and Alan Mayne, *Melbourne: The City's History and Development* (Melbourne: City of Melbourne, 1994), 41.
23. Comment, *The Panorama*, 137–38.
24. Three of the five sheets are dated: the second sheet is dated February 14–15, 1855; the fourth, March 3–5; and the fifth, March 5, 1855.
25. In the mid-nineteenth century, the hillock, at 103 feet above sea level, was the ideal vantage point. I am indebted to Robert Clinch for his analysis of the drawing and the identification of sightlines. James Kearney, *Melbourne and Its Suburbs* (Melbourne: Andrew Clarke, Surveyor General, 1855).
26. Gerard Hayes, "Our Town," *SLV NEWS 47* (Melbourne: State Library of Victoria, July–October 2011), 16.
27. The Melbourne and Hobsons Bay Railway opened on September 12, 1854.
28. Von Guérard visited Purrumbete homestead twice in 1857, on his March–April trip through the Western District and in November, en route to Mount Gambier.
29. Eugene von Guérard, Sketchbook 26, 1857 and 1859, Dixson Galleries, State Library of New South Wales, DGB16, vol. 5, 44–46.
30. See also Comment's discussion of Friedrich's concern with "all-encompassing representation" in *Panorama*, 100.
31. Oettermann, *Panorama*, 30.
32. *Carl Gustav Carus: Nine Letters on Landscape Painting, Written in the Years 1815–1824*, trans. David Brett (Los Angeles: Getty Research Institute, 2002), 138.
33. Ruth Pullin, "The Vulkaneifel and Victoria's Western District," *Melbourne Art Journal 11–12* (2008–9): 7–33.
34. A. W. Howitt to his mother, November 1860 (a letter that Howitt completed on December 3, 1860), Howitt Papers, State Library of Victoria, MS 9356, box 1045/3a, letter 10.
35. Carus quoted in Comment, *Panorama*, 112.
36. Johannes Frisschauf, "Das Panorama als Hilfsmittel der Geographie," *Sonderdruck aus Ausland* 23 (1892), quoted in Oettermann, *Panorama*, 37n86. This argument is informed by Oettermann, *Panorama*, 37.
37. Frisschauf, "Das Panorama," quoted in Oettermann, *Panorama*, 37n81.
38. In 1839 McMillan had led the pioneering expedition over the Alps to open up the Gippsland region for pastoralism.
39. *Ballarat Star*, January 7, 1870.
40. *Ballarat Star*, January 17, 1870.
41. *Ballarat Star*, January 18, 1870.
42. *Ballarat Star*, January 7, 1870.
43. Eugen von Guérard, Sketchbook 35, 1864. I am grateful to Thomas A. Darragh for his assistance with the transcription of von Guérard's notes from the old German handwriting.
44. *Ballarat—Panorama of a City*, 1867, pencil and crayon, 30.8 × 97.6 cm (12 1/8 × 38 7/16 in.), Inscribed January 19–23, 1869, Dixson Library, State Library of New South Wales, Sydney; Eugene von Guérard, *Ballarat from the Tower of the Western Fire Brigade*, 1869, pen, ink, and wash over pencil on paper, 48.0 × 97.0 cm (18 7/8 × 38 3/16 in.), Ballarat Fine Art Gallery, Gift of Thomas Wannliss, 1904; and Roger Butler, "Ballarat from the Fire Brigade Tower, Looking East," *La Trobe Journal*, no. 36, December 1985, 89.
45. *Ballarat Star*, January 7, 1870.
46. For example, Eugene von Guérard, *Distant View towards Yarra Bend from Our Little Tower (Fernsicht nach Yarra Bend von unserem Thürmchen)*, 1871, oil on composition board, 15.6 × 33.6 cm (6 1/8 × 13 1/4 in.), private collection. The house, Little Parndon, still stands at 159 Gipps Street, East Melbourne. Von Guérard lived there from 1862 until 1882.
47. *Melbourne Argus*, September 14, 1881, 7.
48. Ibid.
49. Eugene von Guérard, *Old Ballarat as It Was in the Summer of 1853–54*, 1884, oil on canvas mounted on board, 75 × 138.6 cm (29 1/2 × 54 9/16 in.), Art Gallery of Ballarat, Victoria, Gift of James Oddie on Eureka Day, 1885.
50. Eugene von Guérard, *Vom publick haus zu Ballarat*, February 18, 1854, pencil on paper, 20.0 × 31.8 cm (7 7/8 × 12 1/2 in.), Art Gallery of Ballarat, gift of Mrs. Martell, 1938, 1938.2.
51. Oettermann, *Panorama*, 47; see also Comment, *Panorama*, 144.
52. Friedrich quoted in William Vaughan, *German Romantic Painting* (New Haven: Yale University Press, 1980), 68.
53. Carus quoted in *Carl Gustav Carus*, 138.
54. Georg von Neumayer, *Results of the Magnetic Survey of the Colony of Victoria* (Mannheim: Schneider, 1869), 78.
55. They were in fact at the top of Mount Townsend, the neighboring peak on the Kosciuszko Plateau, one that the party believed was higher than the peak that is today named Mount Kosciuszko, and which they had scaled earlier on the same day.
56. Oettermann, *Panorama*, 38.
57. Humboldt, *Cosmos*, 2:457.
58. Ibid.

KATIE TRUMPENER

7 National Vistas, Peripheral Vision

War and the Making of Nations in Alpine Panoramas

Today nineteenth-century panoramic paintings and the huge buildings housing them survive only in a few locations. The densest remaining cluster is in and near the Alps (themselves a favorite panorama subject): in Thun, Lucerne, Einsiedeln, and Murten (Switzerland); Innsbruck and Salzburg (Austria); and Altötting (Germany).[1]

Across Europe, the painting and installation of these gigantic paintings-in-the-round began in the 1790s to wild acclaim, suffered two eclipses, and enjoyed subsequent revivals of popularity, before losing their audience to the nascent medium of cinema. Local or transnational panorama companies maintained dedicated panorama buildings in most larger European and American cities, built in the round and designed to display a changing, touring series of panoramic paintings.

Over the nineteenth century, panorama painting dramatically changed scale. The earliest extant panorama, depicting the Swiss Alpine city of Thun, was painted in 1809–14 by Marquand Wocher (Swiss, 1760–1830), was widely displayed beginning in 1814, and is now housed in Thun in a modern panorama building. Its surface covers 900 square feet. This essay compares it with the panorama painted in the 1870s by Édouard Castres (Swiss, 1838–1902) and now housed in Lucerne; it covers 12,000 square feet, well over ten times the size of its Thun predecessor.[2]

The panoramas' disproportionate rate of survival and preservation in the Alps results partly from the long-standing regional tradition of tourism based on spectacular vistas.[3] Alpine trains, restaurants, hotels, roads, and footpaths still bill themselves as "panoramic." Present-day tourists to Austria's Großglöckner mountains (Kärnten) can thus stay in Apartment Hotel Panorama (Bad Hofgastein), take the waters at the Panorama Wellness Landscape (Bad Gastein), and travel on Goldeck-Panoramastrasse or Panoramaweg Kaiserstein onto the Kaiser-Franz-Josefs-Höhe, a particularly famous outlook onto the Pasterze Glacier.

As Walter Niedermayr (Italian, b. 1952) demonstrates in his 1997 photographic diptych, *Franz-Josefs-Höhe*, modern visitors to this plaza (commemorating the Habsburg emperor who hiked there in 1856) essentially find themselves on a nineteenth-century panorama-style viewing platform, separated from the surrounding mountains by a low security fence, with benches from which to contemplate sublime views (fig. 7.1).[4] Many viewers sharpen their vision with optical devices: binoculars, camera

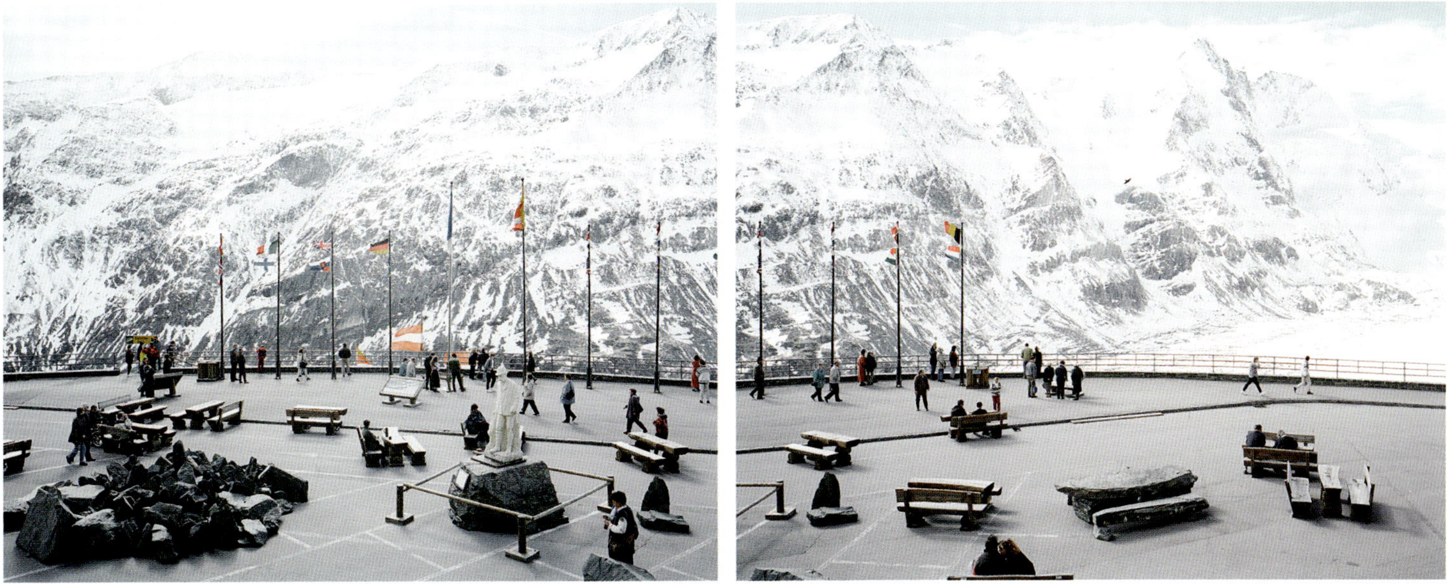

FIG. 7.1. Walter Niedermayr (Italian, b. 1952), *Franz-Josefs-Höhe 1*, 1997. Diptych, photographs, installation: 104 × 265 cm (41 × 104 1/4 in.).

viewfinders, or public viewing scopes (tower viewers). Like nineteenth-century panorama guides, the plaza's four explanatory placards spell out what visitors are looking at, and signs point the way down to the funicular, which potentially enables further immersive, panoramic seeing.

Like the museumgoing photographs of Thomas Struth (German, b. 1954), Niedermayr's diptych meditates on spectatorial experience, the characteristic stances of touristic looking: contemplative, ambulatory, alert, distracted, overwhelmed. Rather than meeting neatly to form a seamless composite, Niedermayr's two photographs overlap slightly in vantage point, while diverging slightly in temporality; the right-hand photograph, taken shortly after the left-hand, reveals further movements by some of the same tourists—now elsewhere on the outlook plaza, or walking away from the scene. Some may be heading toward Hotel Kaiser Franz Joseph's Panoramarestaurant (whose glass "panorama elevator" (*Panoramalift*) offers transport directly from tourist buses to a window-encased dining room overlooking the surrounding mountain range), others to view the Visitor Center's geological exhibits and interactive "Panorama Room."[5]

Niedermayr's diptych is part of his much longer 1985 series, *Alpine Landscapes*, of "serial" photographs—each consisting of two to four consecutive pictures arranged to form a binocular or semipanoramic view, and thereby "to expand the 'horizon' of perception." Both because of our eyes' binocular collaboration and because we see continuously, Niedermayr underscores that "what we see on the retina is never a single image but multiple points of view," and our process of seeing "transforms our peripheral vision into foveal vision" (that is, vision focused on the center of the visual field, where visual acuity is at its height).[6] Niedermayr's serial images at once try to sharpen, focus, and broaden vision, draw attention to our serial perception of stasis, and underscore the natural congruence among vision, still photography, and the moving images that constitute cinema.

Yet despite visitors' movement across the plaza, this particular diptych is calm, almost static; the sublime mountains are peaceful, the viewing platform a safe, civilized, neutral place to watch from. Other parts of the panoramic tradition, this chapter argues, call into question that appearance of safety. During the pivotal scene of *Force Majeure* (*Turist*, Sweden, 2014), for instance, the feature film by Ruben Östlund (Swedish, b. 1974), a family of Swedish ski tourists, lunching together on an overlook terrace in the French Alps, excitedly note the controlled avalanche occurring nearby. The father films it on his cellphone; other diners train their binoculars on the avalanche (fig. 7.2)—until they realize it may not stop before reaching them. As his son screams for his father's help, the father bolts for safety, leaving his family to fend for themselves. Everyone survives, but the film details the emotional fallout from this decisive moment of instinctual cowardice, egotism, and betrayal. Like many filmmakers,

Östlund is interested in the nature of spectatorship, what it means ethically to observe the sublime, to witness potential catastrophe from a place of apparent safety. Nineteenth-century panoramas posed a version of these questions.

In the Alps, as elsewhere, many surviving panoramas became permanent tourist attractions in the places they depict. Like nineteenth-century visitors to the Regent's Park Colosseum panorama of London or present-day visitors to the panoramas of (and in) Gettysburg or Atlanta, tourists in Thun, Salzburg, and Innsbruck can still move between real-life vistas and painted canvases re-creating those vistas.

Nineteenth-century panoramas drew stylistically on visual traditions from cartography, Renaissance Italy's proportionate "ideal cityscapes," and northern Europe's Renaissance tradition of elongated cityscape and riverscape etchings to the Japanese scroll and screen—but also on the theatricality of Baroque trompe l'oeil painting, with its virtuoso perspective and incorporation of realia to blur the line between spectacle and spectator.[7] In the Alps, some panoramas also demonstrate the close interpenetration of what elsewhere appear distinctive panoramic subgenres (alpine, urban, battle, religious panorama) and overlapping painted and performed spectacle traditions.[8] Sometimes a panorama's siting suggests links to other spectacles. Lucerne's panorama building helped anchor a nineteenth-century visual pleasure district; Einsiedeln's Crucifixion panorama was clearly built to attract pilgrims heading for the town's Benedictine monastery, famous for its trompe l'oeil Baroque décor.[9]

Nineteenth-century panorama display was equally theatrical. Viewers walked up a long, increasingly dark staircase, emerging onto a large circular platform, looking out onto the vast, seamlessly circular canvas surrounding them.[10] Atop this wooden deck, spectators looked, stood, perambulated, or sat in relative darkness; the canvas they looked at, in contrast, appeared illuminated from behind (by natural lighting, usually filtering down from hidden rows of windows topping the panorama building).[11]

The painted surface's attempted naturalism—and realia often obtruding into spectatorial space—was thus offset by the panorama's indirect but intensely theatrical lighting, which lent the painted canvas an aura, lit up from within. In turn-of-the-century Crucifixion panoramas, this inner glow helped viewers perceive the panorama as the conduit of, or occasion of, religious experience. Patriotic war panoramas (often evoking religious notions of sacrifice, transcendence, and apotheosis) evoked sublimity to comparable effect.[12]

This chapter considers first Wocher's city-and-mountain panorama of Thun, then two panoramas showing war in the mountains. Innsbruck now houses a 1896 panorama of the 1809 Battle of Bergisel (an important turning point in the struggle for Tyrolean independence during the Napoleonic Wars) by Michael Zeno Diemer (German, 1867–1939). Lucerne, in turn, now houses Castres's panorama depicting the French army's 1871 retreat into Switzerland at the end of the Franco-Prussian War. Panoramic form, these three panoramas demonstrate, is amenable equally to traditionalist and

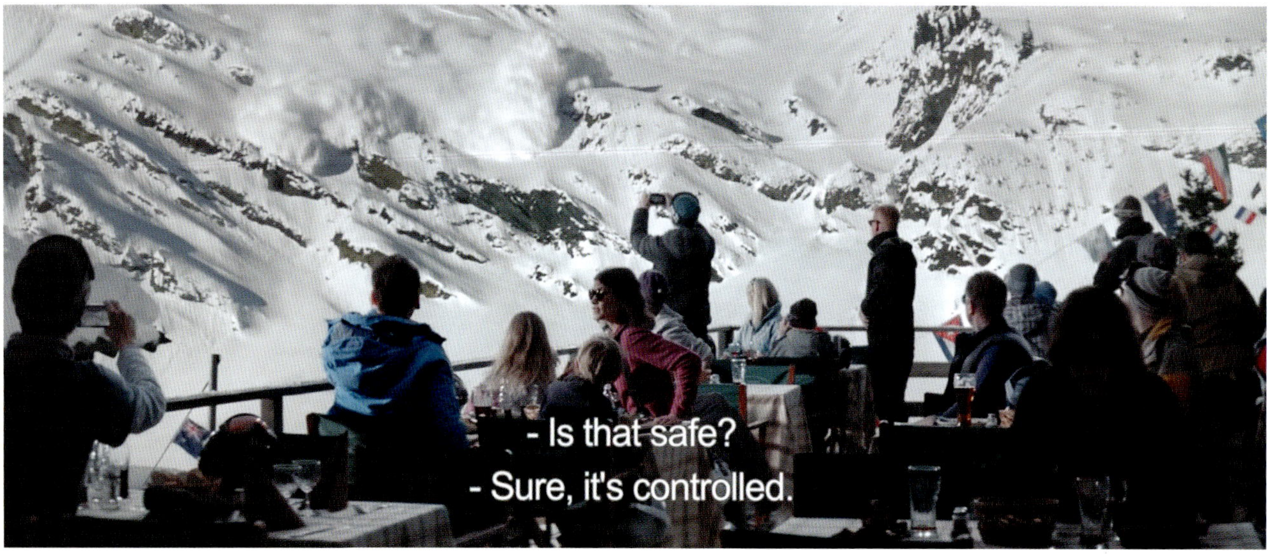

FIG. 7.2. Still from Ruben Östlund (Swedish, b. 1974), *Force Majeure* (Turist), 2014.

radical, protomodernist presentations of history, culture, and nature. Centered on a famous freedom fighter and an organic nationalist uprising, the Innsbruck panorama revives a heroic Romantic nationalism, whereas the Lucerne panorama—with its political ambivalences, claustrophobic use of space, and sense of moral catastrophe—participates in a lineage of political art stretching from Théodore Géricault's *Raft of the Medusa* (see fig. 2.5) to *Guernica* (1937, Museo Nacional Centro de Arte Reina Sofía, Madrid), the famous Spanish Civil War protest painting by Pablo Picasso (Spanish, 1881–1973).

The Thun, Innsbruck, and Lucerne panoramas also grapple with the political and ideological legacies of the Napoleonic Wars. As Oliver Grau, Maurice Samuels, and Katie Hornstein have underscored, the panoramic and the Napoleonic often went together. Both Admiral Nelson and Napoleon recognized the panorama's potential for mass influence; Napoleon planned an eight-panorama celebration of his victories for the park of Versailles.[13] And even in the context of a 1836 memorial tribute to the Napoleonic battle painter Antoine Gros (French, 1771–1835), the permanent secretary of the Académie des Beaux-Arts, Antoine Quatremère, lamented the inadequacy of traditional battle painting to capture modern warfare's complexity and scale: "Only the vast and special expanse of the panorama can suffice."[14]

In Switzerland, the period of Napoleonic occupation inaugurated a new Swiss republic, replacing a regionally anchored federation with a French-style centralized, egalitarian (yet authoritarian) state. Late eighteenth-century Switzerland had seen an upsurge of trans-cantonal patriotism. Yet the Swiss remained deeply divided over France's attempts to modernize and unify their state in its own image. Under the Helvetian Republic, Switzerland adopted a common currency and a national flag, inaugurated a *bureau de l'esprit public*, and forcibly surrendered its traditional political neutrality, becoming a staging ground for Europe's armies. The post-Napoleonic restoration reestablished political neutrality, rescinding currency, flag, and other outward forms of republican federalism. Yet Switzerland remained relatively untouched by the post-Napoleonic nationalist fervor that swept Germany. The Helvetian Republic remained an ambivalent legacy. When Switzerland eventually reconstituted itself as a federalist republic (after a small-scale 1847 civil war), it drew on the American constitution—and its own earlier experiences as an imposed republic.

In its panoramas as in its politics, Switzerland represents a distinctive approach to questions of national cohesion, federation, and collectivity. From the Swiss perspective, the Franco-Prussian War seemed an unhappy replay of the Napoleonic Wars, as Switzerland, now officially neutral, was once more caught up in an ongoing Franco-German struggle. The Lucerne panorama thus visualizes the horrors of that war to defend Swiss neutrality even as it calls into question the possibility of full neutrality.

The Thun panorama, actually painted during the Napoleonic occupation and displayed immediately after the post-Napoleonic restoration, cannily balances the local and the general. It balances ways of seeing rooted in domesticated localized sight with a more abstract, collective vision. Indeed, it juxtaposes a traditional, locally anchored Swiss federalism with a Napoleonic republicanism, intent on forging a more abstract, inclusive modern nation. The panorama also enacts a rapprochement between eighteenth-century modes of allegorizing collective life and a new, Romantic impetus to ground collectivity in everyday life.

Conceived and produced as public art, and asserting Thun's role as gateway to and observation point for the Alps, Wocher's panorama also seeks to connect local affairs to a potential national identity and the Alps' glacial time frame. Its circular form facilitates a sense of boundless organic seeing—and seamless integration between human settlement and natural setting (fig. 7.3). Wocher's panorama, unusually, conjoins two generally distinct types of topographical panoramas, ambitious townscape and detailed survey of an alpine range.[15]

As people inhabit cities, so cities inhabit nature: here a specific Swiss nature is defined by the geological vista at the painting's distant horizon and, in the foreground, the Aare river (originating in an alpine glacier) echoing the shape of the Hauptgasse. Wocher's touristic nationalism is founded on an epic domesticity definable in a relatively short-term human scale but also within the glacial time frame suggested by the rocky contours of the Bernese Alps. The mountains came first; long before Thun became a touristic vantage point for experiencing them at this staged, sweeping distance, urban culture was shaped by their presence.

The painter divides or splits the circle, affording the viewer a series of pointed contrasts. Despite its seamless circularity, this panorama also has two distinct sides. On

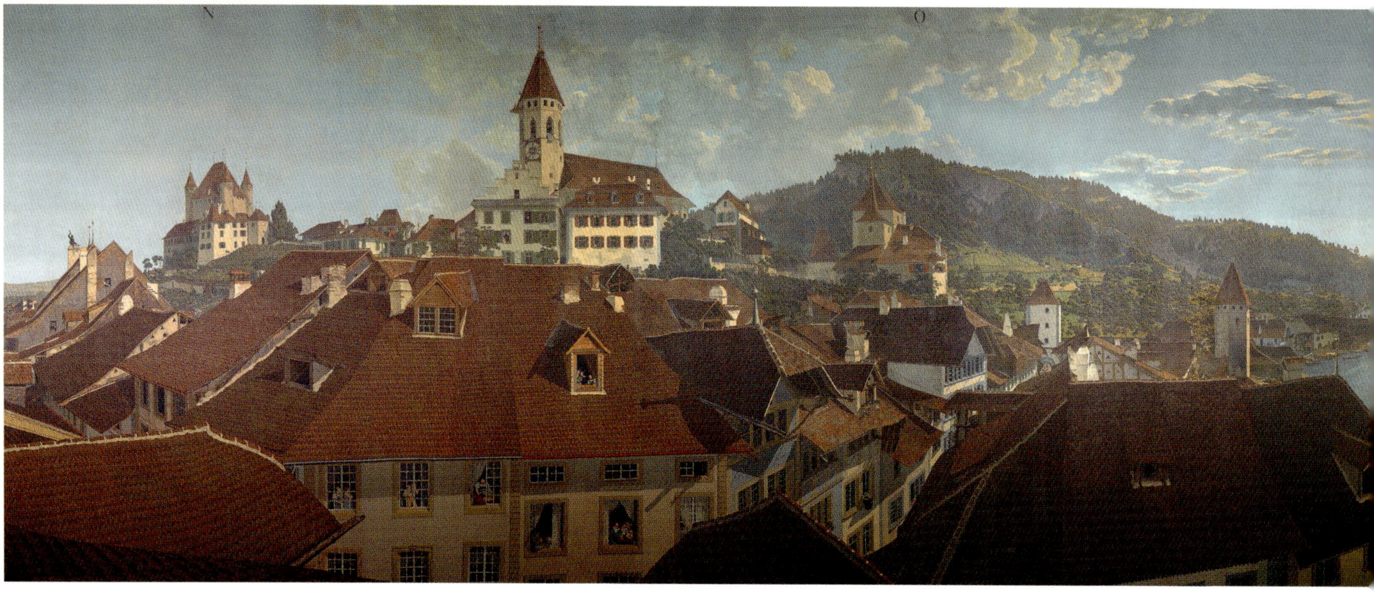

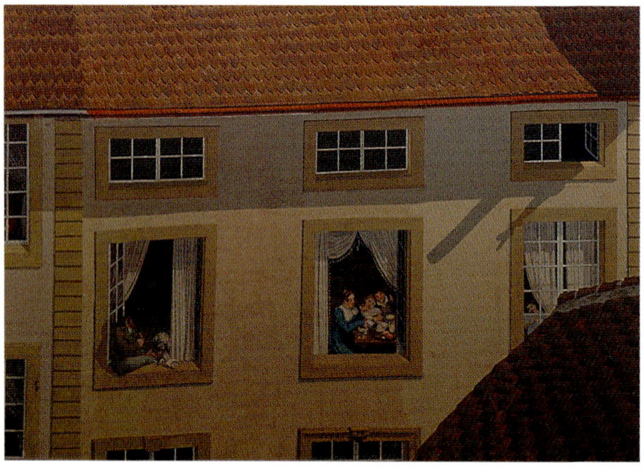

FIG. 7.3. Marquand Wocher (Swiss, 1760–1830), *Panorama of Thun*, 1809–14. Oil on deckle-edged paper, 7.5 × 38 m (24 5/8 × 124 5/8 ft.). Depositum of the Gottfried Keller Foundation, Swiss Confederation, Kunstmuseum Thun, Switzerland.

FIG. 7.4. Detail of fig. 7.3.

the Aare's far shore is a remote cityscape, whose human figures appear only as types—save for the tiny cameo of Wocher and his fellow painter Johann Jakob Biedermann (Swiss, 1763–1830), carrying portfolios, backs to the viewer. On the other shore, an intimate range of houses invites the viewer to look in and observe domestic interactions (fig. 7.4).[16] One side of Wocher's painting is anchored by the distant sublimity of mountains on the horizon, the other side by cats, breakfast tables, and a juvenile viewer-in-the-painting pointedly returning the viewer's gaze. On one side is an Enlightenment collective portrait of a social microcosm, abstracted, comprehensive, busy; on the other are Biedermeier tableaux of daily life and interactions. Like the regional folkloric festivals that inspired it, Wocher's image is designed as an idyll. Yet the idyll remains predominately urban, modern—projecting a future in which Switzerland's Alps will again be controlled by indigenous inhabitants. The panorama's site-specific hyperrealism powers an idealized political and social vision.[17]

Panoramic form initially seems totalizing. Yet it potentially explores contrasting social visions, demonstrating the coexistence of different historical, cultural, and representational epistemes. Sometimes it works to harmonize them.[18] In battle panoramas, however, this sense of conflict, of opposing forces and worldviews, becomes a central subject and organizing principle. Already during the seventeenth century, indeed, the Swedish Regent Hedwig Eleanora commissioned two distinctive galleries on different floors of Drottningholm Palace outside Stockholm to document the respective military conquests of her late husband, Charles X, and her son, Charles XI. The first, a sequence of landscape battle paintings, arrayed end to end in proto-panoramic sequence, displays the 1656 Battle of Warsaw (and further battles won against Poland), shoring up Charles X's kingship. Each painting shows the progress of a specific battle, verging on the diagrammatic (complete with numbers and explanatory key). One floor above, a second battle series, painted in the 1690s by Johann Philipp Lemke, anatomizes Charles XI's 1680s war against Denmark. The Battle of Lund, for instance, is shown in four different paintings, all painted from a semi–bird's-eye view, as four encounters over the same day led to eventual Swedish victory.

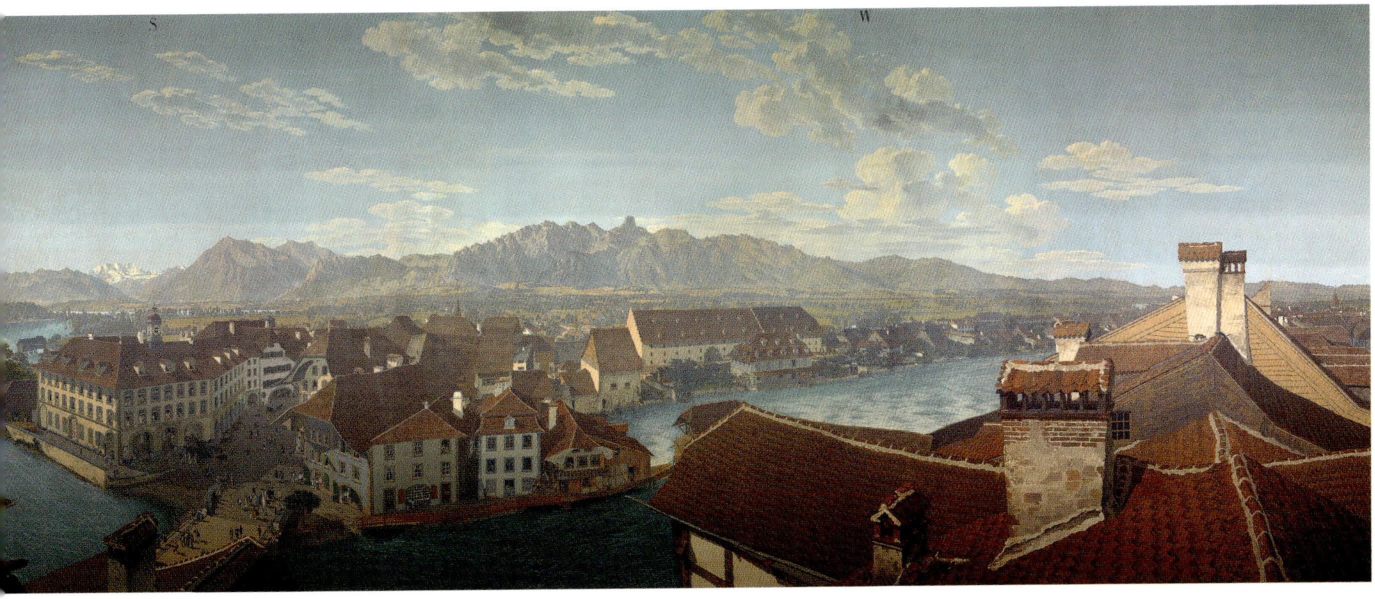

These series form an instructive contrast. The first presents a war's cumulative progress, the second a near-simultaneity of action. Both subgenres became crucial to the later modes of history painting the panorama developed. Already in the seventeenth-century royal dynasties could experience a multiperspectival view of battles and campaigns whose successes grounded their ongoing claims to the throne. These pictures anatomized successful military tactics while narrating progressive phases of a specific battle and of a war as a series of battles. The nineteenth-century panorama, too, joined a series of panels into an interlocking physical surround, inviting viewers to a dual vision and meditating simultaneously on battle's micro-textures and war's large-scale effects. Mid-nineteenth-century French history painters, Katie Hornstein has shown, then revived this contrastive structure in dialogue with contemporary panorama painting: while some displayed series of large-format battle paintings, others displayed groups of complementary paintings or lithographs conceived on different scales of size and detail.[19]

In the Innsbruck panorama, conflict is foregrounded on the level of content. Paradoxically, this licenses a rather static representational strategy. In 1809 Tyrolean partisans' unexpected victory at Bergisel, outside Innsbruck, decisively boosted the anti-Napoleonic cause. The panorama shows a new (yet thoroughly traditionalist) sense of collectivity arising in reaction to foreign occupiers and their republican ideology. Napoleonic and Bavarian troops outnumber Bergisel's local militia, but they are beaten back; the enemy is shown primarily as a distant group, advancing, and sometimes dying, in formation, identifiable but depersonalized by their uniforms. The painting's foreground, in contrast, presents the realia-filled landscape (figs. 7.5a–b) and a Tyrolean peasant militia, often close enough to be individualized, wearing traditional local costumes and armed mainly with staffs and pitchforks, not guns.

In addition to fighting men, the Tyrolean side includes women weeping over the dead, as they join priests in ministering to the wounded, serving communion or spirits. In *Germania* (ca. 98 CE), Tacitus had evoked the Germanic tribes fighting with their families at close proximity, to know what they fought for.[20] The Bergisel panorama likewise underscores that the locals can win their unevenly matched struggle precisely because they are indigenous, belonging to the land, fighting for their families, farms, homes. A piece of realia—the humble wayside shrine—and the painted altar near the farmhouse (with the priest administering communion) face each other across the spectator's space; in this context, the shrine becomes an emblem of their collective religious and national piety, a sanctified national struggle against impersonal forces of cosmopolitanism, republicanism, and imperialism.

The Thun panorama contrasted an older vision of urban collectivity (a collection of classes, groups, *Stände*), framed by physical landscape, with a newer, intimate, domestic vision of familial and neighborhood collectivity. In contrast, the Innsbruck panorama is structured around the opposition between an impersonal, modern "war machine" and a defense force organically rooted in

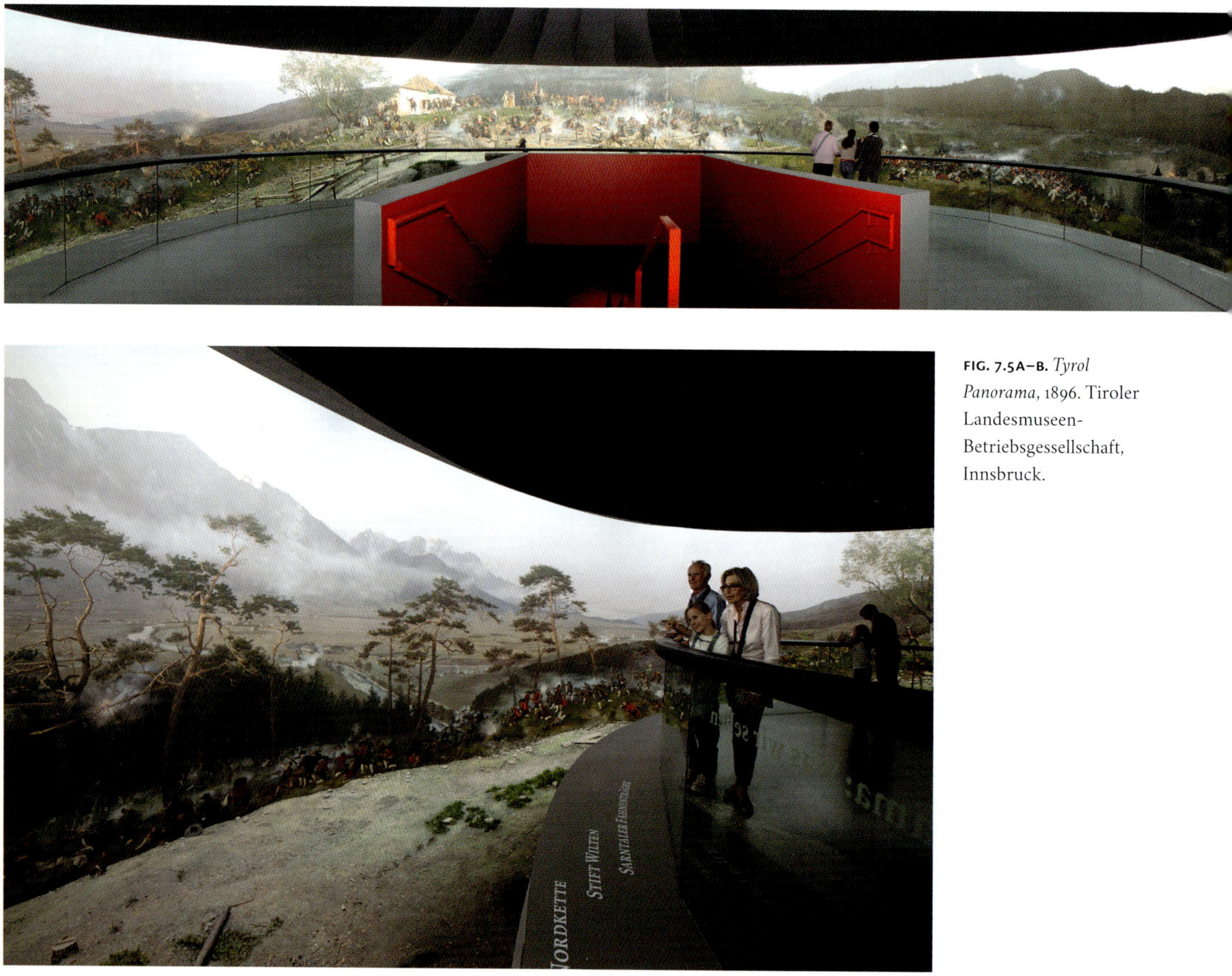

FIG. 7.5A–B. *Tyrol Panorama*, 1896. Tiroler Landesmuseen-Betriebsgessellschaft, Innsbruck.

local terrain—and local things. The space separating the spectator in the middle from the painting's curved surface is filled by a host of real objects: trough, hat, sword, uniform, wheels, guns, barrel, wooden fence, wooden pitchfork, forest terrain (trees, logs, moss, lichen, pine needles, stones, underbrush). These objects evoke a local peasant economy and frame Christianity as the religion of peasants and militiamen: the wooden Virgin Mary shrine is balanced compositionally not only by the valley's formal church buildings below but by vernacular wooden structures, including the broken fence, which initially marked property boundaries and kept out animals and now deters enemies.

Sword, enemy uniform, enemy flag: the few objects of foreign provenance, three-dimensional objects obtruding into the space around the spectator's platform, function as trophies. Abandoned in retreat, they continue to look extraneous. And this contrast between these alien, unassimilable, lethal objects and local, natural landscape underscores the fundamental impossibility of Tyrol under foreign domination: here the landscape itself isolates, rejects, ejects all traces of alien invasion. Here nationalists' ideological grounding rests partly on the realia that surround (or emerge from) the painting. By filling or bridging the space separating viewer and panorama, the realia's dioramic effect situates the viewer in a full, unbroken landscape.

The Lucerne panorama takes the opposite approach in incorporating trompe l'oeil elements as in organizing painterly and physical space. Framing its painted scene are not the comforting supports of a traditional world (branches, shrines, peasant tools) but rifles, telegraph pole, troop train—prophetic signs of an impending, mechanized, depersonalizing modernity.[21] Even the potential sense of harmony, enclosure, protected viewing normally afforded by the painting's rounded shape and the viewer's position on the panorama "bridge" is undercut by this configuration of pictorial space.

Both panoramas still help anchor nineteenth-century tourist districts. Following the 1893 Tyrolean provincial exhibition, the Tyrolean Chamber of Commerce commissioned the Bergisel panorama from Diemer (an academic painter and Munich professor known for previous alpine paintings and panoramic work, including a huge glacier diorama shown at Chicago's Columbian World Exposition). Its 1896 ceremonial opening was held during a major riflemen's festival commemorating "the hundredth anniversary of the Tyrol's being dedicated to the heart of Jesus," a confluence of military display and popular piety strongly evidenced in the panoramic image itself.[22] For years the Innsbruck panorama was situated in a nineteenth-century cyclorama building, a few miles from the events depicted, on a tourist route at the base of the funicular leading to Innsbruck's Alpine Zoo; recently, despite preservationists' protests, the cyclorama was razed and the panorama relocated to the Bergisel itself, placed amid local history exhibits in a regional museum (with a panoramic walking path outside that leads toward mountain vistas).[23]

In the wake of the Franco-Prussian War, both French and German painters produced a new wave of battle panoramas.[24] The French panoramas gathered the public to mourn the collective trauma of French defeat.[25] In Germany, in contrast, Anton von Werner's *The Battle of Sedan* celebrated German victory, depicting the Prussian aggressors as defenders; its 1883 opening, on the battle's anniversary, was a political occasion, attended by the kaiser and key generals, and headlined by newspapers nationwide.[26] The press of both countries reported on spectators so overwhelmed by their respective battle panoramas that they imagined themselves still under fire. (Albert Robida's 1890 French caricature, discussed in the introduction, renders this scenario literal, hence bathetic.)

Lucerne's *Bourbaki Panorama* was commissioned and painted for a French panorama company with Marseilles, Lyon, and Geneva affiliates. In 1881 it became the opening exhibit for Geneva's new panorama building and remained displayed there for eight years (fig. 7.6). The panorama company then considered rotating it with the paintings displayed in their Marseilles or Lyon panoramas but decided its subject would appeal to Swiss more than French viewers. In 1885 Lucerne officials considered erecting a panorama to celebrate the Battle of Sempach's impending five-hundredth anniversary. After financing failed, they instead acquired the Bourbaki painting, erecting a building to house it in the city's visual pleasure district.

It is still displayed within a few blocks of other late nineteenth-century attractions. Across the street, the Alpinorama houses fin-de-siècle alpine dioramas, their painted illusion of depth framed by real objects, from rocks to stuffed mountain goats. A block farther, the Alpineum (a nineteenth-century educational institution established by cartographers and geographers) houses eighteenth-century alpine relief maps, miniature dioramas, a "glacier garden," and a nineteenth-century hall of mirrors. The panorama building's own recent renovation, including a wrap-around addition to the old rotunda built in 2000, foregrounds the panorama as an artifact of pre-cinematic visual culture; the complex now houses a "media, encounter, and cultural center" (*Haus für Medien, Begegnung und Kultur*) encompassing a five-screen cineplex, the médiathèque of Lucerne's public library, a bar-bistro, the municipal art gallery, and an "eco-forum."

In contrast, Lucerne's nineteenth-century visual pleasure district was anchored by the huge thirty-by-twenty-foot relief *Lion of Lucerne* (1821) by the Danish sculptor Bertel Thorvaldsen (1770–1844), carved into the rock wall of a former sandstone quarry then on the city's outskirts. This relief gave its name to the adjacent Löwenplatz, the square where the panorama rotunda was erected in 1889. Thorvaldsen's relief, a lion dying of an arrow shot into his heart, was conceived as a war memorial for the Swiss Guard, Swiss mercenaries killed during the storming of the Tuilleries, while protecting Marie Antoinette; it bears the names of the officers and over six hundred soldiers killed during the skirmish. Still Lucerne's most beloved landmark, the statue is a shrine to Swiss military service, a history of national "neutrality" combined with mercenary activity in other nations' wars, and the monarchist reaction to republicanism (whether revolutionary or Napoleonic).

Next door, in contrast, the *Bourbaki Panorama* weighs the horrors of modern war, thematically and formally, against Swiss neutrality, its subject the Franco-Prussian War's pathetic end. Facing heavy military losses, his retreating army driven toward France's eastern borders, General Bourbaki, commander of France's Eastern Army, attempted suicide to avoid the personal dishonor of surrender. Within a few days, his successor, General Justin Clinchant, tried to save the army by retreating across the

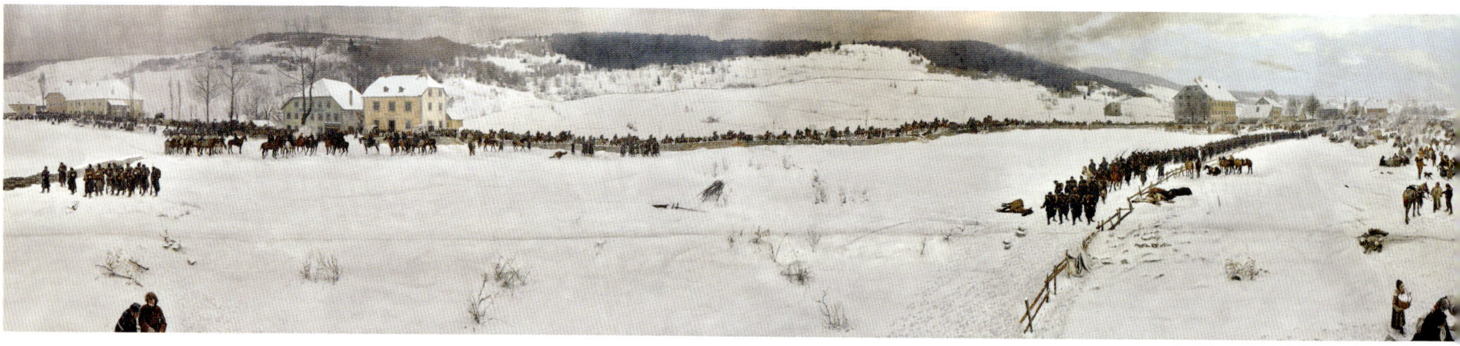

FIG. 7.6. Édouard Castres (Swiss, 1838–1902), *Bourbaki Panorama*, 1881. Oil on canvas, 14 × 112 m (45 × 367 ½ ft.).

Jura Mountains into neutral Switzerland, where international law mandated the soldiers' disarmament, demobilization, and internment until the war ended.

At the war's outset, Castres, then an art student at Paris's École des Beaux-Arts, volunteered as a Red Cross ambulance driver. He thus accompanied—and sketched—the French army's retreat across the mountains, a scene he, like other eyewitnesses, found unforgettably apocalyptic. Some 87,000 exhausted, demoralized, frozen, often wounded French soldiers (and 12,000 horses) crossed the frontier at four crossing points. The vast numbers of French soldiers to be disarmed, succored, secured, fed, and transported posed huge logistical challenges for Swiss authorities. As the war on French soil moved closer to the Swiss border, the Swiss army had partially mobilized—but there were fewer than 20,000 soldiers to guard the entire mountain frontier.

At Les Verrières border crossing, Clinchant met the Swiss high commander, confirming permission for the French army to enter Switzerland to become prisoners of war. Over two days (although depicted in the panorama as simultaneous), 33,500 soldiers then traversed this border crossing, supervised by a few Swiss soldiers. The 64,000 weapons French soldiers surrendered along the frontier had to be dispersed and guarded at various Swiss depots. With great difficulty and delay, the soldiers were transported by train to scattered makeshift internment camps across Switzerland, where they remained for two months, until war officially ended. Individual cantons undertook the huge task of guarding and feeding prisoners; the "Bourbakis" were reportedly deeply grateful for their captors' civil, merciful treatment.

A year later, Castres's painting depicting the Bourbaki retreat, *International Ambulance in the Snow*, won international attention. On its strength, he was hired to design a panoramic rendition of the scene at Les Verrières and, over six months, supervised its execution by a team of Swiss and French painters, including the young Ferdinand Hodler (Swiss, 1853–1918), later a prominent modernist landscapist and would-be dioramist.[27] Painted during the heyday of French Impressionism, the *Bourbaki Panorama* contains individual figures that resemble Paul Cézanne (French, 1839–1906) and Édouard Manet (French, 1832–1883)—and Castres's self-portrait, in a Red Cross armband, among the ambulance men he painted into the panoramic picture. Its crowd scenes are blocked and painted using nineteenth-century realist techniques. The painting's foreground is filled with groups of stricken figures (drawn, production photographs suggest, "from life," that is, posed groups of costumed extras). But the background behind them, across large stretches, is sparse, empty landscape. Both coloristically and in its blocking, the contrast between the patterning of crowds and empty space owes much, in its unbalancing balance, to Japanese screen paintings and French painting influenced by Japanese prints.

The Thun panorama's viewer was situated in the middle of town, could view collectivity, peer into individual households, and, from the comfort of that centered vantage point, look out across the Alps' impersonal beauty. In the Innsbruck panorama, the need to defend country and countryside moved people out onto the hillside, from where they looked back onto the town, their pious battle reflected in the valley's church steeples. In the Lucerne panorama, scattered villagers bring the soldiers food and clothing. Yet its landscape is *not* redemptive but stark, bleak, stony, cold, indifferent to humans and animals struggling, suffering, and dying in its midst. Suffering is not redeemed by patriotism; the landscape is impersonal, the world perhaps godless.

The Innsbruck panorama's inclusion of natural realia helped the viewer feel painted space merging organically into viewing space. Here, presciently, what intrudes into

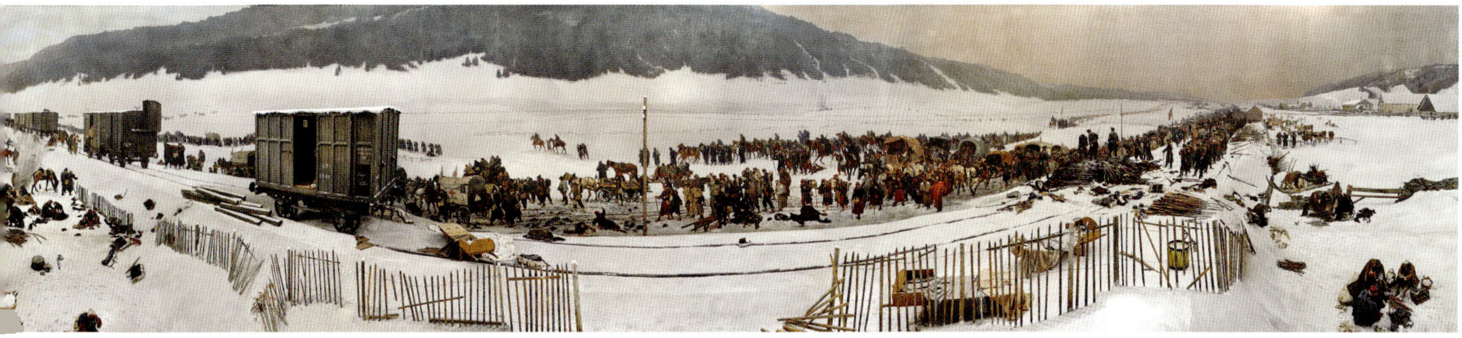

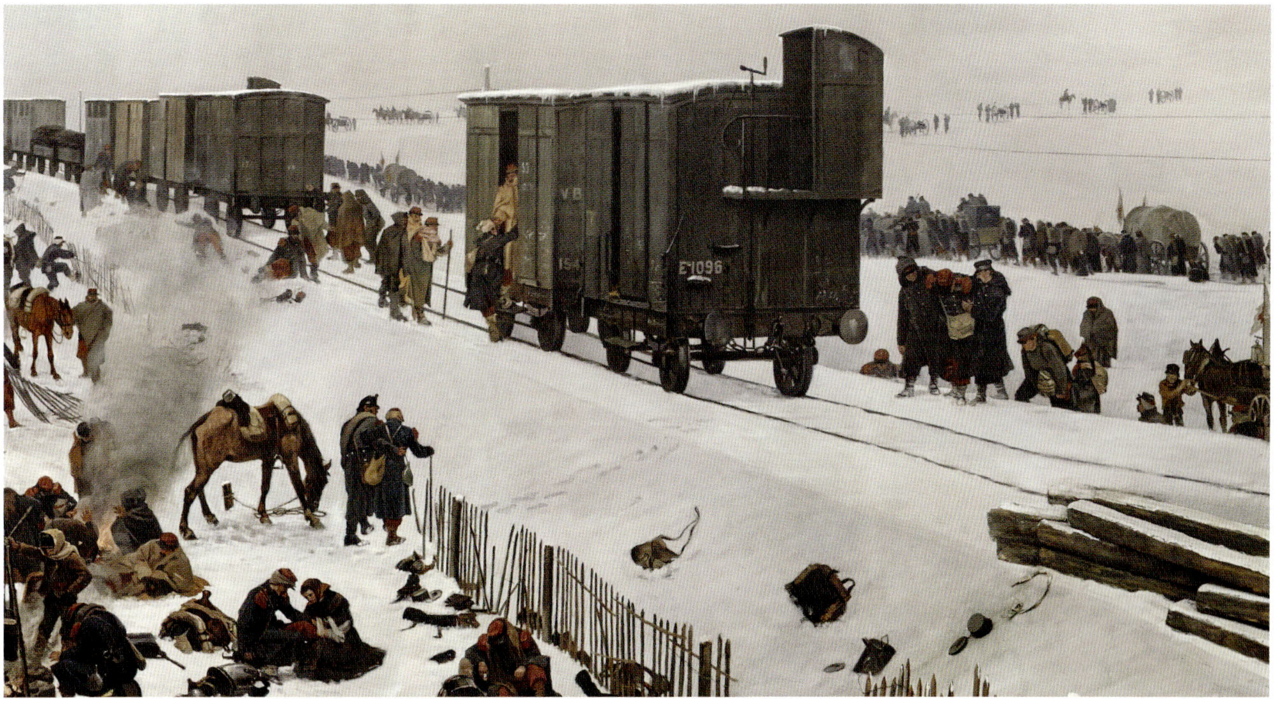

FIG. 7.7. Detail of fig. 7.6.

the spectatorial space are technological objects—telegraph pole, railroad tracks, railroad cars, stacks of guns (fig. 7.7). Railroads played a key role in Switzerland's post-1848 refederation, linking once-distant cantons while eroding citizens' previously exclusive attachment to local sights and terrain. In Gottfried Keller's 1886 novel *Martin Salander*, Switzerland's railroad appears ominous, a harbinger of modernity. In a similar spirit, Émile Zola ends *La bête humaine* (1890) with a runaway troop train heading for the Franco-Prussian front, driverless and on a collision course: the new, technological machine of modern warfare has taken the conscripts, has run out of control, and will not stop running until it has killed them all.[28] The Lucerne panorama, likewise, prophetically sees war's modern mechanization bringing with it new, impersonal, mass death.

World War I, famously, proved unstoppable once mass mobilization began. And once entrenched, tens of thousands of men would die defending small patches of foreign soil, while telegraphs and mobile telephones enabled some generals to remain safely behind the lines, disconnected from the front's horrors. Even at the end of the Franco-Prussian War, General Bourbaki removed himself from defeat's aftermath, attempting to preserve his honor but thereby abandoning his soldiers to struggle without him. In World War II, intensifying technological mediation only increased the gap between those strategizing from a distance and those moved in to kill, or out to be killed. In both world wars, such disconnects led to famous debacles, including Gallipoli and Stalingrad. Generals' and bureaucrats' wish—and increasing ability—to distance themselves physically from the killing operations they planned and directed did not reduce their culpability.

Castres explored the tragic confluence of new forms of technology and the nation-state. In the Innsbruck panorama, patriotic struggle appears fueled by popular Marianist Christianity—and the panorama conceives itself, in the spirit of the mountain shrine, as a shrine to the homeland. Religious imagery plays a different role in the *Bourbaki Panorama*—although here, too, viewers follow a line of crosses around the painting's circle, juxtaposed with machines of communication, transport, and death. A white cross stands beside the French border post. The white cross on a red background appears on flags and emblems decorating the Swiss border post and customs house, on the armbands of the Swiss Border Patrol as they advance to meet oncoming soldiers and supervise their laying-down of weapons. The red cross on a white background appears on the flags and canopy of the Red Cross's horse-drawn ambulances and on workers, like Castres, carrying stretchers, assisting the wounded.

The white cross stands in the distance beside the French border station, flanking one surface, the *tricolore* the other, a now-institutionalized French Revolution mitigated by a return from republican atheism to a religious, Catholic restoration. In the foreground, however, we see the aftermath of a military massacre, as if the Crucifixion is occurring all over again, on a mass scale, full suffering and senselessness made visible—and without Christ's sufferings to explain, redeem, or relativize it. The border patrol, wearing Swiss crosses as emblems of state affiliation, advance toward the limping and dying—but their protection takes the form of imprisonment, mercy tempered by captivity. The Red Cross, in contrast, offers immediate aid to the suffering, carrying them in wagons toward the waiting government trains.

The painting makes much of the way the Red Cross (founded in Switzerland in 1863) reverses the Swiss flag, turning it inside out. Castres's vision of the retreat allows us to see two simultaneous faces of neutrality.[29] We observe a protective yet policing armed force, which refuses to take sides but handles the wounded on the basis of nationality, not needs. Yet we also witness impartial attempts to save lives, regardless of nationality, and a dramatic putting-into-practice of the right of asylum. The panorama was often a form based in, and siding with, national collectivity. Yet this painting dramatizes the emergence of the Red Cross, during the Franco-Prussian War, as a major international institution, deploying a Swiss tradition of neutrality to humanitarian, internationalist ends. Here it is the bearer of mercy and hope in a landscape of hostility and death. Yet even the Red Cross is powerless to halt the composition's relentless motion, from horse carriage to horseless carriage, from ambulatory nursing station to prisoner-of-war camp.

As ideal form, the panorama could represent a frozen present, orchestrated simultaneity. This particular panorama conflates the generals' concordat with mass retreat a day later, forces us to remember the recent past (the moment of defeat and slaughter), and anticipates future cruelties. It also forces us to think about the confluence of macro- and micro-history, visible in the late nineteenth-century convergence of panorama and realist novel. In Tolstoy's 1869 *War and Peace* and Zola's 1892 *Debacle*, war feels overwhelmingly palpable yet horribly senseless. The generals may retain a sense of control, agency; their men cannot. The Lucerne panorama shows us macro-political events made visible, graspable. Tiny figures in the Hôtel Fédérale watch the generals shaking hands, and we, from our opposite vantage point, look out at the same scene. Yet what overwhelms this peaceful encounter, this reconciliation of republic and federation, is the vast, apocalyptic spectacle of an army in retreat.

This questioning of neutrality penetrates deep into this painting's form. Castres's panorama is protomodernist in its work with and against its own shape. Far more than earlier panoramas, the *Bourbaki Panorama* pulls continuously against its own circle. As always, the panorama's viewers stand on a raised platform, looking down and out onto a circular painting surrounding, cradling, or hemming them in. But this painting also works insistently with various horizontal lines: the lines of French soldiers in retreat, trudging along the painting's perimeter, train tracks stretching into the distance, telegraph lines, low fences running along the painting. On one level, these lines pull us away from panoramic centeredness. Without violating illusionistic perspective, its painters manage to pull viewers out of the stop-time of the panoramic moment into the flow, pain, and defeat of history—out of the center's safety and into the trough of suffering.

Yet the painting also describes, again and again, the breaching of its own lines. A dying horse falls on a fence, knocking it down, flattening it with its weight (fig. 7.8). A fallen horse damages another fence. Freezing soldiers dismantle large sections of the wooden picket along the train line, for use as crutches or desperately lit bonfires. A line of cavalry has knocked through a stone fence, presumably to pull through their wheeled cannons. Smaller knots of soldiers circumvent smaller wooden or stone fences, which seem meaningless as markers or barriers, given the crowds trudging along either side and the snow's depth. A whole army passes across an invisible border; their arrival, even in defeat, as future prisoners "brings the war home": they carry the mess of war with them into Switzerland, transforming its fenced, chilly mountainscapes into a theater of war. Neutrality may remain technically possible—the border guards are noncombatants, there not to inflict more death but to protect the border's decorum and, hence, in this instance, to supervise the retreat, register surrendering soldiers, remove prisoners. They are observers and monitors. Yet at least in an ethical sense, they cannot remain uninvolved or unmoved by what they see. Nor can we, panorama viewers on our raised platform at the painting's center. Instead, we find our circle pulled out from under us, caught between the lines, even as the technological realia—weapon pile, train car, telegraph line—obtrude into our space, compromising its separateness and neutrality.[30]

The Lucerne panorama meditates on the advent of modernity, the moral dilemma of neutrality, and spectator complicity. In the process, it critiques the panorama form for simultaneously granting viewers quasi-religious experience and helping them cultivate Olympian detachment. As a self-contained, self-enclosed form of theatrical showing and viewing, the panorama potentially functions as a visual machine whose ideological function partly parallels the new machines of war. In deflating the panorama's circle, piercing the painting's safe center, Castres challenged that alignment, stepping aside from the panorama's apparent ideological centeredness.

Histories of modernism once stressed war's changing nature and renewed trauma as catalysts for twentieth-century art. Yet the Lucerne panorama, this essay argues, registered that shock as early as the late nineteenth century. The broader legacy and paradoxes of panoramic form continue to inform monumentally scaled twentieth-century works—including a late battle panorama and latter-day panoramic photographs and installations.

In 1912, well after the painted panorama's heyday, a new panorama opened in Moscow commemorating the centenary of the Battle of Borodino, that decisive military encounter a hundred miles from Moscow between Napoleon's Grande Armée and the Russian army. Neither

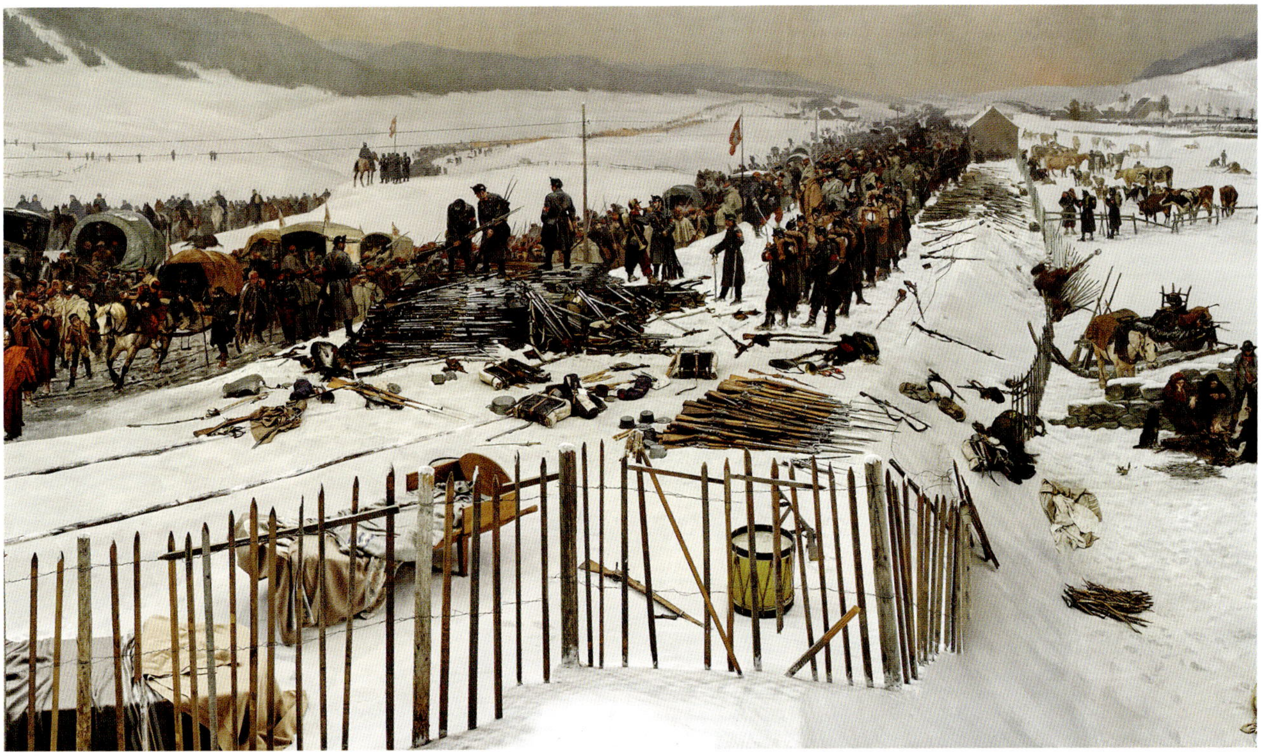

FIG. 7.8. Detail of fig. 7.6.

army routed the other; the Russian army managed to deflect the French attack—but without saving Moscow. Two weeks later, as the Russian High Command evacuated the city and Napoleon's occupying troops arrived, most of Moscow burned to the ground. These events come after the Battle of Borodino, yet this painting by Franz A. Roubaud (Russian, 1856–1928) symbolically anticipates them, in the vast smoke plumes marking Borodino's otherwise almost cloudless sky, in the smoldering farm buildings occupying one panorama quadrant, and in the massive burnt timbers amid the realia surrounding the viewing platform.

To an unusual degree, the Borodino panorama matches its realia to what it portrays. In many places, depictions are elaborately doubled by their (re)incarnation in things: uniform hats, abandoned wheels, horses, weapons, haystacks, earthworks, primitive fences, cannons, even rag rugs (one painted on a hayrick, its embodied twin hung over a nearby fence). Does this reliance on materialized objects suggest that its installers innately distrusted the canvas's eloquence?

Or does it fit the design of this particular painting? Over half the panorama, the streambed running close to the bottom of the image creates a de facto moat between realia and painting. An unusually broad, vast sky occupies fully half the painting's surface. Empty sky above, the horizon blurred a little by battle smoke, cannon fire, and burning farm buildings, below equally vast lands, almost unmarked topographically but at points crowded with large groups of charging soldiers, and then, at the front, Russian dirt and realia: an ordinary place is overtaken by armies and hence history, but it remains anchored by ordinary things, vestiges of rural life, soldiers' gear, cooking utensils.

As always, this panorama is implicitly theological or at least ontological, showing us what life is. The Innsbruck panorama anchored military triumph in a landscape of explicit religiosity. Roubaud's image is evacuated of peasants (and there is only one small church tower, far away). Instead, it offers more abstract meditations on history and groundedness. In one key sector, the French cannons being wheeled along a muddy field have left deep furrows running from the painting's foreground toward the horizon. War literally inscribes the earth, marks field as battlefield. Yet the indentations are also reminiscent of more ordinary furrows left by rural plows. Earlier this season, a nearby hayrick attests, these fields, now trampled to mud, were cultivated. The Grande Armée's passage turns this ordinary hayfield into Freud's mystic writing pad, an apparently erasable surface retaining the imprint of events.

Yet in addition to such passive reactivity, the painting and its terrain seem organized for our understanding as for our gaze. Places are vulnerable: buildings can be burned, streams forded by cannons, but the spectator, nominally landlocked, surrounded on all sides by earth, dirt, burnt wood, is physically elevated above the fray, and slightly above the earth. Viewers' eyeline match is almost with the horizon, remaining (as those painted and embedded deeper in the battle scene are not) in easy contact and alignment with the sky, transparent, luminous, all-seeing—and hence with historical fatedness. The viewer knows the battle and war will come right. Russia will not ultimately fall. The Grande Armée may be within a hundred miles of Moscow, but its soldiers do not get close enough to the viewing platform to discomfit viewers. The Lucerne panorama meditates on the horrors of war, the impossibility of neutrality, the moral price of detachment. Roubaud's panorama instead offers viewers a view from the platform of the sun—and hence composure about events even as they unfold below.

In 1962 Roubaud's painting was reinstalled in a new panorama building in Moscow's newly created Victory Park, in a ceremonial complex designed at the height of the Cold War that commemorates Russia's defeat of Napoleon. The panorama reopened the year of the Cuban Missile Crisis, its celebration of the retroactive inevitability of Russia's endurance more timely than ever.[31] The post-1945 Communist world, with its mandate to bridge the gap between high and popular art, entertainment, and political education, developed its own strong tradition of didactic dioramas and panoramas. Along with refurbishing Roubaud's Borodino panorama, the Soviet Union continued to commission new panoramic paintings, including one of the Battle of Stalingrad, and several panoramas of the 1945 fall of Berlin. (A new panorama on this theme was painted in Russia as late as 1995.)

In East Germany, Werner Tübke (German, 1929–2004) began his *Early Bourgeois Revolution in Germany* in 1976; it opened in 1987 to great fanfare. An enormous epic painting in the round, it is not a true panorama either in perspective or in offering a continuous prospect; in Tübke's distinctive style, it mimics older academic painting yet shades into magical realism, even the psychedelic.[32] Only two years after the panorama's inauguration, the opening of the Berlin Wall profoundly challenged orthodox

Marxist narratives about German history—and in the reunified Germany, they promptly vanished from school curricula. Tübke's *Peasants' War Panorama* (as it is popularly known) nonetheless remains a major regional tourist attraction, attracting close to 100,000 yearly visitors.

In 1994, on the other hand, as the Red Army withdrew all troops from the recently reunified Germany, they took with them a 1970 Soviet diorama of the 1945 Red Army Battle for the Reichstag. Painted in celebration of the Red Army victory over Nazism and intended as a monument to Soviet heroism and antifascism, it was displayed for years in a special rotunda inside an East German Red Army compound. Its placement was presumably intended to motivate Soviet occupation forces in their long mission in East Germany, living and drilling inside their military enclave, patrolling a still-distrustful people. In their post-1989 negotiations with the new German government, conversely, Soviet army officials requested a payment of 800,000 DM to leave the panorama in situ. But Germany's new government felt no stake in the painting and refused to pay. Hence, the painting retreated along with the occupying troops.[33]

Between 2003 and 2007, Susanne Weck (German, b. 1978) and Ulrike Mohr (German, b. 1970) created an installation piece, museum exhibit, and book titled *Lost Panorama: A Project in Stages and Routes*, chronicling their five-year search to locate the subsequent fate of this diorama.[34] Yet the piece also meditates more generally on the panorama in ideological flux. The panoramic, as this volume attempts to show, cannot simply be conflated with the panoptic. Yet in this particular Red Army encampment, triumphalist socialist realist painting displayed in dioramic rotundas enforced nationalist-triumphalist narratives and in the process buttressed different kinds of surveillance states. Its now-empty rotunda points simultaneously to the breakdown of old geopolitical alliances and Stalinist and Cold War rhetoric, and to the internal reorganization of the Second World, as it is reabsorbed into the First.

In 1993, as the introduction to this book describes, the Canadian photographer Jeff Wall spent three weeks at the Lucerne panorama, staging a spectacular semi-panoramic photograph of his own. Photographed on-site, then digitally manipulated, *Restoration* was exhibited in galleries worldwide as a giant slide, illuminated in a giant lightbox (see fig. 0.1). Already well known for posed epic photographs (including elaborately choreographed battle tableaux inspired by the Soviet-Afghan war), Wall reflected on his latter-day attempt to revive key aspects of the panorama. "A panorama," he put it in one interview, "can never really be experienced in representation, in any other medium."

> I made a 180-degree panorama photograph of a 360-degree picture, and so had to show only half of it. . . . The panorama is unrepresentable. Maybe this unrepresentability was one of its great historical flaws. The fact that the panoramas emerged so strikingly, and then died out so quickly suggests that they were an experimental response to a deeply-felt need . . . for a medium that could surround the spectators and plunge them into a spectacular illusion. The panorama turned out to be entirely inadequate to the challenge. The cinema and the amusement park more or less accomplished what the panorama only indicated. The panorama has pretty much always been understood as a proto-cinematic phenomenon, a precursor also of other forms of mass culture. Lately, with "virtual reality" devices, we've come back in a way to a "panoramic aesthetic" which doesn't want to have any boundaries. . . .
>
> *Restoration* has a post-revolutionary, even counter-revolutionary implication. I was interested in the double entendre in the title, the idea that the panorama and the "regime" of representation in which it is involved could be identified with an "Ancien régime," which ironically we are preserving, and even resuscitating, bringing back to life. Why?[35]

On many levels, Wall's *Restoration* pushes forward Castres's demystificatory project: here we move decisively out of the painting's orbit to stand alongside it. We see its dilapidations up close; we watch it being repainted and refurbished. We see, obliquely, its infrastructural skeleton: its templelike dome, its curtains to filter out its windows' light. Its worn realia now blend into the scaffolding supporting the restorers and face the fenced-in viewing platform, which it oddly resembles. The panorama painting's physical and highly theatrical framing become visible, transparent to us as scaffolding. Removed from the "neutral center" where we would usually stand, we instead find ourselves stationed near the casually dressed restorers, who demonstrate an intimate, tactile relationship with this painting. Men in uniforms, women in jeans; an epic painting meant to be seen at a distance, here touched, touched up: *Restoration* offers us a different relationship to history painting, and a different entry point into the panorama than usual.

Yet Wall's demystification depends too much on his sense of Castres's panorama as conservative and antiquated, if still fascinating. As this chapter has argued, the *Bourbaki Panorama* works against itself in protomodernist, not reactionary, ways. Politically, moreover, the panorama's aesthetic seems aligned *not* with a visual ancien régime but with Enlightenment beliefs in the world's knowability and the rational gaze's leveling power, a Romantic faith in the ennobling specificity of place, the French Revolution's belief in ecstatic collectivity. It offers viewers a world transfigured—by the sight of the Crucifixion, by eruptions of nature or war, or simply by sublimities of landscape or cityscape. Emerging at the moment of the French Revolution and a new kind of nation-state, the nineteenth-century panorama is frequently used to evoke the nation as the unique, powerful, even mystical confluence of political, natural, and topographical particulars. Yet all the while, the panoramic form retains a powerful analytical potential; as the *Bourbaki Panorama* demonstrates, the panorama is capable of critiquing the state's emblems and artifices, the arbitrary demarcations dividing one national group from another.

The *Bourbaki Panorama*'s political concerns find renewed resonance in the recent photographs and photo installations of the Swiss photographer Jules Spinatsch (b. 1964), particularly his *Temporary Discomfort* series (2001–3) and overlapping *Surveillance Panorama Projects*. *Temporary Discomfort* documents police protection and security measures undertaken during the 2001 G-8 summit in Genoa, Italy, and successive World Economic Forum gatherings in Davos (2001), New York (2002), and the French border town Évian-les-Bains (2003), on the shores of Lake Geneva (fig. 7.9).

From Genoa onward, global summits have become widely publicized gathering points for a significant range of political protestors. Increasingly, police and security forces have segregated protestors from both politicians and the general public, sometimes assigning protestors to symbolic protest areas miles from the summit.

In 2003 Swiss forces braced for anti-globalization protest spillover into Lausanne and Geneva. Officials worried lest Geneva, given "proximity to the summit," become a cross-border terrorist target. The Swiss coordinating task force declared its interest in establishing "constructive dialogue" with "anti-globalization groups" and allowing peaceful demonstrations. Meanwhile, Swiss "security forces" received "special training on how to avoid violent confrontation, including crowd control measures."[36]

What interests Spinatsch is the ensuing disruption of ordinary civic life and assumptions (local social contract suspended in the putative service of international diplomacy), transforming cityscapes (including his hometown of Davos). Spinatsch's Évian and Geneva pictures document this state of exception: broken show windows, bank and office windows secured with plywood (as if protecting against hurricanes), wrapped monuments. No longer zones of ordinary, collective usage, these municipalities have become musealized, cultural monuments and consumer shrines protectively swathed.

Spinatsch explores the aesthetics of protective shutdown—and the modes of state power they implicitly reveal. Half his cases touch on Swiss political authority, neutrality, and autonomy. For two rather different reasons, Switzerland has repeatedly hosted high-level diplomatic meetings. Its eighteenth-century merchant banks established it as a center of global capitalism; its tradition of political neutrality and long-standing laws protecting bank deposit confidentiality (enacted in 1934, loosened only in 2015) made it a particularly stable tax haven to store individual and international corporate wealth. Swiss banks accumulated a third of the world's "offshore" funds, no doubt including huge illegal gains.

Yet its political neutrality also helped make Switzerland a long-standing center for transnational and internationalist organizations like the Red Cross.[37] During World War I, as resurgent nationalism threatened the Olympic movement, the seat of the International Olympic Committee moved with Pierre de Coubertin from Paris to Lausanne, whose "independent and proud atmosphere" could give the committee its needed freedom.[38] In 1920 Geneva became the seat of the newly founded League of Nations, remaining its "capital" until the League's 1946 dissolution. Later, Geneva remained a center for United Nations agencies, even though Switzerland itself did not join the United Nations until 2002.

Because of its political neutrality during European and global wars (joining neither NATO nor the European Union), Switzerland has been seen, throughout the twentieth and into the twenty-first century, as a symbolically neutral meeting place for world diplomacy, the settling of global economic affairs without recourse to armed struggle. Yet paradoxically, Spinatsch demonstrates, its role as

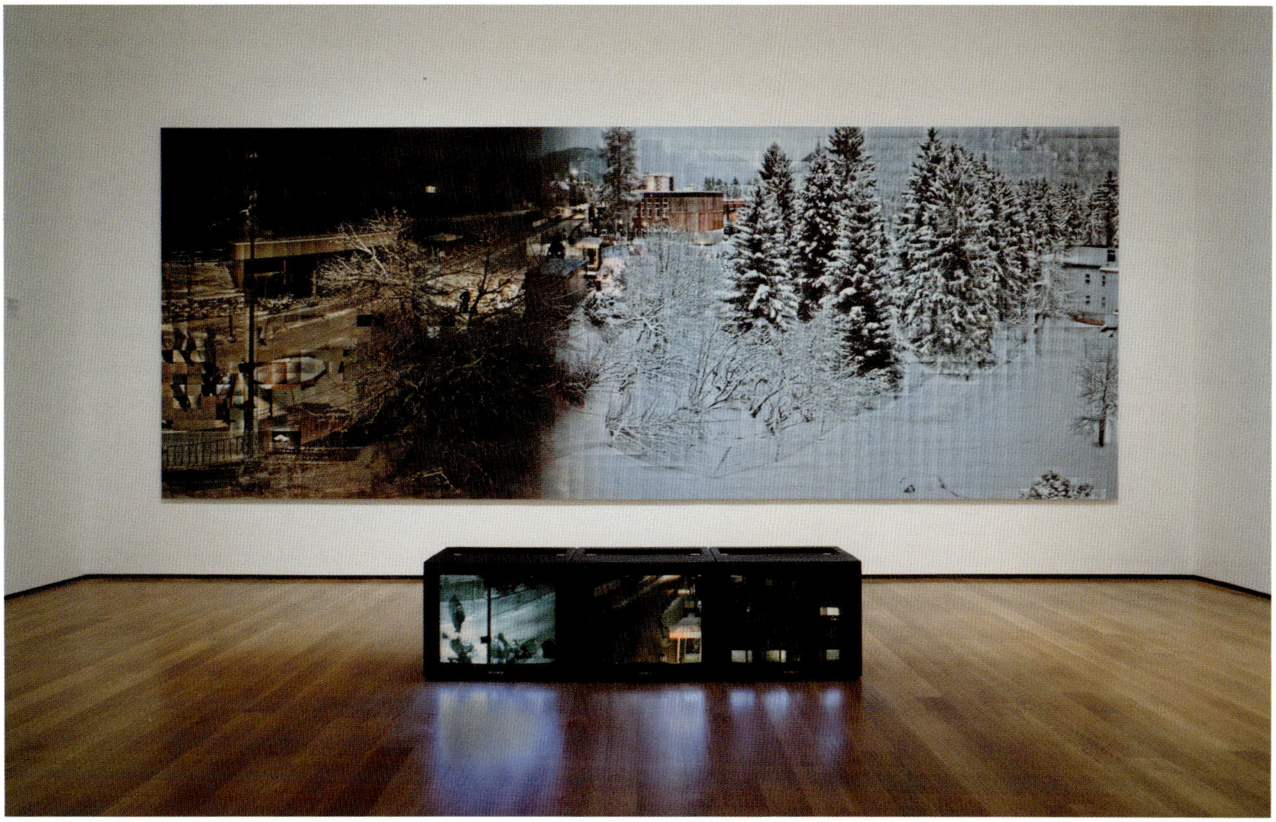

FIG. 7.9. Jules Spinatsch (Swiss, b. 1964), *Panorama: World Economic Forum, Davos*, 2003, from the *Temporary Discomfort* series (2001–3). Camera A, Congress Center North and Middle Entry, 2176 Still Shots, 24.01.03, 06h35-09h30, Hotspots: World Economic Forum, Davos. Hotspot a2/3/5/6.1, parking, Congress Hotel, Carlton, Congress Center. Pigmented inkjet print, 220 × 560 cm (86 5/8 × 220 1/2 in.); and 3 DVDs, each 7 minutes, 28 seconds. Fund for the Twenty-First Century. Museum of Modern Art, New York.

global host increasingly created an adversarial, intolerant attitude toward dissenting locals and visitors—and official anxieties, as during the Franco-Prussian War, that hostilities originating elsewhere might cross Switzerland's borders.

Spinatsch's *TD Pulver Gut, Davos* chronicles police measures to secure Davos's streets and surrounding hills preceding the World Economic Summit, and the continuing urban and natural life within the grid of surveillance cameras. Unlike Spinatsch's other *Temporary Discomfort* case studies, the Davos picture is a composite, assembled from thousands of still shots caught by three surveillance cameras. This particular image makes clear its own composite nature, as night (on the image's left side) somehow morphs into daylight around the picture's middle, even as an unmistakably urban landscape gives way to sylvan tree clusters and powdery snow expanses.

This image alone carries over into Spinatsch's subsequent *Surveillance Panorama Projects* as their first image (and perhaps original inspiration). Subsequent works in the series—huge, elongated, mosaic-like collated surveillance photographs of a football arena, Toulouse City Council meetings, Vienna's Opera Ball, the Frankfurt Stock Exchange trading floor—follow this format. Like the complex, large-scale photographs of Andreas Gursky (German, b. 1955), Thomas Struth, or, indeed, Walter Niedermayr, these works interrogate the surfaces of contemporary social reality and citizens' relationships to their cultural, economic, and political institutions.

Spinatsch's *Surveillance Panorama* photographs also transform imagery produced for practical ends into aesthetic objects, considering their composite, cumulative social ideology, their political effect. The Davos image took shape publicly, in real time. Cameras near Davos's Conference Center were programmed to shoot a thousand frames over the summit's course—and every day, a "live panorama installation" at Zurich's Walcheturm Gallery incorporated two hundred new images into Spinatsch's gigantic panoramic picture, while the public watched the picture's layering.

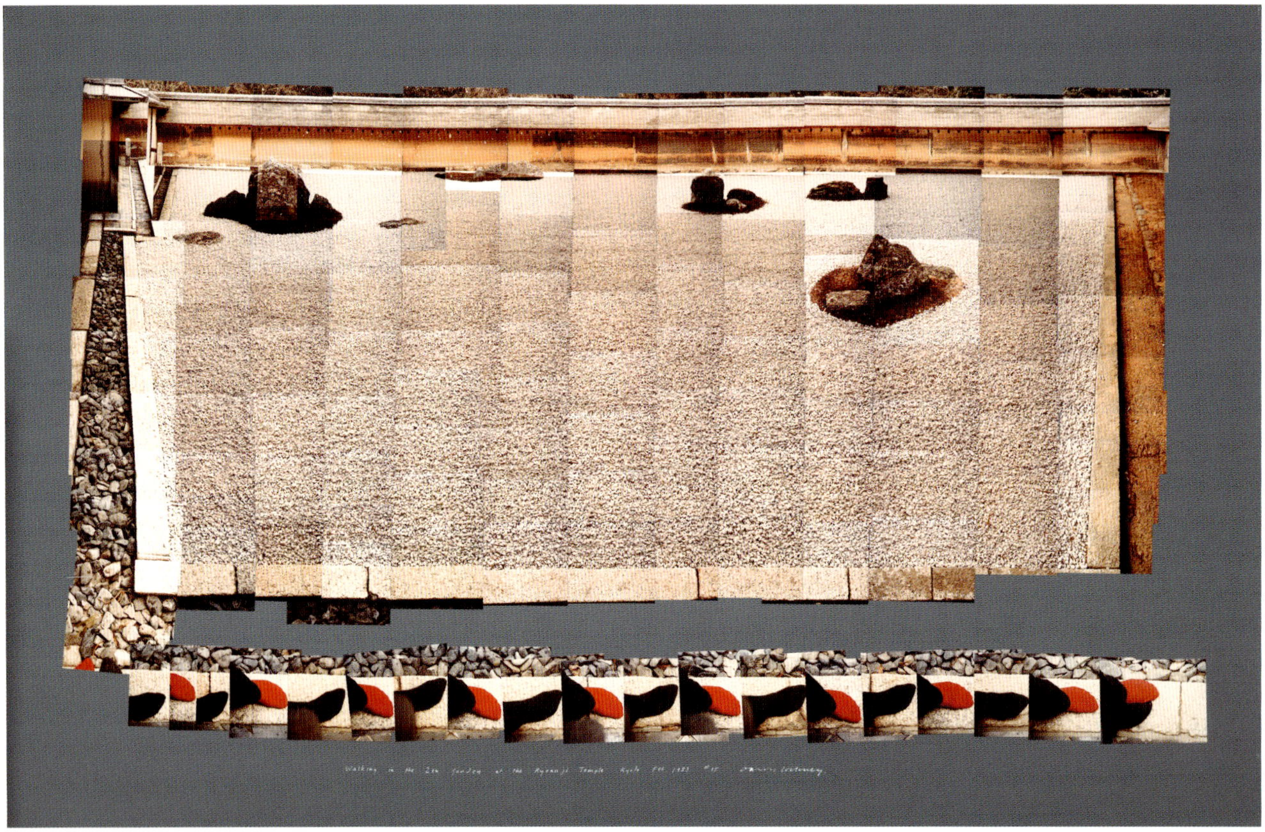

FIG. 7.10. David Hockney (British, b. 1937), *Walking in the Zen Garden at Ryoanji Temple, Kyoto, Feb. 21st, 1983.* Photographic collage (edition of twenty), 101.6 × 158.8 cm (40 × 62 ½ in.).

Surveillance Panorama works have been installed in widely varying ways: mounted flat on the wall, like "ordinary" photographs; mounted in gallery corners, the image spanning both adjacent walls; mounted (in the case of the stadium photograph) as a theater in the round (reminiscent of nineteenth-century panoramic novelty books like Lothar Meggendorfer's *The Circus*); paired with individual video surveillance monitors as a mixed-media installation; and enlarged for installation around a room's walls, like eighteenth-century panoramic wallpaper.

This range suggests Spinatsch's familiarity with panorama composition and exhibition history. Nineteenth-century panoramic photographs often involved (usually invisible) collating or smoothing over a range of angled shots. And in Mussolini's Italy, Jeffrey Schnapp argues, giant panoramic photocollages gained political potency not only from positioning Mussolini the orator in front of a seemingly endless crowd but also from photo editors' and collagers' stretching or contracting famous Italian Renaissance squares to set off Il Duce while collating group photographs into massified group crowds.[39] Spinatsch's work does the opposite: the Vienna Ball panorama assembles hundreds of individually poignant or dramatic vignettes into a vivid collective whole.

Yet Spinatsch's ultimate source is perhaps David Hockney's influential 1980s "cubist" photographic collages, most playful and epistemologically striking in Hockney's composite images of Japanese shrines and Zen rock gardens (fig. 7.10). In Hockney's Japan-based work, the question of composite vision, of viewing's complexity and facetedness, received Buddhist inflection, indexing time's fullness and elasticity. Hockney's 1988 documentary, *A Day on the Grand Canal with the Emperor of China, or, Surface Is Illusion, but So Is Depth* (made with Philip Haas), meditates on China's related scroll tradition, contrasting a 1689 scroll with a 1770 scroll incorporating Western ideas about perspective; more generally, Hockney asks how a social and pictorial composite gathers discrete actors and scenes, the public performance of occupational and social roles.

Spinatsch's work meshes Hockney's preoccupations with the composite questions of temporal fullness, the relationship between movement and calm. Technically, Spinatsch's panorama series involves synthesizing the movements, over time, of thousands of actors, whose

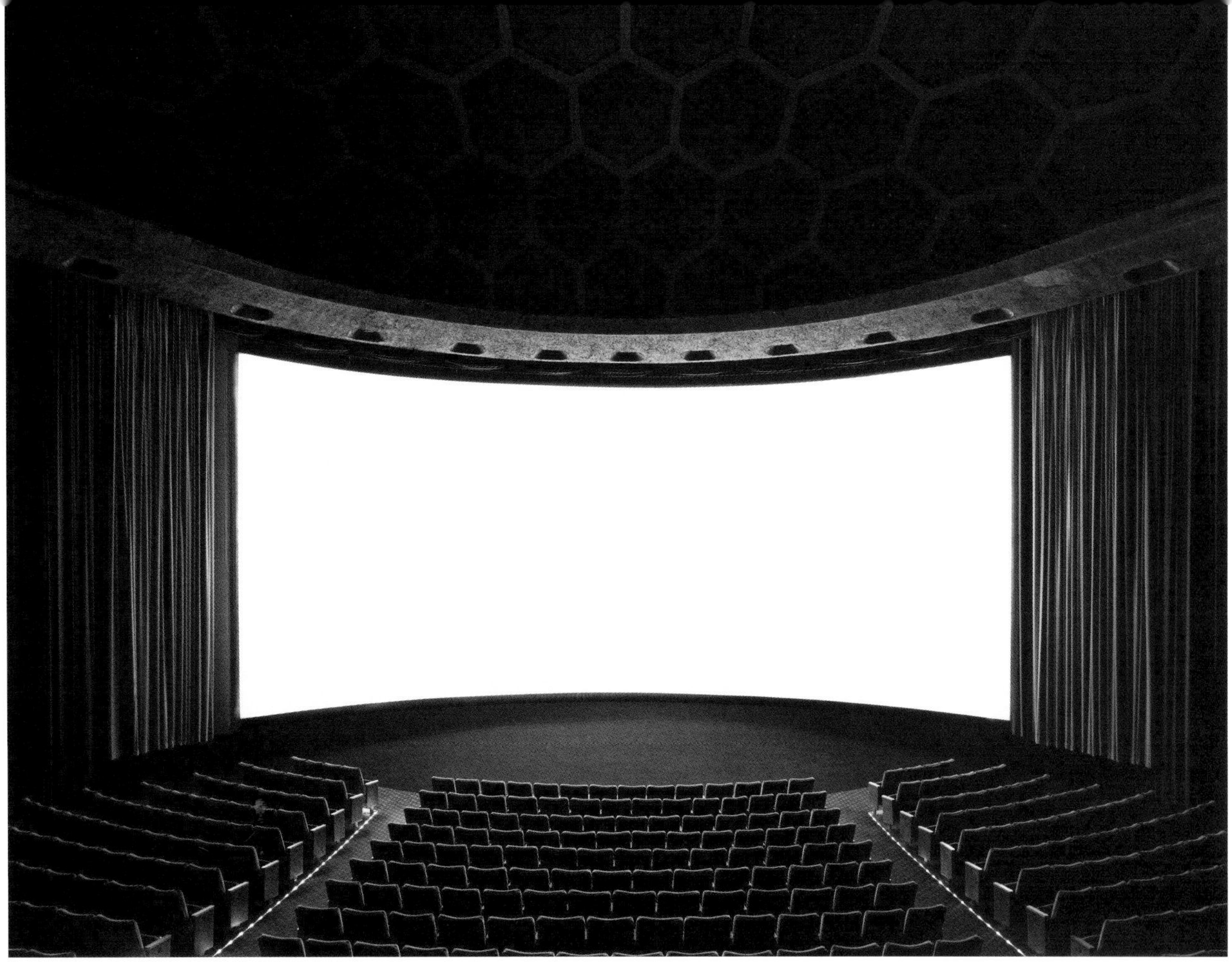

FIG. 7.11. Hiroshi Sugimoto (Japanese, b. 1948), *Cinerama Dome, Hollywood*, 1993. Gelatin silver print, 42.2 × 54 cm (16 5/8 × 21 1/4 in.).

aggregate movements (visible in motion as blurs) might mirror *War and Peace*'s theory of history, as an aggregate of individual decisions and actions. Spinatsch's football stadium picture, *Heisenberg's Offside* (shot over 165 minutes, then collated together from 3,003 still shots into a single large picture) references Werner Heisenberg's uncertainty principle, which established limits to the simultaneous knowability of complementary variables (to the degree momentum can be known, position cannot be known, and vice versa).

The evocative time-lapse photographs of old movie houses made, during the 1980s, by Hiroshi Sugimoto (Japanese, b. 1948) "summarized" a movie's totality, showing in a single layered image all that transpired onscreen, the whole movie, and the absence, presence, then absence of spectators, captured as a single frame (fig. 7.11). Sugimoto introduces a film camera to film an auditorium projecting the previous work of film cameras and editors. Spinatsch's more overtly political work explores the epistemology of surveillance cameras, in place to guard the public sphere against members of the public by recording their movements. In the process, Spinatsch points out, these cameras capture the totality of social action in public. Yet they are also harbingers of a new framing of the public sphere, protecting the powerful while criminalizing those protesting economic and political hierarchies.

During our own politically turbulent yet complacent age (of velvet revolutions and political restorations, renewed nationalist strife, economic globalization, militant anti-globalization protests), visual artists, painters, photographers, and installation artists around the world show renewed interest in the panoramic form, as historical phenomenon and still-live aesthetic possibility. Wall's *Restoration* gives us important new ways of thinking about historical continuities and discontinuities. But other recent panoramic work is equally determined to help us understand the ways individual and collective experience, ways of seeing, are rooted in local specifics of place. As a monumental art form celebrating the emergence of nations, the nineteenth-century panorama is gone, never again to be fully restored. Its legacies, nonetheless, are with us.

NOTES

1. For the Swiss Pavilion at the 1900 Paris Exposition, Giovanni Segantini planned a vast Engadine panorama (with realia including waterfalls, bridges, a stagecoach, and sheep, as well as aromatic air blown through ventilators and cowbells and Alpine horns providing local sounds). Beat Stutzer, *Giovanni Segantini* (Zurich: Scheidegger & Spiess, 2016), 190–94; and Hans Lüthy, "Giovanni Segantini's Panorama for the 1900 Paris World's Fair," *Journal of Decorative and Propaganda Arts* 19 (1993): 34–41. Segantini's proposal included sketches for a massive panorama building (and he installed a 1/10-scale model next to his house). Neither commission materialized. Yet the famous triptych Segantini painted instead, *Life-Nature-Death* (1898–99), echoes panoramic format and vantage point. (Like many previous mountain pictures by Segantini and Giovanni Giacometti, these paintings depict Engadine ranges from immense clearings that form de facto viewing platforms.)
2. The Einsiedeln panorama and its original building were largely destroyed by fire, but they have been reconstructed. Murten's 1893 *Panorama of the [Medieval] Battle of Murten*, painted by Louis Braun (German, 1836–1918), was restored and exhibited during a 2002 Swiss Expo in a "monolith" in Lake Murten built by Jean Nouvel (French, b. 1945); the panorama was subsequently returned to storage. Gaston-François Maillard and Laurence Garey, "Rebirth of the *Panorama of the Battle of Morat*: A Forgotten Memorial to a Crucial Event in European History," *Panorama* 2 (2018): 40–44.
3. Gustav Solar, *Das Panorama und seine Vorentwicklung bis zu Hans Conrad Esher von der Linth* (Zurich: Orell Füssli, 1979); and Tag Gronberg, *Vienna: City of Modernity, 1890–1914* (Bern: Peter Lang, 2007), chap. 5.
4. At the time of Niedermayr's photograph, a Franz Josef statue stood in Europaplatz, ringed by rows of tall flagpoles, flying provincial, national, European, and international flags, implicitly claiming the mountains as a world cultural legacy and for Austria. Europaplatz has been renamed Nationalpark Platz, its statue, benches, and tables removed, and since 2004 recentered on a new anchoring sculpture by Johann Weyringer (Austrian, b. 1949), *Kraft Wellenberg* (a bronze boat on a "sea" of stones, conjuring old mountain legends). A 24/7 live panoramic web feed on the Glossglockner website follows the square and its vista: Grossglockner Hochalpenstrasse, http://grossglockner.panomax.at/. It remains a ceremonial patriotic site: in 2013 the Austrian army commemorated its fiftieth anniversary by pledging six hundred new recruits in a festive ceremony atop the parking garage overlooking the plaza and glacier vista. "Ich gelobe . . . Österreichs höchstgelegene Angelobung auf der Kaiser-Franz-Josefs-Höhe," http://www.meinbezirk.at/neumarkt-am-wallersee/magazin/bundesheerangelobung-auf-der-kaiser-franz-josef-hoehe-am-grossglockner-auf-knapp-2400-meter-hoehe-im-rechten-bildhintergrund-der-grossglockner-ganz-rechts-der-johannisberg-darunter-die-pasterze-m4508199,609958.html.
5. "Panoramarestaurant auf der 'Kaiser Franz-Josefs-Höhe' am Grossglockner," http://www.grossglockner.co.at/index.php?lang=de&mID=2_2.
6. Walter Niedermayr, "Alpine Landscapes," http://walterniedermayr.com/en/alpine-landschaften-eng/1.
7. Solar, *Das Panorama*.
8. Since 1912 Friedrich Schiller's 1804 drama *Wilhelm Tell* has been performed by lay actors every summer in Interlaken's dedicated open-air theater, its setting permitting gripping interaction between the Tellspiel's subject (the Swiss confederation's thirteenth-century consolidation to throw off the Habsburg yoke) and the locale. Horses cross the dirt stage; bonfires illuminate the night air; real rain soaks audiences. In this performance mode, alpine landscape and local climate are more actors than backdrop—appropriately, given the play's attempt to create a national audience. Here the national terrain fought for is literally onstage, before the audience's eyes, under their feet.
9. Altötting, too, was a well-established pilgrimage site; its 1902–3 *Jerusalem Panorama of Christ's Crucifixion* (Gebhard Fugel, German, 1863–1939) likewise catered to religious visitors, as did ten further Crucifixion panoramas inspired by or copied from Bruno Piglhein's pioneering, heavily researched 1886 Crucifixion panorama and executed partly by his former assistants. Annabel Jane Wharton, *Selling Jerusalem: Relics, Replicas, Theme Parks* (Chicago: University of Chicago Press, 2006), chap. 4; and Denise Oleksiszczuk's "*The Cyclorama of Jerusalem on the Day of the Crucifixion*," in this volume.
10. The naval associations are historical; the Napoleonic Wars' decisive sea battles overlapped with the early years of the panorama, providing topical subjects. From 1793 to 1802, half the panoramas exhibited in Britain depicted the British navy, drawing on eighteenth-century marine painting and shore views. Eleanor Hughes, ed., *Spreading Canvas: Eighteenth-Century British Marine Painting* (New Haven: Yale Center for British Art, 2016), 265–67. Fin-de-siècle panoramic attractions attempted ever-greater verisimilitude: like *Battle of Navarino* (1831) by Jean-Charles Langlois (French, 1789–1870), the 1892 panorama *Le Vengeur* by Théophile Poilpot (French, 1848–1915) imitated a ship's deck, yet now the deck moved mechanically; 1900 Paris World's Fair viewers of the *Mareorama* stood on a full-scale steamship deck while a circular moving panorama passed before them. Gabriele Koller, "Panorama und Film: Die Anfänge des Kinos und die Folgen für das Panorama um 1900," in *The World of Panoramas: Ten Years of International Panorama Conferences*, ed. Koller (Amberg, Germany: SPA Stiftung Panorama Altötting, 2003), 76–97; 77.
11. Walter Benjamin's *Arcades Project* (Cambridge: Belknap Press of Harvard University Press, 1999), 532, quotes Émile Labédollière's 1861 description of panoramas of "passage": "spectators, situated on a platform surrounded by a balustrade, as though on the summit of a central building, commanded a view of the entire horizon."
12. Panorama painting and exhibition deployed more localized light effects. Innsbruck's battle panorama heightened dramatic battlefield explosions by affixing reflecting sparkles to the canvas; nineteenth-century dioramas sometimes featured "variations in lighting," compressing a day's shifting light patterns into fifteen or thirty minutes. To Benjamin, such theatrical lighting seemed a "precursor of fast-motion cinematography—a witty, and somewhat malicious, 'dancing' acceleration of time." *Arcades Project*, 881.
13. Oliver Grau, *Virtual Art: From Illusion to Immersion*, trans. Gloria Custance (Cambridge: MIT Press, 2003), 65; see also Maurice Samuels, *The Spectacular Past: Popular History and the Novel in Nineteenth-Century France* (Ithaca: Cornell University Press, 2004), chap. 1. In 1853 the French art critic Paul Mantz again "advocated for the establishment of a panorama museum . . . to educate the French public and transform these public spectacles into enduring monuments to French military history." Katie Hornstein, *Picturing War in France, 1792–1856* (New Haven: Yale University Press, 2017), 107.
14. Quoted in Hornstein, *Picturing War*, 101.
15. Wocher drew on eighteenth-century scientific and cartographic mappings of the Bernese Oberland (including Jacques-Barthélemy du Crest's 1755 *Geometric Prospects* and the geologist Hans Escher's nine hundred topographical alpine prospects, which Escher too used to develop 360-degree panoramic views), as on Basel's contemporary cluster of panoramic watercolorists. Yvonne Boerlin-Brodbeck, "Frühe 'Basler' Panoramen: Marquand Wocher (1760–1830) und

Samuel Birmann (1793–1847)," *Zeitschrift für Schweizer Archeologie und Kunstgeschichte* (hereafter cited as *ZfSAuK*) 45, no. 4 (1985): 307–14. In this *ZfSAuK* issue, Brigitte Meles, "Landschaftspanoramen der ersten Hälfte des 19. Jahrhunderts aus der Umgebung Basels und aus dem Jura," 315–20, and Christine Aieber-Meier, "Blick auf Basel: Die Längspanoramen von Anton Winterlin," 321–24, document nineteenth-century Basel artists' continued production of pencil and watercolor panoramas (partly influenced by Humboldtian "geognostics"), and Johannes Stückelberger's "Charles Girons 'Wiege der Eidengenossenschaft im Bundeshaus in Berlin': Ein Landschaftsbild zwischen Patriotismus, Tourismus und Panorama," 325–30, identifies panoramic echoes in fin-de-siècle alpine landscape and mural painting.

16. P. L. Ganz, *Das Rundbild der Stadt Thun: Das älteste erhaltene Panorama der Welt von Marquand Wocher (1760–1830)* (Basel: Gesellschaft für Schweizerische Kunstgeschichte, 1975), 10. Franz Schmidt (Swiss, 1796–1851) likewise divided his 1827 aquatint *Panorama der Residenz Stadt Carlsruhe* between the star-shaped eighteenth-century fortified city and the flat, wooded riverscape around and behind it.
17. The modern-day *Panorama of Salies de Béarn* (2003) by Roger Hallett (British, 1929–2018) adheres closely to Wocher's model. Ralph Hyde, "Roger Hallett: Panorama Artist," in Koller, *The World of Panoramas*, 102–3.
18. Past and future, pagan and Christian elements, Petra Halkes argues, coexist in the beach panorama Hendrik Willem Mesdag (Dutch, 1831–1915) painted in and of The Hague. Halkes, "The Mesdag Panorama: Sheltering the All-Embracing View," *Art History* 22, no. 1 (1999): 83–98.
19. In his 1856–57 Sevastopol paintings, Jean-Baptiste Henri Durand-Brager (French, 1814–1879) was thus described by a contemporaneous critic as "dividing his mother panorama" to reflect multiple vantage points on the same battle. Hornstein, *Picturing War*, 146.
20. Tacitus, *Germany*, in *Agricola* and *Germany*, trans. A. R. Birley (Oxford: Oxford University Press, 1999), 41.
21. The panorama's mid-twentieth-century exposition involved additional realia (including, most problematically, uniformed dummies representing corpses), removed in the 1970s. One earlier Daguerre alpine diorama likewise included a live goat and a real alpine hut—yet simulating or including live "performers" introduced too much reality into the fictive painted space. Brigit Kämpfen-Klapproth, *Das Bourbaki Panorama von Eduoard Castres* (Lucerne: City of Lucerne, 1980), 16, 50–66. The *Bourbaki Panorama*'s recent restoration nonetheless includes newly commissioned faux terrain, grouping mannequin soldiers and civilians. Heinz Dieter Finck and Michael T. Ganz, *Bourbaki Panorama* (Zurich: Werd Verlag, 2000), 46–53.
22. Franz Caramelle, *Das Innsbrucker Riesenrundgemälde: The 1809 Tyrolean Struggles for Liberation Depicted on 1,000 Sq. Metres of Canvas* (Innsbruck: Athesia-Tyrolia Druck, 1984), 6.
23. Jean-Claude Brunner, "Battle Panoramas Fighting for Revelance in the 21st Century: The *Panorama of the Battle of Murten*, *Tyrol Panorama*, and *The Bourbaki Panorama*, " *Panorama* 2 (2018): 34–40.
24. S. Hausmann, "Die neuste Entwicklung der deutschen Panoramamalerei," *Die Kunst für alle* 5, no. 16 (1890): 257–63.
25. François Robichon, "Emotion et sentiment dans les panoramas militaires après 1870," *ZfSAuK* 42, no. 4 (1985): 281–87; and Frank Becker, "Augen-Blicke der Größe: Das Panorama als nationaler Erlebnisraum nach dem Krieg von 1870/71," in *Das 19. Jahrhundert als Mediengesellschaft*, ed. Jörg Requate (Munich: R. Oldenbourg Verlag, 2009), 178–91.
26. Grau, *Virtual Art*, chap. 3.
27. Jura Brüschweiler, "La participation de Ferdinand Hodler au 'Panorama' de Eduoard Castres et l'avènement du parallélisme hodlèrien," *ZfSAuK* 42, no. 4 (1985): 292–96. Hodler attempted large-format diorama painting in 1916. Finck and Ganz, *Bourbaki Panorama*, 64.
28. See also the Atlanta Cyclorama, painted 1885–86 by F. W. Heine (German-American, 1845–1921) and a team of painters; during the Civil War Battle of Atlanta, one tactical strategy involved tearing up train tracks, disrupting supply lines, and preventing troop mobilization.
29. On the Red Cross presence in Castres's panorama, see Seth Thompson, "Contrasting National Identity through the Lens of the Painted Panorama: The *Bourbaki Panorama* in Lucerne, " *Panorama* 2 (2018): 7–14.
30. This highly self-conscious effect was clearly planned during the painting's execution, for the painters left an empty space on the canvas into which the train car could be inserted, and they half-painted the telegraph pole on the canvas; hence, it lies two-dimensionally flat while emerging three-dimensionally. Ute K. Würthenberger, head of the Bourbaki Panorama's Museum, Conferences and Events, email exchange, July 9, 2014.
31. Konstantin Tsimbaev, "Das Moscauer Panorama der Schlacht von Borodino, Konstruktion von Geschichte und Kriegserinnerung," in *Geschichte im Rundumblick: Panoramabilder im östlichen Europa*, ed. Arnold Baretzsky and Rudolf Jarowski (Vienna Böhlau Verlag, 2014), 128–40. Ju. I. Masepow's pathos-laden Soviet-style "Das Panorama 'Verteidigung Sevastapols 1854–5' und die Stadt Sevastapol," in *Tagungsbericht der Internationalen historisch-wissenschaftlichen Konferenz "Panoramamalerei in der Weltkunstgeschichte" Sevastopol* (Sevastopol: Museum for the Heroic Defense and Liberation of Sevastopol, 2007), 12–18, describes the heroic Soviet defense and "barbaric" Nazi destruction of Sevastopol's panorama building, and the six thousand bullet and flame marks suffered by Roubaud's 1904 siege panorama now triumphantly reconstituted.
32. Harald Behrendt, *Werner Tübkes Panoramabild in Bad Frankenhausen: Zwischen staatlichem Prestigeprojekt und künstlerischem Selbstauftrag* (Kiel: Ludwig, 2006); and Günter Meißner and Gerhard Murza, *Bauernkrieg und Weltgericht: Das Frankenhausener Monumentalbild einer Wendezeit* (Leipzig: Seemann, 1995).
33. P. Kurz (pseud.), "Welcome to the Pleasuredome: Zum Wünsdorfer Panorama-Projekt von Susanne Weck und Ulrike Mohr," in *Panorama: Virtuality and Realities. 11. International Panorama Conference in Altötting, 2003*, ed. Gebhard Streicher (Amberg, Germany: Verlag Koch-Schmidt-Wilhelm, 2005), 98–100.
34. Susanne Weck and Ulrike Mohr, *Lost Panorama: A Project in Stages and Routes* (n.p.: Impressum, 2007).
35. Regina Lange and Renate Buschmann, eds., *Jeff Wall: Restoration* (Basel: Weise Verlag, 1994), 24–26.
36. Anna Nelson, "G-8 Summit in Evian: Lessons from Davos," swissinfo.ch (January 27, 2003), www.swissinfo.ch/eng/archive/G-8_Summit_in_Evian:_Lessons_from_Davos.html?cid=3134756.
37. Caroline Moorhead, *Dunant's Dream: War, Switzerland, and the History of the Red Cross* (New York: HarperCollins, 1999).
38. Cited in "Les origines de la Capitale olympique," lausanne.ch, www.lausanne.ch/thematiques/sport-et-olympisme/lausanne-capitale-olympique/cio/historique-origines-capitale-olympique.html. Although the organization's new location in neutral Switzerland helped it withstand newly fierce nationalist animosities and pressures, the planned 1916 Berlin Games were still canceled. Alan Guttmann, *The Olympics: History of the Modern Games* (Urbana: University of Illinois Press, 2002), 37–38. St. Moritz hosted the 1924 Olympic Winter Games and 1948 Winter Games (the "Games of Renewal," the first post–World War II games after a twelve-year hiatus).
39. Jeffrey T. Schnapp, "The Mass Panorama," *Modernism/Modernity* 9, no. 2 (2002): 243–81.

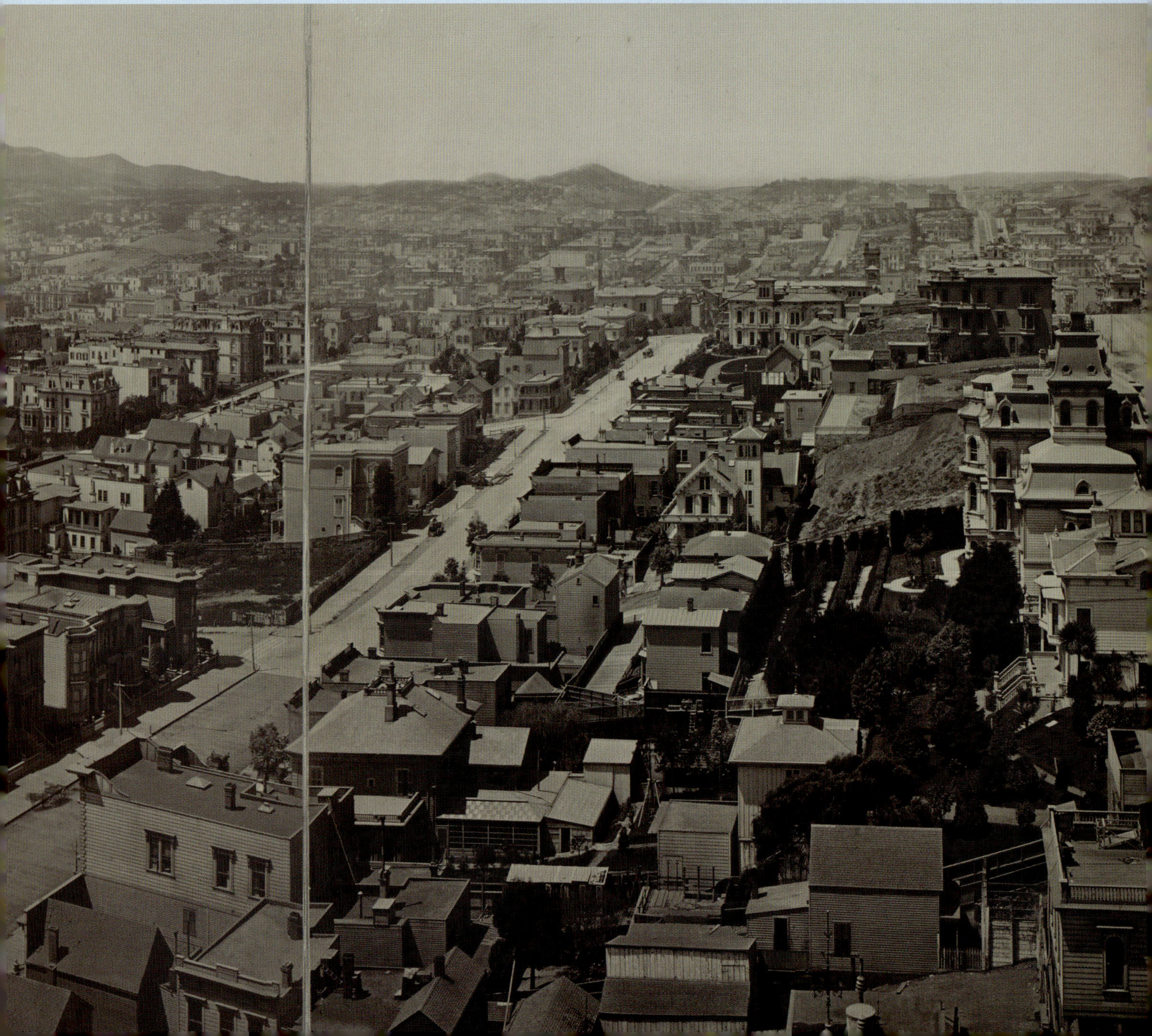

PART II

In (and beyond) the Cinema

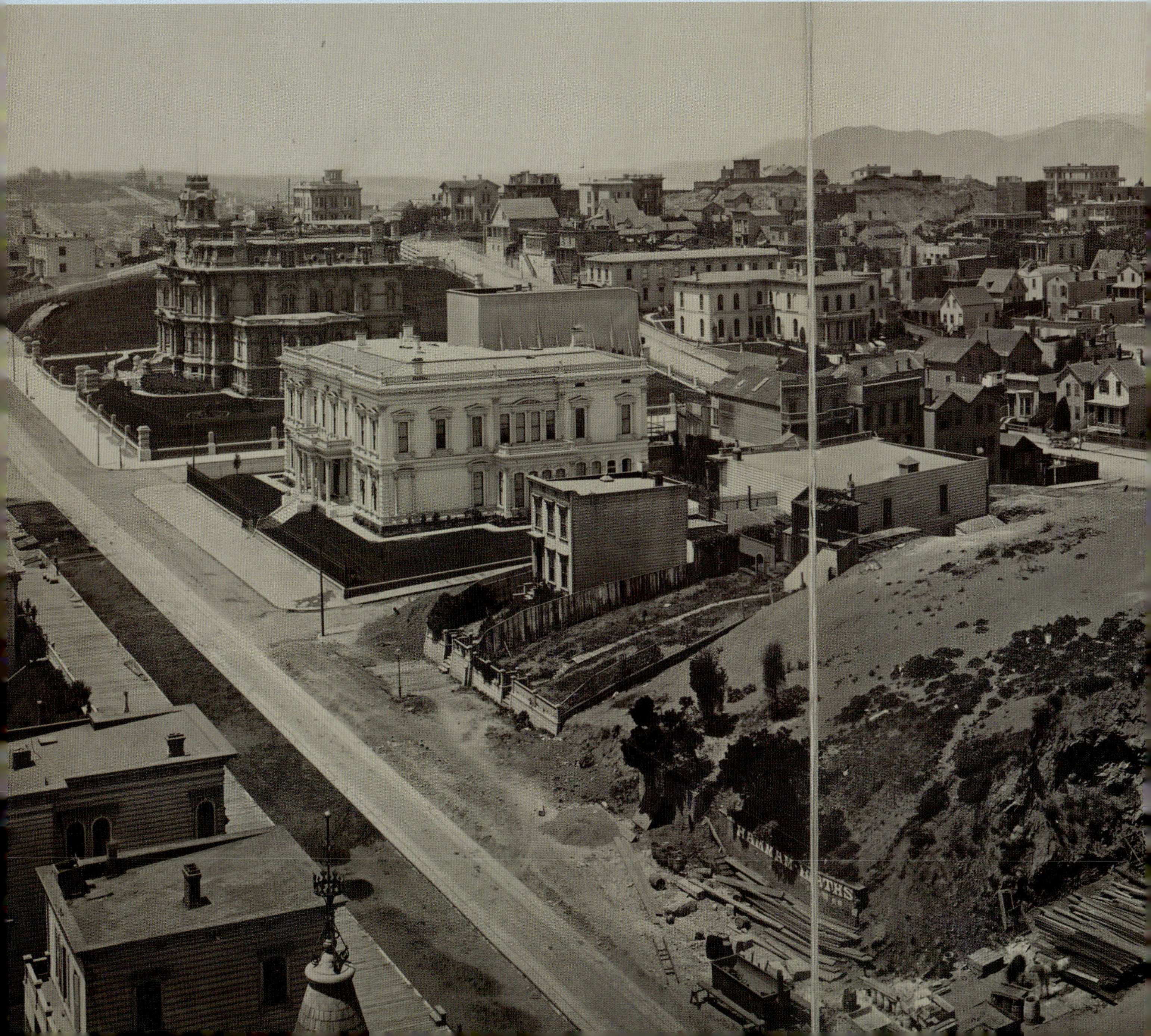

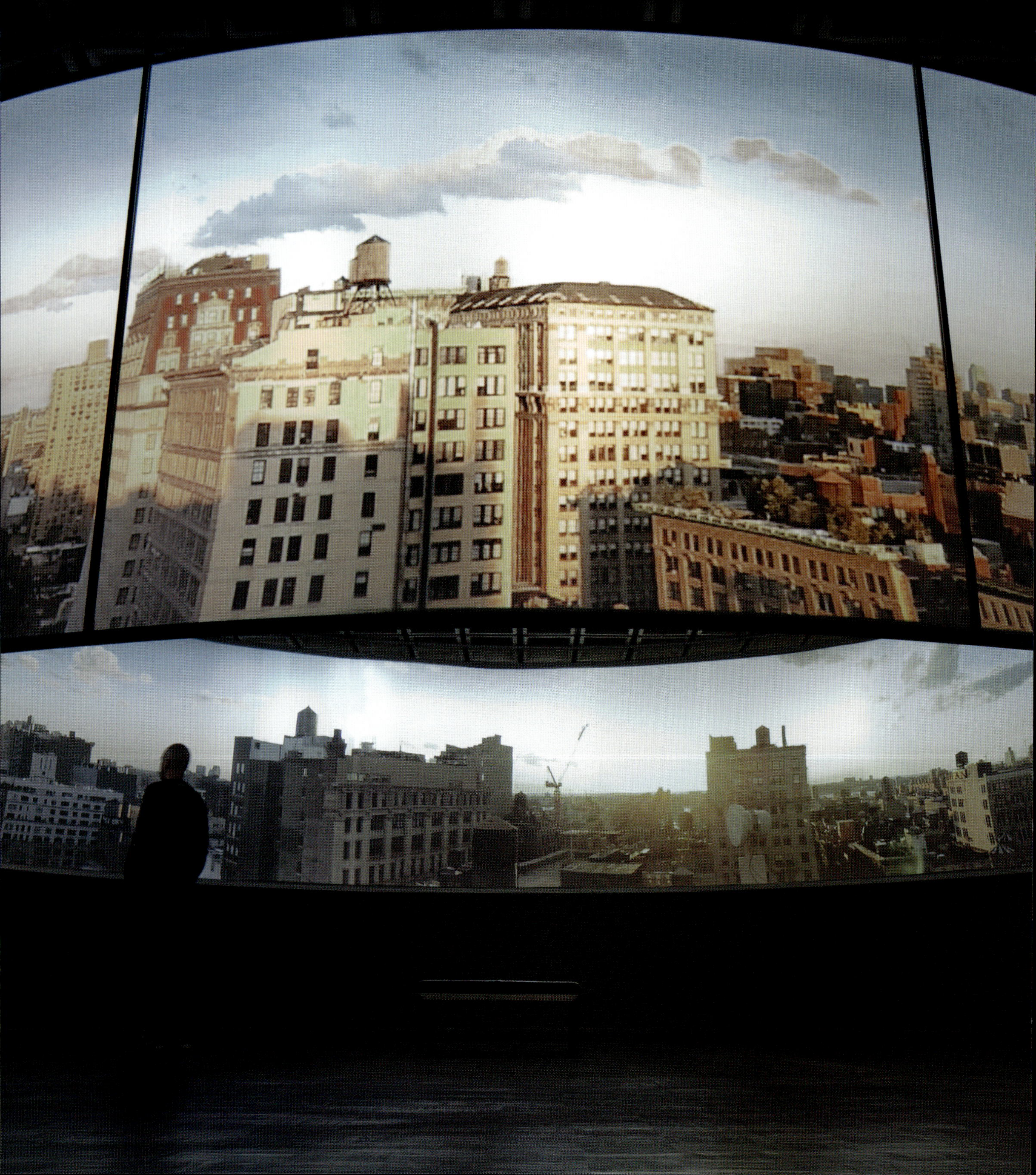

KATIE TRUMPENER

8 Panoramic Journeys, 1900/2000

Documentary Survey in Panoramic Photography, Early Cinema, and Contemporary Installations

All day we sat with our noses glued to the [Pullman car] windows as the incredible panorama unwound itself: plains sprouting wheat; plains sprouting stones; mountains rough and wild.

—Josephine Herbst, "The Magicians and Their Apprentices," recalling her 1896 train ride across the United States

The view through the door of the railroad car or the automobile windshield, in combination with the speed, has altered the habitual look of things.

—Fernand Léger, "Contemporary Achievements in Painting" (1914)

Ben Rose's 1955 photograph *Station Wagon Interior, Utopia Parkway, Queens* (fig. 8.1) looks from a car onto a poetically named suburban street. In 1950s New York, alongside his career in advertising photography, Rose (American, 1916–1980) modified a Cirkut camera and shot a series of experimental, self-reflexive photopanoramas.[1] Rose's *Station Wagon Interior* records a moment of stillness in and for a vehicle of motion. Beyond the windows of the parked car, suburbia's slow, "utopian" rhythms become visible: houses, carports, pedestrians on sidewalks. Yet what Rose foregrounds is the station wagon itself, as a viewing platform.

International Style architecture emphasized glass-centered construction, illuminating interior spaces and producing spectacular vistas. Railway dome observation cars, then tourist buses had featured plate-glass windows, ceilings, even turrets to increase scenic immersion (fig. 8.2).[2] In car design, likewise, windowed wraparounds increased road safety—and enabled panoramic seeing. By the 1950s many cars offered comprehensive, almost 180-degree front-seat views (widened further by side- and rear-view mirrors). Windshields offered an everyday panoramic sublime—and car radios enabled a quasi-operatic, quasi-cinematic landscape experience.[3]

Rail transport had pioneered such panoramic travel.[4] In "new and novel fashion," Dolf Sternberger argues, nineteenth-century engines "opened the world, the lands and the seas."[5] Wolfgang Schivelbusch postulates a new sense of landscape organized by and for transit, seen "*through* the apparatus that moves [the traveler] through the world."[6]

A few key intellectuals (Ruskin, Flaubert), Schivelbusch notes, remained unwilling or perceptually unable to assemble the view from the racing train. Yet for many artists, vehicular vision crystallized new aesthetic sensibilities. Some painters began specializing in "panoramic views of the principal rail-lines."[7] Modernists were inspired by the railway, then the motorcar. A 1892 view through the door of a rolling train inspired Edgar Degas (French, 1834–1917) to resume monotype experiments, to capture the "vague" blur of moving through landscape or a crowd.[8]

facing: Fig. 8.11 detail; previous spread: Fig. 10.1 detail

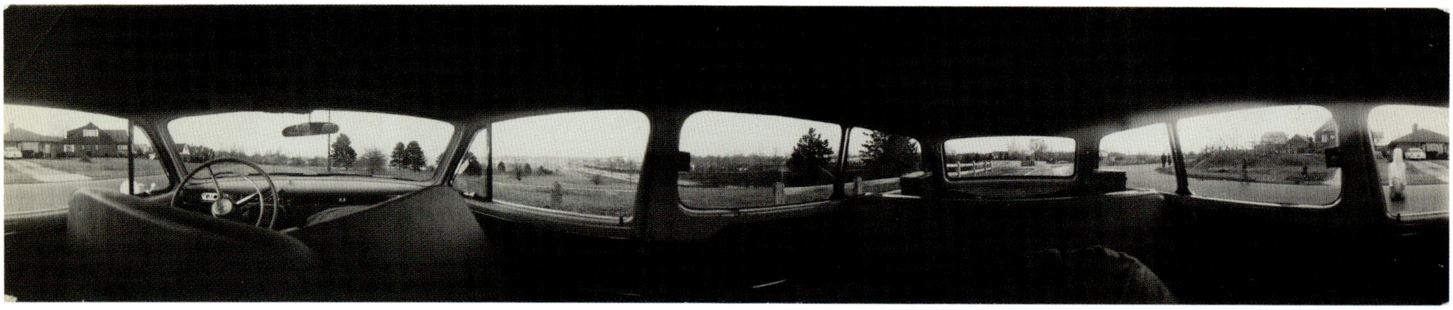

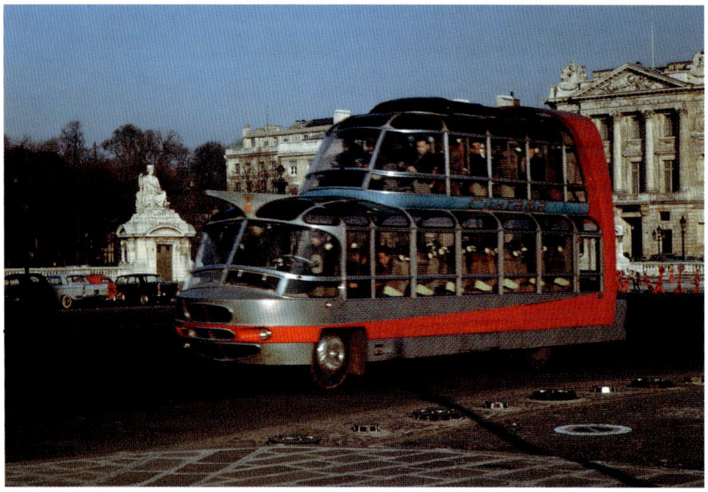

FIG. 8.1. Ben Rose (American, 1916–1980), *Station Wagon Interior, Utopia Parkway, Queens*, 1955. Gelatin silver print, 25.1 × 124.2 cm (9 ⁷⁄₈ × 48 ⁷⁄₈ in.). Museum of Modern Art, New York. Acquired through the generosity of Richard O. Rieger (194.2008).

FIG. 8.2. Citroën U55 Cityrama Currus.

Pierre Bonnard (French, 1867–1947) accompanied Octave Mirabeau on a 1905 trans-European motoring trip, producing sketches from—and of—the driver's seat, eventually published alongside Mirabeau's travel journal.[9]

Henri Matisse's *The Windshield, on the Road to Villacoublay* (1917, Cleveland Museum of Art) depicted the car's front seat as ideal for drawing a rapidly unfolding landscape. Although Matisse conceived the picture while being driven to the airport, this smaller elevation fascinated him. His painting depicts the car as driverless; an early version of his own canvas rests on the steering wheel, occupying the driver's seat. The car's interior presents both a proscenium theater and a new kind of hinged triptych (formed by the car's two-part front windshield and its flanking side windows).[10]

From its inception, cinema was obsessed with moving vehicle views. The train, in Jacques Aumont's memorable formulation, became the place where seated, immobile spectators learned to give themselves over to the framed, mobile view streaming past their windows, "to bear a mobile and organized gaze upon the world"; in recompense, "the cinema gratefully makes the locomotive its first star."[11] Underpinning this cinematic gaze was the ideal of panoramic access. The technical term *panning* (designating a sweeping, horizontal shot) preserves memories of panoramas and moving panoramas as nineteenth-century institutions, even as its gerund form announces new agency and mobility.[12]

Between 1900 and 1910, hundreds of early film titles declared themselves "panoramas." Panoramas were the most "populous film entry by title in the US copyright records," yet thereafter disappeared "almost without a trace" with the development of narrative cinema.[13] In this early film genre, as was true of nineteenth-century photography, moving panoramas, and painted river panoramas, the term designated not only circular, 360-degree movement but any encompassing, sustained unidirectional vertical or horizontal sweep.[14] One filmic subgenre surveyed urban landscapes taken by a stationary camera tilting up and down, or back and forth, clockwise or counterclockwise. Another, the so-called phantom ride (tracking shots from moving vehicles, as if the viewer were a "ghost rider"), records linear stretches of transit routes: train, ferry, tram, horsecar, or cable car.[15] A century later, global auteurs including Hou Hsiao-Hsien (Taiwanese, b. 1947), Abbas Kiarostami (Iranian, 1940–2016), Patrick Keiller (British, b. 1950), and Jim Jarmusch (American, b. 1953) are actively reviving this genre.[16]

This chapter traces the gradual mobilization of the panoramic image, beginning with nineteenth-century panoramic photographers (whose peripatetic image-making journeys radically opened up the seeable world), then with early cinema shot from motorized vehicles. In both media, panoramas reflected the technological transformation of urban, rural, and colonial landscapes, documenting uneven development while arguing implicitly for a technocratic world order. Early cinema's visual mobility and panoramic ambitions simultaneously shaped film aesthetics, producing recurring preoccupation with the distended, information-saturated cinemascopic image. Early documentaries largely eschewed narrative and dialogue, instead foregrounding the experience of moving, the process of looking. The chapter ends with recent, cinematic-based art and web installations that enable spectators to move, virtually or within the gallery space. Today's installations—and web-enabled virtual reality—once again invite viewers to perambulate around fixed yet moving imagery. But even this experience has historical precedents, including the short-lived Photorama developed by Auguste (French, 1862–1954) and Louis (French, 1864–48) Lumière. Patented in 1900 as a "system for stereoscopic cinema," it surrounded viewers on a circular platform with hugely magnified 360-degree panoramic photographs, continuously projected as twenty-foot-tall still images, while viewers pivoted to survey the view's breadth. Modern-day installation artists often explicitly evoke the panorama as institution and revisit early cinema's exploratory journeys. Pushing open the cinematic box, they restore the head-turning, ambulatory freedom, agency, and partial, indeterminate, relatively undirected views enabled by nineteenth-century viewing platforms.

PHOTOPANORAMAS: FRONT AND FRONTIER

The photograph and the panorama are intimately linked. Photography emerged half a century after the development of 360-degree painting, born into an aesthetic climate saturated with panoramic representations. At the 1839 press conference called to publicize the invention of the daguerrotype, Louis Daguerre (already the inventor of the panoramically inspired diorama) displayed photographic samples, including his "panorama" of the Île de la Cité.[17] Daguerre's new method, one Augsburg newspaper averred, was "incomparable" for "buildings, works of art, mountains, panoramas." The *New-York Observer* likewise rhapsodized about photography's potential to produce "perfect and satisfactory panoramas of all the places and scenery on the globe," eagerly anticipating future "panoramas of Jerusalem, Thebes, Constantinople, Rome and other cities of the old world, delineated with the unerring fidelity of the Daguerrotipe [*sic*]."[18]

In 1839 Daguerre's first high-angle "panorama" photographs only hinted at true panoramic formats. Yet already by 1844–45 German and Austrian photographers began patenting cranked panoramic cameras, able to take in extended views of 150 degrees and more. (Later panoramic cameras would boast names like the Pantoscopic [1862] and the Wonder Panoramic [1890].) Not until the late nineteenth century did technology enable photographic prints or projections to grow to a scale rivaling large panorama paintings. Yet from the outset, photographers and their audiences were fascinated by lateral extension of the photographic field.

Following the 1851 invention of the wet-plate collodion process, albumen prints from different negatives and plates were frequently joined, glued, and folded together to produce a single, unbroken, "stitched" or "segmented" panoramic image (known as a "panoramic joiner"). Sometimes, as in Muybridge's *Panorama of San Francisco Taken from the House of Mrs. Mark Hopkins* (1878; see fig. 10.1), shadows shifted visibly between plates and don't quite match up.[19] Some twentieth-century photographers raised such lags to a structural principle. In his photocollage leporello book, *Every Building on the Sunset Strip* (U.S., 1968), Ed Ruscha (American, b. 1937) panoramically surveyed Los Angeles' streetscape from a moving truck bed, recording a vast range of storefronts and cars moving, maneuvering, and parking. Time becomes visible in occasional severing or odd mismatches between panels—and pedestrians' flickering movements.

Many nineteenth-century dioramas used light effects to evoke the passage of diurnal time across the surface of a painted canvas. Long-exposure panoramic photographs, conversely, were on one level able to bake a moment into fixed form. Yet as David Harris underscores, photographers surveying the complex geography of hilly cities like San Francisco sometimes resorted to discontinuous views in the service of a bigger panoramic picture.[20] And Rebecca Solnit reads Muybridge's photopanorama as more like "a movie, edited together out of many discontinuous pieces of time into a plausible but fictitious continuity."[21] Some turn-of-the-century panoramic films, likewise, used dissolves or time lapses to bridge otherwise continuous time and space.[22] By the Constructivist era, S. Svidel's 1935 *Soviet Photo* article, "Volume and Line: Notes on Panoramic Shooting," envisioned photojournalistic panoramas not only rendering a sequence but sometimes showing a scene from multiple simultaneous perspectives.[23]

Like the painted panorama, early photographic and filmic panoramas' reality effects could be understood, on closer inspection, as visibly fictitious, or at least constructed. They nonetheless retained and enhanced the painted panorama's aura of documentary accuracy. Some photographers had previously painted canvas or moving panoramas, carrying "into their new work a keen sense of how to structure sequentially organized narratives."[24]

In the late nineteenth century, conversely, panorama painters began using topographical and panoramic photographs as an invaluable aid to re-creating distant or historical landscapes for their own battle or Crucifixion panoramas. As Max Bernstein apostrophizes the camera accompanying Bruno Piglhein's panoramic research expedition to Palestine: "The photo apparatus, indispensable, the accompanier who notes everything, registering while traveling."[25] Though some artists apparently traced the contours of their own panorama paintings from photographic enlargements, most used photographs as a form of notation, to supplement the sketches that had traditionally extended and preserved artists' visual memory of a scene. In 1855 Jean-Charles Langlois traveled with an assistant to the Crimea, producing photographs later used to compose Langlois's painted *Battle of Sebastopol* panorama.[26] In 1882 Anton von Werner and his team of panorama painters prepared for von Werner's *Battle of Sedan* panorama by photographing, as well as sketching, the 1870 battlefield.[27] During the same year, Paul Philippoteaux, commissioned to paint a Battle of Gettysburg panorama, traveled for several weeks to Pennsylvania to sketch the 1863 battlefield and to supervise a local photographer, whose panoramic site photographs Philippoteaux carried back to France to paint from.[28]

During the Civil War itself, Union generals and engineers had prized the photopanoramic overviews George Barnard (American, 1819–1902) took of fortifications and terrain.[29] As Tim Barringer notes in chapter 1, the drawn and painted panorama was shaped initially by the skills of official military draftsmen and the sponsorship of military strategists before becoming a form of civilian entertainment.[30] Panoramic photography, conversely, developed an existence independent of painted panoramas. Yet throughout the nineteenth century, such photographs were often produced in military and other strategic contexts, as in ordnance surveys; most of these remained unpublished.[31]

The pioneering, globe-trotting British war correspondents Roger Fenton (British, 1819–1869) and Felice Beato (Italian-British, 1832–1909) developed photographic equivalents of the painted battle panorama.[32] Fenton's *Photographic Panorama of the Plateau of Sebastapol* shows encamped armies after a critical Crimean War battle. Beato's photopanoramas, shot after the 1857–58 Indian Uprising, then amid the Crimean and Second Opium Wars, recorded recent ruins, newly abandoned fortifications, army encampments, and cities after occupation. Often the lateral extension of the pictorial field allowed such photography to survey large areas of terrain and to encapsulate the breadth of a battlefield, the sweep of a valley or a desert.

Yet where the painted panorama had attempted to transport viewers into the heat of battle, photopanoramists could depict only war preparations, long-term consequences, or tactical or geographical factors shaping battle outcomes. Photographers traveled with heavy glass negatives (as heavy as four pounds each), chemicals, and dark tents to process the negatives on-site, following each exposure. This cumbersome equipment and development process made it impossible to photograph actual battles in progress.

Mid-nineteenth-century British army officers nonetheless began assembling or shooting panoramic photographs while stationed or campaigning in locations across the British Empire. Viewing from above or afar, their colonial photopanoramas implicitly fostered spectator fantasies of ownership, control, and domination. The panoramic photograph was particularly apt for military or documentary survey since it memorialized the act of surveillance. Photographers—and the camera eyes—turned "quite round" (in Barker's words), 360 degrees from a single point. Such photographs made available a level of detail that fed nineteenth-century data collection programs (ordnance surveys, imperial archives) or informed mercantilist speculation.[33]

In 1860 Felice Beato accompanied British expeditionary forces to Hong Kong and China. His panoramic photographs, Wu Hung argues, are "not innocent records of specific places" but remain "intimately connected with colonial warfare," for "they glorify the point of view of the invading army" and "display the military might of the European forces."[34] In 1867–68 the first team of British military photographers assisted and documented a large-scale military operation, the Royal Engineers' Abyssinian campaign. In the field, their primary function was actually to photograph, print, and disseminate documents (photographic reproduction anticipating the photocopier). Documenting their own expedition was secondary. Yet the resulting photographs, assembled into a commemorative photograph album, were distributed to British government and scientific institutions. During their successful quest to free British hostages, the Royal Engineers had also razed a major city and precipitated the suicide of Abyssinia's king. These events attracted intense British media coverage—yet that coverage successfully sidestepped potential guilt over attacking an ancient Christian nation. Crucially, James Ryan underscores, the Royal Engineers' photograph album depicts no battles and virtually no Abyssinians. Several photopanoramas instead show rugged landscapes dwarfing tiny groups of British soldiers, representing "the art of campaigning as one of subduing the natural world."[35]

Other photopanoramas implicitly advanced colonial agendas. During the late nineteenth century, British panoramic photographers documented military installations, tactically important terrain, and the encroachment of British-built railway bridges and other colonial infrastructure.[36] Other photographs evoked familiar picturesque tropes as they documented crumbling religious monuments or inscriptions. Alternately elegiac and celebratory, tactical (literally occasioned by strategic purposes) and impassive, these photopanoramas often evoke a stillness that belies their own sense of historical momentum and transformation, the ceaseless journeying that enabled their creation and global consumption. Beato's apparently tranquil *Panorama of Lucknow* (1858; see discussion by Maria Antonella Pelizzari in this volume, pp. 52–53) was thus informed by (and viewed with) the knowledge of the role in siege and defense that Lucknow's shattered monumental buildings had played during the Indian "Mutiny."[37]

In 1855 the British army officer Linnaeus Tripe (1822–1902) served as the official photographer for a British mission intended to persuade the king of Burma to accept Britain's annexation of Lower Burma; Tripe's photopanoramas gave British audiences their first broad prospects of Burma, seen on British terms: his sweeping Rangoon photopanorama shows indigenous institutions coexisting with colonial ones, new British military barracks alongside a pagoda.[38] From 1856 to 1859, Tripe served as official photographer for the Madras government. His work there—including his twenty-one-plate, twenty-foot-long photopanorama, *Inscriptions on Tanjore's Great Pagoda* (1857)—documented South Indian historical structures, then subject to British archaeological investigation and preservation.[39]

Like other British photographers in Southern and Southeast Asia, Tripe conveyed both the beauty and putative decay of traditional culture; British civic works represented the future. Yet such photographs remained correspondingly limited in their ability to capture lived reality on the ground, the attitudes and responses of local peoples; unable to depict what went on beneath native roofs, or inside native minds, they sometimes eschewed representing native peoples altogether. Many are shot from great distances, or at dawn, when otherwise teeming cityscapes appeared deserted, abstracting cultural landscapes into lifeless, if harmonious, architectural ensembles.

In colonial India, Christopher Pinney has argued, archaeological photography often showed empathy for and fascination with ancient monuments, in pictures intended to speed their preservation or commemorate their restoration. Yet formally and ontologically, panoramic photography reiterates and encapsulates the process of Westernization and modernization—given the "Cartesian perspectivalism" inherent in these images. Hence, even the most beautiful and most reverent British images of Buddhist temple complexes, Pinney argues, transform the temples' particular forms of situatedness, their way of orienting themselves (and especially their anchoring statues of cross-legged, meditating Buddhas) in relationship to the worshiper's likewise frontally oriented body (whether moving or still). What panoramic photographs do instead is locate each depicted site within a larger framework of terrain and landscape. Their mode is neither intentionally irreverent nor denigrating. Yet in holding the image of a sacred place across a vast, precisely and broadly focused (Cartesian) plane, the panoramic camera creates a representation of Buddhist spaces that is driven by profoundly non-Buddhist philosophical, theological, and ontological understandings.[40] (It is perhaps no accident that the Cartesian grid became a widely used way of dividing up an archaeological site, of tracking what was dug up where, in relationship to what else.) The grid, Pinney implies, remains invisible on the surface of the panoramic photograph, but conceptually it is there, grounding panoramic perspective itself.

Some photopanoramas manifest a colonial geography—and geometry—even more directly. In his photopanorama, *Calcutta from the Ochterlony Monument*, one of seven prints collectively titled *Panoramic View of Calcutta* (ca. 1875–76) (fig. 8.3), Samuel Bourne (British, 1834–1912) showcases the

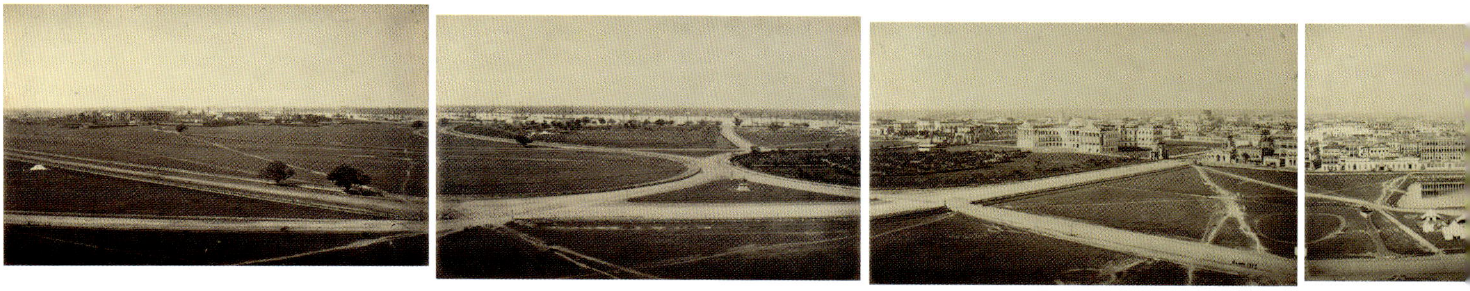

FIG. 8.3. Samuel Bourne (British, 1834–1912), *Panoramic View of Calcutta*, 1875–76. Seven abumen prints, each approx. 19 × 31 cm (7 ½ × 12 ¼ in.). Royal Collection Trust, London (2701698–704).

linear axes and newly ordered topography of British India's capital city; the photographer of *Elphinstone Circle, Bombay* (British India, ca. 1870) showcases the new neo-Georgian crescent around Bombay's Town Hall as a demonstration of Raj cultural power.

In the 1860s, panoramic photographs taken by Sergeant James M. McDonald (British 1822–1885) buttressed Royal Engineer ordnance surveys of Jerusalem and the Sinai Peninsula (surveys themselves shaped by practical, diplomatic, and imperial aspirations, alongside their sense of the Holy Land as British cultural heritage).[41] And in 1920s British Mandate Palestine, photopanoramas provided visual evidence in urban planning reports by the British Arts and Crafts designer Charles Robert Ashbee (1863–1842), then serving as Jerusalem's inaugural "civic advisor": panoramic photographs of Jaffa Road and Gate "in present condition" (ramshackle, crowded with locals) were juxtaposed with sketches of their planned architectural (and demographic) transformation.[42]

Such panoramas were often photographed by army officers, officially "embedded" photographers, and colonial officials. In the American West, South Pacific, and South and Central America, in contrast, the most influential panoramic photographers were peripatetic, fortune-seeking, freelance adventurers. Successive gold rushes lured Bernhardt Holtermann (German, 1838–1885) from Germany to Australia, Muybridge from Britain, and Carleton Watkins (American, 1829–1916) from New York to California. Other itinerant photographers followed rail lines across the American Midwest, taking panoramic photographs of (and presumably selling them to residents of) a long succession of small towns.[43]

Muybridge became renowned not only for the complexity of his *Panorama of San Francisco*, but also for the risks he (and other photopanoramic innovators) took to secure the best pictures.[44] George Lawrence (American, 1868–1938) used kites to capture aerial photopanoramas of post-earthquake San Francisco; Melvin Vaniman (American, 1866–1912), dubbed the "Acrobatic Photographer" and the "Trapeze Photographer," captured panoramic views of San Francisco, Hawaii, New Zealand, Australia, and Rome; he shot his 1904 Sydney, Melbourne, and Australian outback photopanoramas from a hot-air balloon he brought with him from the United States.[45]

In 1873 Muybridge became "the first photographer the U.S. Army hired directly to document a war," producing the widely distributed official photographs of the Modoc War, fought between California and Oregon Indian groups and the U.S. Army. Yet what Muybridge depicted was "not a war unfolding but a war's raw materials: participants and locations."[46] Even these photographs, Rebecca Solnit argues, sustain Muybridge's "act of witness" to the modernization processes transforming North America in ways unflattering to his patrons. Even when "working for railroads and armies, for tourists and easterners he . . . called their attention to . . . landscapes they wouldn't explore, the cultures they wouldn't encounter, the lives they wouldn't live . . . the questions they couldn't answer. Muybridge wasn't neutral. He was independent. He was complicating the record as he made it, inviting doubt into the house."[47]

Other photopanoramists invite comparable claims. The Irish-born John Burke (ca. 1843–1900) financed himself to accompany and photograph invading British forces during the Second Anglo-Afghan War of 1878–80.[48] Burke's nine Kabul photopanoramas include bird's-eye views, landscapes with British encampments, and British soldiers around the looming, ancient Bala Hissar fortress the British threatened to raze—but also picturesque evocations of city outskirts—mosque, cemetery—implicitly lamenting the transformations wrought by colonial intervention. After eight years photographing

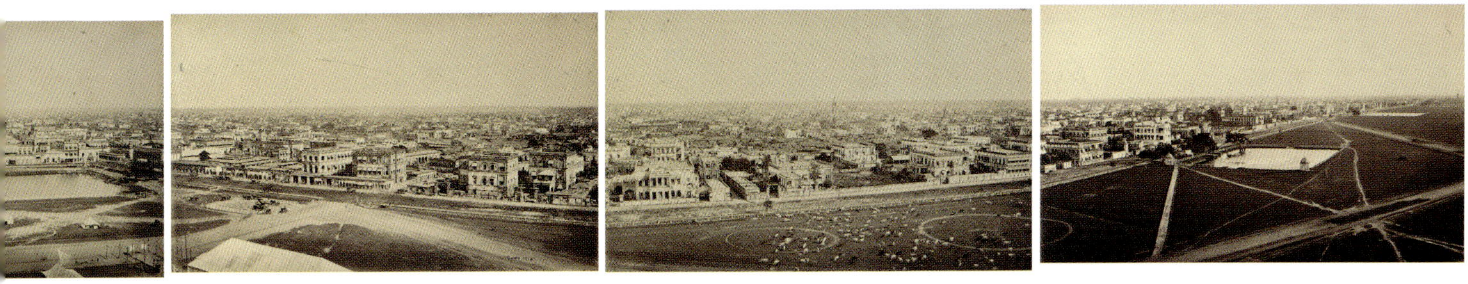

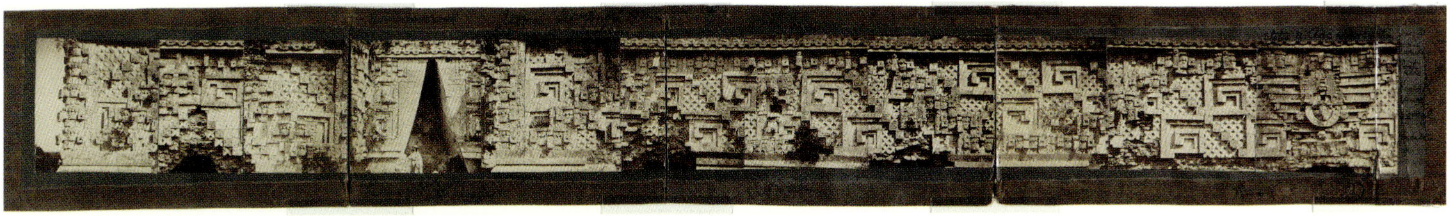

FIG. 8.4. Alice Dixon Le Plongeon (British, 1851–1910) and Augustus Le Plongeon (French-American, 1826–1908), *Panorama of the South Half of the East Facade of the Governor's Palace, Uxmal* (detail), 1876. Eleven mounted albumen prints. Getty Research Institute, Los Angeles. Augustus and Alice Dixon Le Plongeon Papers, 1763-1937 (2004.M.18).

Peru's Incan ruins, the French-American photographer Augustus Le Plongeon (French-American, 1826–1908) traversed Mexico's Yucatán peninsula with his British-born bride, Alice Dixon Le Plonegon (British, 1851–1910), documenting Mayan temple complexes.[49] In Uxmal, they assembled a pieced photopanorama of a 320-foot Mayan frieze (fig. 8.4), supplemented by eighty-three painstaking papier-mâché models of low reliefs and small, hard-to-photograph frieze details.[50] They intended this photography to buttress diffusionist cultural theories, locating Meso-America as the cradle of human civilization—and militating against the colonialist ideologies photopanoramas elsewhere served.

Photography spread almost simultaneously, and relatively evenly, across the nineteenth-century world.[51] Recently, scholars have begun examining early photopanoramas shot by local residents. Like colonial occupiers, local photographers often approached regional landscapes with an eye to Western mercantile and ideological interests. Yet because of their intimate local knowledge, their panoramas also made visible other factors and positions. In Brazil, the photopanoramas of Francisco du Bocage (Brazilian, 1860–1919) thus chronicled the razing of Recife's nineteenth-century architecture and replacement by new industrial infrastructure. Some pictures center on ruins; others juxtapose rubble with the lineaments of new iron construction. In many, including *Porto de Recife—Construção do Armazém* (1910; fig. 8.5), the fish-eye bend accentuates the image's oddly deserted or desolate middle, suggesting peculiar, almost surreal vacancy in the heart of the modern city.[52] Bocage's depictions of urban planning failures and cityscapes of emptiness and randomness anticipate the alienated late modernist panoramic photographs of Josef Sudek (Czech, 1896–1976) and Josef Koudelka (Czech, b. 1938), meditating (as I argue in chapter 12) on Czechoslovakia's soulless Communist-era prefab buildings, political anomie, and environmental degradation.

Recent historians of photography have seen nineteenth-century Chinese photopanoramas as reflecting mercantile and colonial agendas. In his panoramic *General View of Wuzhou* (1860s), the Chinese photographer Lai Afong (Chinese, ca. 1839–1890) thus conveys "the potential of a vast, untapped market for Western goods." And a Chinese photopanorama (1879–91?) of Ningbo, then still closed to foreign residents, "represents an example of data gathering associated with imperialistic enterprise."[53] Western clients commissioning photopanoramas of treaty ports "wanted to show the strength and anchorlike extent of the Western presence."[54] Yet Chinese photopanoramists also pushed the form in new aesthetic directions, reflecting literati sensibilities, following feng shui principles in presenting landscape or conveying the quotidian ordinariness of often-exoticized places.[55]

In Constantinople, three urban photopanoramas Pascal Sébah (Ottoman, 1823–1886) took from the same vantage point, the Galata Tower, enabled a detailed picture of urban transformation from the 1860s to 1880s.[56] In Raj India, Lala Deen Dayal (Indian, 1844–1905) became

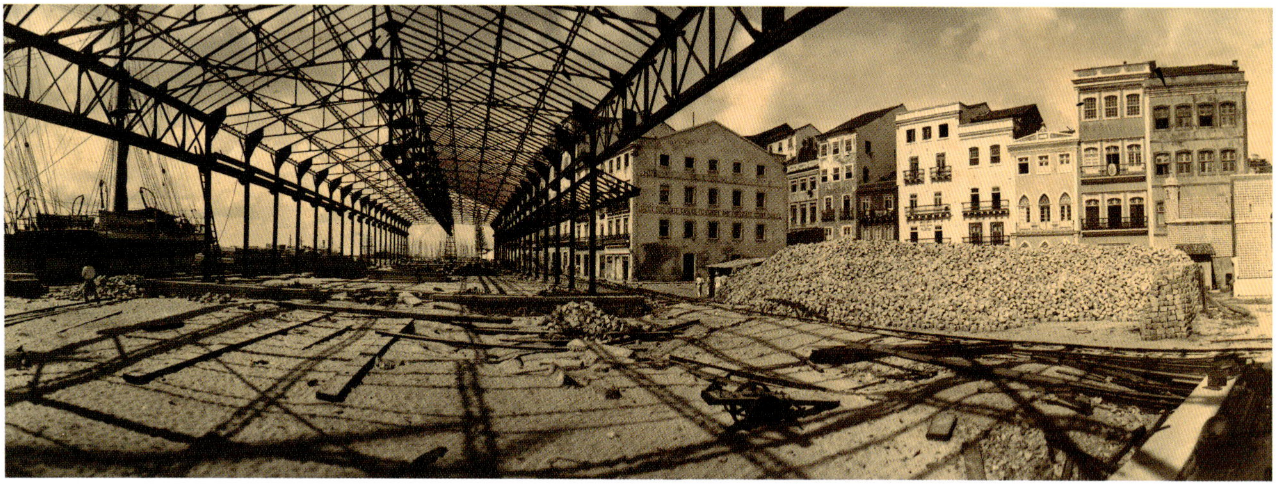

FIG. 8.5. Francisco du Bocage (Brazilian, 1860–1919), *Porto de Recife—Construção de Armazém*. Photographic print, 10.8 × 29.7 cm (4 ¼ × 11 ⅝ in.). Instituto Moreira Salles Collection, São Paulo.

an official photographer to the viceroy and eventually, at a distance, to Queen Victoria herself.[57] Yet alongside his photopanoramas documenting Raj urban reconstruction, others (including his serene two-part *Panorama of Buhj, Gujarat*, ca. 1895, looking across Hamirsar Lake) record vestiges of pre-Raj economic organization and radiate a tranquility bordering on the spiritual.

Smaller and far more portable than their painted counterparts, panoramic photographs enjoyed a wide (and in some cases, worldwide) circulation in the form of prints and commemorative albums. Holtermann's Sydney photopanorama was exhibited in San Francisco and won a medal at Philadelphia's Centennial Exhibition.[58] Muybridge's *Panorama of San Francisco* sold to the public in two formats (rolled scroll, $8; bound, accordion-folded, $10); Beato's multiplate images of Delhi, Yokohama, Edo, Hong Kong, Beijing, and Istanbul entered collections worldwide.[59]

Nonetheless, it might be misleading to think of panoramic photography as an institutionally established practice, parallel to that of salon painting and the beginnings of public museum painting collections. Instead, it seems to have been a diffuse, if at times official and prestigious practice, a form of record keeping and view making as often officially commissioned and ceremonially recognized as commercially circulated. (Most panoramic photographers, indeed, made their living taking more quotidian kinds of photographs, including studio shots.)

Nineteenth-century panoramic photography thus operated as an artisanal, auteurist practice alongside an official mode of recording. And in both capacities, it repeatedly involved attempts to document older, endangered cultural layers and artifacts as well as planning, justifying, and celebrating the infrastructure of modernity.

EARLY PANORAMA FILMS

Following the nineteenth-century precedent of panoramic photography, early film production companies, including Auguste and Louis Lumière, Pathé, Thomas Edison, and Biograph, sent cameramen around the world in search of exotic subjects.[60] And even more than painted panoramas, shuttled around the world, early panoramic films received truly global distribution. Needing physical stability during long camera exposures, panoramic photographers had been forced to follow panoramic painters in working from fixed vantage points, often hills or church towers.

In contrast, turn-of-the-century filmmakers—including the Lumières, Georges Méliès (French, 1861–1938), Edison (American 1847–1931), Alexandre Promio (French, 1868–1926), Billy Bitzer (American, 1872–1944), Sagar Mitchell (British, 1866–1952), and James Kenyon (British, 1850–1925)—shot "panoramas" from moving vehicles: trains, gondolas, streetcars, subways, elevators, funiculars, roller coasters, ferries, steamboats, torpedo boats, and the 1900 Paris Exposition's "moving boardwalk," itself elevated, circular, and panoramic.

Promio's pioneering 1896 tracking shot was inspired by Venice's waterways: "On a boat along the Grand Canal from the station to my hotel, I watched the banks shoot past and thought that *if motionless cinema makes it possible to reproduce moving objects, the reverse might also be attempted by reproducing motionless objects with the aid of moving cinema*."[61] Yet as titles like *Namo Village, Panorama Taken from a Rickshaw* (Gabriel Verye, Lumière brothers [hereafter referred to as LB], France/Indochina, 1900); *Panorama of Cologne, Seen from a Rhine Steamer* (Constant Girel, LB, France, 1896), and *Panorama from Top of a Moving Train* (Méliès, France, 1898) suggest, traveling panorama films drew viewers as much because of the means of transit as for the landscape on view.[62] The vistas of *Panorama of the Banks of the Bosphorus* (Promio, LB, France, 1897) and *Nice: Panorama on the Line from Beaulieu to Monaco III* (LB, France, 1900), indeed, are partly effaced by the steam of the riverboat or train enabling them.

Panoramic films of Europe's colonies sometimes amplified the political agenda of earlier colonial photopanoramas. The Dutch cameraman J. C. Lamster (1872–1954), sent in 1912 by Holland's Royal Tropical Institute to film in the East Indies, launched a tradition of Indonesian phantom ride films (from cars, boats, trains) that lasted through the 1930s, often commissioned or distributed by the Amsterdam Colonial Institute. Like Raj photopanoramas, many showcased colonial modernity's mechanical infrastructure: dams, viaducts, factories, apartment blocks, and, above all, rail tracks, bridges, tunnels, overpasses, and stations.[63]

In Europe and the United States, panoramic films stressed recreational looking, the unfettered eye, the thrill of speed—and sometimes also commercial agendas. Late nineteenth-century American railroad magnates had lent their patronage to Watkins and Muybridge; early twentieth-century train companies publicized their lines by offering filmmakers material support, including free rides, so the resulting films were covertly promotional.[64] In the American West, railroads enabled unprecedented access to spectacular vistas. Muybridge, Watkins, and Vaniman had doubled as stuntmen, risking their lives to capture stunning shots; in the American West or the Alps, where railroads enabled unprecedented access to spectacular vistas, panoramic filmmakers shot from relative safety, conveying mountain and canyon views from moving trains.[65] Yet some films, as Gunning and Keiller stress, nonetheless induce a sense of spectatorial risk.[66] Edison's *Panorama of the Golden Gate* (1902) shows sharp drops near the track; Félix Mesguich (French, 1871–1949) ended his *Panorama of the Cauterets Line III: The Tunnel* (LB, 1899–1900) on a disconcertingly high, wide turn, as if the train will jump the tracks into the abyss. Such train films rhetorically extend the stunting photopanoramic tradition—and tacitly memorialize the many lives lost during railroad construction.

Today's "slow television" rejoins such phantom rides, while greatly extending their duration. Norwegian live broadcasts of *The Seven-Hour Train Journey*, Bergen to Oslo (*Bergensbanen—minutt for minutt*, 2009) and the 134-hour run of Norway's coastal ferry, Bergen to Kirkenes (*Hurtigruten—minutt for minutt*, 2011), attracted record audiences. Half of Norway's population tuned into *Hurtigruten*, as crowds of spectators and dozens of boats began greeting the ferry along its route. These broadcasts gained worldwide media attention. In 2014, indeed, hundreds of British Airways flights began streaming *Bergensbanen* as "hypnotic, calming and entertaining" in-flight entertainment.[67] In the long aftermath of September 11, airline passengers unnerved by aviation risks could be calmed by virtual movement on older, slower means of transport.

During the 2009 *Bergensbanen* broadcast, Norwegian television interpolated historical footage (tracing Bergen Railway's hundred-year history) during the run's 182 tunnels, clearly worried viewers might otherwise stop watching. A century earlier, in contrast, pioneering panoramic filmmakers, enraptured by technology and transportation networks, believed tunnels possessed particular visual interest. Bitzer's five-minute *Interior New York Subway, 14th St. to 42nd St.* (American Mutoscope and Biograph [hereafter cited as AMB], 1905) lingers between stations to showcase New York's elegant new infrastructure and the train's glide from platform to platform.

Like colonial photopanoramas, European-made phantom rides through Middle Eastern, North African, Asian, and East Indian cities foregrounded cross-cultural contrasts, in the ways colonial architecture and urban planning shaped new public spheres. Promio's *Leaving Jerusalem by Railway* (*Départ de Jérusalem en chemin de fer* [panorama], LB, 1897) contrasts the director's ceremonial sendoff by men in elegant European clothing with the mixed public (Franciscan monk, kaftaned men) left behind on the platform.

Promio's Algiers films alternate between static views of Algiers's "Arab market" (traversed by livestock, carriages, indigenously dressed men) and phantom rides through official colonial spaces, arcaded plazas anchored by French statuary, crisscrossed by tram lines, traversed by European women.[68] Colonial Algiers, art historians have argued, exemplified the imperial reorganization of urban spaces and sightlines to acknowledge French power, traditions, and perspectives. Under French colonial rule, Algiers's souks were razed, and the "Governor Square," built in their place, was anchored, European-style, with monumental statuary (itself a tradition aesthetically and politically alien to local sensibilities).[69] Although colonial anxieties persisted about the impenetrability of native neighborhoods (and the visual impenetrability of traditional local women's garments), the new colonial architecture and urban planning were notable for their symmetry and hence ostensible transparency. New boulevards, indeed, made it possible for colonial officials and French settlers to stroll through and experience Algiers as they might along the boulevards of Paris. (The Lumières' 1902 Photorama of Algiers, framed on one side by the colonially constructed Boulevard de la République, gave French virtual viewers the same sense.)

Yet early filmmakers also captured the visual and sociological contrasts in Western cities. American Mutascope and Biograph's three 1904 phantom rides of St. Joseph, Missouri, William Uricchio suggests, may represent "the beginning of a systematic urban mapping project."[70] Harry, Herbert, Joseph, and Earle Miles filmed their thirteen-minute *Trip Down Market Street* (1906) from a slow-moving cable car, surveying San Francisco only weeks before earthquake and fire destroyed parts of what it records. The boulevard easily accommodates an erratic weave of trams, carriages, drays, pedestrians, cyclists, circling motorcars. Pathé's *Vienne en tramway* (France, 1906) traverses Vienna's recently constructed Ringstrasse, designed to provide broad, panoramic views of monumental new national institutions. In sparse traffic, the city appears uncrowded, elegant, architecturally unified.

Urban panorama films are panoramic not only in their sweeping camerawork but in their investigation of street life, social interactions, gender and dress codes. And many seem intensely self-referential, as excited bystanders react to offscreen cameramen atop moving vehicles. In *Barcelona en tranvía* (Spain, 1908), the Spanish film pioneer Ricardo de Baños (1882–1939) showed cyclists crowding Barcelona's boulevards and men running, dancing, and skipping for the camera alongside stretches of tram line. For Alice Guy-Blaché (French, 1873–1968), downtown crowds remained the principal interest in her *Madrid* and *Madrid: Panorama de las ventas* (Gaumont, 1905, cameraman Anatole Thiberville); Madrileños seemed particularly preoccupied with the camera—and perhaps the novelty of its woman director.

Across Britain and Ireland, Mitchell and Kenyon marketed "local films for local people."[71] In Glasgow their 1901 film program (including locally filmed shorts) drew eight thousand spectators daily.[72] The filmmakers sought out newsworthy events—and large crowds that might later pay to see themselves onscreen.[73] *Panoramic View of the Morecambe Sea Front* (1901; fig. 8.6) captures strolling vacationers, tourist groups posing for the camera, children running excitedly alongside the horse tram carrying the cameramen, and, finally, the crowd outside the Winter Garden Theater, waiting to watch the producers' films.[74] In *Ride on the Tramcar through Belfast* (1901), traffic along Belfast's slow-moving, well-spaced high street includes horse trams, serene female and male pedestrians passing well-appointed shop windows—and eight men wheeling advertising boards announcing this film's upcoming premiere at Mitchell and Kenyon's film program, "shown twice daily at Belfast's Ulster Hall." In *Electric Tram Rides from Forster Square, Bradford* (1902), the cameraman gets down from the tram, on-camera, to talk to young women, encouraging them to be filmed to best advantage. Then directors themselves appear, encouraging other Bradford locals to respond to the camera. The filmmakers thus visibly create and stage the bystander interest they ostensibly only record.[75]

AESTHETICS AND POLITICS OF MOVEMENT

In nineteenth-century adultery novels from Flaubert's *Madame Bovary* (1858) to Tolstoy's *Anna Karenina* (1878), vehicular journeys precipitated moral collapse, encouraging untoward social and sexual contact (sleigh, carriage, railway compartment as *chambre séparée*), potentially derailing human lives, rushing them into self-destruction.[76] Early cinema, in contrast, embraced its underlying principle of motion by featuring "traveling" shots to open up new vistas. From the Lumières' earliest films (workers walking or riding through the factory gate; a train arriving in a station), locomotion and vehicular movement proved fundamental subjects—and the implicit ground—for the aptly named "motion pictures," the medium evolved from the motion studies of Étienne-Jules Marey (French, 1830–1904) and Muybridge.[77]

City films fixated on human movement and vehicular traffic. Early dramas—Méliès's *Trip to the Moon* (*Voyage dans la lune*, France, 1902), *The Great Train Robbery* (U.S., 1903) by Edwin S. Porter (American, 1870–1941), *Rescued by Rover* (Britain, 1905) by Cecil Hepworth (British,

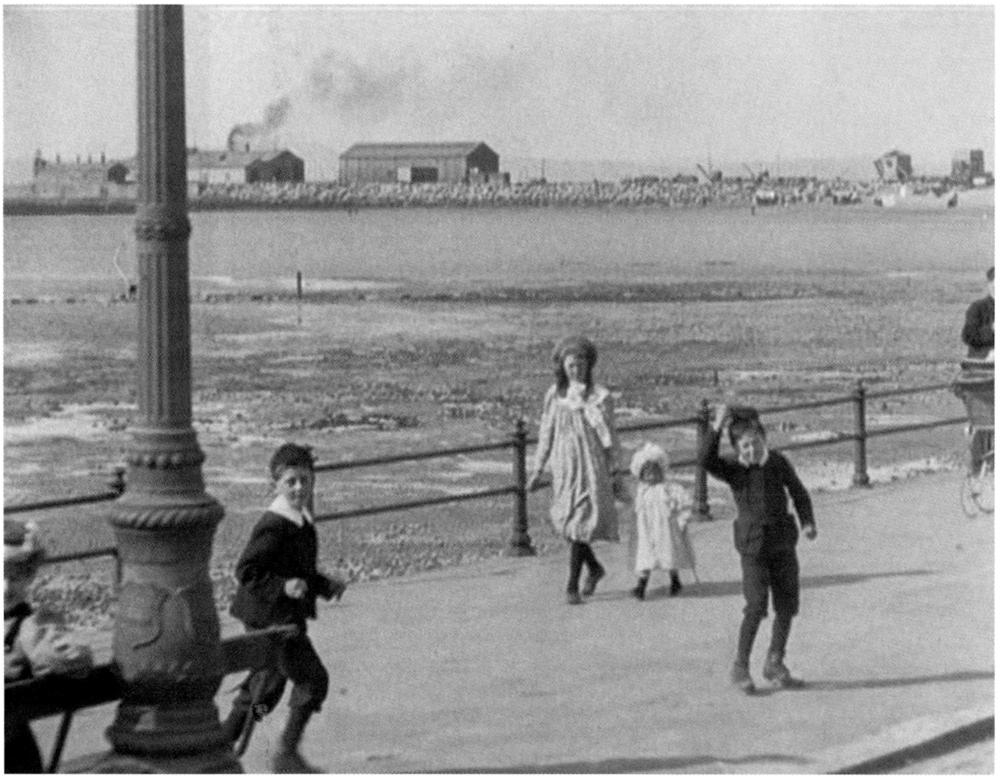

FIG. 8.6. Sagar Mitchell (British, 1866–1952) and James Kenyon (English, 1850–1925), *Panoramic View of the Morecambe Sea Front*, 1901.

1874–1953), the Keystone cops films (U.S., 1912–17) of Mack Sennett (American, 1880–1960)—featured rapid traverses (by rocket, runaway train, getaway car, rescuing canine), chasing, speed, reckless driving, traffic accidents.[78] From these beginnings, a vast international body of road movies, documentary and fictional, used long car, bus, motorcycle, or train journeys to frame quests gone awry, becoming occasions to survey the landscape, sample cross-country conditions, and use random encounters to refocus spectators' vision and protagonists' self-knowledge.[79]

Modernist movements like futurism focused on the dissolution or reconstitution of self in motion. Fin-de-siècle phantom ride films, in contrast, depicted train and tram as new vehicles for realizing agency and conscious vision. Yet these films also focused on the quality of motion, emphasizing alternately the broad, novel vision rail travel made possible, its gliding smoothness, and the dislocation that speed and bumpiness engendered. In Uricchio's words, "Vehicle-mounted panoramas offer traces of the texture of movement."[80] Train movement partly dominates the foreground of Méliès's *Panorama from Top of a Moving Train*; the viewer's eye moves between machinery in motion and stations pulling close, then away. Louis Lumière's *Panorama Taken from the Train of the Arrival in the Perrache Station* (1896) documents landscape along a stretch of track and the train's disorienting headlong momentum. The film opens with a lurch, as the train emerges from behind a wall, enabling a view of scenery and track; its uneven, jolting jogging are the view's ground, the film's most pressing subject. And in Edison's *Panorama of Gorge Railway* (1900), the view's regular interruption by telegraph poles divides the unfolding view into scenes or vistas.

Panoramic waterscapes enable a different mode of terrain and motion study. In Promio's *Panorama of the Grand Canal Taken from a Boat* (LB, 1896), boat and thus camera roll smoothly, unwavering. The Lumières' 1897 *Egypt: Panorama of the Banks of the Nile* is interesting less for its nominal subject, the shoreline, than for its play of lapping water, as the cameramen's boat creates small waves on an otherwise placid surface.[81] Guy-Blaché's *Ocean Studies* (Gaumont, France, 1906) pans over moving tidal water; her *Seville: Panorama of the Port* (1905, France, Gaumont, cameraman Thieberville) moves downstream across Seville's riverfront along the rushing Guadalquivir. Likewise, in the mistitled *Panorama of Calcutta* (1899, actually showing Varanasi), the shoreline view explores the interface between land and water, focusing first on close-range footage of riverside colonnades, ghats (stone steps giving river access), pilgrims immersing and purifying themselves close to shore; gradually we see dense boat traffic, then pull out from shore to see wider Ganges stretches.[82]

Early panoramic films, Gunning argues, display the broadest possible landscape view, apparently unbounded. In the process, they "seem to recreate the actual penetration of space that traveling involves." Differential movement within the scene further deepens the stereoscopic effect.[83] In some panoramic films, contrasting modes of movement lend intense dynamism and visual interest. In *Mills on the Zaan River* (British Mutoscope and Biograph/ Nederlandsche Biograaf en Mutoscope, 1898), Daniel Louis Uyttenboogaart (Dutch, 1872–1947) contrasts the camera's own rapid, smooth (boat-enabled) passage downstream with the huge windmills along both banks, some with steadily turning blades, others immobile. A contemporaneous catalogue description of Edison's *Panorama of Gorge Railway* underscores the intense audience effect of its whirlpool rapids sequence, given "the combined motion of the train in one direction and the water [of Niagara Falls] in the opposite direction."[84] *Panorama of Ealing from a Moving Tram* (British Mutoscope and Biograph, 1901), shot by William Kennedy-Laurie Dickson (Scottish, 1860–1935), turns on the contrast between the tram's gliding movement down a stately street and the unpredictable flapping of the street's many flags and awnings.

"À travers" films like the Lumières' *Panoramic View during Ascension of the Eiffel Tower* (1896–97), Daisuke Miyao argues, "were not simply *actualité*" but were shaped by pictorialist sensibility, their differential spatial and planar organization, their attempt to capture "moments and movements of the environment" influenced by Japanese woodblock prints, Impressionist and Postimpressionist "Japonisme."[85] Panoramic films also reflected other aspects of modernist aesthetics. Unlike traditional, "absorptive" landscape painting, Gunning argues, panoramic films often stress high-speed traverse, their "perception of landscape . . . mediated by speed and technology."[86] Guy-Blaché's fascinating 1905 Spain films panoramically track individual pedestrians' particular, pattern-producing movement, walking a road or traversing a plaza; they amplify Postimpressionism's figure-ground preoccupations and photography-inspired compositions.[87] The Lumières' 1899 *Panorama Taken from an Anchored Balloon*, conversely, unpredictably lifts up and down with the wind, bobbing so rapidly that fairgoers on the ground become unrecognizable, creating disorienting new spectator perspectives and vicarious physical experiences.[88] In their use of aerial perspectives (from towers, balconies, and swings) to abstract urban life, such films inspired first the interwar Constructivist and surrealist photographers like Aleksandr Rodchenko (Russian, 1891–1956), László Moholy-Nagy (Hungarian, 1895–1946), and Josef Sudek, and then, later, the disorienting arcs of 1960s and 1970s experimental filmmaking.

BITZER'S INDUSTRIAL PANORAMA

For all their interest in movement, most early films leave invisible the internal movement enabling projection: the film's own movement through the projector gate. Industrial panorama films arguably come closest to addressing movies' constitutive motion. This small subgenre seems descended ultimately from an early example of the "technological sublime," Robert Barker's pioneering 1792 painted panorama, *London from the Roof of the Albion Mills* (see fig. 1.14), which, in Peter Otto's words, summarized the "commercial, industrial and colonial forces at the heart of modernity."[89]

Bitzer's 1904 AMB series, depicting industrial processes and shop-floor organizations at the Pennsylvania Westinghouse works, evokes ambitious industrial tableaux like *The Iron Rolling Mill* (1872–75, Berlin, Nationalgalerie) by Adolph Menzel (German, 1815–1905). To some contemporary viewers, the mechanized workings of large industrial plants represented their own quotidian reality; to many others, they remained as unfamiliar as Algiers, the Ganges, or the Nile.

Four of these films are panoramic: a phantom train ride between two Pittsburgh factories, and three contrasting panoramas taken inside the Machine Company complex, as cameras moving across the ceiling (suspended from winches normally lifting heavy machine parts) traverse industrial assembly rooms. Unlike other industrial film panoramas, Bitzer's films pan through interiors. In *Panoramic View, Aisle B, Westinghouse Works* and *Panorama of Machine Co. Aisle Westinghouse Co.*, the camera traverses the workrooms above aisles used by manual fitters and supervisors. All have clearly been ordered to ignore the camera. Only one young worker idles in middle of the room, watching the camera pass overhead. Everyone else goes about his business: white-collar workers constantly moving down aisles, some checking how particular assembly pieces are working, overall-clad workmen wheeling equipment or clambering over machinery, wrenches in hand, checking and tightening. Each group's dress and mode of traverse clarifies this workplace's division of responsibility. Despite the factory's noise and potential danger, Bitzer's tableaux convey order and disciplined cooperation between ranks.

Filmed a few weeks earlier in the same factory, *Panorama View, Westinghouse Works, Street Car Motor Room* (fig. 8.7) shows a far more hectic, crowded, visually disorienting workspace that lacks a continuous central aisle. Instead, the camera passes over scrambling workers, patrolling overseers, constantly moving machinery—and a longer line of winches like the one holding it, moving near the ceiling ahead of the camera. We witness men and machinery close to collision, the camera's own progress momentarily halted. Here, too, some workmen hammer in rhythm, as a larger group (completely stationary, vigilant, nonworking supervisors) oversees the filming alongside shop floor discipline.

With good reason, *Street Car Motor Room* remains Bitzer's best-known factory film; the workroom, more overtly stratified and supervised than others, exudes repressed social conflict. The camera's swing through ever-shifting, potentially dangerous industrial space creates suspense; the shooting angle lends the traverse stereoscopic depth. We observe workmen's improvisatory abilities and practiced rhythms as they assemble and move dauntingly heavy machinery. Above all, this panorama film shows us the camera enlisted into the industrial apparatus, suspended like the room's other machinery and inseparable from it.

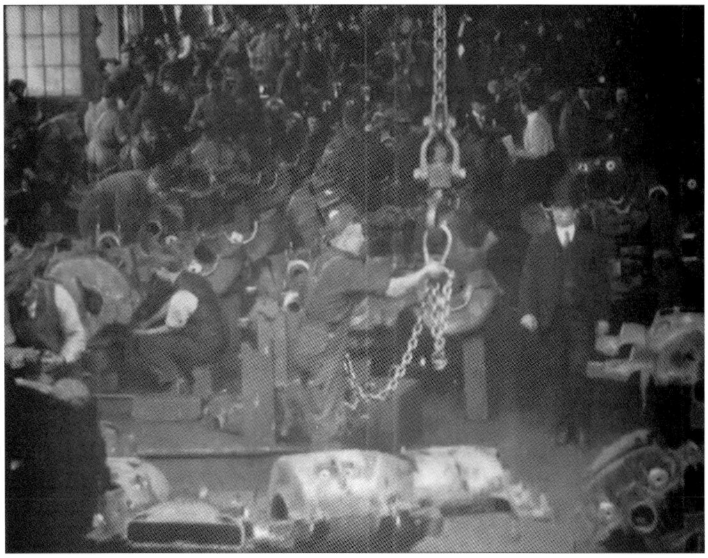

FIG. 8.7. Billy Bitzer (American, 1872–1944), *Panorama View, Westinghouse Works, Street Car Motor Room*. Shot April 21, 1904. American Mutograph and Bioscope. Library of Congress Motion Picture, Broadcasting and Recorded Sound Division, Washington, D.C. (96522105).

PANORAMA FILM AND URBAN ENTERTAINMENT

Many early panorama films reiterated key painted panoramic genres: cityscape, riverscape, seashore, industrial scenes.[90] Like their painted and photographic antecedents, urban panorama films repeatedly took the measure of tall, new structures on the skyline (Eiffel Tower) or surveyed from the high structures themselves, offering bustling cross sections or elevated aerial shots, Olympian, abstracting city views. In fin-de-siècle New York, panoramic cameramen filmed an urban plaza transformed by the new Flatiron Building, rooftop views from the new Times Building, and the Brooklyn Bridge Tower.[91]

Yet panorama films, Keiller argues, were most profound in chronicling subtle, wide-ranging changes in urban movement and transit patterns: the way the advent of the tram, for instance, sped commercial reorganization of the urban core.[92] In other respects, too, panorama films focused on long-term consequences. Like panoramic photographers, early panoramic filmmakers could seldom capture unfolding events, instead recording their traces or aftershocks, their rubble, their commemoration: cyclone, earthquake, and fire damage; executions; emigrant ship launches; building and monument consecration.[93]

What they could chronicle directly and regularly were the many turn-of-the-century expositions (from 1900 to 1904 alone in Paris, Buffalo, Charleston, St. Louis, and Cork), metonyms of an emerging global economic order, which sampled the world's (threatened?) cultural diversity in light of an increasingly interconnected global economy.[94] Panoramic film participated in and showcased these processes: traveling to remote locales and capturing local specificity, they were marketed to global audiences. Like expositions themselves, early ethnographic photography and filmmaking were often implicitly Orientalist, selecting or posing local subjects to resemble European exoticist paintings, thereby producing familiar tropes.[95] Yet filmic panoramas also showed what it was like to live in a "primitive" backwater, or to be caught in accelerated colonial transformation, down to body movements and facial expressions.

Plural in their international gathering of peoples and quasi-ethnographic specimens, world's fairs were also overlap sites for different media, machines, and epochs of panoramic vision; painted panoramas and the final wave of cycloramic entertainments jostled new panoramic and cinematic displays.[96] Paris's 1889 Exposition boasted seven painted (city or battle) panoramas. Paris's 1900 Exposition's two stationary painted panoramas (depicting Madagascar and Mont Blanc) competed with moving panoramas; simulated railway or boat journeys (Stereorama, Transiberiana, Mareorama) were accompanied by painted panoramas: the Tour du Monde, moving panorama views of China, Japan, the Indian and Mediterranean Oceans, and the Suez Canal, and (for two days, until projectors overheated) the Cinéorama, a simulated balloon ride to projected panoramic footage.[97] Hale's Tours debuted at the 1904 St. Louis exhibition; viewers seated in simulated railway cars likewise saw panoramic phantom ride footage, shot from trains. Hale's rides became popular across the United States and Britain and toured in Mexico, South Africa, South America, Europe, and Hong Kong.[98]

Urban pleasure districts likewise showcased panoramas, films, and moving attractions. The Prater housed Vienna's main panorama (1803; rebuilt 1882), a moving panorama (1850), and the double-moving "Pleorama" (1852), with an intervening "ship's deck" viewing platform (inaugural display: Quebec-to-North-Pole voyage). Following the 1873 Vienna International Exhibition, the Prater become dominated by visual attractions: "panoramas, dioramas, magic lantern shows . . . panopticons."[99] Its totemic 1897 Ferris wheel offered citywide vistas; beginning in 1896, it boasted cinemas alongside Carl Hagenbeck's dioramic live polar animal display, as well as "native villages," Wild West shows, peep shows, ethnographic waxworks, a "diorama train" (1895) and a "scenic railway" (1909) running cars alongside painted sets, various "Grotto Trains" (from 1898 onward), and a "Central Train Station" (1919), with changing light and a slide show.[100] Prater nickelodeons thus complemented trips on moving vehicles offering real and virtual views. Such exhibition contexts underscore Gunning's much-discussed notion that early films highlight a "cinema of attractions."[101] Panorama films of pleasure grounds and expositions (and seaside tourism) were implicitly self-referential, rapidly shown across a wide national and international distribution circuit, including the very leisure areas depicted.

PHOTORAMA, COLORAMA

Panoramic film's turn-of-the-century emergence from painted and photographic panoramas included sustained attention to movement as a new, transformative element. Nineteenth-century moving panoramas, unscrolling painted depictions of riverscapes, battles, or allegorical pageants of national history (including American antislavery panoramas tracing abolitionism's momentum), had offered viewers a mechanical dynamism and narrative unfolding. Film went further, effortlessly, mimetically capturing vehicular movement's momentum, rhythm, and consequences, giving viewers a novel sense—simultaneously linear and immersive—of moving deeply through new landscapes.

Yet this apparent breakthrough from relative stasis into full-scale movement, from photography into film, was partial and complicated. Around the turn of the century, panoramic photography began moving toward new forms and institutions. Across Central Europe, "Kaiserpanoramas" (patented in 1890) thus enabled a mode of individualized collective viewing—as viewers, sitting around an octagonal plinth, each looked into individual pairs of eye holes, peering in at and focusing on a succession of stereoscopic slides, rotated at regular intervals on an internal carousel.[102] In Paris, Marey's "chronophotographic" motion studies followed and analyzed the trajectory of moving bodies across space and time.[103]

In 1895 the Chicagoan Charles Chase invented a multi-projector system of projecting a "panorama" of photographic magic lantern slides from a multifaceted central projection column onto a large cylindrical screen that surrounded viewers on a central viewing platform; the pictures thus formed a "homogeneous cycloramic scene without possible discovery of points of joining." The photographs were tinted and projected with an "electric lighting power of 25,000 candles" for an effect "even more grand than the cycloramic paintings."[104] Particularly important was the relationship between the circular screen and the viewing platform. "There are no seats for the audience, the people are on the move, they are a portion of the scene, as if they were travelling in the land viewed. . . . When the scene is projected upon the screen, the floor upon which the spectators stand runs right off into the scene, and it is so real that it seems as if we could step right out into the country viewed."[105]

In France the Lumière brothers, who had so recently begun making panoramic films, likewise patented the

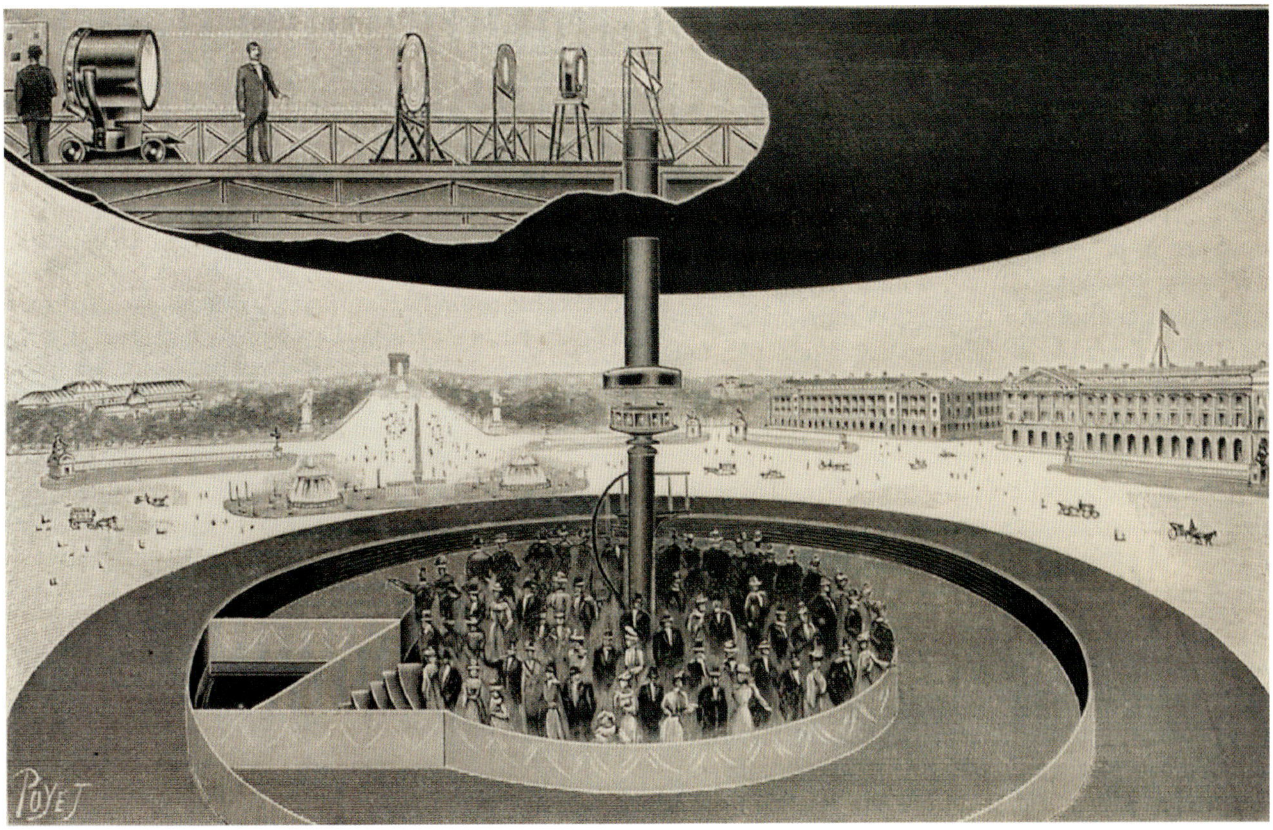

FIG. 8.8. Louis Poyet (French, 1846–1913), engraving of the Lumière brothers' Photorama, Paris, 1902. From G. Mareshal, "Le Photorama: Projections panoramiques de MM. Auguste et Louis Lumière," *La Nature: Revue des Sciences* 30 (1902): 173.

"Photorama," a projected, static, but more immersive form of panoramic photography. Launched during the 1900 Paris Exposition, the Photorama Lumière was exhibited in Paris in a dedicated circular building in 1902–3 (fig. 8.8). Inside, a crowd of spectators stood in the center of the Photorama's huge encircling screen (25 feet tall, with a 65-foot circumference), while a vast, still surround photograph—a landscape, cityscape, or seascape—was projected 360 degrees around them.[106]

Viewers were used to viewing, even holding, small-scale panoramic photographs of vast landscapes. Yet by projecting these on an entirely unfamiliar scale, using them to surround, even dwarf, the viewer, the Photorama tried to realize photography's full mimetic potential—in the process turning the viewing platform into a theatrical, experiential, but virtualized space. Now photoramic landscapes stretched around viewers, capaciously detailed and hence highly realistic, yet existing at a remove, since their black-and-white surface inherently stylized real-life color. Spectators presumably felt on the brink of stepping into a distant locale—and a parallel representational system.

The Lumières' 1901 Photorama *Rome: Toît de l'Église Saint Pierre* (fig. 8.9) showcases the medium's capacity to alternate between sublime and intimate scales; its bystanders and fellow roof watchers recall Eduard Gaertner's painted panorama (see chapters 4 and 5), while offering physical proximity unknown to viewers of earlier panoramic photography. A viewer gazing clockwise from these faces toward the enormous, foregrounded balustrade they stand next to (which appears beyond the small segment reproduced in fig. 8.9) can also admire roof structures, early in the circle: one is shaped like a nineteenth-century panorama rotunda; behind it, the huge cupola of St. Peter's Basilica, the world's largest dome. After surveying the remaining rooftop, the viewer looks over the sharp drop onto St. Peter's vast plaza, with Rome's immensity beyond. The scene encompasses huge, potentially disorienting shifts of scale, yet remains unified, in an extraordinarily full moment, by its sense of suspension. This is, *in nuce*, the eerie, beautiful stillness found in René Clair's *The Crazy Ray* (France, 1925) and Chris Marker's *La jetée* (France, 1962).

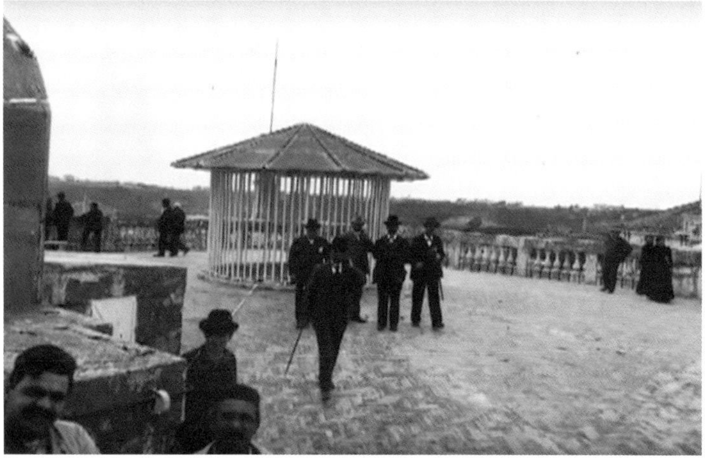

FIG. 8.9. Auguste Lumière (French, 1862–1954) and Louis Lumière (French, 1864–1948), *Rome: Toit de l'Église Saint Pierre*, 1901. This detail shows only a small fraction of the entire composition.

The Photorama is static, yet like Muybridge's zoopraxiscope and the cinematograph, it relies photovisually on continual projection of its compound image. Even more than the painted panorama, the Photorama builds its virtual viewing platform into the photographic image itself. In the Lumières' Dinard Photorama, the spectator looks at the horizon across a vast beach; in the palm-house-like interior of Nice's Municipal Casino Photorama, over a balustrade onto a sea of palms; in their Deauville, Marseille, Algiers, Naples, and Venice Photoramas, onto and from across a pier, a dock, a boardwalk, a shoreline promenade.[107]

Photoramas solved one dilemma of nineteenth-century painted panoramas: the viewing platform's ambiguities, viewers' difficulty in knowing where and how to look, faced with the immensity of the painted circle. Here differences of vantage point—and built-in balustrades—offer us a firmer sense of where we stand; the Rome Photorama even grants us depicted spectators to stand among.

The Photorama closed after a single season. But its influence lingered, in later avant-garde exhibition techniques and in panoramic cinema: Guy-Blaché's *Monastery of Montserrat* and *Grenada: Panorama* (both Gaumont, France, 1905) thus incorporate cinematic panning over city environs and include within the cinematic image architectural features—including the balustrade—that defined the Photorama.

From 1950 to 1990, moreover, in three-week rotation, Kodak's high-profile Colorama series mounted a succession of 565 massive eighteen- by sixty-foot color slides in a billboard-size lightbox suspended high inside New York City's Grand Central Terminal.[108] The lightbox's rectangular format offered the still photograph equivalent of the CinemaScope films dominating 1950s film culture.[109] Yet its scale and broad, collective public viewing echoed the Photorama. Typical images from Colorama's first decade—sometimes involving famous artists such as Ansel Adams (American, 1902–1984) and Norman Rockwell (American, 1894–1978) in their art direction, staging, composition, and cropping—depicted sublime global landscapes or genre scenes of American farmers, suburbanites, or tourists.

Especially during the 1950s and 1960s, the Colorama program showed some propensity for meta-images, particularly scenes where amateur photographers snapped, at a different angle, the same parade, monument, or even the image itself chronicled. Yet Colorama images, seen mostly by commuters (rushing through the station to and from work) also laid great emphasis on the scene's immediate legibility. Colorama images proved wildly, widely popular, but New York's artists protested the airbrushed vacuity and commercialism of Colorama style, which became the satiric target of pop billboard art, such as the panoramic *F-111* (1964–65, MoMA) by James Rosenquist (American, 1933–2017). Over the longer run, however, the Colorama joined the Photorama in inspiring key forms of contemporary artistic practice, from Jeff Wall's lightboxes to installation art.

"TOO MUCH MOVEMENT"? INSTALLATION AS MEDIA HISTORY AND HISTORICAL LOOP

In the nineteenth century, Richard Wagner envisioned a multisensory *Gesamtkunstwerk* directing spectator gaze and affect, building on key effects of the panorama (and moving panorama, crucial to *Lohengrin*). Yet he remained ambivalent about the panorama's overt theatricality, its viewers' relative freedom in controlling and pacing their looking experience, the open-ended interpretations it afforded. Wagner sought a greater degree of integration and subordination of visual effects to the music's pace, drama, and unfolding. Stage sets "are always designed as if they are to stand there alone for their own sake, so that, something like in a panorama, they can be observed at the spectator's will; but I want them only to contribute as silent, enabling background and surround for a characteristic dramatic situation."[110] Modern installation artists, in contrast, design their works to respond to degrees of attention ranging from browsing and milling to careful study. Their attempts to provide immersive experiences aim for a specific range of response, while they are resigned to more aleatory reactions. They create surrounds—and heightened spectatorial self-consciousness—within which viewers experience anew their visual field and environment, sensory apprehension, thought processes, and temporal and spatial embodiment. Their surround is sometimes partial, sometimes complete; at times viewers participate and interact actively with the created environment, and at others they stand outside the created environment, looking across or in at it.

Harun Farocki (German, 1944–2014) turned from film to installations frequently focused on the moment of film editing and montage, a preoccupation rooted in his sense that cinema overused panning, indeed movement itself.[111] For Farocki, the panning shot seemed shallowly rhetorical, movement used to dazzle or provide atmosphere. By contrast, he advocated a frugal, self-conscious deployment of motion: "There is just too much movement in the world. When I make a film, I have to compete with all this movement. So, I try to reduce the level of expectation a little, slow things down a bit. I use still images, in the hope that afterwards, the moving image will acquire a different value. When I show sequences where there is movement, ideally I'd like to produce the same kind of astonishment that occurred when the first Lumière films were shown."[112] Yet the Lumières explored photography's potential not only in movement but in its absence. The Photorama explored photography's surprising ability to hold the viewer in temporal and physical suspension. Like the Photorama, Farocki tried to enable the stillness necessary to absorb the image's complexity.

As an art form, Thomas Elsaesser argues, installation allows temporal reduction and condensation: Farocki freezes and seizes images rather than letting them appear, in their flow, "transparent carriers" of sight and sound. What installation potentially enables is media's historicization, the dramatization and musealization of the cinematic *apparatus*: "What better place than the museum to once more have the cinema confront itself and its history?"[113]

Other key filmmakers—including Michael Snow (Canadian, b. 1928) and Chantal Akerman (Belgian, 1950–2015) (both discussed in chapter 12), Chris Marker (French, 1921–2012), Isaac Julien (British, b. 1960), Werner Herzog (German, b. 1942), and Patrick Keiller—have likewise forayed or moved into installation. Akerman and Marker installed existing films on multiple or competing channels, multiplying montage's effects; Julien creates film for multichannel overlap.[114] Film is normally an art of linear unfolding, enabling only one montage at a time; by contrast, an installation with multiple monitors or projections, showing simultaneously several films or film loops, potentially provides kaleidoscopic ricochet, a dense, singular, nonrepeatable web of cross connections. In *Chelsea Girls* (1966, shown on two nonsynchronized projectors), Andy Warhol (American, 1928–1987) established aleatory juxtaposition as a possible principle of film projection and spectatorship; so did the experimental multiplication, at 1960s world's fairs, of screens and slide or film projectors—sometimes inducing sensory overload for its own sake, sometimes evoking a wide range of places and cultures, in quasi-panoramic global compression.[115]

American multimedia surrounds and "total environments," Fred Turner argues, pioneered under government sponsorship or at corporate expositions, yet they increasingly pushed against Cold War, capitalist ideologies.[116] Recent panoramic installations like Julien's *Ten Thousand Waves* (2010) extend that critical tradition. Before its premiere in China, Julien changed his original title, *Better Life*, since the concurrent Shanghai Expo had adopted the celebratory slogan "Better City, Better Life."[117] Julien's piece, in contrast, elegizes twenty-three undocumented Chinese migrants who, unable to read English-language warnings, drowned in 2004 while cockle picking in Morecambe Bay, off Britain's Lancashire coast. Julien evokes questions of cultural identity (especially vivid in Shanghai, where remains of the cosmopolitan, modernist 1930s are being razed to build freeways and skyscrapers) and the exilic nature of post-Tiananmen Square globalization. Morecambe's drowned migrants epitomize the human and ecological cost of the quest for material prosperity. Mediating between these two moments and places is the mythology created by 1930s Shanghai movies and ancient myths surrounding the Chinese sea goddess Mazu, protector of fishermen.

Although British himself, Julien does little to historicize, contexualize, or mythologize his story's British end. Like other panorama-influenced watercolors, J. M. W. Turner's *Lancaster Sands* (1826, watercolor and body color on paper, British Museum) depicts Morecambe cockle pickers and lobster catchers against broad mudflat expanses. And in 1901 Mitchell and Kenyon's panning

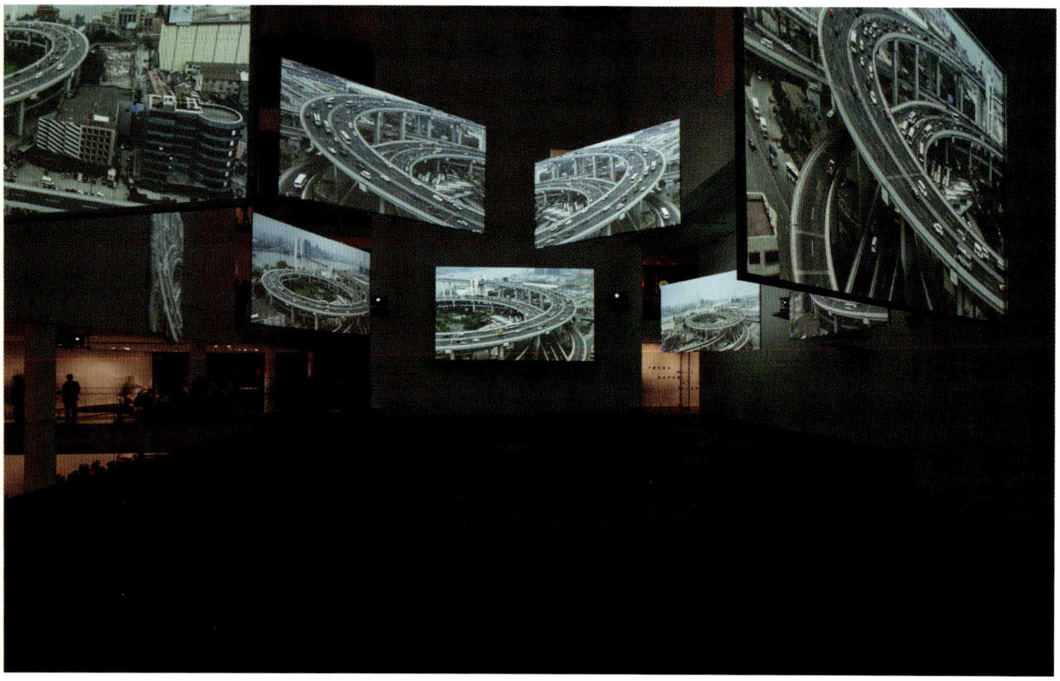

FIG. 8.10. Isaac Julien (British, b. 1966), *Ten Thousand Waves*, as installed at the Museum of Modern Art, New York, 2013–14.

camera recorded vacationers along Morecambe Sea Front. Rather than referencing such images, Julien's installation develops a pictorial countertradition—globalized, queer, postcolonial, diasporic—even as it gestures toward the history of panoramic viewing. Julien's complexly synchronized, layered, interlocking filmic images and scenes are projected onto nine translucent screens installed at intervals and angles, very loosely encircling the spectator. Julien begins with complexly repeated, refracted, often split-screen shots of a Shanghai highway cloverleaf (fig. 8.10).

Traffic scenes, this essay has argued, have always been central to panoramic film. For Julien, traffic indexes an increasingly impersonal public sphere, the human flows globalized commerce enables or necessitates. Julian meditates particularly on historical Chinese urban footage (black-and-white transport shots, rickshaws, bicycles, cars; postwar color photography of Maoist parades and rallies). One newly filmed Shanghai trolley sequence, featuring actors in 1930s clothing, stretches along one side of the gallery, projecting onto multiple screens the vistas from the trolley's front, middle, and end, interspersed with low shots of the trolley track and street at foot level. Revisiting the phantom ride, the viewer receives a faceted yet fractured street view. At moments, adjacent panels add up, satisfyingly, to an integrated whole, like turn-of-the-century peep show "panoramas," offering stereoscopic depth; at others, they cannot be integrated.

Ten Thousand Waves refuses closure. Its screens are installed at angles around a gallery it bisects, making it impossible to follow all screens at once. The panoramic circle does not close; even in the cloverleaf or trolley sequences' occasionally synchronizing circle segments, the effect resembles faceted, neo-cubistic David Hockney photocollage more than continuous image. The piece works by associative montage: modern cityscape with floating goddess; behind-the-scenes footage demonstrating the masking process producing this illusion; fictionalized homages to two classical Chinese films, coexisting with "raw" video and audio shots from a Morecambe helicopter, vainly circling the drowning laborers. The installation's elaborate score, too, assembles a wide range of music and sounds mixed or coexisting in viewers' ears. Even the installation title (elaborated in "The Great Summons," the Chinese American poet Wang Pin's commissioned Morecambe elegy: "Ten thousand waves take us to the shore. Home will arrive under our feet") remains ambiguous about whether waves drowning the immigrants thereby repatriate them or exile them forever. If film is linear, this panoramic installation is multifaceted, nondirective, plural, mixing incommensurate times and places, immigrant and traditional perspectives, 1930s modernist mythologizing, 1960s split-screen spectaculars, 2004 surveillance footage.

Given its ability to create an impersonal, multifaceted view, can panoramic film cameras or installations function as eyes of history? In 1980's *Time Zones*, a Whitney Museum installation by Ira Schneider (American, b. 1939) surrounded viewers with twenty-four television monitors, inviting them to compare footage from around the world, presented as if transpiring simultaneously. Here New York City functioned as an implicit viewing platform from which the rest of the globe became legible.[118]

T. J. Wilcox (American, b. 1965) complicates this perspective by reanimating the Photorama a century after its Paris season. Wilcox's time-lapse, 360-degree composite film *In the Air* (created from six thousand computer-animated still photographs) surveys his New York studio's rooftop view. During its 2013–14 Whitney exhibition, Wilcox's film was projected, mid-gallery, onto a translucent circular screen. Most spectators stood or sat in the circle's center, viewing the panoramic projection from inside—but they could view the projection by traversing its outer perimeter (fig. 8.11).[119] This panoramic scene, appearing photoramically constant (actually subtly shifting through time-lapse), becomes the backdrop for successive left-to-right projections of six short films onto physical locations across the panoramic circle. Like Norway's *Bergensbanen* broadcast, Wilcox's work combines sweeping panoramic survey with interludes evoking historical memory.

Wilcox's interpolated short films meditate on point of view, the ways earlier artists and trendsetters shaped New York's iconic skyline by and for viewing. The Empire State Building once planned a zeppelin disembarking station at its apex, before the Hindenburg crash doomed zeppelin flight. In 1965, myth insists, Warhol launched a phallic silver cloud helium balloon just as Pope Paul VI's motorcade passed Warhol's Factory. The towering Freedom Center inadvertently elicits traumatic memories of the burning World Trade Center, including trapped people jumping to their deaths.

Uniting Wilcox's New York stories are the ways zeppelin, helium balloon, skyscraper enshrine aerial perspective

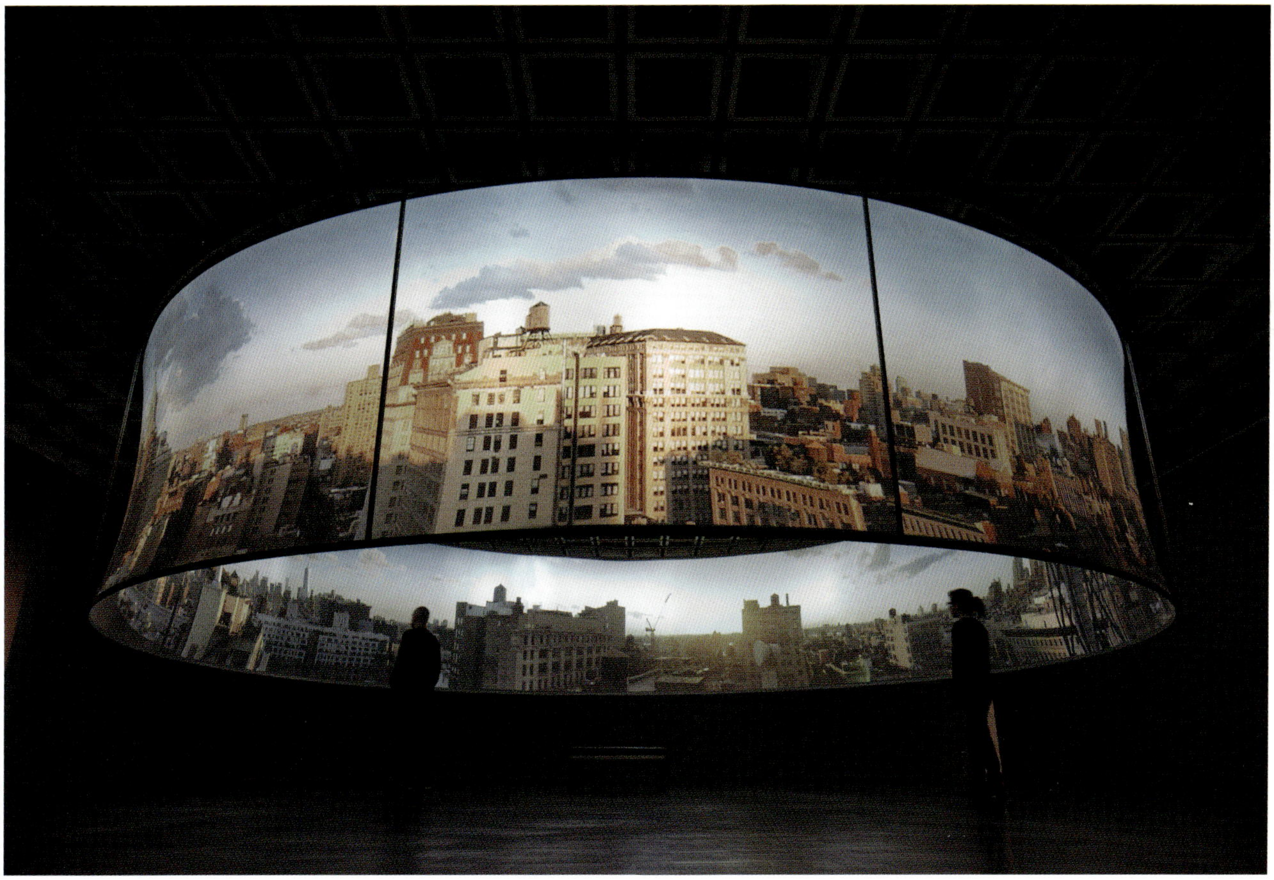

FIG. 8.11. T. J. Wilcox (American, b. 1965), *In the Air*, 2013. Panoramic film installation: Super 8 film transferred to video and HD video, black-and-white and color, silent, dimensions variable; duration: 30 minutes, 42 seconds.

as one precondition of panoramic seeing, offering riposte to earth's gravitational force and power grid—even if limitless, ungrounded, disembodying virtual or visual passage across the sky proves hubristic, an Icarus flight that crashes—homage, and epitaph, to the nineteenth-century panorama.

NOTES

1. "Ben Rose: Panoramas, New York, 1950s," 2008 exhibition, Steven Kasher Gallery, New York, www.stevenkasher.com/exhibitions/ben-rose-panoramas-new-york-1950s/featured-work?view=thumbnails.
2. See, for example, the Leyland Cheetah, Citroën U55 "Cityrama" Currus, and Greyhound Scenicruiser. The Nazis, Hartmut Bitomsky (German, b. 1942) argues in his essay film *Highways to the Third Reich* (*Reichsautobahn*, West Germany, 1985), created Germany's monumental highway system to showcase Nazi reemployment programs and to mark and reorganize the German landscape for the eye.
3. Karin Bijsterveld et al., *Sound and Safe: A History of Listening behind the Wheel* (Oxford: Oxford University Press, 2013).
4. Yet conversely, as Ulrich Giersch argues, early nineteenth-century painted panoramas had helped create the template and need for rapid transportation: "The mobilization and regulation of gazes with the help of new mass media anticipated and reflected the slightly later mobilization of bodies in the new transportation modes and routes." Giersch, "Im fensterlosen Raum—das Medium als Weltbildapparat," in *Sehsucht: Das Panorama als Massenunterhaltung des 19. Jahrhunderts*, ed. Marie-Louise von Plessen and Ulrich Giersch (Basel: Stroemfeld, 1993), 94–104; 96.
5. Dolf Sternberger, "Panorama of the 19th Century," trans. Joachim Neugroschel, *October* 4 (Autumn 1977): 10.
6. Wolfgang Schivelbusch, *The Railway Journey: The Industrialization of Time and Space in the Nineteenth Century*, trans. Anselm Hollo (Berkeley: University of California Press, 1986), 66; emphasis in original.
7. Renzo Dubbini, *Geography of the Gaze: Urban and Rural Vision in Early Modern Europe* (1994), trans. Lydia G. Cochrane (Chicago: University of Chicago Press, 2002), 175. Yet the 1883 Crystal Palace display of Paul Philippoteaux's painted Electric Railway Panorama implicitly competed with railroad-themed rides (London's Great Centrifugal Railway, opened 1842; the Crystal Palace's own switchback railway "panorama" roller coaster, opened 1888). Ana Parejo Vadillo and John Plunkett, "The Railway Passenger and the Training of the Eye," in *The Railway and Modernity: Time, Space and the Machine Ensemble*, ed. Matthew Beaumont and Michael Freeman (Oxford: Peter Lang, 2007), 45–68; 61.
8. Edgar Degas, cited in Jonas Beyer, "Movement and Language," in Jodi Hauptmann, *Degas: A Strange New Beauty* (New York: MoMA, 2016), 176–201; 178.
9. Pierre Bonnard, *Sketches of a Journey: Travels in a Motorcar from Octave Mirabeau's Journal "La 628-E8"* (London: Philip Wilson, 1989).
10. In *Impala* (1968, Cleveland Museum of Art) Alex Katz (American, b. 1927) divides interest between a passenger portrait and angled car windows framing yet bifurcating the view. See also Terry Herndon and Eva Herndon, *Art from the Driver's Seat: Americans and Their Cars* (Lexington, Mass.: Museum of Our National Heritage, 1993).
11. Jacques Aumont, "The Variable Eye; or, The Mobilization of the Gaze," trans. Charles O'Brien and Sally Shafto, in *The Image in Dispute: Art and Cinema in the Age of Photography*, ed. Dudley Andrew (Austin: University of Texas Press, 1997), 231–58; 238.
12. The invention of what the French dub "the traveling shot" remained controversial; Jean-Louis Comolli, "Technique and Ideology: Camera, Perspective, Depth of Field [Parts 3 and 4]" (1971–72), in *Narrative, Apparatus, Ideology: A Film Theory Reader*, ed. Philip Rosen (New York: Columbia University Press, 1986), 421–43, esp. 441–42n13.
13. William Uricchio, "A 'Proper Point of View': The Panorama and Some of Its Early Media Iterations," *Early Popular Visual Culture* 9. no. 3 (2011): 225–38; 236.
14. In early cinema, Tom Gunning stresses, the "extremely polyvalent term" *panoramas* sometimes meant "simply a broad view of a landscape from some 'panoramic' point like a high mountain," but it more often re-created "either the circular effect of the stationary panorama, or the unfolding of a mobile panorama through camera movement." Gunning, "'The Whole World within Reach': Travel Images without Borders," in *Virtual Voyages: Cinema and Travel*, ed. Jeffrey Ruoff (Durham: Duke University Press, 2006), 35. Yet see Uricchio's nuanced perspectival distinctions among painted, photographic, and filmic panoramas (including his notion that filmic panoramas remain dimensionally indebted to stereoscopic photography) in"A 'Proper Point of View.'"
15. Pathé's 1901 catalogue itself made generic distinctions between *"scènes panoramiques du plein air"* and *"vues panoramiques circulaires."* Uricchio, "A 'Proper Point of View,'" 233.
16. See Hsiao-Hsien's *Dust in the Wind* (Taiwan, 1996) and its lateral train views surveying Taiwanese modernity; Kiarostami's Tehran car traverses; Keiller's *City of the Future* installation and DVD; Ruben Östlund's *Force Majeure* (Turist, Sweden, 2014), viewing from the ski lift; Stephanie Spray and Pacho Velez's ethnographic documentary *Manakamana* (Nepal/U.S., 2013), whose cable-car pilgrimages offer mesmerizing glimpses of Nepal's traditions and multifaceted present; and Jarmusch's *Paterson* (U.S., 2016), which follows a poet–bus driver's daily route.
17. Steffen Spiegel, ed., *First Exposures: Writings from the Beginnings of Photography* (Los Angeles: Getty Museum, 2017), 40.
18. "Daguerre's Invention Pertaining to the Fixing of Light," *Allgemeine Zeitung*, January 21, 1839; and Samuel Morse, "The Daguerrotipe," *New-York Observer*, April 20, 1839, quoted in Spiegel, *First Exposures*, 53–54; 85–87.
19. Dimitrios Latsis, "The City View(ed): Muybridge's Panoramas of San Francisco and Their Afterlives in Early Cinema," in *The Image in Early Cinema: Form and Material*, ed. Scott Curtis, Philippe Gauthier, Tom Gunning, and Joshua Yumibe (Bloomington: Indiana University Press, 2018), 205.
20. David Harris, "Eadweard Muybridge and the Photographic Panorama of San Francisco, 1850–1880," in David Harris with Eric Sandweiss, *Eadweard Muybridge and the Photographic Panorama of San Francisco, 1850–1880* (Cambridge: MIT Press, 1993), 40–41. In contrast, Thomas Girtin (British, 1775–1802) made painstaking efforts to preserve coherent perspective in his painted *Eidometropolis* panorama, even at the price of obscuring popular landmarks. Greg Smith, "The 'Connoisseur's Panorama': Thomas Girtin's *Eidometropolis* (1801–1803) and a New Visual Language for the Modern City," *British Art Studies* 10 (Autumn 2018), https://www.britishartstudies.ac.uk/issues/issue-index/issue-10/girtin-panorama.
21. Rebecca Solnit, *River of Shadows: Eadweard Muybridge and the Technological Wild West* (Harmondsworth, U.K.: Penguin, 2003), 161.
22. Uricchio, "A 'Proper Point of View,'" 234–35.
23. S. Svidel, "Объем и Линии: Заметки о Панорамной съемке," *Sovetskoe foto* 2 (1934): 32–33. Svidel instances his own photopanorama of Crimea's Vorontsov Palace, which shows, within a single image, a group of tourists and then, turning, the space they are observing. But

he also warns against the use of panoramic photography to falsify facts, such as a panoramic photograph that repeatedly captures the same five workers over the course of unloading a wharf, which makes it seem that many more workers are present (32).

24. Martha A. Sandweiss, *Print the Legend: Photography and the American West* (New Haven: Yale University Press, 2002), chap. 2, esp. 77. On the long tradition of panorama painters embarking on extensive research tours, see Veronica della Dora, "Putting the World into a Box: A Geography of Nineteenth-Century 'Travelling Landscapes,'" *Geografiska Annaler, Series B: Human Geography* 89, no. 4 (2007): 298–300.
25. Max Bernstein, "Von einem Panorama," *Die Kunst für alle*, 2, no. 7 (1886–87): 109.
26. Although some French artists moved fluidly among painting, photography, and lithography, Langlois relied on his assistant's superior photographic expertise. Yet when the assistant wished to publish some resulting photographs, Langlois threatened legal action. For the "famed panorama entrepreneur" such photographs were not autonomous artworks but "a unique source of information to which other artists were not privy; as the building blocks of his panorama's landscape, akin to preparatory drawings, they needed to be protected from careless dissemination." Katie Hornstein, *Picturing War in France, 1792–1856* (New Haven: Yale University Press, 2017), 139.
27. Oliver Grau, *Virtual Art: From Illusion to Immersion*, trans. Gloria Custance (Cambridge: MIT Press, 2003), 114–15.
28. Chris Brenneman and Susan Boardman, *The Gettysburg Cyclorama: The Turning Point of the Civil War on Canvas* (El Dorado Hills, Calif.: Savas Beatie, 2015), 16–17.
29. Nick Meers, *Stretch: The World of Panoramic Photography* (Mies, Switzerland: RotoVision, 2003), 24.
30. See also Michael Charlesworth, "Thomas Sandby Climbs the Hoober Stand: The Politics of Panoramic Drawing in Eighteenth-Century Britain," *Art History* 19, no. 2 (1996): 247–66.
31. United States Geological Survey Bulletin 657, James W. Bagley's *The Use of the Panoramic Camera in Topographic Surveying, with Notes on the Application of Photogrammetry to Aerial Surveys* (Washington, D.C., 1917), offers a short history of the use of panoramic photography in surveying; it also describes the methods developed by the U.S. Geographic Survey in Alaska, where the vastness of the territory to be mapped and the shortness of the summers made panoramic photography invaluable as an aid to detailed mapmaking. Richard E. Schneider, "Hidden Treasure: Panoramas of the Alaska Territory by Topographers with the United States Geological Survey (1910–1932)," *Panorama (International Panorama Council Journal)* 1 (2017): 27–34. As early as the 1860s and 1870s, during government geological surveys of the American West, Timothy O'Sullivan and William Bell had made panoramic photographs, although their precise intentions remain unclear. Joel Snyder, "Photographic Panoramas and Views," in *One/Many: Western American Survey Photographs by Bell and O'Sullivan* (Chicago: Smart Gallery, 2006), 31–38. From 1894 to 1928, Chicago's Sanitation Department commissioned almost 22,000 photographs (mostly panoramic), recording the erection of the Chicago Drainage Canal and the reversal of the Chicago River. Richard Cahan and Michael Williams, *The Lost Panoramas: When Chicago Changed Its River and the Land Beyond* (Chicago: CityFiles Press, 2011). During World War I, finally, the British army (like other combatant armies) photographed several hundred panoramas of trenches and battlefields, full of tactically vital information and thus officially classified and unpublished. Now housed in the Imperial War Museum, London, they remain a major untapped source for military historians. Peter Barton, *The Battlefields of World War I: The Unseen Panoramas of the Western Front* (London: Constable, 2005).
32. Felice Beato sometimes collaborated with his brother and fellow photographer Antonio (Italian-British, 1835–1906) under the shared artistic name of Felice Antonio Beato; which brother actually photographed a given image often remains opaque.
33. Thomas Richards, *The Imperial Archive: Knowledge and the Fantasy of Empire* (London: Verso, 1993).
34. Wu Hung, "Reading Early Photographs in China," in *Brush and Shutter: Early Photography in China*, ed. Jeffrey W. Cody and Frances Terpak (Los Angeles: Getty Research Institute, 2011), 9; see also David Harris, *Of Battle and Beauty: Felice Beato's Photographs of China* (Santa Barbara: Santa Barbara Museum of Art, 1999).
35. James R. Ryan, *Picturing Empire: Photography and the Visualization of the British Empire* (Chicago: University of Chicago Press, 1987), 74, 92.
36. See *Bird's Eye View of Karachi* (1900, including *Artillery Lines* plate); *Bridge over the Indus at Kotri*, from the public works engineer P. J. Corbett's album *Famine Camp Views in the Poona District and Canal Construction Scenes in Sindh* (both British Library).
37. Narayani Gupta, "Pictorializing the 'Mutiny' of 1857," in *Traces of India: Photography, Architecture, and the Politics of Representation, 1850–1900*, ed. Maria Antonella Pelizzari (New Haven: Yale University Press, 2003), 216–39, esp. 232–36. On the complexity of colonial Indian panoramic photographs, see John Falconer, "The Appeal of the Panorama," in *India through the Lens: Photography, 1840–1911*, ed. Vidya Dehejia (Washington, D.C.: Freer Gallery/Smithsonian, 2000), 34–67.
38. Janet Dewan, *Linnaeus Tripe: Photographs of Burma and Madura in the 1850's* (Toronto: Art Gallery of Ontario, 1995); and Roger Taylor and Crispin Branfoot, *Captain Linnaeus Tripe, Photographer of India and Burma, 1852–1860* (Washington, D.C.: National Gallery of Art, 2014).
39. Janet Dewan, "'This Noble Triumph of Photography': Linnaeus Tripe's Thanjavur Inscription Panorama," in Pelizzari, *Traces of India*, 140–53.
40. Christopher Pinney, "'Buddhist' Photography," in *The Marshall Albums: Photography and Archeology*, ed. Sudeshna Guha (London: Alkazi Collection of Photography, 2010), 178–200.
41. Kathleen Stewart Howe, *Revealing the Holy Land: The Photographic Exploration of Palestine* (Santa Barbara: Santa Barbara Museum of Art, 1997), 29–46.
42. C. R. Ashbee, ed., *Jerusalem, 1918–1920: Records of the Pro-Jerusalem Council* (London: John Murray, 1921), pl. 42–43, and *Jerusalem, 1920–22* (London: John Murray, 1924), pl. 42–43; and Adina Hoffmann, *Till We Have Built Jerusalem: Architects of a New City* (New York: Farrar, Straus & Giroux, 2016), 7–8.
43. Diana Edkins, "An Introduction to Panoramic Photography," in *Panoramic Photography* (New York: Grey Gallery NYU, 1977), 2–7.
44. Harris, "Eadweard Muybridge."
45. Alan Davies, curator, "A Different Perspective: Vaniman the Acrobatic Photographer," State Library of New South Wales, 2009, https://web.archive.org/web/20070219153304/http:/www.sl.nsw.gov.au/exhibitions/vaniman/. On Vaniman's early Hawaii and New Zealand photopanoramas, see *Early New Zealand Photographers and Their Successors*, online blog, http://canterburyphotography.blogspot.com/2013/11/vaniman-chester-melvin.html.
46. Solnit, *River of Shadows*, 104.
47. Ibid., 123.
48. Omar Khan, *From Kashmir to Kabul: The Photographs of John Burke and William Baker, 1860–1900* (Munich: Prestel, 2002).
49. The French panoramic photographer Désiré Charnay (1828–1915) had previously photographed Yucatán ruins. Keith F. Davis, *Désiré Charnay, Expeditionary Photographer* (Albuquerque: University of New Mexico Press, 1981); *Panoramas: Photographies, 1850–1950: Collection Bonnemaison* (Arles: Actes Sud, 1989), 181–85.

50. Laurence Gustave Desmond and Phyllis Mauch Messenger, *A Dream of Maya: Augustus and Alice Le Plongeon in Nineteenth-Century Yucatan* (Albuquerque: University of New Mexico Press, 1988), title page, 71; and Desmond, *Yucatán through Her Eyes: Alice Dixon Le Plongeon, Writer and Expeditionary Photographer* (Albuquerque: University of New Mexico Press, 2009), 188–89, 202–3.
51. By the early twentieth century, panoramic cameras were available to amateur photographers (Czarina Alexandra used one to take family snapshots). A 1912 panorama camera was even designed to take aerial shots strapped to homing pigeons. Jonathan Bayer, "The Panoramic Image in Photography," in *The Panoramic Image*, by John Sweetman et al. (Southampton, U.K.: John Hansard Gallery, 1981), 27–32.
52. Marc Ferrez, Brazil's pioneering photopanoramist (and color photographer), worked on official documentary projects for the Imperial Navy and the Geological Commission, photographing landscapes, cityscapes, train lines, and tunnels. Sérgio Burgi, "From National to Manade: Rio de Janeiro in the Photographs of Marc Ferrez," in Marc Ferrez and Robert Polidori, *Rio*, 2 vols. (Göttingen: Steidl/Instituto Moreira Salles, 2015), 1:234–43; and Burgi, *Marc Ferrez: Fotografias de Brasil, 1860–1920* (Buenos Aires: Ediciones Larivière, 2011), 14–17. Following the tradition of Dutch colonial representations, Ferrez's Rio photopanoramas frame the city for European viewers. Benjamin Moser, "Dreaming Up Rio," *New York Review of Books*, August 11, 2016, https://www.nybooks.com/daily/2016/08/11/dreaming-up-rio-marc-ferrez-belle-epoque-photographs/. Yet they also evoke Rio's underlying rawness, newness, and emptiness—direct results of the city's violent modernization process.
53. Such images extend the logic of the painted panorama of Guangzhou (exhibited in London in 1837), which prepared the British public for the ensuing Opium Wars, "for military confrontations with a distant culture that implicitly threatened British colonial supremacy in East Asia." Jeffrey W. Cody and Frances Terpak, "Through a Foreign Glass: The Art and Science of Photographs in Late Qing China," in Cody and Terpak, *Brush and Shutter*, 58.
54. Ibid., 60.
55. Ibid., 56–57; and Hung, "Reading Early Photographs," 10.
56. Phyllis Lambert, foreword to Harris with Sandweiss, *Eadweard Muybridge*, 11–12. See also Esra Akcan, "Off the Frame: The Panoramic Albums of Istanbul," in *Photography's Orientalism: New Essays on Colonial Representation*, ed. Ali Behdad and Luke Gartlan (Los Angeles: Getty Research Institute, 2013), 93–114.
57. Deepali Dewan and Deborah Hutton, *Raja Deen Dayal: Artist-Photographer in Nineteenth-Century India* (Hyderabad: Mapin Publishing, 2013).
58. "Holtermann Panorama," *Picture Paradise Asia—Pacific Photography, 1840s–1940s*, National Gallery of Art, Canberra, http://nga.gov.au/Exhibition/PICTUREPARADISE/pdf/Holtermann.pdf.
59. Solnit, *River of Shadows*, 159, 170.
60. Antonio Costa, "Landscape and Archive: Trips around the World as Early Film Topic (1896–1914)," in *Landscape and Film*, ed. Martin Lefebvre (New York: Routledge, 2007), 245–66.
61. Quoted in Paul Virilio, "The Last Vehicle," in *Polar Inertia*, trans. Patrick Camiller (London: Sage Publications, 2000), 19; emphasis in original.
62. Biograph's 1902 catalogue distinguished "railroad" films (focused on motion itself) from "scenic" (scenery-focused) films; by 1907 the scenic subsumed the railroad category. Jennifer Lynn Peterson, *Education in the School of Dreams: Travelogues and Early Nonfiction Films* (Durham: Duke University Press, 2013), 79–81.
63. See J. C. Lamster, *Tocht per auto door Weltevreden* (Holland, shot 1912, released 1923); *Molens van de Zaanstreek* (British Mutoscope and Biograph/Nederlandsche Biograaf in Mutoscope, 1898); several *Reis langs de Staats-Spoorwegen op Java* films (Holland, ca. 1920–23) showcase different train lines, intertitles offering train bridge statistics; Dutch East Indies Subcollections, www.eyefilm.nl/en/collection/search-and-watch/subcollections/dutch-east-indies. *A Trip on the Metropolitan Railway* (Britain, 1910) focused on railroad infrastructure (station platforms, bridges); the Swiss Alps phantom ride *From Spiez to Löschberg* (Eclipse, France, 1913) foregrounded dizzying train-track vistas and industrial infrastructure (with moving tunnel and railway bridge close-ups); *Panorama von de Koninghaven te Rotterdam* (Holland, 1925) showed views of, within, and atop Rotterdam's new vertical-lift bridge. On visualizing railroad infrastructure, see Anne M. Lyden, *Railroad Visions: Photography, Travel, and Perception* (Los Angeles: Getty Museum, 2003), esp. "Bridges, Trestles, Viaducts," 37–77.
64. Lynn Kirby, *Parallel Tracks: The Railroad and Silent Cinema* (Durham: Duke University Press, 1979), 21–23. On similar symbiosis between tram and film production companies, see Ian Yearsley, "On the Move in the Streets: Transport Films and the Mitchell and Kenyon Collection," and Patrick Keiller, "Tram Rides and Other Virtual Landscapes," in *The Lost World of Mitchell and Kenyon: Edwardian Britain on Film*, ed. Vanessa Toulmin, Patrick Russell, and Simon Popple (London: BFI, 2004), 181–90, 191–200.
65. Scott MacDonald, "The Attractions of Nature in Early Cinema," in *Unseen Cinema: Early American Avant-Garde Film, 1894–1941*, ed. Bruce Charles Posner (New York: Black Thistle Press/Anthology Film Archives, 2001), 56–63.
66. Gunning, "'Whole World,'" 37–38; and Patrick Keiller, "Phantom Rides: The Railway and Early Film," in Beaumont and Freeman, *The Railway*, 69–84; 72. Some panorama films were deliberately undercranked, inducing dizzying sensations of speed or vertigo among viewers. Tom Gunning, "An Unseen Energy Swallows Space: The Space in Early Film and Its Relation to American Avant-Garde Film," in *Film before Griffith*, ed. John L. Fell (Berkeley: University of California Press, 1983), 355–66; 364.
67. British Airways news release, "Going Slow at 600mph," June 23, 2014, www.britishairways.com/pressrelease/details/86/2014-65/5174.
68. *Arab Market*, 1896; *Government Square*, 1896; *Leaving Government Square in Algiers*, 1903, all LB. On earlier painted panoramas of Algiers, see John Zarobell, *Empire of Landscape: Space and Ideology in French Colonial Algeria* (University Park: Pennsylvania State University Press, 2010), chap. 1; and Frances Terpak, "The Promise and Power of New Technologies: Nineteenth-Century Algiers," in *Walls of Algiers: Narratives of the City in Text and Image*, ed. Zeynep Çelik, Julia Clancy-Smith, and Terpak (Los Angeles: Getty Museum, 2009), 87–133.
69. Zeynep Çelik, "Historical Intersections: The Center of Algiers," in Çelik, Clancy-Smith, and Terpak, *Walls of Algiers*, 198–226.
70. Uricchio, "A 'Proper Point of View,'" 233.
71. Voice-over, *Electric Edwardians: The Lost Films of Mitchell & Kenyon* (United States: Milestone Film & Video, 2006), DVD.
72. Vanessa Toulmin voice-over, *Mitchell & Kenyon in Ireland* (British Film Institute, 2005), DVD.
73. John Widdowson, "Mitchell & Kenyon: Ceremonial Processions and Folk Traditions," in Toulmin et al., *The Lost World of Mitchell and Kenyon*, 137–49.
74. Vanessa Toulmin, *Electric Edwardians: The Mitchell & Kenyon Collection* (London: British Film Institute, 2006), 97. In H. J. Miles's "Panorama of Beach and Cliff House" (AMB, 1903), likewise, California beach strollers and wading children excitedly interact with the camera.
75. Toulmin, *Mitchell & Kenyon in Ireland*.
76. See also Theodor Fontane, *Effi Briest* (1896); Theodore Dreiser, *Sister*

Carrie (1900), and Laura Marcus, "Oedipus Express: Psychoanalysis and the Railways," in *Dreams of Modernity: Psychoanalysis, Literature, Cinema* (Cambridge: Cambridge University Press, 2014), 41–58.

77. Marta Braun, *Picturing Time: The Work of Etienne-Jules Marey (1830–1904)* (Chicago: University of Chicago Press, 1992); and Thom Andersen, *Eadweard Muybridge, Zoopraxographer* (documentary, U.S., 1975). In turn, early phantom ride films inspired panoramic picture books like *Father Tuck's Express Train Panorama with Movable Pictures* (London: Raphael Tuck, ca. 1895).
78. Karen Beckman, *Crash: Cinema and the Politics of Speed and Stasis* (Durham: Duke University Press, 2010), 32–36, contrasts early subgenres of train and car locomotion.
79. On Japan's 1930s leftist bus films, see Sharon Hayashi, "Traveling Film History: Language and Landscape in the Japanese Cinema, 1931–1945" (Ph.D. diss., University of Chicago, 2004).
80. Uricchio, "A 'Proper Point of View,'" 235.
81. J. Hoberman, *Bridge of Light: Yiddish Film between Two Worlds* (Hanover, N.H.: Dartmouth College Press, 2010), 13–14, details the film's odd posterity. Touring the Pale of Settlement in 1898 to exhibit Lumière films, and noting intense interest in the Dreyfus affair, Francis Doublier spliced a French military parade, Paris street footage, Finnish barge footage, and a "panorama of the Nile delta" into a pseudo-actuality about Dreyfus's arrest and captivity.
82. *Barcelone: Panorama du port* (LB, 1896) likewise moves down stone embarkation steps into the river.
83. Gunning, "'Whole World,'" 36.
84. Cited in Nanna Verhoeff, *The West in Early Cinema: After the Beginning* (Amsterdam: Amsterdam University Press, 2006), 283.
85. Daisuke Miyao, "Japonisme and the Birth of Cinema: A Transmedial and Transnational Analysis of the Lumière Brothers' Films," *Journal of Japonisme* 1 (2016): 71–72.
86. Gunning, "'Whole World,'" 36.
87. See Edgar Degas, *Place de la Concorde* (1875, Hermitage Museum, St. Petersburg); Pierre Bonnard's *Nannies' Promenade, Frieze of Carriages* (lithograph, 1899, Museum of Modern Art, New York); and lithographs by Édouard Vuillard (French, 1868–1940), including *Le Jardin des Tuilleries* (1896) and *L'avenue* (1899), both National Gallery of Art, Washington). Dorothy Kosinski and Elizabeth C. Childs, *The Artist and the Camera: Degas to Picasso* (Dallas: Dallas Museum of Art, 1999); and Elizabeth Easton, ed., *Snapshot: Painters and Photography, Bonnard to Vuillard* (New Haven: Yale University Press, 2009).
88. On the confluence of expositions, balloon rides, panoramic views (and photography), see Anders Ekström, "Seeing from Above: A Particular History of the General Observer," *Nineteenth-Century Contexts* 31, no. 3 (2009): 185–208.
89. Peter Otto, *Multiplying Worlds: Romanticism, Modernity, and the Emergence of Virtual Reality* (Oxford: Oxford University Press, 2011), 29–30; on "industrial films," see Peterson, *Education*, 83–84. Mitchell and Kenyon's *Messrs Lumb and Co. Leaving the Works Huddersfield* (1900) likewise opens panning across a riverside factory; Edison's 1903 *Panorama of Riker's Island, New York* and *Panorama Water Front and Brooklyn Bridge* combine shoreline views with industrial operations and infrastructure (pile drivers processing landfill, steam shovels unloading barges, warehouses, bridges, boats).
90. For MacDonald, Niagara Falls films like *Panoramic View of Niagara Falls* (1903, AMB) by F. S. Armitage (American, 1874–1933) and *Circular Panorama of Horse Shoe Falls in Winter* (Edison, 1904), demonstrating the falls' immensity, recall Frederic Church's paintings and nineteenth-century moving river panoramas. MacDonald, "Attractions of Nature," 57–58.
91. Bitzer, *Panorama from Tower of Brooklyn Bridge* (AMB, 1903); *Panorama from the Times Building* (AMB, 1905) by Wallace McCutcheon (American, 1858 or 1862–1918).
92. Keiller, "Tram Rides."
93. *Panorama of Wreckage of Waterfront, Bird's-Eye View of Dock Front Galveston, Panorama of Galveston Powerhouse, Panorama of Orphans' Home Galveston*, and *Panorama of Tremont Hotel Galveston* (all Edison, 1900) describe Texas cyclone destruction (including an orphanage whose inhabitants died). Whereas *Panoramic View of the President's House at Canton, Ohio* (Edison, 1901) shows crowds gathered to view President McKinley's body, stock and panorama shots in *Execution of Czolgosz with Panorama of Auburn Prison* (Edison, 1901) chronicle the execution of McKinley's assassin. Mitchell and Kenyon's *Panorama of Queenstown Harbor* (1902) shows an emigration ship departing County Cork, Ireland; *Panorama of Flatiron Building* (1902) shows New York's recently opened Fuller Building; *Panorama, Union Square, San Francisco* (AMB, 1903) shows President Theodore Roosevelt dedicating San Francisco's George Dewey Memorial (Spanish-American War); *Panorama of Nob Hill and Ruins of Millionaire Residences* (Edison, 1904) and *San Francisco after the Earthquake and Fire of 1906* and *Exploded Gas Tanks, U.S. Mint, Emporium and Spreckels Building* (Edison, 1906) show post-earthquake ruins. For the competing cluster of San Francisco earthquake panoramic films, see Lauren Rabinowitz, "1906: Movies and Spectacle," in *American Cinema, 1890–1909: Themes and Variations*, ed. André Gaudreault (New Brunswick, N.J.: Rutgers University Press, 2009), 158–78.
94. See *Panorama of the Eiffel Tower; Panoramic View from the Eiffel Tower, Ascending and Descending* (*Scene from Tower of the Ascending Elevator*), *Panorama of the Moving Boardwalk* (Paris Exposition), *Panorama of the Paris Exposition from the Seine, Panoramic View of the Champs-Élysées, Panoramic View of the Place de la Concord* [*sic*], *Panorama of the Place de l'Opéra* (all Edison, 1900, directed by James H. White, Canadian-American, 1872–1944); Buffalo's Pan-American Exposition films (all Edison, 1901); *Circular Panorama of Electric Tower*, Edwin S. Porter's *Panorama of the Esplanade at Night, Panoramic View of Electric Tower from a Balloon* (whose camera, despite its title, tilts from ground level); *Panoramic View of the Charleston Exposition* (Edison, 1902); *Official Opening of the Cork Exhibition* (Mitchell and Kenyon, 1902); and *Panorama of the St. Louis Exposition* (AMB, 1904).
95. Malek Alloula, *The Colonial Harem*, trans. Myrna Godzich and Wlad Godzich (Minneapolis: University of Minneapolis Press, 1986).
96. Modern amusement parks likewise stressed the electrification-speed nexus, paralleling cinematic experience. Italy's National Exhibitions occasioned new panoramic displays (Battle of Sevastapol, Milan exhibition, 1881; view of Rome, Turin exhibition, 1884). After 1908, the grounds of Prague's 1891 General Land Centennial Exhibit boasted a cyclorama, housing the 1898 Battle of Lipany panorama by Luděk Marold (Czech, 1865–1898), originally created for an architecture and engineering exposition. Michaela Marek, "Der Untergang tschechischer Demokratie," in *Geschichte im Rundumblick: Panoramabilder im östlichen Europa*, ed. Arnold Bartetzky and Rudolf Jaworski (Vienna: Böhlau Verlag, 2014), 91–113. New York's 1939 World's Fair featured the Perisphere (spectators on rotating balconies circled a huge globe's internal perimeter, gazing down at a futuristic 2039 world) and Futurama ("Highways and Horizons," Norman Bel Geddes, American, 1893–1958), where spectators' small cars flew and drove over futuristic cityscapes. Robert H. Kargon et al., *World's Fairs on the Eve of War: Science, Technology and Modernity, 1937–1942* (Pittsburgh: University of Pittsburgh Press, 2015), 74–75.
97. Silvia Borodini, *Storia del panorama: La vision totale nella pittura del*

XIX secolo (Rome: Officina Edizioni, 1984), 171; Emmanuelle Toulet, "Cinema at the Universal Exposition, Paris, 1900," *Persistence of Vision* 9 (1991): 10–36; Uricchio, "A 'Proper Point of View,'" 230–32; Lauren Rabinowitz, *Electric Dreamland: Amusement Parks, Movies, and American Modernity* (New York: Columbia University Press, 2012), 71–94; Thomas Kuchenbach, *Die Welt um 1900. Unterhaltungs- und Technikkultur* (Stuttgart: Metzler, 1992), 199–208; and Emmanuelle Michaux, *Du panorama pictural au cinéma circulaire: Origines et histoire d'un autre cinéma 1785–1998* (Paris: Harmattan, 1999).

98. Raymond Fielding, "Hale's Tours: Ultrarealism in the Pre-1910 Motion Picture," in Fell, *Film before Griffith*, 116–30; and Angela Miller, "The Panorama, the Cinema, and the Emergence of the Spectator," *Wide Angle* 18, no. 2 (1996): 34–69.

99. Christian Dewald and Werner Michael Schwarz, "Kino des Übergangs: Zur Archäeologie des frühen Kinos im Wiener Prater," in *Prater Kino Welt: Die Wiener Prater und die Geschichte des Kinos*, ed. Dewald and Schwarz (Vienna: Verlag Filmarchiv Austria, 2003), 10–26.

100. Ursula Storch, "Eine Reise um die Welt—Im Wiener Prater," in Dewald and Schwarz, ed., *Prater Kino Welt*, 101–25.

101. Tom Gunning, "The Cinema of Attractions: Early Film, Its Spectator and the Avant-Garde," in *Early Cinema: Space, Frame, Narrative*, ed. Thomas Elsaesser and Adam Barker (London: BFI, 2006), 56–62.

102. Kaiserpanoramas are eulogized in Walter Benjamin's *Berlin Childhood around 1900* (composed 1932–38), Max Brod's "Der Panorama" (*Über die Schönheit hässliche Bilder*, 1913), Konstantin Fedin's *Cities and Years* (1924), Hermann Broch's *The Sleepwalkers* (1931–32), Johannes R. Becher's *Farewell* (1940), and H. C. Adler's *Panorama: A Novel* (1968).

103. Braun, *Picturing Time*. On the contrast between Marey and the Lumières, see Philippe Dubois, "La question du panorama: Entre photographie et cinéma," *Cinémathèque* 4 (1993): 22–39.

104. "The Stereopticon Cyclorama," *Photogram* 2 (April 1895): 91. See also David B. Clarke and Marcus A. Doel, "From Flatland to Vernacular Relativit," in Lefebvre, *Landscape and Film*, 213–44.

105. "The Stereopticon Cyclorama," 92.

106. Auguste and Louis Lumière, "Le Photorama" (pamphlet) (Lyon: A. Storck, 1902); and G. Mareshal ("C.D."), "Le Photorama: Projections panoramiques de MM. Auguste et Louis Lumière," *La Nature: Revue des Sciences* 30 (1902): 171–74. See also "The History and the Discovery of Cinematography, http://precinemahistory.net/1895.htm; and Jean Leborgne, "L'esprit panoramique: Splendeur et décadence d'une utopie holistique" (master's thesis, Paris VIII, 2008).

107. "Le Photorama Lumière," Institut Lumière, www.institut-lumiere.org/musee/photoramas.html. Impressionist precedents include balustrade-based wide fairground views: *View of Paris from the Trocadéro* (Santa Barbara Museum of Art, 1872) by Berthe Morisot (French, 1841–1895) and Édouard Manet's *The World's Fair of 1867* (1867, Nasjonalgaleriet Oslo). Theodore Reff, *Manet and Modern Paris* (Chicago: University of Chicago Press, 1982), 36–39.

108. Peggy Roalf, ed., *Colorama: The World's Largest Photographs from Kodak and the George Eastman Collection* (New York: Aperture, 2005); and François Cheval and Gilles Mora, *La vie en Kodak: Colorama publicitaire des années 1950 à 1970* (Malakoff, France: Éditions Hazan, 2015).

109. John Belton, *Widescreen Cinema* (Cambridge: Harvard University Press, 1992); and Gabriele Jatho, ed., *70 mm: Bigger Than Life* (Berlin: Bertz + Fischer, 2009).

110. Richard Wagner to Ludwig II, May 17, 1881, in Wagner and King Ludwig II, *Briefwechsel*, ed. Otto Strobel, 5 vols. (Karlsruhe: G. Braun, 1936–39), 3:210.

111. In a 1981 essay, Farocki extols the lack of "rhetoric" in the films of Maurice Pialat (French, 1925–2003); they "never leave you observing afterwards: 'well edited' or the like. . . . That is also why his scenes do not begin with a few panorama shots to set the mood." Quoted in Rainer Knepperges, "The Green of the Green: Harun Farocki in *Filmkritik*," in *Harun Farocki: Working on the Sight Lines*, ed. Thomas Elsaesser (Amsterdam: Amsterdam University Press, 2004), 77–82; 79.

112. Elsaesser, "Making the World Superfluous: An Interview with Harun Farocki," in *Harun Farocki*, 185–86.

113. Elsaesser, "Harun Farocki: Filmmaker, Artist, Media Theorist," in *Harun Farocki*, 24–25.

114. Julien's multi-projector installations stress globalized vision: on four screens, *Fantôme Créole* (2005) partially surrounds viewers with historical images of urban Burkina Faso; in three-screen projection, *True North* (2009) illuminates a black Arctic explorer's discoveries. Herzog's five-channel, partial-surround video *Hearsay of the Soul* (2012) bookends enlargements from Hercules Segers's seventeenth-century landscape etchings with music and clips from Herzog's recent documentaries; Keiller's *Robinson Institute* (Tate Britain, 2012) inserted stills from his Robinson film trilogy into an itinerary-based installation of Tate art objects.

115. For Milan's 2015 Fuori Expo, Davide Rampello (Italian, b. 1947) created a 375-square-foot, fifteen-minute *Panorama* multimedia showcase, offering "a unitary vision" of Italian culture: a 360-degree slide show about Italian painting, food, and music, alongside wraparound cityscape and architectural views (Agrigento's Greek agora, Siena and Vigevano's Renaissance piazzas, Trieste's Piazza Unitá d'Italia, La Scala's interior) reminiscent of the Photorama and evoking the panorama's roots and continued preoccupation with public squares, theatrical self-presentation, and the underlying unity of far-flung sites.

116. Fred Turner, *The Democratic Surround: Multimedia and American Liberalism from World War II to the Psychedelic Sixties* (Chicago: University of Chicago Press, 2013), 276–89, links these to the 1955 *Family of Man* exhibition by Edward Steichen (American, 1879–1973). Edgar Reitz (German, b. 1932) exhibited VariaVision, his sixteen-screen, twenty-four-speaker, variably combined multimedia filmic-electronic music at Munich's 1965 International Traffic Exhibit, chronicled it in his film short, *VariaVision: A Filmic Perpetual Motion Machine* (West Germany, 1965), and showcased it in his fictionalized *Second Heimat* (West Germany, 1988–92, episode 11).

117. Christopher Connery, "Shanghai Waves," in Isaac Julien, *Ten Thousand Waves* (London: Victoria Miro Gallery, 2010), 6–11.

118. The New World, suggests Tatzu Nishi (Japanese, b. 1960), saw itself as a neutral space from which to look down at other places. Nishi's 2012 in situ installation *Discovering Columbus* enshrined Columbus Circle's multistory 1893 Christopher Columbus statue in a custom-built apartment, overlooking Midtown and Central Park vistas. The scaffolded staircases to this aerie evoked Robert Mitchell's famous nineteenth-century cross section of the Leicester Square panorama's staircases (see fig. 0.2).

119. In 2012 the *Song 1* installation by Doug Aitken (American, b. 1968) nightly projected music video footage onto the outer skin of Washington's circular Hirshhorn Museum (designed by Gordon Bunshaft, American, 1909–1990), turning the panorama and the museum inside out. Thanks to Caitlin Woolsey for pointing out its panoramic resonances. Kerry Brougher, "Decrystallized Music," in *Doug Aitken, Song I*, ed. Brougher (Washington, D.C.: Hirshhorn Museum, 2012), 24–30, highlights its zoetropic resonances.

RICHARD I. SUCHENSKI

9 Abel Gance's *Napoléon* and the Panoramic Impulse in Cinema

Although the subject has occupied a surprisingly marginal place within cinematic discourse, enterprising exhibitors have attempted to connect the panorama to cinema since the earliest days of film projection.[1] A large number of one- and two-shot films were produced in the 1900s with the word *panorama* in the title, and the lateral movement of the stationary camera, made possible technologically only after 1900, is to this day called a *pan*, acknowledging its debt to the late nineteenth-century moving panoramas. The 1900 Paris World's Fair even featured a demonstration of Raoul Grimoin-Sanson's "Cinéorama," a conscious attempt to construct a cinematic panorama whose visitors watched a system of ten synchronized 70mm projectors presenting images simulating air travel on a curved screen with a circumference of more than one hundred yards (fig 9.1).[2] These sorts of films were all part of what Tom Gunning dubs the "Cinema of Attractions," and, although they continued to be produced until well into the 1910s, they remained popular for only a few years.[3] By 1908 films promising panoramic views of picturesque or exotic locations had largely been supplanted by narrative films, which were then emerging as a major force. Consequently, the intersection points between the two media remained abstract and ill-defined until the connection was made explicit again during the 1950s, with the wave of different wide-screen processes, which often, from Cinerama onward, had titles suggestive of panoramas. Situated nearly halfway between these two historical junctures and anticipating later developments, Abel Gance's *Napoléon* (1927) exemplifies the tensions, contradictions, and potential aesthetic rewards of a panoramic conception of cinema.

Gance conceived his *Napoléon* project as a "giant moving fresco" that would create a new relationship between viewer and image.[4] The original plan entailed the production of a series of six three-hour films—*Arcole, 18 Brumaire, Austerlitz, Retreat from Moscow, Waterloo,* and *Sainte-Hélène*—to begin in 1782 with Napoleon as a cadet at the Royal Military Academy of Brienne and end with his 1821 death. In 1924 Gance expanded his plans even further, envisioning a series of eight linked films of 2,400 meters each; had this been realized, *Napoléon*'s projection time would have been nearly twelve hours.[5] Since the creation of the first film took three years and went heavily over budget, none of the subsequent episodes was made.[6] The finished film, *Napoléon vu par Abel Gance*, ended with the beginning of Napoleon's Italian

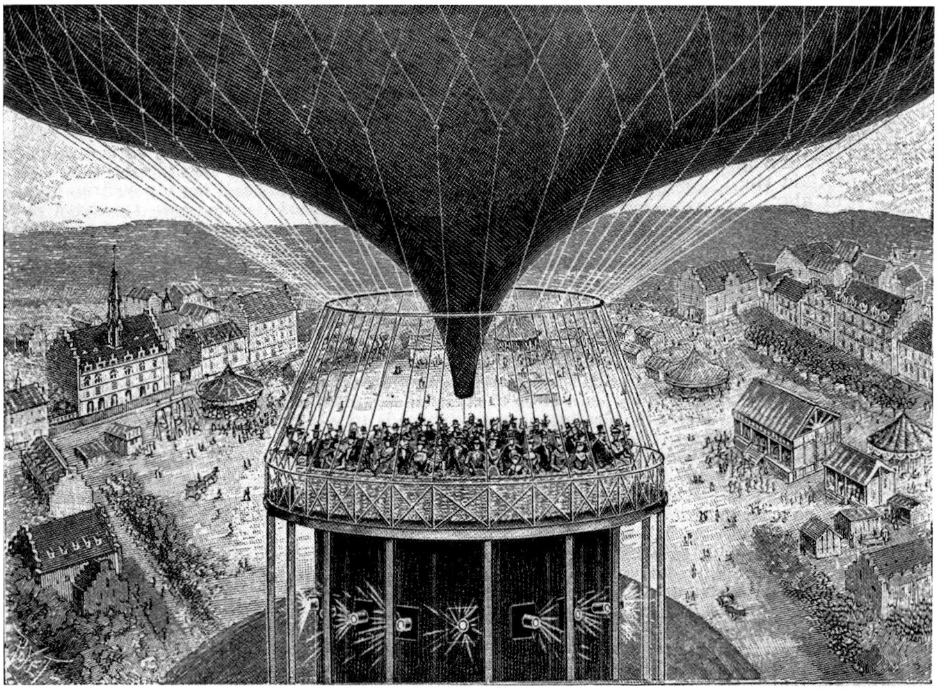

FIG. 9.1. Raoul Grimoin-Sanson's (French, 1860–1941) Cinéorama. From *Scientific American*, supplement no. 1287 (1900).

campaign and included two "triptych" sequences in which three images were projected side by side on an enormous screen.[7] As was true of the panoramas that inspired them, the triptych sequences necessitated special exhibition conditions, and the film was premiered at the Opéra de Paris on April 7, 1927, with an original Arthur Honegger score. Distributed in France and internationally in versions of various lengths, *Napoléon* was later rereleased in alternative sound versions edited by Gance himself. These re-edits, *Napoléon Bonaparte* (1935) and *Bonaparte and the Revolution* (1971), combined new footage with silent-era material and were tailored as responses to their respective historical moments; Napoleon was presented alternately as the embodiment of lost heroic virtues and as a paragon of antiestablishment revolt. Although many contemporary critics regarded them as Gance's most important innovation, none of these shortened versions included the triptychs, which were reintegrated only in 1979 with Kevin Brownlow's first restoration.[8]

Gance's introduction to *Bonaparte and the Revolution* claimed that, with D. W. Griffith's *The Birth of a Nation* (1915), *Napoléon* was one of only two *chansons de geste* in cinema history. Gance met Griffith in 1921, when he traveled to the United States to present his World War I epic, *J'accuse* (1919); Griffith helped Gance secure the film's international distribution and allegedly agreed to abandon his own Napoleon film after hearing of Gance's plans.[9] *The Birth of a Nation* and *Intolerance* (D. W. Griffith, 1916) offered Gance a model of creative ambition and scale, and though films like the Edison company's *Coney Island at Night* (Edwin S. Porter, 1905) used lateral pans as a means of sustaining interest in the gradual disclosure of an electrified amusement park, Griffith's early Biograph shorts used them to forge elegant connections between characters and their environments. *The Country Doctor* (1909) went even further, using a pair of linked, nearly 180-degree movements to frame the human action, discovering the narrative subject only at the end of the minute-long, left-to-right panning shot opening the film and closing with a right-to-left pan that returns to the original landscape. This final shot bears eloquent witness to the spontaneously captured "wind in the trees" that Griffith later described as early cinema's signature achievement and gives the film structural coherence, linking both contingent and planned elements to a single formal device.[10] Implicitly evoking panoramic viewing's slowly shifting spatial perception, Griffith's matched panning movements simultaneously open up and close off *The Country Doctor*'s diegetic world. By contrast, the triptych sequences used in *Napoléon vu par Abel Gance* were designed to radically alter the spectator's conception of cinematic boundaries, promising profound transformations of vision and experience.

Whatever a particular print's length or completeness, Gance's treatment of Napoleon and his era remains unabashedly Romantic. Tellingly, the director's program notes for the film begin with the assertion that "Napoleon is Prometheus."[11] In a speech to his crew at the beginning of production, he explained his overall objective in even more grandiloquent terms: "This is a film which must, and let no one underestimate the profundity of what I'm saying, a film which must allow us to definitively enter the Temple of Art through the giant gate of History."[12] *Napoléon* consists of a series of historically synoptic episodes centered on the figure of Napoleon, associated symbolically with the element of fire and his talisman, an eagle. Like Griffith, Gance attempts to authenticate his narrative by presenting actual historical documents as the basis for many key intertitles, a strategy that presumably helped justify his claim that *Napoléon* would be "the first great French historical film that could enter schools and help children understand that this was how it was, which, in the lycées and colleges, could advantageously replace studies of the emperor by Taine, Madame de Staël, or Chateaubriand."[13] This emphasis on historicity is amplified by the cinematization of iconic paintings such as Jacques-Louis David's *Death of Marat* (1793) and Antoine-Jean Gros's *Bonaparte at the Pont d'Arcole* (1796). The dramatic appearance of the names of figures like Marat, Danton, and Robespierre (the "Three Gods") serves a similar function, synechdocally connecting the film to the collective memory of the history it attempts to represent. For his part, Napoleon (Albert Dieudonné) is portrayed as the self-designated embodiment of the Revolution's principles, heroically saving France from its violent excesses.

In conflating historical process and Romantic genius, *Napoléon* owes a considerable debt to Victor Hugo, whom Gance acknowledged as a model. *La roue* (Abel Gance, 1922) was inspired by a passage from Hugo's poem "At Villequier": "Creation is a great wheel which does not move without crushing someone."[14] And *Napoléon* was influenced on several levels by Hugo's final novel, *Ninety-Three* (1874). Many of *Napoléon*'s characterizations were drawn from the novel, and Hugo's text provided the basis for two crucial scenes. A scene in which Danton speaks about the Revolution's ideals is derived from a passage linking its generative and disturbing aspects: "At the same time as it was giving off revolution, this assembly was also producing civilization. It was a furnace, but also a forge. In that vat where terror was bubbling, progress was fermenting."[15] The "Double Tempest" juxtaposing Napoleon's flight from Corsica with raging debate in the Convention also comes from Hugo:

> To be a member of the Convention was to be a wave of the ocean. And this was true of the greatest. The impetus came from above. There was in the Convention a will that was the will of all and none. This will was an idea, an indomitable and boundless idea which blew into the shadows from the heights of the sky. We call it the Revolution. When this idea passed, it pounced upon one and lifted up another; it carried this man away in foam and broke that man on the reefs. This idea knew where it was going, and drove the whirlpool before it. To impute a revolution to men is to impute the tide to the waves. . . . Truth and justice remain above revolutions like the starry sky above storms.[16]

Gance read this passage to cast and crew before he began shooting the sequence, which used a swinging camera to simulate the effect of a pendulum and which eventually became one of the two triptychs included in the version shown at the Opéra.

Many Hugo novels are animated by a panoramic impulse, an attempt to create and map out an enveloping narrative space charged with historical associations, often by providing a "total" view from a high vantage point. This impulse was thematized directly in both the "Bird's-Eye View of Paris" chapter of *Notre-Dame de Paris* (1831) and the "Top of the Dune" chapter in *Ninety-Three*. In both cases, a character ascends to the peak of an inordinately tall building and stands on a viewing platform of sorts, overlooking a large urban space that functions as a historical palimpsest. *Napoléon* deploys a similarly panoramic approach to historical representation, with "authentic" reconstructions of epochal events passing sequentially before the spectator. Gance and Hugo are also linked through their Homeric sense of narrative and their brazen, sometimes disastrously outsized artistic ambition.

In making *Napoléon*, Gance strove to create a massive film synthesizing all the arts and acting as the "Gospel of the future, a bridge of dreams leading from one era to another."[17] Earlier films such as *Mater Dolorosa* (1917), *J'accuse*, and especially *La roue* had already established Gance as a central figure in French debates over cinema's status as an art. Gance's writings frequently compared his films to symphonies and frescoes, and, like *Napoléon*, many earlier Gance works cited canonical masterworks, such as the Beethoven pieces visually "performed" in *La dixième symphonie* (1918) and the reproduction of Sandro Botticelli's *Birth of Venus* (1485) used as the backdrop for

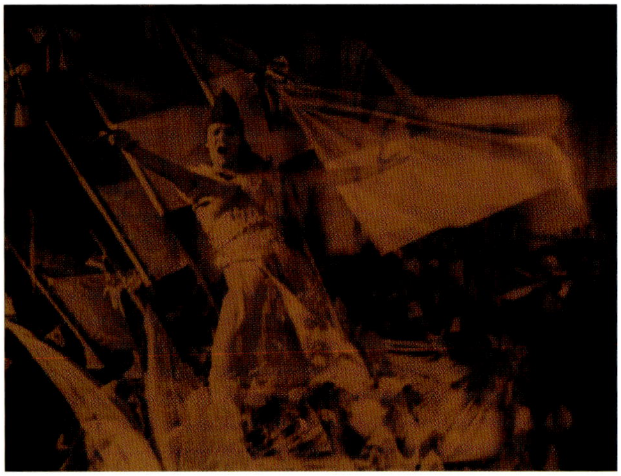

FIG. 9.2. Abel Gance (French, 1889–1981), *Napoléon*, 1927.

the allegorical "Dance of Death" sequence in *J'accuse*. For many of the era's most important theorists and critics (Louis Delluc, Émile Vuillermoz, even Gance's friend Jean Epstein), these were retrograde elements in the work of a prodigious innovator whose main achievement was his control of rhythm and the concomitant liberation of cinematic plasticity from the constraints of narrative.[18] In *La roue*, for example, Gance alternates shots of a train with increasingly brief shots of pieces of the rail and the surrounding landscape, gradually reducing the number of frames per shot until he is finally intercutting barely perceptible images. These montage bursts had an enormous influence on Gance's contemporaries and elicited rhapsodic praise from many of the artists and filmmakers interested in raising cinema's cultural status. Fernand Léger (who designed the film's poster) spoke for many of his colleagues in writing, "With *La roue*, Abel Gance has elevated the art of film to the plane of the plastic arts."[19]

Napoléon employed virtually every technique at Gance's disposal—and he invented several others, including a 360-degree camera mechanism that could be operated from a distance.[20] All these were intended to increase the viewer's affective participation, to, as Gance put it, "make the spectator become an actor . . . to involve him at every level in the unfolding of the action . . . to sweep him away on the flow of pictures."[21] Gance's objective was to enhance collective involvement in the diegetic process, and he frequently used combinations of camera movement and rapid cutting to achieve this effect, thematically connecting them to emblematic events. One striking instance is the scene in which "La Marseillaise" is first performed. Gance rhythmically alternates low-angle shots of individual figures with high-angle shots of the increasingly energized crowd. (Napoleon, having not yet "entered history," is off to the side.) The shots' length is modulated in the manner of *La roue*, as legendary characters like Danton and anonymous faces are intercut at varying speeds, steadily accumulating momentum until finally a superimposed figure representing the Revolution appears in the Convention Hall (fig. 9.2). Although the sequence includes several paroxysmic sections, the complex development of the montage also creates an impression of solidarity that includes the audience watching the film as well as the onscreen characters.

The triptych sequences in *Napoléon* fuse Gance's interest in maximizing the sensory impact of his imagery with his desire to engender a greater degree of spectatorial engagement. Gance had been experimenting with masking and screen proportions since at least 1917; his original idea was to increase the breadth of the image by deploying additional screens to the right and left of the center, creating an "*écran panoramique*."[22] Since Gance initially had no way to see what the three images would look like projected together, he concentrated on creating *triptyque-panoramas* of Napoleon's proclamations to the army in Italy and of the Battle of Montenotte. Gance was able to supplement these panoramic shots with additional triptychs created by combining images shot with a single camera, sometimes amplifying the effect with superimposition (figs. 9.3 and 9.4).

The sequence ending the film begins with Napoleon riding his white horse back and forth among the troops, his movement linking massed units of soldiers as well as the three triptych panels (fig. 9.5). These immense, detailed crowd shots, which often foreground lateral motion as a way of emphasizing their breadth, are overtly panoramic, but they are counterbalanced by triptychs operating on a more symbolic level, such as a set of marching soldier images tinted to look like a Tricolor (fig. 9.6). For the Opéra de Paris, the three images were projected together on a screen fifty feet wide by twelve and a half feet high, with apparently spectacular results.[23] "When the curtains are drawn back, opening out in the wall of the theater that immense breach of light, the effect produced is one of an astonishing power," the critic Émile Vuillermoz wrote: "Gance's triple screen . . . has allowed him to reach effortlessly the highest peaks of the lyricism of the image."[24] The art historian Élie Faure went so far to argue that the use of three images opened the cinema up to "extremely fertile territories," mounting an implicit defense of the "plastic form of film against the continuous encroachments of naturalism."[25]

Virtually all contemporary commentators, including Gance, referred to these triptychs as panoramic, but how closely did they correspond to eighteenth- and nineteenth-century panoramas? In at least one crucial respect, these images do seem more profoundly panoramic than their single-screen counterparts; as in panoramas, the image's sheer breadth makes it extremely difficult to locate the screen's boundaries, removing the trace of reality and thereby allowing for a heightened illusionism.[26] A technical director at Gaumont stressed the importance of obtaining a single unified screen to allow for the creation of a genuinely "panoramic effect."[27] Gance's aggressive editing frequently kept the triptychs from acting as a perfect substitute for the external world, but their very existence seemed to suggest new possibilities for the immersive presentation of filmed images, reinforced on the massive 130- to 145-foot-wide screens he later advocated.[28] Like

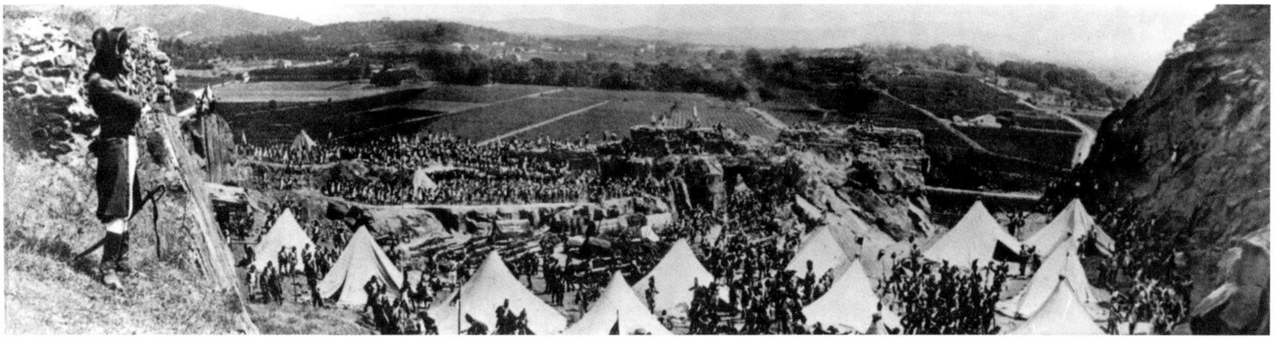

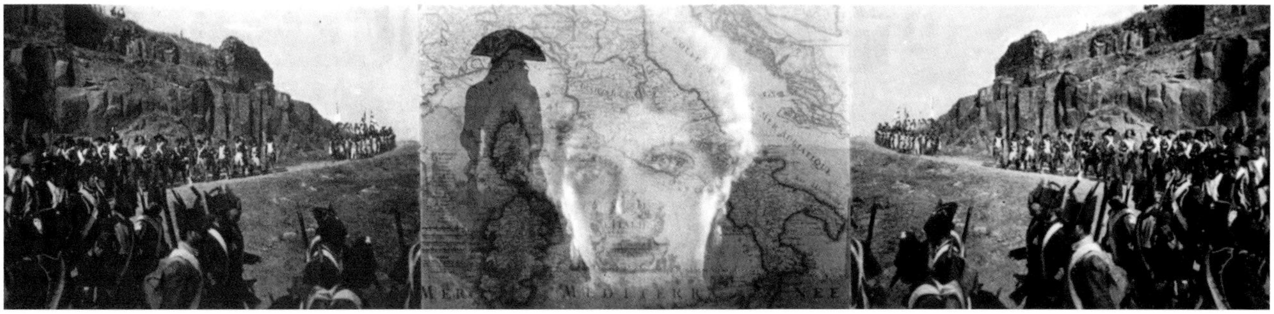

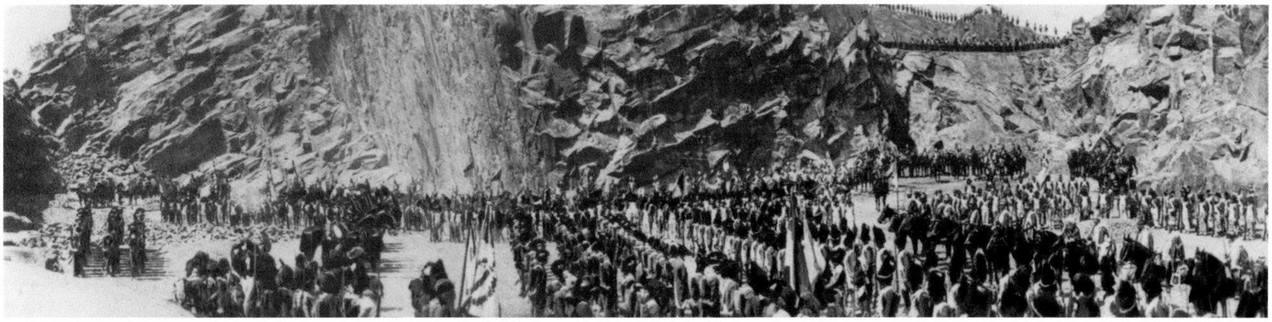

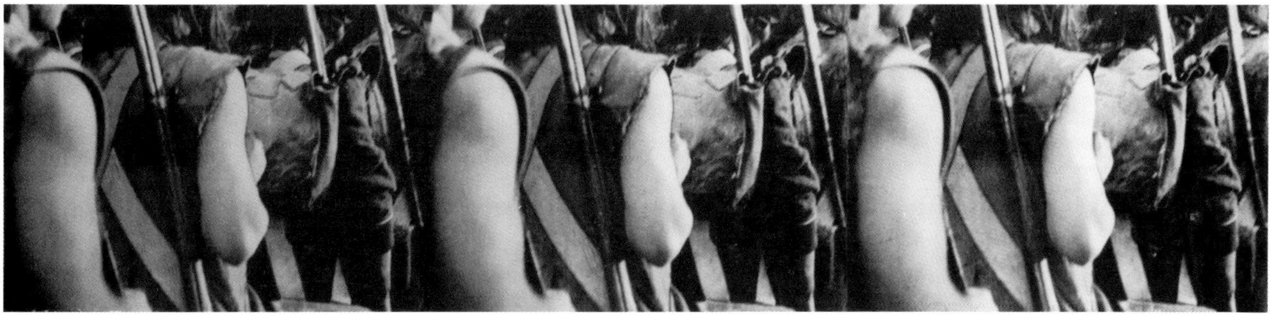

FIGS. 9.3–9.6. Abel Gance, *Napoléon*, 1927.

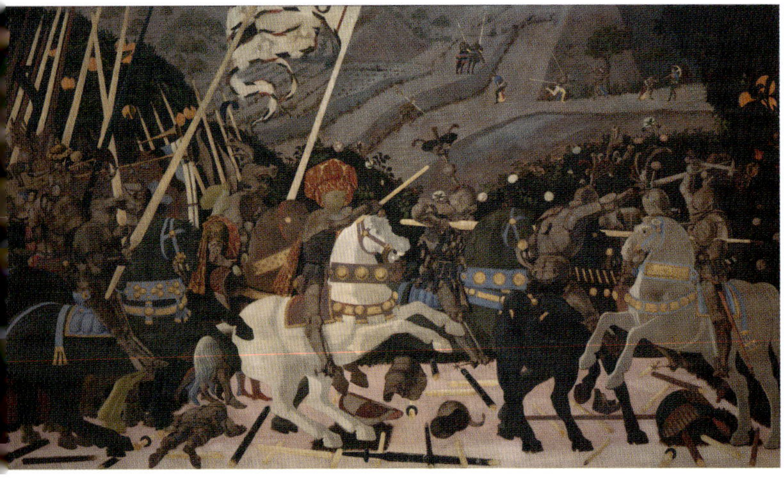

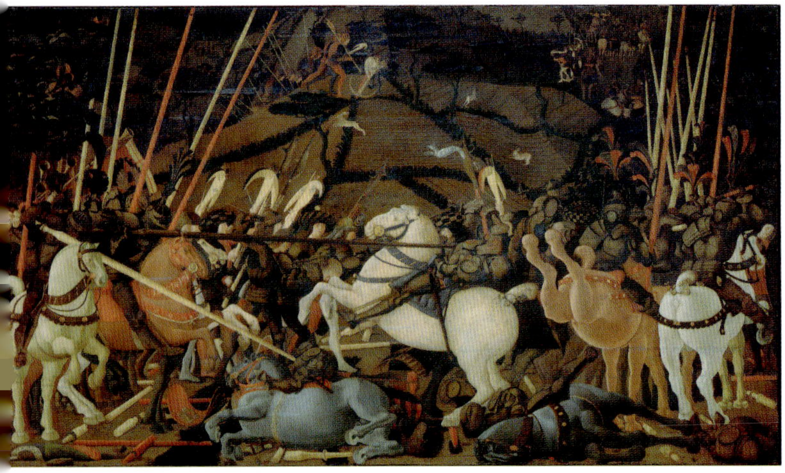

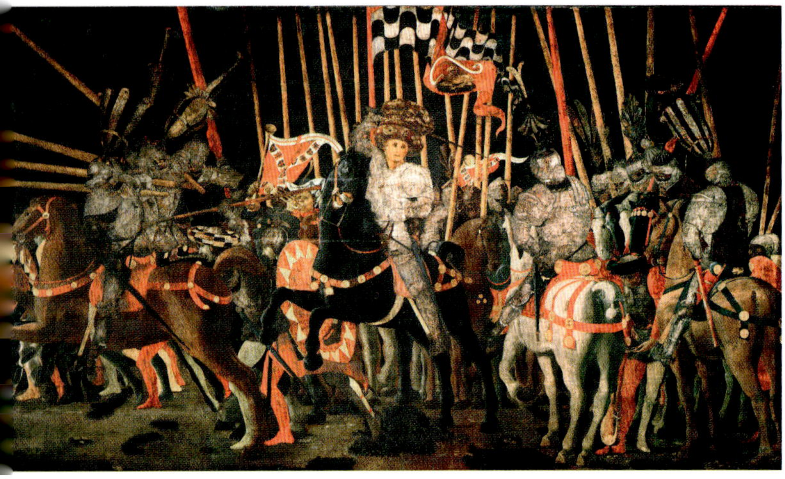

FIG. 9.7. Paolo Uccello (Italian, 1392–1475), *Niccolò Mauruzi da Tolentino at the Battle of San Romano*, ca. 1438–1440. Egg tempera with walnut oil and linseed oil on poplar, 182 × 300 cm (71 5/8 × 118 in.). National Gallery, London (NG583).

FIG. 9.8. Paolo Uccello, *Niccolò Mauruzi da Tolentino Unseats Bernardino della Ciarda at the Battle of San Romano*, 1435–55. Tempera on wood, 185 × 220 cm (72 7/8 × 86 5/8 in.). Gli Uffizi, Florence.

FIG. 9.9. Paolo Uccello, *The Counterattack of Michelotto da Cotignola at the Battle of San Romano*, ca. 1435–40. Wood panel, 182 × 317 cm (71 5/8 × 124 3/4 in.). Musée du Louvre, Paris.

painted panoramas, these projected images also include an overwhelming abundance of details, further encouraging active engagement from the viewer.

Interestingly, some of the violent Battle of Montenotte triptych images seem (perhaps unconsciously) to echo the overall formal design of Louis Dumoulin's 1912 *Battle of Waterloo*, which, Bernard Comment argues, "departs from the normal didacticism of the genre . . . with its [dramatic] array of bodies, horses, smoke, and weaponry."[29] Dumoulin's is a rare surviving panorama of a Napoleonic battle, but they were once among the medium's most popular subjects.[30] In the late 1810s two English panoramas of Waterloo, created by the competing panoramicists Henry Baker and Robert Ker Porter, both drew record-breaking crowds.[31] Pierre Prévost completed a Battle of Wagram panorama in 1810; after seeing it, Napoleon ordered seven rotundas built on the Champs-Élysées depicting the key battles of his career. A propaganda tour throughout the empire was planned, but the rising costs of war kept the project from reaching fruition.[32] After 1815, stationary war panoramas became unpopular in France, yet the first moving panoramas that traveled widely were representations of Napoleonic battles such as Ligny and Waterloo.[33] *Napoléon vu par Abel Gance* shows none of these events, but they would have featured prominently in the multipart epic Gance originally planned.

Gance differs from panoramists like Dumoulin, however, in interlinking multiple perspectives on the same battle, which suggests an affinity with contemporary practices such as Orphic simultaneity and points toward a much older antecedent, Uccello's three-panel treatment of the Battle of San Romano (1435–55) (figs. 9.7–9.9). Uccello's three paintings are now divided between London's National Gallery, Paris's Musée du Louvre, and Florence's Galleria degli Uffizi, but they were intended for display as a group, and the figures' perspectival arrangements create both geometric and metaphoric resonances between the individual scenes.[34] Similarly, Gance used the triple screen to create polyphonic arrangements of distinct but related images, the triptychs serving a musical as well as a structural function (figs. 9.10 and 9.11). As the critic Jean Arroy put it, "One imagines the composer manipulating a giant keyboard under the screen."[35] This approach's symphonic aspects are abundantly evident in the film's final few moments, in which many motifs used earlier are interlaced across the three screens, grounded by arch-Romantic images of Napoleon looking out over the foggy landscape

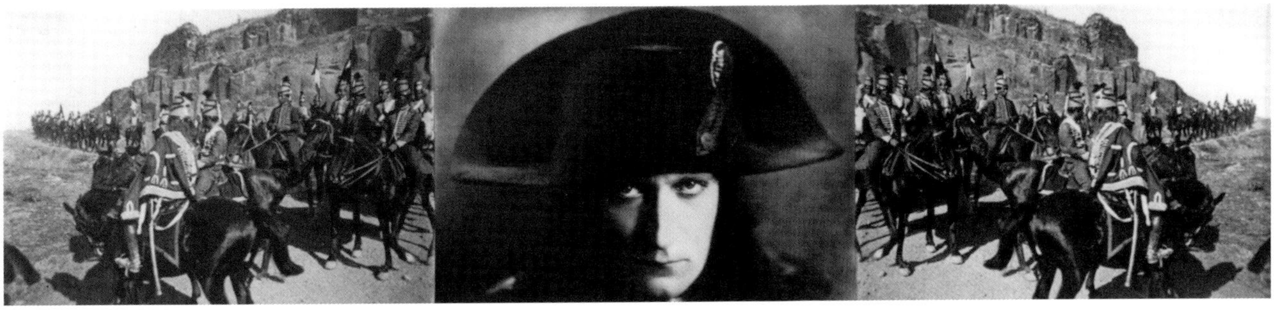
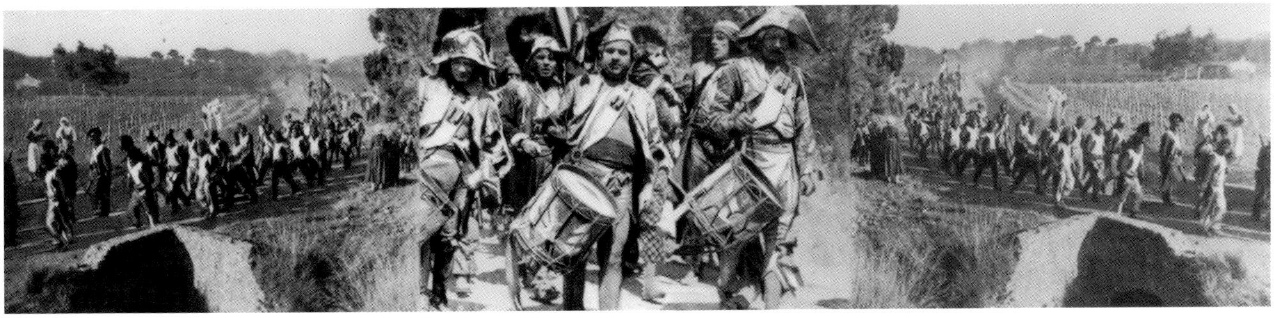
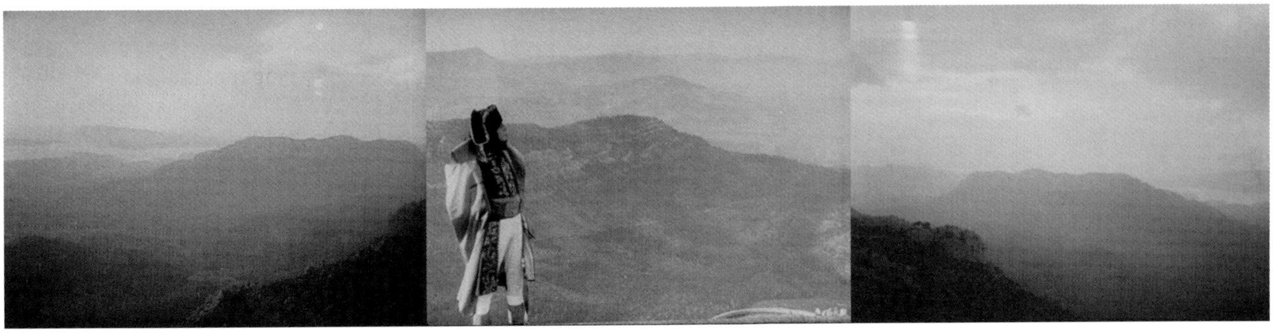

FIGS. 9.10–9.12. Abel Gance, *Napoléon*, 1927.

from a mountain peak, like the figure in Caspar David Friedrich's *Wanderer above a Sea of Fog* (ca. 1817) (fig. 9.12; compare with fig. 0.13). The orchestration of these visual elements builds in intensity until, finally, both the protagonist and the film achieve a joint apotheosis signaled by the cuts from a symbolic eagle flying across all three screens to a series of tinted images connecting Napoleon's face to Promethean flames, mathematical formulas, and the waves of history (figs. 9.13 to 9.16).

The Brownlow versions of *Napoléon* include only this one eighteen-minute triptych reel, but the premiere version included an even more radically contrapuntal triple-screen sequence, the "Double Tempest" montage derived from Hugo's *Ninety-Three*, unfortunately now lost.[36] In Albert Capellani and André Antoine's first film adaptation of Hugo's novel (*Quatre-vingt-treize*, 1914/21), the passage from which *Napoléon* originates had been condensed to a symbolic intertitle—"In Paris, summer of '93, among the tempests."[37] Gance instead used Hugo's text as the basis for an extended montage that deepens the implied relationship between the assembly's disintegration and Napoleon's absorption of its revolutionary energies.[38] The dynamic fusion of superimposition and rapid editing is most acute here, and it was even more pronounced in the original triptych, in which Gance was able to compose "a veritable apocalyptic fresco, a mobile symphony in which, with eight superimpositions per frame, there were sometimes twenty-four interconnected visions."[39] Within this maelstrom of densely layered images, movements were able to resonate with one another across all three screens, and although it would be impossible for viewers to relate all the individual fragments together, the cumulative effect must have been extraordinarily intense. This triptych would also have provided a structural echo of the final sequence, making much more apparent the fundamental interdependence of physical scale (the triple screen) and explosive plasticity within *Napoléon vu par Abel Gance*.

Technical difficulties notwithstanding, Gance believed

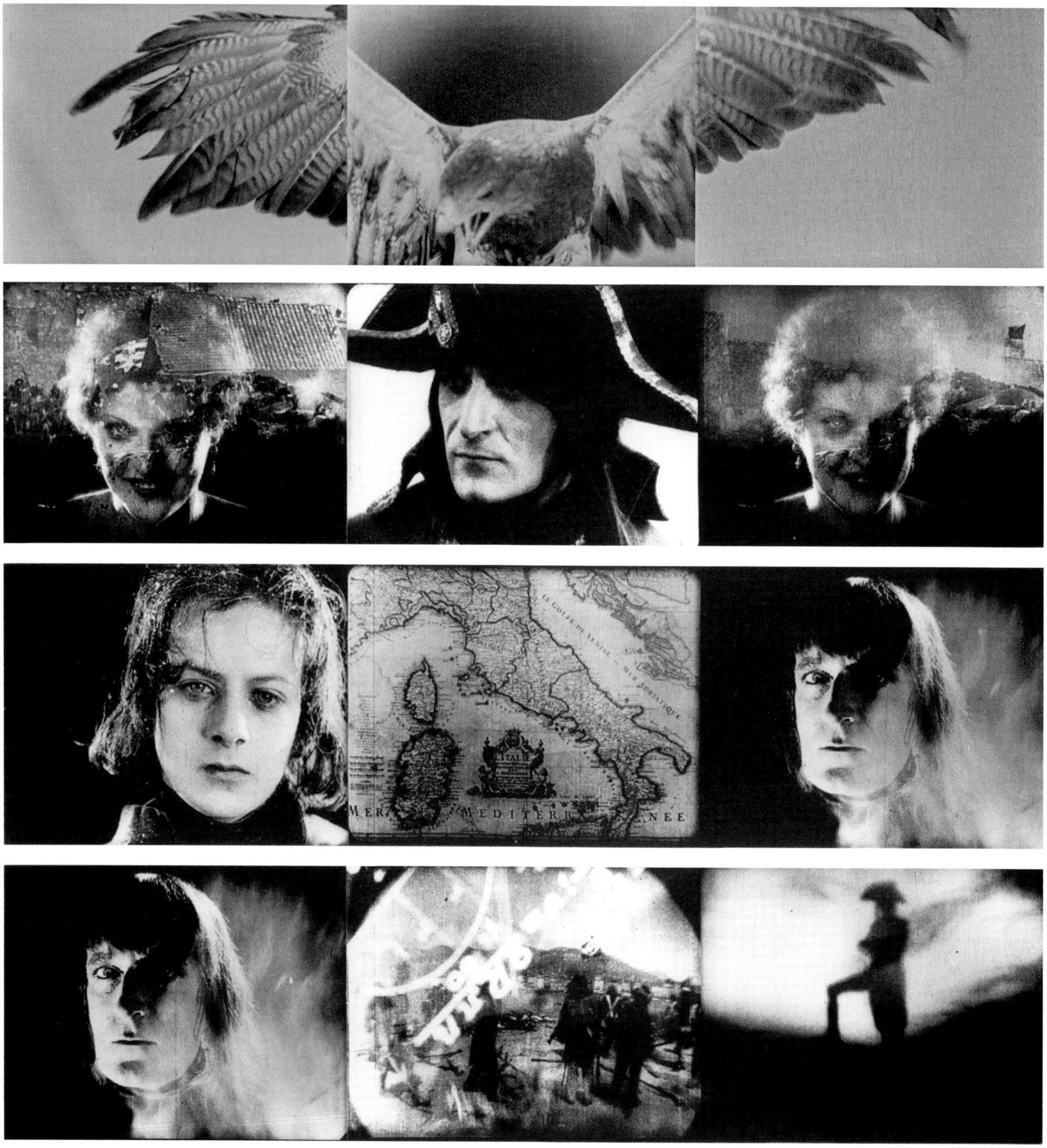

FIGS. 9.13–9.16. Abel Gance, *Napoléon*, 1927.

that the triple screen would serve as the "foundation for a new alphabet for the cinema," as he later put it.[40] In February 1928 Gance arranged for the presentation at Montmartre's Studio 28 of three new triple-screen films created from parts of *Napoléon*: *Galops* (Napoleon's horseback race through Corsica), *Danses* (the "Bal des victimes" sequence), and *Marines* (a montage of production footage and seascapes).[41] Unfortunately, since no other cinema was willing to install permanent triptych equipment, it was virtually impossible for additional films to be produced for the triple screen. Gance nevertheless planned to shoot his next film, *La fin du monde* (1931), an internationalist paean to universal brotherhood, entirely using the new technology, until financial necessity forced him to modify his plans. Undaunted, he also tried to apply it to his unrealized Passion epic, *La divine tragédie*, in the 1940s.[42]

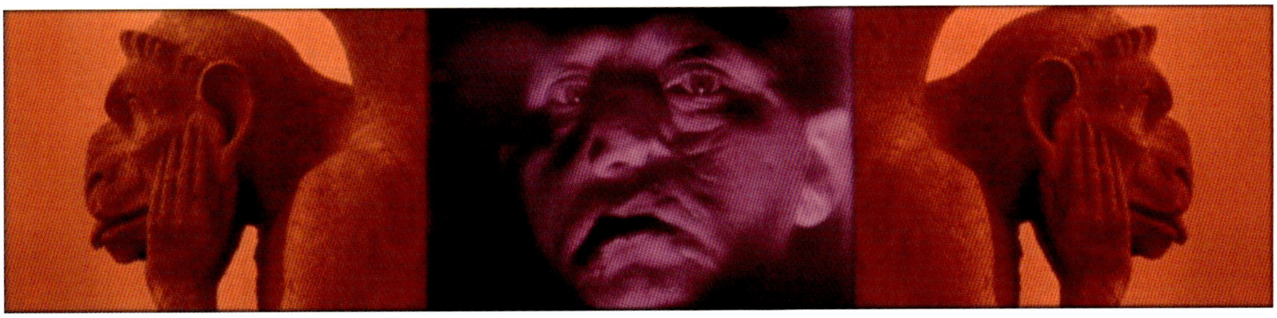

FIG. 9.17. Abel Gance and Nelly Kaplan (French, b. 1931), *Magirama (J'accuse)*, 1956.

Gance claimed to have had the original idea for a triple screen in 1922 and filed a patent for the technical innovations in 1926.[43] *Napoléon*'s triptychs inspired Henri Chrétien's complementary approach, adapting military devices he had been developing to bring "panoramic presentations" to the screen using a single projector and an anamorphic lens called the Hypergonar.[44] Yet since sound had just been introduced, both exhibitors and studios were understandably hesitant to adopt the new technology. Aside from the experimental Jack London adaptation *Construire un feu* (Claude Autant-Lara, 1930) and two short documentaries, no complete films were made and released with an anamorphic lens until, twenty-five years later, Twentieth Century Fox bought the rights to Chrétien's invention and named it CinemaScope.[45]

The Opéra premiere of *Napoléon* also influenced another even more explicitly panoramic invention: the three-projector Cinerama system developed by Fred Waller. In response to the vogue for wide-screen imagery following the international dissemination of these two processes in the early 1950s, the Cinémathèque Française's director Henri Langlois organized a special presentation of the final *Napoléon* triptych at the 1953 Venice Film Festival.

That same year, Gance wrote a short essay outlining his ideas about Polyvision and suggesting ways both panoramic and "variable" triple-screen images could be incorporated into future wide-screen films.[46] Repositioning Polyvision as the precursor to wide-screen cinema and arguing that it offered unique possibilities for expanding the horizons of vision and of art in the 1950s, Gance predicted it would "suddenly open wide the eyes of modern man who no longer believes in miracles. You only need to re-read Nietzsche's *Birth of Tragedy* (1872) to understand that the way ahead is the one I am indicating."[47] Gance never abandoned his belief in the power of the awe-inspiring image, reworking similar themes and sometimes even remaking the same films in the hopes of reaching his audience in more intense ways. In the decades following *La fin du monde*'s failure, *Napoléon* remained Gance's great obsession, but he also returned to his other silent triumphs, incorporating a new version of the rising of the dead in his 1937 sound remake of *J'accuse* and later using that reworked sequence in *Magirama* (1956), a Polyvision anthology film (fig. 9.17).[48]

Thanks largely to active self-promotion, Gance's role in the development of wide-screen aesthetics was belatedly acknowledged, but no studio in France or America was interested in converting to Polyvision. Instead, most major studios began employing their own iteration of either Cinerama or anamorphic CinemaScope. Cinerama appeared first, using synchronized projectors to combine three separate images into a composite with six times the resolution and a width-to-height ratio of approximately 2.59:1.[49] In both its means of production and its final result, Cinerama was remarkably similar to the triple-screen technique used at *Napoléon*'s Opéra premiere, but for one crucial difference: the images were projected on an enormous curved screen that could not possibly be taken in with a single view, which forced the spectator to constantly redirect focus across a panoramic field of vision (fig. 9.18).[50] Lowell Thomas, narrator and coproducer of *This Is Cinerama* (Merian C. Cooper, 1952), described the process as creating a "sweeping panorama in motion" and observed that the activation of peripheral vision strengthened the "impression of reality."[51]

By contrast, anamorphic processes like CinemaScope used special lenses, much like the Hypergonar, to stretch images during filming and expand them during projection, producing onscreen images with a width-to-height ratio of 2.55:1 (later reduced to 2.35:1). Unlike Cinerama, CinemaScope images could be shown on existing flat

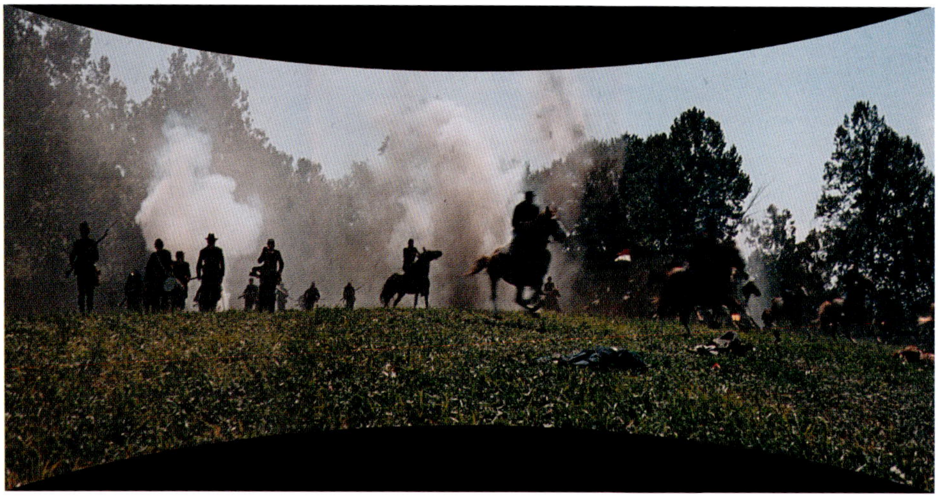

FIG. 9.18. John Ford (American, 1894–1973), *How the West Was Won: The Civil War*, 1962.

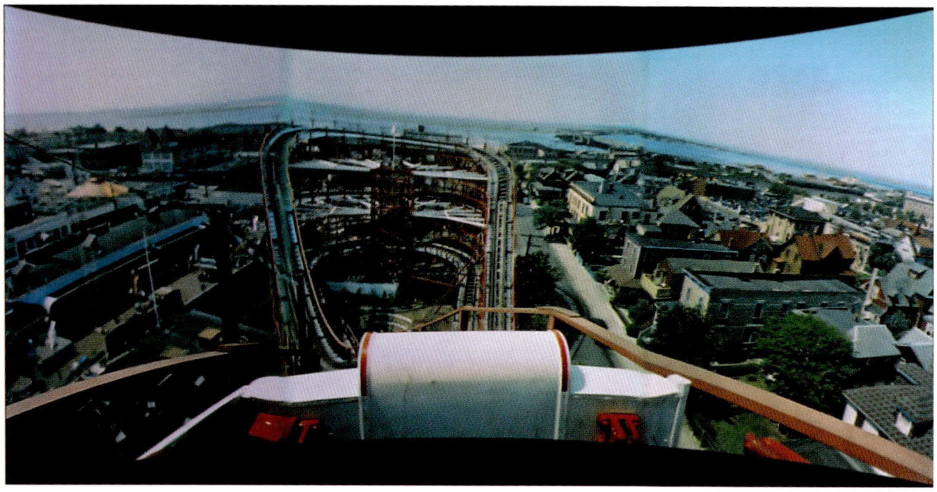

FIG. 9.19. Merian C. Cooper (American, 1893–1973), *This Is Cinerama*, 1952.

screens and, since ordinary theaters needed to replace only their projectors in order to take advantage of the process, this eventually became the standard wide-screen format. Both processes were marketed as techniques facilitating more active participation on the part of the viewer, linked with a sense of presence traditionally associated with live theater and a sense of immersion associated with panoramas.[52]

Many veteran filmmakers, such as Charles Chaplin and Yasujiro Ozu (who famously compared the increased screen space to toilet paper), distrusted wide-screen, insisting that it was useful only for spectacular, impersonal superproductions.[53] Demonstrations of related processes at the 1937 Paris Exposition (Chrétien's Hypergonar, with open-air projections of Jean Tedesco's *Panoramas au fil de l'eau* on a sixty-five-yard-wide screen in front of the Palais de la Lumière) and Disneyland (1955's Circarama, which used eleven synchronized 16mm projectors) helped create the impression that wide-screen's appeal was like a new fairground attraction, an idea borne out by films like *This Is Cinerama* (fig. 9.19).[54] Gance adeptly subverted these associations in his *Magirama* short *Une fête foraine*, juxtaposing shots of bumper cars, Ferris wheels, and roller coasters with blank leader (the contentless black film that precedes the appearance of images at the beginning of film reels), shifting light patterns, and images of various individuals, including the filmmaker, thereby demonstrating that Polyvision could transform even theme-park footage into both a formal game and a phenomenological adventure.[55]

The unbroken wide screen also opened up new compositional possibilities, and by the mid-1950s directors such as Otto Preminger and Nicholas Ray had developed a rich CinemaScope aesthetic built on composition in both width and depth. Unsurprisingly, wide-screen filmmaking's most influential defense was founded on the new format's capacity for a mise-en-scène aesthetic of increased expressivity. For André Bazin, wide-screen made it possible to perform the space-articulating functions typically associated with

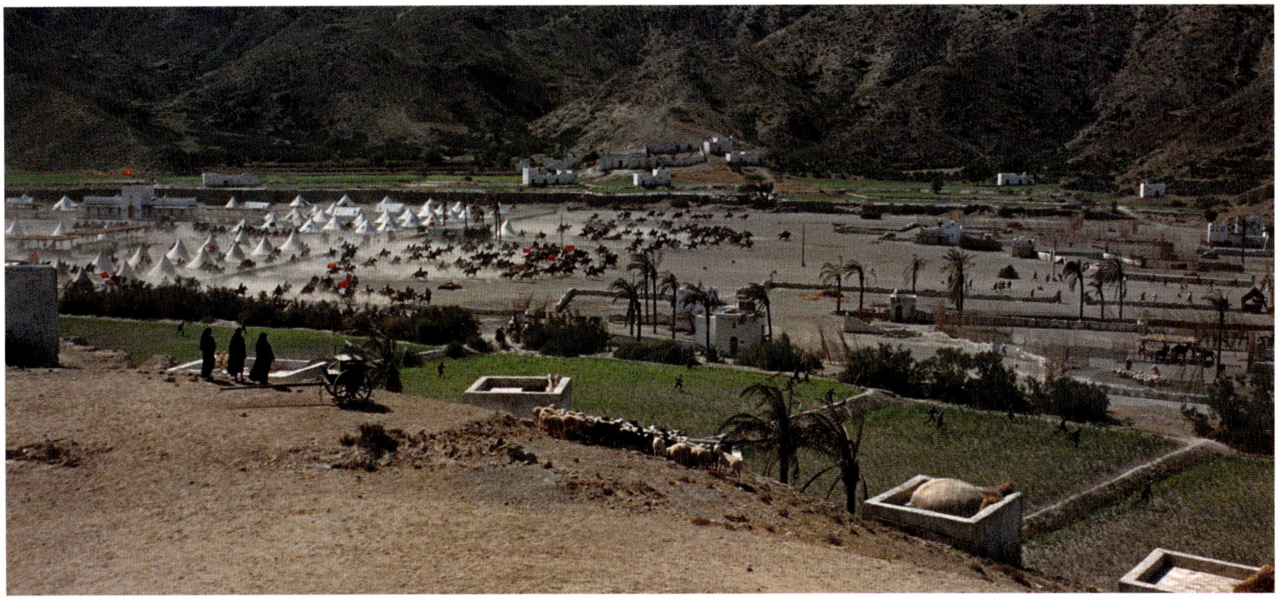

FIG. 9.20. David Lean (British, 1908–1991), *Lawrence of Arabia*, 1962.

shot/reverse shot exchanges within a single shot. This, in turn, enabled filmmakers to use longer takes, which allowed the spectator a deeper perceptual submersion and a "stripping away of everything extrinsic to the quintessential meaning of the image, of all the expressionism of time and space."[56] Elaborating on ideas developed in Bazin's essays (and echoing *This Is Cinerama*'s narrator), Charles Barr argued in 1963 that because it makes use of peripheral vision, the wide-screen image is "more vivid and involves us more directly."[57] In eliminating the need for insert shots that manipulate the viewer's gaze, the wide-screen frame presents images in a "completely natural and unforced" way that requires the viewer to "make a positive act of interpreting, or 'reading' the shot."[58]

Bazin's and Barr's enthusiasm for the new medium was predicated on a deep-seated aesthetic preference for modes of dramatic presentation unmediated by editing and for "open" compositions that encourage the viewer to scan the frame democratically. For adherents of this position, wide-screen simultaneously reified existing strategies for spatiotemporal integration (the long-take, long-shot style associated with directors such as Orson Welles and William Wyler) and activated panoramic possibilities of the film image latent in the Academy ratio. In some cases, the shots themselves simulate panoramic vision. After a major battle in *Lawrence of Arabia* (David Lean, 1962), for example, a slow lateral pan from a high vantage point follows an army's movements into the port city Aqaba (fig. 9.20). This shot structurally parallels Robert Ker Porter's famous 1800 *Storming of Seringapatam* panorama, originally shown in the Lyceum (see fig. 1.25). Porter's panorama was created to celebrate the beginnings of British imperialism in India, and the shot in *Lawrence of Arabia* seems to cite it as an ironic comment on British failures in the Middle East. Like Gance's evocation of Napoleonic battle panoramas, the shot acts as an implicit reminder of the perceptual links (and ontological differences) between nineteenth-century panoramic displays and expansive, wide-screen compositions.

The wide-screen "realism" praised by Bazinian theorists and critics in the 1950s and 1960s had been criticized by Sergei Eisenstein in his eclectic, forward-looking 1931 essay, "The Dynamic Square." Presumably responding to the 70mm Fox Grandeur version of *The Big Trail* (Raoul Walsh, 1930), Eisenstein strenuously objected to "passive horizontalism"; although wide compositions are well-suited to the "nostalgia of 'big trails' [and] 'fighting caravans,'" they are poorly equipped to articulate the verticality of modern urban environments or the overwhelming scale of architectural monuments like Gothic cathedrals.[59] For Eisenstein, the theatrical, horizontal framings that would become typical of early wide-screen filmmaking are linked to a static presentational aesthetic and are thus totally inimical to montage's perceptual dynamism. Eisenstein ends his essay on a surprisingly positive note, proclaiming that the advent of a wider screen should mark yet another stage in montage's development, providing viewers "with a gigantic new

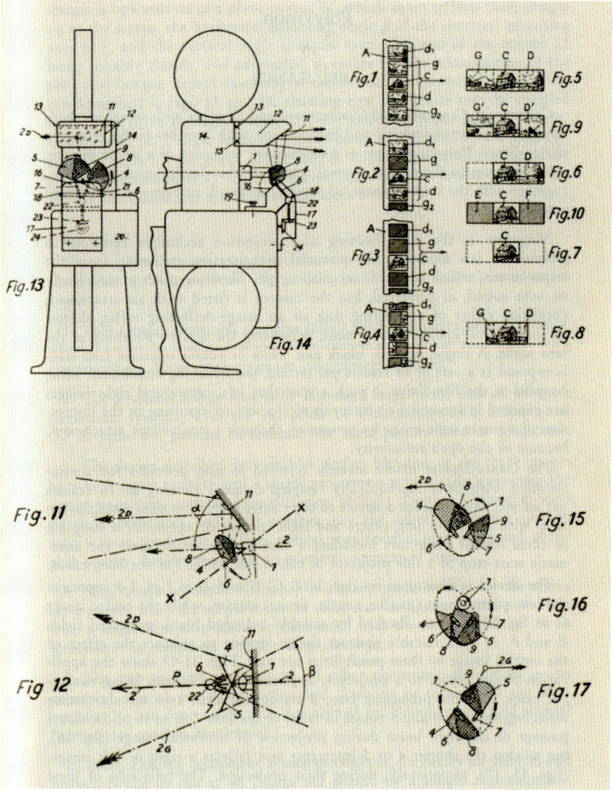

FIG. 9.21. Polyvision diagrams, from Abel Gance, "Polyvision," *Gravesaner Blätter* 4, no. 13 (1959): 101.

agent of impression: the rhythmic assemblage of varied screen shapes, the attack upon our field of perception of the affective impulses associated with the geometric and dimensional variation of the successive possible dimensions, proportions and designs."[60] Although he never mentioned *Napoléon* by name, Eisenstein's call for a dynamic use of wide-screen harmonized with Gance's ideas, and the "Double Tempest" triptych came very close to realizing his objectives.[61] In a 1959 article published in a review associated with the conductor Hermann Scherchen's electroacoustic sound studio in Gravesano, Switzerland, Gance even provided diagrams demonstrating how Polyvision would open up a "vast" array of possibilities for different screen combinations, one of many reasons he felt there was "hardly any comparison between this method and all existing panoramic techniques" (that is, Cinerama and CinemaScope) (fig. 9.21).[62]

Gance maintained that his system could be made to work with a single 35mm projector and even, with an inevitable loss of visual quality, 16mm film, which was rapidly becoming the dominant shooting and exhibition stock for independent and avant-garde filmmakers.[63] Inspired by *Napoléon*, Kenneth Anger presented a triple-screen, 16mm version of *Inauguration of the Pleasure Dome* (1954) at the 1958 Brussels World's Fair, with Gance in attendance (he held a Polyvision demonstration at the same festival).[64] His fellow avant-gardist Bruce Conner developed a triptych version of *Cosmic Ray* (1961) in 1965.[65] During the same period, Gregory Markopoulos attempted to interrelate material shot using three different film gauges and considered using triple-screen projection for early versions of his masterwork *Eniaios* (1947–92).[66] In general, however, the "varied screen shapes" Eisenstein advocated have been used only in the context of split-screen techniques.[67] Jean-Luc Godard argued, in his *Cahiers du Cinéma* review of *Magirama*, that although triple-screen presentations could "provoke supplementary effects in the sphere of pure sensation," he admired directors who "achieve a similar or even superior result by more logical means, breaking the frame but not destroying it."[68] Godard characteristically took this idea to its limit in his *Histoire(s) du cinéma* project (1988–98), layering multiple streams of imagery and sound on top of one another within the space of a traditional 4:3 frame and implicitly suggesting that Gance's polyphonic use of superimposition may be as creatively fecund as his experiments with multiscreen projection.

In this context, *Napoléon* once again takes on critical importance. It can be seen as a pivotal link between the presentational modes of the nineteenth-century panorama and wide-screen cinema. Yet the relationship between cinema and the panorama is not simply a question of a shared set of techniques or even of an approach to illusionistic representation. To cite an obvious example, the mobile, 360-degree camera apparatus Gance commissioned performed profoundly unpanoramic circular movements in *Napoléon*, where its rapid panning was used to capture a barely visible spectrum of battle sensations, and in *La fin du monde*, where it was used to suggest a society spinning wildly out of control. What is panoramic about *Napoléon*, and certain aspects of midcentury wide-screen practice, is the emphasis on an expansive, immersively participatory form of visuality, which courses through the film on every level, attaining its fullest expression in the triptychs. Yet *Napoléon*'s central paradox is that the technique connecting it most directly to panoramic forms is also the site of its greatest, most radical disruptions. The triptychs can legitimately be seen as a progenitor of Cinerama, but they also demonstrated new creative possibilities for interlinking a plurality of rhythms, possibilities that remain largely unexplored. With *Napoléon*'s triptychs, in other words, Gance set the terms for the artistic critique of the panoramic processes he helped invent. At the same time, the complex, symphonic strategies he developed and championed remained grounded within the form of a narrative cinema intended for a mass audience. *Napoléon* thus established a uniquely cinematic idea of space that can be located not only between the panorama and Cinerama but also between gallery-based video installations and virtual reality's interactive projections.

NOTES

1. One notable exception is Béla Balazs, whose *Theory of the Film: Character and Growth of a New Art* (New York: Roy Publishers, 1953), 139–42, devoted a few pages to the panoramic use of mobile long takes. More skeptically, André Bazin alludes to the introduction in the early 1950s of "panoramic screens" created through a "geometrical sleight of hand"—that is, the use of lenses and plates to change the visual proportions of a non-anamorphic film image. Bazin, "Will CinemaScope Save the Film Industry?" in *Bazin at Work: Major Essays & Reviews from the Forties & Fifties*, ed. Bert Cardullo (New York: Routledge, 1997), 77–92; 81–82.
2. See Erkki Huhtamo, *Illusions in Motion: Media Archaeology of the Moving Panorama and Related Spectacles* (Cambridge: MIT Press, 2013), 317–18, for a full account.
3. Tom Gunning, "'Now You See It, Now You Don't': The Temporality of the Cinema of Attractions," in *Silent Film*, ed. Richard Abel (New Brunswick, N.J.: Rutgers University Press, 1996), 71–84.
4. Gance to Princess Clémentine of Belgium, November 1923, reprinted in *Abel Gance, un soleil dans chaque image*, ed. Roger Icart (Paris: Cinémathèque Française, 2002), 69.
5. This version would have been broken into eight episodes: *La jeunesse de Bonaparte, Bonaparte et la terreur, Arcole, Les pyramides, Austerlitz, La Bérénisa, Waterloo,* and *Sainte-Hélène.* (Gance's plans are outlined in a document dated September 4, 1924, and referenced in Jean-Jacques Meusy, "La Polyvision, espoir oublié d'un cinéma nouveau," *1895* 31 [October 2000], 153–221; 163.)
6. With Gance's blessing, the director Lupu Pick made a 1929 German-language film of the *Sainte-Hélène* script. Gance eventually succeeded in making a version of the film intended to be the third part of the *Napoléon* series, *Austerlitz* (1960), but the final result differed greatly from the original conception.
7. Gance told Kevin Brownlow in the 1960s that the premiere version included four sequences in "Polyvision": "Les Deux Tempêtes, the Return to Corsica, Le Bal des Victimes, and the Entry into Italy." Brownlow, *The Parade's Gone By . . .* (Berkeley: University of California Press, 1968), 547. Yet no known version of the film ever included four triptych sequences, and Gance did not begin regularly using the word *Polyvision* to describe his process until the 1950s. As Gance explained in a 1956 radio interview, "I did not see Polyvision, as I make it now, in [the 1920s]. . . . The first idea of Polyvision [came with the triptychs for *Napoléon*], but it was actually elementary in my spirit." "Le bureau des rêves perdus d'Abel Gance, émission radiophonique de Louis Moillon réalisée par Albert Riera le 13 Novembre 1956," *L'Écran*, no. 3 (April–May 1958): 17–22. The "Return to Corsica" and "Le bal des victimes" sequences were presented as triptychs in a 1928 special presentation at Studio 28 (under the names *Galops* and *Danses*), while both "Les deux tempêtes" and the "Entry into Italy" triptychs were included in the version of *Napoléon* shown at the Opéra de Paris.
8. For a history of different restoration and reconstruction attempts, see Georges Mourier, "La comète Napoléon," *Journal of Film Preservation* 86 (April 2012), 35–52.
9. Richard Schickel, *D. W. Griffith: An American Life* (New York: Simon and Schuster, 1984), 457.
10. Ezra Goodman, "Flash-Back to Griffith," *PM*, May 19, 1948, M12–M13, reprinted in *D. W. Griffith: Interviews*, ed. Anthony Slide (Jackson: University Press of Mississippi, 2012), 212–18; 217.
11. Abel Gance, "My Napoleon," translated and reprinted in *French Film Theory and Criticism, 1907–1939*, ed. Richard Abel, 2 vols. (Princeton: Princeton University Press, 1998), 1:400–407; 400.
12. Text reprinted in Icart, *Abel Gance*, 73.
13. The model for Gance's use of documents, as well as much of his Napoleonic historiography, is Jules Michelet, but his treatment is also clearly indebted to the authenticating strategies Griffith employed in *The Birth of a Nation*. Gance, 1923 letter, reprinted in Icart, *Abel Gance*, 69.
14. A more recent translation renders this passage as "Your whole creation is a great wheel which to turn at all must crush someone." "The Graveyard at Villequier," in Victor Hugo, *Selected Poems*, trans. Brooks Haxton (London: Penguin Classics, 2002), 39–49; 43. Hugo's poem was written in 1847 on the part of the Seine where his daughter had drowned four years before; Gance almost certainly cited it with this history in mind, as a tribute to his wife, Ida Danis, who (like the lead actor, Séverin-Mars) died of flu before *La roue* was finished.
15. Victor Hugo, *Ninety-Three* (1874), trans. Lowell Bair (Cresskill, N.J.: Paper Tiger, 2002), 137.
16. Ibid., 140–41.
17. Abel Gance, "Le temps de l'image est venu!" in *L'art cinématographique II*, by Léon Pierre-Quint et al. (Paris: Félix Alcan, 1927), 83–102; 102. Earlier in the essay, he argues that "the cinema silently observes the other arts and, [like a] formidable Sphinx, asks itself which vital parts it will devour" (99).
18. Louis Delluc's 1918 review of *La dixième symphonie* lavishes praise on Gance's formal innovations and calls him a genius, then chides him for the obviousness of the film's dramaturgy and, especially, for the citation of other artworks in a "vision sequence": "Perhaps this will please spectators. Indeed it is quite pretty to look at. But it's no good; it overlays something fine with something pretty but unnecessary. It's simply a mistake. Don't tell me, Gance, that the execution hasn't measured up to the intention. No, you were thinking of the Victory at Samothrace. I wasn't. The Victory at Samothrace suffices unto itself. Leave it where it is, unless you are devoting an essay, a poem, or a play to it. In a film, visibly present like that, it's extraneous. For three-quarters of an hour, you alone kept us interested. Would you have us believe that you aren't sufficient unto yourself? It's too late. We have only come for *La Dixième Symphonie*." Delluc, "Notes pour moi," trans. and reprinted in Abel, *French Film Theory*, 1:143–46; 145–46.
19. Fernand Léger, *"La roue: Sa valeur plastique"* (1922), trans. and reprinted in Abel, *French Film Theory*, 1:272. Jean Cocteau famously said, "There is cinema before and after *La Roue*, just as there is painting before and after Picasso." Cocteau, *The Art of Cinema* (New York: Marion Boyars, 1994), 132. Gance's friend Jean Epstein was equally enthusiastic: "The conviction that pours from *La Roue* is overwhelming. From this film was born the first cinematographic symbol. . . . The cross which turns very quickly takes the form of a wheel. That is why, at the summit of your Calvary, Gance, there is *La Roue*." Epstein, "Les cinéastes—Abel Gance," *Photo-Ciné*, no. 8 (September–October 1927): 153.
20. Nelly Kaplan, *Napoléon* (London: British Film Institute, 1994), 28.

21. Gance, "My Napoleon," 400. Gance detailed his ideas in a letter to Charles Pathé (n.d.): "The most powerful and decisive of all my innovations is that which will consist, finally, of considering the audience not as spectators, but for the first time as actors in the drama, as we are in life. Cinematic pictorialism has had its day. The audience must suffer with the wounded, fight with the soldiers, charge with the horsemen, and command with the leaders, instead of merely watching." Quoted in Icart, *Abel Gance*, 83.
22. "Le bureau des rêves," 22. *J'accuse* and *La roue* used masking to create a variety of screen shapes. Gance also split the screen into three parallel sections in *Barberousse* (1917). Too many early Gance films are lost to outline the pre-1917 development of these strategies.
23. Kaplan, *Napoléon*, 46.
24. Émile Vuillermoz, "*Napoléon*," reprinted in Abel, *French Film Theory*, 1:402.
25. Élie Faure, "Triptyque," in the GANCE386-B90 file at the Bibliothèque du Film, Paris (hereafter cited as BiFi).
26. Bernard Comment argues: "The aim of the panoramic configuration was to produce—using all available means—the illusion of another space, so much that the canvas did not allow its boundary to be seen. The original space (that of the rotunda) was transformed into another space, that of a representation that left no trace of what it really was, becoming the perfect substitute for reality." Comment, *The Panorama*, trans. Anne-Marie Glasheen (London: Reaktion, 1999), 77.
27. "Étude sommaire des conditions à observer pour la projection des scènes triptyques du film 'Napoléon' de Monsieur Abel Gance," BiFi (GANCE396-B90).
28. These large screens would have been able to accommodate both single- and triple-screen projections. See "Projet Abel Gance," BiFi (GANCE387-B90).
29. Comment, *Panorama*, 241.
30. The Russian artist Franz Roubaud's panorama of the Battle of Borodino also survives. The canvas, commissioned by Czar Nicholas II, was publicly debuted in 1912 and stored in 1918. In 1962 it was reinstalled in a new museum built to commemorate the 150th anniversary of the battle.
31. Stephan Oettermann, *The Panorama: History of a Mass Medium*, trans. Deborah Lucas Schneider (New York: Zone, 1997), 110–15.
32. Comment, *Panorama*, 43–46.
33. Ibid., 62–63. Maurice Samuels discusses the form and legacies of Napoleonic panoramas in *The Spectacular Past: Popular History and the Novel in Nineteenth-Century France* (Ithaca: Cornell University Press, 2004), 18–62.
34. Philippe Soupault, author of a book on Uccello, saw affinities between Gance's 1950s Polyvision presentations and the work of the Italian painter, especially in their "desperate desire to get out of the rut of pictorial art," and claimed that Gance's work teaches how to "read and to see the universe in multiple dimensions." Soupault, "Des primitifs italiens . . . au cinéma de l'avenir," *L'Écran*, no. 3 (April–May 1958): 76–78; 77–78. Anticipating Soupault's claims, Gance declared, in a June 1954 statement prepared for a Paris retrospective, that his system would be able to "break out of the cul-de-sac that Modern Art is almost entirely stuck in. . . . The extraordinary, the unusual magic that Polyvision offers us will enable us to escape at will in the fourth dimension, freeing in an instant the cinema from the sensation of visual asphyxiation that the spectator of yesterday suffered through" (BiFi, GANCE379-B89).
35. Jean Arroy, "Le triptyque d'Abel Gance," *Photo-Ciné*, no. 6 (June–July 1926): 98–101; a typed copy (with pages numbered 1–3) is held at the BiFi (GANCE386-B90). Gance quotes this statement in his article "Les nouveaux chapitres de notre syntaxe," *Cahiers du Cinéma*, no. 27 (October 1953): 29.
36. Nelly Kaplan (*Napoléon*, 9) claims that the director inexplicably destroyed it himself during one of his 1940s re-edits of the film. Jean Dréville, who was present at the 1927 premiere, reconstructed this triptych using the existing footage for the Cinémathèque Française restoration. See Bambi Ballard, ed., *Napoléon as Seen by Abel Gance* (London: Faber and Faber, 1990), 58.
37. Shooting on the film began under the director Albert Capellani in spring 1914 and was almost completed before war broke out in August. Concerns about the representation of a French civil war led government censors to order the film's suspension until 1919. Editing was eventually completed by André Antoine and the film finally released in June 1921. See Camille Blot-Wellens, "Le cas de *Quatre-vingt-treize*," *Coffret Albert Capellani*, DVD booklet (Paris: Pathé, 2011), 30–31.
38. This impression is strengthened by the two most dramatic intertitles: "Thus all the giants of the Revolution were swept, one after the other, into the raging whirlpool of the Reign of Terror," followed (after a superimposition of Convention and guillotine) by "And a man, the defiant sport of the Ocean, his Tricolor sail opening to the wind of the Revolution, was being triumphantly carried to the Heights of History."
39. Gance, echoing Jean Arroy's comments, made this argument in a March 22, 1929, lecture titled "Le cinéma de demain," which is reprinted in Icart, *Abel Gance*, 120. For Arroy's virtually identical comments, see BiFi (GANCE386-B90).
40. Gance observed: "From the moment when I sensed the [great expressionist possibilities] of Polyvision, I said to myself that there was a new alphabet for cinema. It would lead me to create a new grammar and I must say that, from that moment, normal cinema was no longer of any interest for me. I thought only that Polyvision would be the language of cinema beginning with *Napoléon*" (interview with Kevin Brownlow used for Brownlow's 1968 documentary, *Abel Gance: The Charm of Dynamite*; interview excerpts reprinted in Icart, *Abel Gance*, 84).
41. Kevin Brownlow, *Napoleon: Abel Gance's Classic Film* (New York: Alfred A. Knopf, 1983), 166. The program also included a scientific film called *Cristaux* and the making-of documentary *Autour de Napoléon* (Jean Arroy, 1928).
42. In a publicity document prepared for *La divine tragédie*, Gance expressed his intention to use triptychs (BiFi, GANCE37-B15). In the 1950s, the aborted project was retrospectively described as the first attempt to make a film in both "Polyvision" and "Sound Perspective" (BiFi, GANCE384-B90).
43. French patent 633 415 was finally processed on October 24, 1927, and amended (35 034) on June 11, 1929.
44. Gance, "Les nouveaux chapitres," 25. Gance later claimed that the Hypergonar was derived from a special lens that he and the cinematographer L. H. Burel invented called the "Diastrephor" ("Projet Abel Gance").
45. Autant-Lara's film included shots presented in the silent 1.33:1 ratio, double and triple images in the manner of *Napoléon*, and sections, on different reels, applying the Hypergonar to create both horizontal and vertical anamorphic effects. The colonial documentary *Une visite aux merveilles de l'exposition coloniale internationale, Paris 1931* also included sections shot using both horizontal and vertical anamorphosis, but these were separated by non-amamorphic shots. Parts of *La merveilleuse vie de Jeanne d'Arc* (Marco de Gastyne, 1929) and all of *La femme et le rossignol* (André Hugon, 1931) were shot using the Hypergonar, but neither film was released anamorphically. On the Hypergonar, see Jean-Jacques Meusy, "Henri Chrétien, Bernard Natan, and the Hypergonar," *Film History* 15 (2003): 11–31; and Jean-Claude Maillet, "G. Bonnerot nous raconte: La grande aventure de l'Hypergonar," *Cinéma Pratique* 21, no. 137 (1975): 75–80.
46. Abel Gance, "Départ vers la polyvision," *Cahiers du Cinéma*, no. 41

(December 1954): 4–9. The term, a visual analogue to musical polyphony, appears to have originated with a review by Émile Vuillermoz of the triple-screen program presented at Studio 28 in 1928 ("Art decorative, sur la 'Polyvision' d'Abel Gance," *Le Temps*, April 28, 1928; a typed copy is included in the GANCE380-B89 file at the BiFi).

47. Gance, "Départ," 4–5. Gance's idea of art as the gateway to universal mysteries was heavily informed by Nietzsche. Like a less ironic version of Nietzsche's *Zarathustra*, Gance wanted to use cinema to "create new psychological values." Gance, *Prisme: Carnets d'un cinéaste* (Paris: Samuel Tastet, 1986), 109.
48. *Magirama* also included a Polyvision version of Norman MacLaren's *Begone Dull Care* (1949), a section from *Napoléon*'s final triptych, and three original shorts: *Châteaux de nu*, *Auprès de ma blonde*, and *Une fête foraine*.
49. The 1.37:1 "Academy" ratio, established in the early 1930s, remained standard until the mid-1950s for 35mm and 16mm sound film as well as television broadcast (in the matching 4:3 ratio). The Academy ratio replaced the 1.33:1 "full aperture" silent-film ratio; the extra 0.04 represented adjustments for the addition of a soundtrack. High-definition televisions use a 16:9 screen ratio that approximates the matted wide-screen ratio of 1.85:1 cinematic projection.
50. In the early 1950s Gance argued that his system could also be used to "embrace and embellish a horizon of 150 degrees." See Gance, "Les nouveaux chapitres," 33.
51. The film begins with a lecture by Thomas tracing a micro-history of illusionistic representations from cave painting to Athanasius Kircher's Magic Lantern presentations to early cinema, finally culminating in Cinerama. Several shots—particularly an aerial view of Edinburgh—are suggestive of panoramas, and near the end Thomas makes explicit the connection (and the relationship between new forms of technological display and military-industrial systems): "Washington, where the sweeping panorama in motion is dominated by the Pentagon, that building famous for its size and the ramifications of office and departments, headquarters of the vast military power of the United States."
52. John Belton, *Widescreen Cinema* (Cambridge: Harvard University Press, 1992), 85–137, describes these processes' marketing.
53. Charlie Chaplin's penultimate film, *A King in New York* (1957), includes a trenchant jab at the wide-screen filmmaking practices then proliferating throughout the Hollywood studios. Chaplin's character is watching a Western in which two characters shoot at one another from opposite saloon sides; to follow the action, he is forced to turn his head back and forth from left to right, constantly reorienting his field of vision. Rubbing his strained neck, the character walks off in dismay, unable to adjust to the more active mode of viewing the new format demands. Similar sentiments are expressed, more ironically, when the Fritz Lang character in Jean-Luc Godard's 1963 film *Le mépris* (a film shot in 2.35:1 Franscope) quips that CinemaScope "wasn't meant for human beings, just for snakes and funerals." David Bordwell quotes Ozu as saying, "The wide screen reminds me of a roll of toilet paper"; *Ozu and the Poetics of Cinema* (Princeton: Princeton University Press, 1988), 6.
54. In this respect, films like *This Is Cinerama* recapitulate the strategies of works such as *Coney Island at Night*. *This Is Cinerama* also positions itself as a successor to early cinema in using a lecturer-narrator who explains a technological novelty and guides a viewer through a series of short sequences from disparate locations, a tradition associated with traveling presenters like E. Burton Holmes. For the open-air presentations at the 1937 Paris Exposition, see Maillet, "G. Bonnerot nous raconte," 78. In 1967 Circarama was replaced with a new system, Circle-Vision 360°, using nine 35mm projectors. A Soviet variant, Krugorama, was launched in Moscow in 1959.
55. A print of each section (left, right, and center) is held at the Centre National de la Cinématographie archives in the Bois d'Arcy.
56. Bazin, "Will CinemaScope Save the Film Industry?" 90.
57. Charles Barr, "CinemaScope: Before and After," *Film Quarterly* 16, no. 4 (1963): 4–24; 11.
58. Ibid., 18.
59. The essay, originally a lecture delivered at a Hollywood meeting of the Academy of Motion Picture Arts and Sciences, was published in the British journal *Close Up* and reprinted in *Sergei Eisenstein: Selected Works*, ed. Richard Taylor, 4 vols. (London: I. B. Tauris, 2010), 1:206–18.
60. Ibid., 218.
61. The triptychs would almost certainly have been removed from any version of *Napoléon* shown in the Soviet Union, yet the "Double Tempest" sequence's montage strategies were discussed there in the late 1920s. John MacKay, "Film Energy: Process and Metanarrative in Dziga Vertov's *The Eleventh Year* (1928)," *October*, no. 121 (Summer 2007): 41–78; 45.
62. Abel Gance, "Polyvision," *Gravesaner Blätter* 4, no. 13 (1959): 101–3.
63. The single-projector system used a strip of 35mm film with nine perforations loaded horizontally. As Gance argued in "Avant-projet d'un équipement complet de matériel spécial de prises de vues et de tirage pour la mise en oeuvre du procédé 'Proterama,'" held in the GANCE379-B89 file at the BiFi, "Recomposition of the full image is perfect with respect to both the uniformity of the light and the stability of the three sections, the one by relationship to the other." Gance envisioned his system allowing for a more seamless form of panoramic representation and greater control over the arrangement of contrapuntal triptychs. Gance initially called this system Proterama, but by the mid-1950s *Magirama* had become his preferred term for the "new shooting and projection technique resulting in Polyvision." Gance, "Polyvision," 102. Gance also claimed (104) that the use of modified 16mm equipment would enable all theaters to create triple-screen images simply by adding "additional screens to cover the whole available width." The GANCE386-B90 file at the BiFi includes a diagram demonstrating how a "*triple écran*" could be created using "anamorphosisx2" and 16mm film.
64. Scott MacDonald, *A Critical Cinema 5: Interviews with Independent Filmmakers* (Berkeley: University of California Press, 2006), 33–34. The 1958 Brussels World's Fair also featured the first European demonstration of Disney's Circarama (with a new film, *America the Beautiful*).
65. The original version used three 8mm projectors. A digital reconstruction called *Three Screen Ray* (or, alternatively, *Eve-Ray-Forever*) was completed in 2006.
66. P. Adams Sitney's *Visionary Film: The American Avant-Garde, 1943–2000*, 3rd ed. (Oxford: Oxford University Press, 2002), 150, includes a section of a 1964 letter outlining the attempt to combine 8mm, 16mm, and 35mm footage in *The Iliac Passion*. Markopoulos included diagrams of double- and triple-screen versions of sections of *Eniaios* in a production notebook (*Chiron Notes*, vol. 3) held at the Temenos Archive in Uster, Switzerland.
67. Split-screen techniques offer one way of supplanting the editing patterns associated with traditional crosscutting by putting multiple zones of action within the same visual "space." Yet far from an "attack upon our perceptive field," they are normally used to smooth over continuity gaps, create suspense, and/or make a scene more legible. The advent of digital projection has made it easier for twenty-first-century filmmakers to introduce shifting aspect ratios, either to demarcate different sections of a film or for dramatic effect.
68. Jean-Luc Godard, *Godard on Godard*, trans. and ed. Tom Milne (New York: Da Capo Press, 1986), 42.

ANDREW VIELKIND

10 Ernie Gehr's *Side/Walk/Shuttle*

Panorama of an Invisible City

Cities, like dreams, are made of desires and fears, even if the thread of their discourses is secret, their rules are absurd, their perspectives deceitful, and everything conceals something else.

—Marco Polo in Italo Calvino's *Invisible Cities* (1974)

In Italo Calvino's novella *Invisible Cities*, the world traveler Marco Polo arrives at Xanadu to inform the aging Mongolian ruler Kublai Khan of the status of his crumbling empire. Polo captivates the emperor with fantastical descriptions of fifty-five cities he once passed through while traversing the Yuan Dynasty's vast expanse. He speaks of one metropolis existing as a subterranean world, one precariously suspended over a dark abyss, and yet another supported by a labyrinthine network of balconies and ladders. The emperor meets Polo's accounts of cities transcending spatial and temporal logic with amusement and skepticism. As it turns out, these exotic tales are all allegories for one genuine city: Polo's native Venice.

Calvino's text approaches the subject of urban alienation through a dichotomy of the city's *visible* and *invisible* aspects. Beneath Venice's superficial, visible facade lies a plurality of mental impressions the city left on the bewildered visitor. Each one of these invisible cities Polo fabricates is a poetic allegory for a past experience of grappling with its disorientating network of canals, bridges, narrow streets, and back alleys. By recounting his exploits to the emperor as a lyrical travelogue infused with his psychological rumination rather than a plainly factual account of what he witnessed, Polo constructs an expansive, *panoramic* portrayal of his personal encounters with Venice.

Ernie Gehr's *Side/Walk/Shuttle* (1991) poignantly foregrounds a similar tension between urban spaces' visible and invisible facets. Rather than Polo's Venice, Gehr's experimental film depicts San Francisco's equally disorienting topography, which he shot with a handheld 16mm camera over numerous ascents and descents in the glass elevator of the Fairmont Hotel on Nob Hill. The perplexing cityscape compositions Gehr accumulated over several months, such as moments when his inverted camera positioning creates the illusion that the laws of gravity have ceased to apply, could have easily been lifted from the pages of *Invisible Cities*. Glistening skyscrapers float gracefully across the screen from all angles and occasionally appear to either rain from the sky or sprout upward, like weeds, from the lower portion of the frame. In some instances, people, cars, and trolleys defy linear time by moving backward in their paths. While each of the film's twenty-five shots is formally unique, they all contribute to a panoramic and palimpsestic representation of San Francisco's uncanny architecture, topography, and arterial flows of pedestrians and automobiles.

The Fairmont Hotel's glass elevator shuttles the spectator between the ground and the top floors, offering a sensation of simulated motion commensurate with the visual tradition of the moving panorama. That nineteenth-century mass media spectacle provided the illusion of traveling through a landscape or seascape by gradually unfurling an elongated, painted canvas mounted on two larger rollers. A more direct antecedent to Gehr's film is the "phantom ride," the cinematic analogue to the moving panorama that became a popular genre during the medium's infancy.[1] Despite a shared namesake, media historians such as Erkki Huhtamo have argued, Robert Barker's original painted panorama and the moving panorama had distinct technological, aesthetic, and cultural identities.[2] Gehr, through the formal structure of *Side/Walk/Shuttle*, nevertheless assimilated discernible features from both the mobile and immobile strains of the panoramic visual tradition.

This chapter considers how Gehr's defamiliarizing depiction of the San Francisco cityscape amplifies those compositional anomalies already implicit in panoramic media dating back to the late eighteenth century. *Side/Walk/Shuttle* exposes a crucial structural impasse that has plagued the panorama throughout its history: the inability to maintain a wholly rational spatial configuration. By pitting the film against other incarnations of the medium—particularly Barker's painted panoramas, Eadweard Muybridge's photographic panoramas, and the cinematic phantom train ride—I isolate what Huhtamo, through his media archaeological excavation, has referred to as the "topoi" of panoramic media.[3] These discursive or stereotypical cultural formulae, such as sensory immersion, multi-perspectivalism, bird's-eye vision, and simulated motion, were constantly remediated in panoramic formats over the centuries, but Gehr's formalist experimentation brings them to the forefront. *Side/Walk/Shuttle* highlights these various topoi and enables us more fully to recognize the limitations (or blind spots) of the different modes of panoramic spectatorship. Emerging as an "afterlife" of previous visual traditions, the film posits that this spectatorship is not unilaterally governed by immersion and direct sensory experience but rather is deeply rooted in the psychological, the personal, the discursive, and often the irrational. Whereas Barker, when designing the painted panorama, made concerted efforts to conceal the seams of the canvas and provide a vicariously convincing illusion of a remote space, Gehr exposes and undermines this artificial reality.

NATURE AT A GLANCE: THE PAINTED AND PHOTOGRAPHIC PANORAMAS

The circular, painted panorama that Barker innovated was the progenitor of several of these tensions in spatial representation. His 1787 patent for the panorama sought to construct "an entire view of any country or situation as it appears to an observer turning quite around" so that he or she may feel "as if really on the very spot."[4] Barker intended that his enormous canvas provide a view of "nature at a glance" (*la nature à coup d'oeil*) through the use of trompe l'oeil and an intricate multi-perspectival system, thereby blurring the boundaries between a natural vista and its simulacrum.[5] Yet as Denise Oleksijczuk points out, these innovations "had a tendency to produce cognitive uncertainty and disorientation as much as a sense of domination and control."[6]

The immense 360-degree canvas of Barker's panorama *View of London from the Roof of the Albion Mills*, opened to the public in its final form in 1791, replicated the view of the London cityscape from the bank of the Thames with such a high degree of verisimilitude that it provoked an astonishing impression of physical displacement (see fig. 1.14). Oleksijczuk argues that it induced a psycho-physiological response: "Inside the Panorama rotunda observers could experience a vertiginous bodily sensation brought about by being simultaneously in a building at London's Leicester Square and within the different space and time of an optical illusion."[7] The composition of the view itself, particularly as rendered by Frederick Birnie in an aquatint facsimile, introduced its own sense of disorientation by flattening the cylindrical canvas out to a two-dimensional image, which denaturalized the vista and exposed the underlying multi-perspectival system—effectively tearing it apart at its seams.

Birnie's six-plate aquatint of Barker's *Albion Mills* has direct formal similarities with the flatness of Eadweard Muybridge's multiplate photographic panoramas of San Francisco. Muybridge, an accomplished landscape photographer before beginning his iconic experiments in analyzing animal locomotion, shot two 360-degree panoramas from Nob Hill in 1877 and 1878. For the 1877 panorama, he erected his tripod on a turret attached to Mark and Mary Hopkins's mansion, at the time still under construction on California Street.[8] The tower's height and the elevation of the land enabled him to obtain a high-angle perspective of the city from about four hundred feet above sea level. Muybridge pivoted his camera on its axis in precise

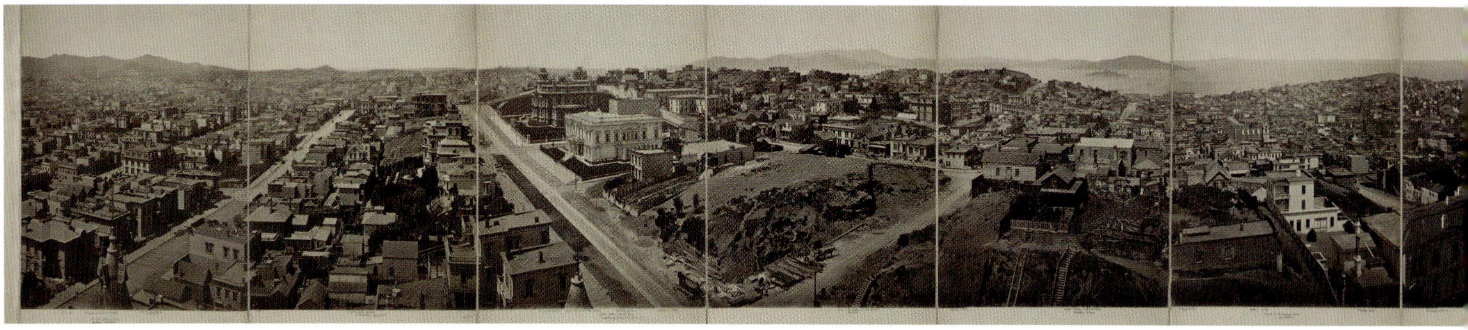

FIG. 10.1. Eadweard Muybridge (American, 1830–1904), *Panorama of San Francisco Taken from the House of Mrs. Mark Hopkins*, 1878. Thirteen albumen prints, totaling 53.3 × 520.1 cm (21 × 204 3/4 in.). The Miriam and Ira D. Wallach Division of Art, Prints and Photographs: Photography Collection, New York Public Library (TL 14.06.3107).

increments to capture multiple wet-plate exposures over a five-hour period; these were developed on the spot and later stitched together as a contiguous series. He mounted the images from the negative in an album as eleven silver albumen plates and also circulated them as 5- by 8¼-inch boudoir cards.[9] In 1878, after returning to the same site in the Hopkins mansion, Muybridge, at 11 o'clock in the morning, angled his camera toward the Twin Peaks in San Francisco's southwestern region and subsequently began rotating his camera clockwise. By roughly four o'clock, he had compiled thirteen prints, which he later mounted on massive plates totaling over seventeen feet in length when arranged horizontally (fig. 10.1).[10]

Since Muybridge's panorama is composed of a series of several exposures taken at various increments over a five-hour period, temporality is inscribed within it. The spectator can experience the passage of time by observing the sizes and the directions of the shadows cast by the moving sun. In viewing the series of plates sequentially from left to right, we first notice the subtle shadows the homes cast in late morning. They dissipate in the center plates as the sun reaches its highest position in the sky but become distended in the final five plates, where the angle of the sun has noticeably sharpened and caused the buildings to shroud large portions of the streets. In this sense, the group of plates amounts to a panorama not only of the cityscape, but also of the dilation of time during the passing day. The panorama encapsulates duration much like Hiroshi Sugimoto's 1978 *Theatres* series, where the photographs of the "empty" screens of movie palaces are in fact each long-exposure condensations of the exhibition of an entire film.[11]

The seventh plate deviates from the Muybridge panorama's pseudo-cinematic, forward progression of time. The orientations of the heavy shadows cast by the chimneys of the local merchant David Porter's home, the building in the immediate foreground at the lower left, are out of sequence when compared to the less pronounced shadows from the sixth and eighth plates.[12] Some scholars, such as Marta Braun, have hypothesized that Muybridge had made an error in developing that plate, which required him to return to that shooting position later in the afternoon to make the necessary correction.[13] The discrepancy in shadow lengths cast by Leland Stanford's stable, the building in the foreground bisected by the margins of the seventh and eighth plates, is also temporally peculiar: the midday sun fully illuminates the left side, but the roof veils the facade of the right side in darkness. While this adjustment undermines a seamless reading of the plates in sequential order, it emphasizes the collagelike and coarsely stitched materiality of the photographic panorama.[14] This interruption of linear time is also a recapitulation of the anachronistic temporality evident in the *Albion Mills* panorama, where the prominent placement of the previously destroyed factory in the foreground troubles the natural sequence of historical events.

The flat, horizontal exhibition format of Muybridge's thirteen plates also produces temporal and spatial anomalies. The photographic panorama, like the aquatint reproduction of *Albion Mills*, resists the immersive experience of viewing that is integral to physically strolling across a viewing platform in a cylindrical rotunda to access all corners of the canvas. The circular panorama depended on this ambulatory spectatorship to achieve its intended effect, but the multiprint portfolio paradoxically takes Barker's notion of "nature at a glance" one step further.

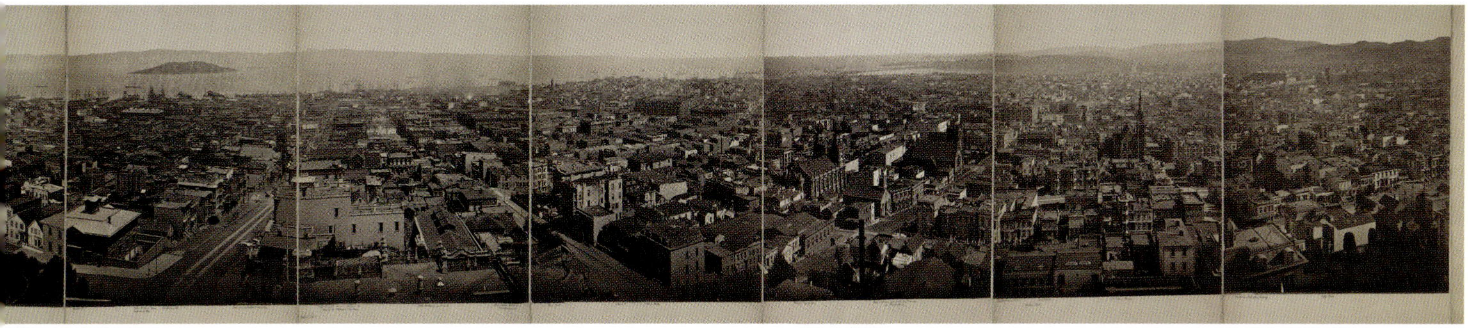

When confronting Muybridge's panorama from a single point in space at the proper distance, the spectator can simultaneously look north, south, east, and west without turning his or her head. In other words, all corners of San Francisco can be seen literally with a single glance. According to the photographer and experimental filmmaker Hollis Frampton, this composition is suggestive of Muybridge's desire to imbue the still photograph with a semblance of time: "Finally, in the great San Francisco panorama of 1877 he condenses an entire rotation of the seeing eye around the horizon (an action that must take place in time) into a simultaneity that is at once completely plausible and perfectly impossible; it is as if a work of sculpture were to be seen turned inside out, by some prodigy of topology."[15] The photographic panorama presents the palpability of time because it condenses the *process* of looking at one's own environment into a single, finite image. It becomes what Frampton refers to as a "tesseract," or representation of a hyperdimensionality that eludes standard human experience of space-time.[16] This "impossible" temporality can be experienced most directly by viewing the seventeen-foot-long array of plates from a considerable distance, so that the left and right edges both rest within the spectator's peripheral vision. At close proximity, the experience of simultaneity is attenuated when the eye must wonder from plate to plate. The spectator performs the mental operation of connecting the first and thirteenth plates in order to restore the unbroken continuity of the cityscape. Each of the cardinal directions carries its own vanishing point outlined by the gradual convergence of two parallel streets toward the horizon. As David Harris observes, these orthogonal lines create "artificial divisions" that permit the spectator to "find his or her bearings."[17] These vanishing points assist the eye in grasping the spatial excess of the image, as did the multi-perspectival system of the painted panorama, by anchoring it to determinate focal points. While the image is partitioned into four distinct quadrants of converging orthogonal lines, its structural logic collapses when we realize counterintuitively that we see each pair of streets twice as they stretch out into the horizon. Since the Hopkins mansion serves as a central terminal, Pine and California Streets recede into the distance in plates 1–3 and again in plates 7–9, when their "left-to-right" configuration is inverted.

The composition of the *Albion Mills* aquatint is even more spatially disorientating in part because the view of London is not divided into a tight grid of orthogonal lines. The recession of Blackfriars Bridge to the opposite bank of the Thames creates the dominant vantage point—the eye's entry position into the image. When the spectator follows the receding lines after an initial glance, the image appears to deceptively adopt a rational landscape composition; the only visible signs of distortion are manifest on the north bank where the Thames appears to wrap itself around and engulf the London urban center. It is not until the eye wanders to the peripheral plates that the radical spatial distortion becomes apparent. The flour mill on which the spectator stands is noticeably bifurcated; the receding row of skylight panels to the chimney's left side in the extreme foreground vanishes at the bottom edge only to continue in the far-left plate. This separation and splaying out of the mill's roof is the root cause of the spectator's directional confusion.[18] With the supporting platform absent, we appear to float above the city sprawling out beneath us in all directions. Consequently, the cognitive reconstructions of the three-dimensional spaces of London and San Francisco from the flat image planes are laborious mental operations.

The spatial and temporal anomalies evident in both panoramas also further convey the urban alienation experienced by the inhabitants of London and San Francisco during periods of rapid modernization and industrialization. The Albion Mills, the world's first steam-powered flour mills, were lauded by some as signs of technological innovation but maligned by others as harbingers of the social ills of modern capitalism, such as the division or reduction of the existing labor force (see chapter 1).[19] The mills' status as a conspicuous symbol of urban modernity is presumably why Barker elected to give prominence to such austere industrial features of the building as the skylights and chimneys, in the immediate foreground. In the fifth and sixth plates in particular, this monument of industrialization obstructs our line of sight to the meticulously detailed vista of London on the south side of the Thames.[20]

Muybridge's panorama does not focus on one particular symbol of industrial progress but instead more broadly reveals the rapid metamorphosis the city of San Francisco was undergoing during the nineteenth century. With the 1848 discovery of goldfields in Northern California, San Francisco blossomed from a remote trading outpost into a vibrant urban hub. Muybridge portrays a booming city extending as far as the water line and the distant hills on the horizon. The mounds of dirt, temporary structures, and network of wooden staircases in the near foreground, which would eventually become the site of a cluster of mansions in the wealthy neighborhood of Nob Hill, most vividly articulate the city's accelerated development. The dominance of this imagery of unfinished dwellings amid the urban sprawl foments the impression that the space still remains distressingly inhospitable.

While famous landmarks, such as churches, ornate homes, and industrial structures are readily identifiable, Muybridge's panorama does not provide a cartographic perspective of San Francisco. Rather than confronting an idealized model of urban planning that distinctly reveals roadways organized into a grid system, the spectator gazes onto a city that is not easily navigable. Furthermore, while the facades of the structures are decipherable, the vitality of urban life within the arteries of the streets and alleys remains concealed from view. The total absence of any human presence on the streets—a byproduct of the long exposure process, which makes people vanish like the actors on Sugimoto's blank screens—saturates the city with ghosts. This erasure of signs of human activity runs counter to the visual tradition of painted panoramas, which, as demonstrated by the heavy traffic crossing Blackfriars Bridge, were typically teeming with life. For the patrons visiting the rotunda, such human figures anchored the believability of landscape's life-size scale.

Muybridge seemed unconcerned with the absence of people in the photographic panoramas, since his primary interest lay in displaying the city's distinctive features, such as its architecture and topography. He distributed his 1877 panorama with a legend identifying 221 observable points of interest, including homes, businesses, and hills.[21] In a prospectus published for *Alta California* in conjunction with the panorama's initial circulation, he explains his intention to create a synoptic image of the city: "Let us imagine a small ant wishing to get a comprehensive view of a painted Japanese dinner-plate. He would succeed if he could get a thimble upright in the middle of the plate, then climb to the top of the thimble and look by turns in every direction. The ant, in that hypothesis, occupies a position similar to that of the man in San Francisco, which represents the saucer, and the palatial dwelling of Mrs. Mark Hopkins, on California street hill, is the thimble."[22] By comparing the human observer (akin to the young man gazing out onto the expansive vista in Caspar David Friedrich's ca. 1817 painting *Wanderer above a Sea of Fog*) to an ant, Muybridge alludes to a notion of the sublime. As he pervasively achieved in his photographs and stereographs of Yosemite Valley, the human body's diminutive stature enters into a stark scalar contrast with the surrounding landscape, which instills feelings of physical uneasiness and disorientation.

SIDE/WALK/SHUTTLE: ERNIE GEHR'S PANORAMIC PALIMPSEST

Before filming *Side/Walk/Shuttle*, Ernie Gehr was already interested in the manner in which the panoramic format could accentuate a sense of urban alienation, particularly given San Francisco's disorienting roadways and physically exhausting hills. He has noted that the film's formal and theoretical aspects were "informed by an interest in panoramas and the urban landscape," particularly acknowledging that "Eadweard Muybridge's photographic panoramas of San Francisco from the 1870s as well as the over-all topography of the city itself were sources of inspiration."[23] These panoramas in fact motivated Gehr to shoot from approximately the same location on Nob Hill, but much of the cityscape that Muybridge had photographed in the 1870s, including the Hopkins mansion, was destroyed by the 1906 earthquake and the ensuing fires. The site of the mansion's wreckage was repurposed for the erection of the opulent nineteen-story Mark Hopkins Hotel, completed in 1926. While the upper floors offered a sweeping panoramic view of San Francisco from almost exactly the same position that Muybridge had photographed, Gehr found the unique design features—particularly the elevator—of the historic Fairmont Hotel to be more aesthetically enticing for filming.

Located on the opposite side of California Street, the future construction site of the Fairmont is prominently visible as a large mound of dirt in the fifth and sixth plates of Muybridge's 1878 panorama. Construction of the nine-story luxury hotel was nearly complete before the earthquake struck in 1906; the structure of the building suffered no significant damage, but its interior was ravaged by the fires. In 1961 the Fairmont also added an adjoining twenty-three-story tower equipped with an exterior glass elevator that connected the street level with an upscale restaurant on the top floor.[24] Gehr sought this transparent elevator for filming because its motion and sightlines surveying the city offered him numerous "visual, spatial, and gravitational possibilities."[25]

The management, however, did not grant Gehr permission to film, which required him to craft a creative solution. During a preliminary planning stage, he rode the elevator repeatedly in order to sketch out the precise angles from which he would later shoot. Once he had a schema of the film's structure in mind, he concealed his handheld 16mm camera under his coat and took repeated trips over the course of several months. Although he was filming clandestinely, he was on multiple occasions caught by security guards and asked to leave under the belief that his presence was disrupting the lunchtime flow of hotel patrons using the elevator to reach the restaurant.[26] Like Muybridge, Gehr had been filming mostly in the middle of the day in order to have ample light and to minimize the size of the shadows cast on the streets below by the downtown buildings.

Side/Walk/Shuttle is composed entirely of twenty-five shots, each roughly ninety seconds in length, recorded from Gehr's trips ascending and descending the glass elevator. The combination of this episodic structure, fixed camera position, and readily legible formal logic situate it within the tradition of the structural films of the 1960s and 1970s. These amounted, in P. Adams Sitney's definition, to "a cinema of structure in which the shape of the whole film is predetermined and simplified, and it is that shape which is the primal impression of the film."[27] Gehr's own

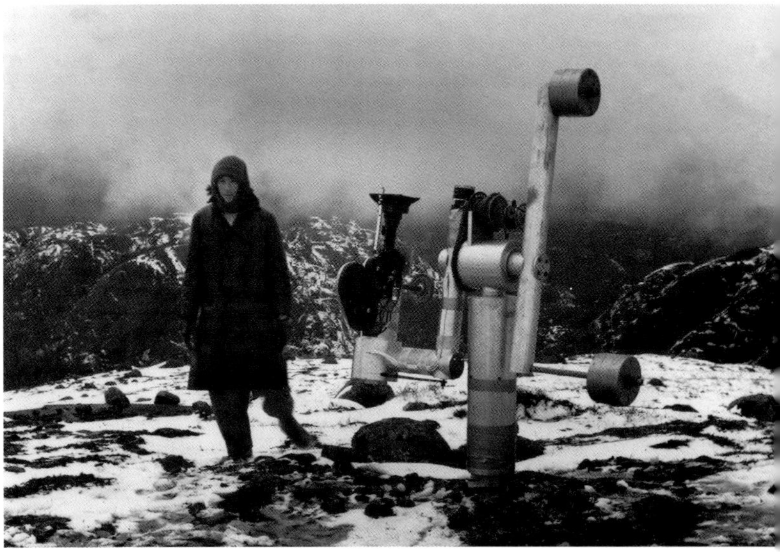

FIG. 10.2. Michael Snow (Canadian, b. 1928), *La région centrale*, 1970. Black-and-white photograph, 12.7 × 17.8 cm (5 × 7 in.).

Serene Velocity (1970), in which he set up a stationary camera in a university hallway and altered the focal length of the zoom lens over several takes to produce the uncanny illusion of flickering motion, is an archetypal example of this mode of experimental filmmaking.[28] In the case of *Side/Walk/Shuttle*, however, it is ultimately the motion of the glass elevator and Gehr's premeditated orientation of the handheld camera that determine the "shape" of the film. He selected his filming angle, but the mechanized "shuttling" of the elevator is what produced the spatial and gravitational anomalies that he was seeking to capture.

The formal logic of *Side/Walk/Shuttle* possesses a cursory resemblance to the structural film *La région centrale* (1971), in which Michael Snow assembled a panorama of the surrounding landscape of the remote Canadian wilderness through a series of gravity-defying camera movements dispersed over numerous shots taken at different hours of the day. After mounting the camera on a remote-controlled robotic arm on a mountainside, Snow established dizzying spectatorial positions where the camera seems to tumble and twirl through space (fig. 10.2). He desired to achieve a "unity of method and subject" by making "a film in which what the camera-eye did in the space would be completely appropriate to what it saw, but at the same time equal to it."[29] As natural features of the environment pass into the field of view and become increasingly familiar, the spectator adapts to a perspective of the landscape adopted by the robotic camera. The essential difference between Snow's and Gehr's films,

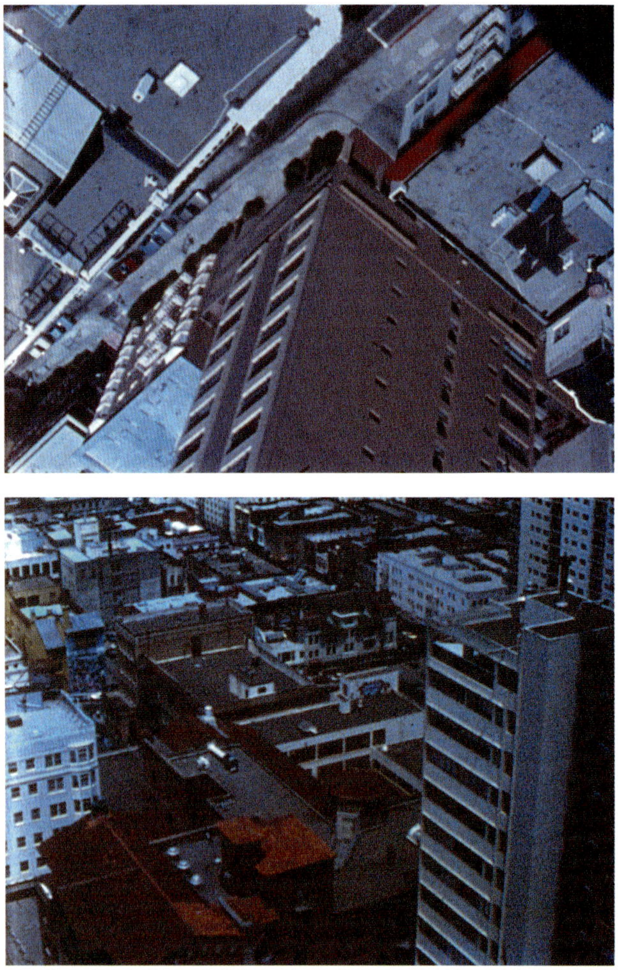

FIGS. 10.3–10.4. Ernie Gehr (American, b. 1943), *Side/Walk/Shuttle*, 1991.

however, is that we identify with the mechanical apparatus when watching *La région centrale*, but we retain our corporeality in *Side/Walk/Shuttle*. Snow algorithmically programmed the movements of his apparatus, but Gehr physically wielded his camera as an extension of his own body. The camera eye in *Side/Walk/Shuttle* personifies *human* vision; it is a mechanized proxy that provides a lens through which the spectator is able to see what Gehr himself was seeing and internalizing. The film reinstates the human presence that Snow deliberately expunged in *La région centrale*.

Side/Walk/Shuttle is an intimately personal film that reflects Gehr's interaction with the urban spaces of San Francisco, from the quotidian to the cathartic. He has underscored the way in which the film embeds an overt sense of subjectivity: "The final shape and character of the work was tempered by reflections upon a lifetime of displacement, moving from place to place, and haunted by recurring memories of other places, other possible yet unlike 'homes' I once passed through."[30] He also recalls that he was initially uncomfortable leaving the familiar confines of New York City to accept a teaching position at the San Francisco Art Institute: "For a long time I thought of New York as my 'home,' but due to economics, I moved to San Francisco in 1988. It's a beautiful city, but I found it difficult to ground myself there. That difficulty was what prompted the making of the film."[31]

Gehr conveys his struggle to acclimate to San Francisco by constructing a panorama of the city that is spatially and temporally disorienting in a manner consistent with the visual anomalies embedded in Muybridge's photographic panoramas. The twenty-five individual shots of the film, alternating between descending and ascending trips in the elevator, challenge prevailing spatial and environmental logic—particularly the stability of our viewing position. Over the course of these trips, Gehr constantly repositions the camera in order to introduce us to new perspectives; we are left in a state of perpetual imbalance as he forces us to reorient ourselves to the new vantage points surveying the shifting orthogonal lines constituting the roadways, shadows, and building facades. The film coaxes us into the realization that our perceptions are easily fooled and that outward appearances of the urban environment are often deceiving—especially to the foreign visitor.

The first four shots of *Side/Walk/Shuttle* adhere to a discernable pattern. The two descent trips (fig. 10.3) have a slightly oblique angle inverted upside-down on the vertical axis, whereas the ascent trips correspond with the camera being positioned firmly right-side up. During the ascent (fig. 10.4), Gehr sustains a level horizon line and gradually unveils an aerial perspective of the city as if seen from the roof of the Fairmont. These more familiar perspectives, such as the hazy vista of Telegraph Hill and Coit Tower seen in the fourth shot (fig. 10.5), are juxtaposed with the exceedingly disorienting descent trips with which he disrupts the stability of the horizon. In several instances, the camera is held at a canted (or Dutch) angle, a tilted-axis framing device commonly used in film noir to externalize the perceptual imbalance and psychological torment induced by the city (fig. 10.6). Gehr uses the canted angle in a similar fashion to unmoor the spectator from the compositional logic of the "flat" horizon and the ordered cartographic grid of aerial perspective. When we trace the intersections of these ubiquitous diagonals, we further lose our directional bearings.

As soon as the eye begins to adapt to these reoccurring shifts in orientation, Gehr discards the pattern. During the elevator's ascent in the sixth shot of the film, in which we expect another high-angle vista, the camera sharply tilts downward to foreground the immense shadows cast by the adjacent buildings on the intersection below. By the ninth and tenth shots, the camera adopts more markedly oblique or "sideways" angles, which rotate the plane of the horizon closer to 90 degrees (fig. 10.7). Gehr anticipates how our proprioceptive faculties would attempt to acclimate to these shifts in perspective, and he undermines them in order to keep us lingering in a state of sensorial bewilderment. He disrupts the formula and laws of physics even further by momentarily reversing the flow of time; pedestrians and vehicles retrace their paths as if they are being guided by an unseen magnetic force.

The directional confusion culminates in the eleventh shot, where the elevator is in fact descending, but the sideways positioning of the camera deceives us into believing that we are actually moving laterally to the left. At this moment the spectator's sense of what can be called "up, down, left, and right" has become muddled. This directional shift occurs again in the twelfth shot; the elevator is physically ascending, but the camera is inverted and held at a canted angle to conjure the uncanny illusion that we are somehow falling from the shadows of the street level toward the sky.

In the fifteenth shot, multiple layers of spatial and perceptual distortion are at play. As the elevator descends while Gehr is holding the camera upside down, a large skyscraper dominates the frame as the visual anchor (fig. 10.8). The building appears to be suspended in midair before gliding against the backdrop of the shimmering waters of the San Francisco Bay and plunging toward the cloudless sky.[32] As he carefully synchronizes the tilting of his camera with the motion of the elevator shuttling downward, the two sides of the horizon line are inverted—the blue waters of the bay are transposed with the lighter blue sky. In the sixteenth shot, the imposing size of the brown building dominates the frame, blocking the horizon (fig 10.9). We see a close-up shot of the building's facade without any environmental cues to aid our orientation. From this perspective, it becomes impossible to perceive whether it is the viewer or the building that moves. This composition permits us again to challenge our own intuition and perceive that the building is gliding past us as we remain stationary.

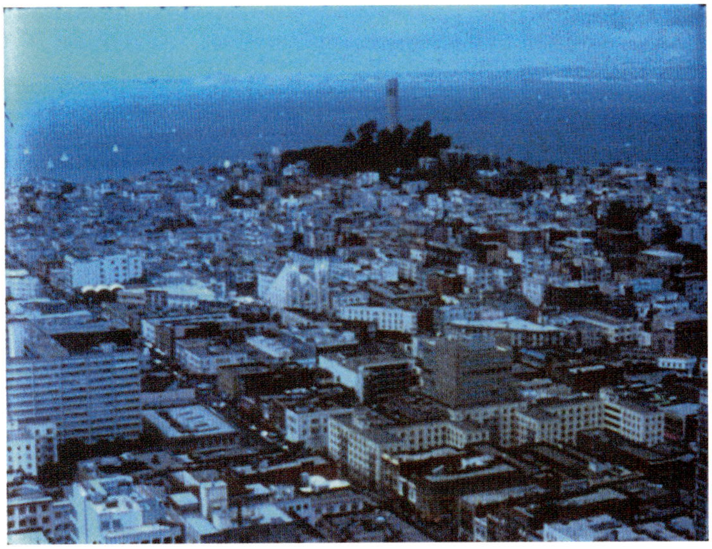

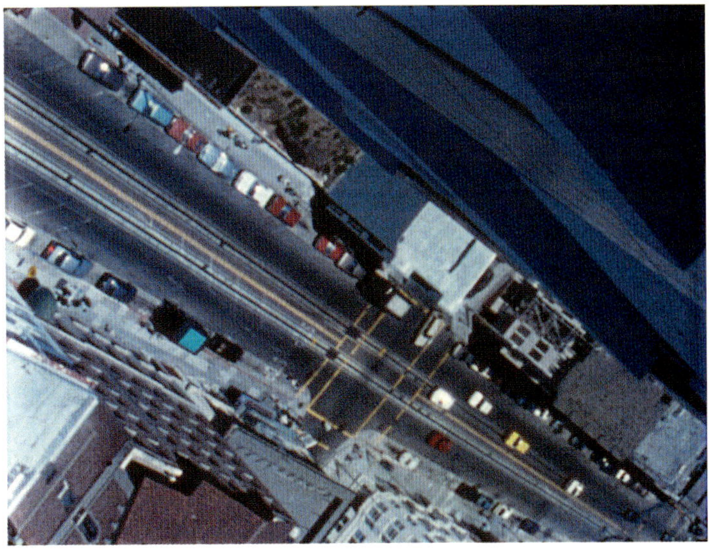

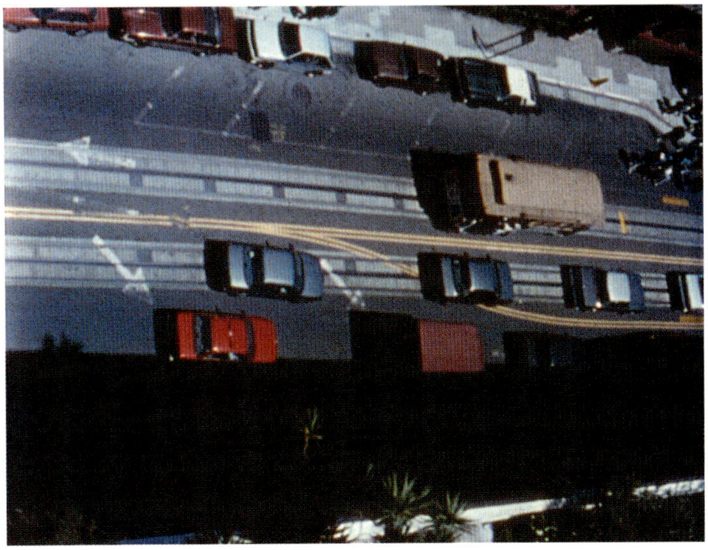

FIGS. 10.5–10.7. Ernie Gehr, *Side/Walk/Shuttle*, 1991.

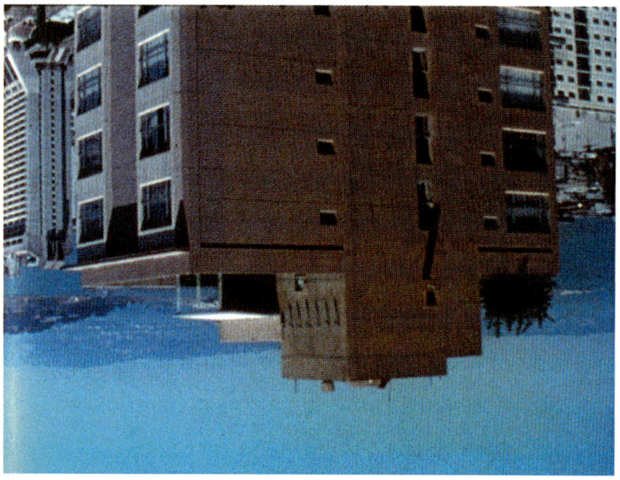

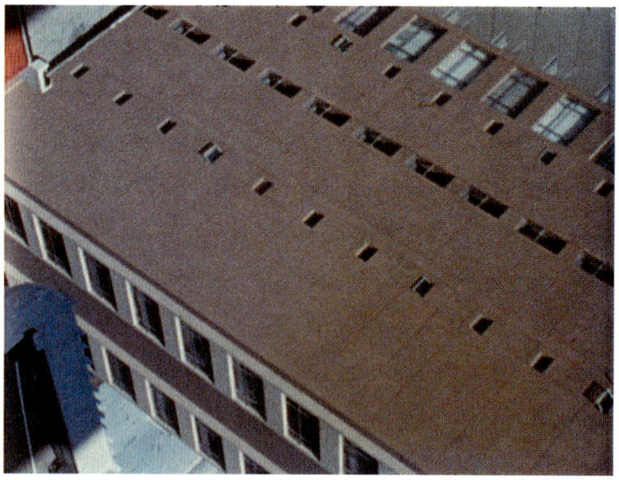

FIGS. 10.8–10.9. Ernie Gehr, *Side/Walk/Shuttle*, 1991.

By the end of the film, our spatial logic has deteriorated to the point that we begin to think that we are floating freely through space. In this respect, the word *shuttle* in the title begins to take on a double meaning. It alludes to the glass elevator, which shuttles people back and forth to the restaurant at the top of the Fairmont Hotel, but it also connotes the gravity-defying capabilities of the space shuttle. This term also references the oppressiveness of the force of gravity that Gehr routinely endured when having to hike up steep hills while returning home with bags of groceries from the market.[33] The title as a whole, with the parsing of the words *side* and *walk*, evokes the fragmented viewing experience that the film presents—particularly our futility in discerning which "side" we are facing.

This decentralization of the spectator was also inherent to the 360-degree painted panorama. As Stephan Oettermann explains, the medium subverted the Albertian model of a single, central perspective of receding orthogonal lines by inaugurating what he calls a "democratic" perspective encompassing "an infinite number of viewing points from which observers can look at the picture without distortion."[34] The myriad of viewing points on a cylindrical canvas also left open the possibility for spatial disorientation. Oleksijczuk references an account of Queen Charlotte allegedly becoming seasick when she "moved her body and eyes along the canvas's surface" of Barker's maritime scene in his 1791 panorama *View of the Grand Fleet*.[35] The panorama carried a "physiologically based mode of perception," which could result in a feeling of queasiness if the eye attempted to process all the various vantage points that solicited attention simultaneously.[36] The multitude of perspectives afforded by Gehr's positioning of the camera and the motions of the elevator facilitate a similar visceral response, since the competing orthogonal lines propagated by the canted camera angles, shadows, and building facades vie for the spectator's attention. These compositions are rendered even more unstable by temporal anomalies such as the cars and people moving backward on the streets and sidewalks.

Gehr's vigilant efforts to conceal the material supports of the glass elevator from the spectator's field of vision intensify the vertiginous compositions of *Side/Walk/Shuttle*. This decision to unhinge the camera from any spatial reference point not only exacerbates the sensation of directional and perceptual imbalance but also emancipates the body from its mechanized confinement so that it feels as if it were tumbling freely through space. This dissociation of the body from the elevator evokes the out-of-body experience that Robert Barker sought to achieve in the painted panorama by figuratively transporting his patrons from the rotunda to the site of the represented vista. Barker made his own attempts to conceal the viewing platform by immersing the spectators in darkness after they ascended the central staircase, when the diffused glow of the canvas from meticulously placed spotlights served as the only points of illumination. The darkened void of the viewing platform and elimination of the canvas frame attain the requisite environmental conditions for integrating us within the illusion, or as Oleksijczuk states, enfold "spectators within a literal figure of the horizon."[37] In other words, while traversing the pitch-black platform, the ambulatory spectators must cognitively acclimate to the painted horizon line, which becomes their dominant proprioceptive reference point. In reference to this process of equilibrium, Oleksijczuk offers the account of the theologian Johann Augustus Eberhard, who, after a disorienting visit to a panorama in 1805, regarded himself as swaying "between reality and unreality, between nature and non-nature, between truth and appearance."[38] Gehr, however, by refraining from filming the elevator itself, unfastens the spectator's contact with the viewing platform and stability of the horizon line, which in turn even further obfuscates his or her ability to discern the real from the unreal.

Despite the "unreality" of its compositions, Gehr's *Side/Walk/Shuttle* is conceptually similar to Muybridge's panoramas of San Francisco in crucial ways. Muybridge considered his "comprehensive" view of the city to be analogous to a "circuit" that had been assembled out of a series of discrete vantage points from a single position in space.[39] In other words, he emphasizes that the panorama must be considered an assemblage or a composite image that is photographed in piecemeal fashion and stitched together for exhibition. The episodic mode of looking and encapsulation of multiple temporalities are mirrored by the structure of *Side/Walk/Shuttle*. Gehr alludes to this similarity to Muybridge's panoramic "circuit" by describing his film as "a horizontal pan of San Francisco broken up into a series of close-ups, each a vertical panorama."[40]

Gehr, in his own writing on nineteenth-century visual media, acknowledges the possibility that Muybridge had been yearning for a teleological leap into cinema all along through his experimentation with panoramas, stereographs, and nature photography. After analyzing Muybridge's eye for dynamism in his compositions and also speculating that contemporary optical toys such as the phenakistoscope implanted him with the spatiotemporal possibilities offered by the persistence of vision, Gehr concludes that "Muybridge's model, guide, and inspiration was cinema *before* photography."[41] The structural similarities between the segmentation of the panorama plates and the individual frames of the filmstrip corroborate this assertion.

In "The Time of the Panorama," Victor Burgin argues that the panorama's temporal continuum is neither a model of pure simultaneity nor a simple chain of narrative events. Because the 360-degree image in the rotunda cannot be consumed in a single glance, it projects "the diachronic onto the plane of the synchronic."[42] Through this uncanny juxtaposition, the panorama establishes a space that is not purely sensorial but is subject to physiological projection, contemplation, and the conjuring of personal memory. In other words, the panorama's configuration opens a liminal space that can be bridged by the mental associations made by the spectator.

Side/Walk/Shuttle (or, rather, cinema in general) departs from the ontology of the photographic panorama by depriving spectators of the freedom to consume the contents of the image on their own terms. While the mammoth size of the Muybridge panorama prevents the spectator from registering its intricate details all at once, the dimensions compensate for this sublimity of scale by permitting anachronistic viewing. One could choose to view the plates out of sequence or possibly spend an extended period scouring one region of the image. The spectator of *Side/Walk/Shuttle*, on the other hand, is constricted by the hard edges of the film frame and the metronomic progression of cinematic time. By succumbing to the point of view and passage of time provided by the cinematic apparatus, we are identifying with Gehr's own personal encounters with San Francisco. The film becomes a means for him to document the idiosyncrasies of his own confrontation with an urban environment that initially seemed alienating to him.

The soundtrack reinforces this notion that *Side/Walk/Shuttle* amounts to a psychological palimpsest, or a multilayered record, of Gehr's subjective interaction with the city. Most of the elevator trips, in no readily apparent pattern, are synchronized with audio that Gehr had previously recorded in other cities throughout the world.[43] Beginning with the sixth shot, we hear a cacophony of voices, footsteps, and a man singing; it is tempting to presume that these sounds were in fact recorded as ambient noise while filming at the Fairmont Hotel, but Gehr has revealed that the sounds were actually taped at a deli within New York City's Grand Central Station. While he considers the voices of the patrons and their specific sandwich orders to be subtly suggestive of the region, the audio does not contain explicit signifiers for Manhattan. The sound carries this specific connection to New York only in his personal memory; the spectator is not able to associate the audio with its original image source until Gehr himself makes the revelation. In the seventh shot, the overheard lyrics of the rhythm and blues song "Walking to New Orleans" echoing throughout the main hall allude to yet another distinct urban center.[44]

Similarly, the images from the twelfth shot of the film are paired with audio that Gehr had previously recorded in Venice. We are able to discern that it is Italian being spoken, but we cannot link it to its precise geographic location. Gehr again resists using audio cues that might be readily associated with Venice, such as the incessant symphony of chiming bell towers or the sloshing of oars against the water in the canals. The recordings of ambient sound from a garden apartment near the center of Geneva are playfully synchronized with the thirteenth through twenty-first shots; no voices are present on the tapes, but we hear the persistent chirping of a flock of birds and the occasional thundering noise of a jet flying overhead. Gehr deems these sounds of flying creatures and machines to pair ideally with the images of the skyscrapers gliding through the air: "I like how sometimes the building we see on-screen takes on the character of an aviary and at times the form of a flying bird or plane, while at all times it also remains what it is: a tall, heavy building that seems to slowly soar through space."[45] The twenty-second shot overlooks the financial district of San Francisco, but the audio was actually recorded in London, where we hear street vendors and their customers discussing in British accents the sizes and prices of clothing. The final shots of the film are matched with the sounds of Berlin, the city that was the home to Gehr's German-Jewish family before World War II, even further suggesting that the disorienting visual compositions of each shot provoke a slew of psychological connections for the filmmaker.

Over the course of his "lifetime of displacement," Gehr maintains that each one of these cities could have been considered his home at one point. He says that "the different sounds may imply different journeys, or perhaps a *memory* of different journeys. Each shot may also be seen as a journey in itself."[46] As a psychological palimpsest, the panorama of San Francisco in *Side/Walk/Shuttle* retains the memories of these previous travels and displacements. Only the first shot of the film, where we conspicuously hear German voices among a multitude of foreign languages, records ambient sound from the actual elevator. This first trip in the elevator gestures to the multicultural identity of San Francisco, but it also sparks Gehr's cascade of memories of cities where he once lived. It also alludes to the diasporic displacement of German Jews, such as those in Gehr's family, in the midst of the Holocaust. This audiovisual pairing marks a continuation of the ancestral reflection Gehr conducts in *Signal—Germany on the Air* (1985), a film that consists of a series of static views of various locations throughout West Berlin, such as the former Gestapo headquarters. This protracted interrogation of physical spaces serves as a haunting meditation on the consistently changing Berlin that still retains the ghosts of the past. Gehr's constant play with duration, image, and audio deconstructs these urban spaces from a subjective point of view, which elicits thoughts of imagined alternative time lines one's life may have followed.

Gehr's lifetime of displacement mirrors the global exploration undertaken by Marco Polo in Calvino's *Invisible Cities*. Like Polo, Gehr finds that each new city he encounters also encapsulates the same impressions, anxieties, and fears that he experienced in previous travels. The film positions the spectator in the role of the emperor Kublai Khan in the sense that he or she becomes enchanted with illusions of a physically implausible city while unwittingly penetrating into the depths of the traveler's psyche. Though San Francisco might initially seem inhospitable, with its rugged topography and deceitful perspectives, it nevertheless begins to bear resemblance to every other city that Gehr had called home. When you travel, Marco Polo says, "you realize that differences are lost: each city takes to resembling all cities, places exchange their form, order, distances, a shapeless dust cloud invades the continents."[47] In this sense, *Side/Walk/Shuttle* cannot narrowly be considered a stitched-together, composite image of multiple perspectives of the city of San Francisco, since it contains visible and invisible traces of all cities. One particular characteristic that is shared pervasively among Gehr's and Muybridge's San Francisco and also Barker's London is the unwavering display of drab and sordid qualities. The austere brown color palette that dominates many of the shots containing skyscrapers on Powell and Sacramento streets recalls the mounds of dirt, construction sites, temporary structures, and factory roofs from the earlier panoramas, suggesting that the artists' collective intent was to unveil all corners of the city—not only those emanating majesty and monumentality.

The dynamic combination of both sound and image is what elevates *Side/Walk/Shuttle* to the status of a psychological palimpsest; it is a panorama that stitches together multiple layers of personal memory. As Gehr succinctly puts it, the film's dynamic combination of elements amounts to "a panorama of the globe."[48] The images of the film record the surfaces of the cityscape, but their unity with the soundtrack is what facilitates penetration beneath the facades to access the invisible aspects of the city or what is contained within our own memories.

Gehr's desire to see beyond the surfaces of the city mirrors the dialectic Roland Barthes finds crucial to

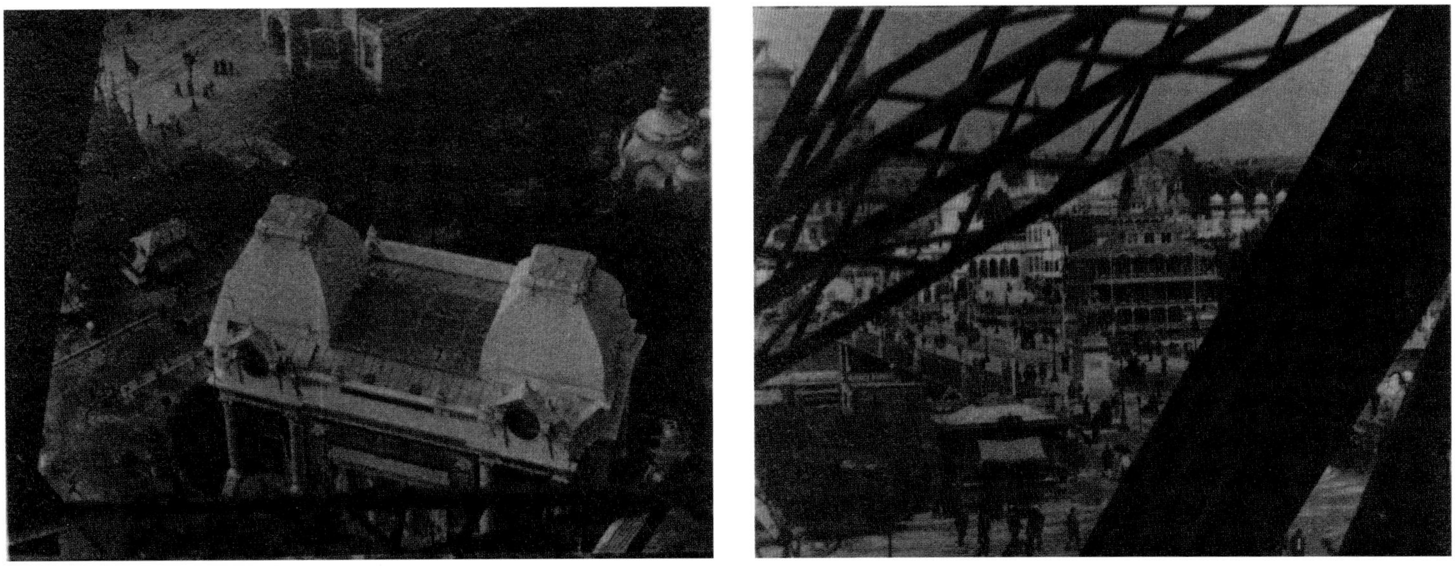

FIG. 10.10. Edison Manufacturing Co., *Scene from the Elevator Ascending Eiffel Tower*, 1900. Library of Congress, Washington, D.C. (00694299).

panoramic vision. In "The Eiffel Tower," Barthes conceives of the panoramic, aerial perspective as creating a tension between the "sensorial" and the "intellectual" means of experiencing our surroundings. Ordinarily when we perceive a sublime landscape, we find ourselves enchanted with its beauty, but we are able to recognize only superficial exteriors of our surroundings. "Panoramic vision," Barthes theorizes, also "added an incomparable power of *intellection*: the bird's-eye view, which each visitor to the Tower can assume in an instant for his own, gives us the world to *read* and not only to perceive."[49] In other words, when we ascend the Eiffel Tower, we decipher the fragmented surfaces of the city and ultimately interpret them in our own personal manner on the basis of individual memories, desires, and cultural associations. The Eiffel Tower is an object of fascination for Barthes because it serves as a vessel for a seemingly endless assortment of hidden meanings: "This pure—virtually empty—sign—is ineluctable, *because it means everything*."[50] In other words, panoramic vision is not just a function of pure sensation or visual pleasure, but it also stimulates our inclination to draw connections between our individual experiences and the objects of our gaze.

PERCEPTION IN MOTION: THE CINEMATIC PHANTOM RIDE

In *Side/Walk/Shuttle*, Gehr creates a compositional tension between the near-ground-level and aerial perspectives and thus never fully sustains the bird's-eye view of the horizon that Barthes deconstructs through his semiotic analysis. Since the elevator is constantly moving in every shot of the film, the vantage point "shuttles" back and forth from just above street level. Although he never places the camera among the crowds outside the hotel, it does glide close enough for us to be able to register both pedestrian and automobile traffic patterns. The mobile, mechanized perspective used in *Side/Walk/Shuttle* has a precedent in the early Edison Studios film *Scene from the Elevator Ascending Eiffel Tower* (1900), which documented the grounds of the Paris Exposition (fig. 10.10). The two-minute film delivers the perspective of a camera attached to an elevator ascending the tower in one trip to overlook the fairgrounds, but unlike Gehr's film, the journey is divided into four different shots.

This Edison short is one example of the expansive genre of early cinema known as the "phantom ride," which embraced the cadences of pure motion by mounting a camera to a moving train or vehicle—a practice that Gehr deconstructs and reinterprets in his films *Eureka* (1974), *Passage* (2003), and *Departure* (2012). The original phantom ride films, however, often contained the word *panorama* in their titles, but, as Tom Gunning notes, they provided the spectator with a simulation of movement through space instead of pivoting horizontally from a fixed position: "These panoramas did not simply show locomotives moving toward the camera, but instead mounted a camera on a train, capturing a mobile view of a landscape."[51] The camera was typically positioned near the front of the train in order to provide an unobstructed view of the landscape.

In these phantom ride films, the locomotive itself becomes a mobile viewing platform and presents the spectator with constantly shifting perspectives.

In the case of *Side/Walk/Shuttle* and *Scene from the Elevator Ascending Eiffel Tower*—both of which are "vertical" incarnations of the phantom ride—the gaze afforded by the movement is more conducive to aerial surveillance than horizontal passage through the surrounding space. The ascents and descents along the vertical axis provide innumerable angles to survey the streets, traffic, and adjacent buildings, but this space cannot be entered or traversed. The laterally oriented phantom ride, on the other hand, as Gunning explains, penetrates the surrounding environment: "The cinematic phantom ride dove straight into the landscape and presented this plunging point of view directly to the viewer."[52] This discrepancy between the vertical and horizontal phantom ride modalities creates a distinction between looking *at* our surroundings and looking *around* them.

In the circular panorama, the spectator is immersed in the illusion of a landscape, but the eye is permitted only to peak into the vast distance on account of the viewing platform's spatial limitations. Oettermann suggests that while the panorama liberates vision by granting mastery over the horizon, it also strictly limits the eye by preventing it from seeing beyond the margins: "At the same time that the panorama celebrates the bourgeoisie's ability to 'see things from a new angle,' it is also a complete prison for the eye."[53] The panorama offers multiple vantage points, but its scalar relationships and proximal distances can never be altered from the physical confines of the viewing platform. In this state of imprisonment, the spectator remains actively pensive while the eye traces the contours of the landscape.

The phantom ride, however, denies the spectator the ability to contemplate the surroundings, especially those in the immediate foreground. As Wolfgang Schivelbusch has postulated, the movement of the train engendered a new kind of "panoramic perception" where the landscape became "evanescent" because "visual perception is diminished by velocity."[54] The view of the foreground out of the train window abstracted the landscape and rendered it unrecognizable to the passenger: "The speed causes objects to escape from one's gaze, but one nevertheless keeps on trying to grasp them."[55] Gehr affirms this observation in *Departure* by placing a camera against the side window of a passenger train as it accelerates along its route, which optically distorts the field of view to the point of illegibility (fig. 10.11). The wooden railroad ties on the adjacent track flicker past us in an indecipherable blur because of the phenomenon of motion parallax, but the mind fixates on them and at times observes that their direction of movement seems to reverse arbitrarily. The pure abstraction of motion is even more pronounced in *Auto-Collider XV* (2011), in which horizontal streaks from a car ride appear that resemble a modernist color field painting (fig. 10.12). While the visual fields of films such as *Passage*, *Auto-Collider XV*, and *Departure* are too fleeting and indeterminate to make sense of one's surroundings, for Gehr they persist as zones of curiosity, contemplation, and personal memory. The dizzying motion blurs of the S-Bahn train zooming through the former East Berlin in *Passage*, for example, again recall his own familial origins but also reflect the city's tumultuous geopolitical history.

In his film *Eureka*, Gehr uses slow motion to reverse this attenuation of visual acuity caused by train travel. He rephotographed and dilated a few minutes of the early film *A Trip Down Market Street before the Fire* (1906), which is believed to have been shot only a matter of days before the earthquake decimated San Francisco, to a total length of just over thirty minutes.[56] Through the camera mounted at the front of a trolley car traversing the length of Market Street toward the Embarcadero, we see rare glimpses of urban life at the turn of the century, such as a city congested with traffic of pedestrians, carriages, automobiles, and other passing trolleys (fig. 10.13). By slowing down the footage to a nearly glacial speed, Gehr decelerates the forces of urban modernity and restores the spectator's ability to recognize the surroundings with visual clarity. As we crawl through this urban space, we can almost distinguish the faces of the men and women who cross our path on the rails ahead.

Side/Walk/Shuttle and *Eureka* exemplify two radically different paradigms of mobility—namely, the vertical surveillance in the former and horizontal penetration through space in the latter—but both strive for the same ends: to render the elusive and invisible qualities of urban life visible. In reference to phantom ride films, Giuliana Bruno argues that the spectator becomes more attuned to the pulse of a city when mobilized: "Traveling with its spectatorship through its shifting positions, [the] travel film created a flowing chart of the city."[57] In the case of Gehr's *Eureka*, the experimentation with the deceleration

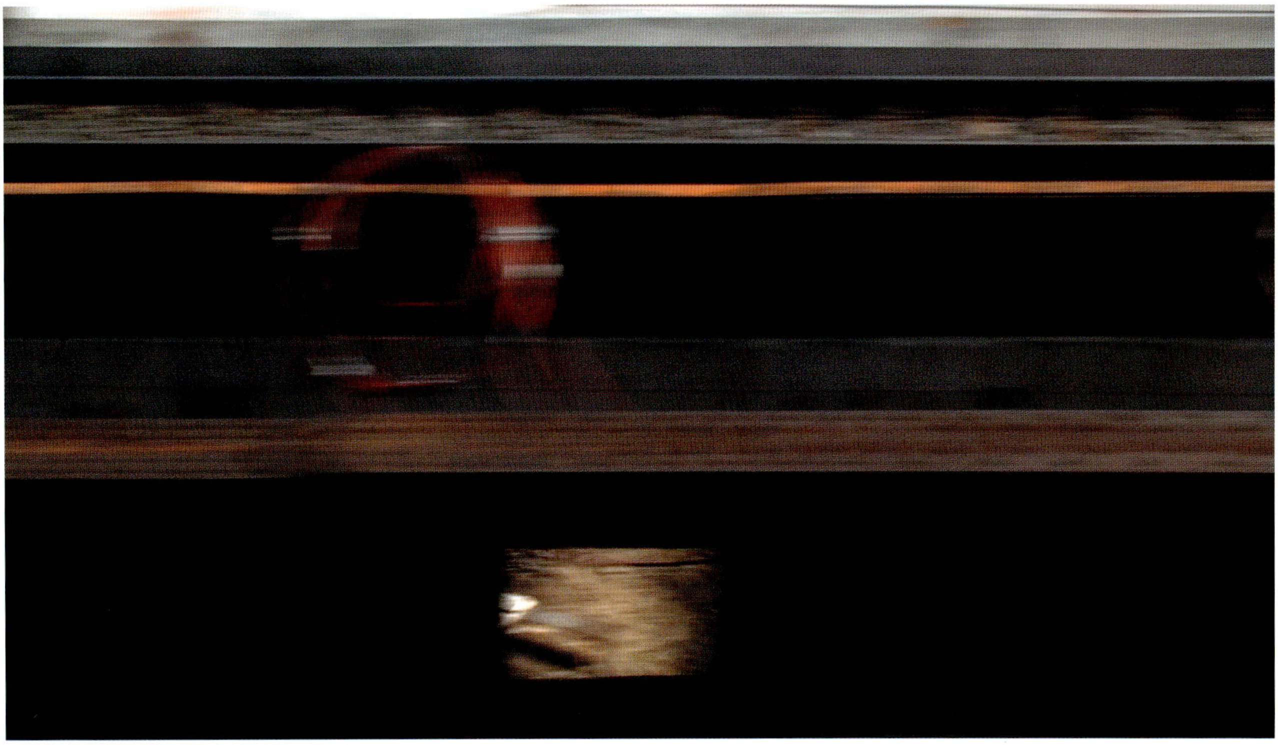

FIG. 10.11. Ernie Gehr, *Departure*, 2012.

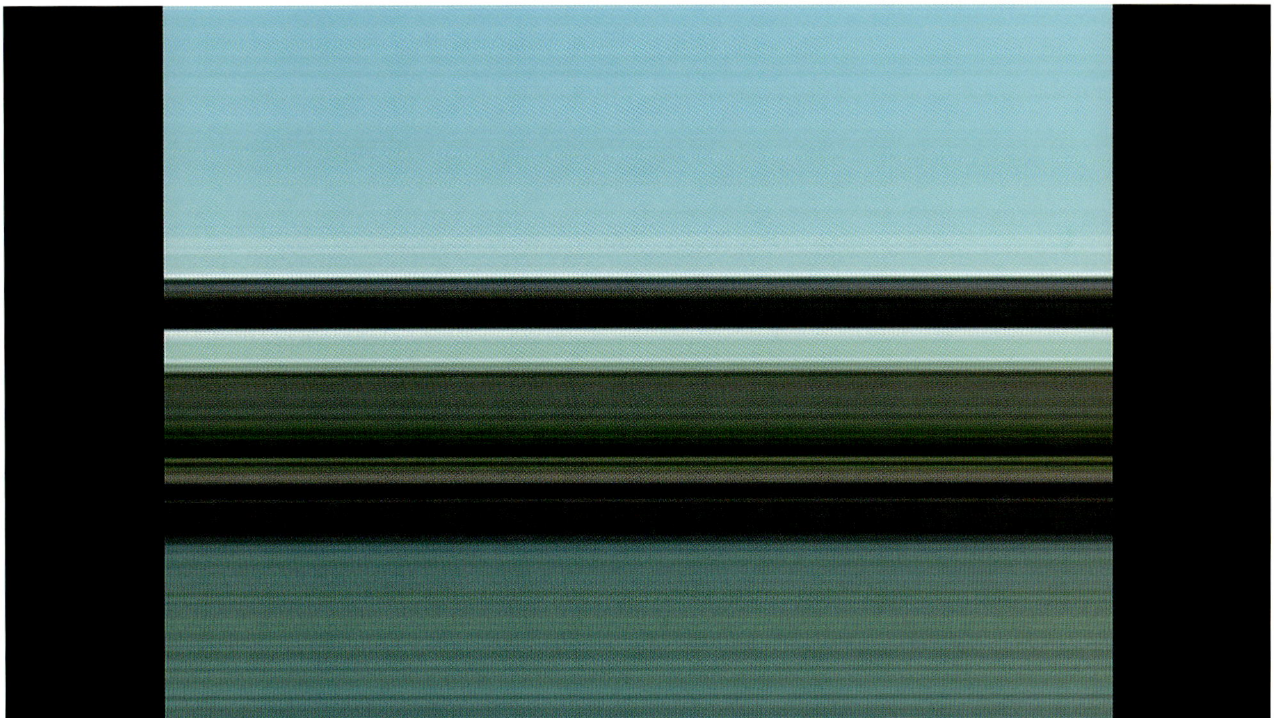

FIG. 10.12. Ernie Gehr, *Auto-Collider XV*, 2011.

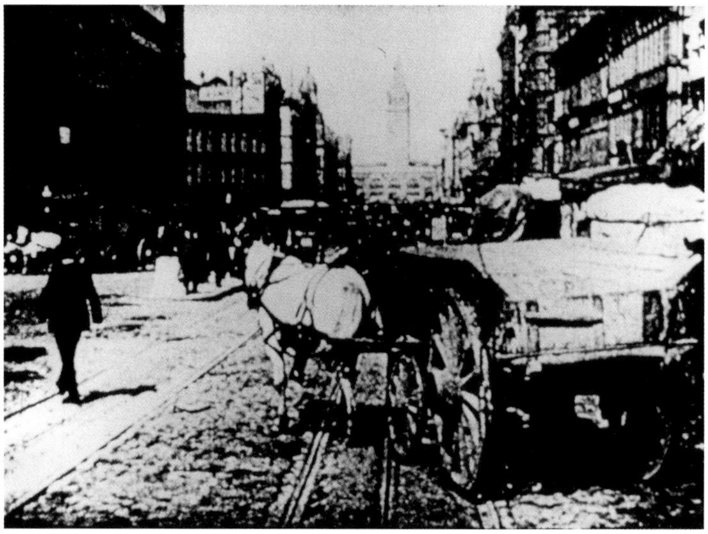

FIG. 10.13. Ernie Gehr, *Eureka*, 1974.

of the bustling city life on Market Street assuages the anxieties induced by the frenzy of urban modernity.

In *The Arcades Project*, Walter Benjamin characterizes the panorama as being a means of escaping the turbulence of congested city life. By entering the rotunda, which serves as a microcosmic representation of the exterior world, the spectator is able to see "the true city—the city indoors."[58] It is through this enclosed, darkened space, with its dizzying simulacrum, that he or she is able to gaze inwardly to reveal the "truth" of urban experience. Gehr's *Side/Walk/Shuttle* functions in the same vein as Benjamin's topology because the glass window of the Fairmont's elevator bridges the human psyche with the alienating aspects of San Francisco. By depicting the confounding features of the exterior cityscape, Gehr constructs a true, but uniquely personal image of the city—a psychological palimpsest that harbors his own memories, desires, and fears. The transparency of the elevator facilitates the internalization of the city and reminds us that that we—like Marco Polo recounting his fanciful travelogue to Kublai Khan—are in fact constructing the panorama ourselves.

NOTES

Thanks to Canyon Cinema, Brian Meacham (Yale Film Archive), Alexis Ainsworth and Kelly Chisholm (Library of Congress), and, most important, Ernie Gehr.

1 For an overview of the "phantom ride," see Tom Gunning, "Landscape and the Fantasy of Moving Pictures: Early Cinema's Phantom Rides," in *Cinema and Landscape: Film, Nation and Cultural Geography*, ed. Graeme Harper and Jonathan Rayner (Bristol: Intellect, 2010), 31–70.

2. For a more detailed explanation of how the moving panorama operated, see Erkki Huhtamo, *Illusions in Motion: Media Archaeology of the Moving Panorama and Related Spectacles* (Cambridge: MIT Press, 2013), 6–8.

3. See Erkki Huhtamo, "Dismantling the Fairy Engine: Media Archaeology as Topos Study," in *Media Archaeology: Approaches, Applications, and Implications*, ed. Erkki Huhtamo and Jussi Parikka (Berkeley: University of California Press, 2011), 27–47; 28–29. Huhtamo appropriated the term from Ernst Curtius as a way to account for the various tropes that recur repeatedly in cultural spheres and media technology. He explains further: "Identifying topoi, analyzing their trajectories and transformations, and explaining the cultural logics that condition their 'wanderings' across time and space is one possible goal of media archaeology."

4. "Specification of the Patent Granted to Mr. Robert Barker of the City of Edinburgh, Portrait Painter; for his Invention of an Entire New Contrivance or Apparatus called by him *La Nature à Coup d'Oeuil*, for the Purpose of displaying Views of Nature at large, by Oil-Painting, Fresco, Water-colours, Crayons, or any other Mode of painting or drawing," in *The Repertory of Arts and Manufactures*, vol. 4 (London: T. Heptinstall et al., 1796), 165–67.

5. Ibid., 165. Barker had originally called his invention *La Nature à Coup d'Oeil* before he ultimately settled on the word *panorama*, meaning "all-sight" in Greek.

6. Denise Blake Oleksijczuk, *The First Panoramas: Visions of British Imperialism* (Minneapolis: University of Minnesota Press, 2011), 11.

7. Ibid., 3.

8. For an account of the production of the panoramas, see Brian Clegg, *The Man Who Stopped Time: The Illuminating Story of Eadweard Muybridge—Pioneer Photographer, Father of the Motion Picture, Murderer* (Washington, D.C.: Joseph Henry Press, 2007), 114–17. Also see David Harris with Eric Sandweiss, *Eadweard Muybridge and the Photographic Panorama of San Francisco, 1850–1880* (Cambridge: MIT Press, 1993), 37–38.

9. For details on the photography and distribution of the 1877 panorama, see Marta Braun, *Eadweard Muybridge* (London: Reaktion, 2010), 120–22. A boudoir card was resilient cardboard material used for mounting the more delicate albumen prints.

10. Ibid., 125–27. Braun also points out that the technology of the 1878 camera had greatly improved from the previous year. Muybridge had printed only nine copies, two of which he gave to Mary Hopkins and Jane Stanford.

11. See Hiroshi Sugimoto and Hans Belting, *Theaters* (New York: Sonnabend Sundell Editions and Eyestorm), 2000.

12. See Eadweard Muybridge, *San Francisco 1878: Portrait of the City* (San Francisco: History Department, Wells Fargo Bank, 1979), for a reproduction of the 1878 panorama and a legend identifying the prominent landmarks. The plates in the reproduction are numbered differently; the seventh plate in my analysis corresponds to the thirteenth plate of this edition.

13. See Braun, *Eadweard Muybridge*, 125.

14. A different kind of discontinuity between plates can be seen in the 1877

panorama where there is some visual overlap between parts of the city on adjacent photographs.

15. Hollis Frampton, "Eadweard Muybridge: Fragments of a Tesseract," in *On the Camera Arts and Consecutive Matters: The Writings of Hollis Frampton*, ed. Bruce Jenkins (Cambridge: MIT Press, 2009), 22–32; 28. It is possible that Frampton was actually referring to the much more celebrated 1878 panorama, but his observations are pertinent to both versions.
16. Ibid., 27.
17. Harris also provides a detailed analysis of visual quadrants constructed by these intersecting streets. See Harris with Sandweiss, *Eadweard Muybridge and the Photographic Panorama*, 50.
18. We can more readily restore the three-dimensionality of San Francisco in Muybridge's panorama in our minds because very few features of the Hopkins mansion—only the tops of the adjacent turrets in plates 1, 3, and 11—are visible.
19. See Oleksijczuk, *The First Panoramas*, 56–68. Also see Brian Maidment, *Reading Popular Prints: 1790–1870* (Manchester, U.K.: Manchester University Press, 2001), 29–30.
20. My analysis of the composition of the aquatint plates is based on the binding of those donated by John Roland Abbey to the Yale Center for British Art. Each of the six is finely numbered in pencil, and the first four contain individual dates from August 18, 1792, through March 27, 1793, in sequential order. The dates on the last two plates are illegible. These notations suggest that this is the intended ordering of the plates, but other reproductions nevertheless have different configurations.
21. See Harris with Sandweiss, *Eadweard Muybridge and the Photographic Panorama*, 50.
22. Reprinted ibid., 49.
23. Ernie Gehr, *1993 Program Notes: Ernie Gehr—A Retrospective* (San Francisco: San Francisco Cinematheque, 1993), 15.
24. For a detailed history of the Fairmont Hotel, see Fairmont Hotel, "Hotel History," https://www.fairmont.com/san-francisco/hotel-history, accessed November 1, 2013.
25. Gehr, *1993 Program Notes*, 15.
26. For these incidental details of the filming process, see Ernie Gehr and Scott MacDonald, "Ernie Gehr," in *A Critical Cinema 5: Interviews with Independent Filmmakers*, ed. Scott MacDonald (Berkeley: University of California Press, 2006), 358–404; 393.
27. P. Adams Sitney, *Visionary Film: The American Avant-Garde, 1943–2000* (Oxford: Oxford University Press, 2002), 348.
28. Drawing from Sitney's taxonomy, *Serene Velocity* is characteristic of a structural film through its fixed camera, loop printing, and strobe effect produced by the rapid alternation of the various focal lengths.
29. Michael Snow, "Converging on *La Région Centrale*: Michael Snow in Conversation with Charlotte Townsend," in *The Collected Writings of Michael Snow* (Waterloo, Ont.: Wilfrid Laurier University Press, 1994), 57–60; 57.
30. Gehr, *1993 Program Notes*, 15.
31. Gehr and MacDonald, "Ernie Gehr," 396.
32. As Scott MacDonald points out, this imagery is evocative of buildings in San Francisco always remaining in a structurally precarious state owing to the looming possibility of earthquakes. See Scott MacDonald, *The Garden in the Machine: A Field Guide to Independent Films about Place* (Berkeley: University of California Press, 2001), 236.
33. These past experiences were conveyed to me during a discussion with Gehr in June 2014.
34. Stephan Oettermann, *The Panorama: History of a Mass Medium*, trans. Deborah Lucas Schneider (New York: Zone, 1997), 31.
35. Oleksijczuk, *The First Panoramas*, 83.
36. Ibid., 84.
37. Ibid., 12. Oleksijczuk explains that the environmental parameters of the panorama rotunda, such as the multi-perpsectivalism, skylights, and sheer size of the canvas, incorporated the spectator into the canvas.
38. Johann Augustus Eberhard, quoted in ibid.
39. Quoted in Harris with Sandweiss, *Eadweard Muybridge and the Photographic Panorama*, 49. Muybridge writes: "The photograph of San Francisco, recently made by putting together a succession of views which, taken from a commanding central point, make a complete circuit of the horizon."
40. Quoted in P. Adams Sitney, *Eyes Upside Down: Visionary Filmmakers and the Heritage of Emerson* (New York: Oxford University Press, 2008), 216–17.
41. Ernie Gehr, "Aspects of Eadweard Muybridge's Photographic Work," in *Radical Light: Alternative Film and Video in the San Francisco Bay Area, 1945–2000*, ed. Steve Anker, Kathy Geritz, and Steve Seid (Berkeley: University of California Press, 2010), 19–25; 21. Gehr is likely to have familiarized himself with Muybridge's work after visiting a retrospective at the New York Cultural Center (May 11–July 1, 1973).
42. Victor Burgin, "The Time of the Panorama," in *Situational Aesthetics: Selected Writings by Victor Burgin*, ed. Alexander Streitberger (Leuven: Leuven University Press, 2009), 293–314; 303.
43. In conversation, Ernie Gehr has informed me that he obtained much of the audio long before he even conceived of making the film.
44. Gehr and MacDonald, "Ernie Gehr," 396. In conversation with me, Gehr has also indicated that he found the overheard request for "turkey with mustard and sauerkraut" to be atypical of San Francisco delis during the 1980s and more suggestive of New York.
45. Ibid., 397.
46. Gehr and MacDonald, "Ernie Gehr," 396.
47. Italo Calvino, *Invisible Cities*, trans. William Weaver (San Diego: Harcourt, 1974), 137.
48. Quoted in Sitney, *Eyes Upside Down*, 218.
49. Roland Barthes, "The Eiffel Tower," in *A Barthes Reader*, ed. Susan Sontag (New York: Hill and Wang, 1983), 242.
50. Ibid., 237; emphasis in original.
51. Gunning, "Landscape and the Fantasy of Moving Pictures," 54.
52. Ibid., 55.
53. Oettermann, *The Panorama*, 21.
54. Wolfgang Schivelbusch, *The Railway Journey: The Industrialization of Time and Space in the Nineteenth Century*, trans. Anselm Hollo (Berkeley: University of California Press, 1986), 55. Tom Gunning in his own reading of Schivelbusch's "panoramic perception" arrives at a similar conclusion: "The pleasures of speed and rapid succession replaced contemplation"; Gunning, "Landscape and the Fantasy of Moving Pictures," 41.
55. Schivelbusch, *The Railway Journey*, 57.
56. Rephotography entails the use of one camera to photograph the projection of another film. This technique was also used by Ken Jacobs in *Tom, Tom, the Piper's Son* (1969). Jacobs, however, was more invasive in his deconstruction of his own source material, whereas Gehr only reduced its projection speed.
57. Giuliana Bruno, *Atlas of Emotion: Journeys in Art, Architecture, and Film* (New York: Verso, 2002), 184.
58. Walter Benjamin, *The Arcades Project*, trans. Howard Eiland and Kevin McLaughlin (Cambridge: Harvard University Press, 1999), 532.

MAL AHERN

11 Playing with Vision

The Panoramic Shot in Laura Mulvey and Peter Wollen's *Riddles of the Sphinx*

> It is said that analyzing pleasure, or beauty, destroys it. That is the intention of this article. The satisfaction and reinforcement of the ego that represent the high point of film history hitherto must be attacked. Not in favor of a reconstructed new pleasure, which cannot exist in the abstract, nor of intellectualized unpleasure, but to make way for a total negation of the ease and plenitude of the narrative fiction film. The alternative is the thrill that comes from leaving the past behind without rejecting it, transcending outworn or oppressive forms, or daring to break with normal pleasurable expectations in order to conceive a new language of desire.
>
> —Laura Mulvey, "Visual Pleasure and Narrative Cinema" (1975)

CINEMA AS A RADICAL WEAPON

In 1975 Laura Mulvey published the essay that would define feminist film theory for decades. "Visual Pleasure and Narrative Cinema" taught a generation of film students to enter the cinema cautiously. The Hollywood film, according to Mulvey, contained within it all the elements of capitalist patriarchy. Every time one of Hitchcock's blondes offered herself up to our gaze, the cinema confirmed that men were active and women were passive—that, as John Berger famously put it, "Men look at women. Women watch themselves being looked at."[1] Mulvey's essay popularized the notion that, from social practices down to our unconscious, masculine language structures our psyches. And the cinema, born of masculine language, shores up those structures.

This was, at least, what many readers remembered from Mulvey's essay. One critic described Mulvey's criticism of gendered looking relations as "so all-encompassing that no form of narrative or visual enjoyment or engagement is exempt." Martin Jay has suggested the Lacanian-Althusserian tradition of film theory that the "Visual Pleasure" essay embodied was essentially "cinephobic."[2] Many still read—and teach—it as a pessimistic essay: an indictment of cinema, even of vision itself.

But these characterizations account for only one part of Mulvey's project. "Visual Pleasure" is surely a polemic, but it is also a program: a rallying cry for radical, avant-garde revisions of cinematic language. Rather than wallowing in "intellectualized unpleasure," Mulvey urges us instead to feel the "thrill" that might come from imagining "a new language of desire."[3] Mulvey practiced what she preached: her own films give us a better sense of what the risks and thrills of experimentation might be.

This essay examines *Riddles of the Sphinx* (1977), one of several films Mulvey made during the 1970s and 1980s with her husband at the time, Peter Wollen. Though the film has five distinct parts, I will focus on its central, longest section, which comprises thirteen panoramic shots.

In each, a camera mounted on a central tripod rotates slowly, taking in a 360-degree view of the mise-en-scène. As we are immersed within this visually disorienting style, we follow Louise, a mother who leaves her husband, gets a job, and undergoes a psychic and political transformation. Louise becomes involved in union politics; she fights for better child care at work; she rejects the patriarchal family structure in favor of coparenting with a close female friend (who may have, by the end of the film, become Louise's lover). All the while, a female voice-over asks unanswerable questions about motherhood, politics, and sexual difference. The story is complex, entertaining, and—dare I say—quite pleasurable.

A rich literature has praised the film's content: its musings on gender, labor, and language. And many critics have understood the panoramic shot as a politically motivated rejection of Hollywood continuity editing.[4] Yet few describe the sensory experience of watching these protracted cinematic panoramas.[5] My analysis of Mulvey and Wollen's film relies not on the mere fact of its divergence from classic cinematic form but rather on a close description of how the camera's panoramic movement shapes visual experience over time.

The pan puts viewers through a playful and challenging cognitive process. Its moving lens stretches and bends the visual field, at times distending the relationship between the shapes onscreen and the words we assign them. This visual experience is, I argue, the very ground on which Mulvey and Wollen hoped to build a new, nonpatriarchal language. Before we create a new language, we first have to *see* the world anew. Rather than assign new words to the same old objects, we must use our eyes and minds to divide the matter before us into yet-to-be-named shapes. Mulvey and Wollen's visual disorientations aspire to the goal Maurice Merleau-Ponty articulated for cinema in his 1964 essay "Film and the New Psychology": "The idea we have of the world would be overturned if we could succeed in seeing the intervals between things (for example, the space between the trees on the boulevard) as objects and, inversely, if we saw the things themselves—the trees—as the ground."[6]

The optical apparatus of mirror, camera, and frame lend their support in this endeavor. But the effort, crucially, is our own. We regard the screen as a philosophical toy, one we can use to exercise our own perception. We sometimes allow the onscreen shapes and colors to cohere into a perspectival narrative space; at other times we choose to regard them as kaleidoscopic patterns. A frame might initially appear as a window or mirror, but soon we learn to let our mind's eye flicker between these two options. The disorientation of the extended panoramic shot transforms the screen: it is no longer a window onto a stage on which characters move, dramas unfold, and events progress. Or it is no longer *only* that. The screen also becomes what Walter Benjamin, essaying cinema's radical potential, called *room-for-play*.[7]

Miriam Hansen has read Benjamin's idea of "play" as a mode of sense perception that might counteract the destructive effects of capitalist modernity by reformulating the relationship between humans and technology.[8] I will use *play* in a similar but slightly different sense. The perceptual play of watching *Riddles of the Sphinx* suggests what it would feel like to be able to restructure the imaginary and thus establish a new relationship between words and things. It is only through playing with both language and vision that we might forge a new, nonpatriarchal relationship to language. *Riddles'* overt politics—its "manifest" content, perhaps—obtains support and significance from its sensory details. In *Riddles*, cinema is equal parts perceptual toy and critical tool. It holds the promise that humans might be able to use machines to reformulate the very process of signification.

RENDERING VOLUME

> The scene is about to yield up its volume. But not without a subtle system of feints.
>
> —Michel Foucault, "Las Meninas," in *The Order of Things* (1970)

Neither the lens nor the mirror recognizes our world of discrete objects, of things with names. Rather, both regard the world as an unbroken field of variegated light. The cinema signifies because we assimilate its visual field to our own abstract systems—much the way we assimilate the visual sensations we encounter whenever our eyes are open. We recognize the shapes the screen offers up, and we call them by their names.

The cinema has also evolved its own language—an abstract, symbolic code. We see a shot of a man and a shot of a woman; if we subsequently understand the couple to be in the same space, gazing at one another, it is due to this system of cinematic language, a set of verbal and visual cues. Inspired by Althusserian Marxism and Lacanian psychoanalysis, post-1968 critics in *Cahiers du Cinéma* and the

British journal *Screen* instigated a thoroughgoing critique of such cinematic codes. Mulvey and Wollen were among the many critics who advocated for a "counter-cinema," a set of aesthetic strategies that would break with the seamlessness of classic cinematic language.[9] *Riddles*, accordingly, rejects traditional editing in favor if its lengthy pans.

Were a film to present one continuous, stable shot, Daniel Dayan argued, viewers would wonder what, or who, had produced the image and to what end; they would think about their own roles as viewers and their relationship to the absent agents constructing the scene. Yet when a reverse shot shows a character's face, the viewer retroactively understands the first shot as motivated by a character's gaze. Thus, spectators learn to assign every shot a cause internal to the film's narrative.[10] Jean-Pierre Oudart used the word *suture* to describe how films thus produce the impression of contiguous space by soliciting the viewer's unconscious cooperation. The classical Hollywood film follows the model of Velázquez's *Las Meninas*, a painting that envelops the space in which we viewers stand, yet erases us in the process.[11]

In the classical Hollywood cinema, editing moves far too quickly and efficiently to let us savor this paradox. It solicits, even exploits, our psychic labor in knitting the film together and sells us back that labor as entertainment. This is how, according to the critics of *Cahiers* and *Screen*, cinematic style produced a *subject*, a living being of illusory coherence shot through with capitalist ideology. According to David Rodowick, many critics in the post-1968 era asserted that "the only valid form of art was one that ruptured the fixity of meaning and decentered or deconstructed the subject."[12] By disrupting the smooth machinations of Hollywood style, it follows that a film might disrupt the subject of capitalist patriarchy too.

It is immediately apparent that the panoramic shot breaks with classical Hollywood style: while classical editing constructs space with crisp efficiency, the panoramic shot unfurls space in time. In this it follows the experience of viewing the painted panorama, one of the founding sites of modern spectatorship. Like cinema, the painted panorama combines multiple two-dimensional, perspectival images to yield an extraordinary sense of volume, a virtual space that is as coherent as—or, rather, more coherent than—the one in which we live. The critics and historians who study these earliest manifestations of the panorama thus engage the same questions of vision, power, and control that were central to 1970s film theory. Stephan Oettermann's now-canonical *The Panorama: History of a Mass Medium* (first published in 1980 as *Das Panorama*), for example, describes how the painted panorama worked on the spectator's eye and body to produce a modern, disciplined subject.[13] Like the Marxist critics of cinema, Oettermann concludes that the painted panorama enslaves vision by offering spectators a sense of visual mastery.

The 360-degree cinematic pan, like its nineteenth-century painted counterpart, makes us acutely aware of the gap at its center, the space from which the spectator sees. Critics of Mulvey and Wollen have suggested that the panoramic shot indulges viewers' fantasies of a centered, coherent self who has a masterful control over his or her surroundings—whereas many 1970s film theorists praised the subject-shattering quality of experimental film style.[14] These debates about vision and volume are essentially about the politics of being—or *not* being—a subject. What are the political stakes to feeling "whole" or "divided," "centered" or "decentered," "constructed" or "deconstructed"? If political modernism could deconstruct the subject, what would it install in its place—or would any stable, nameable self become subject to cooptation?

Already in 1994, Rodowick observed that the question of "*the* subject" had long since retreated in the face of "an ever-widening series of differences defined by complex approaches to gender, post-coloniality, racial and ethnic differences, and queer theory."[15] Yet this necessary development within film studies still engaged questions of the viewer's identity and political agency, or lack thereof. *Riddles* arguably stands at the beginning of radical film theory's acknowledgment of difference. "Visual Pleasure" and other early essays of Mulvey's do not engage racial difference or the fact of queer spectatorship; nonetheless, they grapple with the fact that cinema simply could *not* homogenize its diverse audience, however much it might attempt to do so.[16] Women denied access, under patriarchy, to a stable form of subjectivity were not able to simply adopt the position of the male viewer. Mulvey's appeal to experimental filmmaking suggests that radically new forms of spectatorship might allow women to construct themselves as radically new and different subjects. *Riddles* itself leverages the power of cinema that theory had long critiqued: its power to mold the viewer in its image. Aesthetic forms, *Riddles* suggests, can also build new forms of life.

The thirteen pans that form *Riddles* do not constitute a new cinematic language, an alternative to the shot/reverse shot system that Oudart called suture. Rather, they push back against the abstract, linguistic system of Hollywood editing by emphasizing the visual and sensual registers of cinematic experience. Camera movement—including the panoramic shot—has provided a consistent foil for critics who analyze the "language" of film editing. The camera can follow a potentially infinite number of paths in three-dimensional space, making it impossible to account for camera movement with fully generalizable rules or typologies. Despite our best efforts to subject cinema to a linguistic or structural analysis, camera movement requires us to describe our experience of looking in time. This is particularly important in *Riddles of the Sphinx*, where panoramic camera movement forces viewers to attend closely to the screen as a constantly shifting visual field.

Mulvey and Wollen's belief that visual sensation could serve as the ground for new forms of signification is key to understanding *Riddles*. It is also the direct result of Mulvey's readings in psychoanalytic theory. In the 1970s Lacanian psychoanalysis was a foundational intellectual framework for many film critics. Yet Mulvey's reading of Lacan was distinctive. To understand Mulvey's ideas about gender and language, it is crucial to revisit Lacan's terms *symbolic*, *imaginary*, and *real*. The idea of the *imaginary* deeply influenced Mulvey and Wollen's work on the relationship between word and image and their ideas about how aesthetic experience could transform both.

THE IMAGINARY

"New languages and new forms of representation don't appear like magic just because you hope and want them to," Mulvey stated in a 1979 interview. "Language has to be recognizable; it can't be isolated, just what you hope."[17] Instead, Mulvey wanted *Riddles* to "start making out a space which would not necessarily produce a different language, but force one to think differently"—a necessary step if a new language was ever to emerge.[18] When discussing *Riddles*, Wollen likewise insisted that "it is precisely the interface between image and word that concerns us," specifically "the dialectic of fit and misfit" between word and image.[19] At this interface, *Riddles* performs its initial research into new forms of language and develops a unique audiovisual means of encouraging nonpatriarchal discourse.

Mulvey claimed that *Riddles of the Sphinx* "is really 'about' the imaginary."[20] For Lacan, the symbolic is ruled by presence and lack—that is, we can say what an object *is* only by deciding what it *isn't*. Lacan argues that this structure of presence and absence originates in boys' castration fears: through a traumatic encounter with the female body, the male child discovers both the power and threat of absence, and he uses this knowledge to assert meaning in the field of language. Thus, Lacanian theory could account for only the *male* child's integration into language. Women, according to Lacan, never truly gain entry into "the symbolic order since they never undergo castration anxiety.[21] Girls lack a *stake* in this regime of presence and absence since—as Mary Ann Doane puts it—they literally have nothing to lose.[22]

Lacking access to the symbolic, women, according to Lacan, remain stuck in the realm of the imaginary. Stephen Heath associates the imaginary with the plenitude of the "mother-child dyad," a phase, or relationship, in which the infant does not yet understand where his body ends and the mother's begins—or where objects in general find their boundaries.[23] The female child typically fails to traverse the Oedipus complex, remaining intimate with the mother and failing to internalize the father's "no." Women, moreover, often become mothers themselves, reentering the mother-child dyad from the other side. The imaginary's elastic nature makes it, in Daniel Dayan's words, "the structure through which images are formed."[24] It allows us to organize the visual world into fields of sensation that we later recognize as objects, and to which we append language. It is the adhesive with which we apply words to things. Yet in classic Lacanian theory, to be *stuck* in the imaginary is still to live in the world of plenitude and possibility, in which images emerge from sensation as provisional, always changeable forms, and language lacks the capacity truly to limit perception. In this state, language is correspondingly less effective. Because it lacks the capacity to limit, it also lacks the capacity to signify.

Yet *Riddles* shows how the imaginary gains traction in the world of politics and subjectivity. For Mulvey, "even concrete political activities are shot through with the workings of the imaginary," particularly as women encounter the question of motherhood—"to live it, or to not live it."[25] In the case of Louise, *Riddles*'s protagonist, the concrete activity of child rearing imbricates with her own memories of infancy, influencing her practical, world-altering decisions about labor, unionization, and the politics and practicalities of child care. Rational decision making and inner psychic life appear codeterminate: Louise enters the workplace and negotiates life as a working mother. At the film's literal center—the seventh of its thirteen panoramic shots—the narrator asks, "What would a politics of the unconscious look like?"

The imaginary and the symbolic also serve a *formal* function for the film's visual register, particularly in its thirteen panoramas. In the following section, I will attend closely to these visual sensations, since it is specifically the *pan* that allows Mulvey and Wollen to insist on the imaginary's importance. The pan stresses the "interface between image and word" by distorting the way the film lens divides colors and shapes into objects. As fields of color stretch or float across the frame, they pass from abstract shape to nameable thing, and back again. *Riddles* thus provides a rich visual field that catches the imaginary and the symbolic in an altercation. The fact of panoramic camera movement plays with the links between objects and their signification, suggesting that the imaginary is not simply the unstable ground of a rigid symbolic but the primary site for language's reconstruction.

BENT SPACE

> An image is a stop the mind makes between uncertainties.
>
> —Djuna Barnes, *Nightwood* (1936)

Nearly a decade before *Riddles of the Sphinx*, Jackie Raynal's experimental feature *Deux fois* (1968) also used the extensive pan to interrogate cinematic space in the course of a feminist narrative. One of the film's early shots sets the camera on an embankment in the middle of a four-lane road and executes a lengthy pan that makes several 360-degree loops. Our first journey around with the camera gives us ample time to absorb the scene: a group of pedestrians waits at a crosswalk; a car waits at a stoplight. But by the time the camera makes its second journey around, all these objects have changed position. The pedestrians have disappeared; they have apparently crossed the road behind us while the camera directed our attention away from their trajectory. Our sense of disorientation increases as the speed of the pan picks up slightly, and as we gradually lose track of the number of times the camera has spun around in its place.

In a later scene, the camera pans counterclockwise across a seated group of young adults, who stare back at it. Raynal's own face is one of the last we meet before the camera reverses its 180-degree journey, showing us the same series of young people in reverse. But something has changed: when we arrive back at our starting point, we encounter Raynal's face again. Initially, her appearance is surprising, paradoxical: the young woman appears in this space twice, as if by magic, betraying the viewer's expectation that off-camera space will remain unchanged as it awaits the return of his or her gaze. Within a few seconds, we realize that Raynal simply crossed behind the camera while it was on the midst of its return journey, arriving at the other end of the pan in time to meet us there.

Raynal's experiments illustrate an obvious yet crucial difference between the painted panorama and the cinematic pan shot: the pan necessarily presents 360 degrees in time. Of course, many painted panoramas, particularly battle panoramas, adopt a form of continuous narrative and portray several historical events that do not occur simultaneously. And the viewer of the painted panorama is unable to see the entire work at once; she must encounter it bit by bit over time. Yet the viewer of the painted panorama can still proceed *as if* every part of the artwork is equally available to his or her eye at any given moment. This may be one reason that Oettermann characterizes panoramic spectatorship as a position of visual mastery or enslaved vision, a space both intelligible and inescapable.[26]

The cinematic panoramic shot, on the other hand, displays a world constantly in flux, in which the spectator must cede a great deal of control and mastery over depicted space. Over the course of a 360-degree pan, the viewer sees every part of the landscape in the camera's range of vision, yet sees each part of it only at a particular moment. With the extensive pans of *Deux fois* and *Riddles*, we are often just as aware of what is out-of-field as what we see within the frame.

Riddles plays with the same sense of flux as *Deux fois*, showing objects and characters moving freely in and out of frame. In a sequence set in a playground, *Riddles* plays a similar game to the one referenced in *Deux fois*: Louise and her daughter appear on one side of a spiraling slide (fig. 11.1), then an instant later on the next (fig. 11.2) as the camera mimics the slide's spinning form. In the film's sixth panoramic shot, Louise, who has recently started work as a telephone operator, discusses with her coworkers the possibility of forming a union to fight for free, company-sponsored child care. The camera slowly pans, showing the entirety of the office's break room and its all-female workforce; women pass in and out of frame from one group to another, discussing politics and the everyday in the same breath. Another panoramic shot recalls and

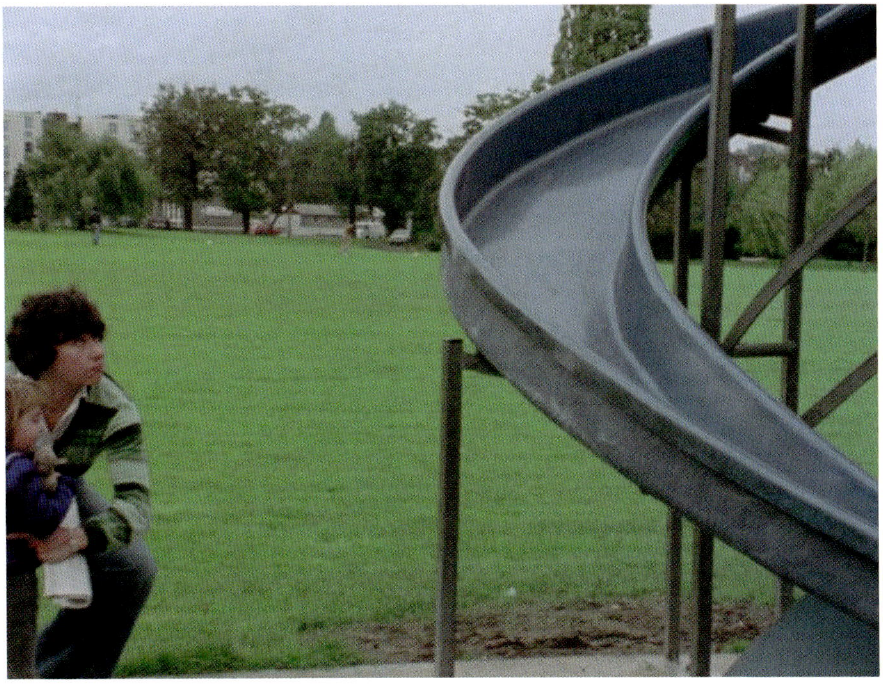

FIGS. 11.1–11.2. Laura Mulvey (British, b. 1941), *Riddles of the Sphinx*, 1977.

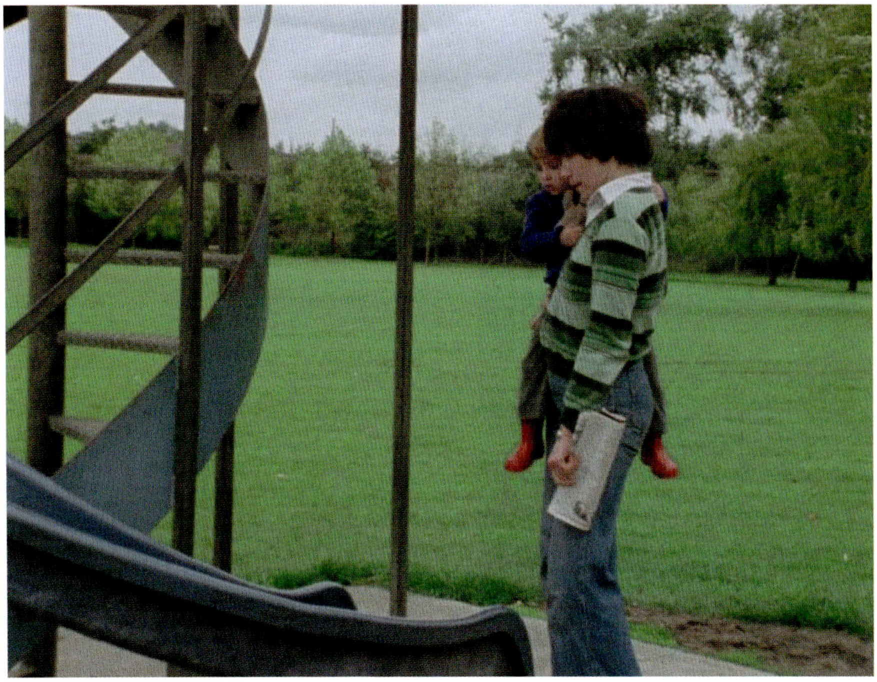

elaborates on *Deux fois*'s vertiginous traffic panorama: it positions the panning camera on top of a moving car. As the vehicle snakes through a series of winding highway ramps, it continues to spin. Miraculously, midway through the shot, our gaze encounters Louise and her friends as they travel in an adjacent vehicle. Throughout the entire shot these women's conversation has played on the soundtrack; until we see their vehicle and thus locate them firmly in diegetic space, it is easy to imagine Louise and her friends riding below us, within the vehicle on which our rotating camera rides. The scene exploits the spatial logic of the classical Hollywood cinema, which often associates the locations of cameras with those of characters. But Mulvey and Wollen play with that spatial logic, stretching it in ways that make us highly aware of how the camera positions us as viewers.

Many of *Riddles*'s most intriguing shots are less obviously virtuosic. In the first few pans, we encounter Louise in the cramped space of her home before she leaves her husband, Chris. In these domestic spaces, we are highly aware not only of our position at the center of the panoramic shot but also of how the movement of the pan slowly guides the camera lens over a series of domestic objects. These familiar *things*—pots and pans, dishes, door handles—all go through several different kinds of perspectival distortion. Camera perspective, of course, automatically renders objects differently depending on where they stand with respect to a central viewpoint: a cuboid object positioned near the camera's central vanishing point might appear nearly square, but move the camera a few inches toward one side or the other, and the orthogonal lines that show its depth will lengthen dramatically. Objects subject to a camera's pan go through even more dramatic transformations, as the camera lens (and, with it, its central vanishing point) moves not only on an X axis with regard to the frame, but also on a Z axis—closer to and farther from the objects before it—as it traces a horizontal arc in space. As objects move with respect to the vanishing point, they also, at the same rate, get closer or farther from the perspectival plane.

In *Riddles*'s panoramic shots, many objects are thus momentarily distorted by perspective, or merely by a shot's framing. Yet because of the constant motion of the pan, these objects always survive their moments of inscrutability. At one point in the first pan a white door fills the entire frame, seeming to swell to a larger size than it was mere moments before. The gray shape at its right briefly loses its iconic relation to its referent: a door handle. This solid color mass, moreover, breaks the continuity between the space we know to lie on the left and right of the white door. But as the pan continues, the door soon becomes a door again: the accident of framing recedes as quickly as it emerged.

Perspective alone rarely distorts objects in *Riddles* into completely abstract forms. But even when the audience can easily recognize the objects onscreen, their subtle changes in shape still alienate. The wide-angle camera lens slightly distorts the objects at the frame's edges, creating a subtle fish-eye effect. With a stable frame, this distortion is scarcely noticeable, but camera movement brings it to our attention. In the initial panorama in Louise's kitchen, we see a straight-on shot of three blue pots sitting on a counter, in a row parallel to the perspective plane (fig. 11.3). The pots are framed on the right side of the shot by the edge of the camera frame, which runs vertically and thus perfectly perpendicular to the counter's level surface. As the camera pans to the right, the appearance of these pots barely changes—yet the appearance of the rectangular counter on which they sit is dramatically transformed.

The right angles of counter and frame that previously dominated the composition—a Cartesian grid framed by cinema's rectangular frame—bends before our eyes when the counter's right edge emerges (fig. 11.4). It is at an angle to the frame's edge; its forms an orthogonal line that recedes in depth toward the kitchen wall. Immediately, our sense of what forms a "right angle" is transformed. Before, the frame's vertical edge and the counter's horizontal plane formed a graphic right angle onscreen. Now,

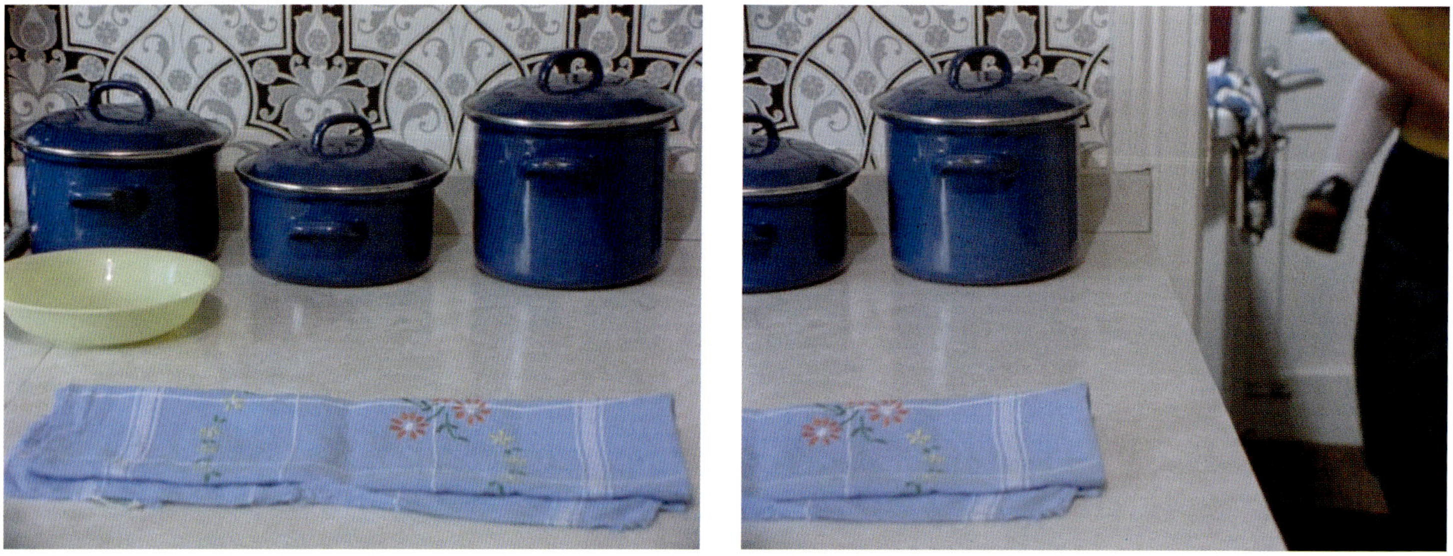

FIGS. 11.3–11.4. Laura Mulvey, *Riddles of the Sphinx*, 1977.

we are aware that a shape that forms right angle in the profilmic world appears as a stretched, warped acute angle when it appears in its graphic, onscreen form. The lens's capacity to render depth comes into conflict with the counter's rectangular shape.

The shape of the counter mutates further as the camera continues to move to the left: its right edge becomes longer, and the distance between it and the left side of the frame increases. Moreover, the actual angle at which the line of the counter stretches across the screen changes with the camera's orientation. We witness this effect in all rectangular objects that the camera closely passes: as its inches past a calendar on the wall, we notice that the frame's lower edge initially matches up with the calendar's horizontal edge (fig. 11.5), but soon the camera's stable movement radically destabilizes the relationship between these two strong horizontals (fig. 11.6). Shapes thus appear elastic. At every given moment each object obtains a different outline, yet without changing dramatically in size and without serving a different function in the mise-en-scène.[27]

In the pan shot, camera perspective thus serves a different function than it does in the Hollywood film. Oudart and Jean-Louis Schefer argue that classical painting, produced according to the figurative codes of perspective, centers the perceiving subject.[28] Since perspective provides a predictable way to model the relative shapes and distances of objects, it presents itself as transparent, effectively hiding its mode of figuration. Moreover, perspectival rendering shows space from a singular viewpoint shared by both the imagined painter and the intended spectator.[29] Dayan similarly argues for Jean-Louis Baudry's apparatus theory as the best argument "that the perceptual system and ideology of representation are built into the cinematographic representation itself."[30] (Though, for Dayan, this argument about the perspectival image remains insufficient to describe cinema's ideological effects since it does not explain how film fiction works.)

While the viewer may be *literally* centered by the pan—in *Riddles*, we observe Louise's room from a fixed point—objects within profilmic space shift as we watch them. The vanishing point of the image changes quickly and dramatically, yet also predictably: the viewer is thus brought into a gamelike relationship with the screen's visual field, predicting how objects may or may not be transformed as the camera traces its path across them over time. Unlike the painted panorama, a cinematic pan does not render space through a discrete number of vanishing points. Instead, it has an infinite number: or, rather, there is one continuously changing vanishing point, locked to the camera's movement. Once Mulvey and Wollen, along with the cinematographer Dianne Tammes, set the focal length and determined the mise-en-scène, there could be no further strategizing about how the space to be represented was to divide. The camera may offer a *rationalized* vision, but it is not necessarily the *human* vision of perspectival painting.

Painters tend to make strategic decisions to avoid perspectival distortion. Artists working on the painted panorama thus chose to place vanishing points at strategic intervals throughout their works to avoid such

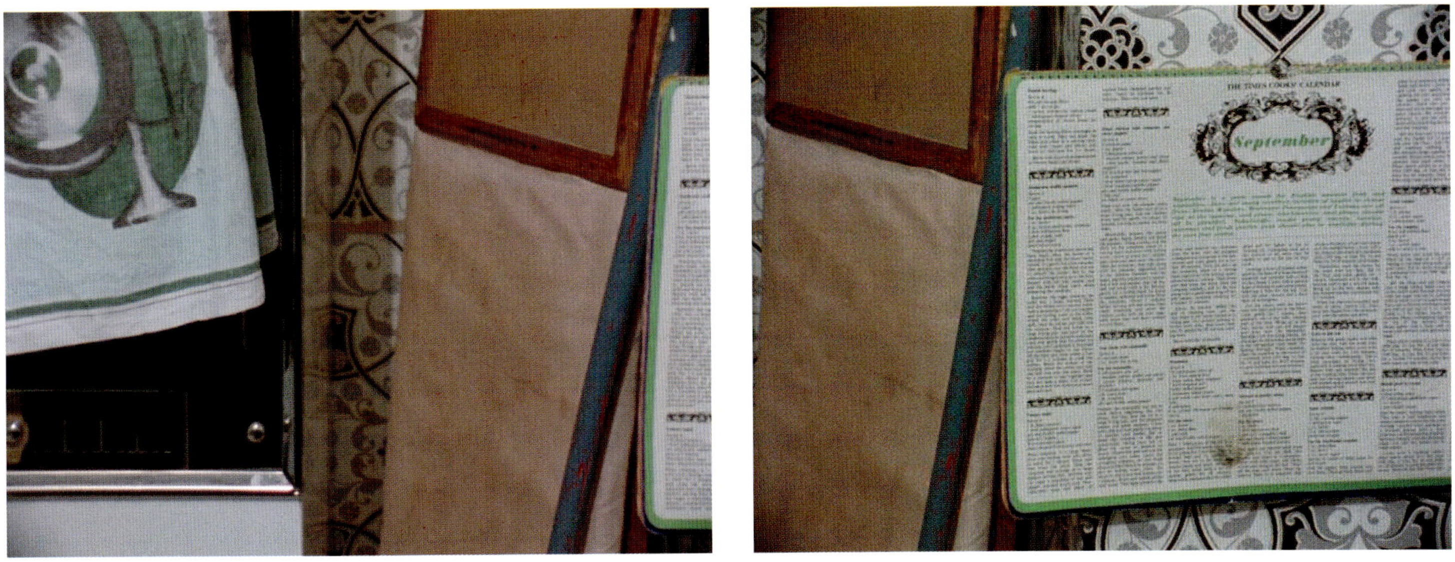

FIGS. 11.5–11.6. Laura Mulvey, *Riddles of the Sphinx*, 1977.

distortions. As E. H. Gombrich has famously observed, painters present to us a world that is filtered through, and thus formed by, human cognition. Gombrich used the term *visual schemata* to describe the mental images we have inherited from past representational traditions and which guide artists' image making. The artist thus "begins not with his visual impression but with his idea or concept: the German artist with his concept of a castle that he applies as well as he can to that individual castle."[31]

Cameras operate differently: rather than creating each object individually with a conceptual framework imposed by words (for example, this is a castle, this is a lion, and so on), lenses address the world not as a plethora of objects but as a continuous field of light. Cameras do not *necessarily* present us with imagery that breaks with our conceptual schemata for objects: on the contrary, most cinematographers go to great lengths to frame and pose objects to render them recognizable, in accordance with the verbal concepts we possess for them. At the same time, we know that camera perspective can warp objects into unconventional configurations that no human would have chosen. Postwar avant-garde cinema often works with this capability: Stan Brakhage's *The Text of Light* (1974) displays abstract imagery that derives from close-ups of a crystal ashtray. The pan, arguably, strengthens the alienating effects of the camera lens: a contemporary camera operators' handbook acknowledges that the "action of a pan" is "an unnatural experience for the human visual system" because a pan, unlike human vision, is not "selective; everything that it 'sees' throughout the duration of the pan or tilt gets equal treatment."[32]

Thus cinema's powers of visual estrangement result from the medium's *temporal* nature. The "panoramic time" of the camera's circular sweep makes both time and space feel elastic. This perhaps explains the overwhelming visual sensation of watching *Riddles*'s panning shots: each shot feels impossibly long, as though it yields far more than 360 degrees' worth of visual information. This plenitude of visual information—the lens's constant regeneration of the objects before it—overwhelms the viewer's ability to assimilate fully the profilmic space. On first viewing, it largely remains extremely difficult to determine precisely when the camera has completed half its transit. And every object before the camera's lens manifests itself as an infinite number of shapes, some far removed from the iconic, verbal-conceptual imagery we associate with them.

If the automatic, mechanical nature of photographic perspective has the power to estrange image from concept, it may also allow viewers to explore the relationship between Lacan's imaginary and symbolic orders. By slowing and distorting the process by which we append words to things, *Riddles*'s pan shots allow the imaginary and symbolic regimes to overlap. Throughout the film, moments of abstraction—such as the white door's complete dominance of the frame—punctuate scenes of recognizable spaces. By slowing our assimilation of the nameable objects appearing onscreen, the film reveals the action of the imaginary and symbolic orders in our minds as we view—and a codetermination of word and image.

"CUT BY CIRCUMSTANCES TO FIT"

One famous shot from *Riddles* plays much more overtly with the idea of the *imaginary*. The twelfth panorama (of thirteen) takes place in the apartment of Maxine, Louise's friend who has helped her develop a feminist, Marxist consciousness. The apartment is a disorienting jumble of curtains and mirrors, and it plays with the spectator's inability to discern tangible objects from their reflected images when both are framed by cinematic projection (fig. 11.7). On the screen, "real" objects are just as flat as their reflections, and we can tell the two apart only if a mirrored surface is clearly framed. As Gilles Deleuze argued of the famous "hall of mirrors" scene in Orson Welles's *Citizen Kane* (1941), cinematic projection renders the "virtual" and "actual" Kane equally present to film viewers.[33] In *Riddles*'s penultimate panoramic shot, tight framing makes it at times difficult to deduce—especially on a first viewing—where each mirrored surface starts and ends. But the camera's panning action also hinders our ability in this regard; it has a leveling effect on the mise-en-scène. Both objects and their reflections appear to inhabit two coeval orders of reality.

The shot begins with Louise: we see her image clearly reflected in an oval mirror as she reads aloud from Maxine's diary. When Louise asks Maxine the meaning of a particular passage, Maxine answers that she does not know, just as the camera passes from the image of an "actual" red curtain to its mirrored reflection. On first viewing, this passage is nearly indiscernible, since the thin strip of the mirror's left frame is almost buried in the red curtain's deep vertical folds. Soon after, we receive a more solid indication that we have entered mirror space, when we see a classical bust doubled onscreen (fig. 11.8). Yet skeptical viewers find no definitive proof that they are not looking at two "actual" busts.

Continuing its right-to-left course, the camera eventually encounters Maxine, who is still listening to Louise (fig. 11.9). On the left, Maxine is framed by the large mirror's left edge—but disoriented viewers who had not realized they were looking at "mirror space" can easily see the frame as a doorframe, and the "virtual" mirrored space as an actual recessed alcove within Maxine's room. Above Maxine's head hangs a landscape painting of an empty blue lagoon. To the left of the mirror frame, we encounter an uncanny repetition of this image. The small rectangle that frames the second landscape may be another mirror, pointing at a precise angle. Yet its matte, square appearance suggests it may, too, be a framed reproduction of the image above Maxine's head.

The entire scene, with its frames within frames and mirrors upon mirrors, recalls Manet's *Bar at the Folies-Bergère*: another riff on *Las Meninas*. The playful viewer has options about how to divide the cinematic image into "actual" space and "mirrored" space. Each part of the frame is only provisionally "mirrored" or "actual"; the viewer labels each with the understanding that further visual data may help her split or collapse these fields of her own creation. Beyond a certain point, it makes no difference whether we look at one of the scene's frames as the border of a mirror or an easily traversed doorframe. The scene does not ask us to define its spaces and objects in terms of negation: the "real" objects as "not reflections," the reflected objects as "not real." Fields of vision coalesce or divide in response to our probings. Here we may be in the Lacanian imaginary Mulvey claimed was the film's setting.

During the scene, Louise and Maxine engage with the text of Maxine's diary in a playful, interpretive way, assigning extreme gravity to the content of their imaginations. Scott MacDonald enumerates how Louise's reading revises the borders between metaphor, dream, and memory spontaneously and at will.[34] One element of Maxine's diary sticks out: the sentence Maxine claims, at the beginning of the sequence, she does not yet understand—"they make a groove or a pattern into which or upon which other patterns fit or are placed unfitted and are cut by circumstances to fit." The phrase initially sounds like nonsense but could in fact aptly describe a mirror: a surface that passively reflects other patterns without adjusting them to fit, merely capturing the incidence of light on it.

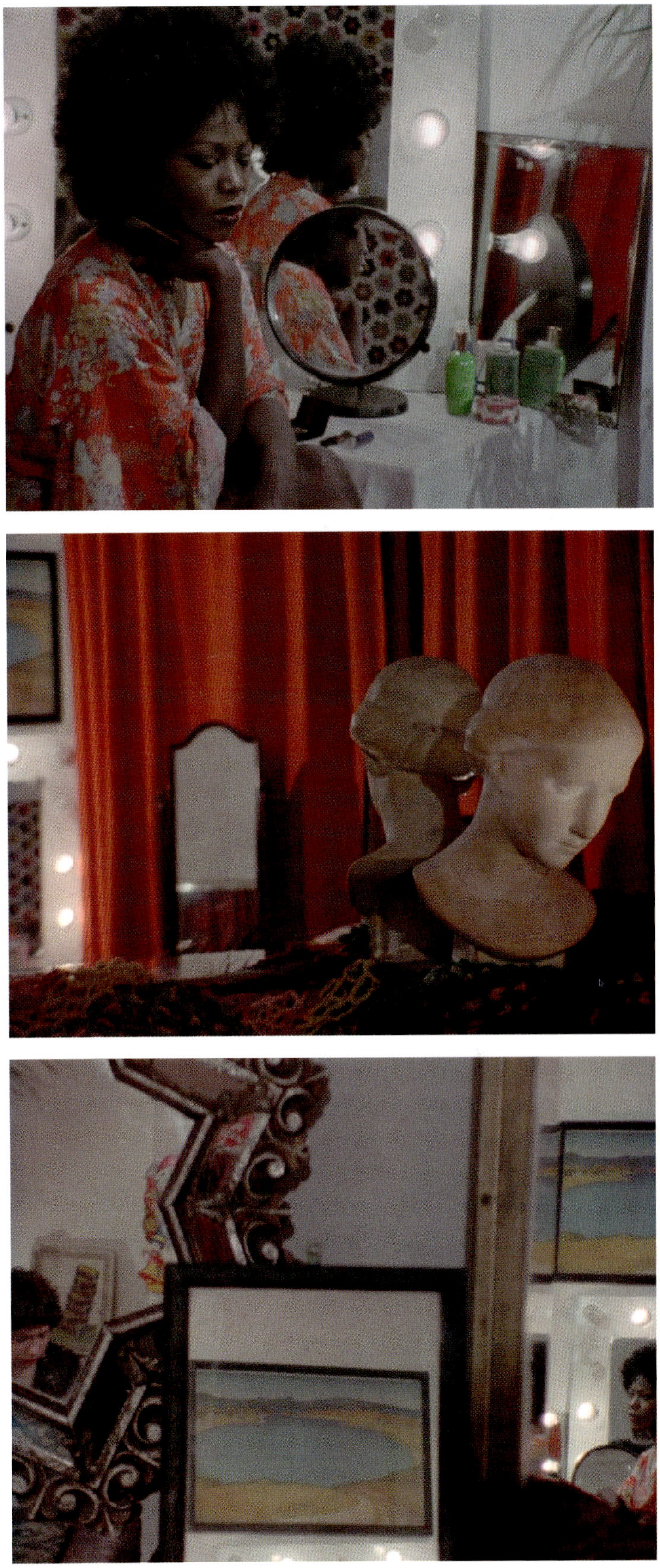

FIGS. 11.7–11.9. Laura Mulvey, *Riddles of the Sphinx*, 1977.

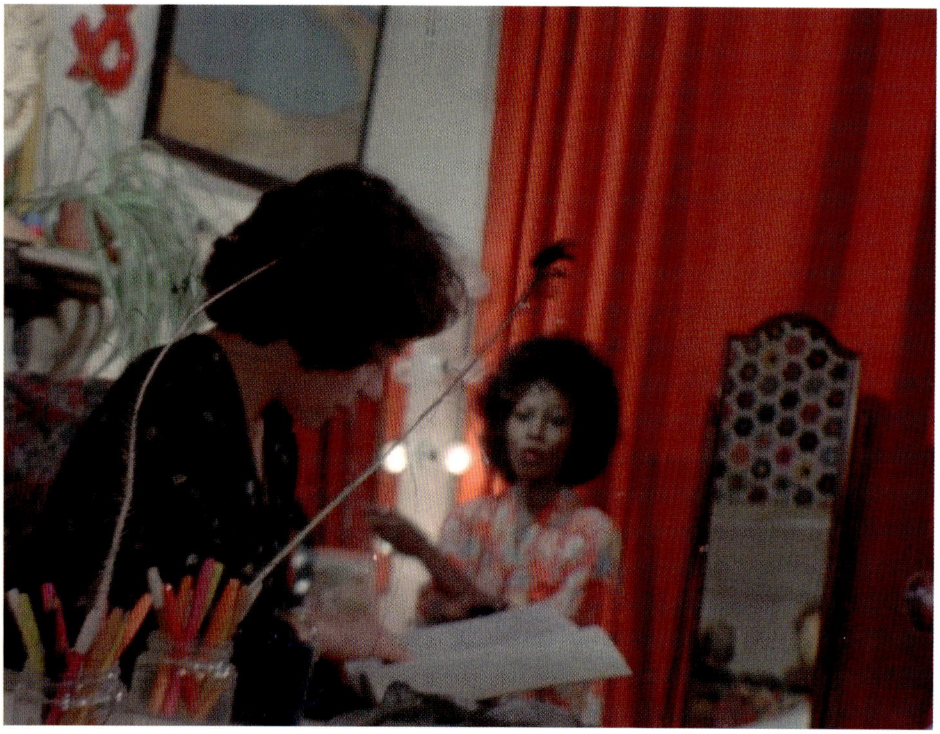

FIG. 11.10. Laura Mulvey, *Riddles of the Sphinx*, 1977.

It could, likewise, describe the film camera's indexical, automatic recording—the very inhuman object that in previous sequences illustrated the imbrications of verbal concept and nonverbal image.

This phrase, in fact, comes from another woman's attempt to reconcile her interests in cinema and psychoanalysis with her lived reality as a woman. It is a quotation from the poet H.D.'s *Tribute to Freud*, an account of the conversations the poet and passionate cinephile held with the aging analyst about a "cinematic" hallucination she saw—or perhaps, she claimed, projected herself—on the walls of a Corfu hotel. She describes these shapes as "hieroglyphics." "The writing, at least, is consistent. It is composed by the same person, it is drawn or written by the same hand. Whether that hand or person is myself, projecting the images as a sign, a warning. . . . Or whether they are projected from outside. . . . For my head is already warning me that this is an unusual dimension, an unusual way to *think*, that my brain or mind may not be equal to the occasion."[35] H.D.'s description of the event sounds remarkably like the psychic uncertainty of writers like Mulvey and Wollen in the face of classical Hollywood cinema: the images onscreen manipulate the viewer's unconscious while appearing to be produced by it. H.D. discussed this experience or "projection" with Freud, who called it "perhaps her most dangerous symptom." Under intense psychoanalytic scrutiny, H.D. insisted on the meaning of this event, her power in the face of it.[36] *Riddles*, likewise, asserts the power and productivity of women's cinematic imagination in the face of more hidebound psychoanalytic readings that treat projection merely as symptom.

Toward the scene's end, the room's elements begin to stabilize: after passing Louise's mirror image—discernible in the reflection of a cup of pencils in front of her—we enter "actual" space (fig. 11.10). But as soon as the "actual" Louise and Maxine pass us, we see another reflection: that of the cinematographer Dianne Tammes, sweeping her camera past a tall, narrow mirror (fig. 11.11). Though one might expect her appearance to read as an ironic assertion of the scene's constructedness, the image strikingly lacks cynicism. Tammes moves the camera with incredible focus and authority but also with lightness. Her hips sway back and forth; she seems to dance, silently and slowly, to maintain the pan's steady rhythm. *Riddles*'s sense of *play* comes to the fore: Tammes smiles while she helps create a world of illusions.

As it was for H.D., cinema is in *Riddles* a powerful tool made by and for women's imaginations. Tammes's camera allows her to create hallucinations, collapse and rebuild the boundaries between spaces—or between two-dimensional reflection and three-dimensional "reality." In

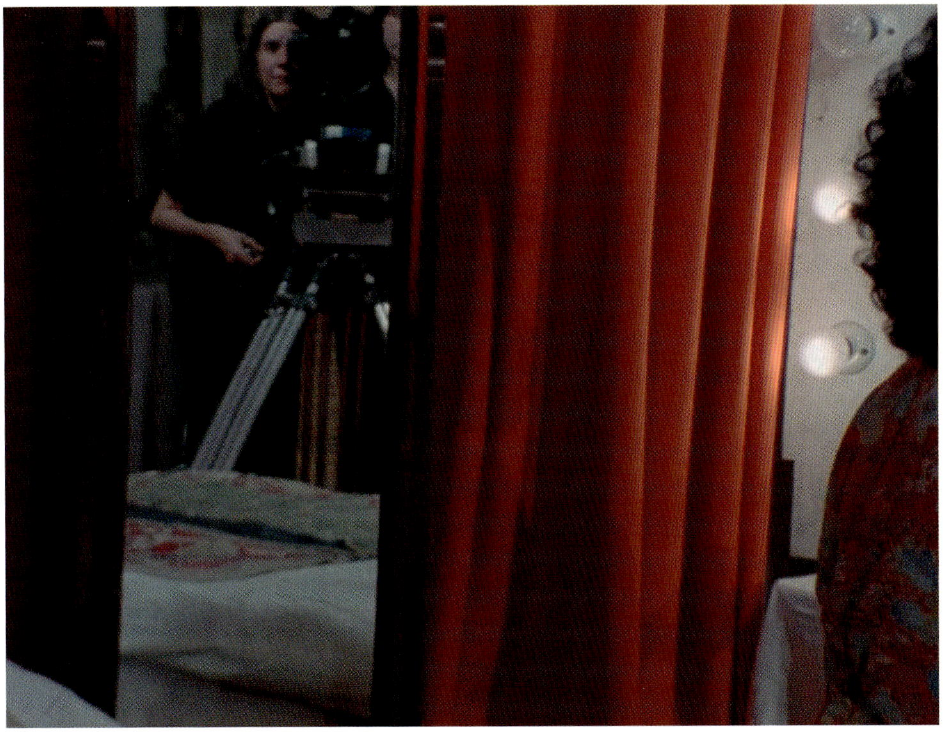

FIG. 11.11. Laura Mulvey, *Riddles of the Sphinx*, 1977.

this panoramic shot, cinema, mirrors, and storytelling all appear as a means by which to access such hallucinatory powers. It suggests the eye might one day literally rearrange reality.

CONCLUSION

> I'm interested in a kind of balance that has some similarity to the way Cézanne equalized the physical facts and the presented illusions in painting. On film the transformation is into light and time and the balance is between the illusions (spatial and otherwise) and the facts-of-light on a surface.
>
> —Michael Snow (1967)

Riddles throws into question the shapes and boundaries of objects, without ever crossing over into pure abstraction: shapes and colors onscreen still maintain their identities as real, tangible things. The film destabilizes the visual codes of illusionist cinema without "destabilizing" the subject (or its "imaginary coherence") in the way many 1970s film theorists advocated. My reading argues, perhaps perversely, that the film in fact secures and stabilizes the female viewer by giving her a sense of playful mastery over the images onscreen. I believe that *Riddles of the Sphinx* encourages us into a playful relationship with space and time, strengthening the identity and capability of the person playing. It is precisely in *aesthetic play* that the viewer senses the potential for a "new language."

Some scholars have criticized Mulvey and Wollen's aesthetic for reflecting neo-Kantian ideals: for Laura Kipnis the film evinces a "conservative reinvestment in aesthetic autonomy," and in their artistic worldview, "one might suspect that the transcendental subject can't be far behind."[37] This critique echoes a more literal complaint that the pan's center stabilizes the viewing subject, reproducing the illusory mastery viewers also experience in Hollywood cinema. But both examples, ironically, provide insight into the way *Riddles* operates: it is precisely *through* being centered, *through* an encounter with modernist aesthetics, that the film's viewers can experience its full political and aesthetic import as a feminist film. *Riddles* makes a centered, subjective cinematic viewpoint finally available to women; at the same time, it establishes this viewpoint as the ground on which we might build a nonpatriarchal language.

Michael Snow's *La région centrale* (1971) offers a useful comparison: another panoramic film that offers viewers similar opportunities to play with, and hone, their senses. The film comprises dozens of 360-degree tilt and pan shots, all taken from the same location: Snow attached his camera to a robotic arm he had erected on a Canadian mountaintop. Over the film's three hours, viewers become intimately familiar with every aspect of the wilderness surrounding the camera, and they come to identify strongly with that camera, arguably much more strongly than they do in *Riddles*. The camera does not just pan along a horizontal plane but performs a series of backflips and tilts—and as we swoop and spin with it, we start to feel as if we are riding a roller coaster. At other times, Snow's camera moves so quickly and wildly on its axis that the onscreen shapes and colors cease to represent an antecedent nature. They are no longer objects outside the window of our spinning vessel—we no longer feel the sensation of moving with the camera but rather find ourselves suddenly back in the theater, sitting in our seats. The colors and shapes have become abstract visual phenomena on a screen. But the best moments in *La région centrale*—the moments that illustrate what Snow has called the "balance" between illusionism and "the facts-of-light on a surface"—come when the camera spins at precisely the speed that allows us to choose between the two. We can, at moments, perform this gestalt switch ourselves and choose how we would like to regard the screen: as window or canvas.

Soon after *Riddles* was made, the critic Annette Michelson wrote a groundbreaking article about *La région centrale* analyzing this very aesthetic experience. Her essay suggests precisely what avant-garde aesthetics might achieve: the creation of a more coherent subjectivity. Michelson inverted contemporary film theorists' critiques of camera perspective, quoting Jean-Louis Baudry's assertion that "the world" of the mobile camera is "constituted not just by [the viewer's] eye, but for it . . . the mobility of the camera seems to fulfill the most favorable conditions for the manifestation of the 'transcendental subject.'"[38] Michelson finds in Snow's film just this formal and psychic significance, as a mobile camera records panoramic views of a Canadian landscape. "It is of course," she writes, "this disembodied mobility of the eye-subject which is *hyperbolized* in *La Région Centrale*."[39]

It is perhaps Snow's *hyperbole* that makes his aesthetic revolutionary: instead of taking for granted our sense of sovereignty over our surroundings and visual apparatus, we obtain a highly self-conscious sense of our perceptual powers. Such playful exaggeration engenders what, in other writings, Michelson has called the viewer's "ludic sovereignty" over his or her own perceptions of space and time.[40] Like the great Soviet avant-garde directors, Michelson believes that playful engagement with cinema could engender "no less than the transformation of the human condition through a cinematic intensification of cognitive accuracy, analytic precision, and epistemological certitude."[41]

Riddles makes its own arguments for the power of the ludic. After Louise's tale concludes, we see series of strong, capable female acrobats, transformed by postproduction processing into abstract splashes of color. The images convey the power and playfulness female bodies can experience, while the video processing makes it difficult to view these women as mere sexual spectacle. Then the film's final section shows an extreme close-up of a child's mercury maze toy. We watch as a bubble of mercury floats through plastic corridors, urged one way and the next by a pair of offscreen hands (Mulvey's).[42] The film ends the moment the game is won, and the silver bubble slips into the hole at the maze's center. We, likewise, have been placed in *our* center; likewise, we have found our way there only through play. The panoramic shots at the center of the film offer many of *Région*'s delights: objects become abstract shapes and then objects again; we guess at the relationships between the screen's spaces. Moreover, the overt political content of *Riddles*, as of Mulvey and Wollen's writings, suggests that intimate links between the transformation of our perceptual and analytic senses and the transformation of our psychic apparatus: that developing the language to speak sexual difference will be an *adventure*, a trip, a radical rewiring of our perceptual apparatus. The film aims at a playful, empowered engagement with the interaction between word and image, object and reflection—between the world as we know it and what it might become.

NOTES

1. John Berger, *Ways of Seeing* (New York: Penguin, 1972), 47.
2. Stephen Shaviro, *The Cinematic Body* (Minneapolis: University of Minnesota Press, 1993), 11; and Martin Jay, *Downcast Eyes: The Denigration of Vision in Twentieth-Century French Thought* (Berkeley: University of California Press, 1993), 479.
3. Laura Mulvey, "Visual Pleasure and Narrative Cinema," *Screen* 16 (1975): 6–18. In 1985 Mulvey described her general project as dialectical: "Visual Pleasure" played a specific role, "a negative challenge to dominant cinematic codes," while her fascination with Lacan offered the means to explore the "logical limit" of sex and gender difference; Mulvey, "Changes," *Discourse* 7 (Spring 1985): 11–15.
4. See, for example, Lucy Fischer, *Shot Countershot* (Princeton: Princeton University Press, 1989), chap. 2; E. Ann Kaplan, *Women and Film* (New York: Methuen, 1983), 162–63; and Scott MacDonald's detailed description of the film in *Avant-Garde Film: Motion Studies* (Cambridge: Cambridge University Press, 1993), 79–92.
5. For many years the film was difficult to find and the extant prints very

faded. With the BFI's recent restoration of the film and its 2014 DVD/BluRay rerelease, *Riddles* has become much easier to write about. One commendable recent essay is Rakhee Balram, "Laura Mulvey and Peter Wollen," *Lux Online*, https://www.luxonline.org.uk/artists/laura_mulvey_and_peter_wollen/essay(1).html, accessed May 2014.

6. Maurice Merleau-Ponty, "Film and the New Psychology," in *Sense and Non-Sense*, trans. H. Dreyfus and P. Dreyfus (Evanston, Ill.: Northwestern University Press), 48–59.
7. Walter Benjamin, "The Work of Art in the Age of Its Technological Reproducibility (Second Version)," in *The Work of Art in the Age of Its Technological Reproducibility, and Other Writings on Media* (Cambridge: Harvard University Press, 2008), 19–54.
8. Miriam Hansen, "Room-for-Play: Benjamin's Gamble with Cinema," *October* 109 (Summer 2004): 3–45.
9. Peter Wollen, "Godard and Counter Cinema: *Vent d'Est*," *Afterimage* 4 (Autumn 1972): 6–17.
10. Daniel Dayan, "The Tutor-Code of Classical Cinema," *Film Quarterly* 28 (Autumn 1974): 22–31.
11. This is Foucault's argument about the painting in his introduction to *The Order of Things* (1960) (New York: Pantheon, 1970). Oudart cites Foucault's essay on *Las Meninas* as inspiration for his theory of suture. Oudart, "Cinema and Suture," *Screen* 18 (Winter 1977): 35–47.
12. David Rodowick, *The Crisis of Political Modernism: Criticism and Ideology in Contemporary Film Criticism* (Berkeley: University of California Press, 1995), xxii.
13. Stephan Oettermann, *The Panorama: History of a Mass Medium*, trans. Deborah Lucas Schneider (New York: Zone, 1997), 31.
14. See Keith Kelly's "Riddles of the Sphinx: One or Two Things I Know about Her," *Millennium Film Journal* 2 (Spring/Summer 1979): 95–100.
15. Rodowick, *Crisis of Political Modernism*, vii–viii.
16. Mulvey writes on the role of the female spectator and the importance of women's films to her thinking in "Afterthoughts on 'Visual Pleasure and Narrative Cinema' inspired by King Vidor's *Duel in the Sun* (1946)," *Framework* 15/17 (Summer 1981): 12–15.
17. Jacqueline Suter, Sandy Flitterman, and Laura Mulvey, "Textual Riddles: Woman as Enigma or Site of Social Meanings?" *Discourse* 1 (Fall 1979): 86–127; 94–95.
18. Ibid., 95.
19. Peter Wollen, "Film in the Field of Language," *October* 17: "The New Talkies" (Summer 1981): 53–60.
20. Suter, Flitterman, and Mulvey, "Textual Riddles," 122.
21. Jacques Lacan, *The Seminar of Jacques Lacan, Book XI: The Four Fundamental Concepts of Psychoanalysis* (1964), ed. Jacques-Alain Miller, trans. Alan Sheridan (New York: W. W. Norton, 1977). See also Jean-Paul Hiltenbrand, "Real, The (Lacan)," *International Dictionary of Psychoanalysis*, ed. Alain de Mijolla (Farmington Hills, Mich.: Macmillan Reference/Thompson Gale, 2005).
22. Mary Anne Doane, "Woman's Stake: Filming the Female Body," *October* 17, "The New Talkies" (Summer 1981): 23–36.
23. Stephen Heath, "Narrative Space," *Screen* 17 (1976): 68–112.
24. Dayan, "Tutor-Code," 24.
25. Suter, Flitterman, and Mulvey, "Textual Riddles," 122.
26. In fact, the repetitions of the shot/reverse shot sequence represent the painted panorama more closely than the cinematic pan: such sequences allow us to feel secure that the space in which a character stands will remain relatively unchanged every time we return to it.
27. These effects, discernible on DVD, appear far more pronounced when the film is exhibited on a large screen.
28. Dayan, "Tutor-Code," 22, draws the connection between Oudart's work on figurative codes in classical painting and on cinematic representation.
29. "The spectator's imaginary can only coincide with the painting's built-in subjectivity"; ibid., 27.
30. Ibid., 28.
31. E. H. Gombrich, *Art and Illusion* (New York: Phaidon, 2001), 72.
32. Christopher Bowen and Roy Thompson, *Grammar of the Shot*, 3rd ed. (Burlington, Mass.: Taylor and Francis and Focal Press, 2013), 172.
33. Gilles Deleuze, *Cinema 2: The Time-Image* (Minneapolis: University of Minnesota Press, 1989), 79–95.
34. MacDonald, *Avant-Garde Film*.
35. H.D., *Tribute to Freud*, 2nd ed. (New York: New Directions, 2012), 46–47.
36. H.D. called the experience the most important in her life—whereas, ever secular, Freud called it the poet's most dangerous symptom. H.D. in turn called Freud's interpretations the film's "narration." Ibid.
37. Laura Kipnis, "Feminism: The Political Conscience of Postmodernism?" *Social Text* 21 (1989): 149–66; 156.
38. Jean-Louis Baudry, "Basic Ideological Effects of the Cinematographic Apparatus," quoted in Annette Michelson, "About Snow," *October* (1979): 111–25; 121.
39. Michelson, "About Snow," 121; emphasis in original.
40. Annette Michelson, "The Wings of Hypothesis: On Montage and the Theory of the Interval," in *Montage and Modern Life, 1919–1942*, ed. Matthew Teitelbaum (Cambridge: MIT Press, 1992), 60–81.
41. Ibid., 62.
42. Personal conversation with Mulvey, spring 2013.

KATIE TRUMPENER

12 Unchained

The Politics of the Panorama Shot in Fiction Film, Experimental Film, and Expanded Cinema

The panorama is an exercise in citizenship.

—Rob Winger, *Muybridge's Horse* (2002)

Tracking shots are a question of morality.

—Jean-Luc Godard, remark during a 1959 panel discussion of Alain Resnais's *Hiroshima Mon Amour*

In *Theory of the Film* (1945), Béla Balázs praised panning shots for their "subtle lyricism," for slowing action into meditative or psychological depths, linking or isolating characters and objects, and enlisting spectators to witness capacious, apparently unedited social landscapes.[1] Panning, as Balázs demonstrates with examples from an international range of 1920s films, can reconnect reactions with original causes (even while forcing the viewer to weigh intermediate space and filmic information) or show a group distancing itself from one member, transforming physically claustrophobic space into horizonless social desert.

This chapter traces the panorama shot's subsequent evolution during the sound era; it works to broaden our sense of film grammar while exploring Balázs's questions of expressivity, the relationship of the psychic to the social. Is there a politics of film form, visible on the micro-level of the individual shot? This chapter surveys the varying uses of the *pan* (both 360-degree full-circle panorama shots and extended tracking shots) to ask what exactly this kind of shot "means."

First, it examines the panorama shot's historical development, focusing particularly on the long tradition of leftist "committed" filmmaking, from the interwar period into the Cold War; the international student movement; and finally the breakup of institutionalized Communism. It considers particularly the politics of space and expanded vision, the public sphere, and Marxist theories of history and revolution. In this tradition, the panorama shot serves not only as the bearer of objective, capacious reality but as a technique for laying bare subterranean political mechanisms or taking in contradictory social forces. As Giuliana Bruno writes (of Robert Polidori's panoramic photography), "panoramic techniques face up to the landscape of social complexities."[2]

Yet this chapter also considers very different uses of the panorama shot. Key melodramas use panorama shots to express complex psychic states—shock, terror, trauma, narcissistic delusion, romantic obsession—and their attendant perceptual limitations, whereas key experimental films use panoramic sweeps to explore vision's objectivity and subjectivity.

These distinct emphases eventually converged. Panoramic shots became central to breakthrough, highly influential New Wave, New Left, and feminist films. Their recurrence can help trace several long historiographical and geopolitical arcs—and the careers of Rainer Werner Fassbinder, Helke Sander, Michael Snow, and Chantal Akerman, whose panoramic preoccupations became entwined with expanded understandings of politics.

Some filmmakers eventually moved into installation art. This chapter ends by considering how Snow, Akerman and Manon de Boer's installations have drawn on panoramic antecedents. As a linear art, unfolding in time, on the screen's fixed space, traditional filmmaking directs viewers' attention, expanding yet delimiting their field of vision. Installations attempt to push open the cinematic box, giving viewers back ambulatory freedom, agency, and those partial, indeterminate, relatively undirected views they enjoyed on nineteenth-century viewing platforms. For some media artists, this gesture too is political, liberating the viewer from traditional film form—in a logical extension of early cinema's "unchained camera."[3]

BETWEEN COMMITMENT AND MELODRAMA

From its inception, chapter 8 argues, cinema was deeply interested in panoramic vision—and its own ability to adapt and extend particular functions of painted and photographic panoramas. Chapter 8 focuses on cinema's first decade and on "panoramas" (short films often consisting of a single panning or circular shot) as a key actuality genre. These important early documentaries surveyed exotic places, commemorated historical events, or conveyed what the world looked like from a moving train, elevator, or rickshaw. The viewing platform from which these films were shot generally remained in motion. Yet cinemagoers, braced in their stationery seats, vicariously took in spectacular sights without physical displacement or physical exposure to danger. "Panoramas" showed the world in sustained glimpses, yet the photographic medium's apparent veracity—and these films' often elegant composition—grounded viewers as they absorbed the look of distant places.

During the 1920s, modernist films made less veristic uses of photography (sometimes using cutouts or animation, or photographing shifts in light rather than material objects). Many key experimental films explored circular motion: swirling carousel and circling figures (Man Ray's *Retour de la raison*, France, 1923), turning letter discs (Marcel Duchamp's *Anemic Cinema*, France, 1926), kaleidoscopic swirling (Hans Richter's *Everything Moves, Everything Revolves*, Germany, 1929), and complex geometrical looping (László Moholy-Nagy's 1930 *Light Play: Black White Gray*, documenting the dappled, bisected light cast by his twirling Light-Space-Modulator).

Early fiction films had used panorama shots for both documentary value (establishing their fictional world's unbounded veracity) and disorienting potential (underscoring dramatic devastations). As Richard Suchenski describes in chapter 9, matching panorama shots across Stillwater Valley frame D. W. Griffith's 1909 *The Country Doctor*.[4] During the opening pan, the doctor, his wife, and their daughter set out on a walk. We then see very high waving grass, the doctor's top hat, mother, and daughter, laughingly fighting their way through the grass, the doctor lifting up Little Edith, then his wife, to pick flowers in a shallower meadow.

Later in the film, Edith dies while the doctor is called away. Griffith's final sequence cuts from Edith's grieving parents to an intertitle: "And the Valley of Stillwater Is Shrouded in Darkness." Yet the final shot gives us light to see by, returning as we came—panning back from the house across Stillwater Valley to where the film began. This opening and closing traverse of landscape is expressive, allegorical, even theological. The tall grass began as documentary detail, only in retrospect metaphorically anticipating loss and death. Nature surrounds human life; in it families lose and find each other. Human life passes; the world endures; wind blows in the grass, the trees, and is gone.

INTERWAR COMMITTED FILMS: POLITICS OF SPACE AND MOVEMENT

In 1909, Griffith's mobile yet impassive camera underscored his film's pathos. By the 1920s, in contrast, feature films showcased "unchained" cameras, swinging in expressive arcs. Forced to marry a drunken brute and to celebrate her wedding on a whirling merry-go-round, the heroine of Jean Epstein's *Coeur fidèle* (France, 1923) cringes as panoramic vistas are reduced to an abstract, Impressionist blur, aesthetically fascinating but deeply disorienting. (Only at the film's close, after her husband's death, can she and her faithful lover ride the carousel more calmly, believing life can now unfold.)

In Abel Gance's *La roue* (*The Wheel*, France, 1923), a phantom ride turns fatal when a speeding train jumps its

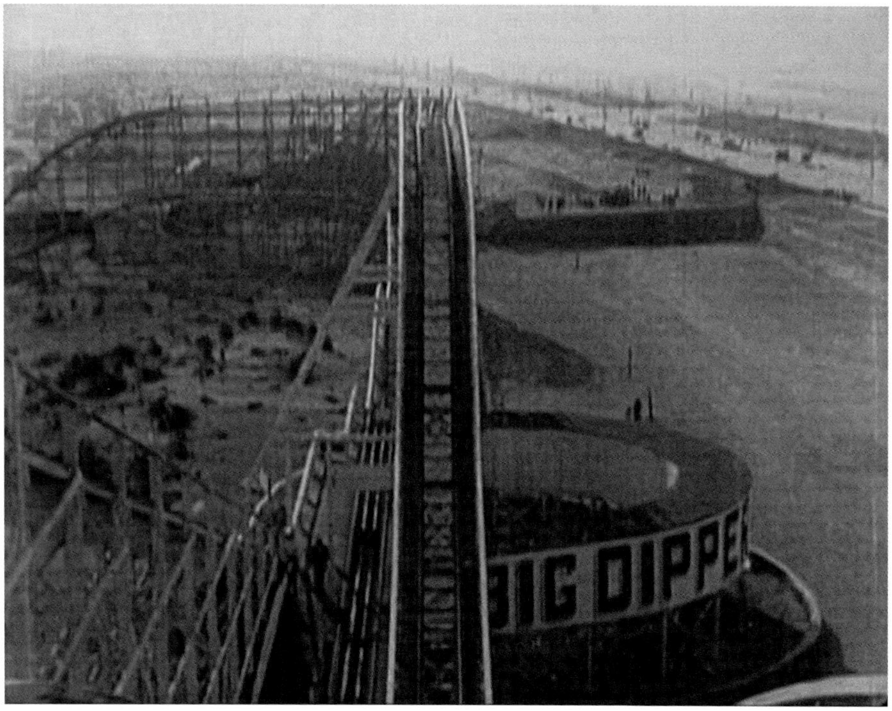

FIG. 12.1. Unchained camera and courtship: riding the Big Dipper, Blackpool. Maurice Elvey (British, 1887–1967), *Hindle Wakes*, 1927.

track. Other films, too, left behind linear plot and angles, exploring more idiosyncratic paths, unsettling sensations, psychic loops. In Evald Dupont's *Variety* (Germany, 1925), a circus performer deserts his family and bourgeois existence for a woman—whom he later discovers is involved with his trapeze partner. In this moment of truth, the room blurrily spins around him, taking on the heady, dizzying movements of circus carousels and trapeze arcs. The panorama shot conveys his loss of moral compass: he murders his partner and finds redemption only in prison.

Tracking shots in Maurice Elvey's *Hindle Wakes* (Britain, 1927), in contrast, represent not the road to perdition but new political departures. On their annual company outing, British mill girls escape shop-floor regimentation, the company town's narrow streets and minds, for Blackpool's dance floors and roller coasters; relishing this unprecedented sensory experience, they make a dizzy bid for sexual freedom. The industrial world must make room, Elvey demands, for sexually emancipated working-class New Women, for the roller coaster's visual whirl, for liberated cameras (fig. 12.1).

From the retrospect of the 1930s, Hans Richter's polemic *The Struggle for the Film* celebrates cinema's liberating potential to change viewers' perception and worldly understanding, lifting them beyond the tyranny of economic conditions. Tenements, 1920s leftists argued, cramped working-class souls. "You can murder someone with an apartment as with an axe," reads the epigraph to Piel Jutzi's *Mother Krause's Journey to Happiness* (Germany, 1929), quoting the leftist caricaturist Heinrich Zille. The tracking shots opening Slatan Dudow's militant *Kuhle Wampe, or To Whom Does the World Belong?* (Germany, 1932, cowritten by Bertolt Brecht) show unemployed workers traversing Berlin on bicycles in their unsuccessful search for work. One becomes so demoralized that he kills himself, jumping from his apartment window into the tenement courtyard.

Alongside commited French and Soviet filmmakers, Dudow and Brecht speculate whether new forms of communal housing might foster political collectivity and solidarity. The protagonist of *Le crime de M. Lange* (France, 1936), Jean Renoir argues most radically, is justified in killing an exploitive landlord to protect the nascent working-class collective his building harbors. At the cathartic moment of tyrannicide, a fluid, empathetic camera moves upstairs, downstairs, avoiding the victim's body to whirl expressively around the courtyard, rhetorically positioned as an agora, now successfully preserved. (The film's original working title was "Sur la cour"/"Into the Courtyard.") This panorama shot arguably becomes a figure for collectivity itself—justifying murder as a political necessity.[5]

Across Europe, film form echoed the left's agonized debates over modernist aesthetics, political tactics of spontaneous political action versus political long

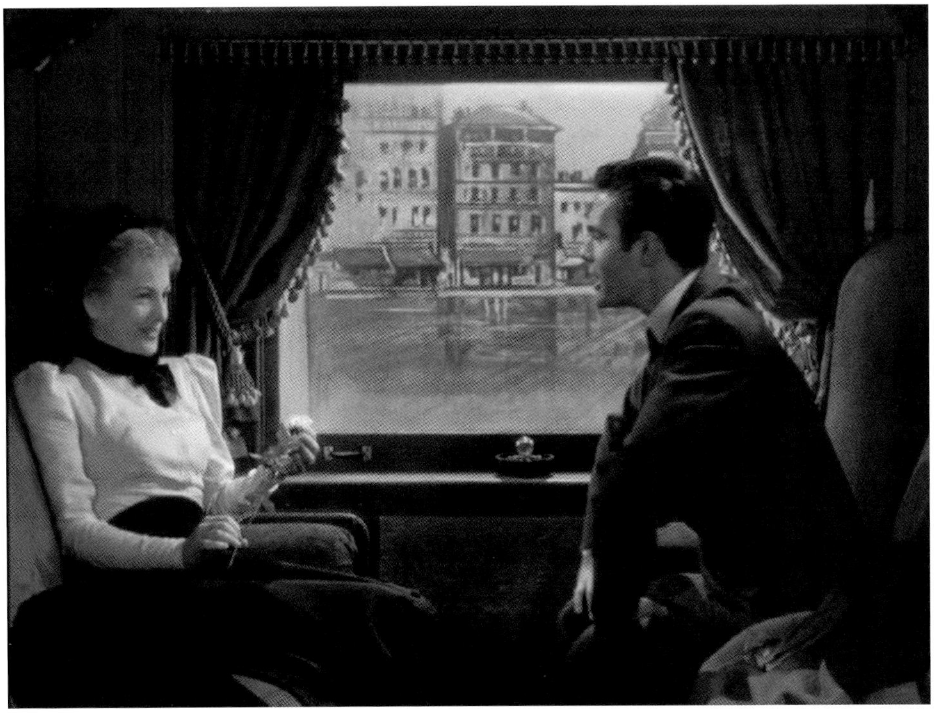

FIG. 12.2. Transported: love in the Prater's Moving Panorama. Max Ophüls (German, 1902–1957), *Letter from an Unknown Woman*, 1948.

marches.[6] Like Elvey's factory girls, Jutzi's working-class Berliners delight in the amusement park, where preciously swirling carousel swings break open their ordinary world of overcrowding. Yet, like Dupont, Jutzi remains suspicious of catharsis provided by sensation, sex, violence, carnival. *Mother Krauss*'s closing tracking shot shows revolutionary change coming not from break-out panoramic moments but the Communist Party's disciplined march.

INNER AND OUTER WORLDS: PANORAMAS AND SUBJECTIVITY

In Hollywood, meanwhile, sound films developed a new formula for depicting conversation. As Jean-Pierre Oudart and Daniel Dayan have influentially argued, this formula—establishing shot; close-up; reverse shots as the conversation moves back and forth—underscore individual characters' distinctiveness and integrity while sewing or "suturing" the viewer into the conversational space between them. In the 1970s and 1980s, psychoanalytic film theorists would decry this suturing process as coercive yet unmooring. Simultaneously oriented and disoriented, they argued, the viewer (forced, in retrospect, to understand each shot grounded in and explaining the shot before) was assigned a space inside the film's psychic force field and yet, splitting identification between two characters, psychically ripped apart.[7]

Hollywood's shot/reverse shot formula directs viewer attention along specific visual paths. Yet during the 1950s especially, Hollywood-based auteurs, including the German émigré Max Ophüls and Alfred Hitchcock, also developed alternative, panoramically oriented mises-en-scène that instead pushed viewers into a vortex, foregrounding not the seamlessness of human communication (and the sewing-up of the viewer inside the projected image) but the messiness of desire, delusions, projection.

In their films, the camera, ostensibly a reliable guide to the external world, instead evoked inner landscapes, compulsions, obsessions. Ophüls' *Letter from an Unknown Woman* (U.S., 1948) lovingly re-creates fin-de-siècle Vienna in the Hollywood studios: in the wintery Prater, a couple, Lisa and Stefan, takes refuge in a "scenic railway" (fig. 12.2) while the shivering proprietor bikes to power a rotating drum, moving painted backdrops (Venice, the Alps) past their "train carriage" window, creating a distant illusion of movement. Lisa and Stefan soon stop looking: trading travel stories, they dissolve into embracing, while the proprietor cycles anew through the landscape roster.

Like cinema, the moving panorama offers imagined transport to various locales, a framework for fantasy, fabulation, love. These lovers will be reunited only when Lisa is dying, forgotten, after a lifetime awaiting Stefan's return (and raising his child). The illusion of motion through the world's imaginary landscapes founded psychic life on memory and masochistic fantasy. The panorama's jerky movement counterpoints Ophüls's characteristically fluid circling shots. This Prater scene recalls cinema's origins in the nineteenth-century fairground, (moving) panorama, and phantom ride, underscoring the myopic, delusional circularity of the protagonists' emotional journeys. The voyage outward, through time and (simulated) space, only indexes psychic processes and projections.

Ophüls's final films (made during the 1950s, after his return to Europe) draw ever more heavily on the metaphorics of circling and encirclement. An adaptation of Arthur Schnitzler's controversial 1897 erotic drama *Reigen*, or *La ronde* (France, 1950), begins its sexual roundelay and establishes the cyclical nature of desire with framing meta-theatrical shots of a turning carousel; *Lola Montès* (France/West Germany, 1955) traces the erotic and political vicissitudes of a famous dancer and courtesan, including key moments on the rotating circular stage of a traveling circus.

Hitchcock's *Vertigo* (U.S., 1958) extends Ophül's investigations into romantic illusion. Its opening credits establish its recurrent spiraling geometrical figures, from camera movement to Madeleine's self-repeating bun.[8] Hitchcock's titular vertigo shot, zooming in and dollying out, flattens three-dimensional into two-dimensional space. Haunted by Madeleine's death, Scotty persuades Judy to dress as—indeed, to reincarnate—Madeleine before swooning into her arms—a misty, redemptive surrender filmed as a double helix. The shot turns without turning: the lovers, dissolved into a climactic kiss, rotate on a lazy Susan, as the camera rotates around them at a different speed, and the neon hotel sign behind them yields to the remembered setting of Scottie and Madeleine's earlier love reverie. *Vertigo* ultimately reveals Scottie's "memories" as delusional, his restaging of lost love as obsessive, pathological. Scottie proves a patsy, Madeleine/Judy a fake; the protagonist has felt his purest desire for a love object that doesn't—and, in her stylization, could scarcely—exist.

Like Ophüls, Hitchcock treated panorama shots as elements in complex film grammars established within individual films and across filmic oeuvres. For them, as for Epstein, the question was how to imbue an ostensibly objective, impartial view with subjectivity, the complex, contradictory imperatives of inner life.

NEW WAVE CIRCLE GAMES: FROM DE-STALINIZATION TO THE STUDENT MOVEMENT

And for such auteurs, melodramas problematizing projection and analyzing mechanisms of desire potentially critiqued the cinematic dream machine. During the same moment, Eastern Europe's nascent New Wave directors were also rediscovering the panorama shot and the unchained camera and resuscitating the visual motifs of the 1920s and 1930s. But they had a more pointed agenda: by giving new primacy to emotional experience, they implicitly reopened old debates about the aims and future of socialism.

Hungary's breakthrough New Wave film, Zoltán Fábri's *Merry-Go-Round* (*Körhinta*, 1956), thus argues for the power of subjectivity—in visual terms (panorama shots, unfettered camera, rapid editing, unprecedented use of soft focus) announcing a departure from Stalinist aesthetics. A village Romeo and Juliet ride a high merry-go-round; at a wedding, their spiraling couple's dance recalls the carousel's circling, thrilling, potentially nauseating disorientation, with its elevated, estranging, liberating view of fairgoers (fig. 12.3). As the dancers speed up, to swirling, Gypsy-inflected music, they focus only on each other; the camera replicates their increasingly blurred view. Their intensity shocks older guests; the music is stopped; the girl faces their opprobrium. Rotation and its unfamiliar purview enable her, for once, to focus on her own desires—indeed for desire to surface—as external authority blurs. Yet this induces profound disorientation; falling in love, she loses sight of other ties; only the beloved stays in focus. Released on the eve of Hungary's abortive uprising, *Merry-Go-Round* is not overtly political, yet its investment in transient psychic states implicitly rejects Stalinist ideas about human happiness, collective norms, the march of history.[9] And like the contemporary films of Mikhail Kalatozov, Andrzej Munk, and Andrzej Wajda, it celebrates the return of an unfettered camera after years of static, dialogue-centered Stalinist "radio films."

In East Germany, too, filmmakers self-consciously returned to the panorama shot and to 1930s thematics, in search of alternative political and aesthetic paths. Yet, given Cold War pressures, even progressive directors sometimes used innovative film language in defense of political orthodoxy. Like *Merry-Go-Round*, Konrad Wolf's East-West love story, *The Divided Heaven* (*Der geteilte Himmel*, East Germany, 1964), uses a dance sequence to

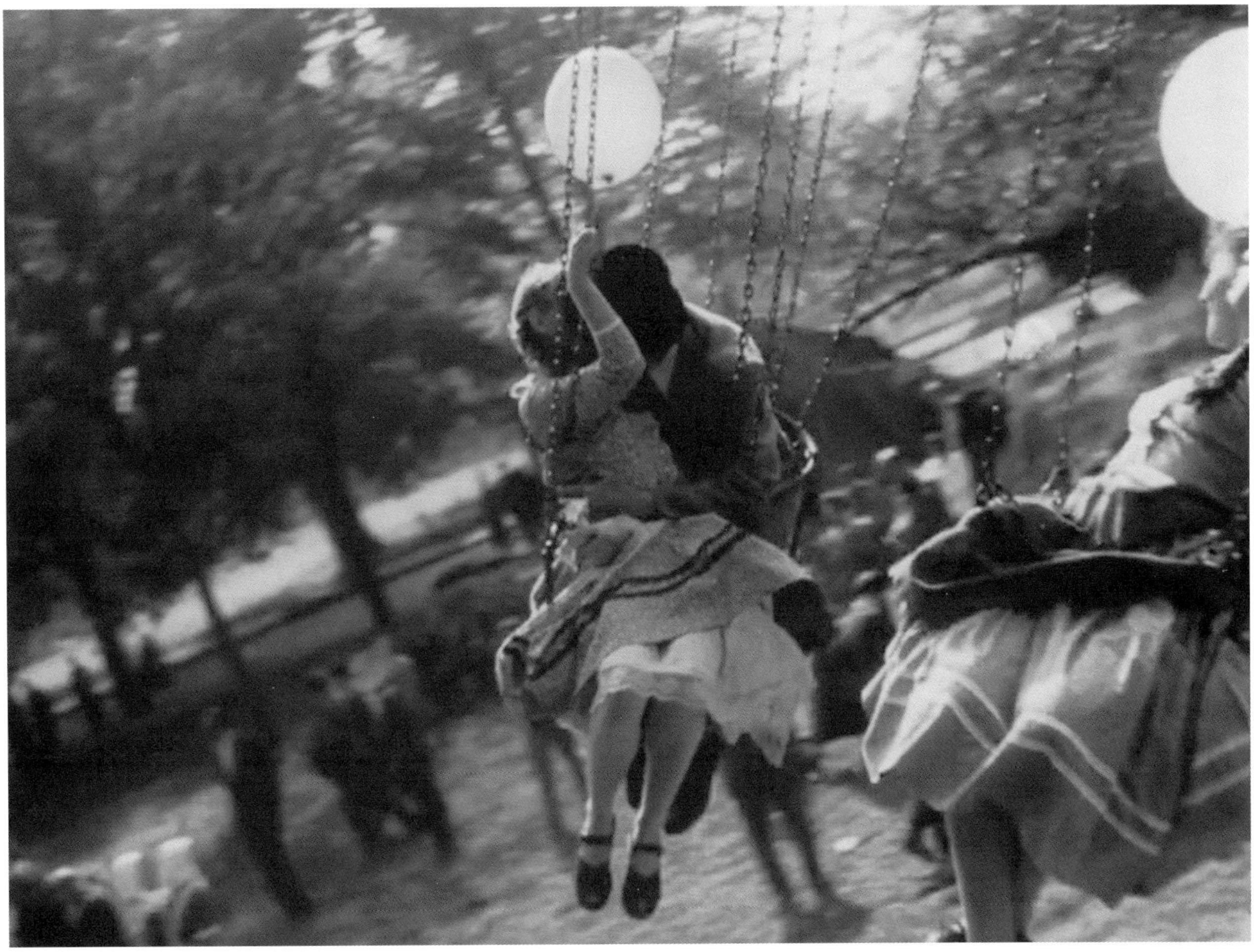

FIG. 12.3. The world blurs as you twirl above it. Zoltán Fábri (Hungarian, 1917–1994), *Merry-Go-Round*, 1956.

stage political and erotic conflicts. Yet here, as the lovers dance, circle, and switch partners in the mirrored ballroom, its reflected surfaces make it hard to distinguish reality from illusion. Love, the mise-en-scene underscores, involves solipsism, projection, and hence political irreality. To defend the Berlin Wall as a political necessity, Wolf condemns the same subjectivism *Merry-Go-Round* championed.

East Germany's most celebrated miniseries, *Country Roads* (*Wege übers Land*, Martin Eckermann, 1968) uses repeated panoramic shots of a country crossroads to locate East Germany at the crossroads of history. The shot first occurs to mark the end of World War II and suggest a woman's still-open future despite her former Nazi complicity. And its repetition, a few years later, benchmarks her firm reanchoring in East Germany's socialist order. Kurt Maetzig's *Banner of Krivoi Rog* (East Germany, 1967) likewise articulates antifascist mythology. Yet its opening credits, panning across mining country, anticipates a later sequence, set in the mid-1930s, where a Communist miner, newly released from a concentration camp, surveys this landscape in fear and despair. Although he is now out in the open again, his unresolved prison trauma induces agoraphobia, claustrophobia. A film ultimately celebrating socialist loyalties nonetheless affords itself the presence of unreliable narrators and panoramic camerawork expressing existential doubt and despair.

In Western Europe, fledgling New Wave filmmakers felt no obligation to provide political or utopian templates, seeing themselves rather as much-needed critics of the postwar order. Formally, their films are deliberately open-ended, resisting all authority or closure. In Alexander Kluge's breakthrough *Yesterday Girl* (*Abschied von gestern*, West Germany, 1966), a claustrophobic open-air panorama shot evokes traumatic Holocaust residues. An East German refugee (and childhood Holocaust survivor) fails to find any secure niche in West Germany. Traipsing from city to city, institution to institution, abandoned, pregnant, suffering recurrent guard-dog nightmares, she flees into an empty landscape as the camera circles and stalks her. Kluge's panorama shot evokes isolation, marginalization, paranoia.

Where interwar leftists sought in the courtyard and panorama shot utopian foretastes of socialist liberation, New Wave panorama shots returned rather to *Coeur fidèle*'s disorienting vision, now figuring the constraints of fascist, capitalist, even socialist society. Young filmmakers chronicling growing anomie registered this social disconnect in fragmented film form; even their tracking shots (potentially a means of absorbing, reconciling, and harmonizing contradictions) conveyed social menace.

The era's most famous tracking shot, in Godard's *Weekend* (France, 1967), traverses a country road as the weekend approaches. Instead of rural harmony, it finds farm vehicles and dozens of urban drivers caught in a seemingly endless traffic jam, some anticipating the weekend (playing ball, playing cards, eating) as they wait but many others gesticulating and honking indignantly at line jumpers. The camera passes numerous car wrecks, some bashed into the rows of trees lining the road, and, finally, at the top of the jam, ruined cars and dead family members lying in the ditch. Throughout France, Napoleon had famously planted rows of trees along the roads to shade his troops as they marched. Now the Napoleonic allée has become a makeshift morgue, witnessing weekly lethal traffic jams, ongoing civil war between drivers in cars, between slick urban cars and farm vehicles.

Yet this comically dystopic shot is also counterbalanced, in Godard's film, against a complex panoramic "Musical Interlude," which (following Godard's long-standing obsession with where "movie music" comes from) locates the source of its non-diegetic music, panning around a farmyard to reveal a grand piano being played alongside tractors and farm animals. Godard uses his panorama shots to establish the complexity and unpredictability of the social universe, opaque in its causality, full of unexpected factors: mechanized death lurks along country roads; concert music fills the barnyard.

Rainer Werner Fassbinder's breakthrough *Katzelmacher* (Germany, 1969), two years later, holds a distinctive panning sequence in structural tension with a different kind of shot. The film's characteristic long-take, frontal, static street scenes showcase the bored dysfunction—and scapegoating tendencies—of disaffected young Munich neighbors. Yet slow fantasy sequences repeatedly undercut these long takes: tracking shots of couples solemnly processing through an urban courtyard, as if present and future hold utopian promise. The juxtaposition between modes renders these scenes poignant rather than hopeful, given the ways real-world relationships habitually disintegrate into power plays. Only in the courtyard can fantasy alternatives hold sway.

The opening episode of Fassbinder's *Berlin Alexanderplatz* (West Germany, 1980), like his melodramas *The Merchant of Four Seasons* (West Germany, 1971) and *Martha* (West Germany, 1974), returns to the urban courtyard as a place where social and psychic pressures converge. Alfred Döblin's 1929 urban collage novel *Berlin Alexanderplatz* had opened with Franz Biberkopf's release from prison into Berlin's inner city; overstimulated by its crowds, cacophony, and advertisement barrage, he flees into an apartment courtyard, beset by apocalyptic hallucinations. Piel Jutzi's 1931 film adaptation omitted the courtyard: instead Biberkopf's overloaded disorientation builds during the tram ride downtown. In Fassbinder's adaptation, in contrast, the courtyard spins to Biberkopf's silent scream, pressing in carcerally as Biberkopf sings a patriotic song, desperate to preserve his sanity.

This Döblinian mise-en-scène also inflects *Merchant*'s opening credits: an itinerant fruit seller hauls his cart into a Munich courtyard to cry his wares. Sales pitches, he later explains, need inviting tones. Yet as he repeats his cry, the camera vertiginously circles the courtyard, building an entrapping round. Like early modern *Cries of London*, Fassbinder's cries of Munich show sellers' public "cries"—and vendor's routines—masking unshed tears over blighted lives.[10]

Like *Merchant*, *Martha* explores masochism and domestic entrapment. It also remakes *Vertigo*'s kiss while underscoring its artificiality and pathology. At their first encounter, in the German consulate courtyard, Martha and Helmut make a (lazy Susan–enabled) double rotation around each other even as the camera movement foregrounds their continuing separateness. They tango toward one another and symmetrically part, their mesmerizing choreography of rapprochement and reseparation inaugurating a torturous sadomasochistic relationship. Like Hitchcock, Fassbinder is coldly diagrammatic; as his emotionally crippled protagonists fall in love, the camera stands apart, yet its swing captures their psychic gyrations, trying to keep their footing as they take in yet avoid each other.

For Fassbinder, as we have seen, this scene is one of his recurrent experiments with panning shots, always linked to questions of power, spectatorship, and abjection. In turn, romantic melodramas like *Vertigo* and *Martha* raise formal and psychological questions informing later feminist and experimental filmmaking—questions later installation art only multiplies. Runa Islam's 1998 multi-projector film installation *Tuin* thus restages *Martha*'s lazy Susan encounter, using surrounding screens to introduce further perspectival close-ups, freeze-frames, variations of speed and color; shattering any consistent narrative perspective, Islam further complicates Fassbinder's ambiguous spectatorial placement. Where painted panoramas aimed for seamless illusion, panoramic film and installation potentially multiply and thereby shatter illusions, enabling epistemological and political breakthrough. In this, they reiterate the liberatory project of interwar committed film and the avant-garde.

During the late 1960s, across the capitalist world, the international student movement framed itself as a vehicle for radical, accelerated social change, systemic political reform, and new forms of collectivity. From the United States to Japan, filmmakers chronicling the movement used panorama shots to suggest its internal contradictions and vulnerabilities. At least in retrospect, their self-reflexivity creates dialogue between the movement's disparate branches. In Ogawa Shinsuke's leftist documentary *Sea of Youth—Four Correspondence Course Students* (*Seinem no umi: Yonin no tsūshin kyōikuseitachi*, Japan, 1966), working students protest potentially prohibitive "reforms" of Japan's open universities, yet they become worn down by tactical debates and uncertainty. By the end, the camera swirls around them as they playfully blacken a political poster, no longer pleading for anything. In Stuart Hagmann's feature *The Strawberry Statement* (U.S., 1970), a student couple watch a twirling zoetrope, which circles long after they've left their dorm. Later, on a merry-go-round, they themselves savor zoetropic movement. But their joyful suspension, like the collective energy leading students to occupy their university, proves short-lived. By the end, as the police clear the occupied building, beating and teargassing terrified students, a poignantly utopian flashback offers swinging, circular shots of events at or before the story's beginning (incoming students touring San Francisco and the university, tasting college life). Joni Mitchell's "Circle Game" ("we're captive on the carousel of time," sung by Buffy Sainte-Marie) links the circling shots to a life cycle: innocence (inevitably) lost, displaced by specters of impotence and death, as adolescents experience adult life's first disillusionments.

In West Germany, key filmmakers criticized the student movement as self-involved, self-destructive. Werner Herzog's *Even Dwarves Started Small* (*Auch Zwerge haben klein angefangen*, 1970) sardonically allegorizes its ambitions and failures; in the closing scene, "dwarf" protagonists leave a driverless vehicle running in circles, filling with exhaust the courtyard the opening credits depicted peacefully, panoramically. Godard's *Weekend* juxtaposes rural traffic jam with panoramic farmyard music; Herzog's vision of civilizational (and vehicular) collapse vertiginously collapses Godard's contrasting layers of film grammar.

In contrast, West Berlin's radical film students offered assured, self-reflexive accounts of their movement. Helke Sander's 1968 student film *Break the Power of the Manipulators* (*Brecht die Macht der Manipulateure*) documents increasingly chaotic clashes between students, working-class West Berliners, and police (exacerbated by the tabloid press's anti-Communist provocations), then pans across a student movement office: students typing, assembling press clippings, posting, analyzing, ripping down newspaper headlines. Sander's Godardian film works to build a new counter–public sphere; her panning camera establishes the critical understanding of media, critical media analysis at its center.

The same year, as a student film exercise, Sander, Gerd Conradt, Harun Farocki, Wolfgang Petersen, Holger Meins, Carlos Bustamante, and Philip Sauber shot a continuous twelve-minute car-window tracking shot of a conceptual art performance. In *Color Test: The Red Flag* (*Farbprobe: Die rote Fahne*), male students relay a red flag along West Berlin's shopping streets; when the final runner reaches Schöneberg Town Hall (home of West Berlin's Senate), he illegally hangs the flag from its balcony—the site of John F. Kennedy's famous 1963 "I Am a Berliner" speech. In the students' seemingly tireless sprint through West Berlin traffic and commerce, homemade leftist emblem held high, to occupy a crucial Cold War symbolic

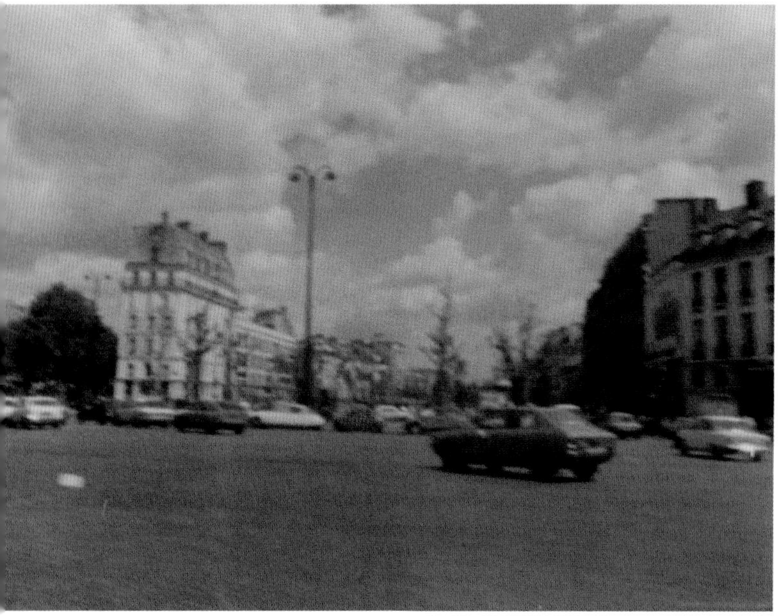

FIG. 12.4. Round and round; emptiness as historical trace: Place de la Bastille as modern-day traffic circle. Jean-Marie Straub (French, b. 1933) and Danièle Huillet (French, 1936–2006), *Too Early, Too Late* (*Trop tôt, trop tard*), 1982.

space, *Color Test* meditates on the continued power and pathos of old revolutionary symbols—and on revolution's increasingly long odds in an age of capitalist prosperity. The Weimar Republic and the Popular Front are important political memories, capable of symbolic animation. But their modes of activism are actually long passed.

HISTORICAL PROCESS AND POLITICAL ART FILM THROUGH THE FALL OF COMMUNISM

In 1970s and 1980s art and essay films, panorama shots often marked the complexity of longue-durée historical developments, patterns, and duration, giving viewers the big picture. Like *Dwarves*, Herzog's *Aguirre, the Wrath of God* (*Aguirre, der Zorn Gottes*, West Germany, 1972) ends in a circle and utter political collapse as Herzog explores absolutism's illusions, the unstable megalomaniac, the imperialist's tenuous power, out of his depth and far from home. In *Aguirre*'s famous opening credits, local guides lead conquistadors down vertiginous Andean passes, the Spaniards' litter, ceremonial clothing, and weapons visibly unfit for their new surroundings. By the film's closing shot, even the camera distances itself, as in *Yesterday Girl*, moving in increasingly large circles around Aguirre, the last dying European survivor, raving while floating helplessly downstream on his now-oarless raft. His fantasy of conquering and controlling a continent proved delusional—like melodrama's masochistic loves, with world-historical consequences. Spanish vainglory may be covered by water—yet for indigenous inhabitants, this violent European incursion will remain a constitutive trauma.

Jean-Marie Straub and Danièle Huillet, Theo Angelopoulos, and Helke Sander used panorama shots to excavate still-tangible political traces. Like *Mother Krauss*, *Weekend*, and *Aguirre*, Straub and Huillet's essay film *Too Early, Too Late* (*Trop tôt, trop tard*, France/Egypt, 1982) juxtaposes circular panorama sequences with very different panning and tracking shots. *Too Early* opens in Paris, with a repeated 360-degree panorama (shot from a car, inducing viewer motion sickness) of Place de la Bastille's traffic circle, where the Bastille once stood, before its storming and demolition began the French Revolution. Yet that only began a nineteenth-century cycle of revolution and restoration: during the car's five-minute circulation around Place de la Bastille, a Friedrich Engels text in voice-over elucidates this circular historical pattern (fig. 12.4). Subsequent panoramic sequences showcase French towns mentioned in prerevolutionary grievance books and very extended tracking down French country roads and along the Nile (past now-unmarked sites of rural unrest) as very intermittent voice-overs describe the jagged, always premature yet also fatally delayed nature of French revolutionary struggle and Egypt's anticolonial movement, juxtaposing first- and third-world histories. The Egyptian footage echoes the Lumières' *Egypt, Panorama of the Banks of the Nile* (France, 1897, see chapter 8) and their inaugural film, *Workers Leaving the Factory* (*La sortie de l'usine Lumières à Lyon*, France, 1895). The Nile's seasonal swelling, flooding its banks, fertilizing, enabling civilization's advance; workers' decisive movement, leaving the workplace that has taken their daylight hours: the film's visual logic links these movements to the movement of history and political destiny.

The Bastille is no longer; razed as a hated ancien régime symbol, this prison vanished from Paris's architectural fabric; only its name—and circling traffic—remains. No external marker commemorates the film's further sites of nineteenth-century injustice or twentieth-century liberation struggles. Viewers often have no way of knowing where they are, lost even aurally in the voice-over's extreme distension, its political astuteness vitiated by its intermittence reaching the viewer's ears. Nothing past, seemingly, can be retained. Yet the film's geometric

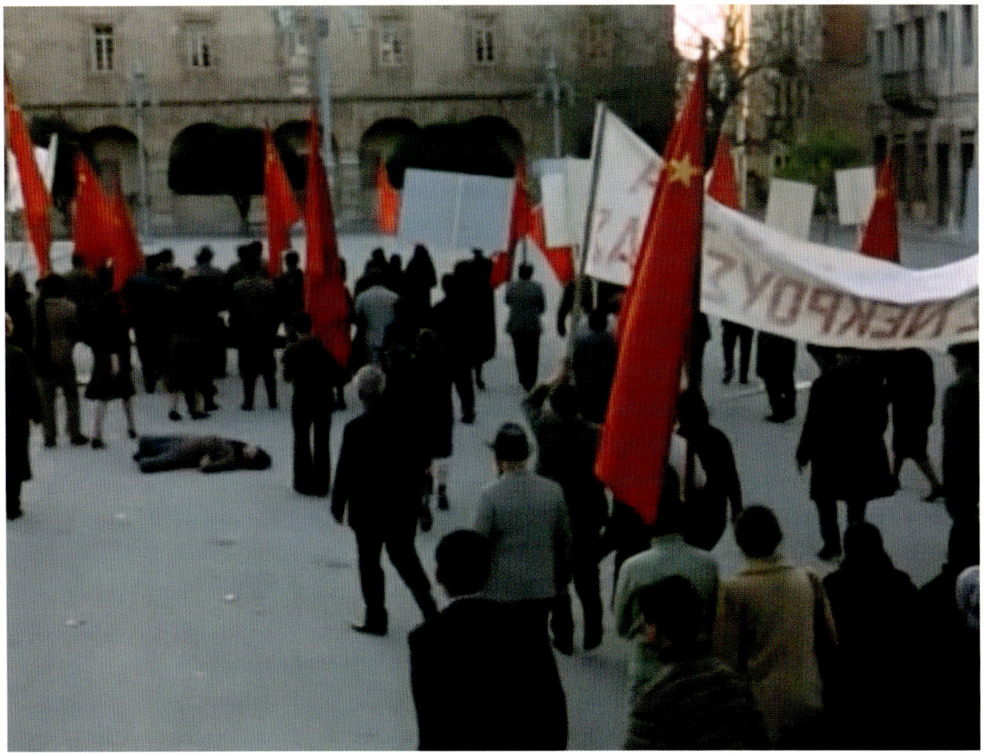

FIG. 12.5. Agora as death trap: a new group of protestors returns to the town hall square where earlier marchers were massacred. Theo Angelopoulos (Greek, 1935–2012), *The Travelling Players (O Thiasos)*, 1975.

mise-en-scène helps viewers viscerally feel the complexities of historical temporality and the long unfolding back-and-forth of political upheavals, cyclical like the Nile's rise and fall.

Angelopoulos's *The Travelling Players* (*O Thiasos*, Greece, 1975) likewise exploits duration and viewers' political and narrative confusion, here to dramatize the rhythm of twentieth-century Greek history. A multilayered ghost story, the film echoes and reechoes scenes of past and present, as an acting troupe—now older, now younger, now in full ranks, now decimated—travels the countryside over many decades, backward and forward in time, endlessly performing the same traditional repertoire while encountering war, civil war, occupation, refugees, coups, dictatorships.

During several panoramic sequences, Angelopoulos overlays two distinct temporal levels. The film's first half ends with a post–World War II public demonstration and clash among pro-Communist, pro-American, and pro-nationalist factions, scattered by violent military massacre—but by the time the camera, circling panoramically around a crowded civic square, turns back on its own tracks, we're in a different temporal layer, witnessing another Communist demonstration, under different historical circumstances, in the same plaza (fig. 12.5). Like Miklós Jancsó in *The Red and the White* (*Csillagosok, katanák*, Hungary, 1967), Angelopoulos stages perspectival switches, reversals of historical fortune, changing political sides, within a single shot. Jancsó's restless camerawork obsessively moves back and forth; Angelopoulos uses the circle, suggesting national space's unbroken coherence, despite historical ruptures.

Straub and Huillet's early films repeatedly circled Rome's hills, by car, in traffic, exhausting viewers, allowing only partial or blocked car-window views past driver and passenger (forms of mise-en-scène later echoed in Abbas Kiarostami's Teheran car dramas). Angelopoulos's traveling players traverse Greece's islands by rail, boat, and foot, carrying luggage uphill and down, town to town, shore to shore. Unlike *Aguirre*'s conquistadors, scaling the Andes, the traveling players traverse their own ground, claiming Greek territory as they walk it, on the most local, tactile scale. Made near the end of the Regime of the Colonels, *The Travelling Players* angrily, lyrically claims an underlying unity to Greek history, despite internecine struggles and political caesuras.

Sander's sardonic *The All-Around Reduced Personality: Redupers* (*Die allseitig reduzierte Persönlichkeit—Redupers*, 1978) considers Germany's seemingly immutable division, the gendered division of social labor, the contradictions

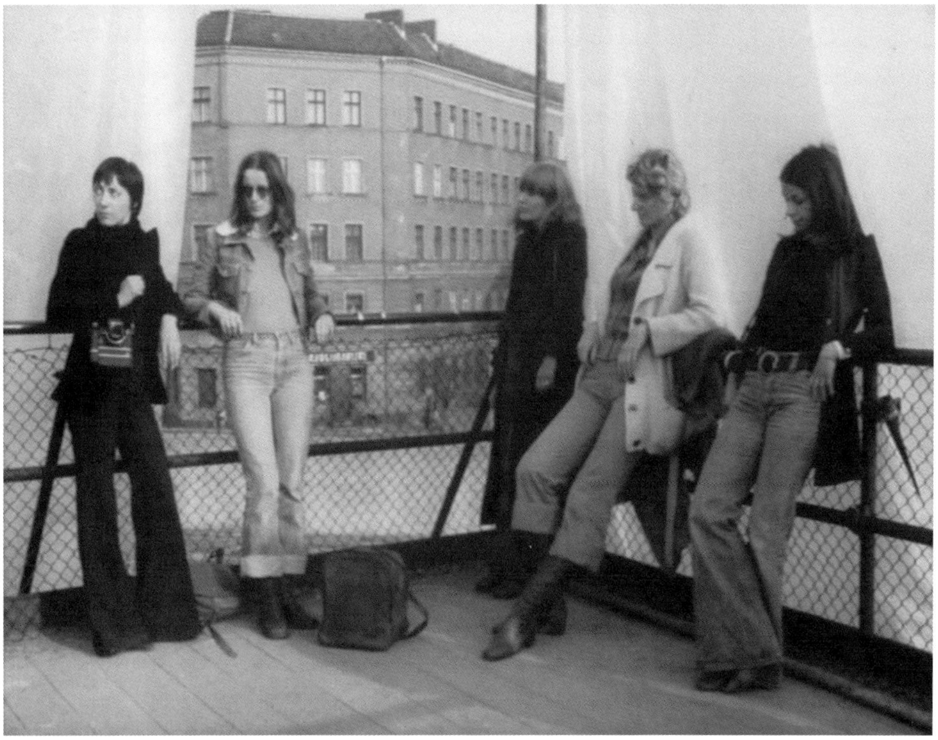

FIG. 12.6. On the viewing platform: a women's photography collective tries to frame East Berlin. Helke Sander (German, b. 1937), *The All-Around Personality: Redupers* (*Die allseitig reduzierte Persönlichkeit—Redupers*), 1978.

of artistic creation, as it follows a leftist West Berlin photographer, eking out a freelance existence and trying to help her feminist photography collective raise local consciousness. Like Godard and Straub and Huillet, Sander opens *Redupers* with long panning shots, driving in a vast circle. Because *Redupers* begins on one side of the Berlin Wall, a full, resolving 360-degree trajectory becomes impossible—there's no way to go *around* the wall, return to where we started, close the circle. The wall's western surface, a de facto wall newspaper, offers Cold War political graffiti chronicling the spectrum of political opinion. Graffiti commemorating Holger Meins (Sander's film-school classmate and *Color Test* codirector who later joined the Red Army Faction and died in prison on a hunger strike) thus balances a memorial tag for West Germans "Kidnapped by the Stasi." This visual political survey is accompanied by aural stocktaking, the car radio surveying Berlin's contradictory radio signals, from East German state radio to Anglo-American occupation forces' networks. The Cold War is audible across the dial, filling the city's air.

Sander underscores the Berlin Wall's paradoxical permeability, tensions between East Berlin Communist aesthetics and West Berlin's New Left. After the wall's erection, viewing platforms built at intervals on its western side enabled now-divided families to see each other. They gradually fell into disuse—or appropriation by Western tourists peering into East Berlin. Now the feminist art collective domesticates the Iron Curtain metaphor, erecting kitchen curtains across a viewing platform (fig. 12.6), summoning an art crowd to watch them drawn. The newly framed view proves anticlimactic: the camera pans across East Berlin's semi-deserted streets, East Berliners going about their business, a quotidian realism apart from Cold War rhetoric; the viewing platforms provide vantages from which both Berlins are visible simultaneously, enabling rare panoramic views of German history and ideology.

In the early 1990s, after the wall fell and the Soviet Union dissolved, Chantal Akerman shot *From the East* (*D'est*, Belgium/France/Portugal, 1993) across an Eastern Europe in radical economic and political transition. Through very long vehicle-based panning, Akerman's wordless documentary explores how Eastern Europeans inhabit public spaces now under reconstruction. Jonathan Crary's *24/7: Late Capitalism and the Ends of Sleep* celebrates *D'est* as "the testament of a social world, however damaged, prior to the imposition of neoliberal financialization, privatization . . . since brutal but crude forms of Stalinist discipline allowed many of the underlying rhythms of social time to persist unchanged." *D'est*'s pans meditate on the "act of waiting . . . something essential . . .

to the tentative possibility of community . . . a tacit acceptance of time shared in common."[11] For Arun Chaudhary, too, Akerman's compositions implicitly convey lost or potential collectivity: *D'est*'s panoramas, pans, crowd shots were major influences on Chaudhary's official videography for President Obama's White House and for Bernie Sanders's 2016 Democratic nomination campaign.[12]

Affectively, however, Akerman's tableaux of waiting, tracking shots of long queues, show sufferers sunk within themselves, without hope that the moment's tedium will be relieved, deeply fatigued by social forms organized around collectivity, and lacking belief in the survival of personality. *D'est* forces its viewer into a meditative stance, close to boredom and exhaustion, to comprehend mute quotidian suffering. Its subjects have spent years waiting: the society of industrialization, full productivity, night shifts, and goods shortages was not conducive to the restorative sleep or social dreaming Crary envisions as capitalism's alternative.

In 1995 Akerman reframed *D'est* as an installation. An initial room screens the entire film; in a second, twenty-four monitors play different *D'est* film loops. On the final room's lone monitor Akerman reads a Hebrew text, then her own French-language text about the film. Her documentary images of Eastern Europeans, waiting, in transition, confront Western museumgoers, themselves forced to stand wearily, uneasily, watching their Eastern counterparts. For those viewing in the first room (or the cinema), *D'est*'s confrontation may feel safely ethnographic; in the second gallery, the piece's slow rhythms, interest in duration, and apparently disconnected, competing loops push viewers to acknowledge their exhaustion or indifference. Akerman's culminating commentary underscores why their ambivalence matters. "Old images of evacuation, of people with packages marching in the snow towards an unknown place . . . faces that vacillate between a strong life and the possibility of a death that would come to strike them without their having asked for anything . . . yesterday, today, and tomorrow, there were, there will be, there are right now even, people that history . . . comes to strike. People who are there, rounded up in herds, waiting to be killed, hit, or starved; people who walk without knowing where they're going; in a group or all alone."[13] For Akerman, Eastern Europeans' forced mass passivity evokes family Holocaust trauma, historical deportations, and genocides on the same Eastern European terrain.

Like Angelopoulos and Akerman, Alexander Sokurov's *Russian Ark* (Russia, 2002) pans to evoke a fragmentary collective history. Yet where Angelopoulos emphasized modern Greek history's ruptures and hauntedness, Sokurov celebrates continuity through a single, unbroken ninety-six-minute tracking shot, the longest to date. Sokurov emphasizes neither Akerman's anonymous crowd nor Angelopoulos's heritage-transmitting theater troupe but the accrual of cultural tradition (despite political reverses) inside elite, imperial institutions. For two centuries the czars' residence, St. Petersburg's Winter Palace today houses the Hermitage, the world's largest art museum. Sokurov follows a visitor down palace hallways as long (fig. 12.7) as a nineteenth-century tunnel book. Tracking across epochs of imperial and Soviet history, he suggests art's capacity to reflect absolutist power while becoming the repository of far more elevated cultural sensibility. Sokurov's film celebrates Russian high culture as it precedes, and survives, the seventy-year Soviet interregnum.

Central European dissidents understand themselves differently, dissenting from post-1989 *capitalism* as from postwar Communism. Karel Vachek's essay films assemble wide-ranging political-artistic collages. *Závis: The Prince of Pornofolk under the Influence of Griffith's Intolerance and Tati's Mr. Hulot's Holiday, or The Rise and Fall of Czechoslovakia* (Czech Republic, 2006) investigates capitalism's and privatization's depredations. From a penthouse overlooking the city, Vachek explains offscreen to his cameraman how to film in a circle, creating a fish-eye cityscape. In a counterpoint scene, intellectuals traverse a Renaissance square despairingly discussing bankruptcy and public distress. Like Francesco Rosi's Neopolitan corruption docudrama *Hands over the City* (Italy, 1963), *Závis* evokes new capitalist puppet masters poised above the city. Yet on the ground, reformers still inhabit a philosophical and architectural landscape reflecting Sienese and Florentine ideals of the well-governed polis.[14]

Czechoslovakia has a significant tradition of dissident panoramic photography. After shooting anonymous photographs of the 1968 Soviet invasion, Josef Koudelka went into self-imposed exile—and began taking panoramic photographs, especially postindustrial landscapes. After the Velvet Revolution, he returned to Czechoslovakia and made his most apocalyptic panoramic series, documenting the Black Triangle industrial mining area between Bohemia, Saxony, and Silesia. In 1994 his enlarged photographs were displayed facing Prague Castle, mute

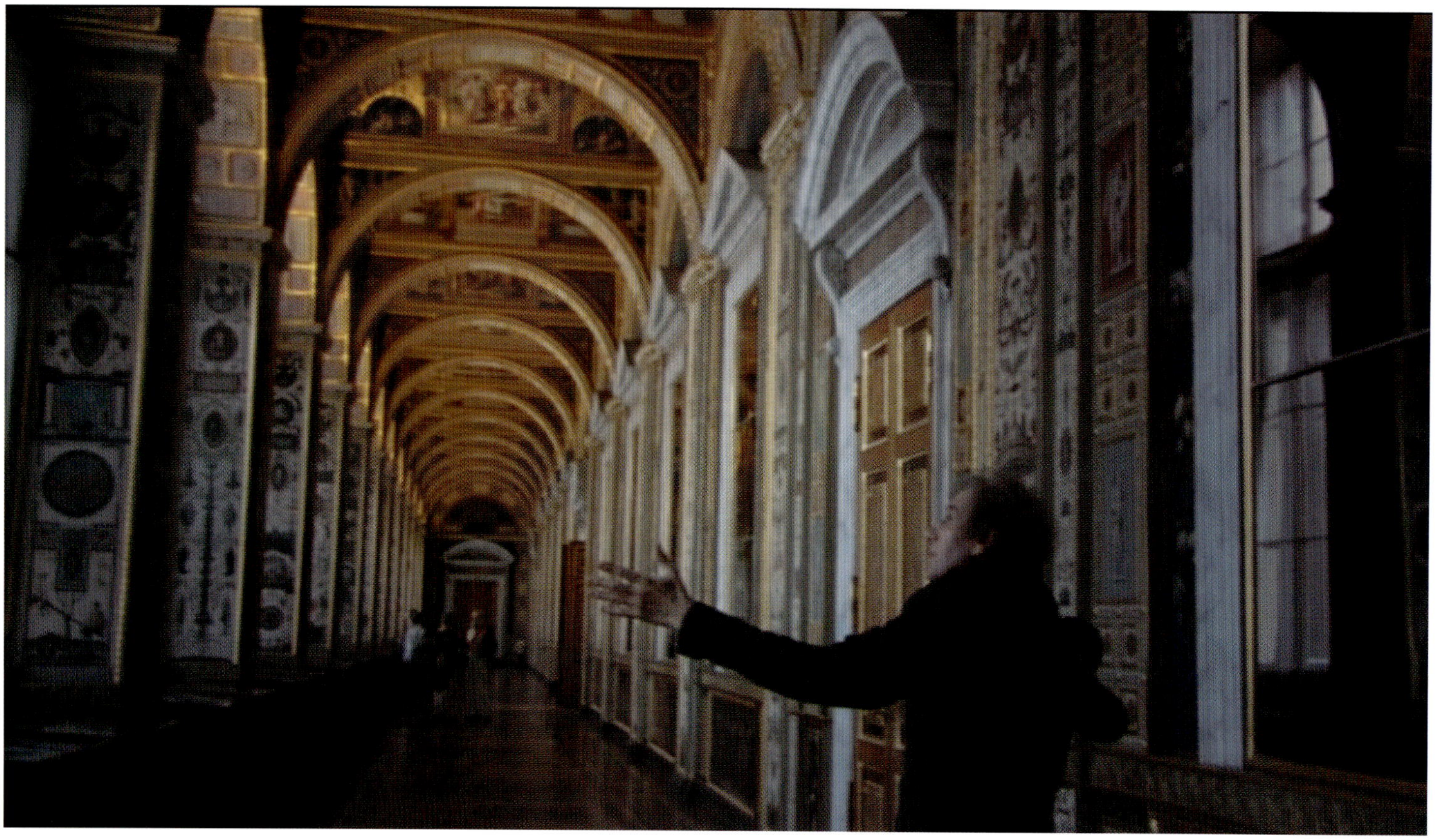

FIG. 12.7. Alexander Sokurov (Russian, b. 1951), *Russian Ark*, 2002.

accusation and environmental witness to Communism's enduring ecological damage.[15]

Four decades earlier, during Stalinism's heyday, the surrealist and poetic realist Josef Sudek traversed Prague with an old flea-market panoramic camera; the black-and-white images collected in his 1959 photobook *Prague Panoramic* (*Prague Panoramaticka*) highlight the uncharacteristically empty city, its unchanging medieval and Renaissance architecture. Sudek's elegiac, classicizing photographs frame Prague as an ideal cityscape in the mode of Renaissance Italian perspectival studies. Like Eugène Atget's Paris—or Koudelka's 1968 Prague—*Prague Panoramic* imagines a city of ghosts, urban fabric intact but drained of people. Yet Prague's architectural survival reminds us that ours is not the only possible political or economic world. Even at Communism's height, Sudek photographed Prague as unchanging, eternal, untouched by current ideology.[16] Even in Communism's wake, Vachek suggests, capitalist social organization remains contingent, not inevitable. History continues; in the panorama's sometimes charmed circle, utopian ideas remain alive.

TWIST, LIFT-OFF: PANORAMA AS EXPERIMENT

Like romantic melodrama, experimental film is often interested in notating fantasy life, visual correlatives for love, emotional states from despair to boredom. From the 1960s onward, panoramically informed experimental film sought to reorient spectatorial experiences of embodiment and peripheral vision. Michael Snow moves from slow continuous zoom-in (*Wavelength*, Canada, 1967) to short tilting and panning (*Standard Time*, Canada, 1967; *Back and Forth*, Canada, 1969) and impersonal panoramic arcs in *La région centrale* (Canada, 1971), as a preprogrammed self-tracking camera on a northern Quebec mountaintop pans and pivots around itself.

Wavelength moves inexorably in one continuous zoom from an apartment-room establishing shot to a close-up of the photograph on one wall. Snow's exploration is rigorous, structural, but dramatic: over forty-five minutes, characters move through the space, and one mysteriously dies. The viewer feels trapped in the fixed linearity of the film's visual unfolding yet mystified about what is occurring, physically grounded certainty balanced against epistemological, even metaphysical ambiguity. This paradox

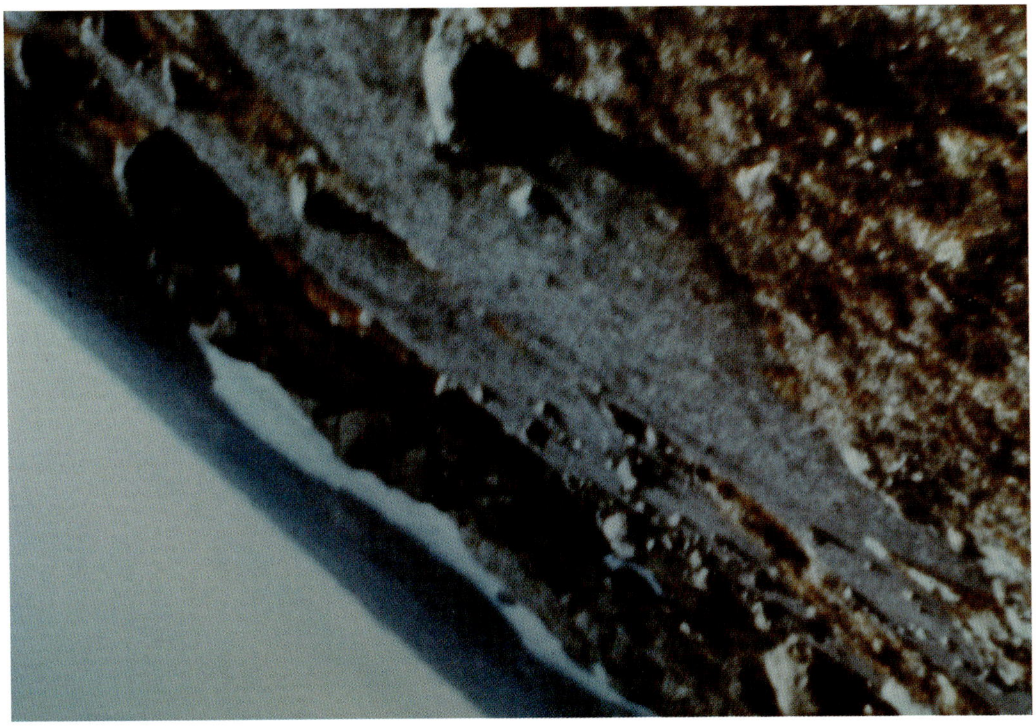

FIG. 12.8. Michael Snow (Canadian, b. 1928), *La région centrale*, 1971.

influenced 1960s and 1970s art films with inconclusive, enigmatic endings. In the climactic shot of Michelangelo Antonioni's *The Passenger* (Italy/Spain/France, 1975, cowritten by Peter Wollen), the camera moves continuously, without stopping or cutting, apparently right through the protagonist's barred hotel window, panning across the dusty courtyard and countryside, eventually coming to rest outside the hotel window, while inside the protagonist has just been found dead. During the seven-minute shot, the movie shifts narrative gear; an already mysterious protagonist (inhabiting a dead man's identity) becomes a corpse, a climactic moment invisible if retroactively palpable. The film risks losing any remaining narrative comprehensibility, but the viewer remains riveted by the omniscient camera's magical passage through walls and bars, retaining its distinctive, authoritative vantage point.

La région's explicitly inhuman camera offers differently confounding views. Over three hours, it pivots in many directions, exploring its surroundings at many scales and speeds, sometimes meticulously examining terrain, sometimes surveying huge swatches of earth and sky. At moments, the camera sees only clouds, gravel, individual pebbles, lichens, light's disorienting passage across hills; it films upside down, in tight circles, or swings outward, in loose, potentially motion-sickness-inducing arcs (fig. 12.8). While in some respects the viewer gains intimate knowledge of the terrain, that terrain becomes complex and slippery—unfathomable not only by night or fog but fundamentally, given the camera arm's whirlygig motion.

Snow's film is almost unbearably concrete yet abstract in conceptual reach. Geologically, the "Canadian Shield," exposed Precambrian rock covering half of Canada (and part of the United States), renders the land above nonarable, hence largely unsettled, barely traversed, rarely depicted.[17] Its name metaphorically evokes bedrock protecting Canada; Snow's "Région centrale" designation suggests this vast wilderness's centrality to Canada's or Quebec's essence (or his own; his French-Canadian mother was born nearby). In an era of intensified Canadian nationalism (and Québécois separatism), the question of what is out there is implicitly political. Snow's epistemological stocktaking is potentially (Canadian or Québécois) nationalist as well. Created in a period of heightened ecological consciousness, Snow's remote-controlled camera, the film's largely invisible center, recalls the 1969 *Apollo 11* broadcast technology—and *Apollo*'s distant earth view from the moon's surface. Inflected by the space program's new sense of planetary scale, Snow's film uses preprogrammed robotic machinery for similarly distancing "central region" views, replicating the god's eye, everywhere, nowhere, impartial.

In a further twist, Snow's 1971 installation, *De la*, mounted his *Région central* camera apparatus in plain view, inside the National Gallery of Canada, videotaping continuously, its live feed displayed on four video monitors. Northern Quebec was ostensibly empty; the National Gallery was often crowded with spectators—sooner or later folded, like the monitors, into the video's purview as the camera whirled. Collapsing the usual separation between artwork and viewer, *De la* created a representational *mise-en-abyme*.[18]

Snow's 1977 photography series *Plus tard* pivoted with a still camera around a National Gallery room displaying the Group of Seven, Canada's most famous modernist landscape painters. Snow's pivot, Johanne Sloan argues, reinvents Group of Seven landscapes as latter-day Canadian panoramas (Snow's dynamism lends their still images movement and depth) while inducing viewers of Snow's blurred photographs to pivot panoramically themselves, as on a viewing platform.[19]

In 1924 two of the Group of Seven painters, Lawren Harris and A. Y. Jackson, had sketched an actual panoramic mural, of the Rockies' Tonquin Valley, to ornament a nearby Canadian National Railways hotel. Preliminary drawings were made on "a hill from which the whole way around the horizon could be seen, a grand panorama of mountains and lakes with stretches of forest and Alpine pastures."[20] The project remained unfinished, even the drawings largely unlocatable.

Snow's more conceptual latter-day panoramic ensemble comments on existing artistic institutions, spectatorship, and national icons. In *Région centrale*, Snow had tried to develop new national icons, a fresh sense of Canadian landscape. Even his resolve to develop the *Région centrale* camera, he recalled, came from "thinking over the history of film. . . . There had been practically no vertical pans that were complete circles. It's just pretty much nonexistent. . . . To try to do this thing I had to invent a machine that would move the camera."[21] Yet (as chapter 8 details) the core of Snow's conceptual "land art," a camera placed to pan in a landscape, was key for actuality films already around 1900.

And already in early features like Griffith's *Country Doctor*, such movement took on emotive force. Later filmmakers return to Griffith's simple but powerful pan. Straub and Huillet use movements of camera, car, wind, and river to explore epochal rhythms of political change. Bruce Baillie's *All My Life* (U.S., 1966) pans to push perceptual limits, regrounding viewers while moving toward the ineffable. During Baillie's single, three-minute right-to-left panning shot, the camera gradually tilts upward, along fence slats, past spectacularly flowering rosebushes (fig. 12.9), up through telephone lines into clear blue sky as Ella Fitzgerald sings "All My Life" (backed by Teddy Wilson's orchestra). Despite potential disconnects between sunny California fields and 1936 nightclub ballad, its lyrics underscore the poignancy, glory, ephemerality of flowers, of love exuberantly blossoming.

Baillie matches the song's slow, syncopated opening piano riff to the slow visual passage past light and dark fence posts—in visual analogue to Wilson's movement up and down the piano keys, joined (right before the panning camera reaches the first flowering rose clump) by a mellow clarinet and Fitzgerald's smoky, joyous voice. In jazz terms, flowers, clarinet, voice each gets a chorus; just after Fitzgerald ends the lyrics, the camera passes the flowers and begins tilting up, to a lilting trumpet and orchestra finale. Song and image end with an upbeat and heavenward swerve. As the screen goes dark, the song ends too; during brief, hand-drawn credits, we hear an old record scratching around and around on the turntable.

Baillie's film meshes landscape, lyrics, jazz, its insistently blossoming, spreading flowers visual correlatives to the emotional discovery of which Fitzgerald sings. Baillie finds additional correlation between panning shot and the single spiraling of the turntable. The song's lyrics present life as totality: giving "all my love," the speaker has belatedly "begun/Living all my life." Love's advent transforms an eternity of waiting into a "sublime" state, given density and meaning. Afraid of the beloved's superiority, the speaker hardly dares lift her gaze: since Sappho, love poetry has involved deification, apotheosis. The camera's final skyward lift is anticipated by the song's elevation of the beloved as a deity whose gaze, warmth, and recognition reorganize earthly existence. The song's emphasis on completeness, fullness, and openness matches the pan's circularity.

When Hollywood romances depicted love, lovers danced, gazed at the moon, wept, sighed—and kissed.

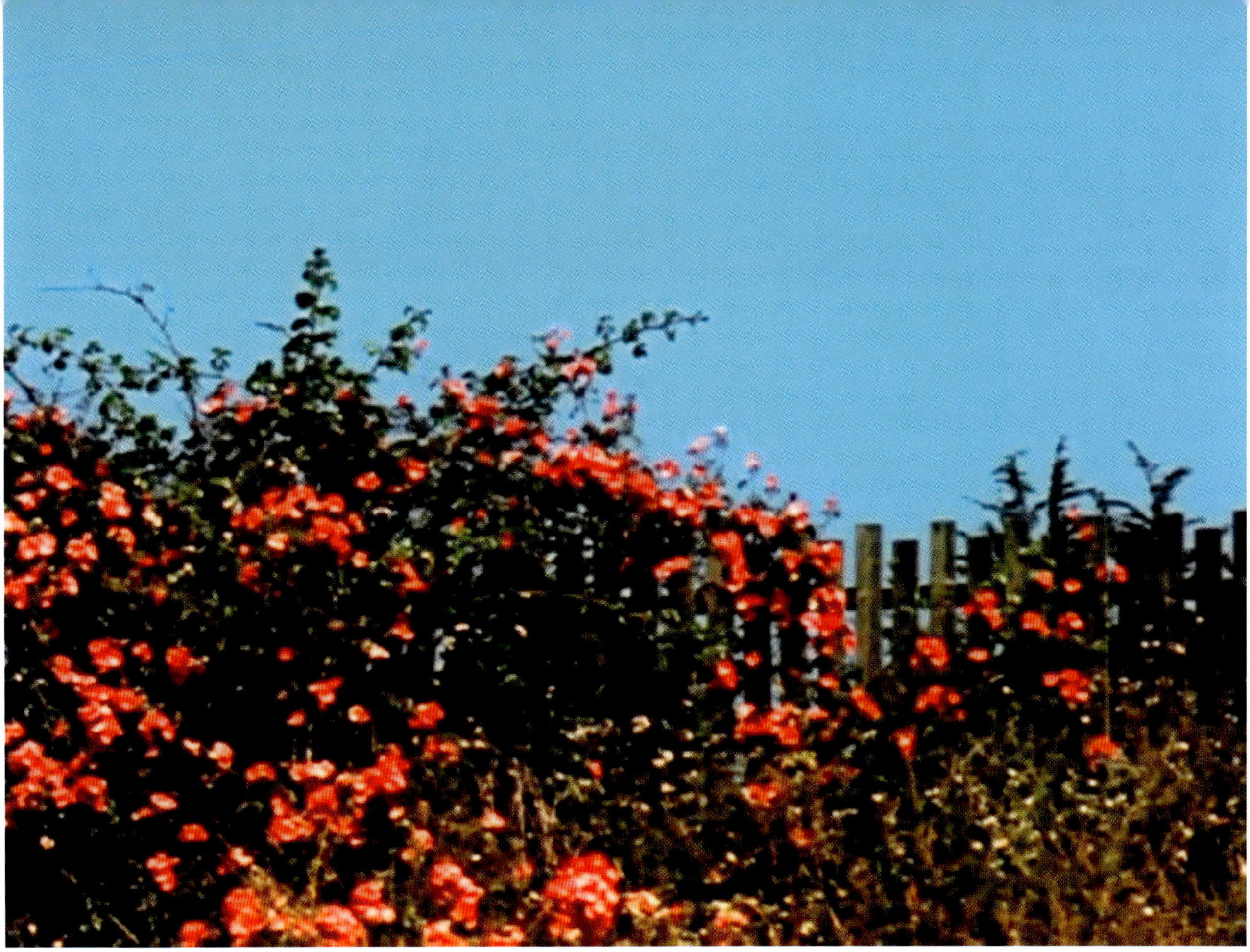

FIG. 12.9. Bruce Baillie (American, b. 1931), *All My Life*, 1966.

The kiss ending many movies abruptly abandoned the previous shot/reverse shot formula; rather than watching one pair of approaching lips in close-up, then the other (mise-en-scène in which the viewer might feel devoured), the viewer watches from a chaste middle distance. Hitchcock's swirling *Vertigo* camera went further: past and present, temporality, visuality collapse as lovers merge in erotic union; "love," however delusional, is dizzying, disorienting, vertiginous. Fassbinder, too, was coldly diagrammatic; as Martha and Helmut fall in love, the circling camera captures their psychic gyrations.

Baillie's panorama film locates love far more diffusely and somewhere else entirely: in timbre, the clarinet's lilt, the trees, the light, the swirl of vision. Love suffuses, transforming subjective experience; Baillie uses color, rhythm, motion, and angle to give this state external expression. He records the pleasure of ordinary vision—and moments, however short-lived, transfiguring, transforming the heart, hence the world. Art records, even catalyzes such moments of profound investment. Art's own processes and media have a mechanical basis—panorama building erected to filter light, needle scraping record—yet offer a means to transcendence.

Feminist avant-garde filmmakers of the 1970s tackled many of Snow's and Baillie's conceptual issues. Akerman met Snow in New York and was deeply impressed with *La région centrale*, which she saw demonstrating "the relationship between film and your body, time as the most important thing in film."[22] Snow's film recorded a textured but uninhabited natural world; Akerman's *La chambre 2* (1972) tracks a lived-in domestic setting. Over eleven minutes of panoramic passes, counterclockwise and then clockwise, the camerawoman Babette Mangolte captures a still life of quotidian objects (kettle, sink, teacups, ornate dresser's curved surface) and Akerman herself, tossing in bed, yawning, eating an apple. Panning as self-determined stocktaking: an independent young woman surveys her domain. Yet Akerman's early films, Ivone Margulies argues, also inaugurated a long preoccupation with claustrophobia, obsession, psychic and domestic residues of her mother's concentration camp internment. Akerman's later films move—often panning—through a wider world,

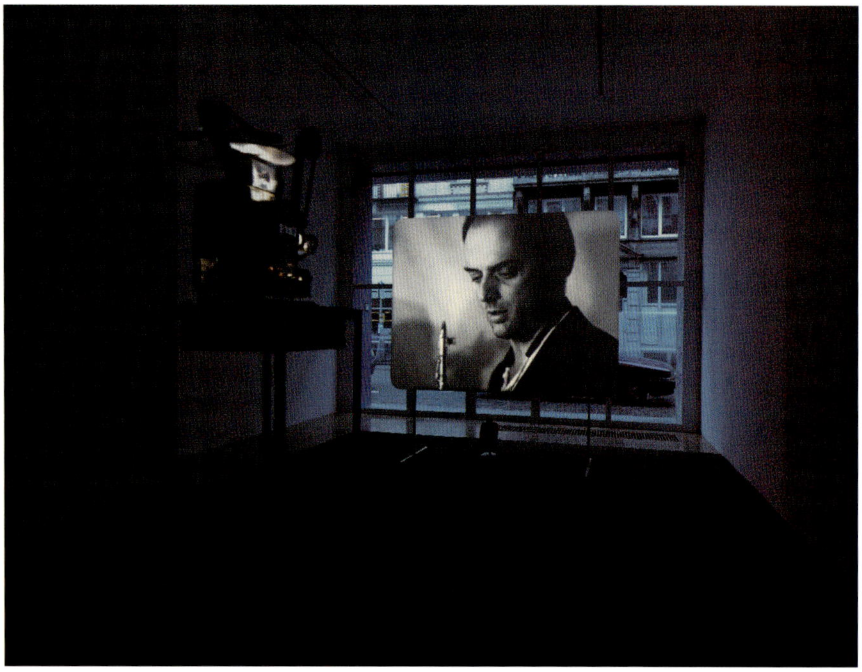

FIG. 12.10. Manon de Boer (Dutch, b. 1966), *Attica*, 2008.

seeking escape yet, like this early "voyage around my room" (the title of Joseph de Maistre's 1794 house-arrest narrative), repeatedly record a circumscribed domestic sphere from which the outer world seems unreachable.[23] The domestic seems self-sufficient, but it cannot divorce itself from external pressures, even as it becomes potentially entrapping. How could women feel at home in a wider world, experience love and attachment, without becoming caught in delusion, claustrophobia, vertigo?

Laura Mulvey and Peter Wollen's *Riddles of the Sphinx* (Britain, 1977) extends Akerman's experiment. As Mal Ahern describes in chapter 11, *Riddles*'s extended series of panorama shots chronicle slices of ordinary London life and environs: domestic locales, workplaces, public spaces, and finally, a film-editing suite, mirrored boudoir, and British Museum mummy room, multilayered places of artistic production, fantasy life, cultural preservation. The film's panoramic tableaux explore the porousness of human attachment; ways city planning, workplaces, even leisure spaces alienate people from each other; and, finally, ways art creates its own dialogue and dialectic of interior and exterior. In *Riddles*'s final panoramas, the multiplication of visual levels, reflections, mummy-casing worlds within worlds forces us to see the complexity of surfaces.[24] Inhabiting the mummy room alongside the camera, we feel embodied and spatially located there—yet erroneously confuse two- with three-dimensional surfaces, gliding along surfaces without resting place.

CODA: *ATTICA* UNCHAINED

Museums and galleries increasingly became locales where viewers might encounter installations or performances alongside two-dimensional paintings, works behind glass; newer, more conceptually based, architecturally modulated art forms pushed viewers to experience their bodies in relationship to gallery space. Installation art interrogates the orchestration—and open-endedness—of aesthetic experience.

Like *Riddles*'s final panoramas, Manon de Boer's panoramic film loop installation *Attica* (Belgium, 2008, fig. 12.10) ponders the nature of surfaces, the tradition of committed art, while laying the ground for a newer, multimedia practice. De Boer films a performance of Frederic Rzewski's 1972 *Attica*, itself a musical setting of a memorable utterance by the Black Muslim leader Richard X. Clark. In 1971 Clark had participated in the Attica prison riots. Outraged by long-standing overcrowding and civil rights violations, one thousand prisoners took fifty guards hostage and seized control of the correctional facility at Attica, New York. Four days later, New York state troopers and National Guardsmen recaptured the prison, killing over forty and wounding more than eighty prisoners and employees. Clark survived (and in 1973 published a memoir, *Brothers of Attica*). Upon his subsequent release on parole, a reporter asked how Clark felt to leave Attica behind. Clark responded, "Attica is in front of me." Rzewski sets that gnomic line, repeated against slow incremental tonal additions and subtractions he described as "squaring."[25] As Chus Martínez explains, "the sentence is spoken six times, from one to six words, until it reaches completion, and then six more times in reverse," while the music "soars and descends within a canonical structure."[26] The effect is of incantatory looping.

De Boer films a latter-day *Attica* performance, visually mirroring this looping canon effect. Rzewski's son Jan plays the saxophone and drones the piece's repeating line. His face, as he begins and ends his recitation, suggests the passage in and out of a quasi-Delphic trance, channeling another voice and sensibility—the more so given that (in Martínez's words), Clark's line itself "transfigures the historicity of the event into a perennial presence for the mind."[27] De Boer's camera first watches each musician playing, then circles the room, including many seconds of "nonrepresentational" wall, then window. But when the camera moves back to the musicians, they have mysteriously changed places. Repeat viewers may eventually identify a mid-film shot of a mirrored wall (briefly visible as blurry seamline), which subsequently reflects the musicians. The camera thus loops once around the room, reaches the mirror, loops back again in a different arc, across the mirror.

This looping structure both orients and dangles the viewer in time and space. For Clark, Attica may be a trauma seared onto his retinas, a haunting place of horrors, a filter through which to see the rest of his life. De Boer's panoramic figure-eight camerawork gives structure to our experience, even as Clark's words defy our usual structures of time, causality, linearity: Attica is never left behind; it always looms ahead, awaiting another pass-through. In Vachek's cinematic traversals, panorama shots evoked the Renaissance ideal city, good government. Memorializing an inhumane prison's catastrophic collapse, *Attica*'s panorama seems designed instead to contain trauma.

Like Rzewski's composition, de Boer's film insists on dynamic forward movement. Yet on its way around the circle, the camera blurs (noticeably pulled back into focus when we reach the musicians once more). In the middle, the circle—and film—becomes abstract, contemplative, non- or barely representational. This resonates threefold with *Attica*'s subject.

First, Rzewski forces our attention to the trauma of the socially marginal, enduring, and unimaginable violence with astonishing dignity and composure. Rzewski's emphasis on marginal experience extends to the text's musical setting and intoning: Attica IS in FROnt OF ME; the sentence's original spoken intonation pattern, rethought as music, repeatedly foregrounds unstressed syllables, giving them equal or greater emphasis. What is background in the sentence's spoken rhythm becomes foreground as chanted. The result is beautiful yet "alienating"; normal signification is suspended, the usual hierarchy of sounds and syllables transformed.

Second, during the spoken preamble, the narrator identifies Richard X. Clark as the historical speaker of *Attica*'s haunting, cryptic sentence, his intonation emphasizing the X in Clark's name. This pronunciation has political implications. A middle initial is normally given less stress than first or last name. But Clark, like Malcolm X and other Black Muslims, adopted X to declare distance from American life's "normal" bureaucratic institutions (from taxation to the census), underscoring slavery's eradication of kinship networks—and evoking the X illiterates use as their signature (since African American slaves were barred from literacy).[28] "X" becomes an empty center—an initial no longer standing for a name, but for a history of brutality suffered into the present by an entire people. And their sense of chiasmus: even when slavery was supposed to be behind them, it always still looms ahead, in new guises, from ghetto to incarceration.

Third, the film's complicated setup echoes the notion of the empty center. What appears a double panorama, two times around a 360-degree circle, proves a 180-degree pan reflected, doubled back on chiasmically, or undone in the mirror. Like *Riddles*'s final panoramas, *Attica* explores issues of self-reflection and mimesis raised by Édouard Manet's *Bar at the Folies-Bergère* (1882, Courtauld Institute) or Diego Velázquez's *Las Meninas* (1656, Prado). What appears to be two worlds is really only one, a world and its reflection. A mirror held to nature stirs meditation on what art can and cannot achieve. De Boer's staging evokes Plato's cave—the musicians stand against a white-sheeted backdrop, and the camera's opening movement back and forth among the musicians focuses on their doubling by their shadows, before beginning its apparently unidirectional, gliding, panoramic movement.

When shown in museum settings, de Boer insists, her film's 16mm projection must be rendered visible, as an eternally repeating, continuous loop. "This projector and its mechanism of continual movement located underneath the apparatus are part of the installation. The looping projection is an element in the content of the work. . . . The text accompanying the music talks of a future that, as a whole, is identical to the past ('Attica is in front of me'). The 360-degree movements of the camera and the repetition of the projection loop give the spectator the sense of being absorbed into an infinite circular movement."[29]

Like Rzewski's composition, de Boer's *Attica* draws its power from its forceful, fundamental political concerns (justice, racism's history, prison-as-deathtrap), formal complexity, and self-reflexivity. It retains an aura of mystery, of unfathomability, even as it pushes spectators toward political home truths, suspending them in the poetic, beautiful, sublime. Like nineteenth-century panorama viewers, *Attica*'s viewers are moved, disoriented, somehow changed. In the 1930s and the 1960s, panoramic film was agitational. Like 1970s and 1980s political art and essay films, de Boer's installation instead moves by indirection, even as the camera rotates, inexorably, in circles.

NOTES

1. Béla Balázs, *Theory of the Film: Character and Growth of a New Art* (New York: Roy, 1953), 142.
2. Giuliana Bruno, "An Urban Panorama," in Marc Ferrez and Robert Polidori, *Rio*, 2 vols. (São Paolo: Institute Moreira Salles, 2015), 1:10.
3. On museumgoers' embodied experience, see Erika Balsom, *Exhibiting Cinema in Contemporary Art* (Amsterdam: Amsterdam University Press, 2014), chap. 1.
4. See Tom Gunning, "An Unseen Energy Swallows Space: The Space in Early Film and Its Relation to American Avant-Garde Film," in *Film before Griffith*, ed. John L. Fell (Berkeley: University of California Press, 1983), 355–66; 365.
5. This pan shot's political and moral implications sparked ongoing debate. See André Bazin, *Jean Renoir*, ed. François Truffaut, trans. W. W. Halsey II and William H. Simon (New York: Simon and Schuster, 1973); Keith Reader, "The Circular Ruins: Frontiers, Exile and the Nation in Renoir's *Le Crime de Monsieur Lange*," *French Studies* 54, no. 3 (2000): 287–97; Colin David, *Scenes of Love and Murder: Renoir, Film and Philosophy* (London: Wallflower, 2009), 58–69; Karla Oeler, *A Grammar of Murder: Violent Scenes and Film Form* (Chicago: University of Chicago Press, 2009); and Martin O'Shaughnessy, "Breaking the Circle: 'Le Crime de Monsieur Lange' and the Contemporary Illegibility of the Radical Text," *South Central Review* 28, no. 3 (2011): 26–44.
6. Gertraude Kühn et al., eds., *Film und revolutionäre Arbeiterbewegung in Deutschland 1918–1932: Dokumente und Materien*, 2 vols. (Berlin: Henshel Verlag, 1975).
7. Daniel Dayan, "The Tudor-Code of Classical Cinema," *Film Quarterly* 28, no. 1 (1974): 22–31; Jean-Pierre Oudart, "Cinema and Suture," trans. Kari Hanet, *Screen* 18, no. 4 (1978): 35–47; and Stephen Heath, "On Suture," in *Questions of Cinema* (Bloomington: Indiana University Press, 1981), 76–112. Philip Shaw's *Waterloo and the Romantic Imagination* (Basingstoke, U.K.: Palgrave Macmillan, 2002), esp. 78–91, uses suture theory to analyze panoramic painting spectatorship. Oliver Grau, too, sees the painted panorama creating a suturing effect, as an "image apparatus" that "fixes the observer in the middle of the circular space" (presumably in the process centering the observer epistemologically and psychically); Grau, *Virtual Art: From Illusion to Immersion*, trans. Gloria Custance (Cambridge: MIT Press, 2003), 107. Yet this fixity assumes a stationary, not a mobile, viewer and view. Panoramas arguably offer alternative metaphors to *suture*: that spot in mid-dialogue is a viewing platform on which the viewer pivots continuously.
8. See my "Fragments of the Mirror: Self-Reference, Mise-en-Abyme, *Vertigo*," in *Hitchcock's Rereleased Films: From Rope to Vertigo*, ed. Walter Raubicheck and Walter Srebnick (Detroit: Wayne State University Press, 1991), 175–88.
9. On *Merry-Go-Round*, see John Cunningham, *Hungarian Film from Coffee House to Multiplex* (London: Wallflower, 2004), chap. 6.
10. Sean Shesgreen, *Images of the Outcast: The Urban Poor in the Cries of London* (Manchester, U.K.: Manchester University Press, 2002); and Katie Trumpener, "City Scenes: Commerce, Modernity, and the Birth of the Picture Book," in *The Victorian Illustrated Book: New Explorations*, ed. Richard Maxwell (Charlottesville: University Press of Virginia, 2002), 332–84.
11. Jonathan Crary, *24/7: Late Capitalism and the Ends of Sleep* (London: Verso, 2013), 122–24.
12. Cited in Rachel Donato, "The Director's Director: Chantal Akerman," *New York Times*, March 27, 2016, AR 16.
13. Quoted in Catherine David, "D'Est: Akerman Variations," in *Bordering on Fiction: Chantal Akerman's D'Est*, ed. Kathy Halbreich and Bruce Jenkins (Minneapolis: Walker Art Center, 1995), 57–64; on the installation, see Shelley Hornstein, "Ornament, Boundaries, and Mourning after Auschwitz," in *Reading Charlotte Salomon*, ed. Michael P. Steinberg and Monica Bohm-Duchen (Ithaca: Cornell University Press, 2006), 126–39.
14. Vachek filmed *What Is to Be Done? (A Journey from Prague to Český Krumlov, or How I Formed a New Government*, Czech Republic, 1996) in a Bohemian town famous for its arcaded Renaissance square and its 1958 open-air "Revolving Theater," an inside-out theater-in-the-round whose tiered audience space moves in a circle. During the 1950s and 1960s, cities worldwide built revolving restaurants; in the Eastern European context, they, like revolving theater, consciously evoked Vladimir Tatlin's 1919 unrealized, eternally rotating Monument to the Third International, conceived as a spur to ongoing revolution and dialectical self-reflection. East Berlin's Television Tower houses a revolving restaurant, overlooking Alexanderplatz's orbit-evoking World Clock (Weltzeit Uhr, both finished 1969).
15. Edward Burtynsky's large-scale photography of contemporary industrial rendering and manufacturing (from Canada to China) extends this critique while exploring a neo-industrial, anti-ecological sublime; Jennifer Baichwal's documentary *Edward Burtynsky: Manufactured Landscapes* (Canada, 2007) opens, in the style of Billy Bitzer's 1904 Westinghouse industrial panorama films, with minutes-long panning across a vast Chinese factory shop floor.
16. Katie Trumpener, "Stalin Boulevard: Panoramic Vistas and Urban Planning in Eastern European Photobooks," in *Remapping Cold War Media: Institutions, Infrastructures, Networks, Exchanges*, ed. Alice Lovejoy and Mari Pajala (Bloomington: Indiana University Press, forthcoming).
17. Annette Michelson, "About Snow," *October* 8 (Spring 1979): 111–24.
18. Jim Shedden and Alexa-Frances Shaw, *Michael Snow Up Close* (Canada, 1995).
19. Johanne Sloan, "Conceptual Landscape Art: Joyce Wieland and

Michael Snow," in *Beyond Wilderness: The Group of Seven, Canadian Identity and Contemporary Art*, ed. John O'Brian and Peter White (Montreal: McGill-Queen's University Press, 2007), 73–84, esp. 83–84.

20. Jackson, quoted in "A. Y. Jackson and Lawren Harris: Jasper/Robson, 1924," exhibition, curated by Lisa Christensen, Art Gallery of Alberta, 2014.

21. Michael Snow interview, "*De La*—Its Origins," clip 13, "Meet the Artist: Michael Snow," National Gallery of Canada, http://cybermuse.beauxarts.ca/cybermuse/docs/SnowClip13_e.pdf. In latter-day homage, the Spanish-born, Brazilian-based artist Daniel Steegmann Mangrané developed a custom-built gimbal camera able to film while rotating 360 degrees and used it to film Amazonian rain forest without disturbing it; recent exhibits have displayed the tripod camera alongside *16 mm* (2009–11) and *Spiral Forest* (2017), the resulting panoramic films.

22. Akerman quoted in Ivone Margulies, *Nothing Happens: Chantal Akerman's Hyperrealist Everyday* (Durham: Duke University Press, 1996), 3.

23. Ivone Margulies, "La Chambre Akerman: The Captive as Creator," *Rouge*, December 2006, www.rouge.com.au/10/akerman.html. *News from Home* (France/Belgium/West Germany, 1977) centers on New York car and ferry panning/tracking shots (site of Akerman's expatriate escape) over which she reads her mother's letters from Brussels. At the end of Akerman's musical *The Golden Eighties* (France/Belgium/Switzerland, 1986), the protagonist leaves the subterranean mall where the film has unfolded as an exterior panorama of Brussels' streets retrospectively establishes its geographical location.

24. One antecedent may be Robert Morris's "Finch College Project" (1969), filming (and then projecting) a partly mirrored surface from a rotating turntable. Chrissie Iles, ed., *Into the Light: The Projected Image in American Art, 1964–1977* (New York: Whitney Museum, 2001), 98–99; this inspired the MIT Media Lab's "Carousel" project (active 2003–4); https://www.media.mit.edu/projects/carousel/overview/.

25. "The compositional techniques employed in both musical scores are similar. The basic device for the generation of melodic and rhythmic sequences is 'squaring.' In this technique, a sequence of notes, measures or phrases is gradually accumulated by adding elements one at a time, and then diminished by subtraction." Exhibition notes for Manon de Boer, *Attica* (2008), Museu d'Art Contemporani de Barcelona (MACBA), https://www.macba.cat/en/attica-3594.

26. Chus Martínez, "Manon de Boer: An Informal Study of the Mind," in *Manon de Boer*, ed. Martínez, Nicolaus Schafhausen, and Monica Szewczyk (Frankfurt: Frankfurter Kunstverein, 2008), 191.

27. Ibid.

28. Malcolm X with Alex Haley, *The Autobiography of Malcolm X* (New York: Random House, 1973), 203.

29. Barbara Dierickx and Rony Vissers, "Entretien avec Manon de Boer" (2008 and 2009), https://www.scart.be/?q=fr/content/entretien-avec-manon-de-boer; translation mine.

KATIE TRUMPENER

13 Envoi

Diurnal Weather

The diorama, a recent invention, which carried an optical illusion a degree further than panoramas, had given rise to a mania among art students for ending every word with RAMA. . . .

"Well, Monsieur-r-r Poiret," said the employee from the Museum, "how is your health-orama?" . . .

"There is an uncommon frozerama outside," said Vautrin. . . .

"Did any of you notice the fog this morning?" asked the official.

"It was a frantic fog," said Bianchon, "a fog unparalleled, doleful, melancholy, sea-green, asthmatical—a Goriot of a fog!"

"A Goriorama," said the art student, "because you couldn't see a thing in it."

—Honoré de Balzac, *Père Goriot* (1835)

In an 1850 essay published in *Household Words*, Charles Dickens profiles a corpulent London retiree who has become a prodigious traveler, able to traverse continents within a matter of days, unburdened by luggage, food, or the need to speak local languages. Along the way, Mr. Booley meets with congenial company, including a boarding school proprietor chaperoning three young students, "two Scotch gardeners . . . two coach-painters" and a host of other "working-people from sundry parts of Great Britain who had conceived the extraordinary idea of 'holiday-making'" in out-of-the-way places, including the icebound Arctic. The secret, of course, is that Mr. Booley and his travel acquaintances are all still living at home, regularly sampling the world—the United States, India, New Zealand, Egypt, Ireland—through London's "gigantic-moving-panorama or diorama mode of conveyance."[1]

Walter Benjamin's *Arcades Project* catalogued panoramic display forms ubiquitous in nineteenth-century Paris. Yet Honoré de Balzac, a key source for Benjamin, articulates even bigger implications. Not only is Paris full of panoramically inspired formal spectacles and urban vistas, but nineteenth-century Parisians came to experience the world, from bodily sensations to daily weather, in terms of panoramic principles, dioramic ways of seeing. Like the arcade, the panorama proposes a way of displaying and contemplating the world that persists into the present moment: the world our viewing platform.

For the self-consciously Benjaminian cartoonist Ben Katchor, modern-day New York likewise contains the mnemic residue of older city formations, an older sense of utopian promise, glimpsed in run-down, half-abandoned industrial and commercial districts. Professor Ayschelle's antiquated Diurnorama (fig. 13.1) was intended originally as a "scientific curiosity." Yet any "orama," Katchor underscores, can become an anchoring tourist attraction (indeed—as several chapters have detailed—centerpieces of urban visual pleasure districts).

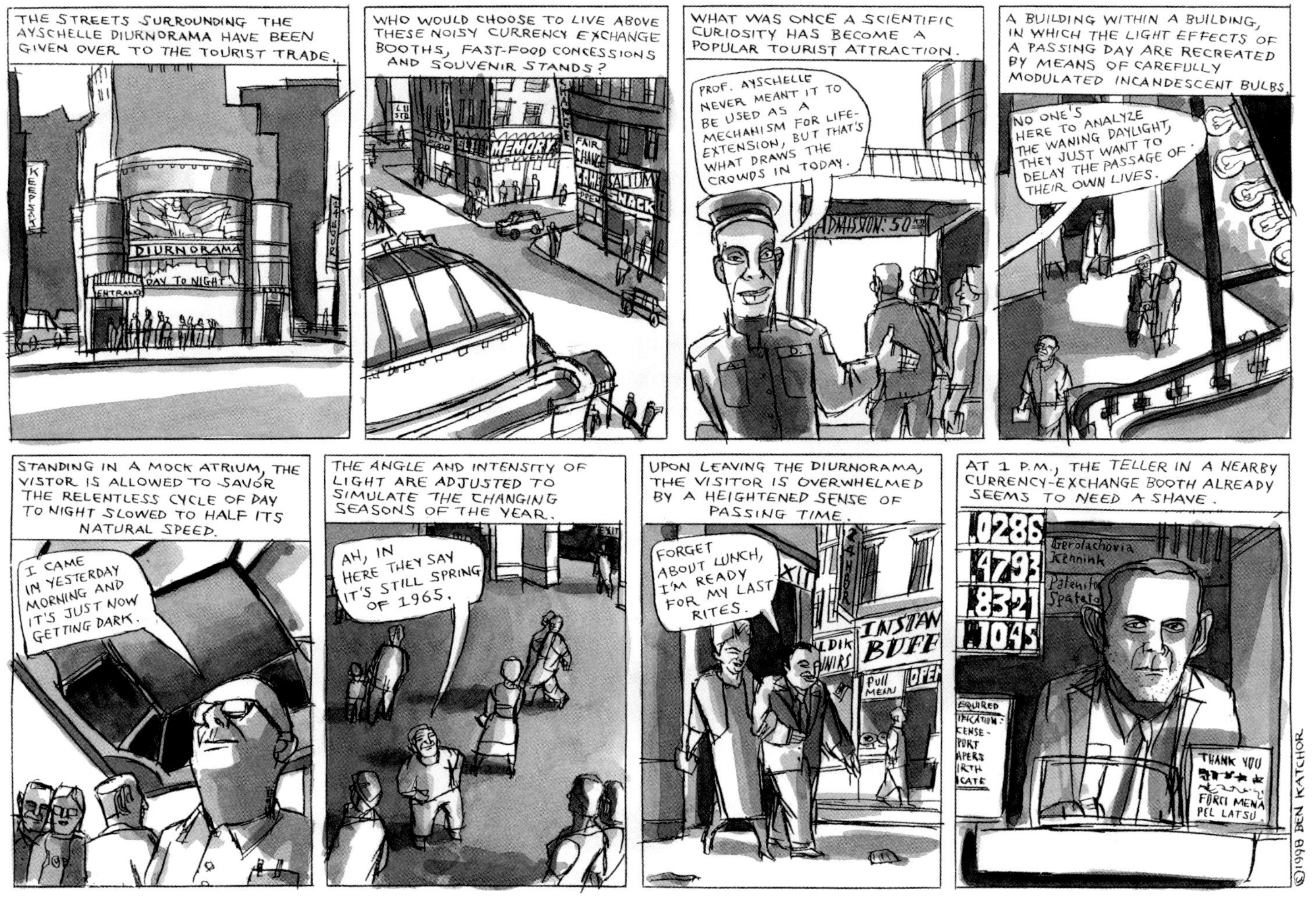

FIG. 13.1. Ben Katchor (American, b. 1951), page from *The Cardboard Valise* (New York: Pantheon, 2011).

In real life, the attraction often proved transient. Many nineteenth-century panorama paintings and buildings have vanished or been recycled. In early twentieth-century Poland and Hungary, panoramic paintings were cut into multiple fragments, many eventually displayed in local museums.[2] In the United States, one version of Paul Philippoteaux's *Battle of Gettysburg* panorama was reportedly cut up to make tents for Native Americans on a Shoshone reservation.[3]

Cyclorama buildings themselves were repurposed as sports facilities, salesrooms, garages, offices. Although recent interest in panorama form has raised the profiles of the few surviving nineteenth-century panoramas, officials still often raze or repurpose surviving cyclorama buildings and "crown" major restorations of panoramic paintings by reinstalling them in new or expanded, self-consciously multimedia buildings. In Lucerne, in lieu of conserving the nineteenth-century cyclorama, the rotunda was deconstructed and retrofitted into a multiplex building, reflecting current media obsessions.[4] Innsbruck's nineteenth-century cyclorama building was recently razed; so, despite fourteen years of preservationist protests, was Richard Neutra's 1962 panorama building at Gettysburg.

Both panorama paintings, in contrast, were restored and rehoused in new structures. At Gettysburg's new visitors' center, groups of viewers now ascend escalators to the new panoramic viewing platform. First, however, they are ushered into a theater to see a short film about Gettysburg and the Civil War, projected on a long, narrow, almost semicircular curving screen and using close-up segments of Matthew Brady's and other Civil War photographs, which creates the effect of the photo-panorama (and, indeed, cumulatively, of the Lumières' Photorama). Without actually indexing the nineteenth century's repeated conjunction of photograph and panorama, this installation manages to evoke something of its effect.

The display of Philippoteaux's painting is more problematic. Like Neutra's predecessor building, the new visitors' center features an exhibition on the history of panoramic display—yet visitors' initial experience of the panorama painting remains marred by a son-et-lumière show, darkening and lightening various parts of the panorama for dramatic effect, rather than letting visitors make sense of it for themselves. From 1982 to 2015, relatedly, Atlanta's *Battle of Atlanta* cyclorama placed visitors in tiered, revolving seating atop the viewing platform, which moved them, carousel-like, in a slow circle around the panorama, allowing them to glimpse only segments of the painting at a time as they watched and heard an explanatory son-et-lumière narration and illumination. A painted panorama was thus transformed into a moving panorama. Again potentially open-ended panoramic seeing, and the painting's insistence on historical simultaneity, was sacrificed to a linear viewing experience, a predigested historical narrative.[5]

Even in places where original installations remain in their original structures, curators sometimes repurpose these spaces to draw public interest. Recent fund-raising to restore the University of Kansas's 1893 *Panorama of North American Plants and Animals* has thus included a "Party in the Panorama"; imaginative curatorial efforts to reinsert Stockholm's half-forgotten 1893 Biology Museum into the local cultural scene have involved contemporary art installations, fashion shoots (models posing amid the stuffed birds), and occasional party rentals. (Since its rotunda is lit entirely by skylight, one winter party unfolded in total darkness, illuminated only by miners' hats: panorama as haunted house.)

Katchor's Diurnorama, in contrast, apparently never stopped drawing crowds, and the infrastructure accompanying every global tourist attraction has grown up around its building: "currency exchange booths, fast-food concessions, and souvenir stands." But (as usual in Katchor's slyly intellectual cartoons) the names of some of these businesses suggest that the Diurnorama centers an emotional as well as economic force field. Inside the "building within a building," one viewer exclaims that the light is still that of the "spring of 1965," a long-ago season somehow fixed against the passage of time. Viewers may end up staying more than a day (or thinking they have) because the passage of time works differently inside the building. As the doorman explains, many viewers linger within "to delay the passage of their own lives."

For similar reasons, of course, viewers of leisure have long attended movies in the afternoon, to revel in yet escape the knowledge that everyone else is working; either way, life inexorably passes. Katchor's Diurnorama viewer who staggers out, disoriented, into the unfamiliar daylight, his sense of elapsed time utterly muddled, can take refuge in the Memory souvenir shop across the street. (As ever, the souvenir offers a fetishized takeaway of otherwise unrecoverable, ineffable experience.) Or to reset the body's now-scrambled internal clock (jet lag in one's own life), the viewer can take immediate physical solace at the "Instant Buffet."

Yet Katchor's cartoon also reiterates nineteenth- and early twentieth-century reactions to the painted panorama. In 1812, when the Anglo-Irish novelist Maria Edgeworth, on a visit to Dublin, visited Robert Barker's Panorama of Edinburgh, she was delighted not only by the verisimilitude of Edinburgh's streets and landmarks but by the staged weather effects, which offered differential illumination—and simulated the passage of time.[6]

In 1882 the caricaturist Albert Robida imagined Paris visitors to a battle panorama held captive on the viewing platform, forced to experience firsthand the intense hunger and temporal attenuation of a siege. Likewise, one of Katchor's viewers, exiting the Diurnorama on a companion's arm, exclaims, "Forget about lunch, I'm ready for my last rites." He is somehow sickened unto death by the feeling his time has passed, overwhelmed by the feeling that during his hours inside he has lived out a whole lifetime.

For the modernist Japanese mystery writer "Edogawa Ranpo," the panoramic represents a solipsistic, aestheticist universe, sickening its creator along with its visitors. In *The Strange Tale of Panorama Island* (1926), a failed writer steals the identity of a rich doppelgänger, marrying his fiancée, and using his fortune to transform a remote island into "a single panorama," made up of a series of discrete panoramic landscapes, all of which remain visible from a single elevated vantage point.[7]

Invited to visit the island, his wife is overcome by "a vague, singularly strange feeling" as she moves between vistas, subtle shifts of perspective inducing the feeling "she were riding the wind, or had lost consciousness," or confronts "a doubly exposed motion-picture film." Yet such disorientation, her husband explains, is central to the panoramic effect: "the bright feeling of waking from a dream that one experiences when one emerges from the dark passageway of a panorama" results from stepping "from one world into a different one," from the passage between fictional and real worlds.[8]

"I have extended and contracted distances in nature just as I wanted," the husband boasts of his creation. Yet the sensation of panoramic enclosure "makes even me . . . feel inexpressibly forlorn and sad, as though I'd been left behind in the middle of an infinite plain. . . . Isn't there in it something eternal that presses in on us with a terrifying force?" As the wife's unease alerts her, indeed, these panoramic spaces are "no longer of the world of human beings, but belonged to the world of demons."[9] While shaping his island, her husband has become increasingly unmoored from reality, from his own past, from conventional morality. When his wife challenges him as an imposter, he murders her orgiastically, kills a further challenger, then dies himself in a scene of striking spectacle.

Ranpo's panorama becomes an aestheticist hall of mirrors, reflecting a twisted psyche, catalyzing tragedy. For Katchor, in contrast, almost a century later, the panorama remains a vehicle for rich philosophical retrospect—on memory, duration, the power of art. Like moviegoers, panorama-goers, and planetarium-goers before them, Katchor's Diurnorama visitors craved passage into and through other worlds. Under the dim light of the atrium, they experience a heightened sense of time and self.

As Katchor's evocation of "last rites" suggests, this experience is a quasi-religious one. Throughout the nineteenth century and beyond, the "oramas" were not just places of amusement but places of transport, stocktaking, ecstasy. In an otherwise secularizing world, they were—and remain—places of enchantment.

NOTES

1. Charles Dickens, "Some Account of an Extraordinary Traveller," *Household Words*, April 20, 1850, 73–77; 76, 77. Veronica della Dora, "Putting the World into a Box: A Geography of Nineteenth-Century 'Travelling Landscapes,'" *Geografiska Annaler, Series B: Human Geography* 89, no. 4 (2007): 298–300, reads Dickens as celebrating the new (virtual, mediated) interconnection of the world. Daniel Martin, "Dickens's Extraordinary Traveller: Immersive Media Forms and the World as Panorama," *Victorian Review*, June 14, 2016, blog post, http://victorianreview.org/?p=1412, offers a darker reading of Dickens's view of virtual tourism.
2. Romuald Nowak, "Polnische Schlachtenpanoramen," in *Tagungsbericht der Internationalen historisch-wissenschaftlichen Konferenz "Panoramamalerei in der Weltkunstgeschichte"* (Sevastapol: Museum for the Heroic Defense and Liberation of Sevastapol, 2007), 73.
3. National Park Service, "The Battle of Gettysburg in Art," December 2, 2015, https://www.nps.gov/gett/learn/historyculture/gettysburg-cyclorama.htm.
4. Christian Marty, "Die Konservierung und Restaurierung des Rundgemäldes von Eduard Castres (Bourbaki Panorama), 1996–2003," in *Panorama: Virtuality and Realities. 11. International Panorama Conference in Altötting, 2003*, ed. Gebhard Streicher (Amberg, Germany: Verlag Koch-Schmidt-Wilhelm, 2005), 102–12.
5. Painted in 1886 by Milwaukee's renowned studio of German panoramic artists, it was (after slight cropping to fit the existing building), permanently installed in 1921 in an Atlanta cyclorama and displayed there for almost a century until the leaking rotunda jeopardized the painting. In 2015 the painting was removed and restored, its lopped-off section reintegrated. It reopened in February 2019 in a purpose-built wing of the Atlanta History Center, while the old cyclorama is repurposed as office space and event venue for the Atlanta Zoo. Atlanta History Center, "Cyclorama: The Big Picture," https://www.atlantahistorycenter.com/explore/exhibitions/cyclorama-the-big-picture.
6. "At first a mistiness, like what there is in nature over a city before the sun breaks out; then the sun shining on the buildings, trees, and mountains"; Maria Edgeworth to Mrs. Edgeworth, October 1812, in *Life and Letters of Maria Edgeworth*, ed. Augustus J. C. Hare, 2 vols. (Boston: Houghton Mifflin, 1895), 1:194. In Edgeworth's *Rosamond* (1801), a little girl reluctantly renounces an opportunity to visit a panorama of Athens; in *Ormond* (1817), an eccentric aristocrat in Ireland's remote Black Islands lives so self-sufficiently that he even paints his own panorama.
7. "Edogawa Ranpo" (pseud. for Tarō Hirai), *The Strange Tale of Panorama Island*, trans. Elaine Kazu Gerbert (Honolulu: University of Hawai'i Press, 2013), 77.
8. Ibid., 78, 74, 71.
9. Ibid., 74–75, 78.

Further Reading

Agathocleos, Tanya. *Urban Realism and the Cosmopolitan Imagination*. Cambridge: Cambridge University Press, 2011.

Aguirre, Robert D. *Informal Empire: Mexico and Central America in Victorian Culture*. Minneapolis: University of Minnesota Press, 2005.

Akcan, Esra. "Off the Frame: The Panoramic Albums of Istanbul." In *Photography's Orientalism: New Essays on Colonial Representation*, edited by Ali Behdad and Luke Gartlan. Los Angeles: Getty Research Institute, 2003, 93–114.

Altick, Richard D. *The Shows of London*. Cambridge: Belknap Press of Harvard University Press, 1978.

Aumont, Jacques. "The Variable Eye; or, The Mobilization of the Gaze." Translated by Charles O'Brien and Sally Shafto. In *The Image in Dispute: Art and Cinema in the Age of Photography*, edited by Dudley Andrew. Austin: University of Texas Press, 1997, 231–58.

Avery, Kevin. "The Panorama and Its Manifestation in American Landscape Painting, 1795–1870." Ph.D. thesis, Columbia University, 1995.

Avery, Kevin, and Peter L. Fodera. *John Vanderlyn's Panoramic View of the Palace and Gardens of Versailles*. New York: Metropolitan Museum of Art, 1988.

Barnard, Edwin. *Capturing Time: Panoramas of Old Australia*. Canberra: National Library of Australia, 2012.

Barton, Peter. *The Battlefields of World War I: The Unseen Panoramas of the Western Front*. London: Constable, 2005.

Belton, John. *Widescreen Cinema*. Cambridge: Harvard University Press, 1992.

Benjamin, Walter. *The Arcades Project*. Translated by Howard Eiland and Kevin McLaughlin. Cambridge: Belknap Press of Harvard University Press, 1999.

———. "Review of Sternberger's *Panorama*" (1938–39). Translated by Edmund Jephcott. In *The Work of Art in the Age of Its Technological Reproducibility and Other Writings on Media*, edited by Michael Jennings et al. Cambridge: Harvard University Press, 2008.

Benosman, Ryad, and Sing Bing Kang, eds. *Panoramic Vision: Sensors, Theory, and Applications*. New York: Springer-Verlag, 2001.

Bermingham, Ann. "Landscape-O-Rama: The Exhibition Landscape at Somerset House and the Rise of Popular Landscape Entertainments." In *Art on the Line: The Royal Academy Exhibitions at Somerset House, 1780–1836*, edited by David Solkin, 127–44. New Haven: Yale University Press, 2001.

Bernstein, Max. "Von einem Panorama: Plauderei." *Die Kunst für alle: Malerei, Plastik, Graphik, Architektur* 2, no. 7 (1887): 105–10.

Borodini, Silvia. *Storia del panorama: La vision totale nella pittura del XIX secolo*. Rome: Officina Edizioni, 1984.

Brenneman, Chris, and Susan Boardman. *The Gettysburg Cyclorama: The Turning Point of the Civil War on Canvas*. El Dorado Hills, Calif.: Savas Beatie, 2015.

Buddemeier, Heinz, ed. *Panorama, Diorama, Photographie*. Munich: Wilhelm Fink Verlag, 1970.

Bull, Gordon. "Taking Place: Panorama and Panopticon in the Colonisation of New South Wales." *Australian Journal of Art* 12, no. 1 (1994): 75–95.

Burgin, Victor. "The Time of the Panorama" (2005). In *Situational Aesthetics: Selected Writings by Victor Burgin*, edited by Alexander Streitberger, 293–314. Leuven: Leuven University Press, 2009.

Byerly, Alison. *Are We There Yet? Virtual Travel and Victorian Realism*. Ann Arbor: University of Michigan Press, 2012.

Byrd, Vance. *A Pedagogy of Observation: Nineteenth-Century Panoramas, German Literature, and Reading Culture*. Lewisburg, Pa.: Bucknell University Press, 2017.

Cahan, Richard, and Michael Williams. *The Lost Panoramas: When Chicago Changed Its River and the Land Beyond*. Chicago: CityFiles, 2011.

Charlesworth, Michael. *Landscape and Vision in Nineteenth-Century Britain and France*. Aldershot, U.K.: Ashgate, 2008.

———. "Thomas Sandby Climbs the Hoober Stand: The Politics of Panoramic Drawing in Eighteenth-Century Britain." *Art History* 19, no. 2 (1996): 247–66.

Charney, Leo, and Vanessa Schwarz, eds. *Cinema and the Invention of Modern Life*. Berkeley: University of California Press, 1995.

Cheval, François, and Gilles Mora. *La vie en Kodak: Colorama publicitaires des années 1950 à 1970*. Malakoff, France: Éditions Hazan, 2015.

Cody, Jeffrey W., and Frances Terpak, eds. *Brush and Shutter: Early Photography in China*. Los Angeles: Getty Research Institute, 2011.

Colligan, Mimi. *Canvas Documentaries: Panoramic Entertainments in Nineteenth-Century Australia and New Zealand*. Carlton South, Vic.: Melbourne University Press, 2002.

Comment, Bernard. *The Panorama*. Translated by Anne-Marie Glasheen. London: Reaktion, 1999.

Dehejia, Vidya, ed. *India through the Lens: Photography, 1840–1911.* Washington, D.C.: Freer Gallery/Smithsonian, 2000.

Dohm, Katharina, et al., eds. *Dioramas.* Paris: Flammarion, 2017.

Dubbini, Renzo. *Geography of the Gaze: Urban and Rural Vision in Early Modern Europe* (1994). Translated by Lydia G. Cochrane. Chicago: University of Chicago Press, 2002.

Dubois, Philippe. "La question du panorama: Entre photographie et cinéma." *Cinémathèque* 4 (1993): 22–39.

Edkins, Diana. "An Introduction to Panoramic Photography." In *Panoramic Photography.* New York: Grey Gallery NYU, 1977.

Ellis, Markman. "'Spectacles within Doors': Panoramas of London in the 1790s," *Romanticism* 14, no. 2 (2008): 133–48.

Field, Hannah. *Playing with the Book: Victorian Movable Picture Books and the Child Reader.* Minneapolis: University of Minnesota Press, 2019.

Foa, Michelle. *Georges Seurat: The Art of Vision.* New Haven: Yale University Press, 2015.

Frich, Arnaud. *La photographie panoramique.* Paris: Eyrolles, 2004.

Frizot, Michel. "Voir le panorama, ou les yeux sont aussi les pieds." *Cinémathèque* 6 (1994): 78–95.

Gallardo, Helena Pérez. *Fotografía y Arquitectura en el siglo XIX. Historia y Representacion Monumental.* Madrid: Cátedra, 2015.

Garrison, Laurie, ed. *Panoramas, 1787–1900: Texts and Contexts*, 5 vols. London: Pickering & Chatto, 2013.

Grand, Karina Lykke, Lise Pennington, and Anne Mette Thomsen, eds. *Gold: Treasures from the Danish Golden Age.* Aarhus: ARoS, 2013.

Grau, Oliver. *Virtual Art: From Illusion to Immersion.* Translated by Gloria Custance. Cambridge: MIT Press, 2003.

Griffiths, Alison. *Shivers Down Your Spine: Cinema, Museums, and the Immersive View.* New York: Columbia University Press, 2008.

Gunning, Tom. "Landscape and the Fantasy of Moving Pictures: Early Cinema's Phantom Rides." In *Cinema and Landscape*, edited by Graeme Harper and Jonathan Rayner. Bristol: Intellect, 2010, 31–70.

Halks, Petra. "The Mesdag Panorama: Sheltering the All-Embracing View." *Art History* 22, no. 1 (1999): 83–98.

Harris, David, with Eric Sandweiss. *Eadweard Muybridge and the Photographic Panorama of San Francisco, 1850–1880.* Cambridge: MIT Press, 1993.

Hausmann, S. "Die Entstehung der Panoramen." *Die Kunst für Alle* 5, no. 13 (1889): 198–202.

Hornstein, Katie. *Picturing War in France, 1792–1856.* New Haven: Yale University Press, 2017.

Huhtamo, Erkki. *Illusions in Motion: Media Archaeology of the Moving Panorama and Related Spectacles.* Cambridge: MIT Press, 2013.

Hyde, Ralph. *Gilded Scenes and Shining Prospects: Panoramic Views of British Towns, 1575–1900.* New Haven: Yale Center for British Art, 1985.

———. *Panoramania! The Art and Entertainment of the "All-Embracing" View.* London: Trefoil/Barbican Art Gallery, 1988.

Kämpfen-Klapproth, Brigit. *Das Bourbaki Panorama von Edouard Castres.* Lucerne: City of Lucerne, 1980.

Koller, Gabriele, ed. *The World of Panoramas: Ten Years of International Panorama Conferences.* Amberg, Germany: SPA Stiftung Panorama Altötting, 2003.

Koschorke, Albrecht. "Das Panorama: Die Anfänge des modernen Sensomotorik um 1800." In *Die Mobilisierung des Sehens*, edited by Harro Segeberg, 147–68. Munich: Wilhelm Fink, 1996.

Kuyper, Eric de, and Émile Poppe. "Voir et Regarder." *Communications* 34 (1981): 85–96.

Lumière, Auguste, and Louis Lumière. "Le Photorama" (pamphlet). Lyon: A. Storck, 1902.

Lüthy, Hans. "Giovanni Segantini's Panorama for the 1900 Paris World's Fair." *Journal of Decorative and Propaganda Arts* 19 (1993): 34–41.

Madeline, Laurence, and Jean-Roch Bouiller, eds. *J'aime les panoramas: S'approprier le monde.* Paris: Flammarion, 2015.

Martin, Carlos, Sergio Burgi, and Julia Kovensky, eds. *Panoramas: A Paisagem Brasileira no Acervo do Instituto Moreira Salles.* São Paulo: Instituto Moreira Salles, 2012.

Maurer, Kathrin. "The Paradox of Total Immersion: Watching War in Nineteenth-Century Panoramas." In *Visualizing War: Emotions, Technologies and Communities*, edited by Anders Engberg-Pedersen and Kathrin Maurer, 78–94. New York: Routledge, 2018.

———. *Visualizing the Past: The Power of the Image in German Historicism*, 27–72. Berlin: De Gruyter, 2013.

Meers, Nick. *Stretch: The World of Panoramic Photography.* Mies, Switzerland: RotoVision, 2003.

Michaux, Emmanuelle. *Du panorama pictural au cinéma circulaire: Origines et histoire d'un autre cinéma, 1785–1998.* Paris: L'Harmattan, 1999.

Miller, Angela. "The Panorama, the Cinema and the Emergence of the Spectacular." *Wide Angle* 18, no. 2 (1996): 34–69.

Mungen, Arno. *"BilderMusik": Panorama, Tableux vivants und Lichtbilder als multimediale Darstellungsformen in Theater- und Musikauffuhrungen vom 19. bis zum fruhen 20. Jahrhundert.* Remscheid: Gardezl Verlag, 2006.

Nouvel-Kammerer, Odile, ed. *Décor de l'imaginaire: Papiers peints panoramiques, 1790–1865.* Paris: Flammarion, 1990.

Oettermann, Stephan. *The Panorama: History of a Mass Medium.* Translated by Deborah Lucas Schneider. New York: Zone, 1997.

Oleksijczuk, Denise Blake. *The First Panoramas: Visions of British Imperialism.* Minneapolis: University of Minnesota Press, 2011.

Otto, Peter. *Multiplying Worlds: Romanticism, Modernity, and the Emergence of Virtual Reality.* Oxford: Oxford University Press, 2011.

Panoramas Photographies 1850–1950. Collection Bonnemaison. Arles: Actes Sud, 1989.

Pinney, Christopher. "'Buddhist' Photography." In *The Marshall Albums: Photography and Archeology*, edited by Sudeshna Guha. London: Alkazi Collection of Photography, 2010, 178–201.

Plessen, Marie-Louise von, and Ulrich Giersch, eds. *Sehsucht: Das Panorama als Massenunterhaltung des 19. Jahrhunderts.* Basel: Stroemfeld, 1993.

Raab, Jennifer. "Panoramic Vision, Telegraphic Language: Selling the American West." *Journal of American Studies* 47, no. 2 (2013): 495–520.

"Ranpo, Edogawa" (pseud. for Tarō Hirai). *The Strange Tale of Panorama Island.* Translated by Elaine Kazu Gerbert. Honolulu: University of Hawai'i Press, 2013.

Roalf, Peggy, ed. *Colorama: The World's Largest Photographs from Kodak and the George Eastman Collection.* New York: Aperture, 2005.

Routhier, Jessica Skwire, et al. *The Painter's Panorama: Narrative, Art, and Faith in the "Moving Panorama of Pilgrim's Progress."* Hanover, N.H.: University Press of New England, 2015.

Ruoff, Jeffrey, ed. *Virtual Voyages: Cinema and Travel.* Durham: Duke University Press, 2006.

Ryan, James R. *Picturing Empire: Photography and the Visualization of the British Empire.* Chicago: University of Chicago Press, 1987.

Samuels, Maurice. *The Spectacular Past: Popular History and the Novel in Nineteenth-Century France.* Ithaca: Cornell University Press, 2004.

Schivelbusch, Wolfgang. *The Railway Journey: The Industrialization of Time and Space in the Nineteenth Century*. Translated by Anselm Hollo. Berkeley: University of California Press, 1986.

Schnapp, Jeffrey T. "The Mass Panorama." *Modernism/Modernity* 9, no. 2 (2002): 243–81.

Schwartz, Vanessa R. *Spectacular Realities: Early Mass Culture in Fin-de-Siècle Paris*. Berkeley: University of California Press, 1999.

Smith, Greg. "The 'Connoisseur's Panorama': Thomas Girtin's *Eidometropolis* (1801–1803) and a New Visual Language for the Modern City." *British Art Studies* 10 (2018), https://doi.org/10.17658/issn.2058-5462/issue-10/gsmith.

Snyder, Joel. *One/Many: Western American Survey Photographs by Bell and O'Sullivan*. Chicago: David and Alfred Smart Museum of Art, 2006.

Solar, Gustav. *Das Panorama und seine Vorentwicklung bis zu Hans Conrad Escher von der Linth*. Zurich: Orell Füssli, 1979.

Sorensen, Jens Erik, Carsten Thau, and Marie Nipper. *Olafur Eliasson: Your Rainbow Panorama*. Exh. cat. Aarhus: ARoS Aarhus Kunstmuseum, 2011.

Sternberger, Dolf. *Panorama of the Nineteenth Century*. Translated by Joachim Neugroschel. New York: Urizen, 1977.

Streicher, Gebhard, ed. *Panorama: Virtuality and Realities. 11. International Panorama Conference in Altötting, 2003*. Amberg, Germany: Verlag Koch-Schmidt-Wilhelm, 2005.

Sweetman, John, et al. *The Panoramic Image*. Southampton, U.K.: John Hansard Gallery, 1981.

Uricchio, William. "A 'Proper Point of View': The Panorama and Some of Its Early Media Iterations." *Early Popular Visual Culture* 9, no. 3 (2011): 225–38.

Wallach, Alan. "Making a Picture from Mount Holyoke." In *American Iconology: New Approaches to Nineteenth-Century Art and Literature*, edited by David Lubin. New Haven: Yale University Press, 1993, 80–91.

———. "The Persistence of the Panoramic." In *Transcultural Spaces: Challenges of Urbanity, Ecology, and the Environment in the New Millennium, REAL Yearbook of Research in English and American Studies* 26, edited by Stefan Brandt, Winfried Fluck, and Frank Mehring, 89–107. Tübingen: Narr Verlag, 2010.

———. "Some Further Thoughts on the Panoramic Mode in Hudson River School Landscape Painting." In *Within the Landscape: Essays on Nineteenth-Century American Art and Culture*, edited by Phillip Earenfight and Nancy Siegel. University Park: Pennsylvania State University Press, 2005. 99–128.

White, Daniel E. *From Little London to Little Bengal: Religion, Print, and Modernity in Early Modern British India, 1793–1835*. Baltimore: Johns Hopkins University Press, 2013.

Wonders, Karen. *Habitat Dioramas: Illusions of Wilderness in Museums of Natural History*. Uppsala, Sweden: Uppsala University Press, 1993.

Zarobell, John. *Empire of Landscape: Space and Ideology in French Colonial Algeria*. University Park: Pennsylvania State University Press, 2010.

Contributors

Mal Ahern is an assistant professor of cinema and media studies at the University of Washington. She has published in *diacritics, Millennium Film Journal, World Picture,* and *The New Inquiry*.

Tim Barringer is Paul Mellon Professor of the History of Art at Yale University. His books include *Men at Work: Art and Labour in Victorian Britain* and *Reading the Pre-Raphaelites.*

Gretchen Holtzapple Bender is a senior lecturer at the University of Pittsburgh. Her chapter emerges from her dissertation on Caspar David Friedrich, landscape practice, and the gendering of space in tourism and visual culture.

Cassius Clay graduated from Yale and studied early-twentieth-century British history at Cambridge on a Paul Mellon Fellowship. He lives and works as a creative director in London.

Jonathan Crary is Meyer Schapiro Professor of Modern Art at Columbia University and a founding editor of Zone Books. His publications include *Techniques of the Observer* and *Suspensions of Perception.*

Noam M. Elcott is an associate professor in the Columbia University Department of Art History and Archaeology, Chair of Art Humanities, and an editor of the journal *Grey Room*.

Carla Hermann holds a Ph.D. in Art History and is a contract faculty member of the Theory and Art History Department of the State University of Rio de Janeiro, Brazil.

Timothy Hyman (elected Royal Academician 2011), a painter, has taught and written widely; books include *Bonnard*; *Sienese Painting*; and *The World New Made: Figurative Painting in the Twentieth Century* (all Thames & Hudson).

Anna Indych-López is a professor of Latin American and Latinx art at the Graduate Center and was the 2018–2019 Stuart Z. Katz Professor in the Humanities and the Arts at the City College of New York (CUNY).

Julia Lum is an assistant professor of art history at Scripps College. Her research centers on art and empire, photography, and landscapes at the intersection of indigenous and British cultures.

Richard Maxwell (1948–2010) taught comparative literature at Yale. His work included *The Mysteries of Paris and London*; *The Historical Novel in Europe 1650–1950*; and *The Demonstration House*, an unpublished historical novel about 1950s Los Angeles.

Denise Oleksijczuk teaches art, performance, and cinema studies at Simon Fraser University. She published the award-winning *The First Panoramas: Visions of British Imperialism* (University of Minnesota Press, 2011).

Maria Antonella Pelizzari teaches the history of photography at Hunter College and CUNY Graduate Center. Current projects include *Print Matters: Histories of Photography in Illustrated Magazines* (Getty) and *Photographs of Italy and the British Imagination, 1840–1900* (Yale Center for British Art).

Ruth Pullin is the author or coauthor of three books on and curator of two major exhibitions on Eugene von Guérard (National Gallery of Victoria 2011; Art Gallery of Ballarat 2018).

Richard I. Suchenski is an associate professor of film and electronic arts and director of the Center for Moving Image Arts, Bard College. He has published *Projections of Memory: Romanticism, Modernism, and the Aesthetics of Film* (2016) and *Hou Hsiao-hsien* (2014).

Katie Trumpener (Emily Sanford Professor of Comparative Literature/English, Yale) has published *Bardic Nationalism: The Romantic Novel and the British Empire* and (co-edited with Richard Maxwell) *Cambridge Companion to Fiction of the Romantic Period.*

Andrew Vielkind is a Ph.D. candidate in the history of art and film and media studies at Yale University where he is writing a dissertation on the intersections between experimental cinema and technoscientific culture. He is also serving as a Mellon-Marron Museum Research Consortium Fellow in the Department of Photography at the Museum of Modern Art.

Marina Warner is a professor of English and creative writing, Birkbeck College, and president of the Royal Society of Literature. Her recent books include *Stranger Magic* (2011) and *Forms of Enchantment: Writings on Art and Artists* (2018).

Index

Note: page numbers in boldface indicate figures; those followed by "n" refer to chapter endnotes.

Illustration Credits

Katie Trumpener: dedication
Scala / Art Resource, New York: p. 44–45, 9.8
John Hammond / Bridgeman Images: pp. 48–49
Schalkwijk / Art Resource, New York. © 2020 Banco de México Diego Rivera Frida Kahlo Museums Trust, Mexico, D.F. / Artists Rights Society (ARS), New York: p. 61
© David Hockney. Photo by Richard Schmidt: pp. 68–69, 7.10
Courtesy of Stan Douglas: pp. 72–73
© 2019 Artists Rights Society (ARS), New York / VEGAP, Madrid. Origin of image: VEGAP Image Bank: pp. 74–75
Photo by Alexander Harding: pp. 78–79
Courtesy of Jeff Wall: 0.1
Courtesy of Bourbaki Panorama, Lucerne: 0.3
Courtesy of Bourbaki Panorama, Lucerne (photo by Gabriel Ammon / AURA): 0.4, 7.6, 7.7, 7.8
bpk Bildagentur / Hamburger Kunsthalle / Elke Walford / Art Resource, New York: 0.13
© 2020 Tate, London: 0.15
© National Gallery, London / Art Resource, New York: 0.16, 9.7
© The Cleveland Museum of Art: 0.18
Tom Schulze © asisi: 0.20
Photo by Ole Hein Pederson. © 2006 Olafur Eliasson. Courtesy of Olafur Eliasson, Tanya Bonakdar Gallery, New York / Los Angeles, and neugerriemschneider, Berlin: 0.21
© 2002 Olafur Eliasson. Private collection. Courtesy of Olafur Eliasson, Tanya Bonakdar Gallery, New York / Los Angeles, and neugerriemschneider, Berlin: 0.22
© Janet Cardiff; courtesy of Janet Cardiff and Luhring Augustine, New York. Image from installation at the Metropolitan Museum of Art, the Cloisters: Fuentidueña Chapel, 2013. Image copyright: Metropolitan Museum of Art. Image source: Art Resource, New York: 0.23
Photo by Tim Barringer: 1.2, 5.2, 5.9, 5.10, 5.11
Nick Cockman / Alamy Stock Photo: 1.7
© British Library Board (Add. MS 15968A): 1.8
Royal Collection Trust / © 2020 Her Majesty Queen Elizabeth II: 1.10, 8.3
Courtesy of the City Art Centre, Edinburgh Museums and Galleries: 1.13
© The Trustees of the British Museum: 1.17, 1.20, 1.23
Reproduced by kind permission of the Syndics of Cambridge University Library: 1.22
© The Fitzwilliam Museum, Cambridge: 1.24
© Museum of London: 2.2
Copyright University of Sheffield Library, National Fairground and Circus Archive: 2.4
Erich Lessing / Art Resource, New York: 2.5, 9.9
Bridgeman Images: 2.6, 2.7, 6.6, 6.7, 6.10
bpk Bildagentur / Stiftung Preussische Schlösser & Gärten, Berlin / Jörg P. Anders / Art Resource, New York: 4.1a, 4.1b
akg-images: 4.6, 4.7
Ingo Schultz / Alamy Stock Photo: 4.8
Stefan Koppelkamm, Berlin: 5.3
bpk Bildagentur / Nationalgalerie / Jörg P. Anders / Art Resource, New York: 5.4
Artokoloro Quint Lox Limited / Alamy Stock Photo: 5.6
Jenni Carter, AGNSW: 6.2
Courtesy of Walter Niedermayr and Galerie Nordenhake, Berlin / Stockholm, and Galerie Johann Widauer, Innsbruck: 7.1
Christian Helmle: 7.3, 7.4
© TLM: 7.5a
© TLM / Alexander Haiden: 7.5b
© Jules Spinatsch. Digital image © The Museum of Modern Art / Licensed by Scala / Art Resource, New York: 7.9
Courtesy of Hiroshi Sugimoto and Marian Goodman Gallery: 7.11
Digital image © The Museum of Modern Art / Licensed by Scala / Art Resource, New York: 8.1, 8.10
Copyright T. J. Wilcox. Courtesy of T. J. Wilcox and Gladstone Gallery, New York and Brussels. Photo credit: Bill Jacobson: 8.11
MixPix / Alamy Stock Photo: 9.1
Courtesy of Photoplay Productions: 9.3, 9.4, 9.5, 9.6, 9.10, 9.11, 9.12, 9.13, 9.14, 9.15, 9.16
© Michael Snow. Courtesy of Michael Snow and Jack Shainman Gallery, New York: 10.2, 12.9
Courtesy of Manon de Boer and Jan Mot, Brussels: 12.1
© 2011 Ben Katchor: 13.1